By the same Authors:

- THE FIRST FIVE-YEAR PLAN
- THE SECOND FIVE-YEAR PLAN
- ARMED INTERVENTION IN RUSSIA, 1918-20
- SCENES FROM SOVIET LIFE
- FROM TSARDOM TO THE STALIN CONSTITUTION
- WORLD AFFAIRS AND THE U.S.S.R.
- RUSSIA, FINLAND AND THE BALTIC
- SOVIET-FINNISH CAMPAIGN, 1939-40 : MILITARY AND POLITICAL
- WHY RUSSIA WILL WIN

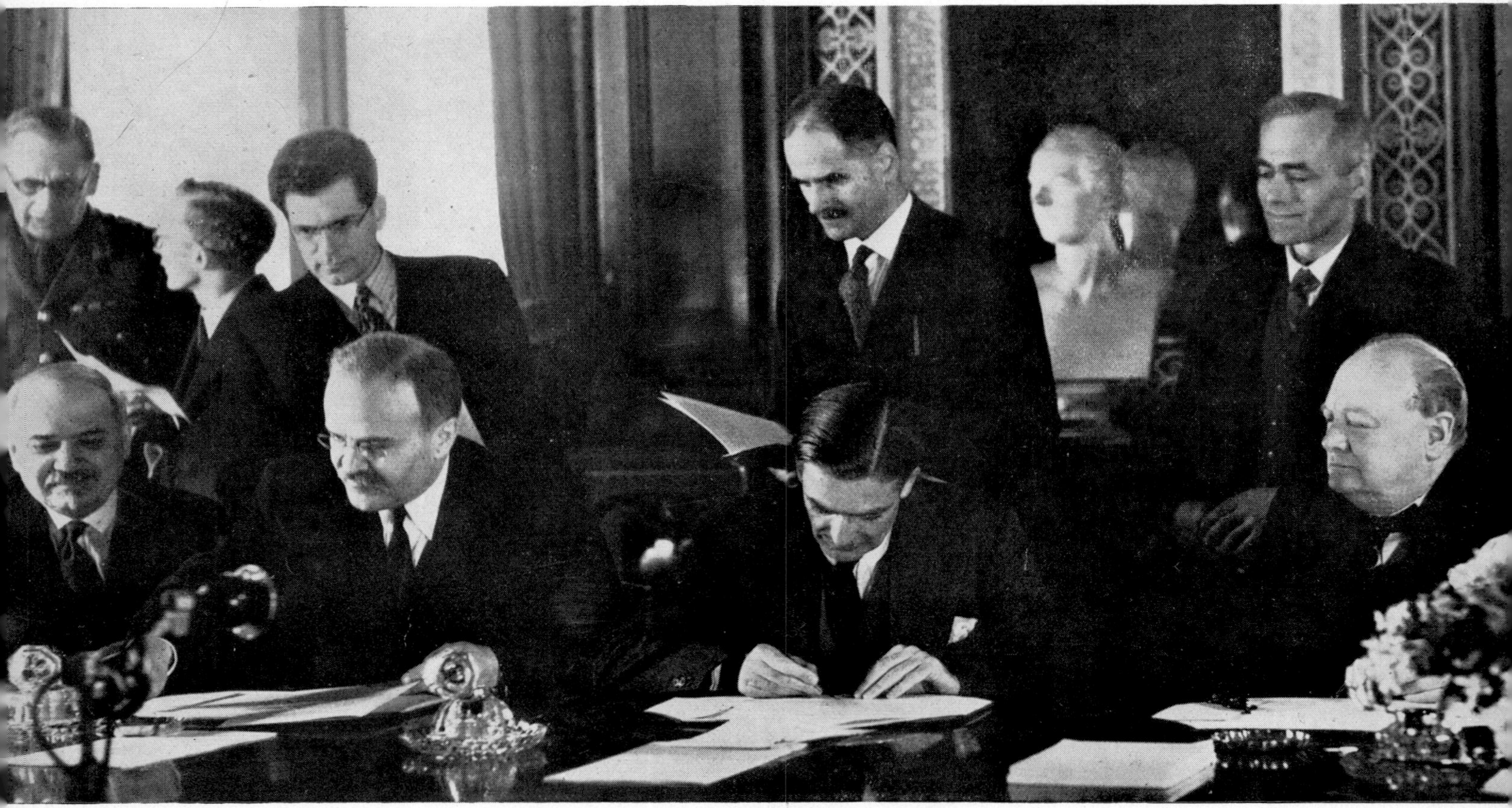

The signing of the Anglo-Soviet Treaty, May 26th, 1942

A HISTORY OF ANGLO-SOVIET RELATIONS

W. P. and Zelda K. COATES

with a foreword by
the Right Hon. David Lloyd George, O.M., M.P.

LAWRENCE & WISHART
AND THE PILOT PRESS

LONDON 1945

First Published . . 1944
Reprinted . . . 1944
Reprinted . . . 1945

BOOK
PRODUCTION
WAR ECONOMY
STANDARD

THIS BOOK IS PRODUCED IN COMPLETE CONFORMITY
WITH THE AUTHORIZED ECONOMY STANDARDS

MADE AND PRINTED IN GREAT BRITAIN
AT THE CHAPEL RIVER PRESS
6.45

CONTENTS

FOREWORD

by

THE RT. HON. DAVID LLOYD GEORGE, O.M., M.P.

WHEN on that memorable day, June 11, 1942, the Foreign Secretary, Mr. Eden, announced in the House of Commons the conclusion of a Treaty of Alliance with the U.S.S.R., I immediately commented: "As one who has laboured for over 20 years to establish a good understanding between Soviet Russia and this country, I felicitate the Prime Minister and the Foreign Secretary and the Government upon the accomplishment of this Treaty. Had it been a fact some years ago many grave blunders in foreign policy would have been avoided. Not only that, this war could never have occurred." There was no exaggeration in these words; I meant every one of them. I might have added that the Covenant of the League would have become an established and irresistible factor in the affairs of nations; the era of disarmament would have begun in earnest, and the age of "peace on earth and good-will amongst men" would have been well on the way.

Mr. and Mrs. Coates have done another fine piece of work in placing on record the course of Anglo-Soviet relations during the past twenty-five years. They have shown themselves to be no respecters of persons, and although they have at times criticised very strongly, they have invariably quoted the subject of their criticism quite fairly and to such treatment none of us who are public men can raise any objection. On the other hand, they are equally lavish with their praise where they consider it was justified. In the main they have allowed the story to tell its own tale by faithful summarising and apposite documentation.

Like the authors, I trust that this volume—which should find a place on the book-shelf of every student of international affairs—will help us to realise our past errors in dealing with Soviet Russia and assist in establishing Anglo-Soviet friendship on an unshakable foundation.

D. LLOYD GEORGE

INTRODUCTION.

WE start our narrative in the first chapter with Mr. Lloyd George's Mansion House speech of November 8th, 1919, i.e. on the day following the second anniversary of the establishment of the Soviet power, but much happened in the relationship between Great Britain and Soviet Russia during the preceding two years.*

Here it is only necessary to put on record the outstanding episodes in the relations of the two Governments in these two intervening years—November, 1917 to November, 1919.

The Soviet Government from the moment that it came into power strove to maintain normal diplomatic relations with the neutral and Allied Governments, including, of course, Great Britain, and soon afterwards it appointed Mr. Maxim Litvinov as Ambassador to Great Britain. But the British Government refused to recognise the Soviet Government *de jure* and Mr. Litvinov as Ambassador ; it also decided to withdraw the British Ambassador, Sir George Buchanan, from Soviet Russia.

However, in the first week of January, 1918—by this date the Soviet Government had lasted much longer than Whitehall, Fleet Street and many diplomatic representatives in Russia had expected—the British Government came to the conclusion that it must establish some sort of diplomatic contact with the Soviet Government and appointed Mr. R. H. Bruce Lockhart† for that work.

It is pertinent to quote what Mr. Lockhart himself wrote regarding his appointment:

> "I was to go to Russia as head of a special mission to establish unofficial relations with the Bolsheviks. Sir George Buchanan was returning home. I was to leave on the cruiser which was to fetch him from Bergen. My instructions were of the vaguest. I was to have the responsibility of establishing relations. I was to have no authority. If the Bolsheviks would give me the necessary diplomatic privileges without being recognised by the British Government, we would make a similar concession to Litvinov, whom the Bolsheviks had already appointed Soviet Ambassador in London."‡

Mr. Lockhart continued: "the situation bristled with difficulties," and added that his next step was "to establish a *modus vivendi* with Litvinov." This he did, thanks to Mr. Rex Leeper of the British

* This period is dealt with at considerable length in our *Armed Intervention in Russia* (Gollancz).

† Mr. Lockhart had been Acting Consul-General in Moscow until September, 1917, and was a strong advocate of coming to terms with the Soviet Government.

‡ *Memoirs of a British Agent*, pp. 200/1.

Foreign Office and Mr. Theodore Rothstein, then resident in London and later Soviet Ambassador to Persia.

Mr. Lockhart continued his narrative thus:

> "A few days later the whole affair was arranged over the luncheon table at a Lyons' shop in the Strand. The two contracting parties were represented by Litvinov and Rothstein on the Russian side and Leeper and myself on the English side. There was to be no recognition—at any rate for the present. Unofficially, both Litvinov and I were to have certain diplomatic privileges, including the use of ciphers and the right to a diplomatic courier."*

At the end of the luncheon "on the rough linen of a standard Lyons' table," M. Litvinov wrote out Mr. Lockhart's introduction to the Soviet Commissar for Foreign Affairs. The following is the translation:

> "Dear Comrade,
>
> The bearer of this, Mr. Lockhart, is going to Russia with an official mission with the exact character of which I am not acquainted. I know him personally as a thoroughly honest man who understands our position and sympathises with us. I should consider his sojourn in Russia useful from the point of view of our interests.
>
> My position here remains indefinite. I learnt of my appointment only from the newspapers. I hope a courier is bringing me the necessary documents without which the difficulties of my position are greatly increased. The Embassy, Consulate, and Russian Government Committee have not yet surrendered. Their relations to me will be determined by the relations of the British Government.
>
> I wrote the other day to the Ministry for Foreign Affairs, asking for a meeting in order to regulate certain practical questions (the viséing of passports, use of ciphers, military convention, etc.), but have not received any reply. I presume the question of my recognition will not be settled until the arrival of Buchanan.
>
> The reception accorded me by the Press is quite satisfactory. I am making the acquaintance of the representatives of the Labour movement. I have issued an appeal to the English working-men in all the Socialist papers. Even the bourgeois press readily accords me its pages to explain our position.
>
> I shall write more fully by the first courier. I have not received an answer from you to my telegram of January 4th, new style,

* *Ibid.*, p. 202.

No. 1. I request you very much to confirm the receipt of all telegrams and to number your telegrams.

The ciphers will, I trust, be delivered to me by the courier. Greetings to Lenin and all friends. I press your hand warmly.

Yours (signed),

M. LITVINOV."*

M. Litvinov and Mr. Lockhart were not to be Ambassadors but diplomatic agents and Mr. Lockhart left Queensferry on January 14, 1918, for Russia.

Two days later, January 16, 1918, the then British Foreign Secretary, the late Mr. Balfour (later Lord Balfour) stated in the House of Commons " His Majesty's Government do not recognise the Petrograd Administration as a *de jure* or *de facto* Government, Mr. Nabokoff [Chargé d'Affaires under the Tsarist and Provisional Governments since January, 1917] will presumably remain at his post until he is superseded or confirmed."

M. Litvinov rented an office as headquarters for the Soviet Diplomatic Delegation at 82, Victoria Street, London S.W., on the door of which he put up a plate with the inscription: " People's Embassy of the R.S.F.S.R."

But this was too much for the owner of the offices, and the " People's Embassy " was given notice to quit.

When M. Litvinov was compelled to leave his Victoria Street office he moved his Embassy to his private address at 11, Bigwood Road, Golders Green, London. A visitor to his home at that time described it thus:

" One cold January evening, in a downpour, I walked along the streets of a northern London suburb seeking the house of the just-appointed representative of Soviet Russia. Row upon row of depressingly similar houses stretched before me. I recalled those occasions on which I came into contact with the Ambassador of the Russian Empire in the days of the autocracy. . . . Finally I found the house I required. The door was opened for me by a simply dressed young woman with short hair. A moment later I entered a small, poorly-furnished room whose only ornament was, apart from the bright fire in the fireplace, a shelf on which were the *Encyclopædia Britannica, The History of the Paris Commune,* and several other English books.

The Soviet representative was dressed in a well-worn brown jacket, drinking tea. The young woman sat down on a small chair and started making toast. This was Litvinov's wife. The

* *Ibid.*, pp. 203/4.

house, the furnishing and all the living conditions of the Russian Ambassador were in no way different from that of the ordinary British worker."

M. Litvinov duly called on the former Chargé d'Affaires of the Russian Embassy, M. Nabokoff, and the Consul-General of the Consulate to hand over their respective premises with their contents, but the representatives of the old régime refused, and in this they were upheld by the British Government of the day. M. Nabokoff probably had a hearty laugh at the absurd policy pursued in the matter by the British Government because subsequently he wrote: "According to international law and all traditions the collapse of the Provisional Government in Russia had put an end to the formal plenary powers of the Representatives of Russia abroad."*

Mr. Lockhart, as already mentioned, was in favour of an understanding with the Soviet Government, but the Government he represented was not, and without any declaration of war, in June-July, 1918, Allied troops, including British, landed in Northern Russia and seized Soviet territory. Further, early in August, 1918, British, Japanese, French and U.S.A. troops were landed at Vladivostok despite the vehement protests of the Soviet Government. The fatal and disastrous policy of foreign armed intervention in Soviet Russia had begun. From this time onwards, stores and military supplies of all kinds were dispatched by all available routes to the Allied armies on Soviet soil and to the Russian counter-revolutionary forces.

At this time and during the intervening months, M. Litvinov and Mr. Lockhart had been acting within the status already mentioned on behalf of their respective Governments, and Mr. Lockhart had advised his Government that the policy of armed intervention would be futile and disastrous, but willy-nilly, he was drawn into the toils of the Allied representatives in Soviet Russia who were carrying out this insane policy.

The Soviet Government quite naturally became suspicious of Mr. Lockhart's activities, and the latter frankly admitted subsequently that these suspicions were justified:

> "The suspicions were well-founded. Almost before I had realised it I had now identified myself with a movement which, whatever its original object, was to be directed, not against Germany, but against the *de facto* government of Russia."†

Further, Mr. Lockhart wrote:

> "Through Hicks [Lockhart's Chief Assistant] I increased my contact with the anti-Bolshevik forces. As far as we were

* *The Ordeal of a Diplomat*, by Constantin Nabokoff, p. 187.

† *Memoirs of a British Agent*, by R. H. Bruce Lockhart, p. 287 (Putnam).

> concerned, they were represented in Moscow by an organisation called the 'Centre,' which was subdivided into two wings of Left and Right, and by the League of the Regeneration of Russia founded by Savinkov. There were constant bickerings between the two organisations. The Centre was in close touch with the White Army in the South."*

The natural result of Mr. Lockhart's very improper and inexcusable activities was that he was arrested in Moscow on September 3, 1918, and three days later, M. Litvinov, purely as a reprisal, was arrested in London.

After prolonged negotiations Mr. Lockhart and M. Litvinov were exchanged in October, 1918, and semi-official diplomatic relations between London and Moscow came to an end. A month later the first World War also came to an end, and a new situation was created.

When the representatives of the Allied Governments met in Paris to formulate the Peace Treaty with the Central Powers and to consider the world situation in general, they soon realised that they could not leave the "Russian question" as it was, viz., that Allied troops should remain on Russian territory and that the Allies should continue to support these troops and to supply the Russian "Whites" with stores, munitions and money.

Mr. Lloyd George and President Wilson saw clearly the sensible course. "Personally, I would have dealt with the Soviets as the *de facto* Government of Russia," wrote Mr. Lloyd George. "So would President Wilson. But we both agreed that we could not carry to that extent our colleagues at the Congress. . . ."† M. Clemenceau, the Head of the French Delegation, was vehemently against.

However, after prolonged discussions between the Allied statesmen, a compromise plan was accepted which came to be known as the Prinkipo proposals. On January 21, 1919, the Conference reached agreement, and on the following day a proclamation drafted by President Wilson was unanimously accepted. The proclamation ran:

> "The single object the representatives of the associated Powers have had in mind in their discussions of the course they should pursue with regard to Russia has been to help the Russian people, not to hinder them, or to interfere in any manner with their right to settle their own affairs in their own way. They regard the Russian people as their friends, not their enemies, and are willing to help them in any way they are willing to be helped. It is clear to them that the troubles and distresses of the Russian people will steadily increase, hunger and privation of every kind become more

* *Ibid.*, p. 291.

† *The Truth about the Peace Treaties*, by David Lloyd George, p. 231 (Gollancz 1938).

and more acute, more and more widespread, and more and more impossible to relieve, unless order is restored and normal conditions of labour, trade and transportation once more created, and they are seeking some way in which to assist the Russian people to establish order.

They recognise the absolute right of the Russian people to direct their own affairs without dictation or direction of any kind from outside. They do not wish to exploit or make use of Russia in any way. They recognise the revolution without reservation, and will in no way, and in no circumstances aid or give countenance to any attempt at a counter-revolution. It is not their wish or purpose to favour or assist any one of those organised groups now contending for the leadership and guidance of Russia as against the others. Their sole and sincere purpose is to do what they can to bring Russia peace and an opportunity to find her way out of her present troubles.

The associated Powers are now engaged in the solemn and responsible work of establishing the peace of Europe and of the world, and they are keenly alive to the fact that Europe and the world cannot be at peace if Russia is not. They recognise and accept it as their duty, therefore, to serve Russia in this matter as generously, as unselfishly, as thoughtfully, as ungrudgingly, as they would serve every other friend and ally. And they are ready to render this service in the way that is most acceptable to the Russian people.

In this spirit and with this purpose, they have taken the following action: They invite every organised group that is now exercising, or attempting to exercise, political authority or military control anywhere in Siberia, or within the boundaries of European Russia as they stood before the war just concluded (except in Finland) to send representatives, not exceeding three representatives for each group, to the Princes Islands, Sea of Marmora, where they will be met by representatives of the associated Powers, provided, in the meantime, there is a truce of arms amongst the parties invited, and that all armed forces anywhere sent or directed against any people or territory outside the boundaries of European Russia as they stood before the war, or against Finland, or against any people or territory whose autonomous action is in contemplation in the fourteen articles upon which the present negotiations are based, shall be meanwhile withdrawn, and aggressive military action cease. These representatives are invited to confer with the representatives of the associated Powers in the freest and frankest way, with a view to ascertaining the wishes of all sections of the Russian people, and bringing about, if possible, some understanding and agreement by which Russia may work out her own purposes and happy co-operative relations be established between her people and the other peoples of the world.

A prompt reply to this invitation is requested. Every facility for the journey of the representatives, including transport across the Black Sea, will be given by the Allies, and all the parties concerned are expected to give the same facilities. The representatives will be expected at the place appointed by the 15th February, 1919."

This was the first attempt by the Allied Governments to discuss peace with the Soviets, and the credit for it mainly belonged to Mr. Lloyd George and President Wilson. How different would have been the history of the world had it succeeded. The communiqué containing this proclamation was issued at 9 p.m., January 22, 1919, and the press were also informed that it would be wirelessed to the parties concerned the same evening. But the official communiqué was never received by the Soviet Government. Why? Up to the present the reason so far as we are aware has never been published. However, we are now in a position to reveal the mystery on the highest authority—the French Government who had all along bitterly opposed any understanding with the Soviet Government simply jammed the wirelessed message to Soviet Russia.

What immediately followed is very instructive. The *Times*, on January 24, 1919, was enthusiastic about the proposed Prinkipo Conference, and in a leading article declared that if the Bolsheviks refused the invitation to attend, "they would have revealed themselves as the enemies of the human race."

But the Bolsheviks did not refuse to attend. Although they had not received the official invitation they did learn of it, and on February 4, 1919, brushing aside all questions of *amour propre*, they sent the following very definite reply:

"The Russian Soviet Government has learned, through a radiogram which contained a review of the press, of an invitation, stated to have been addressed by the Entente Powers to all *de facto* Governments of Russia, to send delegates to a conference on Prinkipo Island.

As the Soviet Government has received no such invitation addressed to it, but has learned—and again through a radio review of the press—that the absence of an answer from the Soviet Government is interpreted as a refusal to reply to this invitation, the Russian Soviet Government desires to remove any false interpretation of its actions. On the other hand, in view of the fact that the foreign press systematically reports its actions in a false light, the Russian Soviet Government takes advantage of this opportunity to express its attitude with the utmost clearness and frankness.

In spite of the fact that both the military and internal conditions of Soviet Russia are constantly improving, the Soviet Government is so anxious to secure an agreement that would put an end to hostilities, *that it is ready to enter at once into negotiations to this end, and, as it has more than once declared, is even willing in order to obtain such an agreement to make serious concessions, provided they will not menace the future development of Soviet Russia.* (Our italics).

The Russian Soviet Government requests the Entente Powers to make known to it without delay the place to which it should send its representatives, as well as the time and the route."

The Governments of Estonia, Latvia and Lithuania also agreed to participate in the proposed Prinkipo Conference. On the other hand, the three Russian "White" Governments, on January 24, 1919, refused the invitation and issued the following statement:

"The three organised Governments of Russia—namely, Omsk, Ekaterinodar, and Archangel—the only lawful groups making for national renovation, refuse to associate with Bolshevism. They will not send delegates to the Princes' Islands."

Did the *Times* denounce these "White" Governments as "enemies of the human race?" Not a bit of it. On the following day it just commented sadly:

"The invitation of the Paris Conference to the scattered members of the Russian Empire has not been well received by those whom it was intended to benefit."

As a result of the intransigence of the "Whites," the projected Prinkipo Conference was not held and civil war and foreign armed intervention continued in Soviet Russia, with all its dire results.

Between the period just mentioned and the date of Mr. Lloyd George's speech of November 8, 1919, with which our first Chapter opens, the Allied Governments not only ignored all the offers* made by the Soviet Government to conclude peace, but they continued to pour munitions, supplies, etc., into Russia through Archangel, the Baltic ports, the Black Sea ports and Vladivostok, to support the counter-revolutionary armies and their own forces. In every way they directed and aided the "White" forces.

* See Chapter 1, p. 5.

During the same period—as dealt with at length in Chapter VI—a vigorous agitation was conducted in Great Britain against the policy of armed intervention in Russia and aid to the Tsarist Generals, and in favour of making peace with the Soviet Government. Although this agitation did not attain all its aims in the period mentioned, it undoubtedly had a considerable effect on the Government's policy, with the result that the last British troops sailed for home from Murmansk and Vladivostok on October 12 and November 1, 1919, respectively.

However, on November 8, 1919, the date of Mr. Lloyd George's speech, there was still a British Military Mission with the counter-revolutionary forces in Southern Russia and the latter, as well as all the anti-Soviet forces in the States on Russia's Western frontier, from Murmansk to Constantinople and in Northern Russia and Siberia, continued to receive enormous quantities of munitions and supplies. The counter-revolutionary forces were under the command of General Denikin in Southern Russia, under the command of General Miller in Northern Russia* and under the command of Admiral Koltchak in Siberia. Japanese troops were in occupation of Vladivostok, and Soviet Russia was subjected to a water-tight blockade on her Eastern and Western frontiers. The Allied Governments, in everything but name, were still in a state of war with Soviet Russia.

About that time a bewildered official at the War Office, part of whose duties was to meet press representatives, was asked one day by a journalist if we were at war with Soviet Russia. The official was nonplussed and took refuge in evasion. He immediately sent a Memorandum to his chief asking if Great Britain was in a state of war with Soviet Russia. He received a written reply stating: "Of course we are at war with Soviet Russia, but as far as the press and public are concerned we are not." That, in broad outline, was the state of affairs in the first week of November, 1919.

Finally, we would draw attention to the fact that so much happened during the period under review in the present book that it would have been far easier to have filled several volumes than to condense the material, as we have had to do, into a single volume. Our method throughout has been to explain the course of events as we saw and understood them, and partly to summarise and partly to quote verbatim from public declarations and official and other documents. Where we have quoted verbatim, nothing has been torn from its context, in summarising we have endeavoured to be scrupulously fair.

There is another point to which we desire to draw attention. In Chapter VI, we deal at some length with the "Hands Off Russia"

* Very soon after the withdrawal of British forces from Northern Russia, the Whites" were decisively defeated, and the entire area passed into Soviet hands.

agitation and the part played in that agitation by the "Hands Off Russia" Committee, but we have not dealt with a number of other organisations whose activities at a later date were also directly concerned with fostering better relations between Britain and Soviet Russia. We have in mind such bodies as the Anglo-Russian Parliamentary Committee (into which the "Hands Off Russia" Committee was transformed in 1924), the Society for Cultural Relations, the Friends of Soviet Russia and the Russia To-Day Society. All these, by the organisation of meetings, the publication of periodicals, books and pamphlets and the organisation of visits to the U.S.S.R. undoubtedly contributed much to the spread of knowledge and understanding of the Soviet Union in Britain, but we considered that a detailed study of their activities was outside the scope of the present book. A number of other organisations have also sprung up since the German attack on the U.S.S.R. on June 22, 1941.

For a quarter of a century we have laboured to explain Soviet Russia to the people of this country, to improve relations between the two Governments and to establish Anglo-Soviet friendship on a solid and durable foundation.

In the hope that this volume will contribute to these aims and will help to prevent a repetition of past blunders, it is presented to the British public.

We take this opportunity to express our thanks to Miss D. Torr and Mrs. D. Poulton for the care with which they read our manuscript and for their very valuable suggestions.

CHAPTER I

THE FIRST BRITISH APPROACH TO SOVIET RUSSIA (1919-1920)

I. November 8, 1919, to March, 1920

Mr. Lloyd George's now historic " Guildhall Speech " of November 8, 1919, marked a turning point in the policy of the Coalition Government *vis-à-vis* Soviet Russia and the beginning of a new tendency which finally resulted in the establishment of trading and diplomatic relations between the oldest capitalist country on the planet and the world's first Socialist Republic.

That speech created a sensation in Great Britain, and important repercussions abroad, and its echoes rumbled over the immense Russian plains from the Baltic to the Yellow Sea, from the Arctic to the borders of Afghanistan.

This was not surprising, because it meant, if not a complete reversal, at least an important change of policy, particularly in view of the fact that just three days earlier the House of Commons had voted an additional £15,000,000 to aid the Tsarist Generals then waging war against the Soviet Government.

The speech made in support of this vote on behalf of the Government by Mr. Winston Churchill (then Secretary of State for War) was uncompromising in character and left the impression on his listeners that the British Government was convinced that the " Whites " would finally be successful, and that Whitehall would support them as long as help was required.

> " Certainly," he stated, " I dispute the title of the Bolsheviks to represent Russia. Indeed I think they would be the first to repudiate any claim to represent Russia. Their views are far greater than the representation of a single country. Their position, if it means anything, is an international position. It may be good or it may be bad, but it has no connection with the Russian State or with the Russian nation which was our ally when the War commenced. Therefore I cannot believe that the title deeds of national Russia will ever rest durably or recognisedly in those hands."*

With sweeping gestures and magnificent largesse, Mr. Churchill declaimed: " The Government had never attempted to argue the matter on the basis of profit and loss, but of right and duty."

Small wonder then that many gasped—some with dismay and others with delight, but all with surprise—when Mr. Lloyd George, after having informed the Lord Mayor and his guests that Great Britain

* *Hansard*, 5.xi.19. col. 1629.

had " sent one hundred million's worth of material and of support in every form " to the counter-revolutionary Generals, added:

> " We cannot, of course, afford to continue so costly an intervention in an interminable civil war.
>
> Our troops are out of Russia. Frankly I am glad. Russia is a quicksand. Victories are easily won in Russia, but you sink in victories, and great armies and great Empires in the past have been overwhelmed in the sands of barren victories.
>
> Russia is a dangerous land to intervene in. We discovered it in the Crimea. But true to the instinct which has always saved us, we never went far from the sea, and we were able to extricate ourselves from there.
>
> But I am hopeful that when the winter gives time for all sections there to reflect and to reconsider the situation, an opportunity may offer itself for the Great Powers of the world to promote peace and concord in that great country."

The Tory papers, although the nominal supporters of the Government, almost without exception furiously denounced the *volte-face.* The *Times* was so indignant that it published a full two-column leader, November 10, 1919, attacking the Prime Minister's declaration. That stately journal had apparently convinced itself, or at least it tried to convince its readers, that if Britain ceased to aid the Russian " Whites " they would turn to Germany, that the " German grip " would be " established upon Russia, Siberia and other regions of Asia," and that the League of Nations would be " turned to the fabric of a dream powerless to act upon so vast a political, military and economic agglomeration."

On the other hand, the opposition press, the Liberal and Labour journals, enthusiastically hailed the new policy as a belated return to sanity.

The Joint Council of the Trades Union Congress and Labour Party at once passed the following resolution:

> " That, having regard to the declarations made by the Trades Union Congress and the Labour Party Conference on the subject, the joint meeting of the Parliamentary Committee and the Labour Party Executive welcomes the Prime Minister's statement at the Guildhall, indicating that the British Government would immediately bring to an end the support now being given to the warfare carried on in different parts of Russia, and seek the means of bringing about peace in that country ; and the joint meeting urges that steps should at once be taken to withdraw all British forces, whether naval, military, or air force, from any warlike

enterprises in or about the territories formerly included in the Russian Empire; and to stop all further supplies of stores, munitions or tanks."

As can be imagined, the subject was immediately raised in the House of Commons. The Prime Minister, on November 13, 1919, to the accompaniment of cheers and laughter, began his reply to a series of questions thus: "With the permission of the House I will answer together questions 47, 52, 54, 56, 60, 63, 64, 66, 70, 72, 73, 74, 75, 76."

This was probably a record in parliamentary history: fourteen questions on the same subject on one day and all answered together. Mr. Lloyd George continued:

"As has been explained, between the date of the Armistice and the end of October, in cash and in kind, the value of nearly £100,000,000 has been spent or sanctioned by the United Kingdom on account of assistance sent to Russia. A substantial part of this sum has been or will be added to the permanent indebtedness of this country. The Government has repeatedly made it clear to the House of Commons that, with the crushing financial burden already cast upon it by the Great War, it cannot contemplate the assumption of new obligations under this head. As the Chancellor of the Exchequer explained in the White Paper and in his speech, there is no provision made for such additional expenditure on Russia. If an addition is to be made to the national obligations under this head it will be the responsibility of the House of Commons to determine the additional taxation that shall be imposed for the purpose.

On the other hand, the Government have an overwhelming sense of the importance of bringing peace to Russia. Not only is Russia a source of unrest and disturbance to all its neighbours, with all the infinite possibilities for mischief which lurk in such a condition over so vast an area, but a settlement of the Russian problem is essential to the reconstruction of the world.

It is proposed to hold, I hope at an early date, an international conference at which Ministers of the Allied and Associated Powers will consider the various grave and outstanding problems which the Peace Conference has so far been unable to settle for one reason or another. Russia will be amongst these problems.

The House, of course, may rest assured that the Government will inaugurate no new policy and commit the country to no fresh action without giving the House the fullest opportunity of discussing it."*

* *Times*, 14.xi.19.

The fact was that the course which Mr. Lloyd George was here enunciating was the beginning of a fundamentally new policy.

Next day the *Times* editorially complained: " The Prime Minister did little yesterday to allay the anxiety aroused by his Guildhall speech." However, the " House " was informed that the subject could be raised " on the motion for the adjournment " four days later. The challenge was accepted and the Prime Minister ostensibly in answer to the Opposition, but really in reply to his own supporters, declared:

> " Looking at the state of the world as depicted by my noble friend,* the unrest in all lands, the questions which are unsettled in all lands, the fact that Britain is one of the Powers which has got the obligation to see that the conditions are established which have been laid down in the Peace Treaty—will anyone advise, will any wise man advise, will any man, a wise man whatever his courage may be, recommend this land to undertake the terrible responsibility of restoring order in a country which is a continent, which is part of two continents, which no country has ever intervened in without landing itself in disaster ? (Cheers). All I can say is I can take no responsibility."†

Next day, the *Daily News* accurately commented:

> " Amid dead silence on the Government benches the Prime Minister announced at the close of his speech in the House of Commons last night that he would no longer take the responsibility of restoring order in a country which was a continent, and financing civil war indefinitely. Our own burdens were too great. His announcement was received with Liberal and Labour cheers."‡

It was a bitter pill for many of the Government supporters, but they swallowed it. Although they made wry faces there was no attempt at this time to depose the Prime Minister. However, the British Government did not, by a long way, immediately abandon their old policy.

The blockade was not raised and in accordance with the decision of the House of Commons, November 5, 1919, military supplies continued to be shipped to the " White " Generals. As can be imagined, Moscow did not delay in expressing its opinion. M. Chicherin (Commissar for Foreign Affairs) in an interview, declared:

> " The impression created among the masses of the Russian people by Mr. Lloyd George's peaceful speeches is such as will enable the establishment of a good understanding between both countries, which our Government warmly desires. . . .

* Lord Robert Cecil. † *Times*, 18.xi.19.

‡ *Daily News*, 18.xi.19.

We have the régime which we find best for ourselves. The British customer and the British purveyor are as necessary to us as we to them. We want peace and the possibility of building up unhindered our internal life, but we also feel the necessity for economic help from more developed and advanced countries like Great Britain, and we are ready to make sacrifices for the sake of close economic connection with Great Britain.

We know that in the long run we will gain more than we shall lose from this economic connection. Great Britain also will gain more than she will lose.

Consequently we welcome the last speeches of Mr. Lloyd George as the first step towards a sane policy answering to the real interests of both countries."*

The scene next moved from London and Moscow to Copenhagen, where the late Sir James O'Grady (then Capt. James O'Grady, M.P.), on behalf of Great Britain, had been negotiating since November 25, 1919, with the then Vice-Commissar for Foreign Affairs, M. Litvinov, for a mutual exchange of British and Russian prisoners of war.

M. Litvinov, on December 10, 1919, sent a copy of a resolution† passed by the Seventh Congress of the Soviets to the Allied Legations in Copenhagen, together with a covering letter stating on behalf of his Government that these constituted a formal offer of peace, and that he was empowered to enter into negotiations respecting all preliminary questions and regarding the date and place of a peace conference. In addition, M. Litvinov made the following declaration to Reuters:

* *Daily Herald*, 1.xii.19.

† This Resolution, adopted December 5, 1919, was as follows:

The Russian Socialist Federative Republic of Soviets desires to live at peace with all peoples, and to devote all its strength to internal constructive work, in order to perfect the production, transport, and public administration on the basis of a Soviet régime, to the work which has hitherto been hindered by the pressure of German imperialism and subsequently by the Entente intervention and the starvation blockade.

The Government of Workers and Peasants has many times proposed peace to the Entente Powers, notably on August 5, 1918, by means of a letter from the People's Commissariat for Foreign Affairs to the American Consul, Mr. Poole; on October 24 by a note to President Wilson; on November 3 to all the Entente Governments, by the intermediary of representatives of neutral countries; on November 7 in the name of the Sixth Congress of Soviets; on December 23 by a circular note addressed by Citizen Litvinov to the Entente representatives in Sweden, and subsequently by wireless messages on January 12 and 17, 1919; by a note to the Entente Governments on February 24; by a draft agreement drawn up on March 12 with Mr. Bullitt, President Wilson's delegate; and by a declaration made on May 7 by the intermediary of Mr. Nansen.

Completely approving these repeated steps, which have been taken by the Central Executive Committee, by the Council of People's Commissars, and by the People's Commissariat for Foreign Affairs, the Seventh Congress of Soviets once again confirms its unchanging desire for peace by proposing once more to all the Entente Powers —to Great Britain, France, the United States of America, Italy, and Japan, to all together and to each separately—immediately to commence peace negotiations, and charges the Executive Committee, the Council of People's Commissars and the People's Commissariat for Foreign Affairs systematically to continue this peace policy, taking all necessary measures for its success.

"Some Allied statesmen have recently intimated that they had received no formal offer from the Soviet Government, although, as has been shown by this Resolution, offers have been made repeatedly. The messages sent by the Soviet Government by wireless, which is their only remaining means of communication with the outer world, are evidently not regarded as sufficient."

In passing it may be noted that this was the ninth peace offer made to the Allied Governments by the Soviet Government since the latter came into power on November 7, 1917. What followed ? M. Litvinov thus explained on the evening of December 10, 1919, to a press representative:

"The British, French and Italian Legations have chosen to return the documents to me, with the remark that they are not authorised to accept communications from the Soviet Government. Should the Allied Governments refuse to receive this formal offer of negotiations, it will reveal the hypocrisy of the complaint that they have never received such offers. How can they receive them if they deliberately refuse to receive them ? "

Asked in the House of Commons, December 15, 1919, to explain this extraordinary procedure, the Under-Secretary of State for Foreign Affairs, Mr. Cecil Harmsworth, replied that as His Majesty's representative at Copenhagen "is not authorised to receive any communication from this source, it was returned unopened."

Commander Kenworthy, M.P. (now Lord Strabolgi), aware that a fortnight earlier the Prime Minister, Mr. Lloyd George, had emphatically declared that no official proposals of any kind had reached the British Government from Moscow, very naturally asked in the House of Commons: "How then is the Soviet Government to approach us with a peace offer ? " but his question remained unanswered.

Later in the day, in reply to further questions, the Prime Minister declared: "If the Bolshevists want to make peace, they must make peace with the people with whom they are making war—the forces of General Denikin and Admiral Koltchak. They have got to make peace among themselves first."*

In the meantime, Mr. Lloyd George was striving hard to bring together the Allied Conference, referred to in his Parliamentary answer of November 13, 1919, for the purpose of discussing the establishment of trade relations between Soviet Russia and the Allied countries.

On the other hand, the opponents of the Government's new policy, because despite all denials such it was, were also busy trying to frighten

* *Daily News*, 16.xii.19.

the country with the apparition of an aggressive and imperialist League, consisting of Soviet Russia, Germany and Turkey, which would rob the Allied Governments of the fruits of victory, endanger the British Empire in Asia, and even create a co-relation of opposing groups of Powers more dangerous to Western civilisation than that which existed on the eve of the world war in July, 1914.

Mr. (now Sir) Bernard Pares who at that time did not in the slightest comprehend the new Russia, warned the Government of the catastrophic consequences which would follow if Mr. Lloyd George succeeded in his new policy.

In a letter dated December 11, 1919, in the *Times,* Mr. Pares declared that if all Britishers were withdrawn from Russia:

> " The Germans will be there and will have the right to be there. But any policy which surrenders Russia to a German monoply, which gives to Germany the Russian raw resources and the Russian man-power, courts a war in which we stand less chance than in the war we have just won. It is equally certain that in ten or 15 years' time the task will have become 50 times harder, and that later we shall have no more chance of refusing it than Belgium had in 1914."

The late Colonel John Ward, M.P., freshly back from Siberia, where he had served under Koltchak as Commanding Officer of the Hampshire Regiment, tried hard to influence a Trades Union Congress held in London on December 10, 1919. He devoted his remarks mainly to what had happened in European Russia, but his statements were so much at variance with the notorious facts that he left the platform discomfited, to the accompaniment of derisive laughter and jeers.

General Sir Charles Briggs, who had been at the head of the British Military Mission in South Russia, returned to England and immediately gave an interview (December 23, 1919) to Reuters in which he stated:

> " There is not the least reason for pessimism as regards Denikin's position. This is the last dying kick of the Bolshevists, as is evident from their repeated attempts at peace. The fact is that anti-Bolshevist movements and risings of all sorts are taking place behind the Bolshevist fronts, and their position is very difficult indeed. The highest military strategists on Denikin's staff believe that the Bolshevists will be driven out of Moscow not later than May, and conditions in Soviet Russia are such as to make this quite possible."

Major General Cherep Spiridovitch, in the *Financial News,* December 31, 1919, stated:

"Scores of English leaders have foretold bankruptcy or revolution or disaster. This has produced a slackness, exploited by the Unseen Hand, designed to alienate the Russians from England, to isolate her, and to thrust Russia into German embraces, to start revolution here and in the Dominions, thus permitting Hindenburg at once to cross the Rhine and crush the Allies, as unexpectedly as promptly."

At this time a number of anti-Soviet Britishers and Russian "Whites" had what they probably thought at the time was a brilliant brain wave. They brought to this country four anti-Soviet Russian "Trade Unionists" to explain to Organised Labour in Great Britain the Koltchak point of view. These "Trade-Unionists" were interviewed by prominent members of the political and industrial sections of the British Labour Movement, but the Russians failed to impress, much less to convince, their listeners. The late Mr. R. C. Wallhead, M.P., after an interview with them, remarked to the writers: "They told us the tallest tale that I have ever yet listened to."

The reception accorded to these four propagandists was very disappointing to their backers. Mr. Bernard Pares regretfully related: "Even the General Federation of Trade Unions, in spite of the good offices of William Appleton and John Ward, was hardly willing to listen to them; there was a campaign against them all over the country, their platforms were rushed and the lights extinguished, and the only helpers that they found were just those whom they did not want, the champions of extreme English Conservatism."*

Mr. Winston Churchill, then Minister for War, and the Conservative press, headed by the *Times* jointly constituted a large part of the opposition to the policy of reconciliation with Soviet Russia. This soldier-politician, speaking at a Coalition meeting at Sunderland, January 3, 1920, said:

"No one could tell what would emerge from the immense, horrible catastrophe of Russia, except that it would probably be something very menacing to civilisation and very dangerous to the peace of Europe and Asia. The Allies might abandon Russia; Russia would not abandon them. The ghost of the Russian bear now sat outside the Peace Conference in silent reproach; now it ranged over the enormous countries leading up to the frontiers of India, disturbing Afghanistan, disturbing Persia, creating far to the southward great agitation and unrest among the hundreds of millions of our Indian population.

Then there was Turkey. A junction of Russian Bolshevism and Turkish Mohammedanism would be full of danger to many States

* *My Russian Memoirs*, by Bernard Pares, 1931, pp. 565/6.

—to none more than to the British Empire, the greatest of Mohammedan States. The armies of Koltchak were almost gone; the armies of Denikin were in serious danger. Were they to disappear—they might—a series of evil consequences, incalculable in their scope, would immediately be set in motion, and by those consequences we of all the countries in the world would be most affected.

"It is even possible," Mr. Churchill added, "according to the information I have received from the numerous officers we have in Germany under the War Office, that there may be some combination between these Kaiser-militarists and Bolsheviks in order to destroy the struggling German Republic. The replacing of the present German Government either by militarist reaction or by Bolshevik anarchy would be contrary both to British and to French interests. It would be a great disaster to the whole world. Either or both would join forces in some way with Russian Bolshevism."*

To-day all this sounds like the ravings of men in the grip of nightmares, but at that date the *Times* accepted them as serious warnings to the nation, commented very favourably on Mr. Churchill's oration and continued:

"People may sneer at Denikin and Koltchak in their defeats, but it is a fact that by their struggles they have helped to keep the peace on the borders of Russia, in Europe, towards Turkey and India, and towards China, and so have supplied the platform from which the doctrine of non-intervention has been preached. If there had been no civil war in Russia we might have had war for interests recognised as unquestionably British. Supposing the Russian loyalists give up the struggle, what will the likeliest sequel be? Not, surely, that Bolshevist Russia will wallow contentedly in the mess until it dies of its own putridity. To suppose that is to misunderstand the whole spirit of the Bolshevist movement. The more it decays at the centre, the more determined will be its pressure outwards. It might decide that China was the best field for its energies. It might seek fresh air, away from its own miasma, towards Constantinople and the Straits or in the highlands of the Asiatic steppes. Or, if Germany were favourably disposed, Poland might be more attractive. What should we do in that case? We could not abandon Poland, nor Armenia and the approaches to India, nor China. We should be brought up against the same problem that we have shirked in the Russian civil war, and this time we could not shirk it. Our lip attachment to peace would

* *Manchester Guardian*, 5.i.20

> have brought us into another war, only in far more inaccessible regions than this war, and our doctrine of indifference to Russian affairs would force us to intervene amid every circumstance of disadvantage and inconvenience to ourselves."*

If the contribution of Mr. Churchill sounded like the ravings of a man in the grip of a nightmare, that of the *Times* resembled the wanderings of a man suffering from delirium tremens.

The result of this agitation was to slow down but not to divert the movement for the re-establishment of trade between Western Europe—particularly Great Britain—and the Soviets.

A close friend of Mr. Lloyd George's remarked to the writers that that gentleman listened to or read what the "Whites," and their British sympathisers, had to say, but despite their advice and admonitions he mapped out his own course and followed it. The probabilities, in fact the certainties are, that the then Prime Minister had made a more correct appraisal of the governing classes of pre-war Europe, and was able to visualise what was happening in Russia more accurately than the "White" Russians and the British "experts."

Mr. J. L. Garvin, editor of the *Observer,* who for a long time had been an ardent protagonist of armed intervention in Russia, now realised that this country had been backing a foredoomed loser, and put his money on the new policy. He declared:

> "The Bolshevists will soon be in effective possession of four-fifths of the former Russian Empire, including the vast bulk of all its agricultural and mineral resources.
>
> We must desire peace with the Bolshevists if possible as with all the world."

This was an important and portentious break in the serried ranks of the Conservative press *vis-à-vis* the Soviet Union.

Meantime, the military position of the counter-revolutionary forces had considerably worsened: by the end of December, 1919, Denikin's army had been cut in two and the Red Army was approaching the Crimea, whilst in Siberia the Czechs had surrendered Koltchak to the Social Revolutionaries on January 15, 1920.

However, there were still powerful forces, it would appear, even within the Government Machinery of Whitehall, which were striving hard to prevent the opening of negotiations with the Soviets.

The Allied Statesmen were sitting in Paris. It was known that the question of Russia was under discussion. Suddenly, on January 15, 1920, the British War Office issued the following semi-official statement to the press:

***Times*, 5.i.20.

"As a result of the Bolshevist occupation of Trans-Caspia, which may now be regarded as practically complete, the situation in the Caucasus has become one of considerable difficulty. Georgia and Azerbaijan are anti-Bolshevist, both as regards their Government and the population, but their armed strength is insufficient to resist invasion, which now threatens them both from the north, where Denikin's right wing is being pressed back, and from the east across the Caspian.

There is a large Bolshevist element at Baku, and a Red landing at that town would probably recruit this element into their ranks immediately on arrival. Daghestan (Northern Caucasia) is even more helpless and could quickly be compelled to throw in its lot with the Reds. A number of Turks, too, are penetrating into the Caucasus from the south, with the object of fomenting trouble.

According to reports received, the Bolshevists continue to pour troops into Trans-Caspia via the Tashkent railway and Askhabad. Mounted troops have already arrived at the latter place in considerable strength. The new arrivals are largely led by old army officers now in the Bolshevist service.

As a result of the large captures of oil fuel from the Volunteers and the occupation of the Kizil Arbat area with its rich oil wells, the railway service is improving. Transport from Tashkent to Askhabad takes only six days and troop trains are coming through at the rate of one a day. The food situation in Turkestan is also improving, thanks to the Bolshevist occupation of Semiretchia (on the Mongolian border).

The Bolshevists are recruiting their forces from the prisoners of war in Turkestan. There are 37,000 of these, mostly Hungarians, and all active Communists. Among the new arrivals at Askhabad are a number of large armoured cars. To the north of the railway the Bolshevists have sent detachments towards Khiva, probably with the object of rounding up the scattered forces of the Siberian Army and the Ural Cossacks driven east and south from Gurieff (on the northern shore of the Caspian).

A party of Bolshevists and Turks are said to have arrived at Herat with two carts containing aeroplane parts, petrol and a wireless set, and have now gone on via Kandahar and Kabul, escorted by Afghan cavalry.

The Bolshevists have opened a large number of propaganda schools in Tashkent, where Oriental languages are to be taught and from which agents will be sent to India, China and all Moslem countries. The Tashkent Soviet, at a recent meeting, determined to concentrate efforts first on India, and it is intended to open propaganda centres there as soon as possible."*

The *Times* accompanied the publication of this statement with a map bearing the caption " Bolshevist Menace to Middle East," according to which the Red Army in Russian Turkestan was threatening Persia, Afghanistan and China.

It seemed at the moment as though this was the overture to a declaration of war particularly because the communiqué was followed by the ominous-sounding postcript:

" Mr. Churchill, Secretary for War ; Field-Marshal Sir Henry Wilson, Chief of the Imperial General Staff ; Mr. Walter Long, First Lord of the Admiralty ; and Earl Beatty, First Sea Lord, left London last evening for Paris to join the Prime Minister and the other British delegates there."

For the first time since the Armistice (November, 1918) there was almost unanimity in the British press and public opinion. Journals of different shades and politicians of various colours declaimed resoundingly against any further British military adventures in Russia. The anti-climax followed with lightening speed. Mr. Churchill and his colleagues duly reached Paris and on the very day of their arrival, instead of a declaration of war, the following decision by the Allied Supreme Council was issued:

> " With a view to remedying the unhappy situation of the population in the interior of Russia, which is now deprived of all manufactured products from outside Russia, the Supreme Council, after having taken note of the report of a committee appointed to consider the reopening of certain trading relations with the Russian people, has decided that it would permit the exchange of goods on the basis of reciprocity between the Russian people and the Allied and neutral countries.
>
> For this purpose it has decided to give facilities to the Russian co-operative organisations, which are in direct touch with the peasantry throughout Russia, so that they may arrange for the import into Russia of clothing, medicines, agricultural machinery, and the other necessaries of which the Russian people are in sore need, in exchange for grain, flax, etc., of which Russia has surplus supplies.
>
> These arrangements imply no change in policy of the Allied Governments towards the Soviet Government."

Naturally the enunciation of two contradictory policies in rapid succession created amazement both here and abroad. Mr. J. L. Garvin made some biting comments:

* *Times*, 16.i.20.

"When is there going to be an end of the intolerable rubbish of the official and semi-official communiqués which are given to the country on the subject of Bolshevism? The other day a statement was allowed to appear which made on ordinary minds an impression worthy of the most alarmist sensationalism of scare-mongering newspapers.

Fortunately we had not long to wait for the anti-climax to super-heated fantasies. For once the anti-climax came with a cold douche of commonsense from Paris. Instead of a new war against the Bolshevists—a war raging from Central Europe, across all the East to the Indian borderlands—it was announced in effect that the Allies, like Lord Grey of Fallodon in 1914—but we hope with better fortune—are at least willing to give every chance to the possibilities of such a Russian peace as is absolutely indispensable to the general peace. For certain specified but extensive purposes the blockade in the Baltic and the Black Sea is to be lifted. Commercial exchange is to be restored 'on the basis of reciprocity between the Russian people and Allied and neutral countries.'"*

Whitehall apparently was still of the opinion that visibility was not yet normal, and decided to disperse the remaining mists by issuing the following declaration on January 19, 1920:

"The particulars given last Thursday in the semi-official statement regarding the Bolsheviks and Central Asia were prepared merely as a matter of routine and had no connection with the movements of any Ministers on that day.

It is a pure coincidence that the Secretary of State for War, the First Lord of the Admiralty, and their advisers left the same night for Paris. Doubtless this gave point for special comment which would not otherwise have been made, for it is a curious fact that a statement on similar lines issued on the previous Thursday attracted little attention."

Next day the *Daily News* facetiously quoted the definition of a coincidence from *Brabb, English Synonyms,* thus: "Something so striking and singular that it can hardly be attributed to pure accident."

The Conservative press led by the *Times, Daily Telegraph* and *Morning Post* (although by now they realised that the country would not tolerate further British military adventures in Russia), vehemently attacked the decision of the Allied Supreme Council on the grounds that to trade with Russia through the Russian Co-operatives was to open commerce with the Soviets. Meanwhile, the British correspondents attached to the "White" Armies were cabling London that

* *Observer*, 18.i.20.

Mr. Lloyd George's change of front, coupled with the decision of the Allied Supreme Council, were having a demoralising effect on the morale—military and civilian—of the anti-Soviet forces and parties.

During all this time the volume of opposition to further military adventures in Russia by Britain was becoming more and more vociferous, particularly in the ranks of organised Labour, and on January 29, 1920, a manifesto appeared in the press warning the Government that " it may be possible for the powerful autocracy which at present in Paris manages the affairs of Europe to begin a new war, but since it would be necessarily a long war it will rest with the forces of Labour to see whether it shall be continued."

The Manifesto was signed by, among other prominent Labour Leaders, W. Brace, M.P. ; J. T. Brownlie ; J. R. Clynes, M.P. ; T. Shaw, M.P. ; J. H. Thomas, M.P. ; A. G. Walkden, etc. etc. This declaration signed by men " who do not subscribe to the theories of the Soviet Government " created a profound impression in Government circles where it was felt that the signatories were voicing the views of millions of workers.

The *Times* furiously denounced the manifesto as " a great infringement of the most fundamental of democratic principles," a criticism which was obviously absurd.

Meanwhile negotiations had been proceeding between the Baltic States and Soviet Russia and peace was signed between the latter and Estonia on February 2, 1920. Estonia is a small country but, nevertheless, the conclusion of this Treaty was recognised by political observers to be of portentous significance. Next day the *Manchester Guardian* editorially commented:

> " While Allied policy towards Russia stumbles uncertainly, Estonia and the Bolsheviks have made a definite peace, and this is a long step towards the general settlement. For one thing, when any one of the five Border States makes peace—Finland, Estonia, Latvia, Lithuania, or Poland—the position of the others is proportionately weakened and the pressure on them to make peace is proportionately increased.
>
> The French policy of a ' barbed-wire ring ' which was to follow the policy of Allied intervention is already dead. The promise to trade through the co-operators, if sincerely meant, struck it a severe wound, and the Estonian peace has given it the final blow. The Allies may continue, if they choose, to refuse to recognise the Bolsheviks, but they should do so with their eyes open to the truth that the Bolsheviks are bursting their bonds and that Russia is coming again into communication with the outer world."*

* *Manchester Guardian*, 3.ii.20.

This extract summed up fairly accurately the reactions of wide circles both here and abroad to the conclusion of the Peace of Dorpat. However, the French Government, although its representatives had been a party to the declaration of the Allied Supreme Council of January 16, 1920, was interpreting that decision in somewhat different terms from Great Britain. M. Millerand, the Premier, stated in the Chamber, February 6, 1920, " that the measures proposed did not entail the reopening of relations with the Soviets, and that the latter would not use the goods sent for equipping the Red Armies. If it were discovered that this was being done, the shipments would cease, and the responsibility would fall on the Soviet Government."*

The French Premier, who could not but have known that he was postulating impossible conditions, apparently was still hoping for the success of the Tsarist Generals. In the same speech he declared: " The three anti-Bolshevist armies had certainly suffered reverses, but there was no indication that these reverses were irreparable."

Whilst these events had been happening the House of Commons was in recess. It was re-opened by His Majesty King George V, on February 10, 1920, who, in the course of his speech from the Throne, stated:

> " In order, however, to assure the full blessings of peace and prosperity to Europe, it is essential that not only peace but normal conditions of economic life should be restored in Eastern Europe and in Russia. So long as these vast regions withhold their full contribution to the stock of commodities available for general consumption, the cost of living can hardly be reduced nor general prosperity restored to the world."

The Prime Minister, Mr. Lloyd George, in the course of his speech justifying the inclusion of this item in the Ministerial declaration pointed out that all efforts to overthrow the Soviet Government had failed, that foreign armed intervention on a bigger scale would rally the Russian people still more firmly behind the Soviets, that there was no danger of the Red Army attacking the neighbouring states, that the Allied Governments were not yet prepared to recognise the new régime, but that it was necessary in the interests of world commerce and prosperity to open up trade with Russia. He added:

> " Europe needs what Russia can give. I wonder whether hon. members have supplied themselves with the figures of what Russia gave to the rest of Europe before the war. If so, the House would realise how the withdrawal of Russia from the supplying markets is contributing to high prices, high cost of living, and to scarcity

* *Times*, 7.ii.20.

and hunger. Russia supplied before the war one-fourth of the whole export wheat of the world—4,000,000 tons. Four-fifths of the flax—it is almost incredible—grown in the world was produced in Russia. About one-third of the total supply of imported butter in Great Britain came directly or indirectly from Russian sources. The grain and flour of Russia of all kinds—maize, barley, oats, etc.—came to nearly 9,000,000 tons. The figures are prodigious in every direction. The world needs it."

The Prime Minister concluded with a solemn warning to the House of Commons and the country:

"The conditions in Europe are serious. Hon. members can see what use has been made of high prices. It has been used to stir up strife, suspicion, and jealousy of existing institutions throughout the land. The dangers are not in Russia, they are here at home. I speak with knowledge, with apprehension and with responsibility, and I warn the House, in the face of things that may happen, that we must take every legitimate weapon to contend against these things, and there is but one way—we must fight anarchy with abundance."*

The Government's decision and Mr. Lloyd George's speech were loudly applauded in the Labour and Liberal press, but the leading Conservative organs scarcely abated their hostility.

The *Times* editorially, without suggesting an alternative policy, commented:

"The House of Commons had to listen yesterday once again to the Prime Minister's Russian speech. Every time he repeats it, and he has repeated it very often, it brings him a little nearer to an avowal that Bolshevism has defeated the Allies and that there is nothing for them but a peace without honour."

The *Morning Post* also editorially declared:

"Last night the Prime Minister explained his Russian policy to a complaisant House of Commons. We say *his* policy because there are signs that he is directing the foreign policy of this country without regard to the advice either of the Foreign Office or of the War Office."

After putting forward the suggestion that Britain should equip Poland and make of her a bulwark against Soviet Russia, the article concluded:

* *Times*, 11.ii.20.

> "Sooner or later we shall have to fight for our lives against these hordes, who are not substantially different from the Huns and Tartars who terrorised Europe in the Middle Ages. It would therefore be wise policy and sound economy to make our first screen and line of defence as far east as possible, and the natural line is Poland."

It would seem that the *Morning Post* was correct in suggesting that the advice of the War Office had been disregarded by the Prime Minister, because a few days later the Minister for War, Mr. Winston Churchill, at a public meeting stated:

> "No one knows what is coming out of the Russian cauldron, but it will almost certainly be something full of evil, full of menace for Britain, France and the United States. It seems to me, therefore, that our dangers, particularly the dangers to France and Britain, have not been finally removed by the war, and that, after a few years, they may come back again in a new, but still in a grave, form. In order to prevent this we ought to try to make a real and lasting peace with the German people and the German Republic. We ought to help and protect the sound elements in Turkish national life. We ought to help Central Europe, particularly Poland, so far as this lies in our power, to recover from the shock of the war."*

Whether Mr. Churchill and those responsible for the editorial policies of the *Times, Morning Post,* etc., honestly believed at that time in the potential dangers with which they were trying to stampede the Government and the country, we cannot say. Perhaps they would plead propagandist licence! Their aims, however, were clear: no relations of any kind with the Soviet Government. At any rate, Mr. Lloyd George knew that these highly imaginative "dangers" had as much substance as a Christmas ghost and he continued to pursue his own policy.

On the day on which the Prime Minister made his House of Commons' speech the news blockade of Soviet Russia was broken. A wireless message from Mr. George Lansbury from Moscow appeared in the columns of the *Daily Herald*. To quote that journal: "The dispatch . . . is the first direct wireless press message which has reached England from that country during the Soviet régime."

Mr. Lansbury, after giving a balanced account of what he had seen, viz., want, privation, order, determination, calm confidence, continued:

> "I earnestly beseech the Government, especially Mr. Lloyd George, to go forward in the big English manner and give the

* *Times*, 16.ii.20.

hand of comradeship to this great people, struggling to its feet after years of pain and loss. Also I urge Henderson, Smillie, Thomas, Williams, MacDonald and Snowden all to unite and, with the authorities, bring about the reconciliation of both nations.

Atrocity-mongering is played out here and in Petrograd. I am as free and safe alone in the streets as in London; indeed more so. True religion is untouched; true marriage is as sacred as ever. The churches are being restored at the public expense. There is nothing here worse than in other capitals; there is much, very much, that is better."*

As can be imagined this message was much discussed at the time and gave an added fillip to the agitation in favour of peace with the Soviet Power.

On February 11, 1920, at Copenhagen, an agreement was concluded between Mr. James O'Grady, M.P. (on behalf of Great Britain) and M. Maxim Litvinov (on behalf of Soviet Russia) for the mutual exchange of British and Russian prisoners of war. The signature of this agreement removed a poisoning irritant and still further improved the atmosphere in Great Britain, *vis-à-vis* Soviet Russia.

M. Maxim Litvinov had been commissioned by his Government to act on their behalf in connection with the decision of the Allied Governments to open trade with the Soviets through the Russian co-operatives. Difficulties at once arose. The co-operators within the frontiers of Soviet Russia were partisans of the Soviet Power, whereas the Russian co-operators living abroad at this time were in the main sympathetic to the defunct Provisional Government. However, after somewhat protracted negotiations it was reported from Copenhagen on February 22, 1920, that a number of these Russian co-operators, in agreement with M. Maxim Litvinov, had left for Moscow to discuss there ways and means of reopening trade between Soviet Russia and the Allied countries.

Support for the policy of peace and trade with the Soviet Government next came from a somewhat unexpected and certainly unusual quarter. The following memorial (it is so important that we quote it in full) appeared in the press, February 23, 1920:

"The signatories do not consider that the crimes committed by the Russian Government in the past should be regarded as a bar to its recognition now. They do not believe that the non-Bolshevist Governments of Siberia and the South have shown themselves superior to their enemies in humanity, while in energy, union and resource they have shown themselves inferior. If the Western Powers are influenced by fear of revolutionary

* *Daily Herald*, 11.ii.20.

propaganda and of the precedent set for direct action by the success of the Soviet Government, the signatories would suggest that no protective measure would be so effectual as the reopening of Russia to commerce, intercourse and observation. The forces of moderation in Russia would be consolidated, the fundamental differences of character, education and economic structure between Russia and Europe would be displayed, and the misery to which the great territories have been reduced would, if once disclosed, be the most impressive of warnings against precipitate and violent social changes.

It is becoming clearer every day that the stability of Europe depends mainly on the Central European States being adequately provisioned during the coming year, and it is impossible to see from what source they can be provisioned except from Russia. As the Russian grain moves westward, the danger of famine and its consequences will disappear.

But without a general peace the resources of Russia cannot be made available. Without the co-operation of the Russian Government and a large concentration of foreign capital there can be no movement of produce on a scale at all proportioned to the need of Europe.

In particular the co-operative project neither relieves the pre-war bondholders nor gives them any inducement to assist in the restoration of Russia. Yet it is believed that the Russian Government is ready, when once relations are resumed, to consider their claims, and it is evident that no class of the community can have a stronger interest in reviving Russian production.

If the Russian supplies are not made available and there is in consequence famine in any region east of the Rhine, there will certainly be disorder, and probably outbreaks of the kind which marked the earlier phases of Bolshevism in Russia.

The longer peace is delayed the more certain it becomes that the German influence will be re-established in Russia, and that Russian policy, both economical and diplomatic, will in consequence take on a character of antagonism to this country. At a time when we shall be at once searching for new markets and leading India and the Middle East through a most difficult period of transition, we cannot afford to see a rival installed in a privileged position and working to make every point of contact between England and Russia a point of friction as well. Once started, they might spread beyond the area of their origin. That the Russian Government, if still at war with the world, would overlook so fair an opportunity of extending its principles is hardly to be supposed. Its natural policy would be to intervene on the side of the revolution everywhere ; with a victorious and seasoned army at its command it could intervene effectively, bringing food as it advances.

In face of the alternatives, we believe that peace with Russia is necessary, both on economic and on political grounds, to save the continent of Europe from catastrophe. But if peace is to come at all, it must come soon, before famine has made itself felt ; and if it is to come soon it must come from England. Being as a nation less exposed than the Continental Powers to a revolutionary infection, we can think with less passion ; having an equal concern with them in the welfare of Europe and a special concern in the peace of Asia, we speak with more authority."

The signatories were:

"Lieutenant-Colonel Sir Hubert Gough, Chief of the British Military Mission, North-West Russia ; Colonel F. G. Marsh, British Military Agent, Caucasus, 1915-17, commanded brigade on the Murmansk front and was Chief of Staff to General Gough ; J. Spencer-Smith, late lieutenant-colonel, Murmansk Force ; F. Lambert, late British Supply Controller and Political Officer in Murmansk ; E. M. Harvey, late Financial Adviser to North Russian Government and to the High Commissioner of the Rhine ; D. Spring Rice, late Financial Adviser to the British Mission, Russia ; and G. M. Young, late Financial Adviser to the North Russian Government."

All the memorialists had at various times within the preceding two years been "engaged in official duties in Russia." This memorial—widely quoted in the press—created a sensation and produced a profound effect on the country. Well it might! It is questionable whether the archives of the British Foreign Office contain a similar document.

The memorial was bitterly attacked by men like the late Mr. Aylmer Maude and their "White" Russian protégés who argued that the "Denikin-Koltchak" group and not the Soviets were supported by the Russian people ; to which Sir Hubert Gough replied by pointing out:

"A further indication of popular opinion in Russia is provided by a circumstance which readers of Mr. Churchill's military communiqués must have noticed. I refer to the fact that when the White generals seemed to be most successful and were in possession of vast tracts of Russian territory (thereby as it was said, freeing the people from Bolshevist tyranny) popular risings constantly took place in their rear, causing hasty retirements which,

> so far as I could see, were not justified by the purely military situation."*

The fact was that the memorialists knew what they were talking about and subsequent developments have proved conclusively that they had an accurate grasp of the then existing realities. On February 24, the day following the publication of the memorial, the Supreme Allied Council, meeting in London, reached the following conclusions:

> " If the communities which border on the frontiers of Soviet Russia and whose independence or *de facto* autonomy they have recognised were to approach them and to ask for advice as to what attitude they should take with regard to Soviet Russia, the Allied Governments would reply that they cannot accept the responsibility of advising them to continue a war which may be injurious to their own interest.
>
> Still less would they advise them to adopt a policy of aggression towards Russia. If, however, Soviet Russia attacks them inside their legitimate frontiers, the Allies will give them every possible support.
>
> The Allies cannot enter into diplomatic relations with the Soviet Government, in view of their past experiences until they have arrived at the conviction that Bolshevist horrors have come to an end and that the Government of Moscow is ready to conform its methods and diplomatic conduct to those of all civilised Governments.
>
> Commerce between Russia and the rest of Europe, which is so essential for the improvement of the economic conditions, not only in Russia, but in the rest of the world, will be encouraged to the utmost degree possible without relaxation of the attitude described above."

The reactions in the French and British press were mixed, but there was a greater volume of opposition to the new policy in France than in Britain. On the following day the Paris correspondent of the *Times* cabled:

> " France, it is observed, was more reluctant than the other Allies to enter into relations of any sort or kind with the Bolshevist Government at Moscow. She could not, however, afford to find herself left out in the cold, and therefore, albeit with grave reluctance, is compelled to acquiesce in the extraordinary formula arrived at in London. With his usual logic and precision of thought the Frenchman refuses to be deceived by camouflage of the existence of which he is only too well aware. Thus one finds

* *Times*, 5.iii.20.

the matter put very tersely and very expressively by the *Liberté*, which declares that the Entente's authorisation of relations other than official diplomatic relations with Soviet Russia is just like the attitude of France with regard to the Vatican."

On one point the British press was unanimous: the decision was a big step in a definite direction and meant more than the words at first seemed to imply.

For instance, the *Daily Chronicle* (then Mr. Lloyd George's organ in the press), commented editorially:

> "The memorandum on Russian policy, to which the Supreme Council agreed yesterday, is a document of the highest importance. It embodies a bigger step forward than it appears to embody; for the Supreme Council is fond of masking its meaning under evasive expressions. Apparently its members cannot bring their minds into agreement in any other way."

The *Times* in a leader declared:

> "It is impossible not to admire the profligate art with which for over a year Mr. Lloyd George has sought for his own purposes to throw a weak, ignorant and reluctant Europe into the venal arms of her Bolshevist seducer.
>
> The next step is to compromise her beyond recall. Then the path will be opened for Lenin, and those who have contrived and toiled to bring them together will have accomplished their task."*

Within the frontiers of Russia, in the meantime, very much had happened. By the end of February, 1920, the whole of Siberia was in the hands of the Soviet Power and Denikin had been driven back to the Caucasus and the Crimea. Outside these two areas the "White" Power had been completely annihilated throughout Russia. It is not therefore surprising that although the *Times* and those who supported its attitude continued to oppose the policy of *rapprochement* with Soviet Russia they had no practical alternative to advance.

II. The first Trade Delegation appointed

Meanwhile the decisions of the Allied Supreme Council of January 16 and February 24 (1920) had been considered by Moscow. Two representatives of the Russian Co-operatives in Paris and London had visited the Soviet capital, explanations had been asked for as to how trade would be permitted and finally the Centrosoyus†

* *Times*, 25.ii.20.

† All-Russian Central Union of Consumers' Co-operatives.

in Moscow appointed the following as their empowered trade representatives—Leonid Borisovitch Krassin; Maxim Maximovitch Litvinov; Victor Pavlovitch Nogin; Salomon Zakharovitch Rosovsky.

M. Litvinov was appointed Chairman of the delegation. Answering a question in the House of Commons, March 8, 1920, the Prime Minister, Mr. Lloyd George, said "it is expected that they (the delegates) will be here shortly." Next day, March 9, 1920, the Allied Supreme Council issued a memorandum stating that the disbandment of the Red Armies was a primary condition of European peace. It laid stress on the need for demobilising the armed forces of the Border States, and urged the importance to Europe of the Russian corn supplies.

The *Daily Chronicle* aptly commented:

> "In regard to Soviet Russia the Memorandum says that the disbandment of the Red armies (estimated at 1,500,000 men) 'is, of course, a primary condition of European peace.' It also lays stress on the need for demobilising the armed forces of the Border States and further on it urges the importance to Europe of the Russian corn supplies. All these points imply the desirability of peace with Soviet Russia, and especially of peace between Soviet Russia and the Border States. But the Memorandum does not explicitly advise such a peace. French comments suggest that it originally did; and that here, too, an important excision was made in deference to French representations.
>
> In both cases, it will be seen, the logic of the original has been largely retained, while its direct conclusion has been dropped. *In the Russian case the logic will triumph, for the need of peace* grows daily more unescapable, however loth French opinion is to face it frankly"* (our italics).

The italicised words deserve special notice. They explain much that happened later in 1920.

Moreover, despite Mr. Lloyd George's reply to the House of Commons, March 8, 1920, a serious hitch arose in connection with the visit of the Soviet Co-operative delegates to Great Britain. Sir Hamar Greenwood (Secretary Overseas Trade Department) replying to a question in the House of Commons, March 11, 1920, declared: "The Government has no objection to admitting the delegation of Russian Co-operators to this country with the exception of M. Litvinov, to whom, in view of the incidents which took place in 1918, they cannot see their way to grant facilities to return to England." (Sir Hamar Greenwood was no doubt referring to the fact that when

* *Daily Chronicle*, 10.iii.20.

M. Litvinov was Minister Extraordinary to Britain in 1918 he, at the express request of the British Labour Movement, publicly explained the internal aims as well as the external policy of his Government.)

Mr. Lloyd George had again bowed to his more recalcitrant colleagues and followers; his weakness delayed the arrival in Britain of the Soviet delegates for over two months. In the interim the curtain had been rung down on Denikin's campaign in the Caucasus. He evacuated the mainland and took ship for the Crimea. His last stronghold and fort on the mainland was occupied by the Red Army on March 7, 1920. The Crimea alone now remained in the hands of the counter-revolutionary Generals.

In the second week of April, 1920, M. Krassin, together with several other Soviet representatives, arrived at Copenhagen where they were met by Mr. E. F. Wise, who, acting on behalf of the Supreme Economic Council of the Allied Governments, negotiated with them. The next decision was taken by the Allied Supreme Council at a Conference at San Remo on April 25, 1920:

> "It was resolved to direct the Permanent Executive Committee of the Supreme Economic Council to meet the Soviet Delegation, headed by Krassin, now at Copenhagen, and take all steps necessary to secure the development of trade relations between Russia and the Allied countries.
>
> The Allied representatives will be prepared to discuss with the Russian delegates the best methods of removing the obstacles and difficulties in the way of the resumption of peaceful trade relations with the desire of finding a solution in the general interests of Europe."

This decision in reality meant that the Allied Governments had decided to enter into negotiations with the Soviet Government. To quote Mr. Lloyd George later in the House of Commons—"We know M. Krassin's position in the Soviet Government. With the full knowledge of these facts the Allies passed this resolution at San Remo. It was decided—if words meant anything—not merely to begin trade relations with Soviet Russia, but to conduct the necessary preliminaries with the Soviet delegation then at Copenhagen, including M. Krassin." (The ban against M. Litvinov was still maintained and the Allies at this stage did not negotiate with him.)

It seemed that at long last the period of quibbling and camouflage was to end and that the Allied Governments had decided to establish forthwith direct trading relations with Moscow which would have had as a first consequence *de facto*, and at a second remove, *de jure*, recognition of the Soviet Government.

Supporters and opponents alike appreciated the great significance of the San Remo decisions. However, no sooner did the sky begin to clear than with tropical rapidity it again became overcast. On the very day of the San Remo resolutions the Polish Army began a wanton and unprovoked attack on Soviet territory, the immediate aim of which was the capture of Kiev. Despite this attack and despite the fact that both the Soviet Government and the Allied Governments regarded Poland as an Allied State, trade negotiations continued between Moscow and the Allies.

The full story of the Polish-Russian campaign has been dealt with in the work referred to in the Introduction. Here we need only treat of it in so far as it affected the immediate course of Soviet Russia's trade relations with the Allied Governments in general and with Great Britain in particular.

A number of important episodes—mutually affecting one another—now followed in quick succession. The Polish Forces occupied Kiev on May 7, 1920, and ten days later the first Soviet Trade Delegates landed on our shores. They were: MM. Nogin, Rosovsky and Klishko. They were met on landing at Newcastle by a representative of the Foreign Office who accompanied them to London. M. Krassin, Chairman of the Delegation, arrived in London on May 26, 1920, and he also was met by representatives of the Foreign Office.

The opponents of relations with the Soviet, who during all this time had been pursuing a daily press propaganda against Mr. Lloyd George's policy now lashed themselves into a fury in which they went from the absurd to the utterly absurd. The *Times* published, among others, a letter signed "Russian Ally" in which the writer urged the *dead* "of one-time smiling Russia" to call out to the British Government with their silent voices: "Remember us before it is too late, lest our blood be on you and your children's children!"

Well might the *Star* protest: "The coming of M. L. Krassin, the Bolshevist commercial delegate is being made the occasion for another of those wild mischievous press campaigns which do their promoters no credit either at home or abroad."

CHAPTER II

THE FIRST ANGLO-SOVIET TRADE AGREEMENT (1921)

I. NEGOTIATIONS IN LONDON. PEACE TERMS. THE RUSSO-POLISH WAR

ON the afternoon of May 31, 1920, two representatives of the Soviet Delegation met representatives of the British Government at 10, Downing Street. The proceedings commenced shortly after 3 o'clock and at 4.30 the following official statement was issued:

> "A conference took place at 10, Downing Street this afternoon between the Prime Minister, Mr. Bonar Law, Lord Curzon, Sir Robert Horne, and Mr. Harmsworth on the one hand, and Mr. Krassin and Mr. Klishko on the other.
>
> A preliminary discussion took place in regard to the reopening of trade relations between Russia and Western Europe.
>
> Mr. Krassin and Mr. Klishko walked from Downing Street by way of the Foreign Office steps into the Horse Guards Parade. The British Ministers left about the same time.
>
> The Premier, accompanied by Captain Evans, motored to Euston, whence Mr. Lloyd George proceeded to Wales to be present to-morrow at the enthronement of the Archbishop of Wales. It is understood that the Prime Minister will return to London on Wednesday morning."*

Whether the draftsman of the communiqué was exercising his sense of humour in the third and fourth paragraphs and indulging in a sly thrust at the opponents of the policy to re-establish Anglo-Soviet relations was never explained. However, next day the *Manchester Guardian* facetiously commented:

> "The blow has fallen. A Bolshevist, a real live representative of Lenin, has spoken with the British Prime Minister face to face. A being, as Sergeant Buzfuz would say, erect upon two legs and bearing the outward form and semblance of a man was seen to approach 10, Downing Street, yesterday, to ring at the door and gained admission. To give this verisimilitude we are informed that Mr. Krassin and his colleage walked from Downing Street by way of the Foreign Office into the 'Horse Guards Parade'. The Bolshevist pretends to go downstairs like any ordinary mortal, but without doubt in doing so he conceals some deep design. Probably if scrutinised his method of locomotion would be found to depend on some inhuman device. Meanwhile, Mr. Lloyd George has seen him and lives. Not only does

* *Manchester Guardian*, 1.vi.20.

> he live, but, whether he walked down any steps or not, we are informed that he motored off afterwards to help to enthrone an archbishop. We trust that the archbishop will receive a double portion of archiepiscopal anointment to avert the evil influences. However, Mr. Lloyd George was not trusted with M. Krassin alone. He was duly chaperoned by Mr. Bonar Law, Lord Curzon, Sir Robert Horne, and Mr. Harmsworth, a combination which might make head against Lenin and all his works. Anyhow, the great contact is made, and the British Empire still stands."

The established contact was warmly welcomed by the Liberal and Labour Press, but vitriolically denounced by most of the Conservative papers. In addition the *Times* with relish quoted some French criticisms. It declared:

> "Our Paris Correspondent emphasises to-day the strength of French disapproval of the negotiations between British Ministers and the Russian Bolshevist delegate, M. Krassin. We understand that this disapproval is by no means confined to France, and that it is shared by members of the British Cabinet, and in more than one Department of State."

When a few days later the matter was raised in Parliament, Mr. Lloyd George, the Prime Minister, thus explained the Government's policy:

> "At San Remo on April 25, the Supreme Council decided to authorise representatives of the Allied Governments to meet M. Krassin and the Russian Trade Delegation then at Copenhagen, with a view to the immediate restarting of trade relations between Russia and other countries through the intermediary of the co-operative organisations and otherwise. It further decided that the 'Allied representatives will be prepared to discuss with the Russian delegates the best method of removing the obstacles and difficulties in the way of the resumption of peaceful trade relations with a desire of finding solutions in the general interests of Europe.' At the same time the names of the Russian delegates were considered, and it was decided that the Allied representatives should meet M. Krassin and the other Russian delegates, except Litvinov, in London at the earliest date. M. Krassin is head of a delegation representing the Russian co-operative organisations, but he is also a Minister of the Soviet Government, and as such he is acting in the name and under the authority of the Soviet Government."

Questioned as to whether French public opinion was perturbed, the Prime Minister replied that he "was not aware that there was perturbation of French public opinion. The mere fact that there may be statements in certain newspapers who are trying to foment trouble between two friendly and Allied countries whose friendliness is essential for the welfare of the world, is no proof that French public opinion is perturbed."*

During all this time the Labour Movement in France had been agitating vigorously in favour of a *rapprochement* with Soviet Russia, but it had not the relative strength of the British Labour Movement and therefore could not influence the foreign policy of the Quai d'Orsay to the same degree as the British Labour Movement affected the foreign policy of Whitehall.

Again the outlook for peace between Russia and Western Europe looked favourable, but two episodes occurred which considerably delayed its realisation. On June 8, 1920, General Wrangel† (on whose behalf Lord Curzon, the Foreign Secretary, had been appealing to Moscow for clemency) burst out of the Crimea and began an advance against the Soviet lines thinly manned by the Red Army. On the other hand, four days later, June 12, 1920, the Soviet troops recaptured Kiev and began a general advance against the Polish Army.‡

These events did not at first affect, at any rate publicly, the continued Anglo-Soviet negotiations in London, and there were several meetings between the two sides. Meanwhile a British Labour Delegation in Russia had been preparing their interim report and this appeared in the press on June 12, 1920. It declared, among other things:

> "We have been profoundly impressed by the effects of the policy of intervention and blockade upon the Russian people. This policy has been pursued by various foreign Governments since 1918, and under various forms, direct and indirect, it is still being pursued to-day. It is at the root of the worst evils which are afflicting Russia at the present time.
>
> While the stoppage of exports from Russia is injurious to the world outside, the stoppage of imports is disastrous to the interior economy of Russia herself.
>
> The problem of food exceeds all others in immediate importance. We are appalled by the conditions of virtual famine under which the whole urban population—the manual and the intellectual workers alike—are living.
>
> A particularly serious effect of the blockade policy has been

* *Daily Despatch*, 4.vi.20. † Who had replaced General Denikin.

‡ This subject is fully dealt with in *Armed Intervention in Russia*, 1918-22.

the cutting off of soap and of medical supplies. Epidemics of typhus fever and of recurrent fever have swept over the whole country. It is true that a great and efficient sanitary organisation has been created by the Commissariat of Public Health.

But despite this organisation the fact that the blockade has cut off soap and disinfectants has been responsible for the loss of thousands of lives by infectious disease."

Respecting the Polish attack. the report stated:

"Perhaps the worst disservice rendered to Russia by the recent renewal of hostilities on the Polish front has been the forcing back of the Russian people, against their will, from the paths of peace into the paths of war. We ourselves have witnessed scores of examples of this baneful process.

The appeal for creative work is being once more set aside in favour of the appeal to military enthusiasm, while war conditions provide new pretexts for restricting individual liberty and preventing freedom of discussion. These conditions cannot be changed while war continues."

Finally the report recommended:

"In view of the above facts, we wish to register our unanimous and whole-hearted protest against the policy whose effects we have described—a policy as foolish as it is inhuman. Russia's supreme needs are immediate peace and free intercourse with the outside world. We recommend that the entire British Labour Movement should demand the removal of the last vestige of blockade and intervention, and the complete destruction of the barrier which Imperialist statesmen have erected between our own people and our brothers and sisters of Russia.

As a first step to attaining these objects, the present Russian Government should be unconditionally recognised. It has shown its stability by resisting for two and a half years the many efforts made to destroy it. It has repeatedly shown its will to peace. We can ourselves bear witness to the fact that it has made vigorous efforts to carry on the work of economic reconstruction."

The report was signed by Mr. Ben Turner, Mrs. Snowden, Messrs. A. A. Purcell, H. Skinner, Tom Shaw, M.P., Robert Williams and Miss Bondfield and "endorsed" by Mr. R. C. Wallhead and Mr. Clifford Allen of the I.L.P.

This balanced and explanatory account of the state of affairs in Soviet Russia was reported and attacked in most of the Conservative press, it was reported and praised in the Liberal and Labour press and was widely quoted on Labour platforms. It acted as an important corrective to the one-sided distortions which had appeared and continued to appear in the majority of the Conservative newspapers and journals.

Whilst the Anglo-Soviet negotiations proceeded in London, M. Krassin explained to the French people, in an interview with a representative of the *Liberté*, the attitude of his government towards the questions of the Tsarist debts and any debts which the Soviet Government might incur.

He declared:

> " People who now hold Russian stocks ought to have known what risks they were taking when they lent their money to the Government of the Tsar. Not only my own party, but all the Russian advanced parties had warned the French investor from 1905 onwards that the Russian people, if they once became masters of their own destinies, would never consent to repay the loans which had been used to crush their efforts to obtain liberty. Our warnings passed unheeded, however, and the French continued to lend money for the purpose of paying the troops employed to fire on the Russian people. French opinion had never believed the Russian Revolution would succeed, and they ought naturally to pay for their blunder.
>
> We are told on all sides that international financial relations would be impossible if, whenever it changed its Government, a nation could repudiate the obligations incurred by the preceding régime. That would be correct in regard to peaceful changes, but history records no instance in which a revolutionary Government has paid the debts of the former régime. The French Revolution of 1789 was itself an instance of this. We consider as sacred the obligations which we incur ourselves, but we cannot regard ourselves as bound by the obligations of the former Russian régime. Juridically, whether you take this word in its broadest or in its narrowest and dogmatic sense, we are not compelled to pay."

This declaration, it is no exaggeration to say, was historic. It expressed a doctrine from which the Soviet Government has never departed. It was published in Paris, June 16, 1920.

Six days later, a Conference of the Allied Governments in Boulogne decided that trade negotiations with Soviet Russia were to be continued " on the understanding that there was no question of political recognition of the Soviet Government." France had again slowed down the pace. The *Daily Chronicle's* special correspondent at the Conference, cabled: "I believe this means that France, seeing Belgium and Italy have preceded her in the path opened by Great Britain, is now more ready to open the trade path, but M. Millerand would not advance further than this."*

On June 23, 1920, the Labour Party Conference meeting at Scarborough, unanimously passed a resolution calling on the Allied Governments "to abstain from all direct or indirect attacks on Soviet Russia and to offer every encouragement to the free development and exchange of her national resources."

Many delegates urged that the resolution should be coupled with a threat of strike action, but it was decided first to find out what could be done by way of a deputation to the Prime Minister.

The Anglo-Soviet talks in London had continued uninterruptedly much to the chagrin, among others, of the *Times*. Unceasingly that journal essayed to belittle the significance of the negotiations and prophesied their inevitable failure. On June 26, 1920, it averred:

> "There is no foundation for the statement that a meeting between the Prime Minister and M. Krassin has been arranged before Mr. Lloyd George leaves for Brussels on Thursday morning.
>
> On the contrary, the British Government are thoroughly disillusioned. Ministers are now aware that M. Krassin is unable to give the guarantees, more particularly with reference to the Bolshevist invasion of Persia, which they demanded as a preliminary to the restoration of trade relations between Great Britain and Soviet Russia. There is accordingly, little prospect of a successful issue of the negotiations.
>
> The opinion is gaining ground in official quarters that the Soviet Government never looked on the Krassin Mission as anything but good propaganda."

On the evening of the date on which this very seemingly definite report appeared, it became known in London that an interview had taken place that day between the Prime Minister and M. Krassin! Next day the *Times* stated:

> "An eleventh-hour interview was arranged between the Prime Minister and M. Krassin at 10, Downing Street yesterday. An observer who saw M. Krassin take his departure after the interview described him as looking 'very cross'. It is understood that no progress was made with the negotiations. M. Krassin is still unable to give the guarantees which the British Government seek as a preliminary to the restoration of trade relations

* *Daily Chronicle*, 23.vi.20.

between this country and Soviet Russia. It is becoming clear that Moscow will agree to no bargain which does not give it in return recognition of the Soviet Government."

The *Times* correspondent, as the sequel will show, deserved to be felicitated more on his imagination than on his accuracy.

M. Krassin left London for Moscow on July 2, 1920, taking with him the British Government's peace terms in a Note dated June 30.

Commenting on M. Krassin's departure the Diplomatic correspondent of the *Observer* stated:

"Mr. Krassin's journey to Moscow to consult his government has given an opportunity to extremists everywhere (whether at Moscow, Paris or Printing House Square) to hail it as a victory for themselves. It is nothing of the kind. The negotiations have not broken down. It would be idle to pretend that Mr. Krassin has not been embarrassed by constant sniping in London as well as at home, but if he fails to bring back with him in three weeks' time the necessary acceptance of Allied political conditions—conditions which are of no importance compared with the vital need of European reconstruction—a catastrophe will result for which all men of common sense will bury their heads in shame.

The political obstacles are (1) prisoners, (2) propaganda. In regard to the former it is significant that Russia has just liberated the Swedish prisoners, and trade with Sweden is forging ahead. Sweden and Russia wholeheartedly want a renewal of trade, and success is the result. The position is slightly different as between Russia and the West. France does not want trade with Russia, nor does a small section of opinion in Britain. They want more ruin, in the blind hope that imaginary enemies will be rendered harmless. It is hard to see what they are afraid of, but they are afraid."*

These comments are very important because they demonstrate that by this date, despite the public propaganda of the *Times*, etc., the drawing-room propaganda of the "White" emigrés, and other influences in high social quarters, an important section of the Conservative Party favoured accommodation with the Soviet Government.

The Labour Delegation had now returned home and issued an appeal to the nation, which appeared in the press on July 8, 1920. The following are a few of the more important paragraphs:

"The British Labour Delegation to Russia, having met to prepare their report, wish to declare at once on the urgent

* *Observer*, 4.vii.20.

necessity of an immediate peace with the Russian Socialist Federated Soviet Republic.

During their stay of about six weeks in Russia, the delegation visited Petrograd, Moscow, Smolensk, and the Polish front, and numerous towns and villages on the Volga from Nijni-Novgorod to Astrakhan. The marks of the cruel blockade and of war were visible everywhere. In the villages, while food was fairly satisfactory, there was a great lack of clothes, coats, household utensils, agricultural implements and machinery. In the towns food was dangerously scarce and the power of work of many workers in the industrial regions was greatly reduced, owing to their obviously miserable physical condition. The transport which should have been bringing food from the country to the towns was taking food, munitions and men to the front. The locomotives, which might have been working stood idle on the rails for want of spare parts for their repair, which the blockade had not allowed to enter Russia. The workshops, which should have been making tools, agricultural machinery and productive machinery, were making guns, bombs and tanks.

In 1918-19 there were over a million cases of typhus fever and no town or village in Russia or Siberia escaped infection. In addition there have been other epidemics of cholera, of Spanish influenza, and of smallpox. The soap, the disinfectants and the medicines needed for the treatment of these diseases have been kept out of Russia by the blockade. Two or three hundred thousand of Russians died of typhus alone. One-half of the doctors attending on typhus died at their posts.

Peace now and at once—that is the great need of Russia and of the world, and in the name of the humanity of the world we call upon our nation to insist that peace be made now and Europe be allowed to turn from the terrible spectres of war, famine and disease to a rebuilding of its homes and a reshaping of its shattered civilisation.

Russia can give much to us from her natural resources, and Russia needs much from us. To pursue a policy of blockade and intervention is madness and criminal folly which can only end in European disaster."

On the same day the Soviet Government accepted the terms of the British Government which M. Krassin had taken to Moscow. They were:

1. An armistice equally binding on both sides.
2. A declaration from both parties that they will in due time

make payment for goods and services actually rendered by the other's nationals.

3. The claims under (2) to be considered at a Peace Conference, for which, however, trade negotiations are not to be postponed.

4. Each party to abstain from interference in the other's internal affairs.

5. Absolute freedom of trade and communication.

The Soviet Note read:

"Complying with the desire of the British Government and with the object of arriving at an early peace between Russia and Great Britain, the Russian Soviet Government accepts the principles laid down in the Allied memorandum transmitted on July 1 by the British Government to the President of the Russian Delegation, Krassin, as the basis of an agreement between Russia and Great Britain, which agreement will be the subject of negotiations, which must begin without delay, between both Governments.

The Soviet Government agrees that the plan proposed by the British Government will have to be considered as a state of armistice between Russia and Great Britain and shares the British Government's expectation that this armistice will pave the way to a definite peace. At the same time the Soviet Government protests against the affirmation, contrary to the real facts, relative to the presumed attacks of Soviet Russia upon the British Empire.

The Soviet Government emphasises once more that as to Soviet Russia in her relations with Great Britain, she desires nothing but peace, and that the absence of the same disposition on the other side was the only cause preventing it from being as yet attained.

(Signed) CHICHERIN,
Commissar for Foreign Affairs."

Now at last it seemed as though these negotiations would be successfully concluded, but suddenly they were brought to a standstill because of happenings quite unconnected with the negotiations. By this date the Polish Army was rapidly falling back. On July 6, 1920, the Red Army occupied Rovno. On July 11, Poland appealed to the Allied Governments for aid to stem the rapidly advancing Soviet Forces, which, on the following day, July 12, entered Minsk.

An Allied Government Conference was summoned at Spa to consider the Soviet reply and the Polish-Soviet military situation. From that town, on July 11, 1920, the British Government, on behalf of the Allies, dispatched a Note to Moscow accepting the Soviet reply to the British offer, but also proposing a Soviet-Polish armistice and a conference between on one side the Soviet Government and on the other side the Governments of the Allies, Poland and the Baltic States.

The Note continued:

> "If, therefore, Soviet Russia, despite its repeated declarations accepting the independence of Poland, will not be content with the withdrawal of the Polish armies from Russian soil on the condition of a mutual armistice, but intends to take action hostile to Poland in its own territory, the British Government and its Allies would feel bound to assist the Polish nation to defend its existence with all the means at their disposal."

The Note concluded: "The British Government, therefore, would be glad of a definite reply within a week as to whether Soviet Russia is prepared to accept the aforesaid proposal for putting an end to further unnecessary bloodshed and giving peace to Europe."

This Note was a distinct breach of faith on the part of the British Government because there was no mention of Poland or of Soviet-Polish relations in the British Note of June 30 to the Soviet Government.

The seriousness of the situation created by the Allied Note was at once realised in responsible quarters here. The *Daily News* next day, in a leading article entitled "The Goose and the Gander," aptly commented:

> "The gravity of the situation created by the Allied Note to Warsaw and Moscow is evident to anyone who will review the course of events which have led up to it. It may be stated in a few sentences. The Polish armies invaded Russia, no doubt against the wish and even the consent of the Allies, but certainly with the aid of munitions and supplies provided by at least one of them. No attempt was made by the Allies in council to stop them and the invocation of the League of Nations was bluntly rejected as visionary. The Polish armies are now retiring in complete disorder before the Bolsheviks, and the Allies promptly intervene in the interests of European peace and order. The Bolsheviks would be less than human if they did not draw the obvious inference from this startling change of front that so long as there was a chance of the Polish adventure succeeding the Allies' love of peace was—shall we say—dormant, and that it awoke to fervid life and vigour only when the Polish cause was hopelessly lost."*

On the same day the "Wireless Press" reported that M. Krassin, together with an augmented delegation, were preparing to leave Moscow for London, and on the afternoon of that day the following dialogue took place in the House of Commons:

* *Daily News*, 12.vii.20.

"*Mr. G. Thorne* (L. Wolverhampton) asked whether a reply had been received from the Russian Soviet Government to the statement of British conditions as to the resumption of trade, and whether any steps had been taken with a view to the termination of hostilities between the Soviet Government and Poland.

Mr. Bonar Law : Yes, the Soviet Government have accepted the conditions laid down by the British Government, and an understanding has therefore been reached as to the principles on which trade agreements will be negotiated. As regards the second part of the question the British Government, after consultation and I understand in agreement with the other Allies, have made proposals to the Soviet Government for an immediate armistice between Russia and Poland on equitable terms, to be followed by a conference to negotiate between Russia and the Border States."*

Next day a specially summoned Trade Union Congress passed unanimously the following resolution:

"That this Congress learns with amazement the new demand submitted to the Russian Government before peace negotiations on the terms of the Krassin document are proceeded with. The Congress is heartily in favour of any and all action which may lead to peace in Eastern Europe, and warns the Government and the Spa Conference that any attempt of a clandestine nature to secure the support of the British democracy in order to give military assistance to Poland is foredoomed to failure. The Congress, therefore, calls upon the Government to adhere to the terms submitted to and accepted by the Moscow Government as a basis of lasting peace between Britain and Russia."

At that time the T.U.C. had an affiliated membership of 8,346,000, and no Government could afford to ignore its definite attitude on this issue. On the following day the *Daily Herald* commented:

"Mr. Lloyd George can still save the day for peace if he will disown the intriguers of Spa and insist on a fair deal with Russia. Our Premier has no principles, but he has intuitions. And if his instinct tells him that the British people are absolutely resolute for peace, he will change his policy in a moment of time. It is the task of the English people to make the Premier forget the diplomats and remember democracy."†

In addition, powerful voices in the ranks of Liberalism were raised

* *Manchester Guardian*, 13.vii.20. † *Daily Herald*, 14.vii.20.

against the British Government's policy. Two deserve special mention: Lord Grey of Fallodon and Mr. Walter Meakin, a well-known journalist. The former, speaking on July 15, 1920, at a Council of the League of Nations Union declared:

> "What I want to point out is this. The Allies are now dealing with the *de facto* Bolshevist Government of Russia, which a few months ago they announced it was their object to destroy. That could have been avoided, in my opinion. In a country like Russia, after a revolution takes place you should at once declare a policy of non-interference. I believe, if that policy had been pursued after the Armistice, Russia would to-day have made some progress through a stage of revolution to a stage of evolution. The result of that policy has been to produce in Russia a national sentiment for Bolshevism. How could it have been avoided? I think by, at the proper time, making use of the League of Nations. That was before the last Polish offensive took place. The time when the Bolshevists wanted peace was the time when we might have had an inquiry by the League of Nations. You must not, first of all, queer the pitch by a policy of interference."

Mr. Meakin had accompanied the Labour Delegation to Soviet Russia, and on their return, in a series of articles in the *Daily News*, he painted an accurate picture of the state of affairs in that country and of the stupendous difficulties confronting the Soviet Government, but explained that the dark colours and serious problems were largely products of the policy of the Allied Governments.

Here it is only possible to quote one typical and illuminating extract from these articles—"Over and over again men said to me in a quiet tone of resignation which was more appealing than bitter complaints: 'It is very hard to carry on. How long will it be before the British workers stop the war and compel their Government to lift the blockade?'"

A new hitch now occurred in the negotiations between the Kremlin and Whitehall. The Soviet Government replied to the Allies, July 17, 1920, stating that if Warsaw applied direct to Moscow, the latter would be willing to discuss an armistice and peace. This was accepted by the Allied Governments who, however, on July 20, 1920, sent an ultimatum to Moscow threatening that in the event of a Soviet invasion of Poland they would give the latter every assistance and support. Cables were also sent from Whitehall to M. Krassin and his colleagues, who had arrived at Reval, stating that they must not proceed on their journey to London until a Soviet-Polish armistice had been negotiated. The Soviet Government understandably resented deeply the new conditions put forward by the British Government and in an interview with the press, M. Litvinov, July 23, 1920, stated:

> "This putting forward of entirely new conditions after an agreement had been reached, following the protracted negotiations and when the delegation was already on its way to London, flouts all international laws and throws a revealing light upon the 'impartiality' of the British Government in the Russo-Polish contest. The delegation does not doubt that British public opinion, especially that of the labouring masses, will very well judge for themselves whether it is in the interests of the British people and of general peace that their Government now causes a new postponement of the negotiations, which has surely been prompted by the French protectors of the beaten Polish adventurers."

The next move came from Moscow. M. Chicherin (Commissar for Foreign Affairs) cabled Whitehall offering to meet the Allied Governments in London to discuss the establishment of peace between the Soviets and the Allied Governments. The Note informed the Allies that:

> "The Russian Government expresses its willingness to meet the desire of the British Government as to its proposal to convene a Conference with the purpose of establishing a definite agreement between Russia and other Powers which participate in hostile actions against her or support such, and is of the opinion that the said Conference ought to be composed of representatives of Russia and of the leading Powers of the Entente.
>
> The Russian Government agree that this Conference should be called together in London. It makes known, at the same time, to the British Government that orders had been given to the military command to meet the Polish *parlementaires* and to begin with *pourparlers* relative to armistice and peace."

Undoubtedly at this time the British Government would have been willing to accept this offer, but the French Government objected.

The British and French Premiers met at Boulogne on July 27, 1920, to consider the Soviet Note. The consultation was a short one only lasting three hours. The *Daily Chronicle's* correspondent thus summed up the agreement reached:

> "It has been decided, subject to the approval of Italy, to send a reply to Moscow, saying that if the Allies are to attend a general Conference certain things must be made clear:
>
> Poland and the other Border States must take part in the Conference, the first and primary object of which is to establish peace in Europe.

Then the Conference could proceed to discuss the questions between Russia and the Allies, with a view to establishing normal relations.

If the Soviet Government replies that it can only make peace with Poland separately, the Conference will fall to the ground.

If, on the other hand, the Soviet Government agrees, there is no reason why the Conference should not meet within a month.

No definite date for the Conference has been fixed."*

After the consultations, M. Krassin was informed that he was free to return to London.

Why Mr. Lloyd George agreed to the Boulogne decisions has never been explained. He can hardly have imagined that they would have been acceptable to the Soviet Government. The latter was more than anxious to conclude peace with the Allied Governments, but it had already explained that it would only negotiate direct with Poland and it was at this time negotiating with Latvia and Finland and had already concluded peace with Estonia and Lithuania.

The French Prime Minister probably anticipated that the Soviet Government would decline the Allied offer, at any rate in the form in which it was put.

The *Times* Paris correspondent cabled on the evening of July 28:

> "Though M. Millerand informed the journalists who met him at the railway station on his return to Paris this morning that he was quite satisfied, and though this morning's Press is in fine feather over the diplomatic victory it considers he won at Boulogne, there are not wanting signs that France is still very uneasy indeed at the new turn given to the Russian situation, which is, in effect, something not very different from the policy of Prinkipo."†‡

The circles, or at least one of the circles, which were opposed to an Anglo-Soviet understanding at this time made, from their own point of view, an exceptionally stupid attempt to discredit the report issued by the British Labour Delegation on their return from Soviet Russia. A Mr. H. V. Keeling had been arrested in Moscow on the charge of being (his own words) "an English spy" and had been sentenced to imprisonment (again his own words) "until the end of hostilities between Imperialist England and the Russian Federated Soviet Republic." Mr. Keeling, according to his own account, had been in Russia in 1914, escaped to Finland and returned to Russia in 1919 "to make further investigations." At a public meeting, July 28, 1920, held under the auspices of the British Empire Union, Mr. Keeling

* *Daily Chronicle*, 28.vii.20.

† *Times*, 29.vii.20.

‡ For details of the proposed Prinkipo conference, see Introduction, p. xi *et seq.*

stated that the British Labour Delegation, before they left Russia, had " to sign an agreement not to attack the Bolshevist Government in any way in England."*

Next day the *Daily Herald* replied " Mr. Keeling is a Liar." The paper continued: " If Mr. Keeling does not know it to be a lie, he can take advantage of the opportunity we now deliberately give him and can proceed against the *Daily Herald* for libel." That was an unequivocal challenge, but no legal proceedings were instituted against the *Daily Herald*.

During the whole time covered by this record, in fact since November, 1917, but particularly during the Russo-Polish war, the most persistent question asked about the Soviet Government was " will it last? "

Mr. Walter Meakin in his *Daily News* articles, which had attracted very wide attention, thus expressed his views on this much canvassed subject:

> "The most positive answer I can give is that after many conversations with men and women holding remarkably diverse opinions, I failed to find any evidence whatever of a vital movement which is likely to bring about a sudden change in the Government of Russia. The old capitalist régime has been completely crushed, and the people remaining in Russia who would still support it have lost all effective means of organising."

It is beyond question that the report of the Labour Delegation and Mr. Meakin's articles made a deep impression on public opinion, and consequently affected the policy of our Government.

M. Krassin returned to England, August 2, 1920. At this date there was something like a crisis in the British Cabinet due to sharp differences of opinion between the Churchill and Lloyd George factions. On July 28—the very day on which a British Note on behalf of the Allied Governments was dispatched to Moscow—Mr. Winston Churchill published in the *Evening News* an attack on the Soviets, equal in savagery to any made on the German Government during the World War.

This meant that Mr. Churchill not only disagreed with the policy of the Cabinet of which he was a member, but that he was violating the tradition of Cabinet unity and Cabinet responsibility for government policy. Because of this aspect of the question—to say nothing of the contents—the article attracted much attention both here and abroad. The matter was raised in the House of Commons, August 2, 1920. The Prime Minister said that the article did not bear the interpretation

* *Times*, 29.vii.20.

sought to be placed upon it and that there was nothing in it cutting across declared Government policy, and that he could not control what his colleagues wrote. The *Times* (in an article signed by a " Student of Politics ") commented:

> " If we stick to that doctrine, Mr. Churchill clearly ought not to remain a member of the Government of whose Peace policy he disapproves ; if he does remain—and evidently he will—it is a clear proof that that old strict discipline has gone by the board, and that members of the Cabinet are to be free to think aloud until the thing becomes an intolerable nuisance and there is a row. Members take a serious view of the matter, for when Mr. Palmer asked leave to move the adjournment only one Coalitionist stood up. Evidently the Coalition was afraid of a Cabinet crisis."*

However, events crowded on one another so rapidly after this date that this probably unprecedented episode was submerged in the public mind. In the meantime the Polish Forces were being rapidly rolled back by the Red Army and the latter, on August 5, 1920, was reported to be within 50 miles of Warsaw. The Polish-Russian peace negotiations had been flagrantly sabotaged by the Polish Government in the hope that the perilous military situation would induce the Allies to declare war on the Soviets.

M. Krassin and some of his colleagues had a two-hours conversation at Downing Street, August 4, 1920:

> " They were received by Mr. Lloyd George and Mr. Bonar Law, the conversations being confined to the subject of the Soviet advance against the Poles despite the overtures made by Warsaw, on the advice of the Allied Powers, for the conclusion of an armistice.
>
> From an unofficial, but apparently trustworthy source, it is understood that the British Ministers indulged in very straight and frank talk with their visitors."†

Two days later, in a leading article, the *Times* shrieked:

> " It is a terrible truth that once more we stand upon the edge of a crisis fraught with possibilities only less tragic than those that lowered over us in this first week of August six years ago."

On the same day the *Daily Chronicle* (which then stood very close to the Prime Minister) in a flaring headline yelled " Blockade of Russia Ordered."

* *Times*, 3.viii.20. † *Times*, 5.viii.20.

II. The Labour Party takes action. Trade Agreement drafted

Fortunately on the same day, Mr. Arthur Henderson, Secretary of the Labour Party, wired to the secretary of every local Labour Party in the country:

> " Extremely menacing possibility extension Polish-Russian war. Strongly urge local parties immediately organise citizen demonstrations against intervention and supply men and munitions to Poland. Demand peace negotiations, immediate raising blockade, resumption trade relations. Send resolutions Premier and Press. Deputise local M.P."

The reply to Mr. Henderson's appeal was tremendous. Enormous demonstrations were held throughout the country at which resolutions were enthusiastically and unanimously carried, protesting against any declaration of war on the Soviets. The Labour Movement did not stop at demonstrations. On August 13, 1920, at a great Conference held in London, a Council of Action was formed which was empowered to take industrial action in the event of a declaration of war against Soviet Russia. The situation created was unprecedented in our history for centuries. The British Government was powerless and this tremendous fact has since been frankly admitted by Mr. Winston Churchill:

> " The British Labour Party had developed a violent agitation against any British assistance being given to Poland . . . councils of action were formed in many parts of Great Britain. Nowhere among the public was there the slightest comprehension of the evils which would follow a Polish collapse. Under these pressures Mr. Lloyd George was constrained to advise the Polish Government that the Russian terms 'do no violence to the ethnographical frontiers of Poland as an independent State,' and if they were rejected, the British Government could not take any action against Russia."*

The *Times* at once realised that the game was up. Next day, August 14, 1920, turning a complete somersault, it blandly stated in a leading article: " The leaders of the British Labour Movement are fully aware that no sane man in this country desires ' war with Russia ' or, if they do not know it, their ignorance does no credit to their intelligence." Comment is unnecessary.†

The Russo-Polish military situation now underwent a decisive change. A battle was fought before Warsaw, August 15, 1920, which resulted

* *The World Crisis: The Aftermath*, p. 269.

† See also Chapter VI dealing with the " Hands off Russia " agitation.

in a Russian defeat, and the Red Army began a general retreat. Meanwhile, the Allied Front *vis-à-vis* the Soviet Union had been broken. The French Government, on August 11, 1920, without any consultation with London, recognised General Wrangel's Government as the Government of Russia. From that date onwards each Allied Government went its own way in regard to the Soviets, and Russo-Polish relations, in the main, became a question solely between Moscow and Warsaw.

The danger of an Allied attack on Russia had definitely passed, but the press and the political circles which had tried to prepare the country for a declaration of war on the Soviets, although they no longer advocated that policy, did not cease their anti-Soviet activities. They continued the campaign against the conclusion of an Anglo-Soviet Trade Agreement, and at this juncture one of the most baseless calumnies which had ever been used against the Bolsheviks was again put into circulation.

Mr. Perceval Landon cabled from Constantinople to the *Daily Telegraph*:

> " Confirmation of the rumour of the ' nationalisation ' of women by the Bolsheviks is now provided by the narrative of a British officer recently escaped from Odessa. This terrible corvee is exacted from the inhabitants of Moscow, Kiev and Odessa, and the officer cites the case of twelve women in the latter town from one block in Chernomorskaya-Street who committed suicide or were shot by their relations rather than submit to the unspeakable outrage."

Needless to say, there was not a word of truth in this accusation, but this did not prevent the calumny being repeated for years afterwards.

In the meantime a draft treaty had been drawn up and this was denounced by the *Times* in a leaderette:

> " We publish to-day the text of the draft agreement drawn up by the Inter-Departmental Committee for the resumption of trade between Great Britain and Russia. It confirms all that we have said about this singular document, and amply justifies the banks in the protest they made last week against its contents. Clause 8 provides that the Soviet Government shall recognise its liability to pay compensation to British subjects in respect of goods supplied or services rendered to the former government of Russia, or to Russian citizens, for which payment has not been made owing to the Russian Revolution. No mention whatever is made of the other and more important debts of the Russian Government, municipalities and private borrowers.

These vast liabilities are simply ignored. Even those debts which it is proposed shall be acknowledged receive recognition in a vague and unsatisfactory manner. These liabilities are not to be recognised as debts to be discharged in full, but as constituting claims to compensation from the Soviet Government.

In short, the proposed agreement is a contract of deliberate repudiation."

However, this journal had another line of attack. The article continued:

"The Cabinet is reported to have postponed consideration of the draft agreement, apparently because the reports as to the disintegration of the Soviet forces grow steadily more persistent. We have all along regarded their dissolution as inevitable sooner or later, but the public's sense of honour would be offended if the document we print to-day were rejected not on the ground of principle, but because one of the parties to it was no more."

The *Morning Post's* denunciation was on similar lines. It read:

"We publish to-day what we believe to be an authentic draft of the proposed trade agreement between the British Government and the Soviet authorities. The draft may, of course, remain only a draft, and the pressure of events may perhaps lead to its annulment altogether. That remains to be seen. But certainly no more inopportune moment could be conceived for the bringing forward of such a treaty. The text we publish bears out what we insisted on yesterday as the crux of the whole 'deal'—the disregarding of Russia's indebtedness to others."*

Like the *Times*, the *Morning Post* was convinced that the Soviet régime was nearing its end. The leader continued:

"All the evidence, indeed, points to the facts that the Bolshevist régime is doomed, and there is some ground for the belief that the end may not be far off.

The phantom of military success is not accepted now even by the Soviet leaders themselves. Indeed, the fatalism of defeat is apparently sapping the energy of the fanatics of Moscow."

The Executive Committee of the British Chambers of Commerce also entered the fray. That body sent the following resolution to the Government:

"That as the maintenance of good faith and the sanctity of contract are the bases of all human intercourse, whether com-

* *Morning Post*, 5.x.20.

mercial, political or social, the Council of the Association of British Chambers of Commerce respectfully inform His Majesty's Government that no agreement between the British Government and the Russian authorities can be supported by the representatives of British commerce and industry unless it provides for the recognition by Russia of all pre-war Russian debts, national, municipal and private."

However, that association would appear to have had some glimpse of realities because it only called for the "recognition of all pre-war debts."

Within the Conservative party itself influential voices were raised in favour of Mr. Lloyd George's policy. "Scrutator" in a remarkable article in the *Sunday Times*, October 10, 1920, addressed not only to the British, but to the French public, declared:

> "Russia is still, next to finance, the master question in our politics. It bears very directly on the relations of Capital and Labour; it stands in close connection with the reconstruction of British foreign trade; and it is in the centre of every eddy in foreign affairs."

Amplifying the last statement "Scrutator" continued:

> "It is not logical, having rejected war, to refuse the only alternative of peace. One other point, for our good relations with France depend on perfect frankness. We sympathise with France's desire to get an equivalent in Poland of the old Russian alliance, and were prepared to go quite as far as France to maintain Polish independence. But France must remember that we have lost not one, but two, alliances in Asia. The Turkish alliance is no more, and Russia, from being a friend, is now actively intriguing with our enemies in Islam. We too, with our enormous responsibilities in Asia, must ensure ourselves, and the natural and best way is by an accommodation with Russia. Otherwise we may have fought to save Flanders only to lose India and the East. Would it not be more considerate of France to remember these anxieties?"

Many business men also wanted the signature of a trade agreement. Mr. A. J. Cummings wrote in the *Daily News*:

> "I have not met a man interested in any of the industries into which I have enquired who is not wholeheartedly anxious to begin doing business with Russia, and who did not express his annoyance—in some cases in very picturesque terms—with the Government for preventing him from doing it."

During these latter months the British Government, partly no doubt owing to internal dissensions, coupled with the perennial hope that some unforeseen set of difficulties would affect the downfall of the Soviet régime, made no attempt to speed up the negotiations.

H. G. Wells returned from a visit to Russia in October, 1920, and in a series of articles in the *Sunday Express* advanced a powerful reasoned plea for an understanding with the Soviets. This, apparently, was too much for Mr. Winston Churchill who, in the columns of the same journal replied:

> "Mr. Wells may, turning this way and that in his evident intellectual pain, say to me, What is the immediate remedy? It is extremely simple. Let the Bolsheviks drop Communism. Let them leave off enforcing this unnatural system which paralyses human effort and dries up the springs of enterprise and wealth. Instantly the recovery will begin. But then they would cease to be Bolsheviks. They would cease to be Communists. . . .
>
> If they will not do so, nothing can save the cities and towns of Russia or the economic and scientific apparatus of the country. For one locomotive they may buy from abroad with stolen gold, two will be worn out on the Russian railways; and the gold will soon come to an end. It will scarcely buy them enough commodities to clothe and equip their armies. We shall soon be increasingly in presence of that complete downfall of every form of life in Russia, except village life, which Mr. Wells foresees.
>
> We must, at any rate, take care that the people of Great Britain, of France and of the United States are not left in doubt or ignorance as to the causes and the character of this frightful catastrophe."

However, an event occurred in November, 1920, which gave a big impetus to the agitation in favour of an Anglo-Soviet commercial agreement. On the 14th of that month the Red Army captured Sevastopol. This meant that apart from some scattered bands the "White Armies" had ceased to exist. In fact, on the same day (November 14, 1920) after a meeting of the British Cabinet, it was reported in the press that "the feeling of the majority of the Ministers" was in favour of the agreement, and four days later Mr. Lloyd George, the Prime Minister, informed the House of Commons that the Cabinet was agreed that a draft treaty should be drawn up for dispatch to Russia. However, there were still many raucous voices raised against it. The *Daily Telegraph* editorially asked:

> "Can this be useful, in any shape, either to Russia or to the

world? Must it not rather be pernicious, since it will delay the inevitable downfall of the frantic despotism which is the cause of Russia's penury?"

On the other hand, Mr. H. G. Wells was persuaded that without immediate outside support Russia would collapse. He wrote in the *Sunday Express*:

"The only alternative to such a helpful intervention in Bolshevist Russia is, I firmly believe, the final collapse of all that remains of modern civilisation throughout what was formerly the Russian empire. It is highly improbable that the collapse will be limited to its boundaries. Both eastward and westward other great regions may one after another tumble into the big hole in civilisation thus created. Possibly all modern civilisation may tumble in."

III. Exchange of prisoners. January 1, 1921, agreement still unsigned

Another matter which had given rise to considerable irritation between Whitehall and the Soviet Government was settled amicably in December, 1920. It concerned the exchange of civil and military prisoners of war, i.e., some British officers and other ranks who had been serving with the "White" Forces in Siberia and the Caucasus, as well as some civilians who had been arrested and detained by the Soviet Authorities, and a number of Soviet subjects who had been arrested and imprisoned in various parts of the British Empire. An exchange had not been easy to arrange. Some of the British prisoners had been arrested in Baku, the Azerbaidjan Republic, and that Republic which was not under the control of the R.S.F.S.R., was hesitant to release them. On the other hand, the Kremlin alleged that Whitehall was not very prompt in supplying a list of the Soviet citizens detained or imprisoned in various parts of the British Empire, and in Constantinople, then in British military occupation. However, the Russian prisoners were repatriated and the Moscow Government having used its good offices with Azerbaidjan, the last batch of prisoners reached England in the course of December, 1920. Thus one serious obstacle, a cynic might with some justice have written pretext, against the conclusion of a Trade Agreement was removed.

One obstacle was gone but another appeared in the form of a judgment by Mr. Justice Roche in the King's Bench Division on December 20, 1920. The issue was whether the British Law Courts recognised as the property of the Soviet Government goods sequestrated in the R.S.F.S.R. by a decree of the Soviet Government and subsequently offered for sale in Great Britain. The material legal point was whether His Majesty's Government had "recognised the Soviet Government." His Lordship giving judgment stated:

> "I am satisfied that His Majesty's Government has not recognised the Soviet Government as the Government of a Russian Federative Republic or of any Sovereign State or Power. I therefore am unable to recognise it, or to hold that it has sovereignty, or is able by decree to deprive the plaintiffs of their property. Accordingly I decide this point against the defendants."

Commenting next day on this judgment the *Times* editorially declared: "In our opinion, the British Government have no option but to terminate at once their negotiations with Krassin and the Soviet."

On the other hand the *Daily Herald* commented, also editorially:

> "What earthly reason can there be for refusing this recognition in name which has already been granted in fact by the negotiations with Krassin? To refuse formal recognition is the last weapon of the obstructionists.
>
> The British Government must be forced to swallow its false pride and face the facts. It must allow trade with Russia, and to do so it must recognise the existing Russian Government."

Three days after the judgment of Mr. Justice Roche, Sir Robert Horne (then President of the Board of Trade) referring in the House of Commons to this judgment averred:

> "If the Russian was a *de facto* Government recognised by the British Government, then we are advised that the British creditor, in these circumstances, would not be entitled to arrest the goods of another Government.
>
> If we make this trading agreement with the Soviet Government then you have an entirely new state of facts. It is obvious that a Government which has entered into a definite trade agreement is in a totally different position, so far as its claim to recognition is concerned.
>
> Accordingly it only requires the matter to be tested in the courts and if decided in favour of the Russian Government, trade will be allowed to flow freely."

A few days later, Sir Paul Dukes, in a lengthy article in the *Times* warned the Government that: "The Border States of Russia share none of the optimism of English politicians in regard to the durability of the Communist régime." In addition, Sir Paul prophesied: "No amount of coercion or propaganda will ever convert the Russian peasant from his ruling passion for personal ownership of his plot of land."

When the bells rang out the old year on December 31, 1920, the proposed Trade Agreement was still unsigned.

Although the New Year opened on the whole in a spirit of hopefulness, there was no slackening in the agitation against the proposed agreement; the agitation in favour of a settlement was more pronounced than ever. Mr. Leslie Urquhart* (Chairman, Russo-Asiatic Consolidated Ltd.) in a letter in the *Times* (dated January 7, 1921) stated:

> "With my intimate knowledge of the Russian peasant, acquired during nearly 25 years' work among them, I am satisfied that they will not much longer rest content with Bolshevist rule. It may be that the serious dissensions which are rife amongst the Bolshevists themselves over these absurd trade negotiations will precipitate a change of rulers very shortly, or that in the spring the peasants will take matters in hand; but, even if it should take a year or even two, one thing is certain—viz., that we shall see a sane Government re-established in Russia. It will be a bitter thing for England in that day to remember that she, alone among the nations, by condoning the unnatural and inhuman methods of the Soviet Government, delayed the restoration of Russia to peace and prosperity."

Negotiations continued, but the vexed questions of "hostile propaganda" and "hostile acts" on both sides were not easily resolved.

However, on January 11, 1921, M. Krassin left London for Moscow, taking with him a draft of the proposed Trading Agreement. That proposed draft Agreement was published in full in the British press on January 25, 1921. Here we are only concerned with the "Preamble" and the "Recognition of Claims," because these were the principal matters in dispute. In the preamble it was stated:

> "That each party refrains from hostile action or undertakings against the other and from conducting outside of its own borders any official propaganda direct or indirect against the institutions of the British Empire or the Russian Soviet Government respectively, and more particularly that the Soviet Government refrains from any attempt by military or diplomatic or any other form of action or propaganda to encourage any of the peoples of Asia in any form of hostile action against British interests or the British Empire, especially in Asia Minor, Persia, Afghanistan and India."

* Died March 14, 1933.

The Soviet reply was cabled on February 5, 1921, to the Foreign Secretary, Lord Curzon. As regards the preamble, the Soviet requested that after the words " especially in Asia Minor, Afghanistan and India " the following words should be inserted:

> " On the other part, the Government of the United Kingdom will desist and refrain from undertaking or assisting any hostile action or propaganda in any form against the interests or the security of Soviet Russia *in the above-mentioned countries as well as in the countries which formed a part of the former Russian Empire,* and which have now become independent States, on the ground of the right of the peoples to self-determination.
>
> The Government of the United Kingdom will also refrain and desist from encouraging or supporting in any way hostile action against Soviet Russia on the part of *Japan, Germany, Poland, Rumania, Hungary, Czecho-Slovakia, Bulgaria, Greece or Yugo-Slavia,* and will not interfere in Soviet Russia's relations with other countries nor hamper these relations.
>
> *The Contracting Parties reciprocally engage themselves to respect the independence and integrity of Persia, Afghanistan and of the territory of the Turkish National Assembly."*

Respecting the " Recognition of Claims " the British draft declared:

> " At the moment of signature of the preceding Trade Agreement both parties declare that all claims of either party or of its nationals against the other party in respect of property or rights or in respect of obligations incurred by the existing or former Governments of either country shall be equitably dealt with in the Treaty referred to in the Preamble."

Regarding this the Soviet reply stated:

> " The Russian Government must also point out that in the new draft handed to Mr. Krassin a stipulation has been inserted referring to the general debts of the previous Russian Governments which was absent in the earlier drafts, and which must be removed at all events."

The Soviet's reply was apparently regarded as reasonably satisfactory by the British Government because in the course of the speech from the Throne, February 15, 1921, the King stated:

> " It is my hope that the negotiations for a trade agreement with Russia will also be brought to a successful conclusion."

IV. The Forged *Pravda*

Whilst the negotiations were continuing an extraordinary action of the British Government came to light. On February 28, 1921, the *Daily Herald* published a photograph of a copy of a forged *Pravda* printed in London. To quote the words of the *Daily Herald*:

> "The paper itself is not the ordinary *Pravda*. It is full of anti-Bolshevik propaganda rather clumsily disguised as news. It is, in fact, a Wrangel propaganda sheet, flying false colours and masquerading as an official Soviet organ."

The *Daily Herald* related that the bogus *Pravda* was printed by a London firm of printers; that to comply with the law it bore that firm's imprint printed at the bottom of the back page; that after having been printed the copies of the paper were taken to the Special Branch printing establishment in Scotland Yard; that in that secret printing office the tell-tale imprint was cut off by guillotining.

Next came what was perhaps a still more astounding part of this amazing business. Once a fortnight these imitation *Pravdas* (there had been a whole series of them) were taken by Special Branch men to Hull or Harwich and despatched to certain British officials in Helsingfors. Thence through the channels established by the "Whites" they were sent into Soviet Russia.

The *Daily Herald's* revelations sounded so extraordinary that at first many hesitated to accept them. However, they were fully admitted in the House of Commons on March 3, 1921, by the then Home Secretary, Mr. Shortt, who excused himself on the ground that the Director of Intelligence had acted without his knowledge. Even accepting Mr. Shortt's disclaimer at its face value, it certainly revealed an extraordinary state of affairs: the Foreign Office and the Board of Trade negotiating with the Soviets and important permanent officials of the Home Office, the Admiralty and the Foreign Office assisting clandestinely—at the British taxpayers' expense—Russian organisations waging, or at least trying to wage, civil war against the Soviets! Not unnaturally this episode increased suspicions in Soviet Russia as to British intentions; and the Chancelleries of Europe, as well as the counter-revolutionary circles, drew their own conclusions.

Happily, the disclosure did not, as it might well have done, shatter the negotiations between the two Governments.

M. Krassin returned from Moscow on March 4, 1921, and conversations with Sir Robert Horne were continued.

However, the negotiations were not allowed to have a clear run. The Russian "Whites" and the French Authorities made another attempt to frighten off the British Government. When M. Krassin was on his way back to London, reports were cabled from the Baltic States to Fleet Street that serious revolts against the Soviet had broken out all over Russia. There was some fire behind the smoke, but the significance of the former was enormously exaggerated. There had been a partial revolt at Kronstadt and some much smaller revolts in other parts of the country, but they did not in the slightest endanger the Soviet régime.

Who and what were behind these revolts? The *Daily Herald's* correspondent, Mr. H. J. Alsberg, cabled from Moscow:

> "I can state definitely that the French Government is concerned in the Kronstadt affair, and that a large sum of money for the use of the mutineers has been sent by them to a certain professor in Viborg.
>
> Supplies are also being sent under cover of the Red Cross."*

And what was the object? The Correspondent continued:

> "Every conceivable pressure is being brought on Mr. Lloyd George to induce him to put off signing the agreement.
>
> If those efforts succeed, it will mean that the agreement will be too late to become operative this summer, and that the opening of trade will be postponed for another year.
>
> It is largely with this object that the fiction factories of Helsingfors and Reval have been working overtime this last fortnight."

V. March 16, 1921, Trade Agreement signed

However, the plot failed. Probably by this time the members of His Majesty's Government had learned to appraise more accurately the value of such reports, and the Trade Agreement was duly signed on March 16, 1921, by Sir Robert Horne, President of the Board of Trade, for Great Britain and M. Krassin for the Government of the Russian Socialist Federal Soviet Republic. The conclusion of the agreement was immediately followed by a much more correct evaluation of the Kronstadt revolt. On March 18, the *Daily Telegraph,* which only a day or two before had been printing scare headlines, published a sober account under the title "The Real Situation," which declared:

> "The Kronstadt affair has been thoroughly misrepresented. The wild rumours about sanguinary encounters, tremendous gunfire, and doughty deeds are exaggerated. They are produced by men who try to replace information they cannot obtain by daring flights of vivid imagination. In loyalty to the public it is high time to bring light to bear upon the situation."

* 12.iii.21.

As for the other revolts—they disappeared for the time being from the columns of the press which had been attacking the Government policy. The agreement was discussed in the House of Commons on March 22, 1921 ; during the debate on the Consolidated Fund Bill, Mr. Lloyd George, the Prime Minister, defending the instrument stated:

> " It is a small world and nations are very dependent on each other. We are dependent on Russia, and Russia is dependent on us. It was done not only in the interests of Russia but of everybody all round."

Referring to the Bolshevik leaders he stated: " They are very able men. I have never doubted it for a moment."

Colonel John Ward, M.P., in the course of the debate, solemnly admonished the House of Commons that " those who thought that in making this agreement they were making friends with the Russian people, would one day find out it was the greatest mistake they had ever committed."

The signature of the agreement legally implied the *de facto* recognition of the Government of the Russian Socialist Federal Soviet Republic. As was to be expected, the settlement had a mixed reception. Papers like the *Daily Telegraph,* the *Times,* the *Morning Post,* the *Daily Mail,* as well as many members of the Conservative Party vehemently attacked the agreement. On the other hand, many Conservative papers such as the *Observer,* the *Daily Express,* the *Evening Standard* as well as many Unionists, and as might have been expected, the Liberal and Labour press as well as the Liberal and Labour Parties, joyously hailed the agreement.

The main provisions of the agreement were: (*a*) that it was a temporary instrument which would be replaced later by a general Peace Treaty ; (*b*) that mutual trade was to be resumed forthwith ; (*c*) that " each party refrains from hostile action or undertakings against the other, and from conducting ' official propaganda ' against the institutions of the other "; (*d*) that the question of claims " in respect of obligations incurred by the existing or former Governments of either country " should be dealt with later in a " Formal General Peace Treaty."

It is necessary to underline here that the Third or Communist International was not mentioned in the agreement and therefore the Soviet Government did not accept any responsibility for the activities of that organisation.

The Trade Agreement was signed, but there were still two hurdles to be cleared before it could be put into operation, viz., the attachability of Soviet goods and Soviet gold by the creditors of Tsarist Russia. The question of goods came before the Court of Appeal consisting of Lord Justices Bankes, Warrington and Scrutton, on May 12, 1921, as an appeal against the judgment of Mr. Justice Roche. In the course of the trial a letter was read, on behalf of the defendants, from the British Foreign Office stating:

> " I am directed by Earl Curzon of Kedleston . . . to inform you that His Majesty's Government recognises the Soviet Government as the *de facto* Government of Russia."

That letter decided the issue. To quote Lord Justice Bankes:

> " His Majesty's Government having recognised the Soviet Government as the Government really in possession of the sovereignty in Russia, the acts of that Government must be treated here with all the respect due to the acts of a duly recognised foreign sovereign State.
>
> In my opinion the plaintiffs had established that the confiscation and subsequent sale of the goods were the acts of a Government which our Government had recognised as the *de facto* Government of Russia."

Lord Justices Warrington and Scrutton concurred, and judgment was given in favour of M. Krassin the head of the Soviet Commercial Delegation to Great Britain.

As to Soviet gold—Mr. Justice Peterson, on May 13, 1921, in the Chancery Division, gave judgment to the effect that a quantity of gold which had formed part of the gold reserve of the late Imperial Russian Government and which was subsequently brought to Britain on behalf of the Soviet Government, was not attachable in respect of obligations of former Russian Governments.

These two complementary court decisions meant that all legal obstacles—but only the legal obstacles—to the development of trade between the two countries were removed.

M. Krassin continued to act as head of the Soviet Trade Delegation in Great Britain and on June 23, 1921, Sir P. Lloyd Graeme* (Minister in charge of the Overseas Trade Department) announced in the House of Commons the names of those composing the British Trade Mission to the R.S.F.S.R. Mr. A. M. Hodgson, C.M.G. (later Sir Robert Hodgson) was appointed Official British Agent. Mr. Hodgson and his staff arrived in Moscow early in August, 1921.

* Later Sir Philip Cunliffe Lister; created Baron Swinton 1935.

CHAPTER III

FROM THE ANGLO-SOVIET TRADE AGREEMENT (1921) TO THE GENOA CONFERENCE (1922)

I. The Volga famine

It is necessary to deal briefly here with the Volga famine of 1921-22 because its repercussions were not without effect on the course of Anglo-Soviet relations. Owing to the primitive methods of agriculture and the lack of irrigation systems, Tsarist Russia was periodically afflicted with famine. It has been estimated that in the Russian famine of 1891 about seven million peasants, including women and children, perished.

The famine of 1921-22 was due to several causes, the most important of which was undoubtedly an exceptionally severe drought, but there were several subsidiary reasons, which intensified the seriousness of the affliction. An American Commission, under the Chairmanship of Mr. A. Johnson, Director of the New York State Institute of Applied Agriculture made a thorough investigation in the provinces affected as to the causes of the famine. There was no doubt in their minds. The report stated:

> "The famine has been due to the destruction of agricultural equipment, loss of draft animals and lack of man power due to our war conditions and finally to the drought of 1920 and 1921. It has not been due in any appreciable measure to a voluntary reduction of production on the part of farmers themselves, for whose industry and courage in the face of adversity the Commission has the highest admiration."

The report added that whereas the average rainfall in the month of May is 38.8 millimetres, it was only 0.3 in May, 1921.

That was not all. Prior to the war Russia imported about fifty per cent. of her agricultural machinery. During the world war, and until the blockade was legally raised by the signing of the Anglo-Soviet Trade Agreement, little agricultural machinery was produced within the country and none was imported. The result was that Soviet Russia, instead of possessing seven to eight million normal ploughs as in 1913, had less than three million badly worn ones in the spring of 1921. In addition, grain seed purchased abroad by the Soviets had been prevented from reaching Leningrad by the British blockade.

The area affected, on this occasion, consisted of the provinces lying in the Volga valley, stretching from the provinces of Viatka (southern half) and Ufa in the north, to the northern shores of the Caspian. The population of this area numbered about 24 millions, of whom about 15 to 16 millions were severely affected by the famine and reduced to dire straits for food.

The news of this terrible visitation became common knowledge in this country in the course of July, 1921, and the subject was discussed in the House of Commons. Speaking in the course of the debate, the Prime Minister, Mr. Lloyd George, said that it had been decided to establish "an International Commission to study the possibilities of rendering immediate aid to the starving population in Russia." He added "this is so appalling a disaster that it ought to sweep every prejudice out of one's mind and only appeal to one emotion—pity and human sympathy."

Admirable sentiments which were responded to by several newspaper proprietors, many public men and thousands of ordinary citizens, but others, politicians, etc., while paying lip service to the need to mitigate the sufferings of the famine victims, sought to use this fearful scourge as a rod with which to beat the Bolsheviks, and as a lever to wring concessions from the Soviet Government respecting the Tsarist debts, without being prepared to meet the much larger Soviet counter-claims for the losses suffered as a result of the millions expended in aiding the counter-revolutionary Generals.

An appeal was made to the British nation by the "Imperial War Relief Fund" on behalf of the Russian peasantry over the signatures of such men as the Lord Mayor of London, the Archbishop of Canterbury, Lord Birkenhead, John Clifford, Arthur Henderson, Gilbert Murray, Field-Marshal William Robertson, H. G. Wells, etc., etc.

Appeals were also launched by other organisations such as the "Save the Children Fund," "Friends' Emergency and War Victims Relief Committee," and "Worker's International Famine Relief Committee."

Sir George Paish and Lord Parmoor in a letter in the *Times*, August 25, 1921, urged that the League of Nations should open "an international credit for Russia for the purchase of food, clothing, boots, agricultural machinery, locomotives, rolling stock, and other things urgently needed. It would, of course, be arranged for Russia to repay the credit when she recovers. In the meantime the nations should guarantee the credit in proportion to their rank or to their wealth, whichever they may prefer, and they should supply food and machinery and other necessaries out of their own stocks, as far as they can do so, up to the limit of the credit they grant. The real need is for things, but clearly, the amount which each nation should contribute must be expressed in terms of money."

The *Times* editorial comment was fairly typical of the Conservative press as a whole. Whilst expressing sympathy with the victims of the famine it continued:

"The whole conception of providing international credits for Russia demands the most careful scrutiny. For it means one of two things. It may mean unconditional and unguaranteed credit for the relief of the victims of famine and the reconstruction of Russia under the present Bolshevist régime. In other words, it would mean maintaining the Bolshevists in power at the moment when their misdeeds have wrought themselves out in their inevitable consequences and are threatening the collapse of the whole hateful and criminal system. To any such attempt we are most emphatically and resolutely opposed."*

Not one word about the drought, nor the extent to which the results of the natural calamity had been intensified by the Allied Government's support of the "White" Generals!

Meanwhile, the Americans, with commendable and characteristic hustle had acted, and an agreement was signed at Riga on August 20, 1921, between the American Relief Administration and the Soviet Government detailing the manner under which the American organisation would work in the famine districts, an agreement which worked satisfactorily until the Americans withdrew some two years later.

The Allied Supreme Council on August 25, 1921, in Paris, appointed a Commission to study the question of giving help to the victims of the Volga famine and the French, British, Italian, Belgian and Japanese Governments appointed delegates to it. Later this Commission appointed a sub-commission to visit the famine districts and for some reason which was never explained, the former French Ambassador to Russia, M. Noulens, was appointed as Chairman. It would have been difficult to make a worse choice because, as the Allied Supreme Council was aware, Noulens was thoroughly distrusted by the Soviet Government, owing to his anti-Soviet activities during the Civil War and the period of foreign armed intervention.

It was generally hoped that the Commission would at once address themselves to the task of raising help for the famine-stricken people, because the urgency of the need was not in dispute. Instead, however, the sub-committee applied to the Soviet Government for permission to visit Russia in order to conduct an investigation.

This application deepened the suspicion, which the appointment of Noulens as Chairman had aroused in Russia, that the Commission's real objectives were ulterior. M. Chicherin replied in terms which by implication were a refusal to admit the Commission. He stated:

"The Russian people remember how, as French Ambassador in Petrograd, M. Noulens worked to bring about Allied interven-

* 25.viii.21.

tion, and how he participated actively in the fomenting of the counter-revolutionary rising. He is as much as any living man responsible for the civil war, the foreign invasions and the blockade. The nomination of M. Noulens is in itself a programme. Now the first steps of his Committee justify all our fears.

The Commission does not propose to aid the hungry. It puts forward instead a complicated plan for investigating the whole internal condition of Soviet Russia. Neither the American Relief Administration, which has already begun to send food to the starving children, nor Dr. Nansen, as High Commissioner of the Red Cross, has thought it necessary or possible to compel the hungry masses to wait for assistance until these profound researches can be completed. While thousands are dying for lack of food, M. Noulen's Commission proposes, instead of collecting food for the hungry, to collect statistics about Russia."

M. Chicherin concluded: "The Workers' and Peasants' Government will give every possible facility and assistance to every practical and serious effort to help the famine-stricken people, but it can only regard the proposals of M. Noulen's Commission as a monstrous gesture of mockery at the expense of men dying of hunger."

Little more was heard of the Noulens sub-commission, but the Commission itself later expanded into the International Russian Famine Relief Commission, to which most of the European Governments sent representatives. It met at Brussels on October 8, 1921, and adopted a lengthy resolution stressing, among other things, the need for additional aid from all sources, the advisibility of a "Commission of Inquiry" visiting the affected areas, and finally it admonished the Soviet Government that if it hoped to obtain foreign credits for the relief of its famine-stricken areas, it "must recognise the Tsarist debts" and give "adequate guarantees" for all future credits. Surely thus to attempt to exploit the famine to extract acknowledgment of the Tsarist debts without any guarantee from the Allied Governments that they would recognise the Soviet's counter-claims was heartlessness and sordidness at its worst. The "International Russian Famine Relief Commission" met occasionally, but made little effort to justify its ostensible raison d'être. No collective assistance by the Governments of Europe resulted from its deliberations.

After a great deal of pressure from members of all political parties in the House of Commons and from many public-spirited individuals outside to send State help to the famine victims, the British Government decided to hand over a quantity of medical stores which were in the possession of the Disposal Board, valued in pre-war prices at £100,000, to the British Red Cross "to be allocated as they believed right," without any conditions whatever. During the course of the debate in the House of Commons, Mr. Clynes bluntly told the Treasury Bench that had the famine occurred under the Tsarist régime " the British Government and the other Governments of Europe would have come more readily to the assistance of the starving people." Some of the stores allocated were a bitter and hollow mockery to the dying peasants. Sir Benjamin Robertson, who visited the Volga district in January, 1922, at the request of the Russian Famine Relief Fund, wrote that these stores contained, among other things, " a large amount of lime juice, some 200 tons." However, fortunately for the credit of this country, the appeals issued by the various famine relief funds were well responded to, and over a million pounds was raised.

Appeals for funds had been issued equally as promptly in other countries and in several the Governments also voted assistance. The U.S.A. Government topped the list with a vote for 20,000,000 dollars. In the course of 1922 it was estimated that about 320,000 children were being fed by the British famine relief organisations, but about 9,000,000 by the " American Relief Administration."

In marked contrast to the British Government's niggardliness in regard to the famine victims, was their relative generosity towards the " White " Russian Refugees. In the financial year 1921-1922 it spent £300,000 on maintaining 5,000 " Whites," a sum which would have saved the lives of 400,000 peasants in the Volga valley.

The parsimony of the British Government in comparison with the generosity of the Government of the U.S.A., the fact that British aid to the " White " Generals, by prolonging the Civil War had intensified the famine, and the generous support (higher than that paid to the British unemployed) given by Britain to the " White " refugees, were all bitterly commented on in Russia at that time. It is perhaps advisable to add here that the Soviet's own efforts to cope with the famine, as well as its most meticulous observation of the agreements with foreign famine relief organisations won for it golden opinions from the foreign relief bodies working in Russia.

The famine naturally had a serious adverse effect on Anglo-Soviet trade. Grain in pre-revolutionary days constituted the biggest single item in Russia's exports and her inability to export grain in 1921 correspondingly reduced her purchasing power abroad. Normally the Soviets might have used a portion of their limited gold reserve for purchases in this country, but this had to be expended on the purchase of seeds and grain in the U.S.A., to help the afflicted districts.

It is notable that in the course of the year the Trade Facilities Acts were passed by the House of Commons, but although Soviet Russia was not excluded from the ambit of the proposals, she was ruled out by an order of the President of the Board of Trade. Under the Act the President of the Board of Trade was empowered to issue such orders with reference to any country whatsoever.

II. Accusations of breaches of the Trade Agreement

When, in the course of October, 1921, the Prime Minister, Mr. Lloyd George, was questioned on the effects of the Anglo-Soviet Trade Agreement, he said that the instrument had given substantial results "though not equal to the anticipations formed in some quarters." This admission was seized on by the Die-Hards of Fleet Street and Parliament to attack the agreement as worthless from a trade point of view. Other matters also gave rise to friction between Whitehall and the Kremlin. It will be remembered that in the preamble to the Anglo-Soviet Trade Agreement signed March 16, 1921, the signatories obligated themselves mutually to abstain from hostile propaganda. The Communist International was not mentioned in the course of the preamble and the Soviet Government neither then nor since undertook any responsibility in connection with the activities of that body.

The Soviet authorities never disputed that the Russian Communist Party was the largest party affiliated to the Communist International and that prominent members of the Russian Communist Party were delegates to the Communist International, but they contended that these Soviet citizens were acting in their private capacity and not as members or representatives of the Soviet Government, in the same way as prominent politicians in Western Europe in their private capacity were members of International Leagues for the defence of the institution of private property."*

On September 17, 1921, Mr. Hodgson in Moscow, on behalf of the British Government, handed a note to M. Chicherin containing a list of alleged breaches of the Trade Agreement. It was complained that the Communist International was carrying on hostile propaganda against the British Empire in Afghanistan, that the Soviet Government was aiding Indian revolutionaries against the British Government; that a well-known Indian anarchist had received financial aid from the Soviet Government; that M. Rothstein, Soviet Minister to Teheran, had been pursuing a policy hostile to British interests in Persia; that a school had been established in Tashkent for training natives of India in anti-British propaganda; that the Soviet Government was supporting the Turkish nationalists, still then nominally at war with the Entente Powers, with money and munitions; that the Soviet Government was assisting the Afghanistan Government with technical and

* There exists an International Entente agains t the Communist Internationa l which has' or had, a British Centre. At the meeting held at Millbank House, Westminster, to form this British Centre, representatives of the anti-Socialist Union and the Economic League (with which many prominent British Tories are associated) were present. (*Times*, 11.vi.28.) See below pp. 60, 306, 334.

financial aid ; that it had established an unnecessary number of consulates in the Eastern districts of Afghanistan with sinister objectives against British India and that border tribes hostile to Britain were being supplied with money and munitions.

All the charges were of a very general nature and in part they seemed to imply that in the opinion of Whitehall the Kremlin had no right to pursue an independent foreign policy in countries adjacent to Russia, if that policy happened to clash with the policy which the British Government was pursuing at that time in these countries.

Needless to say, for strategical and other reasons, Soviet Russia was vitally concerned in establishing and maintaining friendly relations with such contiguous countries as Turkey, Persia and Afghanistan.

M. Berzin, chief Assistant to M. Krassin, replied to Lord Curzon, September 26, 1921, that the charges contained in the British Note were based on false information and that a full reply to the Note would be handed to Mr. Hodgson in Moscow. M. Berzin's reply concluded: " The Russian Government wishes more than ever to promote friendly and sincere relations with his Britannic Majesty's Government."

The comments of the Conservative press hostile to the Anglo-Soviet Agreement could be summed up in the phrase " we told you so." They, as one would expect, underlined the Government's thesis that the Soviets had violated the Agreement and contended that any undertakings given by the leaders of the Soviet Government were, and would be, worthless. The *Daily Telegraph* in an editorial asseverated: " These people, in short, are moral invalids, and the mere notion of entering into an engagement of good faith with them is, and always had been, absurd."

The Soviet Government's full reply was sent to the British Government in the first week of October, 1921. It admitted that some members of the Soviet Government were members of the Executive Committee of the Communist International, but in their individual capacity only, and contended that that fact did not justify the identification of the Communist International with the Soviet Government. The reply continued that the British Government's Note was based on information supplied by a gang of professional forgers and swindlers ; that the Soviet Government, since the conclusion of the Trade Agreement, had had no dealings with Indian revolutionaries ; that there was no propaganda school in Tashkent ; that the Soviet Government was not trying to prevent the Angora Government from coming to an Agreement with the British Government ; that the Soviet representatives in the East had been instructed " to abstain from any anti-British propaganda," and that they were " confining themselves to the protection of Russian interests without infringing upon British interests."

Finally, the reply preferred certain charges of unfriendliness towards Russia, against the British Government. That the British Government had imprisoned and expelled from Constantinople Russian trade agents without trial, and that in collaboration with the French Government it was trying to prevent foreign-relief being sent to the famine-stricken population of the Volga valley.

The next charge of violating the Trade Agreement came from the Soviet Government. On October 26, 1921, M. Krassin, head of the Soviet Trade Delegation in London, handed Lord Curzon, the British Foreign Secretary, a Note specifying several charges against the British Government. It declared that certain officers and men of the "White" Russian armies were being maintained at British expense in Egypt, Cyprus, Mesopotamia and elsewhere, and that troops from these camps had been transported to Vladivostok to serve in the "White" armies.

Lord Curzon replied to M. Krassin on October 31. He freely admitted the existence of the camps, and that 881 men, 106 women and 61 children had been sent to Vladivostok. He justified this on the plea that the Soviet had declined to give these people *en bloc* an unconditional amnesty and that no other country was willing to accept them. In justice to the Soviet Government it is necessary to add here, that in the course of the preceding few months it had offered to send a Commission to visit the camps "to investigate the possibilities of their (the emigrés) return to Russia," which would, of course, have meant granting an amnesty to such emigrés, but this offer was declined by the British Government on the plea that it "would have excluded numbers of persons from its benefit."

Lord Curzon's reply concluded: "There is, therefore, no justification whatever for the interpretation which the Soviet Government has seen fit to place upon the action of His Majesty's Government in sending 881 unarmed men, accompanied by women and children, to Siberia." It may be added that at this time there was no shortage of munitions at the disposal of the "Whites" at Vladivostok and therefore the fact that the 881 men were "unarmed" was pointless.

III. The Soviet Government offers to recognise responsibility for State loans contracted by Tsarist Government

Another big conciliatory offer was now made by the Soviet Government through Great Britain to all States. On October 30, 1921, the Soviet Trade Delegation in London sent a Note to the Foreign Office declaring the readiness of the Soviet Government "to recognise their obligations in regard to other States and their citizens with respect to State loans concluded by the Tsarist Government before 1914 under the express reserve that there be made special conditions and facilities which would make the realisation possible."

The Note concluded that the Soviet Government could only fulfil its promise "if the great Powers conclude with her a definite peace," and to this end it urged the summoning of an international conference "to elaborate a treaty of final peace."

The Soviet Government as already pointed out had throughout insisted that it was under no moral obligation to recognise the debts of a despotism which the Russian peoples had overthrown and this offer was made solely—as Whitehall and Fleet Street cannot but have been aware—on the grounds of expediency. A wise Government and a wise press would have welcomed this offer, which certainly would not be bettered as Russia recovered economically. Instead, the proposal met with coldness, suspicion and a "time is on our side" attitude. Our Foreign Office, not for the first time, covered itself with ridicule in connection with the receipt of the Note. The latter was handed in at the Foreign Office at noon on Sunday and was released to the press on the same evening by the Soviet Trade Delegation. Next morning this Russian overture was naturally given prominence in the press, and the usual enquiries were made by diplomatic correspondents and others at the Foreign Office as to how the Government would react. To the astonishment of all, the Foreign Office replied that the Note had not been received. Finally, it was revealed that the Soviet letter was not opened until 3 p.m. on the Monday, i.e., twenty-seven hours after it had been handed in.

Naturally, the contents of the Note were vigorously commented on in the press.

The *Daily Telegraph's* observations were typical of the Conservative journals opposed to a settlement with Soviet Russia. After arguing that there were other claims besides pre-war loans, viz., sequestrated properties, etc., and that the Soviet Government must give "unconditional recognition" to all "established debts" the paper concluded, "prudence advises us to consider the Soviet Note a step forward on the road to full capitulation and no more."

The opposite numbers in France of our Conservative press saw, for the ten-thousandth time, in the Note signs that the Soviet Government was tottering. The *Echo de Paris* observed: "We see in the offer yet another sign that at the beginning of winter the Bolshevik is at bay, and must seek foreign help for its continued maintenance"; and the *Gaulois* commented: "That the Soviet should make this offer is a sign of progress, proving that the Soviet régime is weakening every day. Let us leave it in peace to its slow death-agony. When it is dead we can talk."

However, some understanding and sane voices, not strictly confined to the "Left," were raised in this and other countries, and the *Daily Herald* admonished the self-delusionists: "We would warn any who, either by this offer or by Lenin's equally realist speech, are led into believing that the Soviet Government is tottering, or that the Bolsheviks are no longer Communists, that they are very foolishly deluding themselves for the hundredth time."

Lord Curzon replied immediately. He luke-warmly welcomed the Note, pointed out that it referred only to State Loans contracted by the Tsarist Government before 1914 and continued:

> "His Majesty's Government wish to know whether recognition of other classes of obligations, e.g., loans to the Tsarist Government since 1914, municipal and railway loans, and claims by foreign owners of property in Russia confiscated or destroyed by the Soviet Government also corresponds with the intention of the Soviet Government at the moment; and they invite that Government explicitly to define their attitude in regard to all such other classes of claims."

This information, declared the Foreign Secretary, was necessary before the British Government and the other Governments associated in the International Commission could decide "what their attitude towards the declaration as a whole should be."

Naturally the Soviets did not want to give away any of their bargaining powers before entering the Conference Chamber and therefore it looked for the moment as if a deadlock had again been reached, but some weeks later it became manifest that Mr. Lloyd George not only did not intend to let the matter rest where it was but that he was determined to make a big effort to effect a general European settlement.

On December 14, 1921, the *Daily Chronicle* published an obviously inspired article entitled "Europe Next" by "Politicus." The Washington Conference had just been brought to a successful conclusion, and the writer asked why should not the two most influential statesmen in Europe, M. Briand and Mr. Lloyd George, agree "to call a European Conference to deal with the European impasse on the same lines as Washington adopted so successfully about the Pacific impasse." The article continued: "The first step is not to abate one jot or tittle of the Versailles settlement, but to summon a new Conference of all the Continental Powers, including both Germany and the other enemy States, and Russia to discuss the basis of a European agreement." The writer concluded: "M. Briand and Mr. Lloyd George have certainly a great opportunity at Chequers next week. Why should not they give a new message of hope to Europe and to the unemployed of all lands by attempting to settle on these broad lines the disputes and suspicions which are slowly strangling the world."

On the following day M. Krassin had a long interview with Mr. Lloyd George and Sir Robert Horne at 10, Downing Street, during which the Soviet's relations with Europe were discussed in their entirety.

The same evening Lord Birkenhead, in the course of a public speech declared:

> "It is for us to gather up the salvage of Europe, and in order to do that you must come to an arrangement with France and with Germany. And you must also come to an arrangement with Russia as well. It is of no use for you to suppose that you can deal with the crisis merely by postponing the collection of the debt. Any settlement must be a settlement of the problem as a whole. And to secure this, and to prevent the possibility of later misunderstandings, we must carry with us the opinion, of French commercial men and French statesmen."*

Further, on the same day, a joint deputation representing the Labour Party Executive, the General Council of the Trades Union Congress and the Parliamentary Labour Party waited on the Prime Minister, Mr. Lloyd George. The Chairman, Mr. J. R. Clynes, on behalf of the deputation, stated that in their view it was essential, in the interests of British trade, that full relations, diplomatic and otherwise, should be established with Soviet Russia. The Prime Minister replied that the deputation was opportune and that he would discuss this question, among others, with M. Briand during the following week.

The two statesmen met in London on December 19, 1921, but little progress was made. There was a wide gulf between French and British policy. London was prepared to recognise the Soviet Government *de jure* provided the latter recognised the Tsarist debts, but Paris wanted to lay down much more drastic conditions before granting *de jure* recognition. A well-known diplomatic correspondent wrote at this time that M. Briand was half-convinced of the soundness of Mr. Lloyd George's views, but that the former had "a very strong opposition to contend with among his officials and his colleagues as well as among his avowed opponents."

IV. The Cannes Conference. Famine continues in the Volga Region

A sub-committee, representative of both Governments, was formed to go into the question of Russian debts and it was decided that the Supreme Council should meet at Cannes early in January, 1922. French opinion underwent little, if any, change between the dates of

* *Daily Chronicle*, 16.xii.21.

the Briand-Lloyd George conversations in London and the opening of the Cannes Conference on January 6, 1922. Four days before the latter event the *Times* correspondent cabled from Cannes:

> " France has been utterly opposed to any steps that may be taken in regard to Russia which imply any recognition of the Soviet Government. Though the tone of the debate in the Senate the other day seemed to show a certain development of opinion, M. Briand, who is much more closely clutched by his Parliament than is Mr. Lloyd George by his, will be compelled to tread perhaps too delicately for the liking of the protagonist of the Prinkipo proposals."*

Shortly after M. Briand had left Paris on the afternoon of January 3, 1922, for Cannes, the *Times* correspondent in the French capital cabled: " Opinion here can never have been less optimistic on the eve of an Allied Conference. Suspicion seems to increase that all ideas on the regeneration of Europe that are in the air can only result in decisions that must be doubly disastrous in that they will not regenerate Europe and that it will be France among the Allies who will have to pay the heavy price for the experiment."†

As usual, whenever the chance of a settlement with Soviet Russia was in the offing, various persons and organisations interested in pre-revolutionary trade and industry or desirous of re-establishing pre-revolutionary conditions, raised their voices. A group of British, French, Japanese, Belgian and Italian bankers and business men met in Paris in the last week of December, 1921, to study ways and means for the restoration of Europe. They agreed on a plan for submission to the Supreme Council at Cannes, in the course of which, to quote the *Times,* they insisted " that there is no hope of prosperity unless private property is respected." The word " Russia " was not mentioned, but it was clear, again to quote the *Times*, that " it is to Russia that this principle chiefly applies."

A few days later a conference of pre-revolutionary Russian manufacturers who had come from all parts of Europe was also held in Paris. These gentlemen were persuaded that foreign capital was " indispensable " to Russia, but they advised foreign capitalists when granting aid to Russia to stipulate conditions which would be " incompatible with the maintenance of Bolshevism."

The Cannes Conference met on January 6, 1922. Mr. Lloyd George in his opening speech sketched a sombre picture of the economic conditions and state of trade in Europe and argued in favour of summoning a European Conference. Referring to Russia, he said:

* *Times*, 3.i.22. † *Times*, 4.i.22.

"If Russia attends, we should make it quite clear to Russia that we can only trade with her if she recognises the honourable obligations of every civilised country—namely, that she should pay all debts, whether incurred by the present Government or by its predecessors, because no civilised country draws any distinction between them; that she will compensate all nationals for loss and damage caused to them when their property has been confiscated and withheld; that she will establish a legal system which sanctions or enforces trade and other contracts with impartiality; that she will refrain from undertaking propaganda to subvert our institutions and social system; and that she will join in undertaking to refrain from attacks on her neighbours.

You must make it quite clear that the last obligation must be undertaken by our own friends. If we insist that Russia shall not attack her neighbours, we must also insist that her neighbours shall not attack her, and if the conditions under which alone trade is possible involve the recognition of the Russian Government, that that also should be done, provided it is made quite clear that the Russian Government will undertake all the other obligations which I indicated."*

The *Times* referred to these proposals as the Prime Minister's "Bombshell," and warned that gentleman in a leading article that the "Soviet régime is tottering on the verge of collapse amid the ruin it has itself created."

Mr. Lloyd George's proposals were accepted and immediately afterwards invitations were issued to all the Allied and European Powers to attend a Conference in March at Genoa, but although M. Briand agreed to the proposals he could not have been certain at that time that the French Chamber would back him. The *Daily Telegraph* correspondent cabled from Cannes: "French public opinion, I find, is aghast at the ease with which M. Briand acquiesced in the conference with Russia, but I believe that at bottom his acquiescence was merely due to a cynical belief that nothing really concrete would result from it."†

M. Briand was suddenly recalled to Paris. He faced a stormy session in the Chamber on January 12, 1922. He concluded his speech with the dramatic declaration: "I have come, and I have told you what I have done. I affirm that nothing in the interest of France has been lost. I relinquish power, and leave to others the responsibility of to-morrow."‡

Immediately afterwards Briand left the tribune followed by his Cabinet colleagues and tendered the Cabinet's resignation to the President.

* *Times*, 7.i.22. † *Daily Telegraph*, 9.i.22. ‡ *Daily Herald*, 13.i.22

M. Briand had not been defeated, but he undoubtedly felt that it was impossible for him to carry on in view of the vehement attacks by the reactionary leaders of the Bloc National led by M. Poincaré. A new government was formed under the premiership of M. Poincaré and at first many quarters doubted whether the proposed Genoa Conference would ever be held. However, a very unmistakable hint was given from circles closely in touch with Mr. Lloyd George that whether France attended or not the conference would take place.

On January 15, 1922, on his way home from Cannes, Mr. Lloyd George had a lengthy conversation in Paris with M. Poincaré, who, in addition to being Prime Minister, had also taken the Ministry for Foreign Affairs. What actually transpired during that conversation the world was not informed; M. Poincaré evidently felt that he could not go back on M. Briand's promise respecting the proposed Genoa Conference, but it was generally understood in Paris that he would do his utmost to make the Conference abortive.

Naturally what had transpired at Cannes and Paris, and the exchanges between the latter city and London were followed with strained attention in Moscow, but the Soviet Government were not by a long way in that yielding—to say nothing of that desperate—mood, in which Downing Street, and still more the Quai d'Orsay, seemed to think they were. On January 13, 1922, a correspondent of the *Observer* cabled from Moscow:

> " Russia is ready to pay almost any price for the right to re-enter the family of nations. Yet it would be a mistake to expect that the Bolsheviks are going to accept any scheme that Europe may propose without a fight. European public opinion would be surprised not only by the shrewdness and sagacity of the Bolshevik spokesmen, but still more by the stiffness of their settled conviction of Russia's ability to assist European peace and economic revival, and not merely to be helped by Europe.
>
> 'The difference between Brest-Litovsk and Genoa,' a Bolshevik leader of the Moderate wing said to me to-day, 'is that there we were faced by a united and determined adversary, while we ourselves represented a country disrupted by revolution and on the eve of civil war. To Genoa we are going as the representatives of a Russia more united than it has ever been during the last century, and imbued with the consciousness of a great position in the world, while the interests of the European nations we are going to face are mutually antagonistic, especially in relation to Russia.' "*

In the same issue of the *Observer*, Mr. J. L. Garvin wrote: "The full recovery of Europe and Russia can do France nothing but good.

* *Observer*, 15.i.22.

Without it Britain cannot recover at all. When British statesmen speak of restoring Germany or Russia they are not using the language of superior wisdom or conscious virtue. It is the language of necessity."

Two days later, in the course of an interview, M. Krassin said: "Without the restoration of Russia there can be no way out of the European world crisis."*

Meanwhile the famine in the Volga Valley pursued its deadly course. In February, 1922, Sir Benjamin Robertson (who had been sent out by the Russian Famine Relief Fund) returned from the Soviet Union and in an interview with the *Times* he painted a very sombre picture of conditions in the famine districts. In passing it may be noted that in answer to a question as to what caused the famine he replied "the failure of the rain originally created it," but he added that it was intensified by "the absence of stocks, the cessation of trade, and bad railway conditions." Commenting on this interview the *Times* editorially declared that the Bolsheviks were responsible for the evils which had befallen Russia and continued: "It is intolerable that European Powers should engage in friendly negotiations with the implacable hostile force whose continued existence will plunge Russia into yet deeper ruin."†

It would be charitable to assume that the *Times* leader writer had forgotten the contents of the interview with Sir Benjamin Robertson when he began to comment on it.

The scene next moved to Boulogne where Mr. Lloyd George on February 26, 1922, had a four hours' conversation with M. Poincaré. According to all reports M. Poincaré was at first against the proposed Genoa Conference pleading that it would serve no useful purpose. Mr. Lloyd George pointed out that one of the gravest problems facing Britain was unemployment which was due to the fact that European markets were closed to British trade, and that it was necessary to make a supreme effort to rebuild the shattered fabric of Europe. Finally, M. Poincaré yielded, but at a price which was revealed in an interview the British Prime Minister gave to the press. He stated:

> "The fact that Russia has accepted our invitation to the Conference does not imply recognition of the Soviet by any means. Everything depends upon the guarantees and safeguards which Russia can give at Genoa. If these are satisfactory then recognition may follow—perhaps immediately.
>
> "But I certainly shall not press for recognition of the Soviet Government if the guarantees forthcoming at Genoa are not satisfactory. I would not do that under any consideration. France and England are in agreement upon that question."‡

* *Manchester Guardian*, 18.i.22. † 13.ii.22. ‡ *Daily Chronicle*, 27.ii.22.

The personal desires of Mr. Lloyd George were no doubt expressed in a leader in the same edition of the *Daily Chronicle.* "Both (Mr. Lloyd George and M. Poincaré) are prepared to meet the Soviet's representatives in conference; neither desires to give them formal recognition until their guarantees are known. This attitude does not alter our own strong conviction that the sooner recognition of Russia can come, the better for peace, present and future."

However, Mr. Lloyd George's opinions were not shared by all his colleagues, although about this time several Cabinent Ministers made speeches in the country stressing the importance of the Russian market to British export trade. Mr. Winston Churchill was still opposed to any relations with the Soviets and Lobby correspondents estimated that fifty to sixty Die-Hards would, if he opposed the Cabinet's policy in the House of Commons, follow him in to the division lobby. The much-anticipated debate took place on April 3, 1922. The Prime Minister, Mr. Lloyd George, submitted the following motion:

> "That this House approved the Resolutions passed by the Supreme Council at Cannes as the basis of the Genoa Conference, and will support His Majesty's Government in endeavouring to give effect to them."

Mr. J. R. Clynes, on behalf of the Labour Party, moved the following amendment:

> "That whilst approving of an international economic and financial conference this House regrets that the scope of discussion at Genoa has been so circumscribed that the Conference must fall short of a settlement of the political and economic evils which afflict Europe, and is of opinion that His Majesty's Government, which has clearly not the confidence of the country and which is responsible for the policy the unfortunate effects of which are to be considered at Genoa, is not competent to represent this country."

It will be noticed that the Labour Party was not opposed to the Conference, but considered that its aims were too circumscribed. A few Die-Hards opposed the Government's policy because they were against any dealings with the Soviets, but the Government's motion was carried by 372 to 94 votes.

The *Times* at that time actually welcomed the assistance of a Russian Terrorist in support of its agitation against the policy of the Government *vis-à-vis* Soviet Russia. On April 7, 1922, it published a lengthy open letter by N. Boris Savinkov, the well-known Russian Terrorist, in which he referred to private conversations he had had with Mr. Lloyd George shortly before the Cannes Conference, during which he had seriously warned the Prime Minister against having any relations with the Soviets. He concluding his hectoring admonition thus:

> " Do not forget, I pray you, that you are conversing with them (the Bolsheviks) upon the eve of their downfall."

The *Times* apparently took Savinkov so seriously that they gave him a full column. However, on the same day as this letter appeared the British Delegation left for Genoa and the stage was now set for the important Conference which was to be held in that city.

CHAPTER IV

THE GENOA, HAGUE AND LAUSANNE CONFERENCES (1922)

I. The Tsarist debts. Treaty of Rapallo

The Genoa Conference opened in the Palazzo di San Giorgio at 3 p.m., April 10, 1922. The following States were represented:

Belgium, France, Japan, British Empire, Italy, Germany, Russia, Albania, Austria, Bulgaria, Czechoslovakia, Denmark, Estonia, Finland, Greece, Holland, Hungary, Iceland, Latvia, Lithuania, Luxemburg, Norway, Poland, Portugal, Rumania, Serb-Croat-Slovene Kingdom, Spain, Sweden and Switzerland.

The British Empire Delegates were: The Rt. Hon. David Lloyd George, The Most Hon. the Marquess Curzon of Kedleston, The Rt. Hon. Sir Robert Horne, The Rt. Hon. Sir Laming Worthington-Evans, Sir Philip Lloyd-Greame. Canada: Sir Charles Blair-Gordon, Professor E. Montpetit. Australia: The Rt. Hon. Sir J. Cook. South Africa: The Hon. Sir Edgar Walton. India: Mr. Dadiba Merwanjee Dalal.

The Russian representatives were: M. George Chicherin, M. Leonid Krassin, M. Maxim Litvinov, M. Adolph Joffe, M. Christian Rakovsky.

The French representatives were: M. Louis Barthou, M. Camille Barrère, M. Colrat, M. Jacques Seydoux, M. Ernest Picard.

The British Delegation was led by the Prime Minister and the Foreign Secretary ; the Russian Delegation included the Commissar and Vice-Commissar for Foreign Affairs, but the French Delegation was led by M. Louis Barthou. The French Prime Minister and Foreign Secretary, M. Poincaré, remained in Paris, determined, as soon became manifest, to sabotage the Conference. Barthou had little in the way of plenary powers. He had continuously to refer to Paris for instructions, a fact which enabled Poincaré coolly and deliberately to bring the Conference to nought.

The explanation of the French attitude was well known. Up to the time of the Cannes Conversations the Supreme Council, which was representative solely of the Allied Powers, had been the chief executive authority in Europe. Russia and Germany were pariahs. France was still struggling with the restoration of her devastated provinces. Impossible reparation payments had been placed on Germany which the latter was unable to meet, and France, the chief beneficiary of reparations, argued that German failure to pay was deliberate. Mr. Lloyd George offered M. Briand the pledged word of Britain to come to the aid of France should the latter be attacked by Germany. This was considered insufficient by the French Chamber and was the main cause of the hurried return of Briand to Paris in the midst of the Cannes conversations, and his subsequent resignation. When M. Poincaré succeeded M. Briand, he strongly pressed Mr. Lloyd George for a full-blooded Anglo-French Alliance, but to this neither Mr. Lloyd George nor British public opinion would agree.

Unemployment in Great Britain, due to the closing down of Britain's pre-war markets, was threatening to rise to the dangerous figure of 2,000,000, and although the British offer at Cannes was made without exacting any *quid pro quo*, Whitehall assumed as a matter of ordinary gratitude that the Quai d'Orsay would support London's efforts to effect a European settlement which was an essential premise for the restoration of Britain's hard-hit foreign trade.

Throughout 1921 the overshadowing problem in Great Britain was unemployment. In June it had reached the menacing figure of 2,178,000, and by December it had only fallen to 1,886,000. These figures explain why British statesmen were so anxious to set the wheels of international trade revolving once more.

However, despite these appalling facts, there were a number of influential circles in Britain who were as hostile as French governmental quarters to the aims of the Genoa Conference. Practically all the London Conservative dailies, stridently led by the *Times*, denounced the protocols of the Conference, and throughout they maintained an unceasing and embittered propaganda against the Conference from the first till the final session.

The Russian delegation was the centre of attention. " What were these terrible revolutionaries like? " " Were they uncouth, unlettered and simple-minded, and would they easily succumb to the honeyed words and insincere flattery of the trained Ministers and Diplomats of Western Europe? "

These were some of the questions which the delegates at Genoa and their Chancelleries at home kept asking. A short acquaintance with the Soviet delegates soon supplied the answers. Mr. J. Saxon Mills, in his book *The Genoa Conference,* stated:

> "There might be different opinions about the political morality of the Bolshevik Delegates, but there could be only one about their ability. They were quite capable of holding their own with the most trained and experienced intellects of the West. They had a happy and disconcerting knack of turning the tables unexpectedly on their adversaries."

The right to attend the Conference was made conditional on the acceptance of the resolutions adopted by the Supreme Council at Cannes on January 6, 1922. Of these the most important were:

> "1. Nations can claim no right to dictate to each other regarding the principles on which they are to regulate their system of ownership, internal economy and Government. It is for every nation to choose for itself the system which it prefers in this respect.
>
> 3. Effective security cannot be re-established unless the Governments of countries desiring foreign credits freely indicate (*a*) that they will recognise all public debts and obligations which have been or may be undertaken or guaranteed by the State or municipalities or by any other public bodies as well as the obligation to restore or compensate all foreign interests for loss or damage caused to them when property has been confiscated or withheld; (*b*) that they will establish a legal and juridical system which sanctions and enforces commercial and other contracts with impartiality.
>
> 5. All nations should undertake to refrain from propaganda from motives subversive to order and the established political system in other countries than their own."

At the opening of the Conference the Russian Delegation accepted these resolutions on condition that they were reciprocal.

On April 13, the Conference got down to serious business. On that date the other Powers represented handed to the Soviet Delegation what was called the "London Experts' Report," which had been drawn up in London some weeks earlier by a Committee of Allied experts. The most important articles referring to financial claims preferred against the Soviet Government were:

"(Chapter 1, Article 1):

The Russian Soviet Government shall accept the financial obligations of its predecessors, viz., the Imperial Russian Government and the Russian Provisional Government, towards foreign Powers and their nationals.

(Chapter 1, Article 2):

The Russian Soviet Government shall recognise the financial engagements entered into before this date by all authorities in Russia, provincial or local, or by public utility undertakings in Russia, with other Powers or their nationals, and shall guarantee the fulfilment thereof.

(Chapter 1, Article 3):

The Russian Soviet Government shall undertake liability for all actual and direct losses, whether arising out of breach of contract or otherwise, suffered by nationals of other Powers, due to the action or negligence of the Soviet Government or its predecessors or of any provincial or local authorities, or of an agent of any such Government or authority."

How were all these numerous and complicated claims to be appraised? The "Report" proposed that the liabilities of the Soviet Government under these three articles should be assessed by a Russian Debt Commission. Annex 1, Article 1, provided:

"A Russian Debt Commission shall be established consisting of members nominated by the Russian Government and members nominated by the other Powers, together with an independent chairman chosen from outside by agreement among the other members, or, in default, named by the League of Nations, either through the Council or through the Permanent Court of International Justice."

With regard to properties sequestrated by the Soviet Government the "Report" (Annex 2, Article 7) proposed:

"Claimants will be entitled to demand the return of the property, rights and interests.

If the property, rights, or interests are still in existence and capable of identification, they will be returned and compensation for their use or for injury thereto during the dispossession will, in default of agreement between the Soviet Government and the private party concerned, be settled by the Mixed Arbitral Tribunals. Agreements for concessions in relation to public utility undertakings shall be modified so as to be brought into harmony with present economic conditions ; for example, as regards charges, duration of concessions, and conditions of operation.

If the property, rights and interests are not still in existence or cannot be identified, or the claimant does not desire their return, the claim may, by agreement between the Soviet Government and the private party concerned, be satisfied either by the grant of similar property, right or interests, coupled with compensation to be agreed, or, failing agreement, to be fixed by the Mixed Arbitral Tribunals, or by any other agreed settlement.

In all other cases claimants shall be entitled to compensation on a monetary basis, to be fixed by the Mixed Arbitral Tribunals."

Respecting the "Mixed Arbitral Tribunals" referred to in this Article—the "Report" proposed that they should be constituted by the "Russian Debt Commission," and that their procedure should be prescribed by that body.

These proposals were naturally quite unacceptable to the Soviet Delegates because, among other reasons, they would have seriously derogated from the status of Soviet Russia as a sovereign state.

According to the theory and practice of International Law a sovereign State has the right to enact any legislation it thinks fit on the territory within its jurisdiction, even when it affects property owned by foreigners and no foreign subject has a claim against that Government provided the law is applied impartially as between native and foreign subjects. This principle was laid down by Mr. George Canning (British Secretary of State for Foreign Affairs) in the following lucid statement as far back as February 27, 1823:

"It is one of the most important principles of the Law of Nations that a stranger visiting a foreign country virtually binds himself to a temporary and qualified allegiance to its laws, and submits to their observance, however unwise such laws may appear to be to him, however harsh and oppressive they really are, and however they may be at variance with his own notions of political liberty or with the impressions of a happier experience. *Such an individual has no right to complain of the operation of the laws of a foreign state upon himself if they are executed impartially and in the same manner in which they would operate upon native subjects.* The fundamental principle is this: an Englishman going into a foreign country accepts the authority of its legislation, abdicates for a time the benefits of British jurisprudence, and subjects himself to all the consequent inconveniences."

This principle, both before and since the Genoa Conference, has not been questioned by any British Government. Referring to the sequestration of British properties in Czechoslovakia and Rumania, Mr. Lloyd George (then Prime Minister) stated in the House of Commons, May 25, 1922: "We have had complaints from our nationals. We have never been able to interfere, because the sovereign rights of these communities were involved."

The proposals of the "London Experts' Report," in two important respects, would have violated Soviet sovereignty: they would have denied to the Soviet Government the right to sequestrate foreign-owned property on its territory; they would have compelled the Soviet Government to submit claims for compensation of nationalised properties to a mixed tribunal consisting of one Russian and four foreigners.

On April 14 and 15, representatives of the British, French, Italian and Belgian Delegations, under the Presidency of Mr. Lloyd George, at an informal meeting, considered with the Soviet Delegation the implications of the report of the London experts.

At this meeting the Soviet Delegation put forward claims amounting to (approximately) £4,067,227,040, for destruction wrought on their territory both by direct foreign intervention and by the aid given to Koltchak, Denikin, Yudenitch and Wrangel.

At the conclusion of the Conversations the following memorandum was handed to the Russian delegation:

"1. *The creditor Allied Governments represented at Genoa cannot admit any liability with regard to the claims advanced by the Soviet Government.*

2. But in view of the serious economic condition of Russia, such creditor Governments are prepared to write down the war debts owing by Russia to them (by a percentage to be determined later); and the countries represented at Genoa would be prepared to consider not only the postponement of the payments of interest upon financial claims, but also the remission of some part of arrears of interest or postponed interest.

3. It must be definitely agreed, however, that there can be no allowance made to the Soviet Government against:

(*a*) Either the debts and financial obligations due to foreign nationals, or

(*b*) The right of such nationals with regard to the return of their property, and compensation for damage or loss in respect thereof."

On the following day an event occurred which nearly brought the Conference to an untimely end. On Sunday, April 16, 1922, the famous Treaty of Rapallo was signed. The terms of this epoch-making instrument were:

"The German Government, represented by Herr Rathenau, and the Government of the Soviet Republic, represented by the People's Commissar Chicherin, have agreed on the following treaty:

Clause 1. The Two Governments agree that all questions resulting from the state of war between Germany and Russia shall be settled between the Reich and the Federal Republic of Soviets in the following manner:

Paragraph A. The Reich and the Republic of Soviets mutually renounce repayment for their war expenses and for damages arising out of the war, that is to say, damages caused to them and their nationals in the zone of war, operations by military measures, including all requisitions effected in a hostile country. They renounce in the same way repayment for civil damages inflicted on civilians, that is to say, damages caused to the nationals of the two countries by exceptional measures or by violent measures taken by an authority of the State of either side.

Paragraph B. All questions of public or private law resulting from the state of war, including the question of the merchant ships acquired by one or the other side during the war, shall be settled on a principle of reciprocity.

Paragraph C. Germany and Russia mutually renounce repayment of the expenses caused by prisoners of war. In the same way as the Reich renounces repayment of the expenses caused by the internment of soldiers of the Russian Army, the Russian Government renounces repayment of the sums Germany has derived from the sale of Russian Army material transported into Germany.

Clause 2. Germany renounces all claims resulting from the enforcement of the laws and measures of the Soviet Republic as it has affected German nationals or their private rights or the rights of the German Reich itself, as well as claims resulting from measures taken by the Soviet Republic or its authorities in any other way against subjects of the German Reich or their private rights, provided that the Soviet Republic shall not satisfy similar claims made by any third State.

Clause 3. Consular and diplomatic relations between the Reich and the Federal Republic of Soviets shall be resumed immediately. The admission of consuls to both countries shall be arranged by special agreement.

Clause 4. Both Governments agree furthermore that the rights of the nationals of either of the two parties on the other's territory as well as the regulation of commercial relations shall be based on the most-favoured-nation principle. This principle does not include rights and facilities granted by the Soviet Government to another Soviet State or to any State that formerly formed part of the Russian Empire.

Clause 5. The two Governments undertake to give each other mutual assistance for the alleviation of their economic difficulties in the most benevolent spirit. In the event of a general settlement of this question on an international basis they undertake to have a preliminary exchange of views. The German Government declares itself ready to facilitate as far as is possible the conclusion and the execution of economic contracts between private enterprises in the two countries.

Clause 6. Clause 1, paragraph B, and Clause 4 of this agreement will come into force after the ratification of this document. The other clauses will come into force immediately."

The Agreement was signed by M. Chicherin and Herr Rathenau on behalf of the Soviet and German Republic respectively. Knowledge of what had occurred reached the various delegations on the afternoon of April 17 and, to quote M. J. Saxon Mills, " the repercussions of this news were formidable."* However, the Russian and German delegations were not in the least perturbed by the impression made on the minds of the other delegations, and it was explained on behalf of the Soviet Republic that negotiations for a Treaty had been proceeding since January and that its signature at Genoa was purely fortuitous. Herr Rathenau endorsed this and pertinently added that the discussions of the Russian question had in practice been removed from the " Political " Commission on which Germany was represented to the residence of Mr. Lloyd George, the Villa de Albertis, where informal conversations were carried on between the other Powers and the Russian delegation, and that under these circumstances Germany was justified in making her own arrangements with the Soviet Republic.

Germany was regarded as the greater culprit and next day a formal protest was sent to Herr Rathenau signed by the representatives of Great Britain, France, Italy, Japan, Belgium, Czecho-Slovakia, Poland, Yugo-Slavia, Rumania and Portugal. The air became thick with rumours of the immediate demise of the conference, but after informal and private inter-delegation conversations it was announced that Mr. Lloyd George would attend a press Conference on the afternoon of

* *Genoa Conference*, p. 90.

April 20. Commentators stated that when Mr. Lloyd George entered the room his whole bearing so exuded confidence that they immediately sensed the crisis would be dissolved. They had not misjudged. He began by stating that some people wanted the Conference to succeed, others hoped it would fail. He was afraid that the latter would be disappointed. Turning to the Russo-German Agreement he said it was not intended to wreck the Conference though it had endangered it, but that it was over and would not, he hoped, further affect the Conference. Finally, he said that the Russian reply to the Note of the Powers was expected in the course of that day and he anticipated that it would be of such a nature as to justify the continuance of the Conference.

The crisis was dissolved. To quote one commentator: "We left the Palace feeling greatly refreshed and encouraged."

After consultation with their Government the Russian Delegation replied on April 20, 1922:

> "The Russian Delegation are still of the opinion that the present economic condition of Russia and the circumstances which are responsible for it should fully justify the complete release of Russia from all her liabilities mentioned in the above proposals by the recognition of her counter-claims. However, *the Russian delegation are prepared to make a further step towards finding a solution for the adjustment of the differences, and to accept items 1, 2, 3 (a) of the above-mentioned memorandum, provided (1) that the war debts and the arrears of interest or postponed interests of all debts are written down, and (2) that adequate financial help is given to Russia assisting her to recover from her present economic state in the shortest possible period.* With regard to 3 (*b*), subject to the above two stipulations, the Russian Government would be willing to restore to its former owners the use of property, nationalised or withheld, or where this is not possible, then to satisfy the just claims of the former owners, either by mutual agreement with them direct or in accordance with arrangements, the details of which will be discussed and agreed during the present Conference.
>
> Foreign financial help is absolutely essential for the economic reconstruction of Russia, and as long as there is no prospect of this reconstruction, the Russian Delegation cannot see their way to put upon their country the burden of debts which could not be discharged.
>
> The Russian Delegation wish also to make it clear, although it seems to be self-evident, that the Russian Government could not admit liability for the debts of its predecessors until it has been formally recognised *de jure* by the Powers concerned."

After considerable deliberation, the representatives of the Powers sent on May 3, 1922, to the Russian Delegation a lengthy memorandum, consisting of a preamble, thirteen articles and an annexe.

It was contended in the preamble that the best, in fact the only, way to bring about Russia's economic recovery was to allow foreign capitalists both to work their old concessions, factories, and businesses and to establish new ones. *There was no proposal whatever to render direct financial aid to the Russian Government,* notwithstanding that the Russian Delegation, in their last note (April 20) emphasised that it could not, without such assistance, discharge the Tsarist and municipal debts and pay compensation.

It was now clear that the interpretations placed on the phrase "Reconstruction of Russia" by the Russian and Non-Russian Delegations respectively, were as the poles apart.

For the Non-Russian Delegations reconstruction meant throwing Russia open to foreign concessionaires, primarily in the interests of the latter.

For the Russian Delegation reconstruction meant improving the economic mechanism of Russia, so as to increase the wealth of the country, primarily in the interests of the Russian masses but also in a way which would enable Russia to acknowledge and discharge certain agreed liabilities to foreign investors.

The thirteen "Clauses" contained in the memorandum were largely a repetition of the "Report" presented to the Russian Delegation on April 13.

The most important ones were:

> "Clause 2, Article 2. *The Allies can admit no liability for the claims against them set up by the Russian Soviet Government for loss and damage suffered during the revolution in Russia since the war.*
>
> Clause 4. In conformity with the general principle admitted *by all Governments, the Russian Soviet Government recognises its obligation to fulfil the financial engagements which it or its predecessors,* that is to say, the Imperial Russian Government, or the Provisional Russian Government, *have contracted vis-à-vis foreign nationals.*
>
> Clause 5. The Russian Soviet Government undertakes to recognise or to cause to be recognised, *the financial engagements of all authorities in Russia,* provincial or local, as well as all public utility enterprises in Russia contracted before this date *vis-à-vis* the nationals of other Powers, unless at the time when the engagement was contracted the territory in which the authority or enterprise was situated was not under the control of the Russian Soviet

Government, or of the Russian Provisional Government, or the Russian Imperial Government.

Clause 6. The Russian Soviet Government agrees to conclude an arrangement within twelve months of the coming into force of this Clause with the representatives of foreign holders of bonds and bills issued or guaranteed by the Russian Soviet Government or its predecessors, for ensuring the re-starting of the service of the loans and the payment of the bills.

If no such arrangement can be concluded, *the Russian Soviet Government agrees to accept the decision of an Arbitration Commission.* This Commission shall consist of a member appointed by the Soviet Government, a member appointed by the foreign holders, two members and a President appointed by the Supreme Court of the United States, or, failing it, by the Council of the League of Nations, or the President of the Permanent Court of International Justice at the Hague.

This Commission shall decide all questions as to the remission of interest, and as to the mode of payment of capital and interest and will take into account in so doing the economic and financial conditions of Russia.

Clause 7. Without prejudice to its freedom as recognised in the Cannes Resolution to regulate its system of ownership, internal economy and government, and to choose for itself the system which it prefers in this respect, the Russian Soviet Government recognises its obligations in accordance with the said Resolution, to restore or compensate all foreign interests for loss or damage caused to them when property has been confiscated or withheld.

In cases in which the previous owner is not enabled to resume possession of his former rights, the Russian Soviet Government will make an offer of compensation. If no agreement is come to between the previous owner and the Russian Soviet Government as to the nature and amount of the compensation, the previous owner shall be entitled to submit to the Mixed Arbitral Tribunal referred to hereafter the question whether the compensation offered by the Russian Soviet Government is just and adequate."

Objectionable though Clause 7 was from the Soviet viewpoint, the Belgian Foreign Minister, M. Jaspar, fought hard to make it still more rigid. He proposed an amendment making the return of foreign-owned property compulsory. Mr. Lloyd George resisted this amendment on the grounds that it went beyond the Cannes Resolution. Against the wishes of M. Jaspar the clause, as quoted above, was finally accepted.

Not content with these demands, the Powers also wished both to lay down the broad principles of Russia's legal system, and even to force on her a system of capitulations. An annexe was appended to the memorandum, from which we take the following excerpts:

"(Article 8):

3. The law to be applied must be known and published; it shall be equal between persons and have no retroactive effect. It shall afford adequate guarantees to foreigners against arbitrary arrests and domiciliary visits.

4. Foreigners shall have free access to the courts, and no disability shall attach to foreigners as foreigners; they shall be entitled to be represented before the courts by counsel of their own choosing.

8. The validity of a clause in contracts for the arbitration of any or all disputes arising therein shall be recognised and rules shall be made for enforcing arbitration awards, including those given in a foreign country.

(Article 11):

Foreigners shall be at liberty to communicate freely by post, telegraph, or wireless telegraph, and to use telegraph codes under the conditions, and subject to the regulations, laid down in the International Telegraph Conventions.

(Article 14):

Foreigners shall have adequate facilities for travelling on Russian railways, roads and waterways, and for the carriage of their goods and merchandise. These facilities shall not be less than those accorded to Russian Government enterprises or Russian nationals, and shall be applied without discrimination."

At this point it is worth while to recall what Mr. J. L. Garvin cabled to his paper from Genoa on the foregoing:

"It is quite impossible for Mr. Chicherin and his colleagues to surrender the sovereignty of Russia. They cannot accept a régime of tutelage, control, capitulations and mixed tribunals. Japan shook off mixed tribunals nearly thirty years ago. Turkey repudiates the old régime of capitulations. It is useless to ask Soviet Russia to accept what even China begins to reject."

As already mentioned, the *Times* was animated by a blind, unreasoning hatred towards the conference. It sent as its special correspondent to Genoa no less a person than its editor, Mr. Wickham Steed, who perhaps with the object of emphasising the journal's support of the French attitude took up his residence at the same hotel as the French

Delegation, namely the Savoia. On Sunday, May 7, 1922, Mr. Steed cabled to London that Mr. Lloyd George was so bitterly disappointed with the French attitude that he had threatened M. Barthou with a rupture of the entente between Great Britain and France. It is true that on that date, in the course of a statement to the British press, M. Barthou admitted that he was supporting the Belgian thesis on the restoration of sequestrated properties, but he argued that although he had sided with Belgium it was not a case of supporting Belgium against Britain but only " a question of public law."

There was no suggestion in the interview that Mr. Lloyd George had threatened the denunciation of the entente.

However, Mr. Steed's cable created an international sensation, albeit a short-lived one. On the same day as it appeared an exchange of letters on the subject took place between Mr. Lloyd George and M. Barthou in the course of which the latter wrote " you did not pronounce one word which could be interpreted as expressing the intention to break the friendship which unites us."

M. Barthou's letter closed that incident but the latter added to the volume of suspicion which made the success of the conference still more problematical.

After careful and detailed consideration of the Powers' Memorandum, the Russian Delegation, on May 11, 1922, handed in their reply.

It was a lengthy document, well worth quoting in full, but considerations of space will only permit of a summary and some of the more important extracts:

1. The Reply maintained that Russia's claim for compensation for the destruction caused by foreign intervention was legally and historically justifiable:

" Without citing other cases we shall limit ourselves to recalling the decision of the Court of Arbitration at Geneva of September 14, 1872, condemning Great Britain to pay to the United States 15½ million dollars for the damages caused to that country by the privateer ' Alabama ' which in the Civil War between the Northern and Southern States gave help to the latter."

2. The Reply pointed out that Governments born of revolutions in the past did not respect the financial undertakings of their predecessors:

" The French Convention, of which France declares herself to be the legitimate successor proclaimed on December 22, 1792, that ' the sovereignty of peoples is not bound by the treaties of tyrants,' In accordance with this declaration, revolutionary France not only tore up the political treaties of the former régime with foreign countries, but also repudiated her national debt. She consented to pay only one-third of that debt, and that from motives of political expedience. This was the 'tiers consolide,' the interest on which did not begin to be regularly paid until the commencement of the nineteenth century."

3. With respect to the proposed Russian debt Commission, Mixed Arbitral Tribunals and régime of capitulations, the Reply stated:

"Clause 7 begins with a fine preamble, recognising the sovereign right of Russia to organise as she thinks fit within her own territory her system of property, her economic system and her Government; but the text of the clause itself is in flagrant contradiction with its preamble. *The sovereignty of the Russian State becomes the plaything of chance. It can be defeated by the decisions of a mixed Court of Arbitration composed of four foreigners and one Russian,* which will decide in the last instance whether the interests of foreigners are to be subject to the restoration, restitution or compensation."

So far the Soviet Government stood firmly on its sovereign rights. Nevertheless, it was no slave to mere legal formalism. The Reply continued:

"Nevertheless, in its desire to reach a practical agreement, the Russian Delegation, as a result of the discussions which took place at the Villa de Albertis, adopted a policy of most far-reaching concessions, and declared itself prepared to renounce conditionally its counter-claims, and to accept the engagements of the former Governments, in exchange for a number of concessions on the part of the Powers, the most important being real credits placed at the disposal of the Russian Government amounting to a sum to be agreed upon in advance. Unfortunately, this engagement of the Powers has not been carried out. The Memorandum says nothing of definite credits which the signatories would be ready to grant to the Russian Government."

Finally the Reply advanced the following proposal:

"If, nevertheless, the Powers desire to examine the solution of the financial disputes between themselves and Russia, inasmuch as this question demands a deeper study of the nature and extent of the claims presented to Russia and a more exact appreciation of the credits that could be placed at her disposal, this task might be entrusted to a mixed commission of experts appointed by the Conference whose work should begin at a date and in a place to be determined by mutual agreement."

The political sub-committee of the Conference met on the morning of May 13, 1922, to consider the Russian reply. Mr. Lloyd George first addressed the commission. He declared that the Russian reply was unsatisfactory but that the suggested mixed commission was helpful and he concluded by urging acceptance of the Russian proposal.

M. Barthou, speaking on instructions from Paris, asserted that the proposed commission would be fruitless, that it would only mean restarting the Genoa Conference in another form. The Italian and Rumanian delegates acted as mediators between the French and British views and finally the sitting was adjourned to permit of informal discussions.

A private conference followed that afternoon between Mr. Lloyd George and M. Barthou, at which many difficulties were removed and when the delegates met again that afternoon it was announced that agreement had been reached on almost all points.

Next day (May 14, 1922) the delegates met again. Finally it was agreed that a new conference should meet at the Hague, that there should be two commissions, one of delegates from the Powers represented at Genoa (excluding Russia and Germany) and the other of Russians, and that the Powers concerned should undertake not to conclude separate political agreements with the Soviets during the interim.

Next day a Note was handed to the Russian Delegation by the Chiefs of the delegations of the Allied Governments. Its substance was: that the Soviet proposal for a meeting of a Commission of Experts should be accepted; that the non-Russian Commission should meet on June 15, 1922, at the Hague "for a preliminary exchange of views"; that the names of the Russian Commission should be communicated to the other Powers not later than June 20; that the two Commissions should meet on June 26, 1922; that "the matters to be dealt with by these Commissions will comprise all outstanding questions relating to debts, private property and credit."

II. "Pact of Peace"

The final plenary session of the Genoa Conference was held on May 19, 1922. The delegations present very wisely recognised that the proposed Hague Conference could only work in tranquillity if there was peace on Russia's frontiers and for that reason the first business of the day was the acceptance by the chief of each delegation present—a few with reservations—of what was known as the "Pact of Peace." This Pact read:

> "In order to enable the work of the Commissions to be carried on in tranquillity, and in order to restore mutual confidence, engagements will be entered into binding the Russian Soviet Government

and the Governments now allied with the Russian Soviet Government on the one hand, and the other participating Governments on the other hand, to refrain from all acts of aggression against their respective territories, and to refrain from subversive propaganda.

The pact to refrain from acts of aggression will be founded on the observance of the existing status quo, and will remain in force for a period of four months from the closing of the work of the Commissions."*

This may have seemed a meagre result for six weeks work, but Mr. Lloyd George said that it had been well worth while. In the course of his speech he admonished the Soviet delegates that Russia without European help could " not recover for a generation "; that Europe was eager to help, but that if Russia wanted her assistance she must first renounce " the doctrine of the repudiation of debts." M. Chicherin was Mr. Lloyd George's equal in retort. He replied: " The British Premier tells me that, if my neighbour has lent me money, I must pay him back. Well, I agree, in that particular case, in a desire for conciliation ; but I must add that if this neighbour has broken into my house, killed my children, destroyed my furniture and burnt my house, he must at least begin by restoring to me what he has destroyed."†

Mr. Lloyd George gave an account of his activities at Genoa to the House of Commons on May 25, 1922. Negotiations with the Soviet Delegates was the kernel of his theme. He told his listeners that the riches of Russia were indispensable to world trade recovery ; that one could only reach the great Russian people through the Soviet leaders ; that Russia was in a deplorable state of want, that she could not surmount her difficulties without outside assistance, but that that would not be forthcoming unless the Soviet Government recognised the debts of its predecessors and restored or compensated for sequestrated foreign-owned properties.

As to the Soviet's counter-claims—Mr. Lloyd George advanced the extraordinary doctrine that France and Britain had each interfered in the other's Civil War and in neither case did the aggrieved party receive compensation, therefore the Soviet's counter-claims were historically unsound. One member, Commander Kenworthy, interjected " Alabama," but the Prime Minister, wisely from the point of view of his brief, ignored the remark.

Mr. Lloyd George continued that the Governments of France, Belgium, Italy and Britain were willing " in view of the serious economic condition of Russia to write down the claims for money

* " Genoa Conference," p. 260.

† *Ibid.* pp. 284, 285.

advanced by Governments during the war," but that private claims, financial and property, would have to be met in full. Mr. Lloyd George did not add, as he might have done, that Great Britain had been the biggest lender to Russia during the war, that France was the largest holder of pre-war private loans, and that Belgium was the biggest claimant for sequestrated properties. Italy's interests were not large under either head. In other words, Britain was willing, in the interests of a settlement " to write down " her claims, but France and Belgium stood for their full pound of flesh. But that was not all—Belgium argued that compensation was not enough, that " property must be restored if that were materially possible " and " France acted with Belgium—not from a grievance—but rather out of general sympathy with Belgium." Mr. Lloyd George might have more truthfully declared that France supported Belgium in the hope of wrecking the Conference. All the rest of the delegations accepted the British point of view.

Respecting the Hague Conference, the Prime Minister said that that assembly would concern itself with practical discussions between experts and he was hopeful of fruitful results because the Soviet Government was in crying need of foreign help and because it did not know what to do with the properties which it had nationalised. On the latter subject he said:

> " They state that a vast majority of the properties—and most of our difficulties came over the property—can, as a matter of fact, be restored. The real reason is, they do not know what to do with them. They had not the skill ; they had not the knowledge ; they had not the workmen ; and they are most anxious to hand these over to anybody who knows what to do with them. That is the fact of the matter. Most of the properties, I understand, are in a position to be restored, and are ready to be restored."

It is difficult to believe to-day that that statement was seriously made only twenty-one years ago.

Preparations were immediately begun for the holding of the Hague Conference. M. Poincaré was too astute to refuse bluntly to send French delegates and thus earn the opprobrium for preventing a European settlement, but he had clearly made up his mind to prevent a successful outcome. The subject, among others, was discussed in the French Chamber, June 1, 1922. To quote the *Manchester Guardian's* report:

> " After a short suspension of the sitting, M. Poincaré referred to the question of the Hague Conference, and said France retained complete liberty of action. Certain obscurities still

existed regarding the programme and the role of this conference. The objection he had formulated in the first instance was now raised by the United States. If America did not go to the Hague this conference could only partially accomplish its work. The French Government, which had accepted no obligation, would examine the situation in complete freedom. It would send experts to the Hague, but only with the consent of Parliament.

In any case, it could not be said that France refused to collaborate in the reconstruction of Europe."*

M. Poincaré's declaration, both in tone and substance, left little doubt that what the French statesman meant by "collaboration" was the demand for submission to the French thesis. This was made clearer on the following day when the French Government sent a Note to all the participating Powers urging that they should lay down, as a condition of the Hague Conference, the principle that the Soviet Government must restore (where possible) to its former owners the foreign-owned property which it had nationalised, and that the right of deciding whether to restore or compensate should not be left to the competence of the Soviet Government.

The French Government were, of course, well aware that the Soviets would not even consider a proposal so derogatory to their sovereignty. Whitehall recognised this and in the course of a lengthy reply dated June 10, 1922, the British Government stated:

"In the matter of private property for instance, the French Government contends that foreign claimants have 'the right to demand its return.' The only exception which it admits to this right is in the case of cultivable land where peasant owners would have to be evicted if the property were to be returned. His Majesty's Government cannot accept this contention. Every State has the right compulsorily to acquire private property, whatsoever its nature, on payment of just compensation. Every State has exercised that right down to the most recent times.

The French Government's argument in this connection is contrary to the first Cannes Resolution, because it contravenes an acknowledged right of Sovereign States throughout the world. Whether the Russian Government makes restitution of private property alienated from its owners or pays compensation for it is a matter solely for the Russian Government. His Majesty's Government would be repudiating British principle and British practice if they took any other view, and they think it hardly necessary to prove that this principle and this practice are com-

* *Manchester Guardian*, 2.vi.22.

mon to the French Government, the Government of the United States, and to civilised Governments in every continent. To attempt to force any other principle upon the Russian Government would be to demand of Russia what no Sovereign State has ever been willing to concede. They entirely agree, however, that the compensation must be real, not shadowy."

The French reply was issued two days later. It made no attempt to reply to the paragraphs just quoted from the British Note, but it made clear that the French delegates would be representatives and not plenipotentiaries and would not be empowered to conclude any arrangements except *ad referendum.*

On the same day, two speeches made in London at a dinner given by the British-Russia Club, one by a leading British delegate to the Conference, Sir Philip Lloyd-Greame,* and the other by a British technical expert, Mr. Leslie Urquhart,† cast a flood of light on the unhelpful state of mind in which even the British representatives were leaving for the Hague. Sir Philip said:

"Russia needed the trade of the outside world more than the outside world needed the trade of Russia. A Russia could exist without the outside world, but it would be a primitive Russia—not one community, but a collection of communities, each living its primitive life. It would be a far different Russia from what the Soviet had pictured."‡

And Mr. Urquhart declared:

"The civilised world could help Russia only through capital, and capital could only function in an atmosphere of public confidence, security and freedom. Should the Soviet Government not be prepared to yield to the demands of economic law, the Hague Conference would fail."§

It is not fanciful to imagine these two gentlemen saying to themselves "Russia is in a very bad way. She will be very complaisant. We shall persuade her to scrap her social system."

The *Times* confidently predicted failure. It declared:

"The French are sending a delegation of experts to show that they have no ill-will. The Hague Conference will meet. It may disperse in ten days' time, probably to the relief of all concerned. It may drag on in obscurity for months. But, at any rate, this dull and formal liquidation of Genoa will leave no deep mark on the history of our time."||

* See Note on p. 54. † See Note on p. 49.
‡ *Times*, 13.vi.22. § *Ibid.* || *Ibid.* 14.vi.22.

III. Preparations for the Hague. The Non-Russian Commission

It had been agreed, despite opposition from the Soviet side, that the non-Russian delegations should meet at the Hague some ten days before the full conference, so as to agree on a joint line of procedure, *vis-à-vis* the Russian delegation. Naturally this procedure was strongly disliked by the Soviet Government because it anticipated that in order to get unity the more reasonable Powers such as Britain and Italy would have to make considerable concessions to the more untractable, such as Belgium and France, and that the upshot would be the presentation of terms wholly unacceptable to Moscow.

However, the non-Russian Powers adhered to this procedure and their opening meeting was held at the Hague on June 15, 1922. All the Powers represented at the Genoa Conference sent delegates except Germany who in the Treaty of Rapallo had made a comprehensive agreement with Soviet Russia.

The Chairman, Jonkheer van Karnebeeck, the Dutch Foreign Minister, in his presidential address declared:

> "The task is arduous on account of the profound divergencies in principle and method which divide Soviet Russia and the other Powers here represented. The problem is more difficult to solve, as the system applied in Russia seems a very real obstacle to the economic restoration of that unhappy country."*

That unhelpful statement, coupled with a blunt interview given by Mr. Leslie Urquhart, one of the British experts, in the Amsterdam *Telegraaf*, in which he spoke of the economic impossibility of the Soviet régime, sounded to competent observers very much like Bolshevik baiting and augured badly for the success of the Conference.

As usual, before the proceedings got properly under way, there were many discussions not only in the Conference Hall but also in the corridors and ante-rooms. In this case an additional difficulty sprang from the intransigence of M. Poincaré: the French delegates were kept waiting for instructions.

On June 19, the non-Russian delegates decided to establish three sub-Committees to deal with (a) Russian debts; (b) private property; (c) Russian credits. The five principal Powers—Great Britain, France, Italy, Belgium and Japan—were represented on all three. The election of the committees would have presented no difficulties had it not been for the sabotaging tactics of the Quai d'Orsay. The *Daily Telegraph's* special correspondent cabled on June 19:

> "The only real point with regard to these Committees was

* *Daily Telegraph*, 16.vi.22.

whether France would agree to act on any of them. As late as mid-day the French delegation had received no instructions from their Government, and the possibility of having to postpone the elections was considered. Shortly afterwards M. Benoist, the French Minister at the Hague, received a telegram from Paris which he read to the meeting. This message directed M. Benoist to state that France would agree to be represented on the Committees subject to the condition that no political questions were discussed with the Russians, that all decisions arrived at should be taken subject to reference to the French Government, and with a reservation to withdraw the French experts from the Committees should the attitude of the Soviet delegates at any time render that course necessary in the opinion of the French Government."

It was next decided to constitute a Standing Orders Committee to organise the work of the non-Russian Commission. This Committee consisted of the President and Vice-President of the Commission together with the Chairman and Vice-Chairman of the three Committees. M. Van Karnebeeck, who, up to this time had acted as temporary President of the Commission retired from the position and M. Patyn, the senior Dutch delegate, was elected permanent President. He was given a mandate to open communications with the Russian Commission and to suggest to its members that they should also select three Committees to negotiate with those appointed for discussion of the subjects referred to the Hague by the Genoa Conference.

The three Committees were to report to the full Commission, and if agreement was reached there was to be a joint meeting of the Non-Russian and Russian Commissions for the adoption of a report to be referred to all the participating Governments. The Russian delegates, headed by M. Litvinov, duly arrived and a meeting of the credits Committee, at which both sides were represented, was held on June 27, 1922. As usual at such opening meetings, some time was taken up in sparring for position.

The Chairman, Baron Avezzano (Italy) asked M. Litvinov what his proposals were, how much Russia needed and for what purposes. Litvinov replied that before discussing Russia's needs it was first necessary to learn whether the various Governments were prepared to give Russia credit and if so to what extent.

Mr. Hilton Young (Great Britain) replied with some heat that there was capital available for investment in Russia upon terms, that they were busy men, that their attendance at the Conference was sufficient proof that credits were possible.

Finally it was agreed that M. Litvinov should draw up a list of Russia's needs under the heads (a) transport; (b) agriculture; (c) industries.

Nominally the three Committees (credits, properties, debts) were to proceed *pari passu*, but the Russians insisted that they could not discuss the other questions until they had received some definite information respecting credits. They were prepared to make considerable concessions, but only in return for the wherewithal to hasten the economic recovery of their country.

Next day, June 28, 1922, the debts Committee met under the Chairmanship of M. Alphand. The latter proposed, and the Soviet delegates agreed, that the Committee should deal with (1) Russian Government loans; (2) railway loans; (3) Treasury bills; (4) other public debts represented by securities.

M. Alphand next read a questionnaire on the Russian budget to which his side wanted detailed answers. This was resisted by M. Litvinov as being outside the Committee's province, but finally he agreed to consider it on condition that the question of a moratorium for Russian debts was included in the subjects for discussion.

On June 30, 1922, at the Credits Committee, M. Litvinov made a lengthy exposition of his Government's point of view, and its foreign credits requirements. He stated, to quote the *Times*, that:

> "Whereas before the war Russia's wealth was 150,000,000,000 gold roubles, with an income of 12,000,000,000 to 15,000,000,000, the European war and the war of intervention had reduced that wealth by five-twelfths. The war of intervention alone had cost the Russian Government between forty and fifty thousand millions."*

He continued that "it was of interest to both parties that the economic reconstruction of Russia should be undertaken as soon as possible."

All the non-Russian Powers represented were asking the Soviets to shoulder heavy burdens, and it was obvious that the Soviets willy-nilly could not discharge such responsibilities unless and until their country's production had been restored. M. Litvinov stated that his Government was preparing to spend enormous sums in reconstructing and developing the country, but they considered that foreign countries should help by providing certain credits for specific services and purposes. He then read the following list:

> "1. Transports: Water transports, railways, Moscow and seaports, harbours (Trans-Siberian not included)—1,050 million gold roubles.

* *Times*, 1.vii.22.

2. Agriculture: Irrigation, new seed, stock and machinery—924 million gold roubles.

3. Industrial reconstruction: Mainly textiles and timber (others, such as oil, practically financing themselves)—750 million gold roubles.

4. Commercial and bank credits—500 million gold roubles."*

These made a total of 3,224 million gold roubles = [approximately] £341,525,000. This sum, large though it was in absolute measure, was relatively small compared with the total which the Soviet Government itself intended to invest in the reconstruction of Russia.

At the same session M. Litvinov promised a complete list of the concessions which his Government was willing to grant as well as the capital sums required for each concession. In addition he presented a questionnaire asking for detailed information on the actual bondholders, their claims, etc. The Soviet thesis in a nutshell was that the Allied Governments, by their interventionist policy, had ruined Russia, and if they wanted any return on their pre-war investments they must be prepared to help in the rehabilitation of the country.

After some additional explanations by the Russian representatives the meeting was adjourned to permit the non-Russian delegates to digest the declaration and to enable M. Litvinov to prepare a further statement. After this session, owing to the business-like declaration of M. Litvinov, the spirits of many of the representatives rose considerably. The *Times* correspondent cabled: "It was the opinion of the British Delegation at the Hague Conference to-day that things are proceeding most favourably."†

On the other hand, the majority of the French papers kept prophesying that the Conference would not have any practical results.

A new factor had arisen which strengthened the hands of the Soviet delegation: it was now July and the Soviet harvest promised to be exceptionally good.

However, the British optimism did not last long. A few days later these ominous words appeared in a *Times* leader: "At the Hague, Great Britain, France and Italy speak with a united voice," which in reality meant that Great Britain had succumbed to French influence, a fact which damned the Conference.

On July 3, 7 and 10, sessions of the various Committees were held. It is sufficient here to summarise what transpired at these meetings. The non-Russian delegation said that they could not reply to M. Litvinov's questionnaire because "the collection of the information would involve an enormous amount of work," but they submitted summary figures of claims under the headings: (*a*) Industrial and

* *Manchester Guardian*, I.vii.22. † *Times*, I.vii.22.

Commercial Property; (*b*) Immovable Property; (*c*) Miscellaneous Groups of Property. However, they admitted that this list was by no means complete.

The Soviet delegation presented a list of properties which its Government was prepared to lease to concessionaires as part compensation for foreign sequestrated properties and added that it was also prepared to compensate financially, but before it could agree as to what extent, it must know definitely what credits it would receive.

At a meeting of the Private Property Committee, July 13, 1922, the representatives of the non-Russian delegation stated that the list of concessions which the Soviets had offered was not nearly adequate and wanted to know how former owners would be compensated where property was not restored. M. Litvinov, in reply, repeated that the Soviet delegation was "prepared to discuss the question of compensation, but you will understand that that is tantamount to the Russian Government undertaking such obligations and this cannot be answered until we know how speedily Russia can be economically rehabilitated and what help foreign countries can give to accelerate its recovery."

Sir Philip Lloyd-Greame replied that the only effective form of compensation would be "the restitution of the property concerned wherever possible," and he asked M. Litvinov what his Government was prepared to restore and what compensation they were prepared to give, but he (Sir Philip Lloyd-Greame) was not prepared to promise anything in the way of credits.

Shortly afterwards the session concluded without having achieved any results.

Next day, July 14, the Credits Committee met. Commander Hilton Young, on behalf of Great Britain, supported by M. Chevilly, on behalf of France, declared that their Governments were not in a position to lend money, that Russia could obtain loans from their respective private holders of capital, and that the only way to achieve this was to restore confidence in Russian integrity by restoring nationalised properties and acknowledging debts. M. Litvinov replied that what the Soviets had been suggesting was not that the Governments should grant loans, but that they should guarantee goods. He pointed out that even "if confidence is restored" there was no guarantee that credits would be forthcoming, and that, therefore, his Government could not acknowledge liabilities and guarantee to discharge them in the future. On July 15 the Chairman of the non-Russian delegation wrote to the Russian delegation asking if it was prepared to improve upon its last offer. M. Litvinov, in the course of a lengthy reply, declared:

> "The Russian Delegation, while rejecting the obligation to restore concessions or leases of property to their former foreign

owners, has repeatedly declared that the Russian Government by no means refuses to discuss concrete forms of compensation which could be given to the former private property owners who have suffered on account of measures taken by the Soviet Government; it merely proposes that the discussion of these forms of compensation should be adjourned until the questions of the financial assistance to be given to Russia and the information concerning the amount of the claims which have been asked for from the Non-Russian Commission have been settled. These latter conditions are determined by practical necessities, for without this assistance and this information the Russian Government would be unable to find the resources or means which can make it possible to give real compensation."

M. Litvinov concluded by stating that the present situation was due to the fact that there had not been a plenary session of the two Commissions and the Russian delegation proposed that the Chairman of the three non-Russian Committees and the Russian Commission should be summoned to seek the means of establishing a basis for the continuance of the Conference.

It was reported the same evening that unless the Russian delegation made some new and better offer the Conference would be wound up.

The two Commissions met on July 19; M. Litvinov recapitulated his arguments in the various Committees that the refusal of credits created an entirely new situation, because the offer made by the Russian delegation was made on the assumption that credits would be forthcoming, but as this was not the case an entirely new situation had been created and it would be necessary for the Soviet delegation to communicate with its Government. He concluded with an offer to refer the following proposals to Moscow, provided the other delegations at the same time referred them to their Governments:

"1. To acknowledge debts due by the Russian Government or its predecessors to foreign nationals;

2. To agree to give effective compensation to foreigners for property formerly owned by them and since nationalised by the Russian Government, provided that the terms of payment of the debts and the terms of compensation, whether in the form of concessions of property or otherwise, are to be left to be agreed between the Russian Government and the persons concerned in the course of two years."

Sir Philip Lloyd-Greame at once replied that he considered M. Litvinov's speech of "the greatest importance" and in reply to a question M. Litvinov said that a reply from Moscow could be anticipated in from four to seven days.

There was no demur to this ; nevertheless, the Standing Orders Committee of the Non-Russian Commission that very same day adopted unanimously a resolution which noted with satisfaction the proposal contained in M. Litvinov's declaration, and added:

> "The Non-Russian Commission does not find in the terms of this declaration itself the basis for an agreement, but notes that the line of conduct indicated in the declaration can, if it is accepted by the Russian Government and loyally carried out, contribute to the restoration of confidence, which is necessary for the collaboration of Europe in the reconstruction of Russia. The Non-Russian Commission also notes that this declaration can help to create a favourable atmosphere for any further negotiations which may be considered expedient by the various Governments."

The acceptance of this resolution was, of course, the signal for ringing down the curtain, or, to change the metaphor and quote the *Times*, for the "evaporation of the Hague Conference."

Next day, July 20, 1922, the Hague Conference formally concluded. Why did the Conference not await a reply from Moscow ? Why were the proceedings so abruptly wound up? The Soviet delegation had their interpretation. On July 21 they declared in a statement:

> "Certain members of the non-Russian Commission—those who at Genoa had raised the greatest objection to the convocation of the Hague Conference, who, in the interval between Genoa and the Hague had tried to render the Hague Conference impossible, who are chiefly interested in continuing the financial and economic blockade of Russia, and who stand out as the main obstacle to the economic reconstruction of Europe, wished to break up the Conference as soon as possible, fearing, if it lasted much longer, the dissolution of their anti-Russian front. They succeeded. The Conference was prematurely interrupted without having completed its labours or fulfilled its appointed role. But the Russian Delegation is firmly persuaded that the problems raised will shortly find a solution through a channel just as favourable, if not more so, for Soviet Russia."

Was this interpretation correct ? A very similar reading of the events was expressed in a section of the Dutch press. It is significant that the *Morning Post* which had been persistently and vehemently opposed to the Conference, stated in a cable from their special correspondent:

> "Some Dutch papers endeavour to blame the French and

Belgian delegates for having brought about the abrupt ending of the Conference and for having more or less persuaded the British delegation to adopt a less conciliatory attitude than might have been expected from them."

This suspicion, which was in substantial agreement with the Soviet interpretation of the facts, was widely shared by press correspondents of all countries who attended the Conference.

On the return home of the British delegation the matter was debated in the House of Commons. The Labour Party speakers stressed that the Russian market was of supreme importance to Britain in view of the serious proportions of the unemployment problem, they charged the Government with subordinating the interests of British trade to the claims of bondholders, and urged the *de jure* recognition of the Soviet Government and the extension of Government guaranteed credits to further British-Russian trade.

Mr. Hilton Young opened for the Government. He said that at the Hague the non-Russian delegations had informed the Russians that they could not hope to obtain any foreign credits or loans until they had "restored confidence" by satisfying the claims of foreign creditors. Later in the debate Mr. Lloyd George, after endorsing what Mr. Hilton Young had said, declared that conditions were becoming so bad in Russia that the Soviets would be compelled to establish the necessary conditions for the attraction of foreign capital. He stated:

> "The factories were becoming derelict. Every month was making them drop into decay. The Russians could not run their factories. They were bound to call in Western capitalists, Western brains and Western skill, which were essential to the running of their manufactures. In regard to the Russian railways, Mr. Lloyd George said that the Russians could not build locomotives. The rolling stock was getting worse and worse, and unless the West came in it would be impossible to run anything along the permanent way. It was worn out, and even if it were all right locomotives and wagons were out of repair, and in a very short time Russia would be short of what was necessary for the very minimum requirements of civilisation."*

Time showed that the two gentlemen were badly informed and were worse prophets. At no subsequent negotiations with any country did the Soviets offer such favourable terms to foreign claimants as at the Hague.

* *Times*, 27.vii.22.

The Hague (1922) Conference was the last attempt made to negotiate a joint agreement with the Soviets. After its close the various Governments represented, each in its own way and in its own time, negotiated direct with Moscow.

Although the Genoa and Hague Conferences did not produce immediate practical results, they were far from a waste of effort. The very fact that they were held and that they were representative of such a large number of nations was a powerful recognition of the importance of Soviet Russia to any scheme of European, and for that matter, world economic recovery, and the fact that personal contact had been established between the Chancelleries of Soviet Russia and the other Powers represented paved the way for individual approaches to Moscow during the following two years.

IV. Russian-Asiatic Consolidated Company Ltd. agreement. Soviet Note on Near East Conference. *Rapprochement* with France

Nothing of importance happened between London and Moscow until September 9, 1922, when the news was flashed from Berlin to all quarters of the globe that an agreement between the Soviet Government and its most important British claimant, the Russian-Asiatic Consolidated Company Ltd., had been initialled in that city. The latter had preferred claims against Moscow amounting to £56,000,000, which represented about one-third of the total British claims. M. Krassin had conducted the negotiations on behalf of the Soviets and Mr. Leslie Urquhart on behalf of the Company.

After initialling, M. Krassin said that the agreement was the result of a compromise, both sides having made important concessions and Mr. Urquhart declared he was confident that the agreement afforded a basis for real work.

Unwisely, from the point of view of British capitalism, the agreement was hailed by the extreme "right" press as a communist capitulation. The *Morning Post*, typical of the others, yelled "that the conclusion of the agreement is a moral defeat for communism, and a great moral victory for capitalism." The real motives which influenced the Soviets were, to be charitable, completely misunderstood. Moscow believed that it was morally justified in refusing compensation to foreign claimants until its counter-claims were met, but as it was anxious to improve its relations with Great Britain it was prepared to make concessions provided it had reasonable grounds for assuming that London would reciprocate.

The Soviets had met the Russian-Asiatic Consolidated Co. Ltd., halfway, not for technical reasons, not because they were unable to work the properties, but for political reasons, because they wanted to improve the atmosphere between Whitehall and the Kremlin. Had these facts been logically faced by the British Government and its Fleet Street supporters, the sequel might, probably would, have been different.

Government circles here welcomed the agreement, yet for some reason which has never been explained, within a few days they openly affronted Russia in a matter of vital interest to the latter. The Greeks had been driven out of Asia Minor, a Conference was being summoned on the initiation of Great Britain at Lausanne to negotiate peace between the Allies and Turkey and to establish a new régime for the future of the Straits, a matter of paramount importance for Russia as the greatest Black Sea Power. Britain was the leading Power in bringing this Conference into being (France had already made a separate peace with Turkey), yet she showed no desire to include Russia, despite the fact that in all previous settlements regarding the Straits, Russia had been a consulted and signatory Power.

On September 14, 1922, the Soviet Government in a long Note to Whitehall stated that the Soviet delegation at the Genoa Conference twice raised the question of the admission of Turkey with a view to bringing the Greco-Turkish war to an end but that its proposals were rejected ; that the Soviets had made their own settlement with Angora in 1921 respecting the Straits ; that Russia, Turkey, the Ukraine and Georgia, to whom belongs practically the greater part of the Black Sea coast, could not admit the right of any other Government to interfere in the settlement of the question of the Straits, and would maintain the point of view set out above, even if the contrary point of view were backed by military or naval superiority.

Moscow was particularly sensitive on the question of her Black Sea coast *vis-à-vis* Great Britain, because it was mainly through the Black Sea ports that Britain had poured in mountains of munitions in 1919-1920 to aid the "Whites," and as one Russian writer picturesquely expressed it "we don't want our open Black Sea towns to live under a constant threat of bombardment by the British Navy whenever Lord Curzon has an attack of indigestion."

No responsible publicist or journalist asserted that the future régime of the Straits was not a matter of vital importance to Russia, yet a month passed and the Kremlin's Note was left unanswered by Whitehall. Moscow drew the obvious conclusion that London had no intention of responding to its conciliatory gesture, and that concession was interpreted as weakness. The result was that the Soviet Government did not ratify the Urquhart-Krassin Agreement. M. Litvinov, in an explanatory interview (October 10, 1922), declared:

> "It was hoped that a deal by which 30 per cent. of British private claims were to be settled would bring about better poli-

tical, as well as trade, relations between England and Russia. What had happened? Shortly before ratification of the agreement became due England refused to admit Russia to the Near East Conference. Russia saw in this decision of Downing Street an act of pronounced hostility and evidence that those members of the British Cabinet who opposed restoration of normal relations with Russia had got the upper hand, and that England was adopting a new and negative policy towards Russia.

The Soviet Government had in vain waited for pronouncements from London. Our Note remained unanswered. The political aim of the Urquhart agreement was thus frustrated by the London Government, and the Soviet Government was accordingly free to judge the agreement from a purely economic standpoint. The Council of People's Commissars felt bound to reject it."

Britain's attitude was all the more suspicious in Soviet eyes as a big change had come over French policy towards Russia. That well-known French statesman, M. Herriot, was in Russia at this time and in an interview in *Izvestia*, speaking with the authority of M. Poincaré, he declared that the new Franco-Russian *rapprochement* was a fact. This was underlined a few days later when the *Temps* stated: "This year Russia has made her diplomatic re-entry into Europe. . . . In any European policy it is necessary in future to take Russia into account."

Britain and France had exchanged roles, but that was not all. Italy as well as France was in favour of Russia being invited to the Lausanne Conference. Britain alone objected. The change in British policy was mainly due to the fact that Mr. Lloyd George's influence had fallen considerably after the defeat of the Greeks, whom he had backed, in Asia Minor, and as his prestige waned, Lord Curzon's frost-bitten policy towards the Soviet Union prevailed. It was common knowledge during all this time that every advance made towards accommodation with Soviet Russia was bitterly opposed by Lord Curzon.

In the third week of October, Russia addressed another Note to this country expressing astonishment that her previous Note had not been answered and stating that "the attempt to confront Russia with the *fait accompli* of decisions arrived at without her participation would compel her to refuse to recognise these decisions."

The tide had begun to flow in Russia's favour, the victory of Turkey (with whom Russia had the friendliest of relations), the change of attitude in France, and her own improving economic position, all constituted a rapid current against which Lord Curzon could not battle. The result was that a clearly inspired paragraph appeared in the press that all the States bordering on the Black Sea have obviously an interest in the future status of the Dardanelles and that therefore delegates representing them, including Soviet Russia, would be heard at the portion of the forthcoming Lausanne Conference dealing with the Straits.

This was so much to the good, but it was very regrettable that Russia's obvious right to be represented was not freely recognised when the decision to summon the Conference was first made. Britain's attitude created a cloud of suspicion in Moscow which was slightly, but only slightly, dissipated by the belated invitation to Russia.

The Conference duly met and Soviet delegates were first admitted to its sittings on December 4, 1922. Meanwhile a general election had taken place in Great Britain, the Coalition Government had ceased to exist, Mr. Lloyd George was reduced to the status of a private member in Parliament; Lord Curzon was no longer subject to any restraining influence, and was able to indulge his anti-Soviet obsession to the full.*

Journalists of all schools and nationalities commented on Lord Curzon's menacing attitude when he and M. Chicherin first crossed swords at Lausanne. A royal encounter of the two protagonists opened on December 12, 1922. The British representative outlined his Government's scheme. In brief he proposed the demilitarisation of the Bosphorus, the Dardanelles and the Turkish Islands in the Ægean Sea, and the establishment of an International Control Commission to supervise the carrying out of the terms of the Agreement. This meant that Turkey would be deprived of physical means to dispute the passage of battleships belonging to non-riparian Black Sea Powers, despite the fact that the Black Sea is a closed sea and not a marine thoroughfare.

Why were the Great Powers, who had bombarded unfortified Russian towns on the Black Sea coast to aid rebel generals against the lawful Government of Russia, and assisted the Greeks to invade Asia Minor, so anxious to have undisputed access for their battleships to this inland waterway? Was it in the hope of reviving these disastrous buccaneering adventures under more favourable circumstances? Russia and Turkey, whose writ covered the greater part of the Black Sea coast line were full of suspicion. They were anxious to prevent the Black Sea ever again becoming the scene of

* On October 19, 1922, Mr. Lloyd George, the head of the Coalition Government, resigned the Premiership and a purely Conservative Government under the Premiership of Mr. Bonar Law was formed. Lord Curzon remained Foreign Secretary. Parliament was dissolved on November 4, and in the subsequent elections the Conservative Party was returned with a large majority.

hostilities. M. Chicherin, December 18, 1922, adumbrated an alternative scheme for the control of the Straits. In brief, the Soviet scheme proposed to restore Turkish sovereignty over the Narrows. The Straits, in peace-time, were to be open day and night to commercial traffic, but closed to battleships, and the passage of light warships was to be permitted in special cases. In time of war the Straits were also to be open to merchant shipping, but Turkey, being a belligerent, would have the right of search. It was also proposed that the scheme should be under the control of an International Board representative of the riparian Black Sea States and the Great Powers, with a Turkish Chairman. It is not our business here to argue the merits and demerits of the two schemes. It is sufficient to add that the Russian proposals were in principle little different from those contained in the Convention signed nearly fourteen years later (July 20, 1936), at Montreux, between Turkey and the Powers.

When the bells rang out the old year on December 31, 1922, the Krassin-Urquhart Agreement was still unratified, the Lausanne Conference had not yet completed its labours and Anglo-Russian trade was still denied the assistance available to British trade with every other country under the different Government guaranteed schemes.

CHAPTER V

THE "CURZON ULTIMATUM" (1923) AND AFTERWARDS

I. Execution of Monsignor Butkevitch. Seizure of British trawlers

During the first three months of 1923, whilst hostility towards the Soviet Union steadily decreased in French Government circles, it steadily grew among British Ministerialists. This was demonstrated in several ways. As regards trade relations, M. Litvinov, in an interview with Mr. Arthur Ransome, stated that "the Canadian Government, obviously under British influence, has refused to admit our trade mission, which they themselves had previously invited"; and that the British Government "now refuses to admit Russian buyers and sellers, representatives of our purely economic organisations, unless vouched for by the particular English firms, thereby committing them in advance to dealing with those particular firms."* And respecting political relations—M. Chicherin, in an interview some three weeks later with Mr. Ransome in Moscow, said:

"I must say in general that I and all my colleagues of the Russian Government have been much saddened by the effect of

* *Manchester Guardian*, 29.i.23.

the Lausanne Conference on our relations with Britain. We saw that the British delegation pursued a policy that must necessarily alienate Russia. The systematic elimination of the Russian delegation from real negotiations on the Straits question ; the absolute absence of any attempt to come to an agreement with Russia ; the obdurate maintenance of those elements in the British proposals which seemed to us to mean not merely passive but also aggressive hostility to Russia—all this convinced us that lack of friendship in the British Foreign Office towards us was no longer restrained by wiser counsels in Downing Street."*

Parenthetically it may be added that Russo-German relations had immensely improved and trade between the two countries had rapidly increased. Less than a week later, Lord Curzon, the Foreign Secretary, gave a comprehensive review of Britain's foreign policy in an address to the Aldwych Club, which occupied more than two full columns in the *Times*. His Lordship's only reference to the Soviets sounded very much like a calculated sneer. He said: "There is the position of Russia, about which I cannot speak to-day ; I have not the time." That was all, but it is not difficult to imagine how it was construed in this country, in Russia and abroad generally. The era of "frost-bitten diplomacy," to quote Mr. Lloyd George, had set in. Certain events were now happening in Russia which Lord Curzon and his supporters in the Cabinet exploited for their own purposes.

During the famine and the subsequent period of recovery the Soviet Government had decreed that the churches should hand over superfluous ornaments to be sold abroad for the relief of the famine victims. Some of the priests defied the law and called on the church members to support them. They suffered the usual penalty for law-breaking: they were arrested, tried and imprisoned.

In addition, Monsignor Butkevitch, a Roman Catholic priest, was condemned to death on March 26, 1923, for high treason. Here was an opportunity which the "Die-Hards" in this country seized with both hands. On behalf of the British Foreign Secretary, Mr. Hodgson in Moscow, on March 30, 1923, handed a Note to the Commissariat for Foreign Affairs stating that the execution of Monsignor Butkevitch "cannot fail to produce throughout the civilised world a feeling of horror and indignation."

Even if the intentions of the British Foreign Office were above suspicion, which many British citizens did not believe, its action could not but lead to results the opposite of those presumably intended, because the Soviet Government, like all Governments, was extremely sensitive to outside interference of any kind.

* *Manchester Guardian*, 22.ii.23.

Mr. Weinstein on behalf of the Commissariat replied briefly to Mr. Hodgson the next day protesting against an outside attempt to "protect spies and traitors in Russia." Further the reply stated that in view of what had taken place in Ireland, India and Egypt to uphold British rule, the Soviet Government could hardly "regard an appeal in the name of humanity and sacredness of life from the British Government as very convincing." Mr. Hodgson replied the following day that he could not accept the Note because it impugned "the sincerity of the British Government in its appeal for clemency."

Mr. Weinstein replied on April 4 that no doubt the British Government were already aware of the contents of the Notes, and it was to be hoped "that in the future it will refrain from attempts of any kind at interfering in the internal affairs of the Soviet Republic."

There the affair could have ended and would have ended had not certain mischief-makers in Great Britain decided hypocritically to work up feeling against the Soviets. Meanwhile, the substance of the Moscow Notes had become known abroad and Monsignor Butkevitch had been executed. This episode was used by the "Die-Hards" to raise the bogus cry of "Religious persecution in Russia."

On the other hand, the affair was appraised in its true proportions in other influential quarters. The *Daily Herald* in a leader declared:

> "In spite of growing opposition to it, capital punishment in many countries exists still. Therefore, if it is 'barbarous,' as many voices are saying, to carry out this execution in Moscow, we are all barbarians together. We are justified, however, in demanding that, so long as the death penalty is inflicted, it shall be inflicted without respect of persons. We in this country have executed bishops, and even an Archbishop, for treason. Why should there be such an outcry over the execution of this Russian Roman Catholic Priest?
>
> He had been found guilty of treasonable correspondence with the enemy in war-time. He was executed for that. To call his execution an attack on religion is nonsensical. The Roman Catholic Church enjoys wider liberty under the Soviets than it ever had under the Tsar and the Holy Synod. But religious liberty does not anywhere include exemption from the law.
>
> Governments are not wont to protest against executions for treason. None of them raised a voice when M. Thiers massacred his prisoners in thousands after the fall of the Paris Commune. None protested when, at the demand of the Catholic hierarchy, Francesco Ferrer was shot by the Spanish Government.
>
> Why do they protest now? They are not moved by humanity, but by class feeling. Governments of the old order—gentlemanly

Governments—may butcher as they will. But if a new kind of Government punishes for high treason a man who was a gentleman, a priest and a monsignor, the cry of 'barbarism' goes up.

The workers, we believe, will not be misled by the spurious indignation. It is important that they should not be misled. For, as we gave warning yesterday, there are war plans afoot. The death of Monsignor Butkevitch may be exploited as part of the 'diplomatic preparation' for a possible new attack on the Soviet Republic."*

The Liberal journalist, A. G. Gardiner, wrote:

"Execution for political reasons is not an innovation of the Bolsheviks. It has been practised, I suppose, by almost every Government of almost every country throughout the ages.

Cromwell practised it on the Stuarts and Charles II took his revenge on the corpse of Cromwell. The French revolutionists murdered the King and then broke up into factions and murdered each other. The Greeks recently executed Gournaris, the ex-Premier who led them into the Smyrna disaster. We hanged Casement and many another traitor during the war, and the Irish Free State Government shot Childers and would probably shoot De Valera if they captured him."†

At the same time the Die-Hards carried on a sustained agitation for a rupture of Anglo-Soviet trade relations. With this in mind Mr. Arthur Henderson, M.P., the Labour Party's Chief Whip, wrote to the Prime Minister, Mr. Bonar Law, on April 17, 1923, pointing out the advantages accruing to this country from its trade with Russia and the future potentialities of that trade. The letter concluded:

"In these circumstances, the Labour Party believes that any rupture of trade relations with Russia would react seriously upon the revival of international trade, and impede the restoration of British prosperity. I hope, therefore, that the Government will not accept the short-sighted policy of those who would undo the work which has already been done to re-establish Russo-British trade."‡

The Prime Minister's reply was disquieting. He wrote that the question had not yet come before the Cabinet, but continued:

"The proceedings of the Soviet Government, however, towards the ministers of religion, the nature and terms of their official

* *Daily Herald*, 4.iv.23. † *John Bull*, 14.iv.23.
‡ *Daily Herald*, 21.iv.23.

communications to the British Government, their seizure of British trawlers, and their violation of the preliminary conditions of the trade agreement, are serious matters, but if we should be forced to take action it will be submitted to the judgment of the House of Commons."*

The "seizure of British trawlers" had reference to a series of events going back to pre-war days. Successive Russian Governments claimed a twelve-mile territorial water limit off the Northern Coasts of Russia. This the successive British Governments refused to recognise. The Soviet Government, like the Tsarist Government, arrested any foreign trawlers, including British, caught fishing within the twelve-mile limit. The only difference was that in pre-war days friendly and not threatening representations were made to the Russian Government. Although the Liberal and Labour press and parties, and individual Conservatives continued to campaign against a rupture with the Soviets, the greater part of the Conservative press (excluding the *Daily Express, Evening Standard* and *Observer*) and party, vehemently advocated, to quote the *Times,* that "Mr. Hodgson ought to be recalled and M. Krassin and his staff in London ought to be given their passports."

On April 25, 1923, Mr. McNeill (Under-Secretary for Foreign Affairs) informed the House of Commons that His Majesty's Government had decided "to address a serious communication to the Russian Government without delay." Next day the newspapers which stood closest to the Government told the country that this meant the abrogation of the Anglo-Soviet Trade Agreement, but that this was a matter of little importance because, to quote the *Daily Telegraph* (which was typical), "the infamy of Bolshevism had best be left to rot to pieces in isolation. It is a process which no action of our own Government can hasten or retard ; and why should its hands be fouled by any sort of contact with that uncleanness?"†

On the other hand (among others) those well-informed men who constituted the Executive Committee of the Union of Democratic Control issued a statement to the nation which, after traversing the case of the Government's supporters, declared:

> "Such a rupture would be a diplomatic step of the gravest kind, tantamount to a declaration not, indeed, of war but of renewed 'hostile activities.' Economically its effect would be in the highest degree damaging to British trade.
>
> The political advantages to both countries of a resumption of friendly intercourse can hardly be exaggerated. Without such resumption conditions making for world-peace cannot be

* *Daily Herald,* 21.iv.23. † *Daily Telegraph,* 26.iv.23.

established. And British policy in Eastern Europe and in Asia must be involved in constant perplexity and in increasing military and naval expenditure.

We cannot conceal our anxiety in regard to the renewed outburst of anti-Russian propaganda now taking place in this country, which seems to bear a suspicious resemblance to that of the years 1919-21, with their successive invasions of Russian territory in large measure financed and supported by the then British Government."

Further, at the "May-Day" meetings held throughout the country by all sections of the Labour Movement, resolutions were carried strongly protesting against the proposal to denounce the Anglo-Russian Trade Agreement and calling on the British Government to establish closer relations with the Soviets.

Which policy would carry the day? At that time competent observers were about equally divided in their forecasts. The subject of the position of religious bodies in Russia was discussed at the Convocation of Canterbury on May 1 and that body, whilst protesting against "religious persecution under the Soviet régime," much to the annoyance of the "Die-Hards" in this country continued, "we must not forget the grievance which Liberalism had against the old régime and the silence of the Orthodox Church when the non-Orthodox creeds, especially the Jewish, were penalised or persecuted."*

II. The British Note. M. Vorovsky shot at Lausanne. Labour Party statement

Finally, a lengthy British Note was handed to the Soviet Government at Moscow on May 8, 1923. It demanded:

"1. The withdrawal of the Russian notes respecting the trials of the priests.

2. The release of the arrested trawlers and crews, suitable compensation and an assurance that British fishing vessels would not be interfered with in future outside the three-mile limit.

3. That in connection with the execution of Mr. Davison and the imprisonment of Mrs. Stan Harding that the Soviet Government should admit their liability and should undertake to pay such equitable compensation as may be awarded by an arbitrator to be agreed upon by His Majesty's Government and the Soviet Government, or failing such agreement, by the President of the International Court of Justice at The Hague, or by some other impartial person of similar standing."

* *Times*, 2.v.23.

4. Further, the Note accused the Soviet Government of having violated the pledge given in the Preamble of the Anglo-Russian Trade Agreement by anti-British propaganda and activities in Persia, Afghanistan and India and in support quoted alleged extracts from cables and reports sent to Moscow by Russian representatives in these countries. It demanded that the Russian representatives in these countries be "disowned and recalled."

5. Finally, the Note declared that unless the Soviet Government "within ten days" undertook "to comply fully and unconditionally with the requests which it contains" His Majesty's Government would "consider themselves immediately free from the obligations" of the Anglo-Russian Trade Agreement.

After delivery the Note was immediately published. In view of its tone, its demands and the ten days' limit (which in itself was a flagrant violation of the Anglo-Russian Trade Agreement) the Note, or as it was immediately named, the "Ultimatum," created the impression both at home and abroad that the Government had decided on a rupture and that delivery of the Note was a sop to legalism.

The *Daily Chronicle*, which stood very close to Mr. Lloyd George, commented:

> "To press for a remedy, to use the utmost pressure, is one thing; to deliver an ultimatum is another. And the ten days' time-limit attached to the British demands, allowing hardly more time than the post permits, makes it an ultimatum. The suspicion is irresistible that Lord Curzon is yielding to the Diehards in his party. Diehardism is not the spirit in which to attack the Russian problem. The Diehards are not so much indignant at British wrongs in Russia as fanatical haters of the Soviet régime. They do not resent, but rather welcome British wrongs, because they tend to bring about the rupture they desire. Lord Curzon should remember that.
>
> Besides, what good does a rupture with Russia bring? It brings us into a complete cul-de-sac, a dead end without any exit. The Russian problem will remain afterwards just where it was before. It will be equally, if not more, insoluble. And yet until some solution is found, it will continue to be out of the power of British diplomacy to frame any intelligible permanent foreign policy, and the reconstruction of Europe, upon which the welfare of this country depends, will be indefinitely postponed."*

* *Daily Chronicle*, 10.v.23.

The *Daily Herald* commented:

> "Such a note sent by one great Power to another would, before 1914, have meant war. To-day, the only hope of avoiding a rupture of relations is that the Soviet Government may display, in the face of provocation, a restraint which the Tsar's Ministers would certainly never have shown."*

Many well-informed quarters believed that the British Government meant much more than a mere denunciation of the Trade Agreement: that its ultimate aim was war. For instance, that very talented authority and writer on foreign affairs, the late E. D. Morel, M.P., stated:

> "Is it (the British Government) hoping to construct an anti-Russian road upon which the shaken Entente can march without friction, and thus renew its sadly impaired vitality?
>
> Is it taking out insurances against any possibility of a Russo-Turkish combination, by making of the Black Sea a prolongation of the Straits so far as the predominance of British sea power is concerned, thus interposing the British navy as a barrier between Russia and Turkey?
>
> *The latter seems the most likely contingency. If so, it would account in itself for the attitude of Lord Curzon on the Straits question at Lausanne and before Lausanne; and a rupture with Russia at this moment would from that point of view be well-timed and intelligible. It would, by a natural sequence, be quickly followed by the assembling of a strong British naval force in the Black Sea.*
>
> This is, of course, a war policy which would complete the economic and political chaos of Europe and ultimately achieve active war."†

Many additional happenings at this period strongly underlined the suspicions voiced by Mr. Morel. Marshal Foch had just inspected the armies of Poland and Czecho-Slovakia and had expressed himself as very satisfied with their efficiency. Lord Cavan, Chief of the Imperial General Staff, had also inspected the Polish Army and had spoken of it in similar terms. A British Military Mission "in plain clothes" had visited Rumania and Lord French had visited Bessarabia.

Poland and Rumania, which were in no way threatened from the west in these days, were certainly not maintaining large armies for the pleasure of increasing their budget deficits.

* *Daily Herald*, 10.v.23. † *Ibid.*

In addition, the Italian representative in Moscow had recommended to his Government the simultaneous withdrawal of all foreign representatives from Russian territory and the rupture of all commercial relations with the Soviets.

All these movements pointed in one direction. War on Soviet Russia. Two days after the delivery of the Ultimatum, and this was not merely coincidental, the Soviet representative in Rome, M. Vorovsky, who was attending the Lausanne Conference as a delegate, was shot dead at the Hotel Cecil, Lausanne, and two of his assistants, MM. Ahrens and Divilkovsky, were wounded. The assassin was a Swiss subject, named Conradi. The conduct of the Lausanne Conference (which had been convened largely on the initiative of Great Britain) was dastardly, and that of the Swiss Government was criminal. When the Conference met next morning no official reference was made to the criminal episode of the previous day. To quote the *Manchester Guardian's* Lausanne correspondent:

> "The Conference this morning resumed its discussions without any allusion to the tragical event.
>
> This diplomatic silence over the assassination is quite contrary to the general feeling here. Ismet Pasha this afternoon published a statement in his own name and that of his Delegation regretting the loss of a very able leader and of a great friend, highly appreciated by Ismet during the Conference."*

In the course of the previous week the Russian delegates had received threats to their safety. They had immediately notified the police but the Swiss authorities took no special steps for their protection. As if all this was not dastardly enough the Swiss Government prejudged the issue. To quote the *Manchester Guardian's* Lausanne correspondent:

> "The Federal Council says the murder is an act of personal revenge. It must be asked whether this categorical statement is not delivered too soon. Many signs, indeed, indicate that Conradi acted only for himself, but it is the task of the Judge, not of the Government, to pronounce an opinion on the guiding motives of the criminal."†

On the day on which M. Vorovsky was assassinated, Mr. Ronald McNeill (Under-Secretary for Foreign Affairs) in reply to a question informed the House of Commons that *H.M.S. Harebell* had been sent to the Archangel district with instructions "to prevent interference with British vessels outside the three-mile limit, using force, if necessary."

* *Manchester Guardian*, 12.v.23. † Ibid.

As the dispute about these territorial waters had been going on since 1910, was not more acute than in previous years, and as no such instructions had previously been issued to a British ship-of-war, Mr. McNeill's reply not unnaturally sent the temperature of uneasiness up to fever point on the opposition benches and there were angry and indignant cries "You want war." There is no doubt that that alarm might have quickly commuted itself into a certainty. Apparently the Government realised that they had gone too far. Later in the evening the Leader of the Opposition, by arrangement, asked the Under-Secretary for Foreign Affairs to make a statement on the subject.

Mr. McNeill replied that "any idea of war with Russia, or a conflict in that sense, had never for a moment entered into the heads of the Government"; it must, however, "insist upon the three-mile limit until we had arrived at an agreement on an international basis."

Finally, he admitted that "the dispute had been going on with Russia for a long time," but in no way explained why a particularly tense moment in the relations between the two countries had been chosen for the despatch of a warship with such dangerous instructions.

Mr. McNeill's second reply somewhat lessened the additional tension created by the despatch of the battleship, but by no means dissipated it. The Parliamentary Labour Party, already alarmed, became more so, and realised that if Russia replied, as most Governments would have done under the circumstances, an Anglo-Soviet rupture, followed at no distant date by war, was inevitable. With these possibilities in mind the Party sent the following telegram to Moscow:

> "Government statement, to-day, that gunboat sent to Murmansk coast with orders to use force if further arrests of trawlers take place causes grave concern, and the Parliamentary Labour Party begs in friendly spirit the Russian Government to refrain from any action which would precipitate resort to force and outbreak of war until further negotiations upon the British Government's ultimatum have taken place. We work here for peace and full recognition of the Russian Government, and view with alarm any possibility of rupture before all means to arbitrate and negotiate have been tried. We are responsible for debate on the Note on Tuesday next."*

Next day the National Joint Council representing the Trades Union

* *Daily Telegraph*, 11.v.23.

Congress, the National Labour Party and the Parliamentary Labour Party issued the following statement to the nation:

> "This Joint Council expresses its strongest disapproval of the terms of the Government's Note to Russia as calculated to bring about a revival of the attacks of the 'White Guards' on the Russian Government, and also a renewal of militarist efforts to resort to force instead of negotiations and justice.
>
> *It declares there may well be faults on both sides, and it calls for a conference, or, in the alternative, a reference of the grievances of the respective countries to arbitration or some International Court.*
>
> It protests against any rupture of trade relations with Russia, which will result not only in increased unemployment here, but also in political unsettlement, which will add to the danger of war. It therefore calls upon both the industrial and political organisations of Labour to protest immediately against the action of the Government.
>
> The Joint Council welcomes the prompt intervention of the Parliamentary Labour Party and expresses its confidence that, in the House of Commons, the Party will defend the interests of our country and the needs of the working classes."*

This declaration appeared in the press on Saturday, May 12, 1923, and formed the subject matter for resolutions and speeches at the hundreds of exceptionally well-attended Labour meetings held throughout the country over the week-end. Mr. J. L. Garvin added his then powerful voice to the rising storm of protest against the Government's policy. He declared:

> "From the first moment when the present Government was formed we feared that Lord Curzon would do what he has done. We expressed the opinion that without a definite agreement between Britain and Russia, no general settlement in Europe and the East ever can be reached.
>
> Lord Curzon's motion as interpreted in the ultimatum is nothing but a policy of cutting off our own nose to spite our face. The Soviet régime has an excellent opportunity. When Lord Curzon demands the unconditional surrender of Russia on all the mixed issues he asks the impossible. Moscow has an ideal opportunity. We are told that M. Krassin is flying from Russia to London. We hope that he has full powers. He and his colleagues, if they are in a wary mood, have the chance of their lives. In reply to the demand for unconditional surrender let them propose unconditional arbitration."†

* *Daily Herald*, 12.v.23. † *Observer*, 13.v.23.

Meanwhile, within Russia, the Soviet Government, in accordance with its customary policy, had frankly and fully explained the situation to its citizens. Mr. Arthur Ransome, describing a mass meeting in Moscow on May 13, 1923, wrote:

> "There was great tension in the air within the theatre, where more than outside the critical character of the situation was realised.
>
> At the end of the meeting an appeal was read to Mr. Ramsay MacDonald and the English Labour Party begging them to do their utmost to prevent any irrevocable step, stating that the Russian nation, which was wholly occupied in economic reconstruction, will do all possible for peace, and regards economic relations as the best guarantee. He then read an appeal to Dr. Nansen, whose name was greeted with tremendous cheers, to use his influence against 'the incendiaries of a new war.'
>
> It is impossible not to feel, in listening to the speeches and watching the demonstrations, that the Russians are determined to do nothing to jeopardise the possibility of a peaceful solution."*

A neutral diplomat present at that meeting remarked to Mr. Ransome:

> "It is a misfortune for humanity that the Western European Governments still believe that war will overthrow the Bolsheviks instead of strengthening them. The people demonstrating to-day were good-tempered enough, because they do not yet realise the real danger of new wars. But if new wars are forced on these same people—and it is pure self-deception to pretend that annulment of the Agreement can have any other effect—you are utterly mistaken if you think that Russia will not fight as a single nation and as a nation bitterly resentful."†

III. The Soviet reply. M. Krassin arrives in London. Conversations at the Foreign Office

The Soviet reply was handed to Mr. Hodgson in Moscow on May 12, and was immediately dispatched to Whitehall. M. Krassin on the same date left Moscow by aeroplane and arrived in London two days later. On that date, May 14, 1923, the Soviet reply was issued to the press. The following were the most important points:

1. It withdrew its notes relative to the trial of the priests.
2. Respecting the arrested trawlers and the three-mile limit the Russian reply pointed out the absence of universally binding international regulations, the varying practice of different countries

* *Manchester Guardian*, 14.v.23. † Ibid.

in this respect, the entire lack of justification for the demand that Russia should accept the same limits as are established by Great Britain, and that not throughout the whole Empire. The Russian Government declared its readiness "to participate in an international conference on this matter, and abide by the decision of such a conference."

3. As regards Mr. Davison and Mrs. Stan Harding, the reply pointed out that both incidents occurred before the signing of the Trade Agreement; and "before the end of the period of British intervention and blockade"; that Mr. Davison was executed "in connection with the activity in Russia of the espionage organisation of the well-known Paul Dukes," and that Mrs. Stan Harding was "accused of espionage by, amongst others, the American journalist, Mrs. Harrison."

The Russian reply further pointed out that during the same period, whilst under British military occupation, twenty-six Commissars had been executed in the Caucasus, and Russian citizens "were detained for several years without any accusation in British and Indian prisons," however, "the Russian Government expresses its readiness to compensate the family of Mr. Davison and Mrs. Stan Harding, if the British Government will express the same readiness in respect of the above-mentioned Russian citizens."

4. In connection with the charges of anti-British propaganda, the reply stated that "the Russian Government considers it necessary to declare that the extracts and quotations cited by the British Government are a combination of invented, falsified, altered and arbitrarily supplemented extracts from deciphered telegrams."

The reply continued:

"It (the Russian Government) is obliged, however, to remind the British Government that it possesses a large number of reports and documents demonstrating the extremely energetic activity of British Government agents to the detriment of the interests of the Soviet Government in the Caucasus, and particularly in districts adjacent to those parts of the Soviet Republics which lie in Central Asia."

5. The Note concluded: "the Soviet Government, therefore, proposes to the British Government to accept the method of a conference and to agree on the place and time at which the authoritative and plenipotentiary representatives of both sides could not only examine and settle secondary points of dispute, but regulate once and for all and to the fullest extent the relations between the Soviet Government and Great Britain."

The conciliatory nature of this reply was incontestable. Such papers as the *Daily Herald, Daily News, Manchester Guardian, Daily Chronicle* and *Daily Express* declared that the Russian reply swept away any justification for a breach with the Soviets. On the other hand, such papers as the *Times* and *Daily Telegraph* still demanded writing finis across the Trade Agreement.

The Soviet Note was debated in a crowded "House" on May 15, 1923.

The discussion was opened by Mr. J. Ramsay MacDonald, the Leader of the Opposition, with a detailed criticism of the Government's policy. "Get into Conference" urged Mr. Macdonald, in effect "Let there be an end on both sides to all these debating society antics and come like men facing realities to the serious consideration of a practical problem." Finally, he warned the Government: "If the Trade Agreement is torn up, there is not the least doubt that a state of incipient war will have been created."

Mr. Ronald McNeill, in reply, said that the Government wanted to maintain friendly relations with Russia, that the idea of war with the Soviets had never entered their minds, that they had much additional evidence of anti-British propaganda on the part of Russia, but despite challenges from the opposition benches, he refused to disclose the source of his information.

"We have negotiated," continued the Under-Secretary for Foreign Affairs, "till we are sick of it." The "Die-Hards" cheered loudly. They thought they could see the ramparts of the Anglo-Soviet Trade Agreement being stormed. They were mistaken. Mr. McNeill's resounding declaration was only the heavy gun-fire to cover the retreat. He continued:

> "Nevertheless I am going to say it. I understand that M. Krassin has suddenly arrived in London from Russia. I presume he has come in order to avert, if he can the consequences that have been foreshadowed in our Note. I do not know whether M. Krassin has asked, or intends to ask, to have an interview with the Foreign Secretary; but I can say this—that, if he does, my noble Friend will be quite ready to see him. He will be glad to have a conversation with him. But I do not want to mislead the hon. Member or the House at all as to the purpose of such a conversation. The Foreign Secretary would be glad to see M. Krassin and to go through the whole of our claims with him, showing him, if he can, where he thinks our claims are reasonable and the way in which we complain of their being met. He would invite M. Krassin, having had that conversation, to communicate with Moscow, if he desires to do so, for instructions, and if it

should be—I do not know whether it would be or not—that, in order to make that communication to Moscow and get instructions back, some certain amount of time would be required, the time limit mentioned in our Note would be given a reasonable extension in order to allow that be done."*

This time the cheers were coming from the opposition benches. The Under-Secretary for Foreign Affairs no doubt felt that a sop was necessary to pacify his own wild men. He concluded:

> " I ought to add this. It must not be taken that we mean to be satisfied with anything less than compliance with our demands."†

One of the most notable contributions to the debate was a short speech by Mr. Lloyd George. He warned the Government that:

> " A quarrel between our two great peoples who have acted together in the greatest emergency in which nations have ever co-operated, between two nations who have made the greatest sacrifices which any nation ever made in the history of the world —a quarrel between two great peoples, whatever the cause may be, is a calamity which is so great that it is really necessary that we should exercise every caution before we come to any decision at all."‡

After pointing out the very dangerous state of Europe and Asia, the ex-Prime Minister concluded: " I ask the Government to enter it with full knowledge of what are the dangers, and to see that a real peace is established with Russia."§

Mr. Asquith warmly associated himself with the strictures and appeal of Mr. Lloyd George, which meant that the whole opposition, totalling about 270 members in a House of 615, were opposed to a rupture with Russia.

That was not all—one of the most serious warnings addressed to the Treasury Bench came from within the ranks of the ministerialists, from that big business man, Sir Allan Smith. Without mincing his words he told the Government that:

> " It is all very well to make a declaration which, under certain circumstances, would justify a declaration of war, and then for another Minister to get up in another constituency, not his own, and say ' Oh, but we have no quarrel whatever with the Russian people. The last thing we contemplate is war and the last thing we desire is an outbreak of hostilities.' If you do certain acts, in accordance with all the criteria of international law, there is only

* *Hansard*, 15.v.23. Col. 318.
† Ibid. Col. 319.
‡ *Ibid.* Col. 320.
§ Ibid. Cols. 323, 324.

one answer to these things and that is that a state of war is *ipso facto* produced ; and if we consider that at this time, when we are so much concerned with the restoration of ourselves, as well as the restoration of Europe, we are entitled to play with fire to such an extent, I say those who are playing with fire will probably get their fingers burnt and they will howl louder than anyone else."*

He concluded on a hopeful note, if patience was exercised " we shall be satisfied that the turbulent period through which we are passing has not been without its reward." Had the Government decided to proceed with the " Curzon policy " it was doubtful whether they would have mustered a majority of seventy in the Commons.

There was a general smile in the " House " when Mr. McNeill said " I understand that M. Krassin has suddenly arrived in London," because as both the Ministers and the Members knew, M. Krassin had been sitting in the Distinguished Strangers' Gallery from the beginning of the debate. As he left the " House " he was besieged by Lobby correspondents who wanted to know how he would react to the Government's offer. He replied, " I have already made known to the Foreign Office that I am in London. I gather from Mr. McNeill's speech that the next step will be to invite me. I have full powers just as I had full powers during the negotiations which preceded the signing of the Trade Agreement."

Although the time limit had been withdrawn and the ultimatum sting had thus been extracted from the British Note, this only meant that the Die-Hards had received a severe battering in the first round, but they were by no means beaten.

M. Krassin had a two-hours' interview at the Foreign Office on May 17, 1923. On the British side there were present Lord Curzon, Mr. Ronald McNeill, Sir Eyre Crowe and some representatives of the Russian Department of the Foreign Office. It was agreed on both sides that no statement should be issued in regard to the conversation, but it was understood that the Notes which had passed between the two Governments were fully discussed. On the same day in the House of Commons on the eve of the Whitsuntide recess, the Government was asked for a pledge that there would be no rupture of trading relations with Russia without the House of Commons being first consulted, but Mr. McNeill refused to give such a promise. This refusal was so unexpected and created such a feeling of anxiety in the minds of the Labour Leaders that both Mr. J. Ramsay Macdonald and Mr. Fenner Brockway cancelled their engagements to attend the International Labour and Socialist Congress at Hamburg in the following week. At the same time the

* *Hansard*, 15.v.23. Col. 361.

National Council of the Independent Labour Party issued the following statement:

> "The I.L.P. views with grave concern the attitude of the Government towards Russia as revealed in the speech of the Under-Secretary for Foreign Affairs in the House of Commons yesterday. It urges that the Russian proposal for a conference on all outstanding issues ought at once to be accepted, and warns the Government that any rupture with Russia will arouse the most vigorous resistance on the part of organised labour. It calls upon its branches to be fully prepared to give effective co-operation in that resistance if it should become necessary, and to maintain a vigorous protest against the unconstitutional disregard of Parliament foreshadowed by the Under-Secretary."

So far no one had revealed for certain what Lord Curzon's exact intentions were at this juncture, but a well-informed Diplomatic Correspondent wrote:

> "It is, in fact, entirely clear that the Foreign Secretary intends peremptorily to break off the negotiations unless M. Krassin comes to him next week with the news that Moscow has surrendered. It is also entirely clear that a complete surrender by Moscow to the Curzon demands is as unlikely as was a complete surrender by Serbia to the Austrian demands in 1914."*

Meanwhile, as one would expect, history repeated itself within the limitless frontiers of Russia. The "Special Correspondent" of the *Observer* cabled:

> "Public opinion of all classes is undoubtedly behind the Soviet Government. Russia wants peace, but not peace at any price. The main interest of the population is the hope of a continuance of the improvement of living and trade conditions. This is the first spring without war, internal disorder or famine. The expectation is widely held of an improved harvest. All classes were looking for a rapid improvement of trade as grain export grows.
>
> Consequently, if a rupture is now forced by Lord Curzon, despite the undoubted attempts of the Russian Government to secure a peaceful settlement, two results seem inevitable. First, Communists and non-Communists alike, now united behind the Government in peace efforts, will support it if peace is nevertheless made impossible. The situation is similar to that of

* *Daily Herald*, 19.v.23.

England in 1914, when national unity was secured by the conviction that the Government, having tried to prevent war, was now resisting aggression."*

In the same issue of that journal, its editor, Mr. J. L. Garvin, in his usual emphatic style, declared:

"While we hope that the conversations between M. Krassin and Lord Curzon may have a peaceful outcome, there can be no kind of certainty about it. Lord Curzon is not only, like the rest of us, anti-Bolshevik—a fact that touches an issue of domestic politics and no more—but he is also fundamentally anti-Russian. His incorrigibly sentimental policy embalms some obsolete ideas from the nineteenth century, and takes little count of the part which our relations with Russia must play for the future in the shaping of Imperial and foreign relations. If Lord Grey, as Foreign Minister, had applied Lord Curzon's principles, he could not possibly have succeeded in developing that mutual friendliness between the two countries which, when it became a war alliance, saved Western Europe from defeat and ruin."

IV. MR. BONAR LAW RESIGNS. MR. BALDWIN BECOMES PREMIER. THE LABOUR PARTY SUPPORTS THE SOVIET REPLY. END OF THE CORRESPONDENCE

Meanwhile an event happened which, although an internal matter as far as Britain was concerned, was not unaffected by what had recently happened between London and Moscow, and was not without influence on Anglo-Soviet relations.

Mr. Bonar Law resigned the Premiership, and Lord Curzon, a notorious aspirant for that office, much to his own amazement and chagrin, was passed over in favour of Mr. Stanley Baldwin. The latter became Premier on May 22, 1923. According to the rumours then current in well-informed political circles the objections to Lord Curzon were that he was not a member of the Commons, that he was out of touch with democratic sentiment and that a manifestation of the latter was his congenital anti-Soviet bias. A personal friend of His Lordship told the writers at that time: "Curzon cannot clear his mind of the superstition that his class were divinely ordained to rule. Democracy and Socialism are anathema to him."

If Mr. Baldwin's elevation did not call forth a sigh of relief in the circles striving for an amicable settlement with Russia, Lord Curzon's failure to secure the coveted prize did.

The "London Correspondent" of the *Manchester Guardian* commented:

"The two questions most in the mind of political students

Observer, 20.v.23.

to-night is the attitude of the new Premier in foreign affairs, particularly as to the maintenance of the Trade Agreement with Russia and towards the French Ruhr policy. There is a general opinion among those who know him that he takes a much more moderate line than Lord Curzon's on the Russian question, which he sees at a rather different angle after his long experience of trade affairs."*

Meanwhile, M. Krassin, after his conversation at the Foreign Office on May 17, had communicated with Moscow, and had received his Government's reply. This he presented to Lord Curzon on May 23, 1923. The following were the main points:

Territorial Waters.

"The Russian Government is ready, in the question of fishing in Northern waters, to conclude at once a convention with the British Government granting to English citizens the right of fishing outside the three-mile limit, pending the settling of this question in the shortest possible time at an international conference; and to pay compensation for the cases in point."

Mr. Davison and Mrs. Stan Harding.

"The Russian Government is ready to pay compensation for the execution of Mr. Davison and for the arrest of the journalist, Mrs. Stan Harding; with the reservation, however, that this willingness in no way signifies that the Russian Government recognises that there was any irregularity in the repressive measures it took against these spies, because their crimes have been proved definitely and by due legal process, and the repressive measures against them were taken before the conclusion of the Anglo-Russian Trade Agreement; in view of which their claims can in no way be regarded as a condition for maintaining the agreement."

Propaganda in the East.

"As to the claims of the British Government on the question of the observation of the conditions of the Anglo-Russian Trade Agreement in the East, the Russian Government, again repelling the charge of having infringed the agreement, does not see, as far as this question is concerned, any other possibility of settling the conflict and preventing future recriminations, and of co-ordinating the different points of view and aims of England and Russia, except by a detailed discussion of them by specially delegated representatives of both Governments."

* *Manchester Guardian,* 23.v.23.

Conference.

"Should the British Government be ready to consider the points at issue between the two Governments, the Russian Government is agreeable to delegate at once the People's Commissar for Foreign Affairs, M. Chicherin, to meet the representatives of the British Government."

Lord Curzon, as transpired a few days later, after he had read the Russian reply, expressed his dissatisfaction with it. He still demanded the dismissal of Soviet representatives in Eastern countries who, in his judgment, were guilty of impermissible anti-British propaganda. This was a point on which the Soviets felt they could not yield "without ceasing" (to quote one of their statesmen) "to be a sovereign state." Finally, the Foreign Secretary said that he would have to consult his Government, but he added that in his opinion "the Soviet Government is losing its chance of preventing the annulment of the Trade Agreement."

Three editorial comments next day are sufficient to indicate how the press reacted:

"It may be said at once that this Note does not comply with the terms laid down by Lord Curzon.

We have no doubt that the Government will insist resolutely on the complete fulfilment of the demands presented by Lord Curzon.*

"The reply of the Russian Government to the British Note, and also to the conversations between Lord Curzon and M. Krassin, issued last night, must remove the relations of the two countries from that condition of tension—we cannot give it a more serious term—which has obtained recently.

There is no reason why the affair should not now be settled swiftly and satisfactorily."†

"This is a Note which, in our opinion, makes any further talk of breaking off relations quite unnecessary."‡

On the same day the General Council of the Trades Union Congress adopted the following resolution for communication to the Prime Minister:

"The General Council of the Trades Union Congress welcomes the conciliatory tone of the Russian reply to the British Government relating to the trading and diplomatic relations of Russia and Great Britain. In view of the abnormal unemployment

* *Times*, 24.v.23. † *Daily Express*, 24.v.23. ‡ *Daily Chronicle* 24.v.23.

prevailing for a long period, the Council, as representing the organised workers, protests against the adoption of any policy on the part of the Government retarding the development of trading activities between this country and Russia. The Council calls upon the Government to act, in further negotiations, in such a manner as will lead to a continuation and extension of the trading agreement, and the complete recognition of the Russian Government."

The Labour Party at the same time sent the following statement to the press:

> "An urgent call has been sent to all the affiliated organisations of the Labour Party to adopt resolutions demanding acceptance by the Government of the latest Russian Note and calling for full diplomatic recognition of the Russian Government, as the best means of ensuring good relations between the two countries. Similar steps have been taken by the Independent Labour Party to bring the whole weight of its organisation to bear on public opinion during the week-end, and urging the adoption of a resolution at every one of its meetings, to be telegraphed immediately to the new Prime Minister. The Labour movement regards the latest Russian Note as a very conciliatory document, and is taking vigorous action to secure its acceptance by the Government."

Owing to the fact that the new Government was not yet fully constituted, matters were allowed to remain in abeyance for a few days. When the subject was raised in the House of Commons on May 28, 1923, the Government would not commit themselves beyond stating that "conversations between the Foreign Secretary and M. Krassin were proceeding."

Two days later, the Prime Minister, in a letter to Mr. Arthur Henderson, admitted that he had received so many resolutions from Labour Organisations on the subject of Anglo-Soviet relations that he could not possibly acknowledge them individually, and he asked Mr. Henderson to accept that letter as a general acknowledgment.

At the same time the two outstanding Liberals, Mr. Asquith and Mr. Lloyd George continued also to pull their full weight against a rupture of relations with the Soviets. Speaking at Buxton, the former declared:

> "The new Government have succeeded abroad, as well as at home, to an unenviable inheritance. There were signs at this moment of a break in the clouds in one quarter which a month ago overhung the international situation. It seemed then that

they were within a measurable distance of a complete rupture of their relations with the Government of Russia. He was glad to believe that through a process of conferences and discussions difficulties were now in the way of being removed, and that the Russian Government were being brought along the only road by which they should be brought to realise that it was, at least, as much to their interest as to ours to comply with reasonable demands."*

On the day on which this appeared in the press, Mr. Lloyd George wrote:

> "It is time we made up our minds that the Soviets have come to stay, whether we like it or not, and that one or other of the formidable men who rule Russia is likely to rule it for some time to come. The sooner we have the courage to recognise this fact the sooner will real peace be established."†

The campaign in the country was having its effect on the Government, and this reflected itself in the next Note, May 30, 1923, handed by the Foreign Office to M. Krassin. It was couched in very different terms from the previous Notes. As regards trawlers—the British Government proposed that "pending the conclusion of an international agreement the Soviet Government shall issue instructions to its maritime authorities to abstain from impeding the operations of British fishermen outside the three-mile limit, and that this shall be recorded in the exchange of Notes."

Respecting Mrs. Stan Harding and Mr. Davison, the Note proposed "that the Soviet Government shall pay the sum of £3,000 in respect of the claim of Mrs. Stan Harding and of £10,000 in respect of the claim of Mrs. Davison."

With regard to the Weinstein-Hodgson letters the Note stated: "His Majesty's Government take note with satisfaction of the unqualified withdrawal of the two letters addressed by M. Weinstein to Mr. Hodgson."

Thus three of the four questions at issue between the two Governments were settled but the important and ticklish question of propaganda remained. The Note asked that the Soviet representatives in Teheran and Kabul "will, within a reasonable space of time, be transferred to some other areas where their duties will not bring them into contact with British interests."

Finally the Note proposed a new "no-propaganda Pledge," and offered:

> "If such a declaration be signed by both parties, His Majesty's

* *Times*, 2.vi.23.

† *Daily Telegraph*, 2.vi.23.

Government will be quite willing in the event of any future infringement of the pledge thus again recorded that the case should be brought immediately to the attention of the Government concerned rather than such incidents, if they are found to occur, should be allowed to accumulate before complaint is made."

The question of recalling the two Soviet representatives was a very difficult one for Moscow because it involved the question of prestige—the prestige of a Government of a great and proud State—and, therefore, when the terms of this Note became known it seemed to many that after all the " Die-Hards " had won.

The Diplomatic Correspondent of the *Daily Herald* wrote: " To assert a right of veto over the personnel of the Diplomatic Corps in Teheran or Kabul, would be to assert a very real British suzerainty over two countries whose complete independence Great Britain has more than once solemnly recognised."

" This demand, then, Moscow is bound to reject—in defence both of its own sovereign rights and of the small nationalities which are threatened by the encroachments of Curzonian Imperialism."*

Further the Correspondent stated:

> " Four papers—the *Hittim,* the *Ittihad,* the *Beharestan* and the *Ikdam* are subsidised from the funds of the British Mission.
>
> Now there is, of course, nothing in that. The subsidising of newspapers by foreign diplomats is common form in most countries outside Great Britain.
>
> But it happens that the British Government is not pledged not to subsidise anti-Russian propaganda in Persia. And it happens that these subsidised papers do carry on very definite and very bitter anti-Soviet propaganda, which is—to say the least—an unfortunate coincidence.
>
> Lord Curzon will need a double portion of effrontery if, in face of facts like this, and of the very definite charges in the *Izvestia* article, he persists in his demand for the recall of the Russian representatives from Teheran and Kabul."†

Whilst Moscow was considering the last British Note, the Soviet Trade Unions, in a lengthy cable to the British Labour Movement, brought out a point which the Curzon Notes studiously avoided, but one which had burned itself into the innermost souls of the Russian people. The cable stated:

> " No mention whatever is made in the Memorandum of the damages sustained from British intervention and blockade by

* *Daily Herald*, 5.vi.23. † *Ibid.* 7.vi.23.

hundreds of thousands of workers and peasants of Soviet Russia and the Commonwealth.

The amount of these damages is very great and we request you to remind the British Government of it."*

On June 11, 1923, the Soviet reply was handed to Lord Curzon. The Russian Government accepted the British proposals respecting the Hodgson-Weinstein exchange of Notes, the compensation to be paid to Mrs. Stan Harding and the widow of Mr. Davison, and the Territorial Waters question.

There still remained the delicate question of the recall of Soviet representatives at Kabul and Teheran. On this point the Soviet reply stated: "The Russian Government invites the British Government to admit that such an exceptional measure, even in the moderated formula of the last memorandum, could be decided upon only as the result of a joint examination of one-sided or mutual accusations."

The Soviets were willing to recall these or any other officers if their guilt were "established by both Governments" as a result of a joint examination, but this proposal "pre-supposed full and unconditional reciprocity." The Russian proposal was certainly reasonable and business-like. It read:

"The Russian Government knows and sees no other way for the settlement of questions at issue between the independent parties—provided one of them has not already decided to bring about a rupture at all costs—except the way of negotiations."†

The final decision in this dispute was taken at a meeting of the British Cabinet late on June 12, 1923. What actually transpired at that gathering has not so far been disclosed by any of the participants, but it was freely rumoured in the corridors of the House of Commons after the meeting that the Prime Minister, Mr. Stanley Baldwin, despite the opposition of Lord Curzon, decided to accept the last Russian reply as satisfactorily terminating the dispute. Next day the Foreign Office sent a Note to M. Krassin, which, after recapitulating the points settled, concluded thus:

> "His Majesty's Government now understand that, in accordance with the normal arrangements governing the movements of members of the Russian diplomatic service, the transfer to another post of M. Raskolnikov, against whom the main charges have been made, has already been decided on. The obstacle which his continued presence in Kabul presents to friendly intercourse will thus be removed. If it is contemplated to leave M. Shumiatsky at Teheran for any further period, His Majesty's Government confidently infer from the undertaking now given

* *Daily Herald*, 4.vi.23.

† Cmd. 1890, p. 12.

by the Soviet Government that it will take very special steps to secure that he complies fully and consistently with the letter and the spirit of that undertaking. In the event of any infringement of it by M. Shumiatsky in the future, they will bring the case at once to the attention of the Soviet Government, and will in such circumstances expect the Soviet Government to take the prompt and severe disciplinary action which it promises in its note.

The Soviet Government having thus complied with the essential conditions of the demands put forward by His Majesty's Government, this correspondence may now be brought to a conclusion."*

The Soviets, on their part, five days later, June 18, replied welcoming the last British Note and agreeing that "the correspondence may be considered at an end." However, Moscow had no illusions. The ship had weathered one storm but there was no certainty that another would not be artificially created at no distant date by Lord Curzon or others who could not accommodate themselves to the idea that Soviet Russia was a sovereign State.

V. M. Rakovsky succeeds M. Krassin. Deputation of business men visits Russia. The General Election

M. Chicherin, in an interview with Mr. Arthur Ransome, in Moscow, on June 21, 1923, declared:

> "I say with full conviction, and we are all persuaded, that Lord Curzon's first Note was planned to bring about a break. It is not the personality of Lord Curzon, but a definite section of the British political world. We have now seen them at work, and it is impossible that hereafter relations should not be colder and more suspicious. We hope, however, that the other and wiser section of opinion will use strong pressure in favour of better relations between our two great countries."†

The Foreign Commissar was convinced that if relations did not improve with Great Britain they might easily become worse, a view which was equally shared by that close student of world affairs, the late Mr. E. D. Morel, M.P. The latter, after consultation with his colleagues of the Labour Party, on the same day as that on which the Moscow interview took place, asked "whether now that the recent dispute with the Russian Government had been satisfactorily ended his Majesty's Government would invite the Russian Government to a conference at which private claims on both sides might be produced and examined in a reciprocal spirit of goodwill, and at which such public issues as might still divide the two Governments might be

* Cmd. 1890, pp. 13, 14.

† *Manchester Guardian*, 22.vi.23.

approached in the same spirit, with a view to the settlement of all outstanding differences and to the resumption of normal diplomatic relations between the two countries."

Mr. Baldwin replied that "His Majesty's Government did not consider that a conference with representatives of the Soviet Government could at present usefully be convoked."

The misgivings of the Soviet Commissar and the British Labour Members were unfortunately only too well founded and another dispute which need never have arisen occurred some six weeks later.

M. Krassin had been appointed to a home post and M. Rakovsky, after the usual enquiries, had been accepted by the British Government to succeed him as official agent in London of the Soviet Republics and an announcement to this effect appeared in the press of July 23, 1923.

At the same time it became known that Messrs. Becos Traders Ltd. (which had associated with it many of the leading engineering firms of Great Britain, viz., Baldwins Ltd., Brightside Foundry and Engineering Co. Ltd., Crossley Bros Ltd., Hadfields, Ltd., etc., etc.), were sending a deputation of business men to Russia headed by Mr. F. L. Baldwin, a cousin of the British Prime Minister.

It looked as though influential British business men were determined at least to try and improve commercial relations between the two countries. This, however, was not at all to the taste of those birds of ill-omen, the "White" Russian emigrés. They had evidently eliminated all scruples from their moral standards and they would seem to have had the utmost contempt for the intelligence of certain British newspaper proprietors, especially those who supported their cause.

For instance, the *Poslednyi Novosti,* a Russian "White" journal published in Paris and edited by M. Miliukov, carried on July 28, 1923, a distorted version of a speech made by the Soviet Minister designate together with a mass of baseless accusations against him. Four days later the *Morning Post* reproduced these accusations without disclosing the source. The question was subsequently raised in Parliament and later the acting British representative in Moscow requested the Soviet Government to delay the departure of their representative. The Soviet authorities, however, had no difficulty in proving the complete falsity of the charges made against their representative and finally, on August 31, 1923, Whitehall announced through the usual press channels that the ban on his entry into Britain was lifted.

After this the agitation died down and M. and Mme. Rakovsky quietly landed in this country on September 30, 1923.

Meanwhile, the delegation of business men who had visited Russia had returned, and their leader, Mr. F. L. Baldwin, in an interview with the press, September 3, 1923, said that "the general impression we have brought back as to the recovery of Russia is one of hope. Recovery will be a long job unless the Government can get outside help, but if they cannot get that I am still confident that they will pull through unaided."

He further stated that Russia had a favourable foreign trade balance, that "there is a trade opening in Russia for agricultural machinery and also for all things connected with transport, both railway and motor." Mr. F. L. Baldwin concluded that Russia was "looking rather to this country for their trade necessities, believing that Britain was in a better position than any other country to extend them credits."*

Mr. J. L. Garvin strongly admonished the Government to put our relations with Russia on a normal basis without further delay. He wrote:

> "We ought to have given full recognition long ago. Instead of that we have maintained the Bourbon etiquette until M. Chicherin has come to hate his fellow-aristocrat, Lord Curzon, and is naturally favouring the French, who have changed their policy and are working as hard as they can to conclude an agreement with Moscow. We ought to sweep away every obstacle to normal relations, political and commercial, with Russia. If we are capable of learning from experience or of applying wisdom and foresight to one of the largest issues in the world, we shall extend full recognition to Russia as a direct result of the Imperial Conference."†

The business men, under the Chairmanship of Mr. F. L. Baldwin, referred to on a previous page, issued their report on November 19, 1923. The following was the *Manchester Guardian's* (November 20, 1923) summary of it:

> "It may be said with justice that the Government of Russia is not only accepted by the people but meets with their approval. Exports are greater than imports, and the Government has decided not to allow anything to interfere with this. Imports are regulated in accordance with the ability to pay for them in exports.
>
> Credit, therefore, is a vital need. The Russian budget is now being balanced by taxation, heavy reduction of Government expenditure, and realisation of Government assets.
>
> Trade prospects with Britain are extremely good, for we manufacture the goods required by Russia. The huge trade with Germany has been lost.
>
> Russia's great difficulty is the absence of credit, and the

* *Daily Telegraph*, 4.ix.23. † *Observer*, 7.x.23.

question of pre-war debts and compensation for property seized stands in the way of complete recovery. The mission is convinced that the Russian Government, if it can be assured of the rapid development of industry, would assume all liabilities, other than inter-Governmental war debts, and fix dates for their liquidation. There is no doubt of her possibility of paying."

It is scarcely open to question that had the British Government at that time shown vision and vigour in assisting British-Russian trade with long-term credits, the Russian market would have been extremely valuable to Britain.

The only other event of importance which had a far-reaching effect on Anglo-Soviet relations in the course of 1923 was the British General Election in the autumn of that year.

The Labour Party's Election Manifesto, November, 1923, stated:

> "Labour's vision of an ordered world embraces the nations now torn with enmity and strife. It stands, therefore, for . . . *the resumption of free economic and diplomatic relations with Russia.*" (Our italics.)

Similarly, the Liberal Party's Election Manifesto stated:

> "Liberals hold that the restoration of Europe is the necessary condition of the revival of our industries, and the re-establishment of peace.
>
> *They would welcome the re-opening of full relations with Russia.*" (Our italics.)

On the other hand the Conservative Party, rather half-heartedly defended their Russian policy. The result of the election was—Conservative 258, Liberal 159, Labour 191, Independent 7. The Conservatives, compared with the others combined, were in a minority of nearly 100 members. There was, therefore, a substantial majority in favour of establishing normal diplomatic relations with Soviet Russia.

CHAPTER VI

I. *DE JURE* RECOGNITION OF SOVIET RUSSIA (1924) AND THE "HANDS OFF RUSSIA" AGITATION (1917-1924)

NATURALLY, as soon as the results of the December, 1923, election became known the question was immediately canvassed as to a change of Government. The Conservative Administration decided to face Parliament, but it was generally accepted that they would be defeated on a vote of no confidence and that a Labour Minority Government with Liberal support would take office.

In view of the Labour and Liberal election pledges quoted in the last chapter, the policy of the incoming Administration towards the U.S.S.R. was universally assumed to be the immediate and unconditional *de jure* recognition of the Soviet Government. This expectation seemed to have been underlined by the Prime Minister elect, Mr. J. Ramsay MacDonald, in his programme speech in the Albert Hall on January 8, 1924. He declared:

> "The pompous folly of standing aloof from the Russian Government will be ended, not because we agree with what the Russian Government has done. That is not our business. I would like to know when a Liberal or a Tory Government, in its international relations, always drew the line at Governments for whose every act they were not prepared to make themselves responsible. But I want trade, I want negotiations. I want a settlement, a settlement from the coasts of Japan to the coasts of Ireland. If I have to protest against what is being done in Afghanistan, how can I protest unless I have channels to use for my protest ? If I am going to say to this man, if I am going to say to any foreign country: 'We are going to deal straight with you ; we are going to treat fairly with you,' how can that be done if I have to whisper to someone behind my back to go and tell somebody to tell somebody to tell somebody to tell Moscow ?
>
> How can you adjudicate or settle the outstanding claims against ourselves or the outstanding claims against Russia: how can these things be settled with half a dozen intermediaries carrying things to each other and at last getting Moscow into touch with a sort of telegraphic work that goes round and round the world before the message is received ? On that I appeal simply to your common sense, to your history, and to the history of the Foreign Office. To that extent we would be no new Government. We would be a Labour Government putting into operation the very principles that have become historical in the operations of our Foreign Office."*

The resounding cheers with which this declaration was received clearly and forcibly demonstrated that the speaker was expressing the desires of the leaders and rank and file of the Labour Movement.

On January 20, 1924, the House of Commons carried a "No Confidence" amendment to the Conservative Government's King's Speech and on the following day the Government resigned. A Labour Government immediately took office.

* *Times*, 9.i.24.

Undoubtedly Mr. J. R. MacDonald intended to apply immediately the policy towards Soviet Russia on which his Party had fought the election, viz., the full, complete and unconditional *de jure* recognition of the Soviet Government. However, certain highly placed circles gave the Prime Minister (who was his own Foreign Secretary) to understand that they would view with strong disfavour the carrying out of this policy, at least in full. Mr. MacDonald hesitated. Definite rumours, arising apparently from nowhere in particular, spread that unexpected and unforeseen difficulties had arisen and that it would be necessary, before proceeding to *de jure* recognition, to send a delegation of enquiry to the Soviet Union.

These reports found their way into the press. To quote just one. In the *Daily Telegraph* of January 29, 1924, "Political Observer" wrote:

> "Mr. MacDonald came to 10, Downing Street with the definite intention to carry out without delay an unconditional resumption of full diplomatic relations with the Soviet Government, being convinced that this is the best way of securing success for the negotiations which will follow as a matter of course. But in the few days which have passed since Mr. MacDonald took office many things have happened ; not to change his original decision—prudence forbids to speak of this yet—but to make his action more circumspect."

Fortunately these rumours had also reached Labour circles and aroused immense indignation. "What did these rumours mean ?" "Had they not been denouncing previous Governments for not establishing normal relations with Soviet Russia?" "Could it be that a Labour Government, now that it had the opportunity, had not the grit to carry through its own policy ?" On the same day as that on which the *Daily Telegraph's* report was published, the following letter appeared in the *Daily Herald*:

> "What is this nonsense about inevitable delays and preliminary formalities and so on before the Russian Government can be recognised ?
>
> What happened with regard to the Greek Government ? On January 11, M. Venizelos took office. On January 16, the British Chargé d'Affaires informed him that his Government was recognised *de jure*.
>
> Nobody devised comic conundrums about old treaties. Nobody suggested that there was a 'problem' or 'administrative peculiarities.' Five days sufficed.
>
> What could be done in the case of Greece could be done in the

case of Russia. If permanent officials pretend otherwise, they are sabotaging, and their sabotage must be stopped, swiftly, firmly, ruthlessly—or this Government is damned.

(Signed) NEIL MACLEAN, M.P."

On the afternoon of the day on which this letter appeared, the following letter was handed to the Editor of the *Daily Herald* for publication:

"The statements appearing in the press as to the Prime Minister's attitude on recognition of the Russian Government have created a feeling of mistrust among active Labour supporters in London. Workers fail to understand why there should be any delay, when both Liberal and Labour candidates were pledged to the policy of recognition; so that there is no danger of a defeat in the House of Commons if an Ambassador were at once sent to Moscow.

Workers have been educated since 1918 by the Labour speakers to understand that reparations and payment of debts by other countries mean the importation of goods without an exchange of exports, thus causing unemployment for workers at home, while the rich enjoy incomes derived by the exploitation of foreign labour; and if a Labour Cabinet were to adopt the quibbles of the Conservative Cabinet in discussing debts and delaying recognition, this would disrupt the movement in the country for years.

(Signed) D. CARMICHAEL,
Secretary,
London Trades Council."

Mr. D. Carmichael meant business. He had provisionally booked a central London hall for a protest meeting. We shall have to wait until certain persons write their reminiscences to learn all that transpired in Downing Street that afternoon and can only record here that the Prime Minister said to an acquaintance that he regarded the two letters "as a lash in the face."

It was not a bad simile. A lash is sometimes necessary and compels the recipient to get a move on. In this case it had that effect. Mr. D. Carmichael's letter appeared next day and in the same edition of the *Daily Herald* its "Political Correspondent" wrote:

"The stories which have been circulating—and have been given great prominence in the press—to the effect that a mission of investigation is being sent to Moscow to examine the possibilities of recognition, may be dismissed as ridiculous.

The Government intends no such step. Nor is such an investigation required. For the question of recognition is already decided."*

We would emphasise here that in our judgment the only man in the Government who hesitated was the Prime Minister. The others were in favour of immediate *de jure* recognition. There was no further delay. Two days later, February 1, 1924, the following Note was communicated to the Soviet Government by Mr. Hodgson:

"I have the honour, by direction of my Government, to inform your Excellency that they recognise the Union of Socialist Soviet Republics as the *de jure* rulers of those territories of the old Russian Empire which acknowledge their authority.

2. In order, however, to create the normal conditions of complete friendly relations and full commercial intercourse, it will be necessary to conclude definite practical agreements on a variety of matters; some of which have no direct connection with the question of recognition; some of which, on the other hand, are intimately bound up with the fact of recognition.

3. In the latter category may be cited the question of existing treaties. His Majesty's Government are advised that the recognition of the Soviet Government of Russia will, according to the accepted principles of international law, automatically bring into force all the treaties concluded between the two countries previous to the Russian Revolution, except where these have been denounced or have otherwise juridically lapsed. It is obviously to the advantage of both countries that the position in regard to these treaties should be regularised simultaneously with recognition.

4. Technically unconnected with recognition, but clearly of the utmost importance, are the problems of the settlement of existing claims by the Government and nationals of one party against the other and the restoration of Russia's credit.

5. It is also manifest that genuinely friendly relations cannot be said to be completely established so long as either party has reason to suspect the other of carrying on propaganda against its interests and directed to the overthrow of its institutions.

6. In these circumstances His Majesty's Government invite the Russian Government to send over to London, at the earliest possible date, representatives armed with full powers to discuss these matters and to draw up the preliminary bases of a complete treaty to settle all questions outstanding between the two countries.

7. In the meantime I have been given the status of Chargé

* *Daily Herald*, 30.i.24.

d'Affaires pending the appointment of an Ambassador; and I am to state that His Majesty's Government will be glad similarly to receive a Russian Chargé d'Affaires representing the Government of the Union at the Court of St. James."

Commenting on the reasons for the delay in extending *de jure* recognition the *Daily Herald* editorially stated, among other things, "susceptibilities in high places had to be smoothed." Many competent observers at the time were persuaded that these "susceptibilities" were the only reasons.

The British Note was welcomed in Moscow as an important international triumph for the Soviet Government and for world peace. The Second Congress of the Soviets of the U.S.S.R., which was sitting at that time, declared, in a resolution, that:

> "Co-operation between the peoples of Great Britain and the Union of Soviet Socialist Republics remains as before one of the first cares of the Union Soviet Government, which, in keeping with all its preceding policy of peace, will make every effort to settle all disputed questions and misunderstandings and to develop and consolidate economic relations which are so necessary for the economic and political progress of the peoples of both countries and of the whole world."

Next followed the official reply which was handed in to the British Foreign Office on February 8, 1924, by the Soviet Chargé d'Affaires. It read:

> "I have the honour, on behalf of the Government of the Union of Soviet Socialist Republics, to inform your Excellency that my Government has taken cognisance with satisfaction of the contents of the British Note of February 1, 1924, in which the British Government recognises *de jure* the Government of the Union of Soviet Socialist Republics, whose authority extends throughout the territories of the former Russian Empire, with the exception of those which have been severed with the consent of the Soviet Government and in which independent States have been constituted.
>
> 2. Expressing the will of the Second Congress of the Union of Soviet Socialist Republics, which proclaimed that friendly co-operation between the peoples of Great Britain and the Soviet Union remained one of the first cares of the Government of the Union, the latter declares its readiness to discuss and settle in a friendly spirit all questions arising directly or indirectly out of the fact of recognition.

3. Consequently my Government is prepared to arrive at an understanding with the British Government to replace those former treaties which have either been denounced or have lost their juridical force as a result of events during or after the war.

4. For this purpose the Government of the Soviet Union is prepared to send to London in the immediate future representatives with full powers whose tasks will also include the settlement of outstanding claims and obligations of one party against the other, as well as the determination of means for the restoration of Russia's credit in Great Britain.

5. My Government, in full accord with the views of the Government of Great Britain, considers that mutual confidence and non-interference in internal affairs remain indispensable conditions for the strengthening and development of friendly relations between the two countries.

6. My Government has learned with pleasure of the appointment of Mr. Hodgson, as British Chargé d'Affaires in Moscow, and has instructed me to inform your Excellency that, pending the appointment of an Ambassador, I have been given the status of Chargé d'Affaires of the Union of Soviet Socialist Republics at the Court of St. James."

II. The "Hands Off Russia" Campaign

De jure recognition was at long last an accomplished fact. At this stage it will be of interest to give some account of the history of the "Hands Off Russia" agitation, which had done so much to bring this fact about.

The "Hands Off Russia" agitation began in this country some weeks after the Revolution of November, 1917, and continued until the Soviet Government was recognised *de jure* on February 1, 1924.

The title does not convey an adequate idea of the aims of that agitation because they were positive as well as negative. Its objectives were in brief: opposition to outside interference in the internal affairs of Soviet Russia; the establishment of normal trading and diplomatic relations between Great Britain and Soviet Russia.

Now, the British Government, although it had dealings within Russia with the representatives of the Soviet Government, refused to recognise that Government either *de facto* or *de jure*, and when M. Maxim Litvinov was appointed Soviet Minister to this country they refused to treat with him as the representative of an existing Government. The British Labour Movement and some Liberal Members of Parliament objected to this unfair and in practice absurd treatment of the representative of a Government which, whether Whitehall and Mayfair liked the idea or not, existed.

The Congress of the British Labour Party was held at Nottingham, January 23 to 25, 1918. M. Litvinov was invited to attend the Congress as one of the fraternal delegates, and on the evening before the Congress a special meeting of the delegates was held to hear the various fraternal delegates.

When M. Litvinov was called on to speak he had a tremendous reception; the delegates, realising, as one remarked, that "history is being made before our eyes," were doubly keen to hear what the diplomatic representative of the world's first Socialist Republic had to say, and an intense silence followed. Speaking in measured tones, in English, M. Litvinov, among other things, said:

> "I am the representative of no ordinary Government. For the first time the working classes have attained supreme power in one of the largest States in the world. The significance of events in Russia has been beclouded by the war and by misrepresentations. I appeal to the British workers to disabuse their minds of the notion that the Bolsheviks have usurped power like a band of conspirators.
>
> They have carried through the revolution in the most approved style with the help of the people and in spite of the hatred of the capitalists and the sabotage of the officials of the Tsarist régime.
>
> The revolution was not only against the Tsar and his régime, but against allied capitalists. The Russian toilers wanted peace as well as freedom and social reforms. They revolted, not against the unsuccessful conduct of the war, but against the war itself. They revolted against the war by revolting against its authors and advocates.
>
> At the time of the March Revolution the Bolshevik leaders were not in Russia. The first Provisional Governments frustrated the policy of the masses and were swept away, and the government was transferred to the Soviets.
>
> Had the experience of the revolution justified itself? The answer was, in one word—Brest-Litovsk. Even if peace did not result from the negotiations, a revolution in Germany and perhaps somewhere else might come within the range of immediate possibilities.
>
> We have placed the German people face to face with two alternatives. Either their Government will accept the Russian democratic formula, or they will continue the war avowedly for territorial conquest.
>
> Will the German people continue to shed their blood to encourage their Junkers and capitalists? I think there can be only one answer. Already we hear the rumblings of the storm

> coming from Austria and Hungary. It will, no doubt, also spread over Germany.
>
> Not only have the war aims of the Central Powers been exposed. The statesmen of the Allied countries have been forced into the open and surely these exposures must have their effect on the minds of the workers of the world."

M. Litvinov then gave details of the social legislation intended by the Bolsheviks. He declared that the Constituent Assembly had demonstrated its opposition to the will of the toiling masses and had therefore been swept away.

In conclusion he appealed to the working class of Great Britain to "speed up your pace" towards peace.

Many of the delegates did not agree with all the declarations of the speaker, but they listened intently, were deeply impressed and his speech was punctuated with volcanic cheers.

On the following day, the Chairman of the Congress, Mr. W. F. Purdy, in his Presidential address, declared:

> "Revolutions are not popular with Governments of any country, and if in the earlier stages of the trouble in Russia, our Government and its Allies had endeavoured to appreciate the real meaning of the Revolution they would not have been so lukewarm over the matter. The suspicion which they aroused as to our aims in this war, their hostility to a free intercourse of opinions has done incalculable harm to the Allied Cause so far as Revolutionary Russia is concerned. Our own Government sent its special representative to Russia to study the situation on the spot, yet it cannot be said that they accepted the advice on the position as he found it, nor adopted the recommendation he made. Even now, notwithstanding all that has taken place, we find no great anxiety on the part of the present Government to recognise those who are acting as representatives of the Russian people."

Protests were at once made both in the House of Commons and in the press against M. Litvinov being allowed by the authorities to make such a speech and under such auspices. His action, it was argued, constituted a violation of the restraints which a diplomatic representative was expected to place on his activities. Strange to say (perhaps not so strange?) these protests came from quarters which were opposed both to the recognition of the Soviet Government and to the recognition of M. Litvinov as a diplomatic representative.

That Conference gave an impetus to a nation-wide agitation (expressing itself in many ways in the House of Commons, in certain sections of the press, on the platform, at Trade Union and Labour Conferences of all kinds, etc., etc.), which did not cease until full and complete diplomatic relations had been established between Soviet Russia and Great Britain.

Here we can only deal with the high lights of this agitation and the events which gave rise to them. We shall start with the genesis. It was rumoured in Moscow in the first days of March, 1918, that the Allied Governments had invited Japan to land armed forces in Vladivostok, and these rumours immediately reached this country together with the definite information that the proposal was abhorrent to practically every section of Russian opinion. The subject was raised in the House of Commons, March 14, 1918, by Mr. Lees Smith, M.P., and others, who clearly realised that this proposal might well be one of those major blunders "which lose campaigns and turn the course of history."* However, the then Foreign Secretary, Mr. Arthur Balfour, if we are to accept his words at their face value, made light of the enormous danger residing in the Russian objection, because, as he contended, "the Japanese would be the friends and not the enemies of Russia." Judging by the speech of the Foreign Secretary, the idea apparently had never occurred to him that the Russian people might hold a contrary, much less a fiercely contrary, view. As a matter of indisputable fact, competent foreign observers in Russia realised that at that time the Japanese were much more intensely hated even than the Germans. "Every class of Russian," reported Mr. Bruce Lockhart in a despatch, dated March 5, 1918, to the Foreign Office, "will prefer the Germans to the Japanese."

However, the opinions of the competent man on the spot were turned down with results which were disastrous to Anglo-Soviet relations and which cost the Soviet Union hundreds of thousands of lives, to say nothing of a stupendous destruction of material wealth.

When the resumed Labour Party Conference was held in London, June 26 to 28, 1918, M. Kerensky, who was then in England, was invited by the Secretary, Mr. Arthur Henderson, to attend the Conference. There was opposition from a number of delegates, but after a strong appeal by Mr. Henderson and the Chairman, M. Kerensky was permitted both to sit with the fraternal delegates and to address the Conference. In the course of his speech, among other things, he declared that the vast majority of the Russian people were opposed to the Soviet régime. He doubtless felt that he had to explain how under such conditions a Government could maintain itself in power. He tried to do so in the following gem:

"Here you might ask the perfectly reasonable question: how

* Words used by Mr. MacCallum Scott on that occasion.

this state of things can be maintained if it is opposed by practically the whole population? This precisely is the question the reply to which reveals the role of that unseverable connection which exists in time of war between the internal state of affairs of a country and the general external situation. I have no desire to attempt an estimate of the personal motives of certain individuals, or to attribute ill-will to causes that have led to great catastrophes—the most imperfect method of explaining historical events. The motives of men are of no importance: it is the actual results of their actions that matter."

Well might many delegates ask on this point, "What on earth was Kerensky talking about?" Next day, M. Kerensky's speech had what is called a "good press." It was particularly welcomed by journals like the *Morning Post*.

Meanwhile, the Allied occupation of Northern Russia, despite the strong protests of the Soviet Government, naturally aroused deep misgivings among some Labour and Radical M.P.'s, who were under no illusions as to the hidden intentions of the Allied Governments. The subject was raised in the House of Commons, August 5, 1918:

"*Mr. King* asked the Secretary for Foreign Affairs whether the declaration of the British Government, made in the press on July 31, that the action of the Allies in Russia was of a temporary character, no menace to Russian sovereignty was intended, and, these objects once obtained, not a single Allied soldier would remain on Russian soil, was made on behalf and with the consent of France, Japan and the United States.

Mr. Balfour: We have made no declaration on behalf of our Allies. What we said on our own behalf was: 'The aim of His Majesty's Government is to secure the political and economic restoration of Russia, without internal interference of any kind, and to bring about the expulsion of enemy forces from Russian soil. His Majesty's Government categorically declare that they have no intention whatever of infringing in the slightest degree the territorial integrity of Russia.' I have no doubt that this is in harmony with the view of all the associated Governments.

Mr. King: Is it not just as well to enforce that admirable statement of war aims with the definite and express consent of our Allies?

Mr. Balfour: Our Allies may or may not think it wise to make a joint declaration. It is sufficient that the various Governments should make their own declaration.

Mr. Snowden: Will the right hon. gentleman explain what he meant by the use of the words: 'To secure the political and economic restoration of Russia '?

Mr. Balfour: They mean that we hope to see Russia in a more orderly condition politically than it is at present. It means that among other things.

Mr. Snowden: Are we to understand that His Majesty's Government and the Allies think that the best way to promote the political restoration of Russia is to accentuate the civil war there?

Mr. Balfour: No, sir. I made it perfectly clear in what I said. We do not propose to interfere with the internal arrangements of Russia. She must manage her own affairs. There is nothing inconsistent with that general statement in anything I have said.

Mr. Lees-Smith: Are we to understand that His Majesty's Government does not intend to assist any of those factions in Russia which are attempting to overthrow the Soviet Government?

Mr. Balfour: Our wish is to secure the object without internal interference of any kind."*

It is hardly necessary to add that the Foreign Secretary's replies increased considerably the misgivings of his questioners—Ministerial evasions usually hide sinister intentions—and these suspicions were not confined to British Labour and Radical circles: they were also shared by the Socialist International. That body, at a meeting in September, 1918, warned its affiliated organisations against the dangers involved in the policy which the Allied Governments were pursuing in Russia.

In various ways, in the House of Commons, in the press and at public meetings, right up till the date of the armistice in Western Europe, the British public were warned that the real aim of intervention in Russia was not " to prevent the exploitation of its immense potential resources by Germany," but to overthrow the Workers' Republic and to re-establish the Tsarist régime. Immediately after the armistice, munitions and military stores of all kinds were poured into Russia to aid the counter-revolutionary Generals. Under these circumstances the agitation against intervention naturally became much more vigorous. All sections of the Labour Movement played their part, as did also the " Free Liberals."

Early in 1919 many members of the political and industrial wings of the British Labour Movement became convinced that some central

* *Daily Telegraph*, 6.viii.18.

co-ordinating body was necessary to rally and give a national lead to the agitation which was being conducted throughout the country against intervention in Soviet Russia and also to issue reliable information respecting both the internal and foreign policies of the Soviet Government, hence the formation of the National "Hands Off Russia" Committee. This Committee was a powerful force in the agitation, and helped to focus attention, particularly the attention of the Labour Movement, on certain specific demands, viz.:

(*a*) The immediate withdrawal of all British troops from Russia.

(*b*) The stoppage of supplies to Koltchak, Denikin and other Tsarist Generals.

(*c*) The raising of the blockade of Russia.

(*d*) The establishment of normal diplomatic relations between Soviet Russia and Great Britain.

The "Hands Off Russia" Committee included among its members some of the most prominent and influential members of the industrial and political wings of the working class movement in Great Britain; it organised meetings and conferences, supplied speakers to other organisations and issued leaflets and pamphlets, but its most important work lay in circularising all local Labour organisations urging them to send resolutions to their local M.P.'s and to the Prime Minister protesting against the Government's Russian policy, and in appealing to Trade Union branches to send resolutions to their Executive Councils and to the Parliamentary Committee of the Trades Union Congress, calling for industrial action to enforce peace and normal relations with Soviet Russia. The Committee's appeals were promptly and warmly endorsed by the local organisations and, no doubt partly as a consequence, the National Organisations made their powerful voices felt.

On April 3, 1919, a joint Conference of the Trades Union Congress and Labour Party was held in London, at which the following resolution was endorsed:

> "That this Conference calls on the Government to take immediate steps to withdraw all British troops from Russia, and to take such action as may be necessary to induce the Allied Governments to do likewise."

Shortly afterwards, the Executive Committee of the Labour Party issued a memorandum to the press in the course of which they stated:

> "The Committee have also taken the Russian situation into special consideration, and, in the name of the politically-organised

> Working-class and Labour Movement, reiterate their demand that a policy of military interference in Russia shall be stopped forthwith; they regret that the inability of the Government to make up their minds regarding their attitude to Russia has meant that British soldiers have been left practically isolated in Murmansk and Archangel, and exposed to attack; the Committee express an emphatic opinion that an arrangement should be made which will lead to the immediate cessation of hostilities and the safe withdrawal of British troops from Russian soil."

A deputation from the T.U.C. and the Labour Party, under the chairmanship of Mr. Stuart-Bunning, waited on the Rt. Hon. Bonar Law and presented a resolution passed at the Joint Conference. In the course of the interview the Chairman said:

> "Supposing an unsatisfactory answer from you, Mr. Bonar Law, and we call a special conference, there is a very strong impression that it is almost inevitable that the conference would decide in favour of a general strike. A general strike, which, in the minds of the people who are supporting this movement, would not be a mere demonstration.
>
> If there is a general strike, it will be an actual strike, not a demonstration, with all that a strike entails."*

Moreover, at this time, resolutions were pouring into Downing Street from all the Trades Councils and Trade Union branches demanding the cessation of all forms of intervention in Russia. The Government could not ignore this huge volume of opinion because, in 1919, the Trade Unions had the biggest membership in their existence and there was widespread support for the sentiments of the then President of the National Union of Railwaymen that "the centre of gravity is shifting from Whitehall to the Offices of the great Trade Unions."

An article which appeared in the *Observer*, June 8, 1919, from Mr. Vernon Hartshorn, M.P., a Miners' Leader, in defence of the threat of the "Triple Alliance" (Miners, Railwaymen and Transport Workers) to use industrial action if the Government persisted in its Russian policy, attracted much attention at that time because Mr. Hartshorn, who was a defender of the parliamentary system, and a moderate man, was believed to be expressing the views of very large masses of Trade Unionists. Respecting the suspicions of the rank and file he averred: "The British workers see nothing in the attack on Russia but an effort on the part of a capitalistic Government to

* From a circular issued by the Parliamentary Committee of the Trades Union Congress to affiliated bodies.

abuse the powers which have come to them through an election on quite another issue, to destroy a community based on Socialism."

Turning to the question of the Government's mandate he stated: "It is true that the majority from which the Government derives its position and power was elected only a few months ago. But the really important question is not when it was elected, but what 'mandates' did the Government receive? . . . Was there a mandate for the wicked and wanton capitalistic war on Russia? Was there a mandate for the attitude of hostility which the British Government is displaying towards any attempt to set up a Socialist Government on the Continent?"

Then defending the workers' right to use industrial action under exceptional circumstances, he declared:

> "It is absolutely useless for the critics of the Triple Alliance to point to the mere mechanism of the Parliamentary system and to argue that the mechanism alone shows that it is a system which is truly democratic. Parliamentary government depends not alone upon its mechanism but upon the spirit in which it is worked. It is quite possible for so-called statesmen to be scrupulously observant of the mere forms of Parliamentarianism and yet at the same time to be false to the spirit and the fundamental principles of democracy. To guard against this particular form of treachery the workers have a perfect right to use their industrial power, whether through the Triple Alliance or any other kind of Labour organisation."

When the Labour Party Conference met in Southport, June 25 to 27, 1919, the question of Anglo-Soviet relations was the high light of the debates. The Chairman, Mr. J. McGurk, in the course of his Presidential address, declared:

> "We must resist military operations in Russia and the perpetuation of conscription at home. There can be no peace so long as we continue to indulge in military adventures in Russia. Russia must be left free to work out its own political salvation, and it would be far better to send to the people the means to stabilise and consolidate the democratic growth of the country than the means for one section to destroy another or perhaps also the Revolution itself. It is useless for Mr. Churchill to say we are not at war with Russia, and that we are only seeking to withdraw our troops already there, and at the same time for this country to take sides in the internal struggles that are presently going on in that country by sending men, munitions and materials to assist Admiral Koltchak to overcome the Bolshevist Revolution. We all deplore the Bolshevist excesses. We all decried the Tsarist

excesses, but the British Government did not assist the 1905 Revolution by sending men, munitions and materials to those who were fighting the battle of democracy against autocracy. The present anxiety of the authorities to assist and support any anti-Bolshevist effort under any leader, regardless of his past associations or future intentions simply because he is anti-Bolshevist, appears to the workers of this country as an indication of a fixed determination on the part of certain sections of the community to use Bolshevist excesses—real or imaginary—as a reason for preventing at all costs the free development of socialistic enterprise in the realm of politics both in this and other countries. So long as this policy of intervention in Russia is pursued, there can be no question of disarmament and the alleged need for retaining conscription in this country will remain."

In the course of the Conference Mr. R. J. Davies moved the following composite resolution:

"This Conference protests against the continued intervention by the Allies in Russia, whether by force of arms, by supply of munitions, by financial subsidies, or by commercial blockade; it calls for the immediate cessation of such intervention; it demands the removal of the censorship, so that an unbiassed public opinion may be formed upon the issues involved; it denounces the assistance given by the Allies to reactionary bodies in Russia as being a continuation of the war in the interests of financial capitalism, which aims at the destruction of the Russian Socialist Republic, and as being a denial of the rights of peoples to self-determination; and it instructs the National Executive to consult the Parliamentary Committee of the Trades Union Congress, with the view to effective action being taken to enforce these demands by the unreserved use of their political and industrial power."

One of the most pointed speeches in support of the resolution and one which well summed up the sentiments of the delegates came from Mr. Neil Maclean, M.P. He said:

"When they understood that they had not yet declared war upon Russia, that no war credits had been voted for Russia, when they understood what were the real reasons of the war against Russia, they ought to be even more embittered against the ruling classes of this country entertaining any idea of the working classes being favourable to it. They were not in that war in Russia for high and noble ideals. They were sending munitions of war, guns and other requisites, because there was in Russia over

£1,600,000,000 of British capital invested. They were sending troops there in order to fight, using weapons manufactured by British armament firms who had money invested in Russia. . . . He, as a workman, as a Member of Parliament, as a Socialist, was going to fight that question either on the floor of the House of Commons or outside, either by constitutional action, or by unconstitutional action until all those boys of theirs were brought back from Russia."

The Conference was unanimously against the Government's policy towards Soviet Russia, but there was opposition to the resolution because many delegates were opposed to using industrial action for political purposes. Finally, it was carried on a card vote by 1,893,000 to 935,000 and the vote was regarded as very encouraging by the elements in the Labour Movement who held that nothing but the serious threat of industrial action would compel the Government to reverse its policy. During the following two months innumerable "Hands Off Russia" meetings were held throughout the country and when the Trades Union Congress met in Glasgow in September, it was expected that the Congress would give powerful expression to the demands of the Movement. The hope was well founded. The most loudly cheered paragraph in the Chairman's (Mr. Stuart-Bunning) address was:

"I had hoped—and I know you had hoped too—that, at this Congress, we could say there was peace everywhere in the world. Unhappily, that is not so, and, still more unhappily, we are involved in a war with Russia which is thoroughly unpopular with the working classes of this country. Their feeling has been illustrated in many ways, and the Government is running a grave risk by ignoring it."

Later in the course of the Congress the following resolution was carried with only one dissentient:

"That this Congress, in view of the general desire of the country, and the repeated declarations of the Government prior to, during, and since the recent general election, as reiterated to the deputation from the Parliamentary Committee which interviewed the leader of the House of Commons (Mr. Bonar Law) on May 22 last, instructs the Parliamentary Committee to demand of the Government the repeal of the Conscription Acts, and the immediate withdrawal of British troops from Russia, and failing this, demands that a Special Trades Union Congress be called immediately to decide what action shall be taken."

Again, it was significant that this resolution was moved by Mr. J. H.

Thomas, M.P.—well-known for his moderate views—who, in the course of his speech said:

> "The resolution calls upon this Congress to endorse two principles. First, it asks you to say in no uncertain voice that the Government's policy with regard to Russia is not only a policy with which the Labour movement as a whole completely disagrees. The unfortunate thing in discussing Russia is that those who take part in the discussion—those who demand some clear statement of policy, those who protest against men being conscripted for one purpose and used for another—are invariably met, not with a defence of the policy, but with a mere gibe as to whether the critics are not really actuated by their sympathy towards Bolshevik rule. Well, I can only answer that point by saying that, so far as this Congress and the Labour movement, as I understand it, is concerned, we refuse to give the right to any Government in any country to interfere with, dictate to, or attempt to mould, the policy which must be the concern of the people themselves."

And it was supported among others by Mr. Tom Shaw, M.P.—equally known for his moderate views—who stated:

> "I am in favour of the resolution. On the vital issues of intervention in Russia and conscription there could be no difference of opinion in the Congress. We should not shed one cup of blood in Russia, or interfere in any way with an internal Russian quarrel, nor should we allow the thing which we had crushed in Germany to be imposed upon us in our own country."

Immediately after the Congress and during October and November, the National "Hands Off Russia" Committee intensified its campaign throughout the organised Labour movement for support of the resolution passed at the Labour Party Conference and the Trades Union Congress, and calling for the cessation of all forms of intervention in Russia and the establishment of normal diplomatic and trading relations with the Soviets. The response was overwhelming. From all parts of the country resolutions embodying these demands were poured upon M.P.'s and into No. 10, Downing Street.

The Committees' platform campaign was strengthened by Principal W. T. Goode, Lieut.-Col. Malone, M.P. (who had recently returned from Soviet Russia) and Commander Grenfell, former British Naval Attaché at Petrograd. The public, eager and anxious to hear from first hand observers, flocked in thousands to listen to these speakers. The largest halls were filled by enthusiastic audiences in London, Glasgow, Liverpool, Manchester, Birmingham, Coventry, Newcastle, Aberdeen, Bristol, Cardiff, Sheffield, Leeds, Swansea, etc., etc.

These meetings were presided over and supported on the platform by prominent local men and women in the Labour Movement; the audiences consisted in the main of Trade Unionists, men who knew what privations were involved in strikes, and yet the sentiment which invariably drew the loudest applause was that industrial action, and not pious resolutions, would alone compel the Government to cease intervention in Russia and establish normal relations with that country.

Meanwhile a deputation from the Parliamentary Committee of the Trades Union Congress waited on the Prime Minister and presented to him the resolution passed at Glasgow and a special Congress was summoned for December 9 and 10, 1919, to hear the report of the Parliamentary Committee. Immediately this became known the National "Hands Off Russia" Committee sent the following circular to every delegate to the Congress and an informative appeal by Principal Goode was handed to each delegate on the morning of the Congress.

To the Trades Union Congress Delegates.

"On Wednesday, 10th inst., the Parliamentary Committee will acquaint you with the reply of the Prime Minister to their requests respecting Russia. Should that reply be unsatisfactory a great responsibility will rest on your shoulders. You will have to make a momentous decision, one involving the lives of millions of men, women and children in Russia, and the welfare, happiness, and even lives of tens of thousands of the unemployed and their dependents in this country. This Committee hopes you will keep three points clearly in mind:

(*a*) The famine in Russia is due in no small part to the blockade.

(*b*) The Soviet Government wishes to place huge orders for manufactured goods with this country so that no worker need be unemployed.

(*c*) The Government had had no mandate from the electors for their policy towards Russia.

You are on your honour. Think of the great issues at stake. Rise to a sense of your responsibilities and use every means at your command to enforce Peace and Trade with Soviet Russia."

The Government's reply was unsatisfactory and the following resolution was adopted:

"That this Congress, having heard the report of the deputation which waited upon the Prime Minister on the question of Russia, expresses its profound dissatisfaction; it calls upon the Government immediately to consider the peace overtures made by the

Soviet Government and, further, to raise the blockade and allow facilities for trade between Russia and the outside world. The Congress demands the right of independent and impartial inquiry into the industrial, political and economic conditions in Russia, and instructs the Parliamentary Committee to appoint a delegation to visit Russia, and to demand passport facilities from the Government for this purpose, and that a further report on Russia be considered at our next Special Trades Union Congress."

In January, 1920, the National "Hands Off Russia" Committee again circularised all Trade Union branches, pointing out that nothing but industrial action would force the hands of the Government and it organised several big demonstrations, including one in the Albert Hall, London, on February 27, 1920. That great hall was literally packed with an enthusiastic audience when Mr. Tom Mann (the Chairman) and the other speakers, Col. Malone, M.P., Mr. Israel Zangwill, Mr. Goode, Mr. Robert Williams and Commander Grenfell walked on to the platform. The temper of that big meeting can be gauged from the following report:

"If any further proof were needed of the failure of the Churchillian policy against Russia it was supplied at the Albert Hall on Saturday evening. 'The object of intervention in Russia,' said Israel Zangwill, 'was to keep Bolshevism out of England. Has it done so?'

His glance swept over the crowded arena and round the loaded galleries, tier above tier, up to the twilight of the dome, and from every quarter came back full-throated the inevitable answer. . . .

Without a single dissentient voice a resolution was carried hailing with satisfaction the successes of the Russian Soviet Republic, demanding the complete and immediate establishment of friendly relations, and calling upon the working classes of Great Britain to enforce this demand by the unreserved use of its political and industrial power."*

Early in March, 1920, Mr. George Lansbury returned from a short visit to Russia. London workers, particularly Trade Unionists, were on tip-toe to hear his impressions and when, on March 18, the *Daily Herald* announced that it had booked the Albert Hall for a meeting on the following Sunday, at which Mr. Lansbury would be the principal speaker, every ticket was applied for within two hours, a record which would take some beating in the annals of that historic hall. Mr. Lansbury, when called on to speak, got such a tremendous reception, that even that veteran of the platform was visibly touched. Then a great hush came over the vast gathering. One and all waited

* *Daily Herald*, 1.iii.20.

to hear about the world's First Socialist Republic. By a happy coincidence, Jean Longuet, grandson of Karl Marx, Lenin's master, was present on the platform. Lansbury gave a long, graphic account of what he had seen in Russia. His audience was spellbound. There was not a word of dissent, but often his sentences were punctuated with volcanic applause. His concluding words aptly summed up his whole discourse:

> "You have been told that Russia is in the grip of a gang of despots. The fact is that Lenin and his supporters have no individual power other than that delegated to them by the Soviets. They are the heads of the largest population in Europe, but they feed, dress and live like the humblest workers."*

When Mr. Lansbury sat down, the vast audience almost cheered itself hoarse. His report justified to the hilt all those who, during the previous two and a half years, had been opposing intervention in, and advocating the establishment of normal relations with, Soviet Russia. Mr. Lansbury was besieged with requests from all over the country to address meetings on his impressions of Russia and told the writers at the time that it was physically impossible for him to accept more than a fraction of the invitations. His platform work stimulated additional interest in the subject of Russia and the demands made upon the National "Hands Off Russia" Committee for meetings, and still more meetings kept on increasing.

Meanwhile, a Labour and Trade Union Delegation had arrived in Russia and the Poles had begun their wanton attack on Soviet territory. Immediately the latter news reached London, the National "Hands Off Russia" Committee, in a circular which was sent to the Executive Council of every Trade Union, and to every Union branch, Trades Council, Local Labour Party and Socialist branch in Great Britain, stated:

> "Russia is attacked solely because our class, the working class, is in power, and they have demonstrated that 'Labour is fit to govern.'
>
> Fellow Trade Unionists, don't allow this fearful crime to go on.
>
> Russia wants peace, the working classes of Poland want peace, the masses of Europe and of the world want peace.
>
> The inhuman Imperialists and Militarists want war.
>
> You can make the British Government give the word which will bring peace to suffering humanity in Eastern Europe.
>
> *Mere pious resolutions won't force the hands of the Government, but resolutions backed by industrial action will.*

* *Daily Herald*, 23. ii.20.

We appeal to you, on behalf of our fellow workers in Poland and Russia, to pass the following resolution and send it to the Polish Legation (address, 12, South Audley Street, London), and to the Parliamentary Committee of the Trades Union Congress, 32, Eccleston Square, London, S.W.1.

That this Executive Council (or Trades Council) (or Local Labour Party) (or Branch) emphatically protests against Poland's wanton attack on Russia, and calls on the Parliamentary Committee of the Trades Union Congress to convene immediately a special National Conference, in order to declare a national strike, to force the British Government to insist on Poland's making peace with Russia and further calls on the Polish masses to take drastic action to frustrate the Imperialist designs of their Government."

In addition, the Committee urged the Local Labour Parties and Trades Councils to include similar demands in the resolutions which would be submitted at the forthcoming May-Day demonstrations.

There was a tremendous response to this appeal. The Labour Movement realised that the Polish action aided by the British and French Governments had brought Europe to the verge of a terrible catastrophe.

Indicative of the intense feeling aroused among Trade Unionists by Polish aggression was an episode at the London docks on May 10, 1920. The S.S. *Jolly George* was being loaded when the dockers noticed munitions among the cargo consigned to Poland. They immediately ceased work and stated that they would not proceed either with the loading of the remainder of the cargo, nor with the bunkering of the steamer until the munitions were unloaded. All that afternoon and the next day the cargo still to be loaded was untouched by the dockers.

On May 12, a report appeared in the press that there was sufficient cargo on the steamer to make a trip worth while and also probably sufficient coal to take her to Dantzig, and that in any case she was fitted with sails and if necessary could make the trip under canvas and that she would sail on May 13 as scheduled. This no doubt was issued in the hope of frightening the dockers. However, they refused to proceed with the loading and on the same day the owners, Messrs. Walford Line Ltd., approached Mr. F. Thompson, the London District Secretary of the Dockers Union and agreed to the men's terms. Afterwards the Chairman of the Company, Mr. J. P. Walford, declared:

"The Walford Line rather than give any colour to the belief that they were doing other than acting quite *bona fide*, and in order that no occasion should be given for creating an industrial dispute, have given instructions for the cargo of munitions to be discharged and the full cargo of general goods may be dispatched at the earliest possible moment.

"The cargo already loaded will be discharged tomorrow morning, and the trade unionists have promised that the work shall be expedited."*

And Mr. Thompson in an interview with the *Daily Herald* stated: "I have received a number of resolutions from London branches of the Union declaring in strong terms that their members would refuse to load war material for Poland or any other enemy of the Russian Republic. We shall keep our eyes open to see that the munitions are not surreptitiously put aboard any other ship."†

On May 22, 1920, a manifesto was printed in the *Daily Herald* and other journals, signed among others by such prominent Trade Unionists as Robert Smillie (President, Miners' Federation of Great Britain), Tom Mann (General Secretary, Amalgamated Society of Engineers), John Bromley (General Secretary, Associated Society of Locomotive Engineers and Firemen), Alex Gossip (General Secretary, Furnishing Trades Association), A. G. Cameron (General Secretary, Amalgamated Society of Carpenters and Joiners), etc., etc., appealing to Trade Unionists

> "to demand that the Parliamentary Committee of the Trades Union Congress, and the Executive Committee of the Labour Party, should convene a National Conference, without a moment's avoidable delay, in order to declare a National 'down-tools' policy of 24 hours to enforce peace with Russia."

The "Hands Off Russia" Committee's ensuing appeal for £2,000 to enable it to print and distribute 6,000,000 copies of the appeal, attracted considerable attention; its activities were denounced by, among others, the *Times*, whose Labour Correspondent, in attacking the Committee, unwittingly paid a high tribute to its work:

> "On May 22, the *Daily Herald* published prominently an appeal from the committee to the organised workers of Great Britain 'to strike for peace' with the Bolshevists. . . .
> The Committee is now advertising for £2,000 for the distribution of 6,000,000 copies of this manifesto, and inviting the workers in the Labour Movement to distribute it in workshops, factories, mines, trade union branches, etc. *The Committee is untiring in its propaganda.*‡ A few weeks ago it sent to the executive council of every union, every union branch, every trade council, every local labour party, and every Socialist branch in

* *Daily News*, 13.v.20. † 13.v.20. ‡ Our italics.

the country, a circular suggesting that resolutions should be passed in favour of a national strike 'to force the British Government to insist on Poland's making peace with Russia.' "*

In the weeks immediately following, the appeal was distributed in hundreds of thousands of copies in working-class centres throughout the country.

The British Labour and Trade Union Delegation returned from Russia early in July, 1920, and the majority of the members were in great demand for public meetings in all parts of Great Britain. The mass agitation continued until the Council of Action was formed and the immediate danger of an Anglo-French declaration of war on Soviet Russia was removed. (See above, p. 42.)

Although the danger of war was removed (at any rate for the time being), nothing resembling normal relations had as yet been established between London and Moscow and the National "Hands Off Russia" Committee continued its agitation on all questions affecting Anglo-Russian relations, until the first Labour Government recognised the Government of the U.S.S.R. *de jure* on February 1, 1924.†

* *Times*, 9.vi.20.

† Commenting on the act of *de jure* recognition the *Daily Herald* stated:

"It is a triumph for International Labour. The credit for its achievement is to be shared, as is always the case with our movement, among very many.

"To pick and choose would be invidious. Yet we should certainly recall to-day the pioneer diplomacy of Mr. O'Grady and Mr. Wise in 1919. And the whole movement will be with us in paying tribute to the work of Mr. Coates and his fellows of the 'Hands Off Russia' Committee. May we of the *Daily Herald* be pardoned if we recall that the first demand in our first number—March 31, 1919—was for full peace and friendly relations with Soviet Russia?"

[*Daily Herald*, February 2, 1924.]

After this milestone had been passed, the Committee changed its name and became the Anglo-Russian Parliamentary Committee. At that time its membership consisted of:—Chairman: A. A. Purcell, M.P., Chairman, British Trades Union Congress; President, International Federation of Trade Unions; Members: John Bromley, General Secretary, Associated Society of Locomotive Engineers and Firemen; General Council, Trades Union Congress; Duncan Carmichael, Secretary, London Trades Council; W. N. Ewer, Foreign Editor, *Daily Herald*; Alex. Gossip, General Secretary, National Amalgamated Furnishing Trades Association; A. W. Haycock, M.P., Independent Labour Party; George Hicks, Secretary, Amalgamated Union of Building Trade Workers; General Council, Trades Union Congress; George Lansbury, M.P., Executive Committee, British Labour Party; W. Lawther, Miners' Federation of Great Britain, Executive Committee, British Labour Party; W. Mackinder, M.P., National Union of Distributive and Allied Workers; Neil Maclean, M.P., Executive Council Workers' Union; J. E. Mills, M.P., Amalgamated Engineering Union; E. D. Morel, M.P., Editor *Foreign Affairs*; Secretary, Union of Democratic Control; John Scurr, M.P., Editor *Socialist Review*; Ben Tillett, M.P., Transport and General Workers' Union; General Council, Trades Union Congress; Ben Turner, M.P., National Union Textile Workers; General Council, Trades Union Congress; R. C. Wallhead, M.P., Treasurer, Socialist and Labour International; Robert Williams, President, International Transport Workers' Federation; Executive Committee, British Labour Party; Secretary: W. P. Coates. The Anglo-Russian Parliamentary Committee continued its very active agitation for the establishment of the friendliest diplomatic relations and the greatest possible development of trade between the Soviet Union and Great Britain. At all crises in the relations between the two countries it has given a clear and sane lead to the nation. It has issued innumerable press bulletins, pamphlets and books on the subjects of the home and foreign policies of the Soviet Union. Its publications are now universally recognised as thoroughly dependable.

CHAPTER VII

THE ANGLO-RUSSIAN TREATIES AND THE GENERAL ELECTION, 1924

I. MEMORANDUM FROM BRITISH BANKERS. ANGLO-SOVIET CONFERENCE, APRIL 14—AUGUST 4, 1924

BRITISH subjects, whose properties had been sequestrated in Soviet Russia, again became very vocal after the diplomatic recognition of the U.S.S.R. and some, even at this date, talked not merely of compensation, but of a return of their properties.

Arising out of the exchange of Notes, dealt with in the last chapter, the British Government appointed a Commission to negotiate a settlement of the issues outstanding between the two countries. The Commission was to work under the control of the Prime Minister and the Under-Secretary of State for Foreign Affairs; it was to be divided into two sections, political and economic; Mr. J. D. Gregory, of the Foreign Office, was to be in charge of the first, and Sir Sydney Chapman, of the Board of Trade, of the second.

Immediately after *de jure* recognition had been accorded, persistent rumour asserted that Mr. James O'Grady, M.P., had been asked and had agreed to go to Moscow as Ambassador. This, in fact, was correct. In some quarters objections were raised. As usual, Mr. J. Ramsay MacDonald got an attack of cold feet. Reports appeared in the press that Mr. O'Grady was not *persona grata* to the Soviets. The *Morning Post*, with evident relish, editorially informed its readers that: "M. Chicherin, himself a servant of the ancient régime, would prefer to have in Moscow a diplomat of the old school instead of a genial proletarian of the type of Mr. O'Grady. And the chances are that the opinions of M. Chicherin on the subject of diplomatists are also shared by our own Foreign Office; perhaps it is the only thing which they have in common."*

There was no truth in this canard as far as Moscow was concerned, and on March 23, 1924, the Russian Telegraph Agency was authorised to state that "the candidature of Mr. O'Grady has never been officially put forward by the British Government, and, therefore, no objection could have been stated."

Mr. O'Grady's name was never put forward to Moscow, but later that year he was appointed Governor-General of Tasmania, and left for Hobart as Sir James O'Grady.

The Soviet delegation arrived in this country on April 9, 1924, and the opening joint meeting was arranged for April 14. On the morning of that day there appeared in the press a manifesto signed by all

* *Morning Post*, 8.iii.24.

the leading British bankers on the subject of Russian debts and possible loans. It was obviously intended as a warning both to the British Government and to the Soviet delegates. According to this document, the essentials for the restoration of Russian credit in Great Britain were:

> "1. That a recognition of debts, public and private, should be agreed upon acceptable to both countries.
> 2. That an equitable arrangement for restitution of private property to foreigners should be made.
> 3. That a proper Civil Code should be brought into effective operation, independent courts of law created, and the sanctity of private contract again firmly established.
> 4. That the Russian Government should definitely guarantee that in future private property shall in all circumstances be free from danger of confiscation by the State.
> 5. That bankers, industrialists, and traders in this country should be able to deal freely, without interference by Government authorities, with similar private institutions in Russia controlled by men of whom they have personal knowledge, and in whose character, word and resource they have confidence.
> 6. That the Russian Government should abandon their propaganda against the institutions of other countries, and particularly against all those from whom they propose to request financial assistance."

When these conditions had been complied with "confidence in Russia will begin to be restored, and the flow of credit will recommence. But the process will be gradual. Credit and confidence can be destroyed at a blow; they take years to restore." And if the Soviets did not comply then "Russia's recovery, which depends upon the resumption of accepted methods of intercourse common throughout the world, will be indefinitely delayed."

To-day, in view of the Soviet's rapid and enormous progress, that manifesto reads more like a proclamation by the Bourbons than a manifesto bearing the signatures of the élite of British banking.

This statement produced a quick and pertinent reply in the following day's press:

> "The London bankers are trying to bring about by economic intervention what has proved to be impossible by military intervention, namely, to dictate to the Russian people what form of government and what form of economic administration the Russian people and their leaders should adopt.
> We, the undersigned, were present with the first authoritative

and official delegation which went to Russia in 1920, and we can testify that Russia's counter-claims upon the British Government are as justifiable as the claims made by British and other investors against the Soviet Government. We have seen for ourselves how railways, bridges, mines, factories and agricultural areas have been laid waste in consequence of the marauding expeditions of the Czechoslovaks and the counter-revolutionary forces of Koltchak, Wrangel, Denikin and Yudenitch in various parts of Russia. We have seen how the means of transport have been destroyed by these counter-revolutionary forces which His Britannic Majesty's Government in 1919 and the early part of 1920 maintained in existence. In fact, much of the death and devastation which was the outcome of the famine in 1921 may be directly attributed to the action of the British Government in its support of the counter-revolutionaries because of the destruction of the means of transport. Had transport been uninterrupted, food could have been brought from the regions unaffected by the drought to the regions so adversely affected."

It bore the signatures of A. A. Purcell, M.P., Ben Turner, M.P., R. C. Wallhead, M.P., George Lansbury, M.P., and Robert Williams, Secretary of the Transport Workers' Federation.

The Anglo-Soviet Conference duly opened at 11.30 a.m., April 14, 1924, at the Foreign Office.

Mr. J. Ramsay MacDonald, in his inaugural speech, summed up the aims of the Conference thus:

"Our first duty will be the liquidation of the past; our second to reach agreement after giving and receiving clear statements upon what in our several views are the rights and obligations actually existing as between the two countries; our third, to provide as far as possible for peaceful and profitable relations in the future.

Under the first head the British Delegation will wish, as you have already been informed, to include considerations of inter-Governmental obligations, the claims of British holders of Russian bonds and of British subjects who have had their properties taken away from them, or who have otherwise suffered losses owing to events and policy in Russia; the claims of British subjects who have suffered personal injury in Russia and so on. Detailed proposals in regard to these will be placed before you presently.

On your side, you have, I understand, a variety of claims of a somewhat similar kind to put forward, and we shall, of course, reciprocate the attention which our own requests will receive at your hands.

On behalf of the whole Delegation, which follows in this the instructions of its Government, I declare that we are imbued with the most sincere desire to use all efforts in order to bring this conference to a successful conclusion.

Proceeding to the economic part of our programme, we consider the most important problem and the one to which all the other problems should be subordinated, to be that of a close collaboration between our two countries in the field of commerce, industry and finance.

The fundamental conditions for this collaboration are in existence; the economic structure of Great Britain and that of the Union of Soviet Socialist Republics are mutually complementary.

On the one hand, a country possessing the most important industry, finance, and shipping in the world; on the other a state with a population of 130 millions in possession of enormous potential riches, which requires for its development large quantities of industrial products and credits."

At that time, in view of the seriousness of the unemployment problem a considerable increase in the export of manufactured goods to Russia would have strengthened the position of the Labour Government. The facilities for such an increase were to hand in the form of the Trade Facilities Acts and Overseas Trade Acts. These acts could have been extended to Anglo-Soviet trade by an order of the President of the Board of Trade. The Prime Minister was strongly pressed to give the necessary instruction. He refused, no doubt calculating that he could use the application of these acts as a bargaining counter in obtaining concessions from the Soviet side. He sacrificed the interests of the unemployed to the interests of the bondholders, and finally lost both. His Government, as a matter of fact, was pledged to extend these acts to assist British exports to the Soviet Union, and had he taken the bold course he would have been supported by a majority of the House of Commons. Commander Kenworthy,* then a Liberal M.P., stated in the course of a debate, and was not repudiated by his leader, that if the Government decided to apply these acts to British-Soviet trade it would be supported from the Liberal benches.

There was widespread dissatisfaction in the ranks of the Parliamentary Labour Party and in Trade Union circles at Mr. MacDonald's ultra-timid policy in this matter, and only the *esprit de corps* of the Labour Movement restrained many from giving full public vent to their dissatisfaction.

In the judgment of the present writers, as they urged at that time,

* Now Lord Strabolgi.

it would have been much to the advantage of both countries had the British Government been willing to make a "Rapallo Treaty," i.e., to restore full diplomatic relations and to agree to a cancellation of all claims against counter-claims. A settlement on these lines could have been effected in a few hours, and then with the application of the Overseas Trade Acts and Trade Facilities Acts to British-Soviet Trade, the whole country would have felt the benefits within a few months.

Apart from a settlement on such lines the questions at issue were extremely complicated and the adjustments called for would, in the nature of things, require many months of negotiations in the coolest of atmospheres. The opponents of a settlement were well aware of these facts, they continuously questioned the Government as to the progress of the negotiations, hoping to create an atmosphere of excitement and nervousness in which the negotiations would come to grief.

Following the inaugural meeting the Conference quickly got down to business and after a meeting at the Foreign Office, under the Chairmanship of Mr. Arthur Ponsonby (Under-Secretary of State for Foreign Affairs), on April 24, 1924, the following official statement was issued:

> "Three Committees were set up, in addition to the Committee which was appointed last week to consider the subject of treaties concluded between the former Russian Empire and Great Britain. The first Committee will examine and prepare facts and figures with regard to debts, claims, counter-claims and means for the restoration of Russian credit in Great Britain. This Committee will form such sub-committees as may be necessary. The second Committee will draft a Treaty of Commerce and Navigation. The third Committee will examine and report on the question of territorial waters. It was decided that the next meeting of the Conference should be held as soon as the Treaty Committee or one of the Committees appointed to-day was ready to report."

As at Genoa, the representatives of the Soviets soon showed that they could easily hold their own with their British critics and those who were negotiating on behalf of our Government.

The Soviet Chargé d'Affaires, on April 25, issued a lengthy reply to the Bankers' Memorandum published on April 14, from which we take the following excerpts:

> "The memorandum demands the re-establishment of private property. The memorandum demands the abolition of the monopoly of foreign trade. The memorandum demands a change of our code. Our answer to such an attempt is a categorical 'never.'

Intervention has failed, although it was backed by a coalition of fourteen States. The same fate inevitably awaits every attempt at intervention in a new form—and that is the end for which the memorandum is actually making propaganda.

Without having received from abroad the loan of a single pound sterling, we have managed by our own efforts, and our own means, to restore 70 per cent. of our pre-war agriculture and 35 per cent. of our pre-war industry in the course of two years. We need just several average crops to have from within increased means for the gradual, although slow, reconstruction of our economic life, but the moment we are faced with the problem of the payment of pre-war debts we should have dealt dishonestly by not saying in advance: 'You want us to liquidate old debts to such or such an extent? You must help us to do it, and give us the possibility of assuming our liabilities. We cannot act like certain other States who have formally recognised their debts but never paid off a penny.'

Unlike all other loans that have been contracted here, we intend to leave the larger part of the sums in England as payment for our orders. We have a detailed plan made of orders referring to different branches of British industry. It is quite possible that out of the smaller part of the loan—the one we should like to get in cash—a considerable part will also remain in England for the purchase of raw material for Russian industry such as wool, cotton, metals, rubber, etc. Our loan will be used, in fact, for the increase of Anglo-Russian trade.

It is false that the monopoly of foreign trade is standing in the way of development of Anglo-Russian trade. On the contrary, it is because of the monopoly that we are such honest payers. There have been no complaints against us in this respect. We are ready to give exhaustive information on that point. We are not afraid of truth, and truth speaks in our favour. In a period of only two years, after the most appalling famine, we have carried out a bold monetary reform in which every unprejudiced witness must see the proof of our solvency.

I must firmly declare that we will not restore property to former owners. This principle, by the by, was done away with in Genoa, and nobody mentioned it again at the Hague Conference. The memorandum of the City bankers goes back, in fact, to the pre-Genoa period. However, on this point too, we could make some practical business offers. One of the practical means of compensating the former owners could be to lease to them on a concessionary basis enterprises which had been formerly their own, and which, according to our economic plan, are given as concessions."

Reverting to the question of the liquidation of pre-war debts, he concluded: "I must say that this question could be solved satisfactorily only subject to a consideration for our counter-claims, that is to say, on condition of real help being extended to us and interested quarters taking into account the ruin brought upon us by intervention, and now being warded off with so much pains."

Scarcely had the Conference got down to work than rumours began to appear in the press that the Soviet delegation was putting forward very heavy claims against the British Government, that the Soviet delegation were not anxious for a settlement, that the Conference had reached a deadlock, etc., etc. These mischievous rumours were so persistent and apparently so circumstantial that the Conference was compelled to take cognisance of them in a public exchange of letters between the Soviet Chargé d'Affaires and the British Prime Minister. The former wrote to the latter on May 6, 1924, declaring that the reports which had appeared respecting the alleged demands of the Soviet delegation did "not in the least correspond with the facts," and that his delegation and Government "adhere most strictly to the mutual undertaking not to publish any information concerning the work of the Conference, except that which is compiled mutually." Mr. MacDonald replied on the following day noting the Soviet denial of the press rumours, affirming that only mutually agreed statements were to be given to the press and declaring that "no attention need be paid to statements recently current in a section of the press."

There is little doubt that much of this anti-Conference propaganda was manufactured in the old Tsarist Embassy, Chesham House, which, with its contents, archives and furniture, was still in the hands of the "White" emigrés.

Chesham House had been leased by the Tsarist Government in the name of its Ambassador. The lease had still some years to run and the Foreign Office had intimated to the "Whites" that they should hand it over to the Soviet representative. The "Whites" demurred and were supported by papers like the *Times* which stated that it was a matter for the Courts to decide. This was obviously absurd, because the British Government of the day was negotiating with the Soviet Government as the legal successor of the Tsarist Government, which naturally implied that it was the lawful owner of all former Tsarist Government property in this country.

The Foreign Office, on May 15, 1924, issued a lengthy statement to the press on the course of the negotiations. It amounted to this. The Conference had met on that morning at the Foreign Office under the chairmanship of Mr. A. Ponsonby and reviewed the work of the Committees up-to-date.

Very definite progress had been made by the Treaties Committee, and its report was presented and adopted. Regarding property claims, the British delegation had proposed:

> "With regard to claims relating to industrial properties and concessions, which should be taken to include factories, mining, oil borings, forestry and any other similar properties and concessions, we suggest that the Union should undertake to give fair and effective compensation, whether in the form of concessions of properties or otherwise, to British subjects or companies, for the industrial properties or concessions previously owned by them or on their behalf which have been nationalised or cancelled; and agree to arrange with the persons in question the terms of compensation in each case.
>
> If in any case disagreement should arise over the terms of compensation, or if for any reason a settlement should not be made within an agreed period, the natural solution would seem to be a reference to arbitration. The constitution of the arbitral body, and its exact terms of reference would have to be discussed."

The Soviet delegation undertook to consider this proposal, but asked for fuller particulars about the extent of these claims and stressed that it was difficult to arrive at a general formula owing to the differences of the British and Soviet social systems. As regards Inter-Governmental claims a discussion led to some divergencies. In view of the technical difficulties involved in assessing these claims, the British delegation suggested their postponement for the present. The Soviet delegation objected to postponement, inasmuch as it would involve the shelving of the only claims which they had put forward, while on their side the British delegation would shelve only a part of their claims.

The Conference adjourned "so as to give the Soviet Delegation the opportunity of studying the various British proposals put forward." The *Daily Herald,* commenting on this report, stated:

> "In view of the enormous complications of the task with which the Anglo-Soviet Conference has to deal, the progress achieved is considered distinctly satisfactory."*

The next official statement concerning the Conference was issued by the Foreign Office on May 27, and related to Russian debts. These were divided into several categories: pre-war debts, nationalised properties and small monetary claims. The statement declared that:

The Russian delegation had pointed out that after the world war Russia had had to defend herself for four years against a coalition of fourteen States; that as a consequence the country was exhausted, that

* *Daily Herald,* 16.v.24.

" the interests of Russia's millions of working people must be considered, as well as those of the few tens of thousands of British subjects " and that the Soviets could not possibly undertake to pay Tsarist Russia's pre-war debts in full.

This statement met with hostility from the opponents of the Government. They alleged that the Government was too yielding towards the Soviets. Three days after it appeared in the press the *Morning Post,* in a leader entitled " A Dreary Farce," stated:

> " Moreover, Mr. MacDonald has no irrefutable evidence that the Bolsheviks are the *de jure* rulers of Russia or that their *de facto* authority is assured for many years to come. The manifesto which we published yesterday from the Grand Duke Nicholas shows that a national movement may spring forth any day in a country where long periods of apathy are so often ended by sudden and dramatic risings."*

The " Grand Duke Nicholas " manifesto, which was given a full column in the *Morning Post,* sounds to-day like fantastic bombast. The " Grand Duke " modestly declared that he had been invited to place himself " at the head of the movement for the liberation of Russia," that under the " future Russian Government " the peasants would be left in possession of the land, but that the landowners who have lost their lands will be compensated, and that industry will be restored to private ownership. The pronouncement concluded: " I will only then consent to place myself at the head of the national movement when I shall have convinced myself that the time and opportunity has come to make a decision in conformity with the wishes and expectations of the Russian people." Apparently this " Pronouncement " was taken quite seriously at that time in many Conservative circles in this country.

An interview with the Soviet Chargé d'Affaires on the state of the negotiations, which attracted considerable attention, appeared in the *Observer* of June 1, 1924. The Soviet representative freely admitted that the Conference was in a very perilous state due to the fact that the viewpoints of the two sides differed widely on the question of debts. The Soviet delegation considered that they were under no moral obligation to accept responsibility for the Tsarist debts, but on the grounds of expediency they were prepared to make a partial payment, provided they received a loan which would enable them to speed up the economic recovery of the country.

The " City's " point of view was that debts were sacrosanct, and that " confidence " could only be restored by a full acknowledgment of these debts, and the restoration of industry to private ownership.

* *Morning Post,* 31.v.24.

One remark of the correspondent who interviewed the Chargé d'Affaires, in view of developments which took place a few years later, has an ironical ring to-day. He said: "You have your debt, and according to British ideas of financial honour, as exemplified in the case of the British debt to the United States, debts are just paid without argument."

The Chargé d'Affaires, in conclusion, said: "I fully understand your difficulties in Great Britain, but you must also understand the psychology of our Russian peasant. Even if he had no principle about paying Tsarist debts, he thinks that he has in fact paid his foreign debts by his blood, by the ruin of Russia and by the damage caused by Allied intervention. He also has his idea of right and wrong. It is no use talking to him of gaining confidence in the City. He must be given something real."

Next day the "Diplomatic Correspondent" of the *Daily Herald* commented: "If the bondholders will not be amenable to reason, if they remain intransigeant, they forfeit their claim to the Government's support. And the obvious course will be to go ahead with the negotiations on other matters and to leave them to settle their own affairs if and when they can."

The *Times* was of the opinion that unless the Tsarist debts were unconditionally recognised, confidence in the Soviet's financial probity would never be created. It declared in its "City Notes":

> "The City is not in the least surprised to learn that the discussions with the Soviet delegates threaten to break down on the question of a loan.
>
> Loans and credits for Russia must necessarily depend upon the restoration of confidence. How can such confidence be revived if she persists in refusing to recognise her debts as a matter of principle? The thing is impossible."*

And even a paper so friendly to the conception of an Anglo-Soviet *rapprochement* as the *Daily News* was convinced that without the abandonment of Communism, Russia could not possibly recover. Mr. A. S. Wade, the "City Editor," who had just returned from Russia averred: "Communism fails because it is an impracticable ideal. During my visit I saw the enormous disadvantages which are to be set against the good results. They will overwhelm Russia in a few years unless a change of policy comes soon."† Mr. Wade concluded "in existing circumstances a loan to Russia would be madness."

On the other hand a Conservative journal, the *Spectator*, was in favour of taking a risk to improve our trade with the Soviets. Mr.

* *Times*, 3.vi.24. † *Daily News*, 3.vi.24.

J. St. Loe Strachey, in an article entitled "Russian Trade: The Key to Employment," wrote:

> "In our opinion, it would be perfectly legitimate for the British Government to intervene, taking, of course, the best precautions they can for payment and to say, 'We will give Russia the credits which she tells us she cannot do without. The initial sum required will not be a very great one. We shall soon get proofs as to whether the Russian Government will keep faith. If they do not, we shall at once 'shut down' and cut our loss. On the other hand, if, as is far more likely, trade begins to revive, our Treasury will certainly be the gainer. We shall get rid of a large amount of unemployment pay, Imperial and local, and the Government will at the same time have a remunerative investment."*

Up to and including June 29, 1924, three meetings had taken place between the chief holders of pre-war Tsarist Government securities and the Soviet representatives, but no progress was made. After the third meeting the *Daily Herald's* Diplomatic Correspondent commented:

> "The Russians have made an offer, which they consider would form a fair basis for compounding with the genuine holders. But they are not prepared to make an arrangement which would put large sums of money into the pockets of speculators who have bought at nominal prices since the Revolution.
>
> These people were, in effect, gambling on the success of Koltchak, Denikin and the rest. Their horses having lost, they still want to be paid as though they had won."†

However, despite the failure to reach agreement with the bondholders, negotiations between the two Governments continued, and by the same date considerable progress had been made by the four Committees into which the Conference was divided. Mr. J. L. Garvin warned the Conservatives that their attitude to the Conference would not have the desired results. He wrote:

> "The credulity of our reactionaries is inexhaustible. The withholding of capital will not bring about that too often prophesied crash in Russia. If it did, no one would be a penny the better off. The persistence of that belief—intervention in another form—calls out an instinctive nationalism on the Russian side."

Turning to the bondholders he warned:

> "We trust that the bondholders will see the necessity, from their own point of view and, in general, from the British point

* 21.vi.24. † *Daily Herald*, 30.vi.24.

of view, of making their own counter-proposals to Russian proposals which they cannot accept. In any case, if the financial negotiations end in failure, there is no reason why a settlement on the other subjects before the Conference should not be reached and recorded."*

II. Negotiations break down. Labour Members intervene. Agreement reached

The House of Commons was scheduled to rise at the end of the first week of August and both sides to the Conference decided to speed up the proceedings with a view to announcing the successful conclusion of the negotiations before the recess. The Conference sat in Committee on Saturday, August 2nd, continued on Sunday, met in a plenary meeting at noon on Monday and continued in session until 7.15 the following morning. Immediately after the Conference rose the following official communiqué was issued (August 5, 1924).

"The Anglo-Soviet Conference, after having sat in Committee the whole of Saturday and Sunday, met in full session on Monday at noon, and sat till 7.15 this morning.

As the Soviet Delegation was unable to accept the amendments and concessions offered in regard to Article No. 14 of the Draft Treaty no agreement was reached. Negotiations broke down, and the Treaty will not be signed."

It immediately transpired that agreement had been reached on all points with one exception and this was the question of nationalised properties. After many formulæ had been suggested and rejected the British negotiators proposed that the Soviets should undertake to give compensation for all "valid claims." The Soviet negotiators proposed the formula "valid and approved by the two Governments." Neither side felt that it could give way and on this issue the negotiations broke down.

The layman may ask what was the material difference between the two formulæ? The "Diplomatic Correspondent" of the *Daily Herald*, who was in close touch with the negotiations, explained thus:

"They (the Russians) objected to the phrase 'valid claims.' It was clear that they felt that the use of the word valid implied that the claims were made as of right, and thus denied the validity of the acts of expropriation. They could not accept it.

They offered the formula 'valid and approved by the two Governments.' That, said the British, made the whole matter one of purely arbitrary selection among the claimants.

* *Observer*, 6.vii.24.

Again and again they tried to find a formula, but the deadlock was complete.

The British delegates had strict instructions on the point from the Cabinet. The Russians were adamant in their refusal to accept any formula which denied or questioned the right of expropriation.

The dawn came, and it was evident that nothing could be achieved. Except on that one point all had been agreed, everything was ready for signature. But it was clearly all or nothing. Reluctantly the weary delegates abandoned their task. They shook hands. The Conference was at an end."*

As can be imagined, the Conservative press was jubilant. The *Times* wrote: "The breakdown of the Russian negotiations was a foregone conclusion: they have failed because of the unbridgeable gap that exists between Soviet and British ideas."

The *Morning Post* declared: "It was with the full knowledge of Communist principles and practice that the Socialist Party in this country gave recognition to the Soviet, and entered into Conference with its representatives. The Socialists habitually and virulently attacked their predecessors in office for 'blockading' Russia, as they expressed the matter, although, of course, there was no blockade. They now find that they cannot themselves agree with the Russians."

The *Daily Telegraph* averred: "The abortive outcome of these months of intermittent discussion was foreseen from the beginning. Indeed, in view of the condition to which the Bolsheviks have reduced Russia, and of their determination not to admit the failure of their revolutionary Communistic theories, any other outcome was impossible."

On the other hand, the *Manchester Guardian* deeply regretted the failure of the Conference. "Unhappily the Conference had broken down over a difficulty which raises a question of principle, and though in negotiations of this kind a breakdown does not forbid all hope, it looks as if this breakdown is due to a difference that is irreconcilable. That it is not due to any want of tact or sympathy in the conduct of the negotiations is clear from the admirable temper in which the final session came to its close."

The *Daily Herald* declined to be downcast: "We refuse to believe that after four months' work, and after coming to agreement on all points but one, there will be a rupture just because that one point has proved more difficult than any other. It would be a crime—yes, and worse; it would be an unexcusable blunder if the inability of tired men, who had been sitting for close on twenty hours, to agree upon

* *Daily Herald*, 6.viii.24.

a form of words, should be allowed to wreck the hopes of all people of good-will."

The *Daily Herald's* faith was justified. Within thirty-six hours from the time of the breakdown of the negotiations, an agreement was reached, owing to the efforts of a number of Labour Members of Parliament.

What actually took place? Many distorted versions appeared in the press. We cannot do better than quote from one who played a big part in achieving the result, the late E. D. Morel, M.P. He explained:

> "A number of back-bench members of Parliament who have played a prominent part for the past four years in the public endeavour to bring about an Anglo-Russian reconciliation which should begin with recognition and be followed by a general Treaty . . . had been following the last phase of the negotiations with anxious attention.
>
> When apprised of the lamentable upshot, six of these members proceeded by appointment to Mr. Ponsonby's room in the House of Commons at 2 p.m., on Tuesday, August 5, heard from his lips an account of the breakdown, and made certain representations. With his knowledge and consent they at once got into communication with the Russians. At 8.30 p.m., these six members, reinforced by some twelve others, met the Russian delegation by appointment in one of the Conference rooms of the House of Commons. Every section of the Party was represented. The proceedings, which lasted over an hour, were conducted partly in English and partly in French. At their close four members were chosen by their colleagues to proceed at once to Mr. Ponsonby in order to place their own views and the views of their colleagues before him. They took with them a formula which seemed to them to make possible the reopening of the shut and bolted door. By that time it was 10 p.m. (August 5). *The Russians, between whom and the British Government there had been no communication of any kind whatsoever since the rupture at 7 a.m.* that day, remained in the precincts of the House. The interview with Mr. Ponsonby then took place with the result that at 11 p.m. the four members who had seen him were able to inform the Russians that, if the latter were willing, official negotiations would be resumed at 11 a.m. the next morning on the basis of the formula submitted. The Russians agreed. The unofficial negotiators went home to bed with the feeling that their intervention had been crowned with success and the disaster had been averted at the eleventh hour.

But these hopes were premature. Official communications were duly reopened at the appointed hour on Wednesday. But, by noon, information came to hand that a deadlock had again occurred. Once more the four members met and were received by Mr. Ponsonby, at 1.30 p.m., one hour and a half before the House was due to meet, four hours before the Government was due to make its declaration to Parliament. Half an hour later the four members were on their way, with others, to the Russian Agency offices, in New Bond Street, carrying with them yet another formula. It was passed across the table to the assembled Russian delegates accompanied by an earnest plea for acceptance,* on the ground that it reconciled the standpoint of both sides. A rapid and earnest consultation between the members of the Russian delegation ensued.

Then the Soviet Representative rose with the words 'I accept.' The long tension was over. Unofficial diplomacy had justified itself. Englishmen and Russians clasped hands.

At 2.45, the Russian acceptance was communicated to Mr. Ponsonby at the Foreign Office. At 3.30, the final details were settled."†

As already explained, the breakdown on the morning of August 5 occurred in connection with the wording of the clause dealing with compensation for nationalised properties. The British side had suggested the words "valid claims"; the Russian side had proposed the formula "valid and approved by the two Governments"; the words finally agreed and incorporated in the Treaty were "agreed claims." The journals which were rejoicing on August 6 were furious on the following morning. The *Times* was typical. It declared: "There has been a sudden and amazing transformation in the history of the Conference with the Soviets. . . . Seldom, if ever, has 'secret diplomacy' effected a revolution so astonishing."‡

On the other hand, the *Manchester Guardian* declared: "The Russian Treaty has been saved after all. It seemed ridiculous that the Conference, after getting over so many obstacles, should collapse over one that was abstract rather than practical in its nature."§

The *Daily Herald*, with pardonable pride, exulted: "With the greatest satisfaction we announce this morning that the negotiations

* Mr. Morel here makes a mistake; actually there was no recommendation to accept. The four members simply stated that in the view of the British Government negotiators the new formula reconciled the standpoint of both sides, but it was made clear that so far as the unofficial British go-betweens were concerned the Russians alone were the judges as to whether the formula was acceptable to them or not.

† *Foreign Affairs*, August, 1924.

‡ *Times*, 7.viii.24.

§ *Manchester Guardian*, 7.viii.24.

were renewed yesterday, and that the form of words was found. The Conference has worked to good purpose. There will be an Anglo-Russian Treaty. A very good stroke of business has been done, both for Russia and for ourselves."*

Mr. Arthur Ponsonby (Under-Secretary for Foreign Affairs) rose in his place in the House of Commons at 7.30 p.m., on August 6, and announced that agreement had been reached ; he gave a general outline of the Treaty and said that it would be signed on the following day. He was violently attacked from the Conservative benches, and to the amazement of many he was also denounced by Mr. Lloyd George, although this was done, as became known on the same evening, without consulting his colleagues of the Liberal Party. Mr. Lloyd George contended that Mr. Ponsonby had only given a very general explanation of the Treaty. He argued that the full terms of the Treaty ought to have been placed before the House of Commons before the Government agreed to sign it, because if the Treaty were finally rejected by the House of Commons after its signature, such an act would create a deplorable impression in Russia; that the British Government had no information regarding the commercial and industrial developments within Russia and therefore could not judge whether there was adequate security for a loan; that Germany had not asked for a guaranteed loan " as a condition of a Great European settlement "; that the amount of the proposed guaranteed loan was not specified; that in any case Great Britain had only about £67,000,000 per annum for new overseas investment. Mr. Lloyd George attacked the whole principle of the guaranteed loan which was a vital point in the Treaty and this afterwards became the gravamen of his attacks on the Treaty. This, as well as the fact that Mr. Lloyd George did not comprehend the Treaty as a whole, will become clear in the following pages.

Next day, the Draft Treaties were presented to the House of Commons and debated. Sir Robert Horne appealed to the Government to allow the question to remain in abeyance until the autumn session. Quietly, but firmly, the Prime Minister, Mr. J. R. MacDonald, replied, " I want to sign the Treaty to-day." His own followers answered with a volley of cheers. He continued: " We pledge ourselves that the Treaty shall lie on the table of the House for 21 Parliamentary days. Is that not enough? Surely it is enough. Is not that the usual practice, or, in so far as it is not the usual practice, is it not evidence that the Government is anxious that not a clause, not a line, shall become operative until it has been sanctioned by the House? "

* *Daily Herald*, 7.viii.24.

III. Reactions to the proposed Treaty. The Campbell Case. The Government falls

Mr. Lloyd George again attacked the Treaty, but with less vehemence than on the previous day, because he learned to his chagrin in the meantime that he could not rely on the Liberal Party to back his attitude. In fact, during the course of this debate a prominent member of the Liberal Party, Mr. William Jowitt, K.C., pledged his support to the Treaty.

There was no vote on the Draft Treaties. The Third Reading of the Appropriation Bill on which the discussion took place was agreed to without a division. As matters then stood, the House of Commons could accept, reject or amend the Treaties when they next came up for discussion. Naturally, the prospects of the Treaties being ratified when Parliament reassembled were immediately canvassed. The Labour Party enthusiastically supported them; the Conservative Party, with equal emphasis, opposed them. What of the Liberal Party? Their support would ensure their ratification. Their opposition would destroy them.

True, Mr. Lloyd George had opposed the instrument, but it was known at that time that he had not the support of the Liberals then present in the Chamber. The *Daily Chronicle* supported the ex-Premier's attitude, but the majority of the Liberal papers supported the Draft Treaties as the best attainable settlement at the time.

The *Weekly Westminster Gazette* commented editorially:

> "If it (the Treaty) did no more than register the assumption that Soviet Russia must be regarded as a member of the European group of nations it would justify its existence. But it goes further than this: and though the main issues between us and Russia are left for further consideration, there are definite concessions of considerable importance in the Treaty itself. The agreement to negotiate with British nationals whose property has been nationalised or concessions cancelled must be recognised as a distinct advance. The conditions of our fishermen have also been improved, and channels of commercial intercourse have been reopened."*

That extract, we believe, reflected pretty accurately Liberal opinion at that time.

In addition, a number of influential, if not popular, Conservative journals also welcomed the treaty. Thus, Mr. J. L. Garvin commented:

> "The Russians made concessions in the matter of compensation to British nationals. Mr. MacDonald agreed that the British

* 16.viii.24.

Government should guarantee a loan as soon as the amount of compensation has been fixed and agreed. Mr. MacDonald took his risk. It is the business of statesmen to take risks. The risk he took is a risk on behalf of peace. The world is still disorganised and its trade stagnant because presumed statesmen have refused to take risks for peace."*

And the *Spectator* (August 9, 1924) declared:

> "The real question, of course, is whether the Government is right in making this very provisional and incomplete settlement instead of letting the negotiations break down completely. For our part, we must say at once that we believe the Government is right. As far as we can see the proposed treaties will not do any harm to any British interest, must benefit some British interests (such as the Bondholders, who will get something instead of nothing, and the Anglo-Russian trader, who gets a commercial treaty and a defined position) and may, by marking the starting-point of the return of Russia to the comity of nations, do, indirectly, great good After all, the alternative is not a better agreement, but no agreement at all."

A week later the editor of the *Spectator* again returned to the subject, and in words which have since proved to be prophetic, asserted:

> "The present attempt to settle Europe is based on the capacity of Germany to pay very large sums to her creditors by means of the plan recommended in the Dawes Report. To do so she must enormously increase her exports. But to whom? Before the war Russia was Germany's largest single customer, while Germany, in turn, was the largest customer of this country. To-day Germany neither buys from us nor sells to Russia anything like the same amount of goods. Is there no connection between these two facts? Is it not possible that the re-establishment of the Russian market is the necessary keystone in the arch of European economic prosperity, and that without it no scheme such as the Dawes Report can have a hope of success?"†

It is not out of place to mention here that in a brochure expounding the Treaties (because as we shall now explain there were in reality two Treaties), issued at that time by the Anglo-Russian Parliamentary Committee, the claimants on the Soviet Union were admonished: "One thing is certain; that bondholders and ex-property owners will lose and not gain should the Treaties be refused ratification."

The warning went unheeded. The claimants thought they under-

* *Observer*, 10.viii.24.

† *Spectator*, 16.viii.24.

stood the new Russia. They thought rejection of the instrument would bring a better offer. As the sequel will show, they scorned the substance, grasped after a shadow and lost all.

Now for an explanation of the Treaties. The instruments signed by Mr. J. R. MacDonald, August 8, 1924, were two Draft Treaties, which would only become operative if ratified by Parliament and the Soviet Government.

No. 1 was entitled " Draft of Proposed General Treaty " and No. 2 " Draft of Proposed Treaty of Commerce and Navigation." The second Treaty met with little criticism. To Britain it ensured " most favoured nation treatment," and to the Soviet Union the extension of the " Export Credit Scheme," and diplomatic immunity to its Trade Representative and his immediate assistants. Respecting the first Treaty, many of its clauses met with little objection. They concerned old Treaties and fishing rights. In fact, the fishing rights were considered as an indisputable gain to this country.

Practically all the denunciations centred round the clauses dealing with compensation to ex-property owners and bondholders.

Briefly, the clauses amounted to this. The Soviet agreed to compensate. A Commission was to " be appointed to examine the validity and ascertain the amount of the claims," and this " Commission shall consist of six persons possessing the necessary qualifications for their task, three being appointed by the Government of His Britannic Majesty and three by the Government of the Union."

When settlements had been reached, according to Article 11, a third Treaty was to be drafted which would contain:

1. The conditions accepted in accordance with Article 6.*
2. The amount and method of payment of compensation for claims under Article 8, which referred to small claims.
3. An agreed settlement of property claims other than those directly settled by the Government of the Union of Soviet Socialist Republics.

Article 12 provided that upon the signature of the third Treaty " His Britannic Majesty's Government will recommend Parliament to enable them to guarantee the interest and sinking fund of a loan to be issued by the Government of the Union of Soviet Socialist Republics. The amount, terms and conditions of the said loan and the purposes to which it shall be applied shall be defined in the treaty provided for in

* Under Article 6 the Russian Government agreed " that by way of exception to the decree of the 28th January, 1918 (concerning the annulment of debts of the former Imperial and Provisional Governments) it will satisfy, in the conditions prescribed in the present Treaty, the claims of British holders of loans issued or taken over or guaranteed by the former Imperial Russian Government, or by the municipalities of towns in the territory now included in the Union, payable in foreign (non-Russian) currency."

Article 11, which will not come into force until the necessary parliamentary authority for the guarantee of the said loan has been given."

It was around Article No. 12 that the storm raged. Few members of the general public have the time or take the trouble to read the text of treaties and, therefore, this article lent itself to easy misrepresentation. It is doubtful whether the politicians and papers which set themselves the task of destroying these Treaties can to-day recall what they then said and wrote without an internal feeling of shame.

Mr. Lloyd George wrote in the *Daily Chronicle* of August 16, 1924:

> "If the Commission set up under its (the Treaty) terms come to an agreement, the Government will be obliged to come to Parliament for a loan of perhaps £50,000,000 of British money to be spent by the Communist Government of Russia.
>
> Some of it must be devoted to the purchase of British goods. But a good deal of it must be handed over in hard cash to the Bolshevik Government to be spent—or squandered—by them. That is the difference between a loan and the financing of British purchases under the Trade Facilities Act. I cannot see this Parliament agreeing to such a transaction."

This was not in accordance with the facts. The Draft Treaty distinctly stated: "The amount, terms and conditions of the said loan and the purposes to which it shall be applied shall be defined in the (Final) Treaty."

Conservative speakers and papers declared that part of the loan would be devoted to compensating British claimants (and that that was all these creditors would get) and that the rest would be handed over to the Soviet Government.

This obviously was utter nonsense. The proceeds of the loan would have been devoted to increasing Soviet productivity which would have enabled the Soviets to compensate British claimants and, of course, in due time to repay the loan.

The attitude of the Conservative Party was understandable, if not intelligent. The Conservatives, as a well-known Soviet diplomat remarked to the writers at that time, "had not yet reconciled themselves to the existence of the Soviet Government." The hope welled up in their minds from time to time that an unpredictable something would lead to the collapse of the Soviet Government and they argued that anything such as the proposed guaranteed loan which strengthened the Soviets, would delay their final collapse.

The official Liberal Party, on the other hand, had never opposed the extension of the Trade Facilities Acts to British-Russian Trade, under which it would have been possible for the Government to guarantee the principal and interest on a number of loans floated in this country for the purchase of capital goods for periods up to twenty-five years and even longer, i.e. for the kind of goods which the Soviets would have purchased with the proposed guaranteed loan.

From the point of view of strengthening the security, and that was a consideration which any British Government naturally would bear in mind, the loan was the more business-like proposition because it visualised a related series of purchases of capital goods, whereas under the Acts each item would have to be considered separately and, therefore, they would have been unrelated.

Under the proposed loan the purchases would no doubt have included agricultural, oil, timber-cutting and other machinery, as well as steamships of all kinds, to enable the Soviets to work on a comprehensive plan to increase their exports, with a view, among other things, to discharging the claims of the bondholders, etc., as well as meeting the interest and amortization charges on the proposed loan; whereas under the Trade Facilities Acts the purchase of machinery for one industry might be sanctioned and for another refused. The loan method alone would have enabled the Soviets to undertake additional financial obligations with the certainty that they would be able to discharge them.

Mr. Lloyd George made a hasty judgment which at first was not welcomed by his supporters in the House. He then applied himself to winning Mr. Asquith over to his side. He succeeded, as we shall see later, and the Liberal Party as a whole fell into line.

Following the debate in the House of Commons on August 7, 1924, the Conservative press, whilst still bitterly opposing the Treaties, rather illogically argued that after all there was little in them. Thus the *Times,* August 8, 1924: "Any business man and any lawyer can judge their value for himself. The general Treaty is only a contract to make a contract upon terms to be hereafter agreed." The *Daily Telegraph* was equally definite: "It may be said, therefore, that there is no need to worry about Article 12, because it is exceedingly problematical whether the conditions will ever be satisfied. That is true, but it only emphasises and underlines the sham. So, again, with the amount, the terms and the conditions of the loan, and the purposes to which it shall be applied—all is hypothetical. Nothing is settled. It is to be defined in the new Treaty provided for in Article 11. There is a fog enveloping all."

The discriminating reader no doubt asked himself: "Then what is all the pother about?" The Liberal *Westminster Gazette* averred: "The Prime Minister was, in our opinion, well within his rights in insisting on signing the Treaty at once. It will have to be ratified by Parliament before it becomes binding on us, and as a matter of fact it commits us to about as little as a major Treaty between two Great

Powers, negotiated after a long breach of relations, could possibly commit us. We are dubious as to the wisdom of giving a State guarantee to a Russian loan, but ample time is available for consideration of the pros and cons of this important matter. When we do come to consider it, a great deal will depend on the amount of the loan and the conditions attaching to it. Until these points are decided it is as well to reserve judgment."

The same issue of that journal published a lengthy interview with the Soviet Representative, in which the latter, explaining the essentials of the Treaties, said: "The British Government will give no guarantee for a loan before we have fixed the amount which has to be paid against pre-war debts, and the claims of private creditors which have arisen in consequence of the acts of the Soviet Government as well as the sum which is to settle the claims of the owners of private property. . . . We have decided in the general Treaty, and I beg to affirm it once more, that the greater part of the loan will be employed in Britain. That the agreement is an advantage for Russia alone is a complete error, for it is equally advantageous to both countries. If there had been no settlement the claims of British subjects could not have been satisfied, and trade between Britain and Russia could not have developed as we desire."

The Treaties were signed at the Foreign Office on August 8, 1924. The ceremony was brief. Then the two delegations warmly shook hands and exchanged hearty congratulations.

After the signature, Mr. Ponsonby sent the following message through the Russian Telegraph Agency to the Peoples of the Soviet Union:

> "I regard the successful conclusion of an Agreement between Great Britain and the Soviet Union with satisfaction and pleasure.
>
> I have always had a great admiration for the Russian people, and throughout my political career I have striven for friendly co-operation between our two peoples. It has been a special privilege, therefore, to have been able to take a part in the renewal of normal friendly relations which have been seriously intercepted for so many years.
>
> I believe our agreement will benefit both countries and will help in no small degree in the general recovery of Europe."

Eloquent of the change which had taken place in France *vis-à-vis* the Soviet Union was the fact that the *Temps* considered that if the Treaties were honestly observed Britain would have put through a good stroke of business. The paper dismissed the denunciations by Mr. Lloyd George and others, with the remark that they are now in opposition, a fact which accounted for their attitude but did not add weight to their arguments. Mr. J. L. Garvin was apparently not impressed with the logic of his political journalistic confrères. Summing up their criticisms, he wrote: "It is said that this is merely an agreement to agree. If that were all it would be better than an agreement to disagree. But that is not all. It is a definite knitting-up of relations with one of the great peoples of the world. It narrows down the issues between two opposed theories of social organisation. It restores what can be restored, and leaves the rest for time and the good-will implied in itself to settle."*

The Tory Party, which always vehemently inveighed against any outside interference affecting the internal or foreign policies of this country, was not opposed to invoking the aid of Russian "Whites" in influencing British policy towards the U.S.S.R. Thus the *Morning Post* (August 19, 1924) quoted with approval the Grand Duke Cyril who, speaking "as the lawful heir to the Russian Throne," declared: "Neither I nor any other Russian doubts that the money will be used to fortify and prolong the waning power of the oppressors of our people."

The Grand Duke went a step further and threatened that when a government of which he approved came to power it would never "recognise treaties or loans or concessions of any sort" concluded between the British and Soviet Governments.

The *Daily News* editorially, on August 29, 1924, definitely denounced the Treaties. It stated: "In their present form the Treaties cannot stand and we cannot conceive that Parliament will pass them."

This was interpreted at that time as implying that Mr. Asquith had been won over to the point of view of Mr. Lloyd George. The *Daily News* was apparently not at all happy about the policy which it had adopted because the article continued: "It is a grave decision, which will be endorsed with great reluctance by the majority of sensible Englishmen; it means at best the postponement of real peace for Europe and at worst the possibility of a very serious immediate conflagration."

The conclusion reached by the *Daily News*, which was, in effect, the decision of the Liberal Party Leadership, as we shall see in subsequent pages, sealed the fate of the Draft Treaties, which in turn constituted a powerful brake on the development of Anglo-Soviet trade. But this decision was much more serious for the Liberal Party itself, because it led inevitably to a general election (a possibility pooh-poohed by the Liberals at the time) at which the Liberal Party received a severe blow, leading to its reduction to a mere "parliamentary group" and from which it has never recovered.

* *Observer*, 10.viii.24.

It is very questionable whether at this time the majority of the Liberal Party rank and file was opposed to the Treaties. The Political Correspondent of the *Manchester Guardian* wrote:

> "A considerable portion of the party are in favour of the treaty, or at any rate are certainly not in favour of turning the Government out on it.
>
> It would be enough, of course, to defeat the Government if the Liberal Party as a body abstain, for the Unionist Party would vote in a body against it, but I do not think that even this is in the least likely. In such circumstances I believe that a sufficient number of Liberals would vote with the Government to outweigh the Unionist opposition."*

Meanwhile, the Trades Union Congress met on September 1, 1924. The chair was, on that occasion, occupied by one of the most capable and powerful personalities produced by the Trade Union movement, Mr. A. A. Purcell (who was a whole-hearted protagonist of the Treaties). In his presidential address he stated:

> "Let me warn the Congress and the affiliated unions that it is well within the bounds of political possibilities that the opposition to this treaty may decide the fate of the Government. I urge the delegates to inform themselves, therefore, of the treaty's importance. It is crucial in the development of Russia's immense resources. The comparatively small amount of trade done with Russia in pre-war days has nothing whatever to do with the present position. The vital point is that Russia has been devastated and her economic organisation in many places destroyed. In the work of reorganisation her demand for goods of all kinds, rendered necessary by the gigantic efforts at reconstruction, makes her at once the largest customer—in fact, the greatest in Europe and Asia—and the smallest of our competitors in heavy industries. Her potentialities as a food producer make her the biggest factor in reducing world food prices. For this reason our entire weight must be thrown persistently on the side of the treaty at all costs."

The Federation of British Industries opposed the Treaties because they failed "to secure to British subjects the facilities, rights and privileges necessary to enable them to carry on legitimate trading activities in and with Russia." That little preposition "in," expressed the real opposition of these gentlemen to the Treaties. They wanted the right to carry on trade not only "with" Russia (which despite their assertions, the Treaties would obviously stimulate) but "in"

* *Manchester Guardian*, 10.ix.24.

Russia. In other words, they wanted the Soviet Government to renounce its monopoly of foreign trade in the interests of British manufacturers and merchants, a proposal which the Soviet Government would not look at.

Finally, Mr. Asquith, in a public letter, came out in uncompromising opposition to the Treaties. Referring to the proposed loan he declared: "Such a proposal finds no warrant (so far as I am aware) in any precedent in our history, and I associate myself without reserve with the protests already made by my colleagues, Mr. Lloyd George, Lord Grey, Sir John Simon, Sir Alfred Mond and Mr. Runciman."*

It is beyond question that Mr. Asquith had been won over slowly and that he took the decision very reluctantly, otherwise as leader of the Liberal Party he would have made a public avowal of his policy much earlier, and he tried to soften his opposition to the Treaties by adding:

> "There is no reason to fear that British Liberals are about to enlist in an anti-Bolshevik crusade. Their object in the matter is that our relations with Russia should be put upon business-like lines, and secured by adequate safeguards—an object which cannot be attained by crude experiments in nursery diplomacy."†

It is eloquent of the divided counsels within the Liberal Party, even at this date, that the *Star* felt moved to declare:

> "We had better be frank and confess our disappointment that Mr. Asquith's letter—clear and decisive like all he writes—contains no reference to Mr. MacDonald's reiterated statement in the House of Commons that the Treaty could be amended."‡

The *Star* went on to contend that the U.S.S.R. should be asked to give adequate security but that if "the Soviet Government will refuse to give the necessary security, we shall keep our money, and the Russian trade of the future will go to Germany. We are going to help to make Germany a loan to enable her to restart foreign trading. One of her first objects will be to trade with Russia, and British money will help to finance that trade, while we, by rejecting the Russian Treaty, will have helped to prevent Russian trade with us."§

Although responsible members of the Labour Government at once took up the challenge and said that they would go to the country if the treaties were defeated in the House of Commons, their warnings were not taken at their face value by the Liberals who, through the mouth of Sir Donald MacLean, declared that if the House of Commons

* *Daily Herald*, 22.ix.24.

† *Ibid.*

‡ *Star*, 22.ix.24.

§ The *Star* was referring to the "Dawes" Loan.

dissented from the treaties "the Prime Minister would be found in a very accommodating frame of mind."

It was widely believed in well-informed political circles at this time that the Liberal Leaders were at first persuaded that Mr. J. Ramsay MacDonald would not have the courage to fight and now they had gone too far to retreat with dignity.

On October 1, 1924, the Liberal Party tabled a motion for the rejection of the Treaties but declaring their readiness "to support any practical and business-like steps for promoting Anglo-Russian trade and for protecting British interests in Russia, and to approve the use of Export Credits and Trade Facilities for assisting trade with Russia on the same terms as with other foreign countries and our Dominions."

This decision, in view of the known attitude of the Labour Party and the certainty that the Conservatives would support the Liberal motion, meant a general election which was not welcomed by many Liberals. The *Daily News,* for instance, stated: "We view the prospect, frankly, without much enthusiasm."

The Tory Party, with a few notable exceptions, denounced the Treaties and the Conservative leader, Mr. Stanley Baldwin, advanced arguments in support of his Party's attitude which implied a complete reversal of the policy advocated by the *Times* with regard to Russia during the world war in 1916.* Mr. Stanley Baldwin said:

> "Whether we like it or not, the natural exploiter of Russian trade is Germany. They have always done the largest trade in Russia because geographically they are the most favourably situated, and they study the Russian language and understand Russian methods of business. In my view, the best thing for world trade, of which we should get our share, would be the development of Russian trade, as and when it becomes possible, by Germany; that she should turn to that market which some day, but not yet, will be a great market; that she should turn to the country the surplus of exports which is to provide for the payment of reparations, and incidentally of some of our interest to America; that she should do that rather than that the bulk of the surplus should be turned either into this country or into our own special markets. . . ."†

Mr. Baldwin's history was not accurate, nor was his reasoning sound. British merchants were pioneers in the Russian market and up to the date of the Crimean War Britain's exports to Russia were nearly double those of Germany. The fact that Britain had lost the leading position in the Russian market, due to several controllable reasons, did

* See the "Times Book of Russia."

† *Manchester Guardian,* 3.x.24.

not mean that she could not regain her lost pre-eminence. As a matter of fact, British exports to Russia exceeded those of Germany in 1923, 1924, 1925 and 1926, and had the Treaties been ratified there is every reason to believe that Britain would have held the lead. This is not all, apart from the fact that under favourable conditions (such as those which were given to many foreign countries under the Trade Facilities Acts) the Soviet market could have been immeasurably developed beyond its pre-war level. Even Mr. Baldwin, in the statement quoted, by implication seemed to recognise this when he said that the Russian market would some day become "a great market."

Although the official Conservative Party was denouncing, or to be more precise, was misrepresenting the Treaties throughout the country, the then most talented journalist in the ranks of Toryism, Mr. J. L. Garvin, was wielding his forcible pen in defence of the treaties. He declared:

> "The restoration of Russia to normal intercourse is essential to every purpose of the League, of disarmament, and of peace both in Europe and Asia. We think that the guaranteed loan would have been a sound transaction, and we regard the whole project as the best no less than the boldest attempt in Mr. Ramsay MacDonald's Premiership."*

It is true that the amount of the loan which would have been guaranteed had never been definitely settled, but circles close to those who had carried on the negotiations assessed it at about thirty million pounds—few members of the general public were aware that Russian gold to the value of £68,000,000 was actually in the possession of the Bank of England at this time. It had been sent to this country during the World War to maintain British currency. Under the Anglo-Soviet Trade Agreement of 1921, the Soviet Government had agreed not to lay any claim to this sum, to which it was legally entitled as the recognised successor to the Tsarist Government, pending a general settlement. This sum alone was about double the amount of the proposed guaranteed loan. The Soviet Chargé d'Affaires wrote:

> "It is not generally known that Russia gave Great Britain 40 per cent. of her gold reserve, or £68,000,000 sterling, to support the British exchange. This fact is absolutely unknown to the general public, but it is not unknown to Mr. Lloyd George, who signed the special convention, with M. Bark, the Russian Finance Minister."†

The Government was defeated in the House of Commons on

* *Observer*, 5.x.24. † *Manchester Guardian*, 10.x.24.

October 8, 1924, on another issue (the Campbell case),* and decided to go at once to the country. Parliament was dissolved next day and polling took place on October 29, 1924.

Politics being what they are the Anglo-Soviet Draft Treaties were not attacked on their merits or demerits. They were misrepresented and distorted. Here we can quote only a few of these distortions. Sir Robert Horne, in Glasgow, October 15, 1924, said:

> "There was not a word in the treaty which provided for a single penny of the loan being spent on British goods. The loan was intended to be used by the Russians in paying off some part of the debt they already owed to British creditors."†

Mr. Asquith, at Paisley, October 17, 1924, said:

> "If there was anything really arranged or approximately arranged that a large proportion—two-thirds or three-quarters of the loan—was to be used in stimulating British trade, there was no hint or suggestion of anything of the kind in the document submitted to Parliament embodying the agreement."‡

Lord Curzon perhaps thought that he ought to outdo both Sir Robert Horne and Mr. Asquith, at any rate, he certainly did. Speaking in the city, October 21, 1924, he said that he found:

> "No mention at all in the treaty of the contention that two-thirds of the money must be spent in this country. As a matter of fact the idea was scouted at Moscow, and the Bolshevik leaders had declared that not a single farthing was to be spent in England."§

As already mentioned, the Draft Treaties distinctly provided that there was to be a third Treaty and that "the amount, terms and conditions of the said loan and the purposes to which it shall be applied shall be defined in the Treaty," and no one in the Soviet Union had said "that not a single farthing was to be spent in England."

* A Crown prosecution had been initiated against Mr. J. Ross Campbell for an alleged seditious article in the "Workers' Weekly"—official organ of the Communist Party of Great Britain—of which he was the Editor. The decison had apparently been a hasty one and on second thoughts the Attorney General withdrew the prosecution because he was convinced he could not get a conviction. In Conservative and Liberal quarters it was asserted that the Government had yielded to pressure from some of its own supporters. This was emphatically denied by the members of the Cabinet. On October 8, 1924, the matter was debated in the House of Commons. The Conservative and Liberal leaders expressed dissatisfaction with the Government's explanation. Finally the Government was defeated by the carrying of a motion by 364 to 198 calling for the appointment of a "Select Committee" to investigate the affair. Next day the Government announced the dissolution of Parliament.

† *Manchester Guardian*, 16.x.24. ‡ *Times*, 18.x.24.

§ *Daily News*, 22.x.24.

Despite all these distortions and misrepresentations the Treaties on their merits constituted such a sound business proposition and the Labour Movement had so vigorously taken up the challenge of their opponents that up to October 24, 1924, the Labour Party was not only not losing but was winning considerable additional support in the country.

A number of their Tory opponents apparently came to the conclusion that some new element must be introduced into the fight to prevent the Labour Party from coming back in increased numbers. They found it in a notorious forgery, the "Zinoviev Letter." This document, which changed the course of a critical general election, is so important that it demands a chapter to itself.

CHAPTER VIII

THE "ZINOVIEV LETTER"

ALL the circumstances surrounding this notorious letter are not at present public property and perhaps never will be, because those who know best about them have good reasons to keep silent.

Many of the facts recorded in this chapter came to light gradually between October, 1924, and May, 1928, but for the convenience of our readers we shall deal with them in chronological order, indicating either in footnotes or in some other manner our authorities.

It is necessary to retrace our steps a little. It was common knowledge that up to the date of the *de jure* recognition of the Soviet Government (February 1, 1924) by the British Labour Government, and despite Mr. Lloyd George's *de facto* recognition of the Soviet Government on March 16, 1921, many Russian "Whites" in London, influential figures in the old Tsarist régime, had been in close personal touch with some of the most highly-placed permanent officials in the British Foreign Office. However, it was hoped that with the *de jure* recognition of the Soviet Government, these permanent officials would refrain from further dealings with rebels against a foreign government with which Great Britain was in full diplomatic relations.

The "White" Russians and some permanent officials had other views on the subject. On May 1, 1924, the *Poslednie Novosti* (a "White Russian paper published in Paris by M. Miliukov) stated:

> "When recognition became a fact, on the initiative of E. V. Sablin,* the Russian diplomatic representative in London, the

* M. Sablin had succeeded M. Nabokoff at Chesham House.

> chairmen of fourteen Russian public organisations, were summoned, and a decision was unanimously adopted to 'request E. V. Sablin to protect their rights and interests, and to be mediator in all matters which it would be necessary to submit for the consideration of the British Government.'
>
> E. V. Sablin handed a copy of this resolution to the Foreign Office, where satisfaction was expressed with the fact that the Russian non-Bolshevik Colony had extended its confidence to the old diplomatic representative.
>
> Mr. Gregory, the chief of the Northern Department of the Foreign Office, has sent M. Sablin a letter informing him that he would be glad to see him at any time to discuss unofficially any questions concerning the interests of Russian organisations. Further, Mr. Gregory assured M. Sablin that the attitude of the British Government towards Russian emigrés will, in future, continue to be as courteous as before.
>
> At the same time, E. V. Sablin sent the resolution of the meeting of the Russian organisations to a number of persons who were sympathetic to Russian emigrés, and in a covering letter he pointed out the motives of the emigrés in continuing not to recognise the Soviet Government."

At that time, Mr. Gregory was not only a highly-placed official in the Foreign Office, but he was also a member of the Committee of that department which was negotiating in London with the representatives of the Soviet Government.

Why should Mr. Gregory, an important official of the Foreign Office, have relations with Russian "Whites"? They were aliens in this country and, therefore, the appropriate Government department to deal with them was the Home Office. Conversely, why should these Russian "Whites" desire to keep in touch with the British Foreign Office? Why were they not content to deal with the Home Office like all other aliens? Were there covert motives behind all this?

At present, we can only recount the facts and happenings in the following pages and let readers make their own deductions.

As already mentioned (p. 180), Parliament was dissolved on October 9, 1924, and by a remarkable coincidence on the following day the "Zinoviev Letter" was received by the Foreign Office. The first vital fact to note in connection with this document is that the original letter was never produced or seen by any Government Department.* It was only claimed that the original document which came into the possession of the Foreign Office was the *typed* copy of a letter which the Department had never seen.

* Statement issued by the Labour Government after investigation, 4.xi.24.

Copies of the "copy" were circulated to four Government Departments, but it was such a clumsy forgery that not one of the Departments treated it seriously.*

The "Zinoviev Letter" was dated Moscow, September 15, 1924, and was addressed to "The Central Committee, British Communist Party." It instructed that Party to carry on a constitutional agitation for the ratification of the Anglo-Soviet Treaties; to form "cells" in the Army; to attract ex-servicemen into the ranks of the Communist Party and to prepare for "an armed insurrection." The forger displayed his unskilfulness by over-emphasis, which so often betrays the inapt novice.

The letter was headed "Executive Committee, *Third* Communist International." (Our italics.) Had it been a genuine letter it would have been headed: "The Executive Committee of the Communist International." The names "Third International" and "Communist International" were well-known; when this International was first formed it was called "Third International" and later took the name "Communist International." The forger, apparently to make doubly sure, headed his forgery "Executive Committee Third Communist International." There had been two Internationals prior to the establishment of the "Third International," but neither of these had been designated "Communist."

Moreover, the body of the letter showed that the author was unfamiliar with Communist literature and phraseology. For instance, he referred to a "military section" and "military cells." The Party had no military section or military cells. The document, as mentioned above, was addressed to "The Central Committee, British Communist Party." The official title of the Party was "Communist Party of Great Britain."

The letter concluded:

"With Communist greetings,
President of the Presidium of the I.K.K.I.
ZINOVIEV.
Member of the Presidium: MCMANUS.
Secretary: KUUSINEN."

Mr. Zinoviev was not "President of the *Presidium* of the I.K.K.I.," but "President of the I.K.K.I." He would never have signed himself "President of the Presidium," nor in an English letter would he be

* Mr. J. H. Thomas (a member of the Labour Cabinet) speaking in the House of Commons, March 19, 1928, said: "This document was circulated to four departments we know and every Minister on that side who has investigated the case knows that it was not only not treated seriously in some departments, but it was not shown even to the military heads of one department."

likely to have used the Russian initials IKKI in place of the English "Executive Committee of the Communist International."

Further, he invariably signed himself not "Zinoviev," but "G. Zinoviev."

Mr. McManus was certainly a "member of the Presidium," but he always signed himself either "A. McManus" or "Arthur McManus"—not, as in the "document," "McManus."

Nor was Mr. Kuusinen secretary of the Executive Committee, or entitled to sign himself as such. The secretary was Mr. Kolarov. Mr. Kuusinen, as a subordinate member of the secretariat, always signed "For the Secretariat," not "Secretary." Further—he never signed "Kuusinen," but "O. W. Kuusinen."

On October 14, 1924, the letter came before Mr. Gregory. By this date the election was in full swing. Mr. J. R. MacDonald was speaking in the provinces and Lord Haldane was deputising for him at the Foreign Office. On the following day, Sir Eyre Crowe (Permanent Under-Secretary of the Foreign Office), without consulting Lord Haldane,* sent the "Letter" to Mr. MacDonald. On October 16, the Prime Minister, in the midst of the stress and excitement of a general election, read the "Letter." It is self-evident that the atmosphere in which he was then working was not conducive to a cool and juridical examination of the document. He replied immediately, and his letter reached the Foreign Office the following day, instructing that the greatest care should be taken to test the authenticity of the document and that pending the investigation a draft protest should be prepared by the Foreign Office.

Apropos of nothing in particular the name of "Zinoviev"—whose estimate of Mr. J. R. MacDonald had for a long time been well known—now began to appear on the platform and in the press. On October 20, 1924, Mr. Baldwin, speaking at Southend, said: "It makes my blood boil to read of the way in which M. Zinoviev is speaking of the Prime Minister of Great Britain to-day."

This appeared in the press on October 21, and on the same date the Tory Head Office had a mysterious visitor:

> "There called at the Conservative Central Office yesterday, a man who had been sentenced to death† by Zinoviev."‡

> "Among the callers at the Conservative Central Offices, Bridge

* It is not an unreasonable assumption that had Lord Haldane been consulted he would—competent lawyer that he was—have come to the conclusion that the letter was a forgery. At most he would have seen the Soviet Chargé d'Affairés, and the latter would have had no difficulty in demonstrating that the "Letter" was a forgery. That would undoubtedly have been the end of the matter and the outcome of the general election would in all probability have been very different.

† Zinoviev had never been in a position to sentence anyone to death.

‡ *Morning Post*, 22.x.24.

> Street, Westminster, yesterday, was a man who had escaped from Russia after being sentenced to death by Zinoviev, the Bolshevik leader."*

On the same day as these reports appeared in the press, the London correspondent of the *Manchester Evening News* wired his paper: "There is a report here to which much credence is attached that before next polling day comes, a bombshell will burst and it will be connected with Zinoviev."

Meanwhile, the "Letter" was being dealt with by the Foreign Office. On October 21, Sir Eyre Crowe sent a draft protest to the Prime Minister, addressed to his constituency at Aberavon, but the latter was in his son's constituency at Bassetlaw and did not receive it until the 23rd. He amended the draft and immediately returned it uninitialled. It reached the Foreign Office on October 24, 1924.

The fact that the Draft was not initialled meant that it was not finally approved and that it was not, as yet at least, to be communicated by the Foreign Office to the Soviet representative in London. Yet on the afternoon of October 24, 1924, without consulting either Lord Haldane or Mr. Arthur Ponsonby, M.P.† (the Under-Secretary of State for Foreign Affairs), without any authority in writing from Sir Eyre Crowe and in flagrant defiance of the Anglo-Soviet Agreement of June, 1923, a strong letter‡ of protest was sent to the Soviet Chargé d'Affaires signed by Mr. J. D. Gregory. The protest, among other things, stated:

> "I have the honour to invite your attention to the enclosed copy of a letter which has been received by the Central Committee of the British Communist Party from the Presidium of the Executive Committee of the Communist International, over the signature of M. Zinoviev, its President, dated September 15. The

* *Daily Mail*, 22.x.24.

† Mr. J. Maxton, M.P., speaking on behalf of the Labour Party, in the House of Commons, March 19, 1928, said: "During the four days when this matter must have been the subject of common discussion among the responsible officials in the Foreign Office my hon. friend, the Member for Brightside Division (Mr. Ponsonby), who was then Under-Secretary, was actually sitting in the Foreign Office on one of those days in conversation with M. Rakovsky. Round about him in the office were responsible officials discussing the whole of the happenings connected with this business and never once did one whisper of it reach the ears of my hon. friend. Although the officials concerned knew that their chief was away in a far distant part of the country, and moving about, and difficult to get into contact with, they deliberately, designedly and with malice aforethought, concealed the knowledge from the Under-Secretary, who, as Under-Secretary, had been the man in charge of all the negotiations with reference to the Russian Treaty." (*Hansard*, 19.iii.28, columns 77-78.)

‡ "On the 21st the draft—the trial draft—was sent to me at Aberavon for my consideration. I was away in my son's constituency at Bassetlaw. I did not receive it until the 23rd. On the morning of the 24th I looked at the draft. I altered it and sent it back in an altered form, expecting it to come back to me again with proofs of authenticity, but that night it was published. (Cries of 'Shame')." (Mr. J. R. MacDonald speaking at Cardiff, 27.x.24). (*Manchester Guardian*, 28.x.24.)

letter contains instructions to British subjects to work for the violent overthrow of existing institutions in this country, and for the subversion of His Majesty's armed forces as a means to that end.

It is my duty to inform you that His Majesty's Government cannot allow this propaganda and must regard it as a direct interference from outside in British domestic affairs.

I should be obliged if you would be good enough to let me have the observations of your Government on this subject without delay."

Further, the Foreign Office, in defiance of international usage, on the same afternoon sent copies of this letter to the press without waiting for the Soviet reply. On the same afternoon the *Daily Mail* sent copies of the "Zinoviev Letter" to the press. We shall explain later the source from which, according to the *Daily Mail*, they obtained it.

The correspondence appeared in the press next morning and naturally caused a sensation, but the man who was probably the most astounded and nonplussed in Great Britain was the Prime Minister, because he knew that he had not given instructions to send the protest, and because the Foreign Office could quite easily have telephoned him on the afternoon of October 24, 1924, but did not do so. To quote himself:

"I cannot to this day quite understand how for six hours when it was known I was at the end of a telephone at Aberavon, I was not informed of the *Daily Mail's* intention or of the Foreign Office's intention to send a note to Rakovsky."*

However, the correspondence was published and the whole country, on the afternoon of the following day, Saturday, October 25, 1924, was waiting for Mr. MacDonald to explain. What was he thinking? What struggle was going on within him before he mounted the platform? His bosom friend, Mr. J. H. Thomas, told us:

"I say that on the Saturday afternoon when he (Mr. J. R. MacDonald) was expected to deal with the document and was, in fact, going to deal with it, he had telegraphed to the Foreign Office to ascertain the facts concerning its publication and that he received a reply from the Foreign Office saying 'You initialled it.' He knew he had not, and he had to face that audience and the country saying to himself, 'I am told I did something, but if I dare act I shall throw the Civil Service over.'"†

* In an interview with the *Times*, 5.iii.28. † *Hansard*, 19.iii.28, col. 104.

Let us say at once that we do not share in the slightest degree Mr. Thomas' solicitude for his friend; for at 2 p.m. on that Saturday, the Soviet Chargé d'Affaires had handed a Note to the Foreign Office declaring that the "Zinoviev Letter" was a forgery, a fact of which Mr. MacDonald was aware before he mounted the platform.

In our judgment the honest and bold course would have been the wisest, particularly in the midst of a general election when people as a rule think in terms of black and white. The Prime Minister ought to have disavowed the action of the Foreign Office and on the strength of the Soviet Note and the internal evidence in the document itself declared that the letter was a forgery. Had he done so he would have rallied and put fresh heart into his Party. Instead he maintained a stony silence on the subject on that fateful Saturday afternoon and evening and on the following day; consequently he left his Party in a state of uncertainty and confusion as to his own opinion of the "Letter."

The Soviet Note to the Foreign Office was immediately released to the press and the characterisation of the "Letter" as a forgery was accepted by the majority, if not all, of the Prime Minister's Cabinet colleagues and by probably all Labour candidates and speakers, but the Prime Minister's muteness when strong leadership was doubly necessary, naturally weakened the fervour with which they replied to the assertions from their opponents that the document was genuine. Mr. MacDonald broke his silence on October 27, 1924, at Cardiff, but even then he gave the country to understand that he did not know whether the "Letter" was a forgery or not, despite the fact that in the meantime the Soviet Chargé d'Affaires had sent a second Note to the Foreign Office conveying an offer from his Government to submit the authenticity of the "Zinoviev Letter" to an impartial arbitration court.

The Prime Minister's hesitancy was fatal because it naturally encouraged his opponents to repeat that the document was genuine, and the rest of the Labour Party were hamstrung in their endeavours to convince the country that the "Letter" was a forgery to say nothing of the fact that the electors were presented with the spectacle of a Party differing from its leader on the issue which then dwarfed all others.

Polling day was on October 29, 1924. The Labour representation was reduced from 191 to 151; but the Liberal Party, which precipitated the election, was reduced from 159 to 40 and the Tory Party came back with a working majority. It is hardly necessary to add that the Liberal Party has never recovered from the effects of this election.

The Labour Government resigned office on November 4, 1924, but before doing so they issued a statement to the effect that after hearing the evidence of the various departments they could not come to any positive conclusion on the subject of the "Zinoviev Letter," but that the original had never been produced or seen by any Government Department.

Sir Austen Chamberlain, the new Foreign Secretary, sent a Note to the Soviet Embassy declaring that in the British Government's opinion the "Zinoviev Letter" was authentic. The Soviet Chargé d'Affaires, on behalf of his Government, again informed the Foreign Office that the "Zinoviev Letter" was a forgery, and again offered to submit the matter to independent arbitration.

Sir Austen Chamberlain informed the House of Commons that the Government was convinced that the "Zinoviev Letter" was authentic, but it could not disclose the source of its information for fear of imperilling the safety of persons who supplied the document. The Soviet Embassy sent another Note to the Foreign Office, offering on behalf of its Government to guarantee if necessary the safety of the persons who supplied the British Government with the "Zinoviev Letter." The Soviet offer, dated December 22, 1924, was declined by the British Government.

Early in 1925, the Parliamentary Labour Party set up a Committee to investigate both the authenticity, and the circumstances surrounding the publication of the "Zinoviev Letter," and shortly afterwards the following sworn statement was presented to the Committee:

> "Through a registry office in July, 1924, I obtained a situation as housemaid for Mrs. Bradley Dyne. I started at Birchington, near Margate, where she had a furnished house. We left there and went to Glencoe, Cedar Road, Hythe, and stayed there two-and-a-half months. Mr. Gregory used to come to Hythe for week-ends. He stayed almost all one week and came almost every other week-end. I gathered he was an official at the Foreign Office. We left some time in September, 1924, and came to live at Kenway Cottage, Kenway Road, Earl's Court. Mr. Gregory came in about 10 a.m. every morning. Mrs. Dyne used to see him in private. Mrs. Dyne told me they had lost a lot of money through speculating in francs, that Mr. Gregory would have to leave the Foreign Office and get a job elsewhere. She also said she was going to get work. This was about October 21. On a number of occasions I heard her telephoning to a firm named Ironmonger about keeping them waiting for certain funds. Mr. Gregory pretty well lived there during that week. They went out to lunch together and generally came to tea and left about seven.

On Saturday, October 25, Mrs. Dyne called attention to Mr. Gregory's photo in the paper. She went out to lunch. On the same day Mrs. Dyne spoke to the bank manager on the telephone and asked if he would wait. She mentioned the sum of 60,000 francs, and said it would be all right. About this time Mrs. Dyne said Mr. Gregory did it when the Prime Minister's back was turned. On Monday, October 27, Mrs. Dyne said that Mr. MacDonald had got thrown out and Mr. Gregory had made his name. Mr. Gregory should have come to London, but Mrs. Dyne said that he had 'phoned up to say he had gone to Cardiff to see Mr. MacDonald.

On Tuesday night, October 28, Mr. Gregory came with a man aged about 40, a foreigner. Mr. Gregory said, laughing, 'Come into the plot.' They went into the room together, staying until about nine, when the Russian left. They appeared to be very pleased, and coming out Mrs. Dyne said, 'Come, we are fifty-fifty in the situation.' "*

After considering the sworn statement the Labour Party Committee decided that the honourable course was to acquaint Mr. Gregory with its contents and ask for his comments and they placed the matter in the hands of Mr. J. H. Thomas. The latter related:

"This document was in my possession in February, 1925. What did I do with it? I sent for Mr. Gregory, and I said, 'Now look here Gregory, this is the kind of thing that is going about, and it is only fair you should know it, and I am taking the straightforward course of showing it to you right away.' He thanked me for it, and his answer was, 'there is not only not a vestige of truth in it, it is not only absurd and ridiculous, but the facts are that Mrs. Dyne's husband was a college chum of mine and I merely visited the house.' I said, 'I accept that unreservedly.' "

As Mr. Thomas remarked, he accepted Mr. Gregory's word and there the matter was allowed to rest, and apparently the public had heard the last of the notorious "Letter."

Before proceeding further there are a few pertinent matters on which we would comment.

The late Mr. Arthur McManus was supposed to be a joint signatory of the "Letter," yet no legal proceedings were taken against him. In the course of a speech in the Ardwick Picture Theatre, Manchester, on October 26, 1924, attended by the police and press, he definitely challenged the authorities to prosecute him, but they never made a move. It is inconceivable that Mr. McManus would not have been

* Extracts from the Statutory Declaration read to the House of Commons, March 19, 1928, by Mr. J. H. Thomas. *Hansard*, cols. 99-100.

placed in the dock if in the judgment of the Law Officers of the Crown the authenticity of the "Zinoviev Letter" could have been proved.

As we have pointed out above, a scrutiny of the document itself, apart from everything else, would have been sufficient to convince anyone conversant with the history, aims and tactics of the Communist International that the "Letter" was a transparent forgery.

The competent British Government departments cannot but have been aware of these truths and, as already mentioned, all these departments, with the sole exception of perhaps some officials of the Foreign Office, readily recognised that the document was not worthy of serious consideration.

This did not, however, prevent the use of this document for ulterior objects.

For a long time it looked as though the "Zinoviev Letter" had retired for good from the political arena, but suddenly it again leaped into the centre of the stage. The London evening press of January 26, 1928, reported the opening of the trial of a Mrs. Aminto M. Bradley Dyne before Mr. Justice Horridge and a special jury in connection with some currency deals. The plaintiffs were a City firm of bankers, Messrs. Ironmonger & Company, of Angel Court, Throgmorton Street, London, E. C., who claimed £39,178, which they said was owing to them by the defendant in respect of foreign currency sold by her to the bank and resold by the bank to her. In the course of the trial, on January 27, 1928, a partner in the plaintiff firm, in cross-examination, divulged the fact that Mrs. Dyne had been introduced to the firm by Mr. J. D. Gregory, a permanent official at the Foreign Office, and that he had been a partner with Mrs. Dyne in some of her transactions. Judgment was finally given for Messrs. Ironmonger & Co., and immediately afterwards there was a demand for an enquiry into the matter in so far as it affected Mr. Gregory and two other Civil Servants.

On February 1, 1928, the Government appointed a Special Board of Enquiry, consisting of Sir Warren Fisher, Permanent Secretary to the Treasury, Sir Malcolm Ramsay, Controller and Auditor-General, Mr. M. L. Gwyer, H.M. Procurator-General and Solicitor to the Treasury, to investigate "certain statements made in course of the case Ironmonger & Co. v. Dyne affecting Civil Servants."

The Statutory Declaration, quoted on a previous page, was placed by Mr. J. R. MacDonald before this Special Board which in its report (Cmd. 3037), dated February 25, 1928, referring to the affidavit and its implications stated:

> "Presumably, the idea must have been to bring about a state of things likely to produce a marked effect upon the course of foreign exchanges, so that an astute speculator, knowing in

advance what that effect would probably be, would be enabled by extensive and timely sales or purchases to reap the benefit of his act. As soon as the act was done and the effect produced, the opportunity would be gone."

We submit that the Statutory Declaration does not by any stretch of imagination suggest this deduction.

However, the Special Board added one absurdity to another; having drawn a ridiculous conclusion from the Statutory Declaration they devoted five pages of their report to demolishing the product of their own imaginations, a task which could have been performed in a few lines by quoting the value of the franc on each day, from October 10 to October 24, 1924.

The implications of the Statutory Declaration are, in our judgment, crystal clear and we have no doubt that our readers will draw the same conclusion as we have made in our minds.

Was it because these deductions were so evident and so damning that the Special Board put up their inflated man of straw and then demolished him?

Immediately after the publication of the report of the Special Board, the Labour Party decided to press for a full enquiry "by a body empowered to take evidence on oath, to send for witnesses and papers," a proposal on which the Conservative Press, with the sole exception of the *Express,* endeavoured to pour scorn. Suddenly, to the amazement of the country, some light came from an unexpected quarter as to how the *Daily Mail* secured copies of the "Zinoviev Letter."

Mr. Thomas Marlowe, who in 1924 was Editor of the *Daily Mail,* contributed a letter to the *Observer* of March 4, 1928, in the course of which he stated:

> "I first heard of it, the 'Zinoviev Letter,' on Thursday, October 23, when I found on the writing table at my office the following telephone message, which had been received late on the preceding evening, Wednesday, October 22, from an old and trusted friend:
>
> 'There is a document in London which you ought to have. It shows the relations between the Bolsheviks and the British Labour Party. The Prime Minister knows all about it, but is trying to avoid publication. It has been circulated to-day to Foreign Office, Home Office, Admiralty and War Office.'
>
> The problem thus put to me was a comparatively simple one. The last sentence of the message was almost a solution of it."

The last paragraph is daylight clear and practically the whole of the press attributed to it the same meaning, viz., that Mr. Marlowe had friends within the Government departments who kept him informed as to the documents circulated therein, and who could, when needed, supply him surreptitiously with copies, an implication which cast an exceedingly grave reflection on the integrity of the four departments mentioned. Thus:

> "The Foreign Office can hardly be expected to be so helpful if editors insinuate that their friends can find out what documents are circulated to Foreign Office, Admiralty and War Office and can get them."*

> "The gravity of this carefully precise statement, the good faith of which there is no need to doubt, lies in the suspicion it casts upon the integrity of the Civil Service and particularly upon members of the four Departments of State enumerated in the statement. It is a fairly obvious inference that the information on which the *Daily Mail* acted was communicated outside by some person or persons who had official access to the information from within."†

> "It is considered that the editorial statement throws aspersion on the whole Civil Service."‡

It was now acknowledged, albeit grudgingly, by the Tory Press, that in view of Mr. Marlowe's disclosures, the Government could not or ought not to refuse the Labour Party's request for a thorough investigation:

> "The resolve of the Labour Party to press for an official exhumation and inquiry will be confirmed by Mr. Thomas Marlowe's account of the circumstances in which a copy—indeed two copies—of that document came into his possession as editor of the *Daily Mail*, and of the use which he made of it."§

> "After the events of the week-end one finds a growing feeling among Conservatives that the Government would be well advised to grant an investigation."‖

> "No reason . . . seems to exist why the demand should not be granted even though the subject was most elaborately ventilated at the time. A refusal might conceivably confirm some lingering suspicion that the present Government . . . had something sinister to hide."**

> "We fear an inquiry is necessary."††

Mr. Baldwin had already announced, on February 29, 1928, in response to the pressure of the Labour Party, that the Government

* *Spectator*, 10.iii.28.
† *Daily News* and *Westminster Gazette*, 6.iii.28.
‡ *Daily Chronicle*, 6.iii.28.
§ *Daily Telegraph*, 5.iii.28.
‖ *Morning Post*, 6.iii.28.
** *Times*, 7.iii.28.
†† *Spectator*, 10.iii.28.

would give half a day for a discussion of the report of the "Special Board" in connection with the "Francs Case," and it was generally anticipated as late as March 10, 1928, that the Prime Minister, in the course of the debate, would declare that the Government had decided to accede to the Labour Party's request.

On the morning of the debate (March 19, 1928), however, the Leader writer in the *Daily Telegraph* stated: "The Government can only say 'No' this afternoon to the demand for another Zinoviev enquiry."

Mr. Ramsay MacDonald, opening the debate on behalf of the Labour Party, moved:

> "That, in the opinion of this House, certain disclosures contained in the Report of the Board of Inquiry appointed to investigate certain statements affecting civil servants, and other disclosures made subsequently, regarding what is known as the Zinoviev Letter, are of national importance and concern and should be made the subject of an inquiry by a body empowered to take evidence on oath, to send for witnesses and papers, and to report."*

Mr. Baldwin, the Prime Minister, replying for his Party, said that "the Government refuse to lend themselves to an inquiry which can serve no national end and is foredoomed by its very nature to futility."

Continuing, Mr. Baldwin read a statement which he said had come to his notice within the previous forty-eight hours, signed by a Mr. Conrad Donald im Thurn, the most important passages of which were:

> "On the afternoon of October 8, 1924, at about 6 p.m., I met in London on business matters, a gentleman with whom I had had business transactions in the past, and who was, as I knew, in close touch with Communist circles in this country.
>
> At the conclusion of our business conversation he mentioned to me the fact that he had learnt of the arrival in this country of an extraordinary letter from Moscow, a letter which had been sent to British Communist Headquarters by an individual called Zinoviev, whom he knew as 'Apfelbaum.' I asked him if he could obtain for me the complete text of it. He said 'Yes,' and gave me the complete text at approximately 9.30 a.m. on the following day, October 9.
>
> I thereupon decided to do two things:
>
> 1. To bring the facts to the notice of the Government Department mainly concerned, which I did, and

* *Hansard*, 19.iii.28, col. 47.

2. To communicate this information to the electorate of this country through the press, as soon as my informant was able to settle his affairs here, and to get to a place of safety, for he assured me that his life would be in danger.

When the necessary arrangements for the safety of my informant had been made, I handed my copy of the letter, not to the *Daily Mail* direct, but to a trusted City friend whom I knew to be in close touch with that newspaper, and requested him to arrange for its publication.

At no stage in these transactions did I receive any assistance from anyone employed in any capacity in any Government Department."

Even if we accept without question every assertion in this declaration, *it only accounts for one copy of the "Zinoviev Letter,"* but the then Editor of the *Daily Mail* received two. In his letter to the *Observer*, from which we have already quoted, he stated:

"Telephonic soundings soon put me in touch with another friend, whom I invited to come and see me without delay. He called early in the afternoon and, although he knew of the document, and was disposed to be indignant at the Government's reluctance to allow publication, he did not think he could help me to get a copy of it. I insisted that I must have it, and at length he promised that if he could obtain the approval of a third person he would send me a copy through the post.

Half an hour after he had left me another friend called. He had the thing in his pocket, and what he wanted was my advice as to the best method of publication. I had no doubts on this subject, and gave him my opinion promptly. It was to the effect that he should hand his copy of the Letter to me, whereupon I would give it the widest publicity and issue it to the other London newspapers.

But it seemed that he also had a friend to consult, whose decision could not be made known till the following mid-day. I told him that I should probably receive a copy from another source before then, and that if it came during that evening, I should certainly publish it next morning. I arranged in any case to meet him at mid-day, and early on the Friday afternoon I had the Letter in my possession.

I returned with it to my office, and there on the table was another copy which had just come by post. I compared the two copies and found only such trifling differences as would arise from any lengthy document being transcribed by different hands.

The only important difference was that in one copy the name of McManus, to whom the letter was written, appeared immediately under the name of Zinoviev, as if McManus were the co-signatory." (The italics are ours).

In passing, we may observe that this last paragraph is in itself sufficient to discredit the authenticity of the "Zinoviev Letter"; in one case Mr. McManus was an addressee, in another a signatory; had there been a genuine original such discrepancies could not have arisen. However, Mr. McManus, in the course of his speech at the Ardwick Picture Theatre, on October 26, 1924, referred to on a previous page, stated that he had arranged to leave Moscow about September 15, the date of the "Zinoviev Letter"; that he was unexpectedly detained in that city until a month later; that during the interregnum he lived next door to Zinoviev and met him frequently. The probabilities are that the forgers and their confederates in the plot were not quite certain of Mr. McManus' movements and they tried to provide for all eventualities by making him a signatory in one case and an addressee in the other, intending to use the one which corresponded with Mr. McManus' movements.

But to return to Mr. im Thurn's statement, it throws no light on the source from which the *Daily Mail* got a second copy, and it in no way disposes of the grave reflections cast by implication on the integrity of the permanent officials in the Foreign Office, Home Office, War Office and Admiralty by Mr. Marlowe's disclosures, yet the Government seized on this statement as an excuse for refusing the Labour Party's request, and the Conservative press, in endorsing this decision, added that the declaration exonerated the Civil Service. For instance:

> "Mr. Baldwin blew the whole charge against the Civil Service sky-high by reading a signed statement, from an English gentleman unconnected with politics, who had actually sent a copy of the Letter both to the *Daily Mail* and to the Government of the time."*

> "But really all these matters have been threshed out so often and so fully that the public regard them first as *choses jugées*, things that are finally settled, and secondly as an intolerable bore. Although Mr. Baldwin confesses that he thinks discussion on Zinoviev and his letter always interesting and that it 'can never fail to do us good,' it is to be hoped that we have now heard the last of the subject for some time to come."†

And Mr. im Thurn was equally concerned that the matter should not be discussed again: "I think it is in the interest of everybody

* *Morning Post*, 20.iii.28. † *Times*, 20.iii 28.

that the matter should now be dropped and buried. So far as I am concerned it is done with."*

If the Conservative Party and its press were convinced that the "Zinoviev Letter" was genuine, why were they so anxious to hush up the matter? The fact is that they were well aware that the famous (or infamous) "Letter" was a patent forgery and that an exhaustive enquiry would reveal this and other unpleasant circumstances.

We would in particular draw attention to a number of remarkable coincidences:

On October 8, 1924, the Labour Government was defeated on the Campbell case; on the afternoon of the same date Mr. im Thurn was informed by his mysterious business friend about the existence of the "Zinoviev Letter."

On October 9, 1924, the Labour Government resigned; on the same day Mr. im Thurn received from his friend a copy of the "Zinoviev Letter."

On October 20, 1924, apropos of nothing, Mr. Baldwin, speaking at Southend, said: "It makes my blood boil to read of the way in which M. Zinoviev is speaking of the Prime Minister of Great Britain to-day." Mr. Baldwin's concern for Mr. MacDonald was very touching.

On October 21, 1924, a Russian "White," "who had been sentenced to death by Zinoviev," called at the Conservative Central Office, and according to the *Daily Mail* and *Morning Post* of the following day he gave to a representative of each paper a lengthy statement of the life history of Zinoviev.

It is, of course, possible that the synchronising of the resignation of the Labour Government with the receipt of a copy of the "Zinoviev Letter" by Mr. im Thurn is a mere coincidence.

It is, of course, possible that Mr. Baldwin's reference in his speech of October 20, 1924, to "M. Zinoviev" had no relation to the "Zinoviev Letter."

It is, of course, possible that the visit of the "White" Russian, "who had been sentenced to death by Zinoviev," to the Conservative Central Office on October 21, 1924, and the lengthy statement which he gave to the representatives of the *Daily Mail* and *Morning Post*, concerning the life history of M. Zinoviev had no connection with the "Zinoviev Letter."

Can all these happenings have been mere coincidences?

To return to Mr. Gregory. The Special Board of Enquiry, referred to on page 190, made the following comment on his conduct:

* *Evening News*, 20.iii.28.

"We find it difficult to see any circumstance of extenuation. He was an official of wide experience, the head of his department when these transactions began, and before they were discontinued an Assistant Under-Secretary of State; yet he encouraged, instead of checking, speculative transactions on the part of those junior to himself, and even shared transactions with them. The extent and duration of his speculations were such as to involve him in serious financial embarrassment.

We cannot doubt that he was conscious of the impropriety of what he was doing, and we do not regard it as any sufficient excuse that he did not at any time make use of official information for his private ends."*

As a consequence, the Secretary of State for Foreign Affairs directed that "Mr. Gregory be dismissed the Service." Some months later, the latter wrote a book,† in which he dealt, among other things, with the "Zinoviev Letter." It is very significant that he admitted by implication that the Foreign Office never saw the original and he did not state that the document was authentic. In cavalier terms he declared that "It doesn't in the least matter" whether the Zinoviev Letter was "a copy or a facsimile or a clever imitation."‡

We have narrated the outstanding facts and we are convinced that these facts clearly point to a very definite conclusion and that had the Tory Government adopted and acted on the Labour Party's motion of March 19, 1928, the findings would have revealed the existence of an unholy alliance of Russian "Whites," the Conservative Party or an influential section of this Party and others to destroy the Anglo-Soviet Draft Treaties (1924) and the Labour Government of that year.

CHAPTER IX

AFTER THE "ZINOVIEV LETTER" (1924-1926)

I. THE CONSERVATIVE GOVERNMENT REFUSES TO RECOMMEND RATIFICATION OF THE TREATIES. THE SOFIA OUTRAGE. MORE FORGED DOCUMENTS

AFTER the Conservative Government took office in the first week of November, 1924, the question of their attitude towards the Soviet Government was much discussed in the press and in business and political circles.

* *Daily Express*, 28.ii.28. † *On the Edge of Diplomacy*, 1928.

‡ J. D. Gregory, *op. cit.*, p. 216.

The fate of the Draft Treaties was soon settled: on November 21, 1924, the new Foreign Secretary, Mr. Austen Chamberlain, sent a Note to the Soviet Chargé d'Affaires, stating:

> "His Majesty's Government have had under review the treaties negotiated by their predecessors with the Government of the U.S.S.R. and signed on August 8 last.
>
> "I have the honour to inform you that after due deliberation His Majesty's Government find themselves unable to recommend the treaties in question to the consideration of Parliament or to submit them to the King for His Majesty's ratification."

British subjects who had lodged claims against the Soviet Government—or those who presumed to speak for them—were jubilant, apparently little realising at the time that they were throwing away the bone of a percentage liquidation of their claims for the shadow of a full settlement. Contradictory rumours were circulated and canvassed in political circles and Fleet Street respecting the Government's further intentions. According to some, the Government intended to send a strong Note to Moscow respecting propaganda, others declared that they contemplated the "review" of *de jure* recognition,* and still others that they would allow relations to remain as they were.

There were no doubt differences within the Cabinet, but finally they decided to allow things to remain as they were, at least for the time being, and the year 1924 ended without any further change in Anglo-Soviet relations.

What would happen in 1925? In political circles many thought that before the spring was out the Government would have effected a drastic change in our relations with the U.S.S.R., although they were not clear as to what form that change would take.

Many of Mr. Baldwin's supporters were hoping that the Government would take advantage of the "Zinoviev Letter" incident to sever diplomatic relations with Moscow, but this would not now have been a simple matter, because in the course of 1924 the Government of the U.S.S.R. had been recognised *de jure* by (in addition to Great Britain) Italy, Norway, Austria, Greece, Danzig, Sweden, China, Denmark, Mexico, Hungary and France.

In addition, Japan recognised the U.S.S.R. *de jure* in January, 1925.

The year 1924 had been called the "year of recognition" and as a consequence the international position of the U.S.S.R. was much stronger in the spring of 1925 than ever it had been before.

* International jurists asserted that this was impossible, claiming that once a Government was recognised *de jure* such recognition could not be withdrawn so long as that Government lasted.

This the new Tory Administration could not ignore, quite apart from the fact that many of the cooler and less prejudiced heads in the Government were influenced by the tradition of the "continuity of foreign policy" and important manufacturing and exporting interests would have been hostile to any diplomatic changes which might react unfavourably on trade relations between the two countries.

However, it soon became evident that certain Tory groups both within and without the Government were determined on one pretext or another to bring about a worsening in Anglo-Soviet relations. On the other hand, it was clearly evident that the British Labour Movement was equally determined to try and effect closer relations between the two countries.

On February 18, 1925, Mr. Arthur Ponsonby, M.P., asked the Foreign Secretary whether the Government had taken any steps to bring about an Anglo-Soviet claims settlement, to which Mr. Austen Chamberlain replied that they had had no approaches from the Soviet Government. Moscow lost little time in replying. On March 4, M. Chicherin (Commissar for Foreign Affairs), in the course of a speech, declared that no State was in conflict on so many points with the Soviet Union as Great Britain and that, therefore, an earnest attempt should be made to reach agreement. He referred to a statement made in the British House of Commons that the Soviets must take the first step and added: "I do not know what they mean by the first step, for we are always ready for negotiations."

There was no response by Mr. Austen Chamberlain and a fortnight later (March 18, 1925) Mr. Ponsonby asked the Foreign Secretary whether the Government would inform Moscow to what points in the Draft Treaties it objected. Mr. Chamberlain replied that the Government had no intention of doing so and added: "In my opinion the time has not come when His Majesty's Government can advantageously take any new step."

The British Foreign Secretary's reply was an unambiguous rebuff to M. Chicherin's offer and another opportunity of improving relations between the two countries, universally recognised as essential to European reconstruction, was ungraciously refused.

British Trade Unionism was thoroughly dissatisfied, if not alarmed (in view, among other things, of the serious dimensions of unemployment at home and the general instability abroad), at the Government's *non-possumus* attitude and the General Council of the Trades Union Congress, March 25, 1925, issued the following declaration:

> "That in view of the abnormal and prolonged unemployment now existent in the United Kingdom, and the impossibility of restoring its pre-war foreign trade so long as Russia is not

admitted to the Comity of Nations, this General Council calls upon the British Government to reopen immediately negotiations with the Government of the Union of Socialist Soviet Republics, with the following objects:

1. Complete* diplomatic recognition of the Soviet Government of Russia;

2. The encouragement and support of trade relations with Russia by the application of the Trade Facilities Acts and the Overseas Trade Acts to Russian trade.

The Council also desires to emphasise the importance of including Russia in the Family of Nations as a means of more firmly establishing the possibility of peace in Eastern countries, and declares that through Russia, as part of the Confederation of Nations, a powerful influence in this direction will be secured."

The appeal and admonition of the Trades Union Congress fell on closed minds and not only did the Government take no steps to bridge the gulf between London and Moscow, but one of its members, Lord Birkenhead (Secretary of State for India), took steps to widen the chasm. At a Primrose League banquet, April 3, 1925, he declared, to the accompaniment of cheers, "We, at least, do not desire to have any contact at all with elements of Soviet Russia."†

At this time the shipbuilding industry was very badly hit by the slump and although it had been known that the Soviets were in the market for ships, our Government refused to help, a fact which Mr. A. B. Swales (then Chairman of the General Council of the Trades Union Congress) brought pertinently to the notice of the industry. He wrote: "It might be worth while for some of the shipowners to examine their own consciences, to examine the political prejudices of their friends in the Cabinet; to discover how the said Cabinet has by its refusal to apply the Trade Facilities Act to Russia contributed not a little to the starving of the shipbuilding industry here."‡

Moreover, it became clear towards the end of April, 1925, that a section of the Tory Party had decided to start an agitation for a diplomatic rupture with the Soviets.

No stick was too rotten to be neglected as a weapon against Moscow. A case in point is the use made by the anti-Soviet press in Britain of a bomb explosion in the Cathedral of Sveta Nedelia, Sofia, on April 16, 1925, during the funeral service of General Gheorgieff who had been assassinated in a street of the Bulgarian capital a few days earlier.

In Bulgaria the Tsankoff Government had for a long time been conducting a reign of terror against the agrarians and other opposition

* See pp. 133-134 and 206-207. † *Daily Mail*, 4.iv.25. ‡ *Daily Herald*, 17.iv.25.

elements. There had been a number of assassinations of Government supporters on the one hand and of Communists and other opponents of the Government on the other, as well as fierce repressions and executions by the Government; the Left elements had even been deprived by the Government of their seats in the Sobranye.

The Tsankoff Government, which had come to power by force and only maintained itself by the constant use of force, was anxious to obtain permission from the Council of Ambassadors for an increase in the Bulgarian army which had been limited to 20,000 by the Treaty of Neuilly. The pretext employed was the alleged danger of a Communist rising and the Bulgarian Government, like the Nazi German Government later, set itself up generally as a barrier against Bolshevism. In such circumstances it was, of course, natural that the Sofia outrage should at once be attributed by the Bulgarian Government to the machinations of Moscow and "documents" purporting to prove the "hand of Moscow" in this as in other crimes duly made their appearance. All this was eagerly lapped up by the anti-Soviet elements in Britain, as well as by the reactionary press throughout Europe, and a great anti-Soviet hue and cry arose.

The Diplomatic Correspondent of the *Daily Telegraph** declared that "The fount [of terror and revolution] has already been traced to Moscow, operating through propagandist agencies and sub-agencies in various localities, of which Vienna and Varna are respective and notable examples." And after stating that Austria, which maintained normal relations with the U.S.S.R. was perhaps too weak to offend the latter, declared: "Sofia and the 'Little Entente' Powers are expected to make individual and collective representations to Vienna on that account. Then it might be advisable that other and greater civilised Powers should join in a collective *démarche*. The safety and solidarity of the civilised world are felt to be deeply involved in some combined action to that end."

The *Daily Mail* (April 20, 1925) headed its reports from Bulgaria thus: "Moscow's Massacre in Bulgaria. Plotters Unmasked. Many Reds Arrested and Some Killed. Zinoviev's £400,000 Subsidy." And in a leader the following day it drew the moral:

> "There is a plain moral for the people of this country to draw from this ghastly episode. When they used to read of the old Nihilist outrages in Russia English people shuddered and were thankful that they did not happen here—though, to be sure, we had our own abominable Fenian outrages from time to time. But St. Petersburg, at any rate, was remote from London—the news seemed to come from a long way off. There is not that

* 18.iv.25.

sense of remoteness to-day. The Sofia explosion sounds very loud in our ears. Why? Because the same arch-conspirators are at work against the peace of this country also. Moscow sends its emissaries to London as well as to Sofia. There are many dangerous Russians here at this moment who never ought to have been allowed to enter, and who ought to be sent packing at the earliest moment."*

The *Morning Post* similarily threw all restraint to the wind and roundly declared in a leading article:

"Let us make no mistake in this matter. We are again in times when Christendom is threatened by an Eastern invasion of barbarians, who are in this case assisted by secret allies and agents in our midst. We might trace the outline of various attempts—risings in Germany, outrages in France and Italy, all directed by the same hand. And why not in England? Is there no danger here? Have we not had warnings enough—in the Zinoviev letter, in the Campbell prosecution, and in many other events, such as frequent discoveries of arms and explosives, which we have reported from time to time? Need we refer to the evidence, disclosed in judicial proceedings, of Communist activities also in Ireland, in Egypt and in India?

". . . The most notorious Bolsheviks are allowed to enter Great Britain, to consult with their dupes and tools in this country, and to maintain elaborate organisations, under the guise of trade, manned by experts in all the dreadful arts of revolution. In such circumstances, are we not courting such outrages as we have already seen in other countries? If the Bolsheviks are equal to blowing up a Cathedral in Sofia they are equal to blowing up a cathedral in London."†

The Communist International categorically denied any connection with the Sofia outrage, an act which was altogether at variance with their principles, and the Soviet Government denied the allegations that it was supporting financially or otherwise the organisation of insurrection, etc., in Bulgaria. These denials were, of course, swept aside by our Diehards and indeed were only used as the basis of renewed outbursts against the Soviet Union.

In Bulgaria itself the arrest and massacre of Government opponents of all shades increased—thousands were arrested, hundreds were shot, many without even the semblance of a trial. Others who had been tried and condemned were hanged publicly.

Then came the *dénouement* of the whole affair. In the first place,

* 21.iv.25. † 21.iv.25.

the Bulgarian Government, having obtained permission for an increase in their armed forces toned down their accusation against Moscow and began to blame Serbia for instigating the Communist movement in Bulgaria. Later, however, when the Bulgarian Government desired an understanding with Yugoslavia—they again took up the Moscow bogey.

As for the "documents" incriminating the Communist International and the Soviet Government, their make-up and contents proved them to be transparent forgeries—a veritable "Zinoviev Letter." To give but one instance, the Diplomatic Correspondent of the *Daily Herald*, having seen a photograph of the document said:

> "The notepaper may be genuine or a careful imitation. But the forger has added to the heading 'U.S.S.R. People's Commissariat of Foreign Affairs,' the words 'Kremlin, Moscow.' Presumably he thought that the Moscow Foreign Office was in the Kremlin. But the effect is to produce a document bearing an address of which the English equivalent would be 'Foreign Office, Buckingham Palace!'
>
> "The letter—which purports to sanction payments for secret couriers—is addressed to a fantastic and quite imaginary 'Plenipotentiary Embassy of the Comintern.'"*

And so on.

Later still, the actual forger of the "document" was revealed by the *Berliner Tageblatt* to be a notorious forger of letters, etc., a certain Drujelowski, who had been arrested for forging documents early in May. This was reported fully in a cable from their Berlin correspondent by the *Manchester Guardian*, June 27, 1925, who said that he himself could corroborate in the main, the statements in the *Tageblatt* from "a source that is absolutely authoritative and entirely disinterested."

On April 25, 1925, the *Daily Mail* published a leader entitled: "Clear Them Out; The Bolshevik Plotters in Our Midst," and this agitation was maintained on and off until the severance of relations two years later. Although the raucous voice of the *Daily Mail* was constantly heard and its name was associated with this agitation, we doubt whether it had any great influence on the course of Anglo-Soviet relations, because that journal has started innumerable stunts and agitations, which more often than not have come to naught. Probably that section of the Conservative Party believed, or had persuaded themselves, that the Soviet Government was so weak that a serious diplomatic set-back would face it with insoluble problems.

* 5.v.25.

This view was vigorously contested by Mr. Phillip Kerr (the late Lord Lothian) who, in the *Observer*, April 26, 1925, stated:

> "It is quite a mistake to believe that the present Government of Russia is a weak Government, liable to be easily overthrown. It is an exceedingly strong Government. Not only has it all the weapons of the State at its command. It rests upon very firm foundations. It rests upon the peasants, who regard it as the guarantee of their possession of the land as against the old landlords. It rests upon the industrial workers, who are now the privileged class."

Despite the efforts of the *Daily Mail* and other Tory papers, the Government as a whole, it would appear, continued to keep its prejudices under the control of its head, and on May 6, Reuter cabled from Moscow:

> "Mr. Hodgson, the British Chargé d'Affaires, when passing through Baku on his way to Teheran, is reported to have stated to a correspondent of the Rosta Agency that the considerable, although perhaps unremarked, work which had been going on in the direction of resumption of economic relations between Britain and Russia, gave reason for the belief that the commercial relations of the two countries had entered on a period of improvement and strengthening."*

This was followed five days later by the following note in the *Daily Telegraph* (May 12, 1925) from its "Parliamentary Correspondent":

> "A number of Unionist M.P.'s, including Sir W. H. Davison and Captain Victor Cazalet, waited upon Sir Austen Chamberlain at the Foreign Office last evening, in order to discuss with the Secretary for Foreign Affairs the relations of the British Government and the Soviet Government. What the deputation urged, in effect, was the suspension of all dealings with the Soviet Government until that Government has met its obligations, and has given definite proof that it is prepared to abstain from any share in revolutionary propaganda in this country.
>
> It is gathered that Mr. Chamberlain was by no means prepared to go to such lengths. He pointed out that the Labour-Socialist Government accorded recognition to the Soviet Government, and that it would be a serious step to suspend relations with that Government without grave cause. He reminded the deputation that far-reaching consequences might ensue, and showed them clearly that, in the circumstances, he could not advise such action."

* *Daily Telegraph*, 7.v.25.

Apparently, the Die-Hards had not by this time made very much progress.

In passing, it may be mentioned that another legal suit was decided May 13, 1925, in favour of the Government of the U.S.S.R. Its representative in London claimed the possession of certain property, including archives, books, documents, furniture, etc., which were housed at the old Imperial Consulate at 30, Bedford Square. The claim was resisted by M. Onou, who had been appointed by the Provisional Government. He advanced the extraordinary defence that the Soviet Government was not the successor of the Provisional Government. Mr. Justice Acton, in the King's Bench Division, giving judgment in favour of the Soviets, remarked that "M. Onou had no real answer to the claim" of the Government of the U.S.S.R.

It soon became evident that Mr. Chamberlain's somewhat reassuring statements did not reflect a united Cabinet opinion, for Sir W. Joynson Hicks, the then Home Secretary, at a public meeting, May 15, 1925, made a general attack on "Bolshevism" and on the activities of the Communist International, which he identified with the Soviet Government. He concluded with the threat that the Government would have to deal soon with "the man who comes over in disguise, very often to ruin, if he can, by fair means or foul, the Constitution of the country which has given him succour." Who that mysterious "man" was the Home Secretary, apparently, left to the imagination of his audience, and as far as the writers are aware his identity was never revealed and the speaker never clearly explained what he meant.

A few days later, rumours reached London from Berlin, Rome, Paris, the States of the Little Entente and the Baltic countries, that British diplomacy had proposed to the Allies the despatch of a joint Note to Moscow demanding the immediate repudiation of the Communist International and the removal of the headquarters of that organisation from the Russian capital. No sovereign state would even consider such a request, because it would have meant a flagrant interference in its internal affairs, and, therefore, these rumours created great uneasiness in Liberal, Labour and moderate Conservative circles in this country. When the matter was raised in the House of Commons, May 20, 1925, the Foreign Secretary denied that the Government had any such policy in mind. The reply allayed anxiety; however, later rumours averred that soundings had actually been made in the various European capitals, but that the replies had not been encouraging for Whitehall, and that in consequence, the attempt had for the time being been abandoned.

Certain city interests were anxious for an improvement in trade with the Soviet Union. "Our exports to Russia," said the *Financial News*, March 20, 1925, "are only about a quarter of what they were before the war. It is an important loss. We are concerned, therefore, that the conditions of her restoration should be clearly defined and steadfastly maintained."

The journal no doubt honestly wished for a big increase in Anglo-Soviet trade, but it laid down, among others, as a condition "that the Soviet Government should cease to claim the monopoly of foreign trade," a condition which the Kremlin could not and would not consider for a moment.

II. Mass demonstrations. The Chinese National Movement. Trade Union Delegation to the U.S.S.R.

The British Labour Movement was not idle. It organised an "unemployment Sunday" on June 21, 1925, when mass demonstrations, held throughout the country, were devoted solely to the question of unemployment. In the course of a resolution submitted at all the demonstrations, the following clause was included:

> "This demonstration calls on the Government:
>
> 'To take every step to assist international trade, and in particular to reopen immediately negotiations with the Russian Government with the object of encouraging and supporting trade relations by the fullest possible application of the Trade Facilities Acts and the Overseas Trade Acts to Russian Trade.'"

The meetings were well attended and no item in the resolution was received with louder cheers than this one. The demonstrations were followed up two days later by a T.U.C. Delegation to the Prime Minister to urge, among other things: (1) Complete diplomatic recognition of the Soviet Government of Russia; (2) the encouragement and support of trade relations with Russia by the application of the Trade Facilities Acts and the Overseas Trade Acts to Russian Trade.

According to the official statement issued at the conclusion of the interview:

> "The Prime Minister stated that Russia had never taken more than a very small percentage of the export trade of this country, but its return to the sphere of world trade would be of considerable value to this country.
>
> Mr. Chamberlain said that the assumption that recognition was incomplete was not well founded, and the fact that both countries were represented by Chargés d'Affaires and not Ambassadors made no difference whatever. He was quite sure that trade was not at all fettered by diplomatic considerations.
>
> Sir Philip Cunliffe-Lister* expressed doubts as to whether

* See p. 54.

extension of the Acts would actually stimulate the development of long-term credit business with Russia."*

The Government's reply was not convincing: if it made no difference to the relations between two great countries whether they were represented by Chargés d'Affaires or Ambassadors, then why appoint Ambassadors at all? The fact that only Chargés d'Affaires had been appointed lent colour to rumours which constantly cropped up, that Whitehall had doubts as to the stability of the Soviet Government, and this created an atmosphere of uncertainty, detrimental to the development of trade.

As to the Trade Facilities Acts, etc.—successive Governments claimed that they greatly assisted the development of foreign trade with all parts of the world. Why should they not have helped to increase British-Russian trade? Five years later, the successor of these acts, the Export Guarantee Scheme, was extended to Anglo-Soviet trade with admittedly satisfactory results.

About this time the National Movement in China was rapidly growing in numbers and influence, and, as had previously happened in Japan and Turkey, it was challenging the whole system of capitulations. The Soviet Government, which had freely renounced all the privileges and concessions extorted from China by the Tsarist Government, openly expressed its sympathy with awakening China, and a Soviet citizen, M. Borodin, was at that time acting as adviser to the Nationalists.

There was nothing improper, in fact, there were plenty of precedents for this. Britain in the past had not hesitated to express her sympathy "with nations rightly struggling to be free," and British subjects as well as nationals of other countries had often acted as advisers to foreign Governments.

However, the Chinese Nationalists were demanding that the Treaty Ports (in which about £250,000,000 of British capital had been invested) should be transferred to Chinese sovereignty and that the whole system of capitulations should be suppressed, demands to which the British Government were not prepared to accede.

Whitehall seemed to think that the U.S.S.R. should have had no foreign policy of its own if it happened to clash with that of the British Government.

Up to this time there had been isolated ministerial attacks on the Soviets, but on June 28, Lord Birkenhead, Sir Douglas Hogg and Sir Robert Horne all bitterly denounced the Soviet Government, accusing it of working against British interests in Asia and infecting British Trade Unionists who visited Russia with its doctrines.

* *Daily Telegraph*, 24.vi.25.

Commenting on these speeches the *Westminster Gazette* declared that they "would undoubtedly be held to presage very serious events, if this part of our foreign relations were subject to pre-war rules and conventions. But from the end of the war onwards the relations of all the Powers with Soviet Russia have been in a wonderland of their own, to which no conventions and not even common logic seem to apply."

The seriousness of the situation created by these and other diatribes was realised in Moscow and M. Chicherin, Commissar for Foreign Affairs, at once replied in an interview. He said:

> "Lord Birkenhead appears to be aiming at breaking off diplomatic relations with the Union of Soviet Socialist Republics, and the next step can only be war. It is clear that Lord Birkenhead and his colleagues are merely looking for a pretext, the consequences of which cannot be foreseen. As Commissar for Foreign Affairs, I must call the serious attention of all responsible persons to the grave consequences which will ensue, if Lord Birkenhead's threats materialise."

Referring to the position in China, the Foreign Commissar stated:

> "The pretext for severing relations is the recent outbreak in China, which is really due to the revolt of the Chinese against political and economic oppression on the part of the Great Powers. Prominent statesmen like Senator Borah, Chairman of the Foreign Relations Committee of the American Senate, have stated that there would be no trouble in China if foreigners would respect the rights of the Chinese people."

As regards the general charges, M. Chicherin declared:

> "Lord Birkenhead accuses the Soviet Government and its agents of aiming at the destruction of the British Empire and of supporting any movement directed against mankind in general. From the very beginning, the Soviet Government has proposed to the British Government that all questions at issue between them should be settled to the mutual advantage of the two countries."

Finally, the Foreign Commissar made a business-like offer. He said:

> "Lord Birkenhead should blame his own Government, however, inasmuch as an agreement had already been reached between Great Britain and Russia, which was afterwards repudiated by Great Britain. I, for my part, have declared

many times that we are willing to come to an agreement with any State in order to promote the cause of world peace. This is the best reply to the attacks made upon us in connection with the happenings in China."

The dangerous position created by the outbursts of Lord Birkenhead, Sir Douglas Hogg and others, was also realised in Labour circles. When asked his opinion, Mr. J. R. Clynes, M.P., who had the reputation of always measuring his words, said:

"They constitute a monstrous repudiation of the statements made by the Government when Parliament was opened this year. In the King's Speech the desire was clearly expressed not to interrupt normal intercourse between Russia and Great Britain, and definite references were made for friendly international relations."*

As to what should be done, Mr. Clynes declared:

"Nothing has been proved against Russia to justify any widening of the breach between the two countries, and the willingness of Russia to attest her friendship before any impartial tribunal should at once be accepted, and an end put to the deplorable tendencies which make towards ruinous hostilities between the two countries. It is time that the war-mongering talk of the last few days was ended."†

The question of M. Chicherin's offer was raised in the House of Commons, July 6, 1925, when the Foreign Secretary was asked if he intended taking advantage of it, to which Mr. Chamberlain replied "the answer is in the negative." It is difficult to divine what the Government did want at this time, because although the Foreign Secretary gave an emphatic refusal to the offer from Moscow he made "an appeal to everyone in circumstances which are critical to refrain from language of any kind to make them more dangerous than they are," which seemed very definitely to imply that he was anxious for accommodation with the Soviet Union, yet he unhesitatingly rejected the one method, the method of conference, which offered the possibility of success.

It was axiomatic that differences could not be ironed out by platform exchanges between London and Moscow. The General Council of the Trades Union Congress, with a keen appreciation of the critical situation existing, wrote to the Prime Minister, July 7, 1925, regretting the Government's decision to reject "the cordial offer of M. Chicherin to discuss any question at issue between the two Governments" and

* *Daily Herald*, 4.vii.25. † Ibid.

strongly urging the Government to avoid " any action likely to provoke a breakdown in diplomatic relations."

On the following day Mr. Austen Chamberlain informed the House of Commons " that no proposal for the severance of diplomatic relations between London and Moscow, is under consideration by the Government."

It may be as well to recall here that, as we have seen, throughout this period the British Trade Union movement was, in general, decidedly friendly towards the Soviet Union and a Trade Union Delegation consisting of representative Trade Unionists with A. A. Purcell, a former Chairman of the T.U.C., as Chairman of the Delegation and F. Bramley (Secretary of the T.U.C.), as Secretary to the Delegation, visited the U.S.S.R., leaving London on November 7 and returning December 19, 1924.

The report they issued subsequently* as to conditions in the U.S.S.R. was very favourable and still further strengthened the sympathies for the Soviet Republic amongst wide circles of Trade Unionists and labour supporters.

Between April and July, 1925, a number of representative British Trade Union women made a visit to the U.S.S.R. in order to supplement from the women's point of view the information gathered and the impressions received by the men's Trade Union Delegation of 1924.

The British women Trade Unionists travelled widely over the U.S.S.R., visited numerous factories, crêches, hospitals, sanatoria, Rest Homes, schools, etc., and were immensely impressed by all they saw. In September, 1925, the women Trade Unionists published their findings,† including reports of conversations with men and women workers, peasants, teachers and children in different parts of the Soviet Union.

Although the report was attacked in the Conservative and Liberal press—the *Daily News* called it " sheer audacity "—it undoubtedly had a considerable effect in strengthening the sympathy with which the British Labour Movement had throughout viewed the progress of the young Soviet Republic.

Labour opposition to a diplomatic rupture backed by Liberal support coupled with the fact (if rumour spoke correctly) that M. Briand had returned a firm refusal to a British proposal for a joint move against the Soviet Government, apparently meant, for the time

* " Russia," the Official Report of the British Trade Union Delegation to Russia in November and December, 1924. Published by the Trades Union Congress General Council, 32, Eccleston Square, London, S.W.1. Price 5s.

† " Soviet Russia." An Investigation by British Women Trade Unionists—April to July, 1925. Published by the Anglo-Russian Parliamentary Committee, 6/7, Buckingham Street, Adelphi, London, W.C.2.

being, the defeat of the Die-Hard anti-Soviet elements in the Cabinet. The Soviet Chargé d'Affaires (who had been absent in Moscow) returned to London, July 8, and on behalf of his Government (partly, no doubt, with the object of placing relations between the two capitals on a more solid footing) offered to place orders in this country to the value of £15,000,000 for machinery, etc., provided reasonable credit terms could be obtained.

British manufacturers were then keen to accept the orders and some British financial interests were known not to be averse from financing them, but the atmosphere of uncertainty which hung over the Government's Russian policy brought the balance down on the adverse side in financial circles, with the result that little came of the offer.

As regards the line-up within the Cabinet, according to the London correspondent of the *Manchester Guardian,** there was a minority in favour of a rupture of relations with the Soviets. Becoming more specific, the correspondent continued: "Lord Birkenhead, Sir Douglas Hogg and Sir W. Joynson-Hicks arc said to be the chief who are ready for a breach with Russia." Judging by the public utterances of this trio, we are persuaded that the correspondent's information was well founded.

Asked for his opinion on the then existing situation, Mr. J. Ramsay MacDonald, M.P., replied:

> "Until the Treaty which the present Government rejected without ever having explained why—I suppose the only explanation they could have given to Russia was 'we hate you,' and that would hardly have been a decent thing to say—is put on its feet again there can be no satisfactory political or trade understanding. On this point the Labour Party stands firm. Let there be no doubt about that!"†

III. Crisis. Soviet "Buying Commission" arrives. Credits refused

The Soviet Chargé d'Affaires had had a long interview with Mr. Austen Chamberlain, July 13, 1925. No joint communiqué was issued, but after leaving the Foreign Office, he said: "The crisis is not yet ended."

On the next day he issued the following statement to the press:

> "There is still a crisis. Indeed, it is chronic. Our opinions differ only when the question arises as to the character and causes of this crisis. Our public opinion considers that, while in Russia there is not a single individual who does not desire the establish-

* 11.vii.25. † *Daily Herald*, 11.vii.25.

ment of completely normal relations with England, whilst there is not a single paper which conducts a campaign for the rupture of relations; in England, on the contrary, a section of public opinion is constantly pointing a loaded pistol at the Soviet Union. Every incident, real or artificially created, is utilised for the purpose of carrying out this policy of a rupture with the Soviets. *For this purpose, this section of public opinion stigmatises as propaganda everything done by the Soviet Government, including the natural and legitimate efforts of the latter to protect the interests of the greatest Continental State, possessing extensive Asiatic and European frontiers.* For this section of British public opinion, the existence of the Soviet Union is undoubtedly inconsistent with the existence of Great Britain. Therein lies the danger. This is one of the causes of the existence of a chronic crisis."* (Our italics).

We emphasise the words italicised because they draw attention to the most important issue then in dispute between London and Moscow. The U.S.S.R. is a great European and Asiatic State. She was naturally interested in happenings in the countries bordering on her far-flung frontiers (just as much as Britain was in developments in say Belgium and China), but Whitehall seemed to think that the Soviet Union should subordinate her own interests to those of Great Britain. The British Government would not have dreamt of making such a demand on any other Great Power, and it is difficult to believe that it could really expect that Moscow would, or could, comply. It is interesting to note that a few days later, at a public meeting, Lord Birkenhead declared: "The theories of Moscow are irreconcilable with the safety of the British Empire."

Before the House of Commons adjourned, August 7, 1925, the Labour Opposition warned the Government that they were deceiving themselves when they calculated that if they ignored the Soviet Government the latter would come to them cap in hand, and the Labour spokesmen urged the Government, for diplomatic and trade reasons, to accept the Soviet Government's many offers for a round table talk.

Mr. Ronald McNeill's† reply was not helpful. He repeated the usual charges of anti-British propaganda, demanded that the U.S.S.R. should abolish her monopoly of foreign trade, come to an agreement with the creditors of Tsarist Russia, and, by implication, brushed aside the Soviet's counter-claims. Finally, Mr. McNeill said:

"If the Soviet Government choose to approach us in a perfectly friendly spirit, and make proposals for the resumption of trade,

* *Times*, 15.vii.25.

† Under-Secretary of State for Foreign Affairs. Later became Lord Cushenden.

> they will receive very careful and quite sympathetic consideration, but so far as we are concerned, after what has passed and after what is within our knowledge of the policy and the methods of the Soviet Government, it would be merely waste of time and inviting a rebuff for us to approach them."

Mr. McNeill ignored the fact that the Soviet Government, as already recorded, had made several approaches to Great Britain and had been rebuffed. Nevertheless, *Pravda* commenting on Mr. McNeill's speech declared: "The time has arrived to give up threats and intrigues, and to begin to talk with Soviet Russia in a business-like manner." The journal concluded with words which were prophetic:

> "There is only one course: either to derive real economic advantages from trade with Russia, or progressively to lose economic influence in the East."

Towards the end of August there arrived in England a "Buying Commission" from the Soviet Textile Trust with powers to place orders here for textile machinery to the value of £5,000,000. The Lancashire manufacturers were anxious to accept the orders, but the difficulty of credit again rose and the British Government showed no inclination to help. This attitude drew some severe strictures from the Secretary of the Trades Union Congress, Mr. F. Bramley, who said:

> "The Act has been utilised for trade with countries with which we do not agree regarding their economic and social arrangements, but there seems to be a special antipathy in Government circles against Russia. If the boycott of Russia is continued much longer, we shall be bound to assume that influence in high places is responsible."*

Eventually, some six orders in all were placed with Lancashire firms, because these particular manufacturers were in a position to grant the credit terms,† which the Soviet Delegation asked, but the sum total of these orders fell far short of the £5,000,000 which the Delegation would have liked to place. On the eve of the departure of the "Buying Commission," the Chairman, Mr. J. G. Eremin, stated:

> "We must note with deep regret that up to now we have been unable to place in England the £5,000,000 worth of orders it was intended to place. As a matter of fact, we have succeeded up to now in placing only a small proportion of the orders we brought with us. This is due primarily to the following reasons: practi-

* *Daily Herald*, 21.viii.25.

† "Averaging two years, and payments to be made by instalments." (*Manchester Guardian*, 31.viii.25. Interview given by Chairman of the Delegation.)

> cally all firms with which we were negotiating were unanimous in pointing out to us that in accepting our orders they have to meet considerable financial difficulties. They would be prepared to meet us on the question of credit required provided the banks would grant them the necessary accommodation. But the banks refuse to do it.
>
> Our general impression is that so long as this root obstacle remains it is impossible to expect a speedy and successful placing of orders by us in this country. This fact is of particular importance, because next year we intend building new textile works, which will require machinery and appliances. We intended ordering these in England, but the difficulties which we experienced in placing our orders make us seriously consider the advisability of looking for the machinery required by us in Germany, France or the United States."*

The *Financial News,* although it approved the decision of the banks not to finance the orders, admitted that: " Our industry is by no means in a position to reject an order of £5,000,000 without due consideration of the arguments for and against. It is not at all surprising that some of our manufacturers were inclined to run some financial risk for the sake of increasing the activity of their half-employed plant."†

The financial houses themselves were none too happy at this loss of trade. " The bankers were, in fact, wavering," wrote the Diplomatic Correspondent of the *Daily Herald* (September 10, 1925). " I am informed by a high banking authority that several of the biggest banks were inclining in favour of accepting Russian bills, and ending the boycott on British trade. But, before they decided, they asked the advice of the British Treasury. And the Treasury gave its verdict against credit for the Russians."

The Trades Union Congress was naturally very concerned to learn that these orders, which would have meant work and wages for thousands of their unemployed members, were lost. Unanimously, at a session of the Congress, September 10, 1925, it urged:

> " The British Government to use its influence with all commercial and financial interests to secure these orders for British firms, and to extend to trade with Russia the operations of the Trade Facilities Acts in the same manner as these Acts had been applied to other countries, believing such action to be in the best interests of British trade, and that the national burden of unemployment could be materially alleviated by the fullest use of the economic resources of the community."‡

* *Financial News,* 31.viii.25 † *Ibid.*1.ix.25
‡ *Daily Herald,* 11.ix.25.

Meanwhile, despite lack of assistance, not to say discouragement, from Whitehall, Anglo-Soviet trade struggled on. The Chairman of the Soviet Trade Delegation in London, at a business dinner at the Connaught Rooms, September 18, 1925, stated:

> "The total exports from Great Britain to the Soviet Union, which in 1921 was only £3,400,000 sterling, reached in 1924 £11,100,000 sterling, and in the first six months of 1925 it was £9,400,000 sterling. We have another four months of the current year to run, and the second six months are usually the most productive for trade. We, therefore, have every reason to think that the British exports to Russia during the current year will be not less than £15,000,000 sterling and possibly even more.
>
> A feature of the British exports this year is the increase in that part of our exports which represents goods of British manufacture On the whole, Soviet imports from Great Britain form 20 per cent of her total imports. I know that this figure does not really satisfy British industrial circles. They would like to see Great Britain at the head of the importing countries to the Soviet Union. I may say, on my side, that this figure does not satisfy us either. Great Britain could play a much more important part than it is playing at the present time in the trade of the Soviet Union and in the economic life of the latter generally. Our agriculture, our industry, our transport, marine, river, railways and so on—the development of our mining industry, our electrification scheme, our building programmes—all require equipment, with which British industry could well supply us."

He concluded:

> "At first we estimated the value of our orders in England at £15,000,000 sterling, and at the present moment we have no reason to anticipate a decrease of this estimate, but to the contrary, provided necessary credits are granted, the orders will be increased. The question of credits is one of the most important for us at this moment."*

Later in the evening, replying on behalf of the British guests, Sir James Kemnal stressed the potentialities of Russia and declared that the relations between his firm and the Soviet Union had always been satisfactory because the Trade Delegation and Arcos had always fulfilled their obligations to the letter.

It was eloquent of the interest now being taken in the Soviet market that the company present included, among many others, Sir Robert Hadfield, Sir James Kemnal, Sir Charles Stewart, M.P., Capt.

* *Financial News*, 19.ix.25.

Boyd Carpenter, M.P., Mr. Robinson (Chairman of the Russo-British Chamber of Commerce), Major L. B. Holliday, Mr. Handley Page, etc., etc. Perhaps the atmosphere of this dinner and the interest which the speeches created led the Soviet Government to believe that the time was opportune for another approach to this country; at any rate it made a further attempt to induce British manufacturers and bankers to devote added attention to the Soviet market.

The President of the All-Russian Supreme Economic Council came to this country in October, 1925, and visited many factories and shipbuilding yards in Northern England and Scotland. He was immensely impressed with what he saw, and, like his predecessors, found that the manufacturers "were deeply interested in the proposed Russian orders . . . but they pointed out that the banks were unwilling to facilitate the granting of necessary credits to us." He continued: "In this connection I may point out that the conclusion of the Soviet-German trading agreement has opened up a wider field for us. Thus, we have recently received a loan from Germany, and succeeded in arranging acceptable credit terms there. Other countries, too, are not averse to granting us similar terms. I consider that it will only be possible to organise normal trading relations with British manufacturers providing British banks are prepared to facilitate the granting of acceptable credit terms."*

The reader may ask how it was that impoverished Germany was in a position to grant these credits. The explanation is that the German-Soviet bills were in the main rediscounted on the London market. Later, British bankers had, in effect, to write down the value of German debts to this country, whilst at the same time the Soviet Union honoured all its obligations to the Reich.

Had our bankers, instead of rediscounting Russo-German bills, been prepared to accept Russo-British bills, they would have received *their money in full*, found work for unemployed British workers and saved the national exchequer considerable sums in unemployment pay.

IV. The Locarno Pact. The trial of the twelve Communists. Further developments in China

Meanwhile, a number of complementary instruments, comprising the Pact of Locarno, were initialled, October 15, 1925. Under these agreements, Germany, Belgium, France, Great Britain and Italy guaranteed the Franco-German and Belgo-German frontiers; arbitration agreements between Germany and France and between Germany and Belgium and arbitration treaties between Germany and Poland

* *Manchester Guardian*, 23.x.25.

and Germany and Czechoslovakia were concluded ; a Franco-Czechoslovak and Franco-Polish treaty of mutual assistance in case of German aggression were negotiated.

The Soviet Union was completely excluded from the scope of the Locarno Pact and, not unnaturally, Moscow was very distrustful of this instrument.

Their suspicions were confirmed when the Under-Secretary of State for the Colonies, at a public meeting, said:

> "The struggle at Locarno, as I see it, was this: Is Germany to regard her future as being bound up with the fate of the Great Western Powers, or is she going to work with Russia for the destruction of Western civilization? The foreign commissar was brought from Moscow to try to prevent that. The significance of Locarno is tremendous. It means that, as far as the present Government of Germany is concerned, it is detached from Russia and is throwing in its lot with the Western Party."*

Many observers realised that the Soviet Union could not but look with suspicion on the Locarno Pact, unless it was complemented by her inclusion, and Mr. J. L. Garvin argued strongly for this policy. "Mr. Chamberlain," he wrote, "has found that where correspondence is futile or alienating, personal meetings work wonders. Why should not M. Chicherin come to London and Paris as naturally as to Berlin and Warsaw? Anyone acquainted with them both would wager that if the British and Russian Foreign Secretaries could converse face to face for one hour—utterly different men though they are—misconceptions would fall away, they would shake hands by impulse at the end, and after that the world's interests would go better and better."†

The German Government of that time would have heartily welcomed the completion of the Locarno Pact by the inclusion of the Soviet Union. On the eve of the Pact, it had concluded a new Trade Agreement with the U.S.S.R. and had established a State Bank credit of 100 million gold marks for the purchase by the Soviets of German manufactured goods.

However, instead of an approach to Moscow, the Home Secretary, Sir W. Joynson-Hicks, speaking at Bournemouth, November 4, 1925, accused the Soviet Government, without advancing any proof, of being responsible for the unrest in India, China, Persia, Afghanistan and even Africa.

It was, of course, very easy to make sweeping statements of that kind. Hearing them, one wondered whether the Home Secretary had ever heard of the Indian Mutiny, the Boxer Rising, the various Persian revolutions, the Anglo-Afghan wars, and the Zulu, Sudanese

* *Observer*, 25.x.25. † Ibid.

and Boer wars, etc. In passing, we may note that on one occasion, Lord Curzon, in the course of a speech in the House of Lords, blamed the Soviet Government for the Irish Rising of Easter, 1916, an episode which occurred a year and a half before the November Revolution!

The Home Secretary's speech was followed by two patent acts of discourtesy to the Soviet Government. The Chargé d'Affaires gave a reception at Chesham House which was attended by a large number of M.P.'s, business men, literati, etc., etc., but which was boycotted by the Foreign Office. Shortly afterwards, M. Rakovsky was transferred from London to Paris, but the Foreign Office was not represented on the railway platform at his departure.

It would seem that at this period the Government had a bad attack of the "jitters." Many of their followers were pressing for legislation on the question of the Trade Union political levy in the hope of crippling the Labour Party financially. The conditions of the working classes had been and were worsening. "During the past twelve months economic and social conditions in this country have become increasingly serious," stated Mr. A. B. Swales in his Presidential address to the Trades Union Congress, September 7, 1925. "The working people have been called upon to make enormous sacrifices during the period of depressed trade, and have been unable to withstand all the encroachments of the employers upon Trade Union standards of wages and working conditions." Further, the mineworkers of Great Britain were being warned that the industry could not continue to pay the even then low level of wages—some 11 per cent. less than in 1914—a proposal against which the miners and organised Labour generally strongly protested, and there was a danger of a stoppage of work in the mining and other industries.

On November 25, 1925, twelve members of the Communist Party of Great Britain were sentenced at the Old Bailey to periods of from six to twelve months imprisonment on charges of conspiracy. During the period between arrest and conviction the Home Secretary, Sir William Joynson-Hicks, took the unprecedented course of making two public speeches, which to put it mildly, read as though intended to affect the course of the trials. After the second speech Mr. Pringle—one of the defending counsel—called attention to the speech in court and remarked that "if it was not contempt of court it was very near it."

The whole proceedings were regarded in Labour and Liberal circles to be such a travesty of justice that after sentence had been pronounced, the following motion was placed on the Order Paper of the House of Commons in the names of Messrs. Ramsay MacDonald, J. H. Thomas, Philip Snowden,* Arthur Henderson, Tom Shaw and

* Later Viscount Snowden.

C. P. Trevelyan:—

> "That the action of the Government in initiating the prosecution against certain members of the Communist Party is a violation of the traditional British rights of freedom of speech and publication of opinion,"

and a group of Liberals, including Mr. Runciman,* handed in a motion stating:

> "That this House reaffirms its belief in the right of free speech, writing and opinion; regrets that in the recent Communist prosecution the Attorney General appeared to base his case rather upon the denial of these rights than upon evidence and specific acts of violence or incitements thereto, and further regrets the atmosphere of prejudice created in connection with this and other trials by the speeches of members of his Majesty's Government."

It is thus evident that the Government, as we have just stated, were suffering from a bad attack of the "jitters," and they seemed to think that the Soviet Government was responsible for their nerve trouble. The speeches of the Home Secretary, etc., the exclusion of the U.S.S.R. from the Locarno Pact and the studied discourtesies were to a slight extent offset by a speech of the Foreign Secretary, Sir Austen Chamberlain, on November 20, 1925. The atmosphere in which he spoke is important. He was being fêted at the Savoy Hotel to celebrate his success at Locarno, and in the course of a lengthy address, he said:

> "But the spirit which took the British Government to Locarno must and will inspire the British Government and its representatives in its relations with all other nations. We are pursuing a policy of appeasement, reconciliation and peace. We will do all we can to find a method of solving any difficulties that may exist between us and any other countries. Though we have no pretension to dictate and no desire to impose a policy on any other country, we will work in other spheres as we worked at Locarno, to secure the peace of the world, to give European civilisation a chance to survive and to secure that our sons and our grandsons shall not again live through the tragedy through which we have lived."†

He did not mention the U.S.S.R., but it was thought by his listeners that he was alluding to that country. "Most of his hearers," wrote the *Daily Express*, "and the company included a remarkable repre-

* Subsequently Viscount Runciman. † *Manchester Guardian*, 21.xi.25.

sentation of politics, art, literature and the drama, interpreted one passage as a significant gesture in the direction of Russia."

Whatever may have been in the Foreign Secretary's mind, his "gesture" was not followed by any diplomatic *démarche* in Moscow. Some weeks later, M. Chicherin was spending a holiday in France; he met M. Briand, then Premier of France, and was entertained to lunch by that statesman, December 12, 1925. On the same day, in the course of an interview with a representative of the *Observer*, the following dialogue took place:

> "Have you, M. Chicherin," I asked, "modified in any way your very uncompromising criticism of the spirit of Locarno?"
>
> "I am afraid," replied M. Chicherin, with a smile, "that I shall have to disappoint you. We still regard Locarno with apprehension, for we don't yet see Locarno's contribution to the cause of peace. I, for one, readily accept the assurance of the participants in the Conference, that Locarno is 'a beginning.' But a beginning of what? That only time will show.
>
> Locarno or no Locarno, we want real peace and a removal of the antagonisms which would tear the world to pieces, and we are whole-heartedly ready to make our contribution to this end.
>
> We realise quite readily that no settlement can result from a situation in which one party gives all and the other takes all. Settlement is a matter of give and take; and we are realists enough to allow full play to this fundamental principle of negotiation. This principle is, I believe, fully recognised by the British people who, more than any other, put their confidence in facts. The Union of Socialist Soviet Republics is a fact, and a considerable one. If only this is borne in mind, an accommodation between Great Britain and Russia should not be difficult."*

It will be noticed that M. Chicherin did not indulge in a vague "gesture." He mentioned Britain by name and expressed the readiness of his Government to negotiate with this country on the principle of give and take. International diplomacy being what it is, one could hardly expect the Foreign Commissar to go further than he did. Not for the first time an advance by the Soviets to this country was interpreted as a sign of internal weakness. The *Times*, a few days later, argued that the Soviet was facing internal difficulties and that "these difficulties may explain the pilgrimage of M. Chicherin and his attempts to confuse the real issue with the pretext that the Soviet Government is in some way aggrieved by British aloofness." Not only was there no advance from the British side,

* *Observer*, 13.xii.25.

but on the contrary, Mr. Churchill jumped in with another abusive attack on the Soviet Union which drew the apposite comment from the *Westminster Gazette* that a "policy which alternates between the abuse of Mr. Churchill and the timid advances of Sir Austen Chamberlain is neither sensible nor consistent."

The *Times*, in view of what it had asserted, must have been somewhat disappointed to read a few days later the impressions of Mr. A. W. Golightly, a director of the C.W.S., who had just returned from a business tour of the U.S.S.R. He said:

> "It is four years since I last travelled in Russia, and I am literally amazed at the progress which has been made in the intervening period. I am not exaggerating when I say the openings for successful trading have increased tenfold. From what I saw, Russia will recover economic stability and prosperity more quickly than has appeared possible."*

Regarding relations between the two Governments, Mr. Golightly declared: "Our inquiries had in every case to do with industrial and commercial development. What we saw makes me hope that the British and Russian Governments will speedily arrive at mutual agreement in relation to liabilities and international trade."

Questioned respecting credit for Russian trade, he replied: "We have now done a lot of trade with Russia, covering a considerable period. It has been done through our banks. Never once have the Russians failed to meet their obligations to the full."

Despite the fact that London had not vouchsafed any reply to the interview given in Paris by the Foreign Commissar, and notwithstanding that he must have known that another approach would be interpreted in some influential quarters in London as weakness, M. Chicherin gave the British Government another opening. In an interview at Berlin, December 31, 1925, he stated:

> "We cannot make fresh proposals to Britain until the British Government informs us which points of the agreement reached with the Ramsay MacDonald Government are unacceptable. We regard a settlement of the differences between Britain and the Soviet Union as very desirable, but we have the definite impression that the British Government does not desire at the present moment such a settlement."

Asked if he would welcome a meeting with Mr. Chamberlain,† he replied with an emphatic affirmative. However, again there was no response from London and M. Chicherin returned to Moscow.

To sum up, throughout 1925, Anglo-Soviet relations steadily

* *Daily Herald*, 19.xii.25. † Became Sir Austen Chamberlain, Dec. 1925.

deteriorated, and the British Government treated with ill-concealed contempt every advance from Moscow. It seems incredible to-day that responsible statesmen should have acted with such levity towards the solution of serious problems at issue with a great nation.

Before proceeding further, it is necessary to turn our attention again to happenings and developments in China, because they had serious repercussions on Anglo-Soviet relations. During the period under review the peoples of Central and Northern China, groaning under the yoke of the various War Lords, were turning more and more towards the Canton Government established by the famous Chinese leader, Dr. Sun Yat-Sen; and the Chinese National Party, the Kuomintang, inspired by Dr. Sun's teaching, grew rapidly in strength and influence throughout the length and breadth of that vast densely-populated country. The aims of the Party were the denunciation of the Unequal Treaties, the complete restoration of Chinese sovereignty, the development of constitutional democracy and the economic and cultural amelioration of the Chinese masses.*

These principles had been proclaimed even before the overthrow of the Manchu Dynasty by the Peoples' Movement. The old "unchanging East" had gone. China, among other Asiatic countries, was on the march. Had the Western European countries with big investments and business interests in China been wise they would have welcomed this new natural and healthy awakening of a great people.

True, the realisation of the aims of the Kuomintang would have meant many readjustments of foreign interests in China, the unconscionable exploitation of Chinese labour would have had to go, but a strong, prosperous and friendly China would have been a far better market for the products of Western industry than a weak, impoverished and sullen China.

No doubt certain foreign interests would have suffered. Profits coined out of the tears and suffering of children† of tender years in

* Briefly the "Three Peoples Principles" enunciated by Dr. Sun Yat Sen and which constituted the aims of Kuomintang have thus been translated by an authoritative member of that party: "National equality outside the state ('of the people'), a political equality in the state ('by the people'), and an economic equality corresponding to Lincoln's 'for the people'". ("China and the Nations," p. xii.)

† The following are extracts from the Report (1924) of the Child Labour Commission appointed by the Municipal Council of the Shanghai International Settlement—a mainly British body, with no Chinese representatives. The Child Labour Commission had nine members, one of whom was Chairman of the Cotton Mill Owners' Association of China, and another three were also employers:

> "*Cotton Mills.*—In normal times, night work is the rule. There are two 12-hour shifts. On occasions when there is no night shift, the length of the day's work is frequently 13 hours, or even more. In some mills, there is a regular one-hour interval for meals, whilst in others, the employees take their meals as best they can. The children . . . in the great majority of cases have to stand the whole time they are at work. The Commission saw many children at work who could not have been more than six or seven years of age."
>
> "*Silk Filatures.*—The regular hours of work are 12 hours a day . . . many of the children employed are very young, certainly not more than six years of age.

the cotton mills of Shanghai would have been a thing of the past. On the other hand, there would have been big possibilities for business of a more savoury kind.

The Soviet Government, because it opposed Imperialism, the domination of one nation by another, was naturally fully sympathetic to the Peoples' Movement of China. The Soviet Government voluntarily renounced all extra-territorial rights in China and all privileges wrung from that country by the Tsarist Government, and on May 31, 1924, concluded an agreement with China on terms of complete mutual equality. It had hoped that other countries would follow its example. Had they done so and helped China to develop her resources and her defence forces, the probabilities are that China to-day would be strong and free from the scourge of Japanese invasion.

M. Chicherin, in an interview with Mr. Arthur Ransome in February, 1926, explained his Government's point of view *vis-à-vis* China. He said:

> "When in the beginning of the nineteenth century the South American Republics carried on a war of national liberation against Spain, and when, further, in Spain and in Italy parliamentarism struggled against absolutism, the English Government gave open diplomatic help to these movements. It helped the national liberation movement in Poland, it helped Hungary, then struggling to create a national State, and it gave very decided support to the movement for liberation and unity in Italy.
>
> The Soviet Government consider that the Chinese people have no less right than these to national unity and independence. The Soviet Government and its agents are far from trying to develop in the Chinese people any hatred towards foreigners. On the contrary, a free, democratic China, the creation of which has our sympathy, will present far more favourable relations with all countries than a China enslaved and exploited, under the burden of unequal treaties. The national movement of oppressed peoples, with which we sympathise, must in general lead to the greatest cultural efflorescence of these peoples."

Turning to the question of the Soviet's relations with the East as a whole, the Foreign Commissar said:

> "In general, our relations with the peoples of the East are based on mutual friendship and on a perfectly peaceful policy free from

---

They earn from 20 to 25 silver cents a day (about 6d.)."

"*Match Factories.*—Young children, certainly not more than five years of age seen working. . . . Many babies and infants who could hardly stand slept or played on the floor whilst their mothers worked. White phosphorus is used in some of these factories."

Extracts like these might be multiplied many times.

any sort of aggressiveness. Looking over the history of the development of these relations, one may observe that we were all the time the object of attack on the part of Imperialist Powers in Asia, and that our friendly relations with the national movements of the peoples of the East developed in the course of our struggle against the aggressive policy of Imperialism directed against ourselves."*

Turning again to China, M. Chicherin said: " In China itself, at our first coming into touch with the Central Government in Peking we were brought up by the hostile attitude of the Chinese Government towards entering into diplomatic relations with the U.S.S.R., and the reason of this was pressure from Imperialist Powers, and it is only in the process of *rapprochement* with the Chinese national movement that we have succeeded in breaking through these obstacles set up by England and other Western Powers."

It is difficult to imagine how the Soviet Government, if it remained true to its principles, could adopt any other policy towards China, and it is equally difficult to imagine how any Government which accepted the right of " self-determination " (so loudly proclaimed by the Allies during the war) could cavil at the Soviet Government's attitude, particularly in view of the fact that China herself was an Ally.

We must now return to the course of Anglo-Soviet relations. On September 3, 1925, five British Labour M.P.'s, together with the Secretary of the Anglo-Russian Parliamentary Committee, left London for the U.S.S.R., where they carried out an investigation as to the possibilities of Anglo-Soviet trade. They stayed in the U.S.S.R. up to October 13, visited Moscow, Nizhni Novgorod (now Gorki), Kharkov, the Donetz Basin, Rostov-on-Don, many villages in the Don and Kuban Cossack regions, Armavir, Grozny, Baku, Tiflis, Erivan, Leninakhan, Vladikavkaz and Leningrad.

They had numerous interviews with Soviet economists and the heads of the Commissariats for Finance, Foreign Trade, various Industries and other important Soviet statesmen. Their report, issued in March, 1926,† showed the rapid progress then being made in the restoration of the Soviet economy, the stability of the Soviet Government and the enormous possibilities of an extension of Anglo-Soviet trade, given normal friendly political economic relations between the two countries. Unfortunately, these relations were, and continued for a long time, anything but normal, still less friendly.

A vote for the Export Credits Acts was before the House of Com-

* *Manchester Guardian*, 27.ii.26.

† "Possibilites of British-Russian Trade." An Investigation by British Members of Parliament. Published by the Anglo-Russian Parliamentary Committee, 6/7, Buckingham Street, Adelphi, London, W.C.2. Price 1s.

mons, March 1, 1926. Mr. A. V. Alexander, the well-known co-operator, and Mr. Walter Runciman,* the well-known Liberal, advocated the extension of the Acts to British-Russian trade. To the chagrin of the Government and the pleasure of the opposition parties, Sir Philip Pilditch (a member of the Advisory Committee administering the Acts) declared that he was as willing to support transactions with Soviet Russia as with any other country. This was considered a big advance on the part of the Government, and, as the *Times* correspondent remarked, "speech followed speech, and there were few, even among those of the Conservatives, who did not support the backing of Russian bills."

It looked for the moment as though sound business sense had overcome political prejudice. But, alas, unreasoning bias won in the end. The Home Secretary, at the end of a tense debate, declared that the Government was not willing to risk the taxpayers' money (which naturally occurred in every application of the Acts) in Russia. Feeling in the House can be gauged from the fact that the Opposition was only beaten by 197 to 109 votes.

As our readers know, Mr. Winston Churchill had been a bitter opponent of relations with Soviet Russia, but he was now Chancellor of the Exchequer and apparently the exigencies of his budget somewhat overcame his antipathies. In the course of a debate on Inter-Allied debts, March 24, 1926, after he had boasted that "we always have in this country our own unbroken tradition of never defaulting" and after he had explained the debt settlements with the U.S.A. and France, he turned to the question of the U.S.S.R.:

> "Russia has repudiated her War debts as well as her civil debts, but perhaps this is not the last word that we shall hear from Russia. Things are changing in Russia. The importance of world credit to that vast community is dawning upon the rulers of that country. We do not abrogate any of our claims, but this I do say, that if at any time the initiative in raising this question comes from Russia we should not treat Russia with less consideration than we have treated other debtors."†

These were probably the friendliest words which the Chancellor of the Exchequer had up to that date applied to the U.S.S.R. and they moved Mr. J. L. Garvin to comment:

> "Mr. Churchill's invitation to Russia was unexpected and welcome. He has opened no door as yet. The occasion proposed for the visit is austere. But Russia has been asked to knock and is promised a courteous welcome. It is something that the

* Subsequently Lord Runciman.

† *Hansard*, 24.iii.26, col. 1251

Government should have begun to take account again, officially, of the existence of Russia, even as a debtor."*

As to the terms which Whitehall would accept the diplomatic correspondent of the same paper stated:

> "It is now taken for granted that if the Russian Government made a funding offer of £4,750,000 a year for sixty-two years the offer would be accepted, for such an offer, representing about one-sixth of Russia's obligation, would be commensurate with the Anglo-Italian settlement."†

The correspondent added: "Mr. Churchill's statement is understood to be supported by the Big Five Joint Stock banks, whose support is a matter of some importance."

These terms were, no doubt, considerably milder than a Tory Government would have offered a few years earlier when its members were calling for a settlement in full, but more reasonable though they were, they contained no recognition of the Soviet's counter-claims and no provisions for a loan and, therefore, were quite unacceptable to the U.S.S.R.

The British Government of the day was still hoping that the Soviet Government would come to an arrangement with British private claimants in the expectation that after such a settlement the Soviets would be able to float a loan on the London market without the guarantee of the British Government. This was made clear in a letter, dated April 7, 1926, from the Foreign Secretary to the London Chamber of Commerce. *Izvestia,* commenting on this letter a few days later, stated that the Soviet Government was anxious to conclude a debt settlement, but despite the presence of a Soviet diplomatic representative in London, no approach had been made to him. The paper maintained that in any case an indispensable condition of a settlement was a guaranteed loan.

Meanwhile, an unexpected episode attracted considerable attention. Four Conservative members of Parliament left for Soviet Russia on April 17, 1926. They were: Sir Frank Nelson, Capt. R. C. Bourne, Mr. R. J. Boothby and Lieut.-Colonel T. C. R. Moore. The object of the visit was summed up by Lieut.-Colonel Moore as he and his colleagues were boarding their train at Liverpool Street:

> "I certainly hope that our visit may result in a better relationship between Russia and this country, because I believe not only that the welfare of each country is necessary for the good of the whole world, but also that Russia has far more to gain by cultiva-

* *Observer*, 28.iii.26. † Ibid.

ting relations with Britain than with any other country. Further, I think that settled and fair Government in Russia would react upon us to a greater extent than upon any other nation."*

The report of these M.P.'s was issued at the end of May. As regards the masses of the people, it stated:

> "Information as supplied to us from many sources tended to indicate that the bulk of the workers and peasants are better off since the revolution than before. This statement, detached from its context, might be supposed by some to show that we consider Communism, as such, to be a success. Nothing is further from our minds and, therefore, we would point out once more that the present system of the government is not Communism as we understand it, but an autocracy, and that the so-called dictatorship of the proletariat is nothing more or less than extremely efficient dictatorship over the proletariat. The system of class and caste (socially speaking) has been largely broken down, and the fact is accepted. Those who suffer have given up the hope, or indeed, we think, the desire for any radical change which might upset such immunity as they are at present accorded, believing, as we also do, that evolution is the best hope of lightening their lot; and it is our conviction that closer sympathy and understanding between the other European countries and Russia would do much to assist this happy development."†

Respecting finance, etc., it declared:

> "Those responsible for the administration of Soviet finance and currency have had immense difficulties to contend against since June, 1924, when a wholesale reorganisation took place, and have still in front of them a formidable problem, but we have no hesitation in stating that, whilst the position generally bristles with complexities, the situation is in no sense dangerous, and that the Government is very far removed from imminent bankruptcy, which latter view has been given voice to, of late, in several quarters. The present financial policy is sound and, in fact, almost austere."

It used some terms which turned out to be truly prophetic:

> "Soviet Russia makes no secret of the fact that it wants to trade with Great Britain, and that in order to do this a loan or long-term credits or both are necessary. In the meantime, Great Britain may be losing an immense advantage; we have evidence

* *Financial News,* 19.iv.26. † *Manchester Guardian,* 1.vi.26.

in our possession as to how her competitors are getting ahead of her in Russia, and once the next decade or so in Russian finance has been successfully surmounted, a chance of making fair terms for those of our nationals whose property was confiscated in 1917 and good terms for any loan the City of London may wish to make may have passed."

This report was little to the liking of their fellow Tories. The reactions of the *Daily Telegraph* were typical. It declared that "many of the judgments" which the four members of Parliament "formed are little likely to be welcomed in Conservative circles," but the leader writer, apparently, felt constrained to admit "they are probably right as to the firm establishment of the Soviet Power and its unassailability from without."

V. The General Strike. Support for the Miners from Soviet Trade Unions

In the meantime an event had occurred the consequences of which had serious results on Anglo-Soviet relations. Early in May there was a general strike in Great Britain in support of the British miners whose then very low standard of life was threatened with a further reduction. After the general strike had been called off, the miners' dispute continued and the Trade Union Movement of this country appealed for national and international support for the miners, and sent representatives to European countries and the U.S.A. to support this appeal. Help came from many countries, including the U.S.S.R.

The leaders of the Soviet Trade Unions appealed to their members to levy themselves, which they did enthusiastically, and the proceeds were sent to the British miners. In all, the Soviet Trade Unionists raised over £1,250,000. The total sum was large absolutely, but not relatively compared with the amounts received from Sweden, Latvia and Czechoslovakia, and it worked out at only a little over 2/- per member of the Soviet Trade Unions.

But a hue and cry against the Soviet Government was again raised in this country by the papers and politicians who had always opposed relations with the U.S.S.R.; they alleged that the Russian money sent to the British miners had been raised by a forced levy and that it was Government and not Trade Union money. This was a canard.

In an interview published in *Izvestia* of June 1, 1926, the Secretary of the General Council of the Soviet Trade Unions, stated:

"All classes of workers in the U.S.S.R. responded very heartily to the call of the T.U.C. We had to restrain members of the

Unions who, at general meetings, decided to contribute one-half of a day's wage, instead of the quarter asked for by the T.U.C."

Many foreigners present in Russia at that time confirmed this statement. Thus the *Daily Herald* of June 17, 1926, published the following extract from a letter which Mr. F. Buckley, of Rochdale, received from the acting chief of the Quaker centre in Moscow:

> "There is much interest and sympathy here for the miners. The way the workers in the various factories and other places are levying themselves is very fine."

The same issue of the *Daily Herald* published the following extract from a letter, dated May 13, 1926, which Mr. George Lansbury, M.P. had received from his daughter in Moscow:

> "I can see the eagerness and spontaneousness with which the workers in the various unions suggested a levy to help the British workers."

Mr. A. Oliver, Treasurer of the N.U.R., who travelled widely in Russia during the general strike in Great Britain, sent the following telegram to the *Workers' Weekly* (June 11, 1926):

> "*Daily Mail* story on forced contributions to Russian Relief Fund absolutely untrue."

Mrs. W. Horrabin, Secretary of the Plebs' League, wrote as follows in the same issue:

> "We know exactly what value to place on the tales of the poor worker in Russia whose hard-earned penny the miners are now spending. To anyone who was in Moscow and saw the enthusiasm of the workers there to help the British workers, the whole thing reads like a farce."

There can be no doubt that the British Government's own sources of information agreed with these testimonies, but this did not prevent members of the Government from making the most unfounded accusations.

Thus Lord Birkenhead, speaking at a luncheon, June 9, 1926, stated: "These monies are being paid not by the miners . . . but are officially contributed by the Russian Government."

As if this absurdity was not enough, the noble Lord went one better and added that the object of the Soviets was "to filch from the British coal trade as large a share as they can in the interests of the Russian coal trade."

Lord Birkenhead was talking arrant nonsense, to give it the kindest interpretation. The following figures show why:

Britain's coal production in 1925	247,000,000 tons
Russia's total coal output in 1925 (nett)	14,979,000 tons
Russia's estimated production for 1925-26 (nett)	21,361,000 tons
Britain's coal exports in 1925	50,000,000 tons
Russia's coal exports in 1925	319,116 tons

Thus, it was clear that the legend about Russian competition with Great Britain was absolutely ridiculous. In point of fact, owing to the rapid development of Russian industry, her coal output was insufficient to meet existing requirements, and the small quantities of coal exported from South Russia were sold abroad solely because it was cheaper to do that and buy foreign coal with the proceeds for importing through the northern ports, than to transport the coal across Russia to the industrial areas in the north.

If Lord Birkenhead believed what he said, and we would not cast reflections on his honesty, it shows to what an extent members of the British Government had lost their nerve at this time.

There was nothing improper in the fact that the Soviet Trade Unionists were sending financial aid to the miners. British Trade Unionists had on innumerable occasions helped financially foreign Trade Unionists involved in industrial disputes. "It is not easy," wrote the political correspondent of the *Westminster Gazette,* "even for the Law Officers, to say how the receipt of this money can be stopped". . . . "The Belgian miners are also sending their contribution to the British miners, but it is only the Russian money which is being questioned."

The upshot of all these events was a renewed agitation against the maintenance of diplomatic relations with the U.S.S.R. The British Government apparently felt that they must do something to pacify their right wing; accordingly, the British Foreign Secretary, Sir Austen Chamberlain, speaking in the House of Commons, declared:

> "I instructed His Majesty's Chargé d'Affaires in Moscow to inform the Soviet Government that His Majesty's Government cannot pass over in silence the action of the Soviet Commissariat of Finance in giving special authorisation for the transfer to this country of funds destined for the support of the general strike. He is to point out that the general strike was an illegal and unconstitutional act constituting a serious threat to established order, and that the special action taken by the Soviet Commissariat of Finance in its favour does not conduce to the friendly

settlement which the Soviet Government profess to desire of the questions outstanding between the two countries."*

Mr. Ramsay MacDonald asked:

"Has the money that has been transmitted, been transmitted from Soviet sources, or resources, or was it merely with the sanction of the Financial Commissariat of the Soviet Government ? "†

Sir Austen Chamberlain replied:

"What is within our knowledge, and was the ground of my protest, is that the stipulations of the law in force have been waived in order to permit the transmission of this money in support of an illegal and unconstitutional strike."‡

In passing, it may be observed that the General Council of the T.U.C. declined the offer of financial aid from the Soviet Trade Unions during the existence of the general strike. As regards the money transferred by the Soviet Trade Unions to the British miners, no "special authorisation" was necessary, as the acting Soviet Chargé d'Affaires in London stated in an interview published in the press of June 17, 1926:

"The regulation governing the transfer of money above 100 roubles (decree of April 14, 1926) grants to the Commissariat for Finance the right of control over such transactions *in order to suppress speculation in the transfer of currency*. According to established precedent, permits for the transfer of money abroad are granted without any difficulty by the currency conference in cases which cannot be suspected of being of a speculative nature."

The British Government apparently demanded from the Soviet Government conduct that it did not ask from any other Government, i.e., that it would take special measures to prevent aid being sent from its nationals to the British miners. At this time Trade Unionists and others of practically every European country and the United States of America were sending money to the British miners. The *Manchester Guardian* pertinently commented:

"It is absurd to suppose that the Russian Government could have prevented these things happening even if they had felt disposed to do so. The Russian Trade Unionists look up to the British Trade Union movement with a sort of romantic devotion. England is the classic land of Trade Unionism, where Trade Unions can do what Trade Unions can do nowhere else. The

* *Hansard*, 14.vi.26, col. 1960. † Ibid. ‡ Ibid., col. 1961.

amounts contributed make a good show when they are reported, as in the Russian papers, in seemingly interminable detail, but they are naturally small in detail and can hardly amount to anything very effective in the aggregate.

It is pointed out—and it is a relevant point—that so long as the Russian Government refrains from contributing there is no diplomatic precedent for calling upon it to stop the contributions. For years American money from private persons and from organisations poured into Ireland to finance an openly seditious movement, yet no protests or threats were ever addressed to the Government of the United States."*

The Soviet Government handed its reply on June 15, 1926, to the British Chargé d'Affaires in Moscow. The Note stated:

"There exists in the Soviet Union no prohibition against the remittance of money abroad, the only restriction on such remittances being the obligation of obtaining a permit in every case.

Expressing as it does the will of the workmen and peasants of the Soviet Union, the Soviet Government could not prohibit the trade unions, comprising millions of workers of Soviet Russia, from sending money abroad in aid of trade unions of another country.

The Soviet Government at the same time calls the British Government's attention to the incompatibility with real facts and with normal relations between Governments of the statements of some of its members, alleging that the sums remitted to the British Trades Union Council were sent by the Soviet Government when in reality they had been forwarded by the Central Council of Trade Unions of Soviet Russia in agreement with the Control Committee of the Trade Unions of the Union of Socialist Soviet Republics."

Apparently Whitehall regarded these assertions as indisputable, a fact which led the Parliamentary Correspondent of the *Daily Telegraph* to comment:

"Some Unionist members express considerable doubt as to whether it will have been possible to trace any direct connection between the Russian donations for the miners and the Soviet authorities. Failing clear proof that Russian State funds have been used for the purpose, the British Government, of course,

* *Manchester Guardian*, 14.vi.26.

will be unable to take any action, and in any event, it is gathered that such step as the repudiation of the recognition accorded to the Soviet Government, which is being pressed for in some quarters, would not be taken. It is the belief in well-informed quarters that the Government as a whole is not disposed to contemplate such drastic action."*

The whole matter was debated in the Lords on the following day, and the Earl of Balfour, speaking on behalf of the Government, although he criticised severely the Soviet Government's attitude towards this country added:

> "I think that nothing is to be gained by breaking off relations with the Soviet Government. In the sensitive conditions of the world to-day, it would be the height of rashness, except in the face of really serious danger, to introduce a new disturbing element."

However, the Conservative politicians were not the only ones who were concerning themselves regarding relations with the U.S.S.R. Less prejudiced minds realised the importance of Soviet Russia in the Comity of Nations. Mr. Lloyd George, speaking at the Oxford Union, June 15, 1926, declared:

> "You will never know peace in Europe or peace in the world until Russia is included in the fraternity of nations. I know it is not a popular thing to say, but unpopular things are not always untrue, and popular things are not always true."

Three days later, Viscount Grey expressed the same ideas in slightly different terms. He averred:

> "Unless you get Russia into the League of Nations, bona-fide, in favour of disarmament she will always be an obstacle in the way of disarmament. So far as the constitution of the Government is concerned, whether it is a despotism or whatever it is, I would treat it as we have always done other Governments, whose constitutions we did not approve."

After Lord Balfour's statement in the Lords, many hoped that it reflected a definite decision of the Government and that henceforth there would be no further ministerial attempts to bedevil relations between the two countries. They were soon disillusioned. A few days later, Mr. Winston Churchill, with or without Cabinet authority,

* *Daily Telegraph*, 16.vi.26.

made a declaration calculated to ruin trade with the U.S.S.R. He admonished:

> "Persons who lend money to Russia, as they are entitled to do, must be alive to the risks they run, and must understand that in no circumstances will the British Treasury accept any responsibility if they are defrauded. Should the Government find it necessary at any moment to expel the Soviet agents, no claims for losses will be entertained by the Treasury. My advice to traders is to make sure they get paid, or get full security before their goods leave this country. If they lend money and lose it they will have no one to thank but themselves, and the Government must remain absolutely free to take any action they think necessary in the public interest."*

This warning could not but produce an atmosphere pernicious to Anglo-Soviet commerce, yet at this date there were 1,700,000 unemployed in Great Britain. Mr. Churchill's statement drew a pointed reply from the late Mr. E. F. Wise, who, in an interview, stated:

> "Mr. Churchill warns anyone inclined to adventure in Russian trade that he is to expect no help from the Government or the Treasury if he gets into trouble. At no stage has there been any question of Treasury guarantee or other support. On the contrary, the Trade Facilities Act and Export Credits Act, which have been available to every country in Europe except Russia, have been deliberately withheld from Russia. The attitude of the Foreign Office and of Ministers like Mr. Churchill has been consistently unfriendly to the development of trade, except for the brief period when the Labour Government was in office.

* It is possible that Mr. Churchill, apart from his anti-Soviet prejudices, had taken seriously a letter by Sir Henri W. A. Deterding (Director-General of the Royal Dutch Petroleum Company and a director of the Shell Transport and Trading Company), which had been published in the *Morning Post* some six months earlier. In this letter, Sir Henri, replying to an article in *Izvestia* flung in turn unfounded accusations and various innuendos against the Soviet Government, followed by threats and then by fatherly advice, to the effect that unless the Tsarist debts were recognised and private properties (more particularly the formerly foreign-owned Russian oil plants), nationalised by the Soviet Government were returned—they (the Soviet Government) would never get credits from abroad, and without this they could not possibly rehabilitate the country. He concluded with the following exhortation: "Why not admit that you share with me the faith that you are near, very near, the end of your tether, and that, before many months, Russia will come back to civilisation, but under a better Government than the Tsarist one? Be men, and admit, like Lenin did, that Bolshevism does not work, that you have made a mistake. You will save millions of lives and restore happiness to millions. All your articles against me will not diminish by one iota my conviction that Bolshevism in Russia will be over before this year is, and as soon as it is, Russia can draw on all the world's credit and open her frontiers to all willing to work. Money and credit will then flow into Russia, and what is better still, labour." (*Morning Post*, 5.i.26.)

Sir Henri flattered himself—the Soviet statesmen were not in the slightest interested in his convictions and the sequel shows how wise they were to be indifferent.

Yet British trade grows with Russia at a faster rate than with any European country. Here are the figures:

	Sales on the British market. £	*Purchases in Great Britain.* £
1920	—	2,809,641
1921	1,866,375	7,281,258
1922	5,933,283	9,432,936
1923	10,458,066	4,658,592
1924	19,443,669	14,800,956
1925	26,907,678	31,170,995
Total	£64,609,071	£70,154,378

These figures, so far as purchases are concerned, include goods of British origin, mainly machinery, tools and textiles, re-exports, chiefly of colonial produce normally marketed in this country, and purchases made in London from British firms of colonial and other goods shipped direct to Russia, such as tea grown in Ceylon and shipped direct to Siberia, or wool shipped direct from Australia to Russia."*

In the meantime, the dispute in the mining industry continued well into November, 1926, and all the Tory fulminations did not frighten Soviet Trade Unionists into withholding help from the British miners. The Conservative gentlemen were slow to apprehend the nature of the new Russian citizen. Lessons learnt under compulsion are usually painful, and however beneficial they may be in the long run, they are apt to irritate in the process and make the pupils angry. That is exactly what happened in the case of our Tory statesmen-students. The Workers' and Peasants' Government ought to have trembled before their fulminations, instead of which it answered their arguments point by point and continued unperturbed to exercise its undoubted rights.

It is piquant to recall that in France, in particular, they had great difficulty in understanding why members of the British Government should consider severing relations with the U.S.S.R., because of the aid which was being sent by Soviet Trade Unions to British miners; they recalled that before the war the Tsarist Minister in Paris financed the Paris press opposed to the Government. The French Secret Service undoubtedly kept the Government fully informed about these matters, but the question of severing diplomatic relations was never raised.

The *Daily Mail* announced, June 28, 1926, that "a committee of

* *Manchester Guardian*, 22.vi.26.

Conservative M.P.'s has been formed . . . to maintain watch over Soviet activities." It was now clear that a number of Tory members had decided on a persistent agitation to force the hands of the Government. A meeting was held in the Albert Hall, London, July 15, 1926, attended by about 7,000 people. Colonel John Gretton, M.P., presided, and to quote the *Times*, the gathering included "many representatives of both Houses of Parliament." Among the speakers were Commander Locker-Lampson, M.P., Sir Hamar Greenwood, M.P., Mr. Mitchell Banks, M.P., and Sir Henry Page-Croft, M.P.* The degree to which the orators and audience had worked themselves into a state of hysteria, to use no stronger term, may be gauged from the following extract from the *Morning Post*:

> "The General Strike, Sir Henry Page-Croft continued, was announced by Zinoviev in Moscow six weeks before it took place as due for the first week of May. I want to warn you, he added most seriously, that the Government of Russia is making war on our country day by day. Mr. Cook ('Shoot him! Lynch him!') has declared that he is a Bolshevik and is proud to be a humble disciple of Lenin. He is treating the miners of this country, whom we all respect and honour—(cheers)—as 'cannon fodder,' in order to achieve his vainglorious ambitions. If, however, we desire to help our own kith and kin, we desire to help them after Mr. Cook has told them that his policy will be to throw some 400,000 of them on the streets for good. We are met here to-night to tell the Government that we support them in any step that they think necessary at the present time. Give the Arcos and all those others who have come to make trouble in our midst 48 hours' notice. (Loud and prolonged cheers)."†

Not for many years had such threats been hurled at a responsible Trade Union official. It is hardly necessary to add that the general strike was not, and could not have been announced in Moscow six weeks before it took place.

Not one of the speakers who had such "respect" for the miners mentioned whether he had contributed anything to the miners' funds during this long dispute.

The *Daily News* report of the gathering stated:

> "The speakers vied with one another in coining choice epithets to apply to Soviet agents and supporters. These were samples: Hired vilifiers; purveyors of sedition; scum of our gutters; outpourings of foreign sinks; mercenaries of Moscow;

* Subsequently Lord Croft.

† *Morning Post*, 16.vii.26.

mad Mullahs of Socialism; swindling syndicate; aliens and criminals; microbes of Bolshevism."*

To the credit of the *Daily Express* be it said that journal could not stomach the proceedings at this precious meeting. The paper reported:

"Commander O. Locker-Lampson, M.P., referred to the attempt of the Socialists in the House of Commons to institute an inquiry into the commercial connections of Cabinet Ministers, denouncing the efforts which, he declared, had been made to besmirch British honour and hold this country up to ridicule in the eyes of the world.

'They had a right to!' came a shrill cry from the back of the hall, and an uproar followed. There were shouts of 'Put her out!' as a slim, fair-haired girl stood up. Then a squad of young stewards hastened along the passage towards the girl and escorted her to the exit.

'I am not a Socialist or a Communist,' the girl said to a *Daily Express* representative outside the hall. 'I am a Conservative, but I think the Socialist Party has a right to do what it did.'

She burst into tears. 'I have never been treated so shamefully before in all my life,' she said. 'Some of the things the people said to me when I was leaving the hall made me sick.'"†

An additional aim of the organisers of this meeting was, we think, revealed next day by the *Westminster Gazette*. It stated: "It is quite clear that Mr. Locker-Lampson and Sir Hamar Greenwood—a suitable mugwump for this galley of flag-wagging incoherents—are using this campaign as an argument for an attack on the rights of sober-minded trade unionists; and that is the only point of danger in these hysterical antics at the Albert Hall."

The House of Commons rose in the first week of August, 1926, and the anti-Soviet platform agitation died down, whilst the grouse were being slaughtered. However, the stream of absurdities continued in the press. The *Daily Mail* of August 9, 1926, carried a long story of revolts in all the main centres of Russia. The authors, who were in Russia at that time and visited many of the centres mentioned, heard nothing of these "revolts" until their return some weeks later to London.

Sober minded and clear sighted business men were apparently little influenced by all these neurotic outpourings. The assistant-secretary of Messrs. John Hetherington and Sons Ltd., in his report to the annual general meeting of the shareholders declared:

* *Daily News*, 16.vii.26. † *Daily Express*, 16.vii.26.

"Now with regard to the Russian contracts of which I spoke last year. In view of the general attitude towards Russian affairs which until recently it was the fashion to adopt, you will probably wish me to say a word or two. The contracts have been kept punctiliously both in the letter and in the spirit. We are, in fact, very pleased with the way the business has been transacted. Our experience of the scrupulous exactness with which the Soviet authorities have regarded their contracts is not, of course, unique, but has evidently been quite general."

VI. Shakespeare's Birthday at Stratford-on-Avon

An amusing incident which occurred a week or so before the outbreak of the General Strike forms a good illustration of the depth of anti-Soviet prejudices then prevailing among sections of the governing classes of Britain. It happened in April, 1926, when in the absence of a Soviet Ambassador, M. Maisky was functioning as Chargé d'Affaires *ad interim.*

As is well known on April 23, a ceremony is held at Stratford-on-Avon commemorating the anniversary of Skakespeare's birth. Up to that time the Soviet representatives had never been invited to participate in the ceremony, but suddenly some time early in April the Soviet Embassy received an invitation to the 362nd Shakespeare Anniversary ceremony. Later it transpired that the invitation had been sent as the result of an error on the part of the clerk concerned who, not being well versed in high politics, simply addressed invitations to all the Missions included in the official Diplomatic List.

Immediately on receipt of this invitation M. Maisky replied accepting it, expressing great pleasure in view of the high esteem in which Shakespeare is held in the Soviet Union. The letter of acceptance seemed to have the effect of a bombshell when it reached Stratford-on-Avon. Tremendous commotion ensued. Members of the Shakespeare Club (and there were about 2,000 in a town of about 15,000 population) felt scandalised, held a meeting of protest and sent a petition to the higher authorities demanding that the Soviet delegation be prevented from appearing and unfurling the Soviet flag at the approaching anniversary ceremony. At the head of this movement of protest was Mrs. Melville, wife of the Vicar of the church situated in the cemetery where Shakespeare was buried.

Soon afterwards M. Maisky received a telegram from the Mayor and Town Clerk of Stratford-on-Avon (the Mayor was at the same time President of the Shakespeare Club) to the effect that they would like to come to London to talk over the situation. This was agreed to and the Mayor tried hard to persuade M. Maisky not to come to Stratford-on-Avon, explaining that while they would be delighted to see them at the ceremony they had so many unruly elements in the town that an unpleasant incident might occur. M. Maisky who had gone through many much more difficult and dangerous experiences, was naturally not to be frightened by the possibility of an hypothetical unpleasant incident at Stratford-on-Avon. He pointed out that they were the hosts and the Soviet representatives the guests ; if they withdrew their invitation naturally the latter would not go, but that as long as the invitation stood he felt it his duty to accept. The suggestion that the invitation might be withdrawn put the Mayor and Town Clerk in a quandary for never in the history of the Shakespeare Club of Stratford-on-Avon had there been such a precedent. Once an invitation was sent out it could not be withdrawn.

A few days later M. Maisky was invited to the Foreign Office. As a matter of fact it was the only " business visit " that he had made to the Foreign Office during his two years' stay in London as Counsellor to the Embassy. Such were the relations that existed then between the Soviet Embassy in London and the Foreign Office! The Foreign Office Official who received M. Maisky, having ascertained from the latter that he had received and accepted an invitation from Stratford-on-Avon, explained at great length that the situation was a little difficult, that the local people were greatly incensed at the prospect of a Soviet delegation attending the ceremony, that there might be some unpleasant incidents, that a great crowd of people could not be properly controlled, etc., etc. Therefore he felt constrained to inform M. Maisky in advance of this feeling and suggested that perhaps, under the circumstances, in order not to create complications in the relations between the two countries, it might be better if he were to abstain from going to the Shakespeare anniversary celebrations.

However, M. Maisky replied in the same strain as he had done to the Mayor and Town Clerk a few days before, saying that having gone through many untoward experiences in his life and not being a naturally panicky man he was not afraid of any unpleasant happenings, and that, moreover, he had full confidence in the ability of His Majesty's Government to maintain order in territories under their control. Thereupon the Foreign Office Official intimated that, though naturally they would take all precautionary measures for the protection of the Soviet representatives he, M. Maisky, had been warned and had had the situation explained quite clearly.

From the middle of April the question of Soviet participation at the Shakespeare ceremony was given great publicity. It became a topic of the day. Newspapers began to publish articles, even leading ones, on the subject. The Conservative press referred to the great indignation prevailing at Stratford-on-Avon and demanded that the

Soviet appearance at the ceremony should be prevented. The Labour and Liberal press took the opposite view. All sorts of rumours started to circulate that there might be disturbances on the day of the ceremony, that some untoward incident might happen, that the Soviet flag might be torn down, that the Soviet representatives might be physically assaulted. The consequence of all these rumours and polemics was that many workers of Birmingham, particularly Trade Unionists, held several meetings of protest against such malicious intentions on the part of the Conservative elements, and decided to muster in force at Stratford-on-Avon (which is not far off) on the day of the celebrations, to guard the Soviet flag and Soviet delegation.

The whole question began to take on such proportions that the Home Office became uneasy and found it necessary to tone down somewhat the widespread agitation and reports which appeared in the press by announcing that with a view to maintaining perfect order Scotland Yard would send a special flying squad to Stratford-on-Avon to prevent any untoward incident occurring.

Meanwhile, M. Maisky ordered a large and excellent Red flag bearing the Soviet emblem to be made for the occasion, and he made all the necessary arrangements to go to Stratford-on-Avon on April 23. On the eve of the celebrations, i.e., April 22, this flag was sent to Stratford-on-Avon with one of the Embassy officials as all flags had to be there in time for them to be affixed to the flagpoles and unfurled at the ceremony. On his return to the Embassy the official related that he gathered there was great consternation among the officials of Stratford-on-Avon and a feeling almost of despair.

Next morning the Soviet delegation travelled to Stratford-on-Avon in a special coach attached to a morning train put at the disposal of all diplomatic representatives going to the ceremony. The Soviet delegation consisted of four people: M. and Mme. Maisky, the Soviet Consul-General in London and the Russian poet, Nicolas Minsky, who was living in London at that time. When they arrived at Stratford-on-Avon there was a great crowd at the station. All the diplomats who came on the same train were met by the town officials, shown into waiting cars and taken straight from the station to the avenue where the celebration was to be held. The flagpoles were already in their place bearing the folded flags. The Soviet flag was the last one in the row facing the market place. The whole street and in the adjacent houses, the windows and housetops, were filled with a tremendous crowd. Later the Soviet representatives discovered from the local people that they had never had such a crowd in any of the many years this ceremony had been performed. Under thousands of inquisitive eyes the Soviet delegation marched along the street to its allotted place. There was complete silence—tense and obviously unfriendly—as they went to their place at the foot of the flagpole bearing the Soviet flag. But it was significant that the whole market place was full of a great crowd of workers who had come from Birmingham. Here the atmosphere was quite different. The workers smiled to the Soviet representatives and waved their caps. It was evident that whilst the street behind might be full of Soviet enemies, in front of them stood good friends.

At 12 o'clock sharp the trumpet sounded and the representatives of the different countries pulled their strings unfurling their flags. This act was performed by Mme. Maisky for the Soviet delegation, and the Red flag was swept up immediately at full length by the strong breeze. The workers assembled in the market place greeted the unfurling of the Soviet flag with a storm of applause. This evidently came as a great surprise to the officials who no doubt had not expected anything of the kind.

Then followed the march of all the delegations, headed by the Mayor and other Town officials, to the tomb of Shakespeare. As the Soviet representatives took their place in the procession the workers immediately surrounded the Soviet flagpole and kept guard there. Each delegation carried a bouquet of flowers or a wreath to place upon the tomb. M. Maisky carried a large wreath of violets.

On reaching the church the flowers and wreaths were received by the Vicar, Mr. Melville, and placed by him on the tomb of Shakespeare. When M. Maisky gave him his wreath Mr. Melville's face was said to have resembled that of a petrified dragon, but he could not refuse to take it and place it on Shakespeare's tomb. From the cemetery all the delegations went to Shakespeare's house.

Then followed luncheon at the Town Hall. At that time it was the custom for the diplomatic representatives to say a few words after lunch. First there was an official speaker, an Englishman, and then followed the tributes of the diplomatic representatives who were present, made in order of their precedence of seniority. Just before lunch M. Maisky informed the Mayor that he wished to say a few words. The Mayor obviously did not like the idea, but he could do no other than put down the name. When the time came for the speakers to pay their tributes it was notable that in spite of this, M. Maisky had been overlooked. M. Maisky again sent up a note to the Mayor who on receiving it, looked embarrassed and showed it to those sitting near him. A hasty discussion followed but still representatives lower in seniority than M. Maisky continued to be called on. Finally, M. Maisky sent the Mayor a third note. There was more embarrassment, a further whispered consultation, and in the end the Mayor rose, and with an expression on his face as of a man about to plunge into cold, deep water, called on M. Maisky to speak.

When the latter rose he received a mixed reception. About half of those present started to hiss and the other half cheered. He waited for a minute or two until the noise had subsided and then began to pay his tribute. There was nothing political in his speech. He just spoke of Shakespeare and how he was esteemed in his country, and that many of his tragedies were performed there. During the whole time he was speaking a distinct division was obvious in those listening. Roughly half applauded and the other half were hostile and there were continual interruptions.

The lunch ended, and after it the Soviet delegation decided to return home. Just as they were on the point of going back the town officials, with unexpected kindness, invited them to make a tour of some local and neighbouring places of interest. They agreed, and were shown into the car accompanied by guides. Next to the chauffeur, as they learned afterwards, sat the head of the local police in mufti. They were driven round to various places of interest and eventually arrived at a small railway station about 10 to 15 miles from Stratford-on-Avon, on the way to London. Then their guides very kindly suggested that they might catch their train there instead of losing time returning to Stratford-on-Avon, explaining that if they missed this train it would mean waiting for several hours for the next one. The reason for this " kindness " now became quite apparent, and it was confirmed the next day in the press when it was stated that the authorities were afraid that at the departure of the Soviet delegation there might be a demonstration at the station and a clash between the two currents of local opinion. Therefore they had decided that the delegation should be taken to a nearby station and put on the train.

One little sidelight on the whole affair is particularly amusing. When they arrived at Stratford-on-Avon, Mme. Maisky had with her a little attaché case containing her personal belongings. M. Maisky naturally carried it for her during the whole of the ceremony, etc. But a Birmingham evening paper in which the whole ceremony of the day was described in most glowing terms, with photographs, etc., also contained a paragraph saying that all through the ceremony Mr. Maisky looked and acted just like an ordinary peaceful citizen, but that they had only had one doubt, and that was that a certain suspicious feeling was aroused in the minds of many onlookers by the fact that he carried a small attaché case. Many thought that bombs might be hidden in it!

CHAPTER X

PREPARATION FOR A RUPTURE OF RELATIONS (1926-1927)

I. APPOINTMENT OF M. KRASSIN AS CHARGE D'AFFAIRES IN LONDON. DEATH OF M. KRASSIN

TOWARDS the end of September, 1926, M. L. Krassin, who had been appointed to the Soviet Embassy* in London, took up his post. M. Krassin, during his previous term of office in London had made a very favourable impression, especially in business circles, and was regarded in this country, first and foremost, as a business man. His re-appointment to the London Embassy was interpreted as a sign that another effort would be made by Moscow to improve relations, particularly commercial relations, with this country. "Although it would perhaps be premature," commented the *Financial News*, "to regard his arrival as the turning-point in Anglo-Soviet diplomatic, commercial and financial relations, there is good reason to hope for an improvement. M. Krassin is easily the most sympathetic Soviet statesman, and inspires more confidence in the City than anyone else Moscow could send here."

M. Krassin did not disappoint those who were anxious that efforts to improve relations between Whitehall and the Kremlin should be continued, but he did disappoint those who expected him to come with a cap-in-hand demeanour. He gave a lengthy interview to the press, October 1, 1926, in the course of which he declared that when he first came to London certain circles regularly predicted the collapse of the Soviet Government in a few weeks or at most in the next few months. "We are now," he added dryly, "probably the most stable Government in the world."

Turning to the Soviet's economic recovery, M. Krassin stated:

> "Agriculture, in which over 80 per cent. of the whole population were engaged, was developing rapidly—grain exported in 1925-26 amounted to 125,000,000 poods, against 73,000,000 in 1922-23; the cotton bought from the peasants by the industrial trust totalled 9,643,000 poods this year, against 2,373,000 poods in 1923-24; and in three years the number of tractors on the land had increased from 300 to 25,000—'more than in this very rich and progressive country.' The gross production of the big industries, which in 1913 stood at 7,010 million roubles, had now reached 95 per cent. of that figure, while the gross productions of agriculture had attained to 89 per cent. of the pre-war record."

* Officially the British Government did not designate M. Krassin's official residence as an Embassy, but most people invariably referred to it as such.

The following dialogue then took place:

"*A Press Representative*: Would not the request for credits have a greater chance of success if Russia acknowledged her debts to Great Britain?

M. Krassin: That is a very complicated question. The question of debts cannot be decided in a one-sided way. Our Government was quite willing to consider the problem of debts in the negotiations of 1924, and, lately, the official representative of the Soviet Government has declared its willingness to deal with this question.

A Press Representative: Is it not the aim of the Soviet Government to make all capitalist countries like Russia?

M. Krassin: Our aim is to restore our proper estate.

A Press Representative: In your request for credits are you not, in effect, asking capitalist countries to help in cutting their own throats?

M. Krassin: The fate of the capitalistic system does not depend on the granting or refusing of a loan to the Soviet Government. Business is business. Armstrongs are selling locomotives to the Soviet Government. Possibly that means help for the Soviet Government and for Communism. But I don't think you would say to Armstrongs, 'You are helping revolution in sending your locomotives there.' It is the same with America, which is sending us tractors. It was a very important thing to get credits from Ford. Business is business.

M. Krassin added that the Soviet Government obtained credits on better terms in Germany, France and Italy than in England; France and Italy were building big ships for Russia. From his point of view this was unfortunate, because it was to his interest to place as many orders as he could in Great Britain. He had yet to begin negotiations in the City; he had seen nobody there since he left England three years ago."*

One could hardly expect M. Krassin to go further because at this date he had not yet presented his credentials to Sir Austen Chamberlain, but his statements, taken as a whole, did constitute a basis for negotiations, had a desire for a reasonable agreement existed in Whitehall.

However, a few days later, October 7, 1926, the Conservative Party Congress adopted a resolution calling for the severance of all diplomatic and trading relations with the U.S.S.R. It is true that the speakers to the resolution were of the more irresponsible type, but it was not without significance that the motion was carried unanimously.

On the other hand, the Labour Party Conference, October 14, 1926,

* *Daily Telegraph*, 2.x.26.

adopted a resolution unanimously calling on the Government to "take the fullest advantage of the arrival of M. Krassin in this country to reopen negotiations for the establishment of political and economic relations with Russia." The late Mr. C. T. Cramp, moving the resolution, said: "I believe on excellent authority that M. Krassin is prepared to enter into such negotiations if we can force the Government to take a hand."

In the meantime, M. Krassin had had a conversation with Sir Austen Chamberlain during which he expressed a strong desire for better relations between the two Governments, but the Foreign Secretary intimated that the only conditions in effect acceptable to London were complete surrender on the part of Moscow; recognition and funding of Tsarist debts; renunciation of counter-claims; a foreign policy subservient to Great Britain.

It was now autumn and the indoor meeting season had begun again. The "Clear Out the Reds" campaigners held a mass meeting in the Albert Hall, October 15, 1926, at which the chief speaker was Commander Oliver Locker-Lampson. This gentleman, who had apparently convinced himself that he understood everything about Russia, told his credulous audience, to the accompaniment of loud cheers, that "the vast idol of enemy Bolshevism is cracked and rocking." The Commander went further. "He appealed to Russian refugees, who were present in large numbers at the meeting, to be of good cheer. He would ask them to remember that faith, freedom and order were coming back to a released and holy Russia again. (Cheers)."*

Another choice morsel from Locker-Lampson's harangue was: "The time had come to seize Bolshevism by the throat, and face Mr. Cook (cheers) and all other parasites of the Soviet."

There was an interesting aside which conveys some idea of the state of nerves of this audience:

> "A reference to Krassin's ambition to become a landed proprietor in England evoked from a man on the balcony, the ejaculation: 'Good luck to him.' The interrupter was promptly ejected by the stewards amid cheers."†

In passing, it is hardly necessary to add that Mr. A. J. Cook had never received a penny piece from the Soviets, that M. Krassin had never bought and never intended to buy any property in this country, and that at any meeting of sane persons, no one would be flung out for making a perfectly proper interjection. A Mr. N. A. Rowe, who attended the meeting, wrote:

> "From the commencement of the meeting until the conclusion

* *Morning Post*, 16.x.26. † *Daily Mail*, 16.x.26.

> of Commander Locker-Lampson's speech the air was rent at frequent intervals with vulpine cries of 'Down with the Jews!' from certain rabid ladies in the audience—and were suffered to go unchecked.
>
> At the conclusion of Commander Locker-Lampson's speech a member of the audience rose, and, in a very decent manner, protested against a section of the community being condemned in this wholesale fashion. That his protest had the sympathy of a large number of people in the hall was shown by the instant applause which followed. This did not prevent his being seized and thrown out."*

This anti-Soviet agitation continued up to the date of the Arcos Raid.

Meanwhile, after his conversation with the Foreign Secretary, M. Krassin was preparing to get busy in other spheres. He informed a representative of the *Financial News*:

> "I have been away from this country for three years, so that I have rather lost touch with opinion here. My first task is, therefore, to get into touch with financial, industrial and commercial circles, so as to ascertain their views about a possible solution. Within the next few weeks I hope to meet a great number of business men and financiers, and it is only after an interchange of views with them that I shall be able to have some idea as to what might or might not be done in the settlement of outstanding questions between the two countries."

On one point M. Krassin was insistent. His Government was prepared to negotiate a comprehensive settlement but he added:

> "We are not prepared to restore pre-war property. Moreover, I believe that in most cases the old owners themselves are not very keen on having such property restored to them.
>
> In certain individual cases my Government is prepared to negotiate with former property owners for the granting to them of concessions."

Within these limits there was ample room for compromise and settlement. However, there was no advance from the side of the British Government to create a better atmosphere in which negotiations could take place. In fact, certain members of the Government were apparently determined that such an atmosphere should not materialise.

Sir William Joynson-Hicks, addressing his constituents, November 2,

* *Westminster Gazette*, 18.x.26.

1926, actually stated: "That the conduct of the leaders of the Miners' Federation is largely in accordance with the wishes of the governing party in Moscow."

No one who understood in the slightest the mentality of the leaders of the British Miners' Federation could entertain for a second this absurd assertion, yet it was seriously stated by the British Home Secretary.

There would seem to have been at this time a rivalry between Sir William Joynson-Hicks and Lord Birkenhead as to who could prefer the most inane charges against the Miners' Secretary and the Soviet Government. Next day, the noble Lord, in a speech which was humorously described as "Birkenhead's Gallop," said:

> "Let us face the plain indisputable fact. Mr. Cook, who is the humble disciple of Lenin, is bound to accept, and does accept, the orders of Moscow. There has never been an occasion in the whole history of England in which any trade unionist leader who claims allegiance to any considerable body of English workmen has proclaimed and admitted that he was a slave and a serf of a foreign Power. And of what a foreign Power! A foreign Power of whom I do dispute and have disputed the right under existing conditions to be recognised at all in this country."*

Others took a different view of the generous help sent by the Soviet Trade Unionists to the British Miners. The Albert Hall was crowded on November 7, 1926, to celebrate the ninth anniversary of the November Revolution.

Sir Charles (then Mr. C. P.) Trevelyan, M.P., in the course of a speeeh, stated:

> "The Russian people had forgotten what other Governments had attempted to do to their country, they had forgotten the hundred millions that was spent against Russia by this country, but they had remembered that the people of this country were never their enemies.
>
> Their gift to the miners of this country was *the biggest that had ever been given by the workers of one country to the workers of another country.*"†

Concluding, he said, amidst loud cheers:

> "After that million pounds it is quite impossible that our people will ever be dragged at the heels of even the worst Government to quarrel with the Russian people."

* *Times*, 4.xi.26. † *Daily Herald*, 8.xi.26.

It is worth recording that this meeting was as well reported even in the Tory press of London as the anti-Soviet meeting in the same hall, despite the fact that this meeting did not lend itself to "good copy," because no one was thrown out by "gentlemanly" stewards.

When the House of Commons reassembled in November, Sir Austen Chamberlain admitted that M. Krassin had told him that his Government would welcome negotiations to put relations with Great Britain on a better footing, but that he (Sir Austen) had informed him that negotiations were unacceptable until the one political condition (propaganda) embodied in the Trade Agreement was being observed.

This was trifling with the subject; the two sides were not agreed as to the interpretation of that political condition and obviously the only way to settle the dispute was by the method of conference.

The Soviet Government naturally could not agree that the British Government should be the sole interpreters of that clause. *Izvestia,* after declaring that the Soviet institutions operating in Great Britain had faithfully abstained from propaganda, asked whether the British Government seriously expected the Soviet Government to deny the right of existence in Moscow to the Communist International and to prevent Russian workers from aiding British miners. The journal concluded: "In putting out this absurd unfulfillable condition, Sir Austen Chamberlain shows that he does not want an agreement with the Soviet Union."

Unfortunately, there were no further negotiations between M. Krassin and Sir Austen Chamberlain because the former, who had been in delicate health for some time, died suddenly in London on November 24, 1926. The same afternoon, in the House of Commons, the British Foreign Secretary stated: "I hope I may be permitted to express my regret at the death of M. Krassin, the Soviet Chargé d'Affaires, to whom reference is made here."

M. Krassin had made a very favourable impression in Great Britain and his passing was mourned by many, both in business and political circles. The *Financial News* commented:

> "In M. Krassin the Soviet Government loses an able servant and one faithful to its strange ideas. His untimely death is undoubtedly a great loss to the Government and the cause for which he worked.
>
> He had a strong intellectual conviction that communal ownership was the best basis for the organisation of modern industry and this theory he pursued almost fanatically."

A joint meeting of the National Executive of the Labour Party and the General Council of the Trades Union Congress passed a resolution of condolence for transmission to his family. Mr. J. R. Clynes, M.P., after expressing in the name of the Parliamentary Labour Party their deepest sympathy with Mrs. Krassin and her family, added:

> "This is a tragic and untimely end to a life of great public service. This country as well as Russia has lost something by his sudden death. I believe that, if M. Krassin had been spared, his great diplomatic and business abilities would have enabled him to compose some of the differences which exist between Great Britain and Russia."

The *Daily Herald* declared:

> "He died, as he would have chosen to die, at his post. And his passing is a loss, not only to the Soviet Union, but to the Socialist and Working Class Movements throughout the world. His work at home in the reorganisation of Russian industry, abroad in establishing more friendly relations between the Soviet Union and the Western Powers, will endure.
>
> It is to his family, to his comrades, and to the many friends who feel the irreparable loss, that the sympathy of the British Labour Movement goes out to-day."

The body of M. Krassin lay in state in Chesham House until November 28, an event which attracted much attention and many reminiscences. To quote just one:

> "In a blaze of brilliant lights from cut-glass chandeliers, which refracted them in prismatic hues—surrounded by magnificent flowers in which red prevailed—the pale figure of M. Leonide Borisovitch Krassin, Chargé d'Affaires of the Union of Soviet Socialist Republics, lay in state in the regal reception hall of Chesham House, Belgravia, from 5 to 10 p.m. yesterday.
>
> At each corner of the bier stood a silent figure with bowed head—two girls and two young men from the Russian colony in London.
>
> These guards were relieved every hour. They wore their everyday clothes, and the only sign of mourning they displayed was an armlet of black edged with red.
>
> From the adjoining ante-room the subdued music of an orchestra penetrated the hall of death—throbbing, sobbing strains, which accorded with the melancholy picture seen by those who came to pay a last mark of respect to the memory of one of the makers of modern Russia.

The body, clad in black, lay in a coffin with heavy brass fittings on a dais covered with a red pall. The features, framed in head and beard of snowy white, were nobly calm in death.

Visitors of every class passed up the beautiful staircase, where in the days of the Tsars brilliant throngs ascended to the splendid room now occupied by the mortal remains of an implacable enemy of Tsardom."*

Up to a late hour on November 27, 1926, men and women of all classes and creeds, as well as many foreign visitors, came to pay their last tribute to a man from whom none could withhold respect. The members of the Diplomatic Corps and representatives of the British Foreign Office paid their last respects to the great diplomat on the morning of November 28, and on the afternoon of the same day the body was conveyed from Chesham House to Golders Green Crematorium. A large crowd numbering several thousands, among whom were many public men and women, had gathered at Golders Green Station, from which the cortege proceeded slowly to the crematorium. The accommodation in the chapel is limited to a few hundreds and only a fraction of those present could gain admission.

Before the ceremony, which consisted of speeches and Russian revolutionary songs, began, the large crowd was marshalled in semi-circular form around the entrances so that they might hear something of the proceedings inside. High and moving tributes were paid to the deceased by representatives both of the Soviet colony in London and of all sections of the British Labour Movement. The wreaths, which came from many individuals and organisations, filled two motor coaches. One, with a pick and shovel design, attracted special attention. It bore the inscription "From the Miners' Federation of Great Britain, in revered memory and deep gratitude: Herbert Smith, Tom Richards, W. P. Richardson and A. J. Cook."

The same evening, two members of the Soviet Staff in London left for Moscow to convey the ashes, which were later interned in the walls of the Kremlin. A great figure had passed, not only Soviet Russia but the whole world was the poorer.

A few days later, in Moscow, M. Litvinov, then deputy Commissar for Foreign Affairs, paying a warm tribute to the work and memory of M. Krassin, recalled amongst other things, that the latter in his last report expressed confidence in his ability to bring about better relations between Great Britain and the U.S.S.R. But this was not to be. His passing was the signal for an intensified agitation not for the bettering but the severance of relations between the two countries.

* *Westminster Gazette*, 27.xi.26.

II. Anglo-Soviet relations again deteriorate. Developments in China. The R.O.P. incident

After the death of M. Krassin, this country and the world was not left long in doubt as to the desire of Soviet Russia to continue the work which M. Krassin had left uncompleted. M. Chicherin, then in Germany for a cure, gave a statement to the press in Berlin December 6, 1926, in the course of which (according to the press report) he pointed out that the attitude of Britain to the U.S.S.R. was based on the principle of the old French proverb: "This animal is very wicked, when attacked it defends itself."

M. Chicherin cited a writer in the *Fortnightly Review* as saying that Sir Austen Chamberlain had once told Krassin that there was not one British agent in the East who did not report about anti-British activities by the Soviet Union. M. Chicherin's reply to this was that neither in the East nor in the West was there a Soviet agent who did not report the systematic hostility of British diplomacy.

"The deciding factor," said M. Chicherin, "remains that our Government has always offered England an arrangement and still offers one, but without any success. We stretch the hand of friendship and peace towards England, but the hand remains in the air."

The outstretched hand was not only not taken by Great Britain, but it was reported that "to an influential deputation in the House of Commons, the Prime Minister, on December 14, is known to have shown greater sympathy than on any previous occasion, with the view that England should be rid of the Soviet agents."*

When the old year drew to its close, the outlook for Anglo-Soviet relations looked blacker than ever. January, 1927, was a dead month as far as Anglo-Soviet relations were concerned, but on February 1, the late Mr. Leslie Urquhart, Chairman of the Russo-Asiatic Consolidated Ltd., circularised the shareholders of that Company asking them to write their M.P.'s urging the latter to support any action in Parliament designed to sever diplomatic relations with the U.S.S.R. The circular made the extraordinary assertion that "We see to-day our troops sailing East to protect British lives and interests in the Chinese tragedy foisted on us by Soviet Russia."

The circular urged that the British Government should sever diplomatic relations with the U.S.S.R. until the Government of Russia "makes a satisfactory agreement on all outstanding matters, including the settlement of claims."

As was pointed out in an earlier chapter, Mr. Urquhart, when there was a prospect of a settlement between his company and the U.S.S.R.

† *Daily Mail*, 29.xii.26.

had advocated the *de jure* recognition of the Soviet Government. Why had he changed his mind? Was it because of events in China? Hardly. This is what Lord Rothermere's paper declared:

> Mr. Urquhart stated to a *Daily Mail* reporter last night that while M. Krassin was alive some hope had been entertained by Russo-Asiatic Consolidated Limited regarding the company's claim for £56,000,000 in respect of its properties in Russia. Since the death of M. Krassin, who was the Soviet Chargé d'Affaires in London, the company had been definitely informed by the Soviet that no compensation whatever would be granted."*

Business reactions were divided:

> " In the City the attitude of mind which this agitation reveals is growing quickly. There is a strong political tinge in it, although Russo-Asiatic is not concerned with the political side of the question.
>
> As the movement is growing, the longer sighted men deplore the raising of the demand for cutting Russia off, especially as it is known to have powerful supporters in the Government. They would rather see a conference between representatives of the two countries on much more realistic lines than the last."†

As one of the reasons advanced by Tory statesmen and editors for their bitter attacks at this time on the Soviet Government was that the latter, so they alleged, was responsible for the genesis and the continuation of the dispute in the coal industry, it is important to recall the authoritative statement of the Secretary of the Miners' Federation, Mr. A. J. Cook. He said:

> " The Russian Government are blamed because the Russian workers answered our appeal, not with coal to defeat us, but with levies to keep our people from starvation. For this they have earned the everlasting hate of the Government and the capitalist class.
>
> The *Daily Mail* stated (as everyone knows, untruthfully) that ' At home we have had the coal strike instigated and financed from Moscow'. . . .
>
> It is true that the Russian workers, together with the workers in all other countries, sent help to us during our struggle, but they had nothing at all to do with the starting of the lock-out—the Government and the coalowners were entirely responsible for that —nor had they anything whatever to do with the control of the miners' policy, which was decided on all points by the M.F.G.B. at their conferences.

* *Daily Mail*, 2.ii.27. † *Daily News*, 2.ii.27.

We received over £1,000,000 unconditionally from Russia, in answer to our appeals for help, which were sent to every country where there was an organised Labour and Trade Union Movement.

Since the end of the lock-out we have received over £50,000 more, while the Women's Committee under Dr. Marion Phillips has also received several thousands. Every penny of this was collected voluntarily from the workers of Russia.

It is quite clear that the British Government intends, if we allow them, to break with Russia because of this assistance the Russian workers have given us. The miners, their wives and children will never forget who were their friends in their time of need, and we shall trust those who stood by us."*

The dispute in the coal industry was now at an end but events and developments in China were focussing attention and Tory statesmen and editors found another pretext for attacking the Soviet in the attitude of the Chinese Nationalist Movement towards the Imperialist Powers. The Nationalist Movement was in control of Southern China, in occupation of Hankow, astride the middle Yangtse and threatening Shanghai. Whitehall, as already explained, very shortsightedly, feared this new spirit and movement in China, because it threatened certain privileges which had been extracted at the bayonet's point from a weak China. What was the aim of this Movement ? The Foreign Minister of the Chinese Nationalists, M. Eugene Chen, explained:

"It is the recovery of China's full independence. And until this act of historical justice has been done there can be no real peace between Chinese Nationalism and British Imperialism. A nation that is not dying can never be at peace with its conqueror. It will strike at a selected moment."*

Should this have frightened Western Europe ? Mr. Chen continued:

"Great Britain or any other Power has nothing to fear when China, under Nationalist leadership and rule, recovers her lost independence. . . . The Government whose existence is implied by the modern state in China will necessarily work out the specific foreign issues involved in the recovery of China's full independence along the lines which, while asserting and enforcing Chinese authority and preserving vital Nationalist interests, will not disregard the considerations of right and justice due to foreign nationals. But in this connection a great and impressive fact must be grasped. To-day, the effective protection of foreign life and property in China does not stand and can no longer rest on foreign

* *Daily Herald*, 3.ii.27. † *Times*, 25.i.27.

> bayonets and foreign gunboats because 'the arm' of Chinese Nationalism—the economic weapon—is more puissant than any engine of warfare that a foreigner can devise."

The Nationalists wanted to settle the disputed issues by negotiations. He concluded:

> "It is, however, the view of the Nationalist Government that the liberation of China from the yoke of foreign imperialism need not necessarily involve any armed conflict between Chinese Nationalism and the foreign Powers. For this reason the Nationalist Government would prefer to have all questions outstanding between Nationalist China and the foreign Powers settled by negotiation and agreement.
>
> To prove that this is no idle statement of policy the Nationalist Government hereby declares its readiness to negotiate separately with any of the Powers for a settlement of treaty and other cognate questions on the basis of the economic equality and of mutual respect for each other's political and territorial sovereignty."

As already explained, Soviet Russia, true to its principles, was sympathetic to the new spirit in China and some Soviet citizens, in their private capacities, were serving in the Nationalist Forces. The Soviet Government did not prevent their subjects from so acting if they desired, just as the British Government took no steps to hinder General Sutton, a British subject, from serving with the ex-brigand and War Lord of Manchuria, Chang Tso-Lin.

The Chinese Nationalists were demanding the recognition of China's sovereignty and were not prepared to barter it. Whitehall found this new Chinese dignity and uncompromising spirit very unpleasant and attributed what it termed Chinese obstinacy to Soviet influence.

It is significant to recall to-day that the *Frankfurter Zeitung* at that time had an expert on Chinese affairs on its staff who attributed the attitude of the Chinese Nationalists towards Great Britain, not to Soviet influence, but to the mistakes of British policy.

On February 4, 1927, Mr. Winston Churchill, Sir W. Joynson-Hicks and Mr. Amery, all made speeches blaming the Soviet for the attitude of Mr. Chen towards this country.

More reasonable voices, however, were also raised in British public life. Speaking on the same day, Mr. J. R. Clynes said:

> "I consider it rather unfortunate that Sir Austen, while admitting the out-of-dateness of those treaties, should have spoken about meeting the Chinese half-way. In this matter I feel we shall have to choose between an indefensible effort at further

conquests in China, or a full concession of Chinese rights based upon a proper conception of equity and justice."

Considerable additional bodies of British armed forces had been landed in the foreign concessions which not unnaturally, in view of China's past treatment by this country, inflamed passions in China and destroyed any prospect of the development of an atmosphere of conciliation in which alone a durable settlement could have been negotiated. This was greatly regretted in the Soviet Union. Speaking to a press conference in Moscow on the same day as that on which the speeches just referred to were delivered, M. Litvinov declared:

> "The proposals of Mr. O'Malley seemed to create a basis acceptable to the Canton Government, and it is a matter of regret that the coupling of these peace negotiations with threats, intimidation, and military intervention have, judging from Mr. Chen's statement, caused a breakdown.
>
> British Conservative circles are trying to shift their own mistake on to the shoulders of the Soviet Government, on the basis of ridiculous legends, and to explain the greatest liberative movement in history among China's millions by the 'machinations' of Soviet agents."*

Rumours which had never quite died down became more pronounced now that the Cabinet were again considering a rupture with the U.S.S.R., without any attempt to settle differences around the table. Mr. J. Ramsay MacDonald, M.P., like many others, realised that the Conference method alone offered any prospects of success.

"We have been firing guns at one another," said the then leader of the Labour Party, "at very long range whereas we ought to have come closer together and brought the Russians up against our complaints and their own iniquities. I think we are very much to blame ourselves for having allowed the thing to go on, but to imagine that it is going to be stopped or that we are going to be put in a better political or economic position by breaking off relations is to me sheer madness."†

Other sane voices in the columns of papers like the *Daily News* and *Observer* were raised in similar accents. The Editor of the latter wrote: "It is still quite possible that our negotiations with Chinese nationalism may end well and that our relations with Russia may be permanently improved. Let us keep cool heads."

Mr. Leslie Urquhart who, as our readers know, had joined the agitation to hand their passports to the Soviet representatives, now invoked an extraordinary reason for withdrawing the British Mission

* *Daily News*, 5.ii.27. † *Daily Herald*, 5.ii.27.

from Moscow. He declared: "However vigilant may be our representatives in Russia, they are unable to penetrate the intentions of the Russian Communist Party represented by the Soviet Government, and therefore are useless for the purpose of information."*

Presumably that meant that a Diplomatic Mission which could not pierce the defences of the Secret Services of another Government was worthless. We wonder if it ever occurred to Mr. Urquhart that if that doctrine were applicable to British Diplomatic Missions abroad, it would also be applicable to foreign Diplomatic Missions in London.

Mr. O. Locker-Lampson, M.P., was easily the equal of Mr. Urquhart in advancing postulates which were the negation of common sense. He wrote: "Millions of Englishmen want to know why the Government sends thousands of soldiers overseas to compel yellow rioters in the Far East, when by expelling certain Red elements at home England would be mistress of her destinies."†

Presumably this meant that if the Soviet representatives were expelled from London, the Nationalist Movement in China, the uprising of a great and ancient nation against the bondage of foreign tutelage, would cease. One is tempted to ask: "Do some people ever read history?"

Apart from the public agitation, undoubtedly considerable pressure was being brought to bear on Ministers behind the scenes (in the Lobbies of Parliament, in Tory clubs, Mayfair drawing-rooms, and at week-end country house-parties) in favour of severing relations with Moscow. "Ministers will secure no peace," wrote the Political Correspondent of the *Daily Mail* (February 14, 1927), "from a large mass of their followers so long as they persist in their present passivity."

The fly in the ointment, according to this correspondent, was the Foreign Secretary, Sir Austen Chamberlain, whose "cogent" arguments against drastic action were reported to "have had a marked effect on many of his Cabinet colleagues."

This rumour was confirmed two days later when, after a Cabinet meeting, reports appeared in papers standing close to the Government to the effect that no immediate action was contemplated.

The Labour Movement, industrial and political, realising the serious repercussions which an Anglo-Soviet rupture would bring in its trail, in a statement to the nation, declared:

> "The National Joint Council of the British Labour Movement regards as a positive danger to world peace the renewal of agitation to break off official relations with Russia. The Labour Movement pledges itself to oppose any such step being taken, as that would only increase our difficulties, both industrial and political. The Labour Movement calls for a closer relationship

* *Daily Mail*, 10.ii.27.

† *Daily Herald*, 12.ii.27.

with Russia so that grievances may be dealt with so soon as they arise and thus prevent illwill being engendered.

The National Joint Council therefore expresses the hope that a representative of the Russian Government will be appointed to London forthwith and the discussion and removal of mutual grievances begun at once."*

Strange though it may appear, whilst Anglo-Soviet diplomatic relations were worsening, commercial relations between the U.S.S.R., and the U.S.A. and Germany improved.

" In the last week, in the middle of this agitation against Russia," stated Mr. E. F. Wise, Economic Adviser to the Centrosoyus, " the German Government has substantially increased its guaranteed credits to Russia for the purchase of machinery in Germany. I have just returned from the United States and in the last month and a half I have succeeded in doubling the credit facilities enjoyed by the Russian Co-operative organisations from American banks."†

Up to this date much had been splashed in the press, said in the House of Commons and shouted from the platform about Soviet violations of the Trade Agreement, yet strange to relate, M. Litvinov‡ could with truth aver:

> " Neither the Soviet Government nor its Embassy in London has once received from the British Government the slightest indication of a single practical case of violation of the Trade Agreement of 1921. Naturally there were plenty of general and unsubstantiated charges in Parliament and in the public utterances of British Ministers, as well as in Sir Austen Chamberlain's conversations with our representatives. However, all our suggestions that such accusations should be based upon real concrete facts have invariably been declined."§

Turning to the question of the political campaign for a rupture of relations, M. Litvinov said:

> " Several members of the British Government are openly adhering to this campaign. Unfortunately, the British Government as a whole, by its ambiguous conduct, contrary to the usual forms of diplomatic relationship, has given ground for the belief that it encourages this campaign by making unfounded general statements, alleging the violation by the Soviet Government of the Trade Agreement of 1921.
>
> At the same time it must be remembered that as far back as

* *Daily Herald*, 19.ii.27. † *Manchester Guardian*, 19.ii.27.

‡ M. Litvinov was speaking to the Central Executive Committee, 21.ii.27.

§ *Morning Post*, 22.ii.27.

1923, after the well-known British ultimatum, Lord Curzon undertook an engagement on behalf of the British Government to inform the Soviet Government without delay of alleged cases of violation of obligations so that such cases should not accumulate without preferring charges."*

The Deputy Commissar did not shirk the question of China. He added:

> "We could but welcome the establishment between China and other countries of new relations based on equality of rights. In this connection, as distinguished from the attitude of the British Government, the actual position of Japan should be noted. We welcome the idea of the Japanese Foreign Minister that 'every attempt forcibly to establish peace under pressure from outside may do more harm than good.'"†

No one could deny that M. Litvinov's declaration constituted the basis for a round table conference at which existing differences and a *modus vivendi* could be threshed out, but the offer was spurned by Whitehall and on the following day reports appeared that another Note of protest in general terms was to be sent to Moscow. This was not all. The British Government wanted if possible joint international action against the Soviet Union. "Another question recently discussed," wrote the well-informed Diplomatic Correspondent of the *Daily Telegraph*, "concerned the opportuneness or otherwise of sounding other Powers as to the prospect of joint diplomatic action at Moscow." The anticipated Note was handed to the Soviet Chargé d'Affaires on February 23, 1927. After dealing with a series of alleged breaches of the non-propaganda pledges in very general terms, the Note concluded:

> "His Majesty's Government consider it necessary to warn the Union of Socialist Soviet Republics in the gravest terms that there are limits beyond which it is dangerous to drive public opinion in the country, and a continuance of such acts as are here complained of must sooner or later render inevitable the abrogation of the Trade Agreement, the stipulations of which have been so flagrantly violated, and even the severance of ordinary diplomatic relations."

There was no reply to the Soviet Government's offer to discuss outstanding differences, and it therefore left the position worse than it was before.

The Note was no doubt the result of conflicting views within the

* *Daily Herald*, 22.ii.27. † *Westminster Gazette*, 22.ii.27.

Cabinet: some were anxious to negotiate a durable settlement whilst others wanted a repetition of the Curzon Ultimatum of 1923. This was reflected in the Tory press on the following day. The Labour and Liberal press was unanimous in condemning the Note. The warning of the *Daily Chronicle* is worthy of special mention. It stated:

> "Those who preach breaking off relations and 'expelling the Reds,' should be seriously asked whether they want another Great War. For that is what their policy would lead to. Russia is a Great Power with a great future; she covers a large fraction of the earth's surface; and it is difficult to think of anything more perilous than that this giant State and the British Empire should not even be on speaking terms, should have no channels of intercourse, no possible germs of amity for time to ripen."*

The terms used by the Liberal journal would, undoubtedly, have been endorsed by the majority of public opinion at that time.

The *Daily Express*, although a Conservative paper, had no use for the hysteria of many of the Tory journalists and politicians. It declared:

> "The British Note to Russia was received with hysterical disfavour, especially in that section of opinion which desires a complete break with the Soviets. For a long time these extremists have been beating their drum with a combination of persistency and fury which should have worked the Government up to the breaking point—even as the tom-tom is used to rouse the blood of the savage warrior."†

Although in the Note to the Soviet, the British Government wrapped itself in a white sheet, the Home Secretary, Sir William Joynson-Hicks, was compelled to admit in the House of Commons, on the day following its presentation that he had been in touch with an ex-Tsarist diplomat, M. Sablin. The following dialogue then took place:

> "*Mr. Mosley:* Does the right hon. Gentleman consider that it is proper to receive a Russian who, in the words of the Trade Agreement, is fomenting rebellion against the Government of Russia?
>
> *Sir W. Joynson-Hicks:* It is a long tradition of the Home Office to be courteous, and I always receive, as far as time permits, those who desire to see me."‡

Naturally, the Home Secretary's quibble about courteousness

* *Daily Chronicle*, 24.ii.27. † *Daily Express*, 25.ii.27. ‡ *Hansard*, 24.ii.27, col. 1895.

deceived nobody. His action in conferring with M. Sablin was a distinct breach of the letter and spirit of the Trade Agreement.

Asked for his opinion of the British Note, Mr. J. Ramsay MacDonald replied: "I think that the dispatch is more like the leading article in a newspaper than a Foreign Office document."*

It is significant that although certain British traders who had preferred claims against the Soviet welcomed the threat to Anglo-Soviet relations, the *Financial News* wrote: "On the whole there is little belief in the City that the position of the Russian creditors would be improved by breaking off relations. Their best hope must lie in an improvement in Anglo-Russian trade."†

Izvestia pertinently commented:

> "The Note was published in the British press before it reached the Soviet Government, contrary to the usual forms of international amity. The Note misses its mark. It contains no specific charges which could justify either representations or the threat of the abrogation of the trade agreement, or even the severance of ordinary diplomatic relations."

The Soviet's official reply was handed to the British Chargé d'Affaires in Moscow on February 24, 1927. It denied the general charges made in the British document, declared that the only instance deduced in the last four years was the forged "Zinoviev Letter"; charged certain British Ministers with making unjustifiable attacks on the U.S.S.R., and declared that if the British Government severed diplomatic relations, it must take full responsibility for the consequences. In striking contrast to the British Note, the Soviet reply ended with an appeal for reconciliation. It stated:

> "On its part the Soviet Government confirms that the statements of the late M. Krassin, quoted in the Note of the British Government, concerning the desirability of removing all difficulties existing between the two countries and everything giving ground for mutual complaint and of establishing quite normal relations, actually correspond to the immutable and sincere wishes of the Soviet Government. In accordance with the decision for peace of the toiling masses of the Soviet Union, which are in entire conformity with the same aspirations of the popular masses of Great Britain, the Soviet Government will in future also pursue its peace-loving policy, which excludes all aggressiveness towards other countries. *It will welcome the British Government sincerely, if it will go to meet it on this path.*" (Our italics.)

* *Daily Herald*, 25.ii.27. † *Financial News*, 25.ii.27.

Here was an opportunity for a round table conference, but it was thrown away with both hands: the British Government announced that it did not intend to reply to the Soviet Note. Apparently nothing but complete surrender on the part of Moscow and a British interpretation alone of the mutual obligations of the Anglo-Soviet Trade Agreement would satisfy Whitehall.

The exchange of Notes between London and Moscow naturally attracted much attention abroad, particularly in France, and it is worthy of note that in that country, at least a big section of the press held that M. Litvinov had had the best of the argument. The Paris correspondent of the *Manchester Guardian* cabled:

> "The press of the Left, and even some neutral papers, say openly that Russia has the best of it in what the *Ere Nouvelle* calls this 'diplomatic game of poker,' and the *Petit Journal* declares M. Litvinov's Note to be 'a masterpiece of diplomacy.' The quotations from speeches by Mr. Churchill and other members of the British Government are considered very telling, and it is felt that the proverb about the inhabitants of glass houses applies."*

Much to the regret of those British manufacturers who were executing Soviet orders, the atmosphere created by the exchange of Notes was detrimental to the development of trade between the two countries.

The exchange of Notes was discussed in the House of Commons on March 3, 1927. On the morning of that day the *Morning Post*, in a leader which attracted considerable attention, declared:

> "We may safely assume, then, that the Government are in earnest; and that their present hesitation merely relates to choice of the policy best fitted for the end in view. We have opposed both recognition and the Trade Agreement, but we cannot see much practical service in the denunciation of these instruments. It is a great cry, but very little wool, and would leave the danger very much as it is at present. What would be of service, if it could be attained, would be a European understanding directed to the end of disinfecting the world from Bolshevism, and, in particular, confining it to its chief plague-spot of Russia. If the Government were to induce the rest of Europe to combine with them in such a policy, then we might really get to business."†

The debate largely resolved itself into a duel between the Foreign Secretary, Sir Austen Chamberlain and Mr. Lloyd George. The former first defended himself against the Die-Hards in his own party:

* *Manchester Guardian*, 1.iii.27.

† *Morning Post*, 3.iii.27.

"You cannot have, whatever the provocation, whatever your own interests, a sudden breach between this country and Russia without its having its repercussions on the whole European situation. It is for that reason that I have urged upon His Majesty's Goverment patience and forebearance, under circumstances of continued provocation such as we have never endured at the hands of any other nation, such as, indeed, I believe there is no parallel for in the international relationships of any other two countries."*

Turning to the British Note, he declared: "We thought that before we proceeded to any extremity, it was right to call the world to witness the serious nature of the complaints which we have, and to give the Soviet Government one more opportunity to conform their conduct to the ordinary rules of international life and comity."†

Regarding the Soviet reply, he stated:

"The Soviet reply to the Note of His Majesty's Government misses the point. We have no desire, and we have made no attempt, to interfere with them within their own boundaries; we have carried on no diplomatic campaign against them in any part of the world; we have lived up, not merely to the letter, but to the fullest spirit of the mutual engagement which we undertook with them. What we ask of them is not that they shall change their domestic institutions, not that they shall refrain from preaching to their own people that their own institutions are superior to those which are preferred by the rest of the world, but that they shall henceforth make their policy conform to the ordinary comity of nations, and abstain from the effort to promote world revolution and from all interference in our internal affairs."‡

Mr. Lloyd George followed. Respecting the gravity of the situation, he declared:

"I agree with the right hon. Gentleman in all he said in his very grave words about the danger of a rupture with Soviet Russia, having regard to the present condition of the world. It would have repercussions in Asia and in Europe of a very grave character indeed. Lord Balfour called attention to that in his great speech in the House of Lords, in July last, upon this situation, and I thought that meant that the Government had definitely made up their mind not to address a minatory note to the Russian Government."§

* *Hansard*, 3.iii.27, col. 633.
† Ibid., col. 634.
‡ Ibid., col. 633.
§ Ibid., col. 635.

Referring to the Foreign Secretary's complaint of hostile speeches in the U.S.S.R., Mr. Lloyd George countered:

"The Chancellor of the Exchequer has been delivering speeches which are certainly very improper to deliver against a country with whom you are officially on good relations. Those are speeches which certainly ought not to be delivered unless you break. The language is violent language, and it is obviously directed against the Government, and he says so—against those who are sitting in the Kremlin. He has said so in so many words. And so has Lord Birkenhead been delivering speeches of that kind."*

Then, turning to the complaint of unfriendly attacks in the Soviet press, he retorted:

"The Rt. Hon. Gentleman quotes newspapers in Russia. Has he quoted a newspaper which is supposed to be semi-official now, the *Morning Post?* The *Morning Post* has run away from its old position now that the Government have taken up their present line. Its truculence is always the truculence of the faint-hearted. When it comes right up against it, it is not going to put an end to recognition, it will not determine the Trade Agreement, but what does it propose? The Right Hon. Gentleman complains that the Soviet Government are under the impression that we are organising a Federation of Europe against them. Would he mind reading the *Morning Post* article this morning—if he can find time—reading the end of it? It is an appeal to Europe, practically inviting the Government to get a federation of that kind against Russia and Russian Bolshevism. How can he complain, then, if Soviet Russia, with all shades of revolution, and the darkness and the suspicion of revolution, should come to the conclusion that we also are in a conspiracy with regard to her?"†

Mr. Lloyd George continued that it was clear from the Soviet Note that the U.S.S.R. wanted to keep on good terms with this country and he strongly urged the Government to reply in the affirmative "to the invitation of the Soviet Government to talk over these difficulties." However, the Government was adamant in this matter and stubbornly refused to meet the Soviet representatives in Conference. Commenting on the debate the next day, the *Daily Express* averred that the Note to the Soviet Union was a "concession to hysterical pressure from the Right," whilst the *Times* declared:

"The Bolshevist leaders have received a clear warning from the British Government, and it is for them to justify themselves before Great Britain and before Europe."

* *Hansard*, 3.iii.27, col. 638. † Ibid., cols. 639-640.

This debate took place on March 3, 1927. Had the members of the Government sincerely believed in their case against the Soviet Union and had their Note and Sir Austen Chamberlain's speech been intended as a "warning to Moscow," they would at least have given the Kremlin time for reflection before resorting to challenging and provocative action themselves. Yet four days later two Cabinet Ministers delivered vehement attacks on the Government of the U.S.S.R. Lord Birkenhead, speaking at Portsmouth (March 7, 1927) regarding the U.S.S.R. exclaimed:

> "There is no freedom of life. There is neither justice nor law, there is no protection for religion, there is no sanctity for marriage in this home of the proletariat, in the spiritual home from which our leading Communists draw daily and weekly refreshment. They have one of the richest countries in the world. They have very nearly destroyed it. They have done more harm to the resources and to the wealth and to the trade of Russia in ten years than the Tsarist Government, with all its admitted incompetence, was able to do in one hundred."*

In passing we may remark that the economy of Russia which had been ruined by the world war, the subsidised civil war and the blockade, had been more than restored by the Soviet Government by this date. However, it is only fair to add that Lord Birkenhead, in another connection, admitted that statistics were not his strong point.

Sir William Joynson-Hicks tried his hardest to emulate Lord Birkenhead. He shouted:

> "Here in our own land, as everywhere, we had the machinations of the Russian Government seeking to destroy all that we held dear. Not content with the misery of their own country, they were seeking to extend that misery to other countries, seeking to destroy civilisation, seeking to destroy what they called the 'capitalist system' and because we were the head and forefront of civilisation throughout the world it was the people of Great Britain who had to bear the brunt of the first attack of the Soviet Government."†

Sir Austen Chamberlain presumably thought that it was incumbent on him to do something to counteract the ravings of his Cabinet colleagues. On the following day, in an interview at Geneva, he declared that Britain was not trying to organise an anti-Soviet bloc. "We have never tried to do it and never shall."‡

It is indicative of the effects produced abroad by the policy of our

* *Daily Telegraph*, 8.iii.27. † Ibid.
‡ *Daily News*, 9.iii.27.

Government towards the U.S.S.R. and to the anti-Soviet tirades of members of the British Government that Sir Austen completely failed to convince his foreign audience. The *Times* correspondent cabled from Geneva, March 8, 1927, that despite the Foreign Secretary's denials "the main body of the foreign journalists at Geneva are convinced that the British Note to the Soviet Government was a sort of declaration of diplomatic war, and that since then Great Britain has entirely revised her policy with regard to Poland and Rumania and is busily stirring them up against the Soviets."*

Cables which arrived at the same time in London from various European capitals demonstrated that the scepticism of Geneva was shared by the entire Continent. France was particularly suspicious of the value of the Foreign Secretary's disclaimer. The *Manchester Guardian's* correspondent cabled from Paris:

> "Sir Austen Chamberlain's denial at Geneva that the British Government is trying to form a combination against Russia is received here with general scepticism, equally shared by persons and papers favourable to such a combination, and by those opposed to it. One cause of this scepticism is the Italian decision to ratify the declaration of 1920 by confirming the annexation of Bessarabia by Rumania, which is universally attributed to British influence and regarded as proof that Italy is ready to join with England against Russia."

Germany, through the lips of her Foreign Secretary, Herr Stresemann, warned Great Britain that "the economic life of the world cannot be restored to the normal while a country with a population of 150 millions is left outside the pale."†

On the other hand, fearing that Sir Austen's disclaimer at Geneva might, perhaps, gain some measure of credence, his colleague, Lord Birkenhead, eight days later made another speech, in which he described the Soviet leaders as murderers and assassins.

It was widely believed at this time that Sir Austen was anxious to maintain relations with the Soviet Union, but that others were determined to defeat his efforts.

Despite this most unpromising atmosphere, Moscow apparently decided to make another effort to persuade the British Government to meet its representatives. The Chairman of the Council of People's Commissars in the course of a speech in Moscow, April 19, 1927, after referring to the unsatisfactory relations between the two countries, stated: "The Soviet Government, as before, was ready to proceed with the negotiations and held it to be desirable and possible to remove the present strained relations."

* *Times*, 9.iii.27.

† *Daily Chronicle*, 11.iii.27.

Again there was no response from Whitehall. On the contrary the Government was now guilty of an act which could not be construed other than as a calculated affront to the Soviet Government. Russian Oil Products Ltd., which was a selling agency in this country for Soviet oil, had had an advertisement inserted in the Telephone Directory (a medium of advertising open to all firms registered in Great Britain) on the usual trade terms. When this matter was raised in the House of Commons, May 3, 1927, the Assistant Postmaster-General, Viscount Wolmer, gave the amazing answer that the advertisement would be withdrawn from future issues.

It is very significant that despite the dangerous political atmosphere created by the speeches of some Tory Cabinet Ministers and the partial financial boycott of the Soviet Union, trade between Britain and the U.S.S.R. had reached its high-water mark in 1925. In that year Soviet sales in Great Britain amounted to £31,412,000 and Soviet purchases to £35,645,000. It is true that due to the worsening relations, sales in 1926 fell to £24,415,000 and purchases to £16,627,000. This retrogression was not at all to the liking of certain financial interests in this country. Moreover, the Soviet Trading Organisations had steadily built up a reputation for financial integrity. All this and other factors resulted in the conclusion of an agreement between the Soviet Trade Delegation and the Midland Bank on May 11, 1927, under which the latter would have financed Soviet orders in Great Britain to the amount of £10,000,000. One of the terms of this agreement was that it did not preclude the Soviet Trade Delegation from reaching similar understandings with other banks. Had it been allowed to operate, this agreement (which would certainly have been followed by others) would have been of tremendous historical importance, because it would have meant the end of the financial blockade of the U.S.S.R. British exports to the U.S.S.R. would have risen enormously and Soviet orders would have provided a livelihood for hundreds of thousands of persons in this country. May 11, 1927, might have constituted a turning point in the history of Anglo-Soviet relations.

It was a case of now or never for those who had been working for a diplomatic rupture. The Agreement would have been announced to the world a day or two later and would have had an effect on the electorate that no Government could ignore. The members of the Cabinet and their Russian "White" friends knew of the agreement. Some quick thinking must have been done in certain quarters. On the following day, May 12, 1927, the famous (or infamous) "Raid on Arcos" took place, which shattered the agreement and led to a diplomatic rupture between Great Britain and the U.S.S.R. That subject, however, is so important that it deserves a chapter to itself.

CHAPTER XI

THE ARCOS RAID (1927)

I. MAY 12, THE RAID TAKES PLACE. QUESTIONS ARE ASKED IN PARLIAMENT

BEFORE proceeding to the question of the police raid on Arcos, it is necessary to recount some pertinent facts.

The premises of Arcos Ltd., and of the Trade Delegation of the U.S.S.R. in Great Britain were housed in one building, 49 Moorgate, London, E. C. 2. Arcos was a joint stock company registered in Great Britain in accordance with British laws. The activities of the Trade Delegation were based upon the Trade Agreement concluded in 1921 between His Majesty's Government and the Soviet Government.

The Chairman of the Trade Delegation was the Official Trade Agent of the Soviet Government, and his offices enjoyed diplomatic immunity as provided in Clause 5 of the 1921 Trade Agreement. Further, the Agreement guaranteed the right to the Official Trade Agent to use cypher codes in his communications.

It is particularly important to note that the Trade Delegation, although housed in 49, Moorgate (premises belonging to Arcos Ltd.), occupied offices which were self-contained and on all the entrances of which were notices in large type, both in Russian and English, "TRADE DELEGATION OF THE U.S.S.R."

It was, therefore, quite impossible to confuse the premises occupied by the Trade Delegation with those occupied by Arcos.

In view of the hostile attitude of leading members of the British Government and powerful sections of the press towards the Soviet Government, and in view of the fact that an unauthorised or, for that matter, a strictly forbidden act of an employee might be construed as an authorised instruction of a responsible official, the then plenipotentiary representative of the U.S.S.R. in Great Britain sent the following instruction, dated December 29, 1926, to all the departmental managers of the Trade Delegation and subordinate organisations:

> "You are asked to inform all employees under personal signature of notification, of the following Instruction issued by the Embassy and the Trade Delegation of the U.S.S.R. in Great Britain on December 16, 1926.
>
> Supplementary to previous instructions and orders, we once again categorically request that all employees, without exception, of the Embassy and Trade Delegation of the U.S.S.R. in Great Britain, refrain from any actions which might be interpreted as

interference in the internal affairs of Great Britain. In particular, the English employees are requested to refrain from any political work within the limits of the territory of the Embassy and Trade Delegation. They are also forbidden to form any organisations in any way connected with political parties.

You are notified, that in the event of any employee violating this instruction in any way, he or she will be immediately dismissed.

This instruction is to be shown to every employee, who must attach his personal signature."

In addition, a pledge was required from all Soviet citizens employed in these organisations that whilst in this country they would not participate in the activities of any organisation or society pursuing political aims.

Naturally, neither the Trade Delegation nor any other employer could vouch for the honesty of all its employees, nor guarantee that they would carry out its instructions to the letter. The Trade Delegation did what was humanly possible, and it is difficult to conceive how they could have done more.

On May 12, 1927, at about 4.30 in the afternoon, a considerable force of uniformed and plain-clothes police (the press report stated about 200) entered No. 49, Moorgate.

According to the evidence of people who were present, the raid was carried out in the following manner:

The police, immediately on entering the building, took possession of the telephone exchange, disconnected all the telephones and occupied the lift and all the entrances to the building. Various groups of the police occupied the entrances to all the floors and rooms belonging both to Arcos and the Trade Delegation. Within a few minutes the whole building was in the hands of uniformed and plain-clothes officers.

The warrant authorising the search was not presented before the search began. The Acting Chairman of Arcos Ltd., in spite of repeated demands, was only allowed to see the warrant an hour after the search had commenced.

The warrant authorised not only a search of the premises occupied by Arcos Ltd., which was subject to British law, but also of those of the Soviet Trade Delegation, which was a flagrant breach of the Trade Agreement.*

* According to Article 5 of the Trade Agreement, the Chairman enjoyed all the rights and immunities enjoyed by the official representatives of other Foreign Powers in Great Britain. The right of the Chairman to the above-mentioned privileges had been confirmed shortly before by a Foreign Office Note, dated February 16, 1927.

All persons found by the police on the stairs, corridors and landings of the huge building were detained by the police. The employees of Arcos and the Trade Delegation who were in their offices were ordered to leave them and go into the corridors. *Only the police remained in the offices, and all the demands of employees to be permitted to be present during the search were refused and they were not allowed to enter the offices then occupied by the police.*

One group of police officers rushed immediately to the Cypher Room of the Chairman of the Delegation of the U.S.S.R. At that time, there were in the room the Cypher Clerks. One of them told the police officer that this room was one of the Trade Delegation offices where the cypher communications of the Chairman of the Delegation were kept, and that they, the Cypher Clerks, were not allowed to permit anyone into the room or to show the cypher communications to anyone without the express permission of the Official Trade Agent, or of one of the members of the Trade Delegation or responsible official of the Trade Delegation.

No notice was taken by the police of the protests of the Cypher Clerks, and the attempts of the latter to prevent the police officers from access to the cypher communications resulted in two of them being assaulted by the police, one receiving several blows on the face.

This was an additional breach of the Trade Agreement because under Article 4 of that instrument the Trade Delegation was entitled to communicate freely by post, telegraph and wireless telegraphy, and to use telegraph codes under the conditions and subject to the regulations laid down in the International Telegraph Convention of St. Petersburg, 1875 (Lisbon Revision of 1908).

At about 5 o'clock, the police entered the chairman's office.

Those employees (among whom was Mme. Maisky, who was in charge of one of the departments) who were detained in the corridors were questioned, the majority were told to turn out their pockets, and some underwent a personal search by police officers.

An hour later, the women were gradually allowed to leave the building, the men were detained longer, some of them till late at night.

About an hour after the commencement of the raid, the police gave permission to the Secretary of the Trade Delegation to examine some of the rooms. Similarly, the Acting Chairman of Arcos Ltd., was allowed at about the same time to enter the various rooms in the company of a police officer.

Naturally, the subject of the raid was at once reported to the Soviet Embassy. The First Secretary called immediately on the Director of the Northern Department of the Foreign Office, Mr.

Palairet, "who expressed complete ignorance even of the fact that the raid was taking place."*

From there, the First Secretary proceeded to the premises of the Trade Delegation, but was refused admission by the police. He next called (about 6 p.m.) on the Superintendent of the City Police. What happened is related in his own words:

> "Our interview lasted for about a quarter of an hour. At first, when I stated that I desired to be admitted to the premises of the Trade Delegation, the Superintendent refused to grant such permission. I replied that he had no right to refuse my admittance to the premises of the Trade Delegation which, being the offices of our Official Trade Agent, enjoys the privilege of extra-territoriality in accordance with the 1921 Trade Agreement. Thereupon, he seemed rather puzzled and finally said he would grant me the desired permission providing I gave a promise to take nothing away from the building.
>
> I interrupted and stated that we were not discussing as to what I should or should not do, the point was that when I arrived at the premises of the Trade Delegation the police had refused to admit me. Considering that I am a member of the Embassy, this constitutes, in my opinion, a breach of my diplomatic privileges as well as of the diplomatic privileges of the Trade Representative, whose offices, according to the Agreement of 1921, enjoyed diplomatic immunity. I applied to him because he was in command of the police guarding the entrance. Since he could not give me a permit to enter the Trade Delegation, I requested him to tell me to whom I must apply. I added that I had come direct from the Foreign Office, where I had had an interview with Mr. Palairet, who, on the contrary, had stated that he thought it necessary that I should witness how the search was proceeding.
>
> After exchanging a few more remarks, the Superintendent ordered one of his men to go with us, and we were admitted into the premises.
>
> On returning to the Trade Delegation and Arcos, and after waiting another twenty minutes downstairs, I was admitted to the Trade Delegation. I proceeded immediately to the room of the Chief of the Trade Delegation. I found there some of our colleagues, and several detectives. I asked the chief officer on what authority they were making the search. He presented a warrant to me which stated that he was authorised to make a search in the premises of Arcos Ltd., and the Russian Trade Delegation. I told him that according to the Trade Agreement of 1921,

* Extract from a statement issued by the Press Bureau of the Soviet Embassy dated May 15, 1927.

the premises of the Russian Trade Delegation are the premises of the Official Trade Agent, who, according to this Agreement, enjoys all the privileges of diplomatic immunity, and that, in consequence, in having entered the premises of the Trade Delegation and proceeded with a search there, the police had committed a breach of the Trade Agreement of 1921. The chief officer answered that he did not know anything about the Trade Agreement, but that he was in possession of a warrant which authorised him to proceed with the search of the premises of the Trade Delegation. With that search he was now proceeding and would carry it out to the end. Then I said to him, 'Do you mean to say that you will make a search in all these premises and safes belonging personally to the Soviet Trade Agent?' The Chief Detective Thompson replied curtly, 'Yes.' Then I repeated that I protested against the search which was a breach of the Agreement between Great Britain and the U.S.S.R. signed in 1921."

At about 7 o'clock the same evening, the First Secretary rang up Sir Austen Chamberlain's Private Secretary requesting him at the instruction of the Chargé d'Affaires *ad interim* of the U.S.S.R. in Great Britain, to arrange an immediate interview between him and Sir Austen. It was explained that the question which the Chargé d'Affaires desired to discuss with Sir Austen was the raid on the premises of the Trade Delegation and the violation of the 1921 Trade Agreement.

The Secretary replied that he could fix an appointment for 11.30 a.m. next day, but not earlier.

The Soviet Representative then requested that Sir Austen Chamberlain's Private Secretary should be so good as to arrange an interview for the Chargé d'Affaires immediately with some responsible member of the staff of the Foreign Office. Sir Austen's Secretary promised to give a reply by telephone a little later. Without waiting for a reply, however, the Chargé d'Affaires called personally at the Foreign Office, but when ten minutes after the telephone conversation he arrived there, he found neither Sir Austen Chamberlain's Private Secretary nor any responsible member of the Foreign Office staff. Thus all the attempts made by the Chargé d'Affaires to communicate with the Foreign Office during the evening of May 12 were without result.

The Chargé d'Affaires saw Sir Austen Chamberlain on the following morning and handed him a Note which read:

"Sir,

At half-past four this afternoon the premises of Arcos and the Trade Delegation of the Union of Soviet Socialist Republics at 49, Moorgate, were occupied by armed police; this, in spite of the fact that in accordance with the Trade Agreement of 1921, the premises of the Trade Agent of the U.S.S.R. in Great Britain enjoy diplomatic immunity.

During the raid, which is still in progress at the time of writing, an employee of the Trade Delegation, who had refused to give up the key of a safe containing the personal papers, cyphers, codes, etc., of the Official Trade Agent, was assaulted by the police. The post addressed to the Official Trade Agent, which had just been brought by the couriers, was carried off by the police.

These proceedings are a flagrant violation of Article 5 of the Trade Agreement which includes the following passage:

'Official agents shall be at liberty to communicate freely with their own Government and with other official representatives of their Government in other countries by post, by telegraph and wireless telegraphy in cypher, and to receive and despatch couriers with sealed bags subject to a limitation of three kilograms per week which shall be exempt from examination.'

Moreover, in accordance with Article 1 of the Trade Agreement the British Government has undertaken 'not to exercise any discrimination against such trade as compared with that carried on with any other foreign country or to place any impediments in the way of banking, credit and financial operations for the purpose of such trade.' But the very fact of the occurrence of the raid must inevitably injure Anglo-Soviet trade.

In addition, I must point out that during the raid, the most elementary guarantees and demands of common decency were violated.

The search was begun before the presentation of the warrant, which was handed to the Assistant Director of Arcos an hour after the commencement of the search. In nearly the whole of the premises the search proceeded in the absence of representatives of the institution raided.

All the employees of Arcos and of the Trade Delegation, both men and women, were detained and subjected to a personal search. Among those detained were women possessing diplomatic passports, as for instance, the wife of the Chargé d'Affaires, and the wife of the Financial Attaché. The personal search of the women was carried out by male police officers.

I beg to state that I have informed my Government of all that has occurred, but, whilst awaiting their decisions and instructions, I consider it my duty to protest most emphatically against the violation in the above manner of the obligations undertaken by the British Government in accordance with the Trade Agreement of 1921."

Later the following statement was issued by the Press Bureau of the Soviet Embassy:

> "When the Note protesting against the raid on the Trade Delegation was handed to Sir Austen at 11.30 a.m. on May 13, his attention was especially drawn to the fact that the raid was a direct and seemingly deliberate violation of the 1921 Trade Agreement, since the premises of the Official Trade Agent had been raided and the police on entering 49, Moorgate had first of all seized the cypher-code and documents which were the personal property of the Official Trade Agent. Such actions cannot but make relations between the two countries more strained and would seem to be directed to that end. At the same time, it was pointed out that the manner in which the raid was being carried out was such that the interests of the institutions raided were in no way taken into account and gave no guarantee that the documents and materials which the police might allege to have been found on the premises of the Trade Delegation were really there before the raid took place."

On the same day the General Council of the Trades Union Congress sent a vigorous protest to the Prime Minister, the Rt. Hon. Stanley Baldwin, in which the secretary stated:

> "The General Council is unable to discover that any complaint of any kind had officially been made to the diplomatic representatives of the U.S.S.R. in Great Britain which would justify the extraordinary proceedings taken by the Home Office.
>
> The General Council find it difficult to believe that the representatives of any other important national state could be treated in this summary fashion, and I have to record their protest against a step which cannot fail to have an injurious influence upon the relations between Great Britain and the U.S.S.R."

There was no question that the Chairman of the Trade Delegation and his offices enjoyed diplomatic immunity and one well-known legal authority declared that such a flagrant breach of International law had not taken place in British history in the previous 200 years. However, the Foreign Office, to whom the Soviet Trade Delegation naturally looked for protection, took no steps to call off the raid.

The Trade Delegation had been asked by the police to hand over to them the keys of the safes in the offices of the Trade Delegation. This the latter declined to do because these offices were extra-territorial.

At the time of the raid no information was disclosed as to what the police were seeking, but reports appeared in the press that their objective was an important British state document. The Soviet Trade Delegation immediately issued a statement to the press declaring "in view of the report in the Press that the object of the search was to find a certain official State document which had been lost a few months ago, the Trade Delegation considers it necessary to declare that it knows nothing of any such document, that it has never seen it, and that there never was, and there is not, such a document in the files, archives, or safes of 49, Moorgate."

When the matter was raised in the House of Commons on May 13, the Home Secretary made a very significant admission. He said: "I know that I directed that application should be made to the magistrate for a warrant to search the premises of Arcos Ltd., and that warrant was granted."*

Questioned as to whether the premises of the Trade Delegation had also been raided he lamely replied: "I cannot answer a question as to the exact portion of the building where the Trade Delegation is."†

On the evening of May 13, expert safe-breakers were brought to the premises of the Trade Delegation to break open the safes. The safe-breaking and search continued until the evening of May 16, 1927, when, to quote a press report, "the police paraded in the hall of the Arcos premises and were dismissed. Immediately they left the caretaker locked the iron gates."‡

Meanwhile, before the results of the search were known, the Tory press was loud in its congratulations to the Home Secretary. They believed that this meant the end of relations with the U.S.S.R. Their satisfaction, however, was not shared by that prominent Conservative, Sir Allan Smith (Chairman of the Engineering and Allied Employers National Federation), who declared:

> "It is very regrettable that the police raid on Arcos Limited should have occurred just at this time. It may do good eventually by clearing the air, but it has delayed the placing of orders in this country which will result from the agreement."§‖

The Home Secretary was again questioned on the matter in the House of Commons, May 16, 1927. He declared that from information received he had reason to think "that a certain official document was or had been improperly in the possession of a person employed in the premises occupied by Arcos Limited, at 49, Moorgate." That,

* *Hansard*, 13.v.27, col. 803. † Ibid., col. 800.
‡ *Westminster Gazette*, 17.v.27.
§ Sir Allan was referring to the Agreement with the Midland Bank.
‖ *Manchester Guardian*, 16.v.27.

after consulting the Prime Minister and Foreign Secretary, a warrant had been issued which " authorised the search of the premises occupied by Arcos Limited, and the Trade Delegation, and the search was carried out in strict conformity with the warrant. I am informed that the search only came to an end at 12 o'clock last night. The document in question was not found, but the police have taken possession of certain papers which might bear upon the matter, and the examination of those papers is still proceeding."*

The occupants of the Treasury Bench looked decidedly uncomfortable when a Tory back-bencher, Major MacAndrew, appositely asked: " Have any steps been taken to deal with the person responsible for this document, which has apparently been stolen ? "

Ironical Opposition cheers followed the Home Secretary's reply: " At present I am not in a position to make a statement in regard to that."

In reply to a series of other supplementary questions drawing attention to the gravity of the matter, Sir William Joynson-Hicks promised to make a full statement a few days later.

The Government was now in a dilemma, albeit one of their own creation. The missing document, if it ever existed, had not been found. What could they do ? If they admitted that the search had been fruitless they would have looked ridiculous in the eyes of the country and the world, and the Home Secretary, who had many friends in the Cabinet, might have had to resign. Big men would not have been afraid to acknowledge their mistake or to put the interests of the country and world peace before mere face-saving. But they were not big men. They resolved to make a mountain out of a mole-hill and to use that product of their own creation to justify a diplomatic rupture with the U.S.S.R. On the day following the Home Secretary's answers in the House of Commons, the Soviet Government handed a strong Note to Sir Robert Hodgson in Moscow. After dealing exhaustively with the circumstances of the Raid the Note continued:

> " However, the absolutely unprecedented and unrestrained hostile campaign of hate which culminated in the raid on the premises of the Trade Delegation and which also lately was meeting with growing encouragement by members of the British Government, compels the Soviet Government with all earnestness and frankness demanded by the alarming situation created, to put the question to the British Government whether it desires the further preservation and development of Anglo-Soviet trade relations or whether it intends in the future to hamper them.
>
> For its part the Soviet Government categorically declares that

* *Hansard*, 16.v.27, cols. 915, 916.

the conduct of trade relations is possible only on condition of the strict observance by the British Government of the Trade Agreement and of the guaranteeing to the economic organs of the Union of Soviet Socialist Republics the possibility of uninterrupted, quiet and normal work.

The Soviet Government feels it has the right to demand from the British Government a clear and unequivocal reply from which it may be possible to draw due conclusions. At the same time it reserves the right to present demands for satisfaction for the violation by the British Government of its treaty obligations, for insults suffered, and for material losses caused by the action of the police."

The effects produced in the U.S.S.R. by the Arcos Raid and the Soviet Note of protest were a great surprise to those in this country who thought that the prestige of the Soviet Government at home would be weakened as a consequence. The opposite was the case. The people rallied round their Government more enthusiastically than ever. *Izvestia* was not bragging when it declared:

"While the peoples of the Soviet Union are ready to receive a favourable reply with sincere satisfaction they will face rupture without astonishment or anxiety, at the same time firmly believing in their right and strength. The international situation is not at all such as to warrant Sir Austen Chamberlain's expectation of a broad and sympathetic response in the event of a rupture with the Union of Soviet Socialist Republics."

As already mentioned the Cabinet was in a dilemma. To quote the Diplomatic Correspondent of the *Observer*:

"Students of diplomacy feel some concern that an important issue in foreign policy should be forced upon the Cabinet by the Home Office and the War Office, not by the Foreign Office and to the embarrassment of the Foreign Office. It is commonly assumed that something has now to be sacrificed to the principle of Cabinet solidarity, and the fear is growing that the victim will be the Foreign Office.

The strength of those members of the Cabinet who advocate a break with Russia is the accomplished fact of the raid on the Trade Delegation, which in their view makes a rupture inevitable. Although the issue is not yet settled, and although it is surmised that Sir Austen Chamberlain has not yet given in, one has to be prepared for the possibility of a Government announcement on Tuesday that relations have been broken off, an announcement that would have incalculable effect on British interests in many parts of the world."*

Between May 13, when the Home Secretary first answered questions in the House of Commons respecting the Raid, and May 24, when the Prime Minister declared the Government's decision, most of the Rothermere and other Tory journals were working frantically to inflame public opinion against the Soviet Government and to create an atmosphere which would make it difficult for a weak Government to resist the pressure of its irresponsible elements. In addition it was freely rumoured that the British Government had now resolved to try to organise an international bloc of Powers aiming at isolating the Soviet Union with all the sinister motives that that implied. "On this question the British Government has now definitely assumed the leadership of Europe," wrote the Diplomatic Correspondent of the *Westminster Gazette*. "Other countries are prepared to follow its example."

The Prime Minister's much awaited statement was made to a crowded House on May 24, 1927. Its substance was that:

(*a*) Soviet agents in Great Britain had been endeavouring to obtain by illegal methods secret information respecting the armed forces of the Crown.

(*b*) A highly confidential document was found to be missing and that there was reason to think that it had been conveyed to Soviet House. Hence the search of that building.

(*c*) Documents were found on the persons of two men, employed in the cypher department of the Russian Trade Delegation, proving that they were in communication with the Communist Parties in Great Britain, U.S.A., Mexico, South America, Canada, Australia, New Zealand and South Africa.

(*d*) The Soviet Chargé d'Affaires in London had wired his Government asking it to send information to various organisations in this country and to enable him to support a political campaign in this country against the policy of the British Government in China.

(*e*) The Government of the U.S.S.R. was carrying on propaganda in China against British interests in violation of the terms of the Anglo-Russian Trade Agreement of March 16, 1921.

However, the only evidence advanced was an alleged cablegram, which, to use the words of Mr. Baldwin "is in the possession of His Majesty's Government," from the Russian Foreign Office to the Soviet representative in Pekin.

The Prime Minister concluded that the Government had "decided

* 22.v.27.

that unless the House expresses its disapproval on Thursday, they will terminate the Trade Agreement, require the withdrawal of the Trade Delegation and Soviet Mission from London and recall the British Mission from Moscow. The legitimate use of Arcos is unaffected by these decisions and His Majesty's Government are prepared, whilst terminating the privileges conferred by Articles 4, 5 and 6 of the Trade Agreement, to make all arrangements necessary for ordinary trade facilities between the two countries."

On the following day, the Press Department of the Soviet Embassy issued a categorical reply over the signature of the Chargé d'Affaires. The charges (*a*) and (*b*) were denied. As no evidence had been advanced by Mr. Baldwin there was and could be no detailed reply. As regards (*c*) the reply stated: on being questioned, one employee declared categorically that he never had in his possession a list of secret addresses. As to the documents stated to be found in the possession of another employee, these having been evidently taken by the police out of his pocket, the circumstances under which the search took place made it quite impossible to determine whether they were really taken by the police out of his pockets, or whether the police came into possession of them on some other occasion.

Respecting (*d*) the reply declared: "It can be proved from the copies of all the telegrams kept in the files of the Central Telegraph Office that no such telegraphic correspondence passed *en claire*,* and Mr. Baldwin must have been referring to some alleged cypher telegrams decoded by a department of the British Government. An admission of this character in itself sounds very strange on the lips of the head of a Government which accuses the Soviet Government of meddling with British official documents. But let that pass. I declare categorically that neither I nor anybody else from the staff of the Embassy ever received or sent such telegrams."

Referring to (*e*) the reply averred:

> "The Embassy has had no time to make inquiries with respect to the telegram from the Commissariat for Foreign Affairs to the Soviet representative in Peking dated November 12 last, but the contents of the telegram, as quoted by Mr. Baldwin, bear on their face all the signs of an invention (particularly the construction of the phrases, the terms used, and the references to non-existent bodies)."

It will be noted that the British Government, which set such store by its plighted word (no "scraps of paper" for it), in deciding to sever relations in this way was violating flagrantly the terms of the Anglo-Soviet Trade Agreement to which it had set its solemn signa-

* *I.e.*, not in code.

ture. Article 13 declared: "It is agreed that before taking any action inconsistent with the Agreement the aggrieved party shall give the other party a reasonable opportunity of furnishing an explanation or remedying the default." Russia was not given "a reasonable opportunity of furnishing an explanation or remedying the default" if default there was. On the contrary, she was sentenced and banished without trial.

The Parliamentary Labour Party, when it met next day, had before it the Government's declaration and the Soviet reply. It had no means of knowing where the truth lay, and it very wisely moved the following motion on May 26, 1927:

> "That, having heard the statement of the Prime Minister, this House is of opinion that the termination of the Trade Agreement with Russia and the severance of diplomatic relations would have serious international consequences and close a promising avenue to the restoration of trade and industry, and is, therefore, a policy to which the country ought not to be committed until a Report of a Select Committee, based upon an examination of all relevant documents and a full inquiry into the facts, has been submitted to this House."*

Concluding a powerful speech in support of the motion in which he stressed that the Government by their decision had themselves violated the Trade Agreement, Mr. J. R. Clynes said: "We press for this inquiry, convinced that no good results could accrue to our interests from the application of the Government's decision."†

Sir Austen Chamberlain, the Foreign Secretary, followed for the Government. He refused the Labour Party's motion for the setting up of a Select Committee and then, no doubt unconsciously, he proceeded to justify not only the Labour Party Motion, but also the Soviet Government's right to conduct espionage activities against this country, because he gave to the House a string of information collected by the British Secret Service: alleged instructions sent by the Commissariat for Foreign Affairs to its representatives abroad, etc. The gravamen of Sir Austen's indictment could be summed up thus: "Our Secret Service has been active and successful in obtaining Soviet Government secrets; their Secret Service has endeavoured to do the same *vis-à-vis* us; we are entitled to act in this way, they are not."

The Government's case was riddled by one who had been in an unique position to know the facts, Mr. Lloyd George. He declared:

> "What is the first charge brought by the Prime Minister in his document? It is espionage for the purpose of obtaining informa-

* *Hansard*, 26.v.27, col. 2203. † Ibid., col. 2212.

tion about our Army and Navy. Are we not doing that? If the War Office and the Admiralty and the Air Force are not obtaining by every means every information about what is being done in other countries, they are neglecting the security of this country. Foreign Secretaries know nothing about it. It is not their business, but it is our business to get information. Foreign Governments are getting information about whatever is happening here. As a matter of fact, when the Great War broke out there were no secrets with regard to the machinery of the enemies we fought that we did not know. We knew the number of ships, we knew their guns, we knew their calibre. We knew even their spies and could have laid our hands on them at any moment, and we did so at the right moment when it suited us. These things cannot be done in one country without the Government knowing it. All the same, it is the business of Governments to find out exactly what is being done about armaments in every part of the world. It is their business to do it. If the Soviet Government are doing it they are offending in common with every other Government in friendly relations with us in the world."

Mr. Lloyd George was ably reinforced by Mr. Arthur Ponsonby, who had been in the diplomatic service and had been Under-Secretary of State for Foreign Affairs, February-November, 1924. He said:

"We must really face the fact, when we are getting on our high moral horse, that forgery, theft, lying, bribery and corruption exist in every Foreign Office and every Chancellory throughout the world. The recognised official attitude is to put on a mask of impassable piety, which means that you ignore the whole thing. Of course you must. This weapon is used during war because it is valuable. It is used during so-called peace because peace is used for making preparations for the next war.

I say that I have during my career seen a document which was taken from the archives of a foreign country. I have also travelled with a spy and heard what he had to say. He travelled with me because he wanted to get information from me, and he also wanted to get from me the despatches that I carried. The more friendly he became, the more tightly I had to cling to the despatches. He was on a mission to this country in order to get a newspaper to take up the cause of a particular foreign Government that he was supporting."

Mr. Ponsonby's exposure was too much for Mr. Austen Chamberlain. He accused Mr. Ponsonby of talking nonsense, wrote something on a slip of paper, threw it across to Mr. Ponsonby and then, angry and flushed, he ostentatiously walked out of the Chamber. His actions were an insulting performance, which evoked much comment in the Lobbies.

A little later, Mr. Tom Williams asked blandly "where that £146,000 goes which is spent each year on the Secret Service? We never get to know from Ministers how this money is spent." Needless to say the Treasury Bench was silent. The Rt. Hon. Arthur Henderson, winding up for the Labour Party, pointed out: "In the present instance, with such a proportion of supporters as the Prime Minister has behind him, the Government would have been able to place on the Committee of Inquiry a very considerable majority of their own Members." A remark which evoked unwilling cheers from the Government benches.

Sir William Joynson-Hicks, the Home Secretary, winding up for the Government had, of course, to admit that the State document which was the ostensible object of the search had not been found, but he declared that one of the Soviet employees was known by them to be a Soviet spy, and described him as a "human document."

The House waited! What next! Had this man been arrested? Espionage is a very grave charge! Would he be indicted on that count? To the amazement of the House, the Home Secretary dropped the subject and proceeded to other matters until he was sharply brought back to the subject. To quote Hansard:

> "*Mr. R. Morrison:* I am sure the House has been waiting to hear what the right hon. Gentleman proposes to do with the human document.
>
> *Sir W. Johnson-Hicks:* Will the hon. Member leave the human document to me? I do not think it desirable that I should announce what will be done. The conduct of the Government has not yet been approved by the House of Commons. The despatch has not yet been sent to the Chargé d'Affaires which will be sent to him to-morrow if the House passes the Amendment, as I hope it will. After that, the Home Secretary will be in a position to decide what course he intends to take in the other matter."

After the Home Secretary's speech the vote was taken and the Labour Motion was defeated by 367 to 118.

II. The Soviet Chargé d'Affaires requested to leave. Charges of espionage. Demonstrations of friendship at Victoria Station

On the following day, a Foreign Office Note (dated May 26, 1927) was delivered to the Soviet Chargé d'Affaires, declaring that the

British Government regarded itself as free from the terms of the Trade Agreement; that "the existing relations between the two Governments are suspended"; but that the Government "will raise no objection to the continuance of the legitimate commercial operations of Arcos Limited, in the same conditions as those applicable to other trading organisations in this country."

Finally, the Note requested the Chargé d'Affaires and his staff to withdraw "from this country within the course of the next ten days," and informed him that the British Mission had been instructed to leave the U.S.S.R.

On the afternoon of the day (May 27, 1927) on which this Note was delivered, an event took place which had probably no parallel in British Diplomatic history. The Chargé d'Affaires and the principal members of his staff were entertained to lunch in one of the private dining rooms of the House of Commons by leading members of the Labour Party and the Trades Union Congress. The room, which had seating accommodation for about 50, was uncomfortably packed. No attempt was made either to advertise the lunch or to keep it secret. The arrangements were made in the ordinary way. However, about half an hour before the appointed time several of the convenors were approached from the Tory side and asked to cancel the lunch, and there were even hints at unpleasant consequences if they persisted in keeping to the arrangements.

The suggestions were rejected and the threats ignored. It was not a question of braggadocio. The convenors considered that they were justified in demonstrating to the world that at least a considerable section of public opinion in this country was hostile to the Government's decision. The lunch was duly held and passed off without incident. The Tory press was furious at this "effrontery" and finally the matter was raised on the floor of the House, but the Speaker replied that it was not the practice to enquire "as to the guests members propose to entertain." We would add that there was no effrontery, calculated or otherwise. The hosts were emphatic that they had done nothing improper.

Opposition members, apart from being opposed to the Government's policy, were dissatisfied with the evasive replies from the Treasury bench on May 26, and they raised these matters by questions in the course of the following week. The Government, it will be remembered, claimed that it knew the contents of private despatches which had passed between the Soviet Foreign Office and its Embassy in China. On this subject the following dialogue is illuminating:

> "*Lieut.-Commander Kenworthy:* May I ask, then, how the documents that passed between Moscow and Peking were obtained

—on territory not under the jurisdiction of His Majesty's Government ?

Sir A. Chamberlain: I cannot prevent the hon. and gallant Member from asking, but I must, respectfully, decline to reply.

Lieut.-Commander Kenworthy: Are we to understand, then, that that part of the Trade Agreement, which referred to mutual abstention from propaganda and interference in neutral territories, has been broken by His Majesty's Government ?

Sir A. Chamberlain: No, Sir, the hon. and gallant Member is not entitled to understand that, which is absolutely contrary to the facts.

Lieut.-Commander Kenworthy: If that be the case, how is it possible for communications passing between Russia and another country to come into the hands of the right hon. Gentleman without such interference ?

Sir A. Chamberlain: That is a question which I have respectfully declined to answer, and I again decline, on grounds of public interest.

Mr. Thurtle: Is it not a fact that these documents to which reference is made were obtained by espionage on the part of the British Government ? "*

No answer was returned to the last question. It is easy to divine why.

Mr. Thurtle asked the Financial Secretary to the Treasury if any record is kept of the amount of the Secret Service Vote which is expended abroad and the amount which is spent at home ; and, if so, will he state how much of last year's Vote was expended at home and how much abroad during the last financial year ? Mr. McNeill replied: "It is not in the public interest to give details of this expenditure."†

It will be recalled that on May 26, the Home Secretary declared that he was not then in a position to state what would be done in the case of the "human document"—the subject was raised on June 2, 1927, when the following dialogue took place:

"*Lieut.-Commander Kenworthy:* May I ask the right hon. Gentleman why this alleged spy was not arrested and proceeded against ?

Sir W. Joynson-Hicks: The hon. and gallant Gentleman must know that in the history of our country it has not always been found desirable either to arrest spies or proceed against them at any particular moment."‡

* *Hansard,* 30.v.27, cols. 17, 18. † Ibid., col. 22. ‡ Ibid., 2.vi.27, col. 523.

For some reason which was never explained, the "human document," who was arraigned in the House of Commons on one of the most serious charges known to the criminal code, was allowed to leave these shores without let or hindrance.

These were not the only questions left unanswered. It will be recollected that on May 16 the Government had been asked by one of its own supporters whether any action had been taken against the British Government official responsible for the original "document," and the Home Secretary replied that he was not then in a position to answer. That question was not subsequently answered and still remains unanswered.

It may be asked how one can explain the zigzag policy of the British Government towards the U.S.S.R. from the end of 1924 till May, 1927, and why did Whitehall finally sever relations with the Kremlin ? The series of episodes recorded in this and the previous chapter seem to supply the answer.

Within the Cabinet there was a section determined to effect a diplomatic rupture whatever the consequences. There was another section siding with Sir Austen Chamberlain, which desired to maintain, perhaps even to improve, relations with the U.S.S.R. Up to the date of the Arcos Raid neither side had won. The Birkenhead-Churchill-Joynson-Hicks section had had sufficient influence to prevent an Anglo-Soviet round table conference being held ; on the other hand, the Chamberlain-Balfour section had been sufficiently strong to prevent a rupture, but not powerful enough to force the Cabinet to accept one of the many Soviet offers to negotiate a settlement of outstanding issues. In our judgment, had the Foreign Secretary acted more courageously the Government would have met Soviet representatives in conference, an agreement would have been reached and a rupture prevented.

Finally, on the balance of probabilities, Sir Austen Chamberlain had to bow or resign. On this matter Mr. Lloyd George had little doubt. Speaking in the debate, May 26, 1927, he said: "I think the Foreign Secretary has had his hands forced in regard to this breach of relations. I think that is quite evident. If I may say so, I do not think the Foreign Secretary spoke with the same fervour to-day as he did when he was defending the policy of Locarno. In my judgment, I do not think the Foreign Secretary came to the conclusion before the Home Secretary acted that the time had arrived to have a rupture with Soviet Russia. I think that is rather important, and, if I may say so, I think he was right, and I do not think the time was well chosen."

As our readers are aware, the most serious charge preferred against the Soviet representatives was that of espionage. It is piquant to recall the comments of two Tory papers on this point.

The *Evening Standard*, in its issue of May 28, 1927, stated:

> "The French take the rather cynical view that no Government in fact lives up to Sir Austen's ideals, and that, *if the conduct of the Bolshevik agents was a valid reason for breaking off diplomatic relations, there would be many such ruptures.*" (Our italics).

The *Sunday Express* of May 29, 1927, in a leading article, stated:

> "The rupture is now defended on the ground that there has been a discovery of a system of espionage practised by the Russians. But espionage has been practised by civilised and uncivilised nations from time immemorial. All Governments practise it. Espionage has never been used as a pretext for breaking off relations."

The fact, of course, is that espionage has been and is practised by all Governments, and is not made a pretext for severing diplomatic relations. Those proved guilty of espionage could have been dealt with by the Law Courts. Lord Parmoor (a very distinguished lawyer), speaking on this point in the House of Lords on May 31, 1927, said: "If, however, incriminating documents had been found the Courts were open to the ordinary course of criminal procedure, and anyone implicated would have been liable both to punishment and deportation."*

No sooner had the Tory press and the more irresponsible Ministers achieved their object than doubts began to arise in their minds as to the effects it would have internationally and on the future course of Anglo-Soviet relations.

On the day following the Commons debate, the Prime Minister declared:

> "I wish, therefore, to state emphatically that our rupture of diplomatic relations does not in any way mean or imply war against Russia. The utmost it appears to mean is that we do not intend to have any further political dealings with Moscow. But we are wholly in favour of the pursuit of legitimate trade between the two countries."†

And journals which up to then had argued as though diplomatic relations with the Soviets were undesirable and unnecessary at once

* House of Lords Debates, 31.v.27., p. 681.

† *Times*, 28.v.27.

began to talk of re-establishing them on a new basis. Thus the *Times* declared:

> "No one in this country in any party dreams of relegating the fact of Russia to oblivion. Since the Revolution a very serious attempt has been made to maintain relations with Russia through the observance of diplomatic relations with the Soviet Government. Those relations have been proved to be a sham because the Soviet Government has persistently defied their implications. No relations with any country can be based upon make-believe. That phase is over, and the next task is to build a Russian policy upon sounder and more permanent foundations."*

Next day the *Daily Telegraph* supplemented:

> "It is not by truckling to the Bolshevik temperament that one gains its respect, and when official relations are restored it will have to be on quite new terms with respect to the Trade Delegation, and on the understanding that British diplomatic patience will not be so long-suffering of broken pledges as it has been in the last six years."

As for Mr. Lloyd George, second thoughts confirmed his opinion of the seriousness of the Government's action and its immediate cause. Speaking at a Liberal demonstration, May 27, 1927, he declared:

> "To bring about a diplomatic rupture with one of the greatest powers in the world is not a thing to throw caps about. It is a thing to bend knees about. Why have they quarrelled? Quite frankly, they never intended it. They just glided into it and tumbled into it. It was an affair of the police. The Ministerial head of the police of this country was made the director of foreign policy, and, quite frankly, he is not up to it. This is the most serious decision we have taken since August, 1914, and yet the Cabinet was never called together to decide whether the step should be taken. But the rupture with 150 millions of the most formidable people on earth has been decided upon."†

The ex-Prime Minister's opinion as to the immediate cause of the rupture was also shared by another publicist with good sources of information, Mr. J. L. Garvin. He wrote:

> "The raid by itself was a fiasco as regards the discovery of new and decisive evidence. But this being so, Parliamentary

* *Times*, 27.v.27. † *Manchester Guardian*, 28.v.27.

considerations forced the total breach in order to defend the raid."*

Mr. Garvin was convinced that the Government had not thought out the implications of its policy. He further declared:

> "Do we expect the Anglo-Russian question to remain simply in the air? And for how long? Have we no conception of what are to be the ultimate relations between the British and Russian peoples? And have we no considered view about the standing and irremovable problem of Britain, Russia and the world as affecting the prospects of the League, disarmament and peace? Who can see in Ministerial declarations a shadow of significant thought on any single one of these searching questions?
>
> We doubt whether the 'anti-Reds' know the extent and meaning of their own success. The last bang has burst the drum they have beaten so long and so loudly. In other terms, Arcos was their cake and they have eaten it."

Mr. Garvin, like many others, bemoaned the fact that the severance of diplomatic relations meant the destruction of the agreement with the Midland Bank. He continued:

> "As it is, we have over a million unemployed in the middle of the Conservative Government's third year of office. And we have thrown away £10,000,000 worth of orders for British manufacture—orders that in our opinion would have been actually placed had a more discriminating policy been tried. We should like to have seen some real effort to keep those orders and to reduce our unemployed. We think this might have been done. We are sure it ought to have been attempted."†

We would add that in the absence of normal relations only a Government guarantee would have saved the agreement with the Midland Bank, and that was not forthcoming.

Not unnaturally the question at once arose as to the future of Soviet contracts already entered into. The Soviet Trade Delegation had no intention of venting their resentment at the action of the Government on British traders.

The Soviet Chargé d'Affaires, on May 30, 1927, informed the Foreign Office that the Soviets were anxious to fulfil all the contracts which had been entered into and to settle all outstanding accounts, and asked whether sufficient staff would be permitted to remain here for that purpose. The Note concluded:

> "In the event of a refusal to issue such permission orders will

* *Observer*, 29.v.27. † Ibid.

be given for the immediate liquidation of all the Soviet trading institutions and British companies in which the money of Soviet citizens and organisations is invested, and the responsibility for all damages which may arise for Soviet institutions and citizens as well as British citizens as a result of such a speedy liquidation will rest with the British Government."

Meanwhile the British Note had been communicated to the Kremlin and the reply of the latter was handed to the British Chargé d'Affaires in Moscow, May 28, 1927. After pointing out that the raid on Arcos had been without result, the Note protested:

> "The Soviet Government declares that the British Government had no legal ground either for the first violation of the Trade Agreement of 1921, namely, the police raid on extra-territorial premises of the Soviet official agents, or the second violation, namely, the terminating of this agreement without six months' notice, as provided by the agreement."

Turning to the reasons for the British Government's decisions, the Note went on:

> "It is evident to the whole world that the fundamental cause of the rupture is the defeat of the Conservative Government's policy in China, and an attempt to mask this defeat by a diversion directed against the Soviet Union, while the direct reason is the British Government's desire to divert public opinion from the failure of the absurd police raid on the Arcos and Trade Delegation premises, and to save the British Home Secretary from the scandalous position in which he found himself owing to this raid."

The Note concluded in optimistic terms:

> "At the same time, it (the Soviet Government) firmly believes that the time is near when the British people will find ways and means for the unhampered realisation of their aspirations for peace and the establishment of normal friendly relations with the peoples of the Soviet Union."

Mr. Baldwin had declared that the Government would permit trade between the two countries to continue. The question at once arose "how ?" The Soviets could neither sell nor buy here without a staff of technical and commercial experts. The Government, now somewhat sobered, seemed anxious to expedite an acceptable agreement on this question. The Home Secretary informed the House of Commons, June 2, 1927, that:

> "The Government have no desire to place any difficulties in

the way of trade between Russia and this country, and Russians desiring to come here for the purpose of *bona fide* trade will have the same facilities accorded to them as the nationals of any other foreign Power. The same machinery with regard to visas and all other matters will apply as heretofore with only this exception, that there will not in future be a British Passport Control Officer within Soviet Russia."

In reply to a further question he said:

> "The Home Office has been in constant communication with the Foreign Office and the Passport Department, and I hope very shortly to be able to announce the complete arrangements which will be necessary to enable the passage of Russian Nationals to this country for that purpose."*

The greater part of the Soviet staff left London by boat on June 2; but the Chargé d'Affaires and his wife as well as M. and Mme. Maisky left Victoria Station at 11 a.m. on June 3, 1927. A huge crowd of friends and sympathisers, among them Mr. Arthur Henderson, Mr. Walter Citrine, Mr. Ben Tillett, Mr. George Lansbury, etc., etc., were gathered on the platform, many of the women laden with bouquets. The appearance of the Russians at the barrier was the signal for a great outburst of cheering and the singing of the "International." As the crowd pressed around the departing Russians, bouquets were showered on the Soviet women. Again and again the party had to pose for the photographers and ever louder, the strains of the "International" rang throughout the station, intermingled with cheers for the Soviet Republic. As the party reached their carriage, the policemen, in order to keep a gangway for them, had to link arms to keep back the surging, cheering throng. The guard's whistle sounded, the doors were closed and the train slowly moved out of the station, the big crowd cheering and singing, and the Russians bowing and waving. Was this to be the last? Suddenly a voice shouted: "You'll soon be back." The Russians were still within earshot. They heard, smiled and waved back. The whole crowd suddenly seemed to realise that these were the words for which they had been waiting. They shouted them again and again until the waving figures at the windows were lost to sight. "They" (the Russians), wrote the *Morning Post,* "were accorded a send-off by their British Labour friends such as would have been worthy of illustrious and heroic allies."

The final act in this drama was played two hours later at Dover. The *Kent Evening Echo* recorded that the acting Chargé d'Affaires

* *Daily Telegraph*, 3.vi.27.

with his wife and two children, together with M. and Mme. Maisky, Counsellor to the Embassy, merely stepped off the train from Victoria at the Marine Station, exchanged farewell greetings with Mr. W. P. Coates, the Secretary to the Anglo-Russian Parliamentary Committee, who had travelled with them on the train, the steamer's whistle was blown, and they had left the country.

The Chargé d'Affaires told a *Kent Evening Echo* representative that he had nothing to communicate for publication, but Mr. Coates expressed the firm opinion that the rupture was of a temporary nature, and that there would be an early resumption of relations. Any other course, he said, was impossible.*

The diplomatic wires between the British Empire and the U.S.S.R., covering a fourth and a sixth of the world's surface respectively, were severed. The Die-Hards had achieved their aims. What next? The Soviet representatives left on Friday morning. Saturday is a favourite day for Tory fêtes and speechmaking. Surely this particular Saturday would be devoted to party " Mafeking." Yet *mirabile dictu* there was nothing of the kind. On the contrary, Lord Birkenhead, speaking at Leicester on Saturday, June 4, 1927, to the amazement of the country declared:

> " Some of our opponents have said that it is not possible that two communities so great in numbers and in geographical extent as Russia and Great Britain can remain permanently estranged—permanently without diplomatic representation, the one at the Court of the other. We never made that claim. If for a reasonable period of time the present Russian Government or any Government that may succeed it, shows that it has learned the elementary decency of international conduct, there is no reason at all why the position should not be reconsidered. There is nobody in our party who thinks it conceivable or helpful to the tangled interests of a war-worn world that antagonism of a semi-permanent character should exist between two great populations."†

Well might the *Daily News* comment: " This new note of melancholy regret tinged with hope is the chastening of experience. Lord Birkenhead may not be the happiest official choice for even a timid gesture of conciliation ; but it will be welcomed not less sincerely by men of good-will in all parties who have bent their energies to healing the wounds of a disorganised and disrupted Continent."‡

It only remains to add that after the respective departures of the British Mission from Moscow and the Soviet Mission from London, Norway took charge of British interests in the Soviet capital and Germany took charge of Soviet interests in Britain.

* 3.vi.27. † *Manchester Guardian*, 6.vi.27. ‡ 6.vi.27.

CHAPTER XII

THE AFTERMATH OF THE DIPLOMATIC RUPTURE (1927-1928)

I. "No Russian Oil" campaign. Criticism of the severance of relations

Before proceeding further we want to deal here with one of the most ludicrous and futile press stunts conducted by a British newspaper against the U.S.S.R., the *Daily Mail's* "No Russian Oil Sold Here" campaign.

In May, 1927, that journal started a press attack on the sale of Russian oil in Great Britain. It appealed to all firms using oil to pledge themselves not to purchase Soviet oil and it also strongly urged garages to boycott Soviet oil and to display posters:

DAILY MAIL
NO
SOVIET PETROL
SOLD HERE.

Day after day the *Daily Mail* appealed in flamboyant terms to all and sundry to disdain the use of Russian oil and on October 31, 1927, it triumphantly announced that British firms, etc., using in all petrol to the amount of 51,651,000 gallons per annum, had pledged themselves not to "use petrol of Soviet origin." Surely this was a tremendous achievement for six months of campaigning! Lord Rothermere's triumph was short-lived. On the following day in a letter signed by W. P. Coates in the *Daily Herald* it was pointed out that:

> "The *Daily Mail,* after months of agitation, boasts that 'Government departments, municipal authorities, great business firms and others,' whose sum total annual consumption of petrol amounts to '51,651,000 gallons,' have pledged themselves not to buy 'petrol of Soviet origin.'
>
> At first sight the figures look impressive, but, last year, we, as a nation, imported 677,000,000 gallons of petrol, and the *Financial News* of July 8 last, in a special article, estimated that the 'consumption of petrol in Great Britain, will increase to about 800,000,000 gallons' for 1927.
>
> As 51,651,000 is less than $6\frac{1}{2}$ per cent. of 800,000,000, the *Daily Mail* has unwittingly advertised the utter failure of its boycott campaign."

The *Daily Mail* continued its agitation, but henceforth dropped all reference as to the quantity of oil consumed by the firms, etc., who had agreed to boycott Soviet petrol. The Rothermere organ had already received a shock some two months earlier, when it became known that the sale of Russian oil in this country had risen considerably. The *Financial News* editorially stated: "According to its own published statements the R.O.P.'s* sales have shown a considerable increase since last year; recent press attacks on the marketing of Russian oil in this country have drawn public attention to the commodity, and the R.O.P. have been astute enough to utilise this notoriety as the jumping-off ground for an extensive publicity campaign."†

The late Mr. E. F. Wise (Economic Adviser to the Russian Co-operative organisations), in a statement to the press, said:

> "The quantity of Russian spirit sold direct in Great Britain by the Russian organisations was approximately fifty per cent. higher in the twelve months ending October, 1927, than in the previous twelve months. A temporary set-back immediately after the rupture in June has been succeeded by increased sales in Britain, and in each case they exceeded the corresponding figures of previous years."‡

Gradually the *Daily Mail* posters disappeared from the garages throughout the country and the space given to the agitation in the columns of that journal became smaller and only intermittent, until by July, 1928, the agitation had practically ceased.

We do not pretend to know what took place in the editorial offices of Northcliffe House, but perhaps the following figures published by the Board of Trade in July, 1928, of British imports of oil from the U.S.S.R. for the first halves of the corresponding years had given them to think furiously:

LAMP OIL

	Gallons
1926	10,282,000
1927	19,339,000
1928	25,386,000

MOTOR SPIRIT

1926	12,998,000
1927	17,876,000
1928	18,015,000

* Messrs. Russian Oil Products Ltd.

† 26.viii.27.

‡ *Evening Standard*, 1.xii.27.

LUBRICATING OIL

1926	1,158,000
1927	3,443,000
1928	3,772,000

Other figures given for the first halves of 1927 and 1928 were:

GAS OIL

	Gallons
1927	2,466,000
1928	4,218,000

Moreover, by this date circumstantial rumours had appeared in the press that negotiations were afoot to settle outstanding differences between the Soviet Oil Syndicate and the Oil Combines. The negotiations were not immediately successful but the sales of Soviet oil in this country continued to rise. In 1928 the total import of various descriptions of Soviet petrol was 32,000,000 gallons more than in 1927. The increase was due to several factors, but undoubtedly one was the free advertisement given to Soviet petrol by the *Daily Mail.* The Soviet official who was in charge of the great oil producing area in Baku, said that he would have been willing to pay for the *Daily Mail's* agitation at advertisement rates. One factor, among others, which the Rothermere journal apparently left out of account was the very large number of Trade Unionists—to whom the *Daily Mail* was anathema—engaged in road transport. Very many of these drivers to our personal knowledge not only did not boycott Soviet petrol, but boycotted the garages which displayed the *Daily Mail* posters. The boycotters were boycotted and the *Daily Mail* posters disappeared.

On February 28, 1929, the following Reuter message was cabled from Moscow:

> "The signature of an agreement between the Anglo-American Oil Combine and the Russian Oil Products is announced here to-day.
>
> The agreement will last for three years. The Russian Oil Products will be given an equal share of the British market with other companies.
>
> The agreement also provides for the supply of large quantities of Soviet kerosene, crude oil, and petrol to the companies entering the combine, which is led by the Royal Dutch Shell Group.
>
> The newspapers, commenting upon the agreement, point out that it marks the end of the bitter campaign against Russian oil which has been conducted for a number of years.

They state that the agreement does not provide for any compensation to the owners of Russian oilfields which were confiscated by the Soviet Government."*

This was published in the British press next day and at the same time the Oil Combines announced that the price of petrol would be raised forthwith by 2¼d. per gallon.

Without a single dissenting voice the leading Conservative dailies admitted that the competition of Soviet oil had kept prices down in this country:

"A message from Moscow, which we published yesterday, reported that an agreement had been signed between the 'Anglo-American Combine' and the Russian Oil Products. The message is vague in character, and the companies chiefly concerned are silent on the matter. That an agreement of some sort has been arrived at is indicated by the fact that the price of petrol was advanced by 2¼d. per gallon, *for there can be little doubt that it would have been raised sooner but for Russian competition.*"† (Our italics).

"Consumers expressed the conviction yesterday that the increase in price could not have taken place without some sort of undertaking on the part of the Russian interests *not to undercut prices in the future.*"‡ (Our italics).

"The result of the agreement has been to put the entire petrol supply of this country into the hands of one group, as formerly R.O.P., *and the Power Petrol Company were the only opposition to the combine consisting of the 'Big Three'—The Anglo-American Oil Company, Shell-Mex Ltd., and B.P.*"§ (Our italics).

"*The inclusion of Russian petrol in the new charges has caused grave concern amongst petrol users.* Now that the Russian product has come more or less into line with supplies of the other concerns, *fear is expressed that further increases may be made.*"|| (Our italics).

The *Daily Mail* made no comments on the benefits which R.O.P. competition had conferred on British motorists, due no doubt to the fact that the proprietors of that journal considered they had done quite sufficient to advertise gratis Russian petrol during the previous twenty months. So much for this agitation which was a grotesque failure.

* *Morning Post*, 1.iii.29.
† *Financial News*, 2.iii.29.
‡ *Times*, 2.iii.29.
§ *Morning Post*, 2.iii.29.
|| *Daily Telegraph*, 2.iii.29.

The diplomatic wires had been cut between London and Moscow. What next ? Did the Government sit down and think out a clear-cut policy ? Our record of the course of events will supply the answer. Abroad the rupture had a disturbing effect, especially as it was generally held that Great Britain would not have severed diplomatic relations on what were universally regarded as very trivial grounds, unless she intended to follow that up with some far-reaching action. The disclaimers of Lord Birkenhead and the Prime Minister were not taken seriously.

Mr. H. Wilson Harris aptly related:

> " In the last ten days or so I happen to have been meeting a number of foreigners of different nationalities, and every one of them, with hardly an exception, has had waiting on his lips a question about British relations with Russia. What everyone wanted to know was what lay behind the breach of relations. What was it leading to ? What policy was it a part of ? How was it going to affect other nations ? Was a general offensive against Russia in contemplation ? "*

Mr. Wilson Harris replied to his interlocutors that, in his judgment, the Government had blundered into the matter and would not go beyond what had been done but he failed completely to convince them.

The working class Movement and prominent Liberals continued to denounce the action of the Government. The General Council of the T.U.C., in a detailed reply to the Government's case, stated:

> " The Government seeks to justify this drastic step by documents published in its White Paper. The secret document stated to have been stolen and which furnished the pretext for the raid on Arcos, Ltd., has not been discovered, nor is anything revealed in the White Paper which in the minds of reasonable men can warrant the extreme steps taken.
>
> The General Council believes it imperative that agreements freely entered into between nations should be observed, both in the letter and in the spirit, and it considers that any complaints which the British Government may have had against the Russian Trade Delegation or the Russian Embassy, could properly have been dealt with under Clause 13 of the Trade Agreement of March, 1921, which declares: ' It is agreed that before taking any action inconsistent with the Agreement, the aggrieved party shall give the other party a reasonable opportunity of furnishing an explanation or remedying the default."†

The statement concluded: " The General Council expresses the hope

* *Daily News*, 7.vi.27. † *Daily Herald*, 11.vi.27.

that Russia will rise superior to retaliatory desires, and will, by the conduct of her international relationships, inspire the confidence of the people of the world and play her full part in the establishment of peace, security and progress amongst the nations."

At the Co-operative Congress at Cheltenham, June 8, 1927, the 2,000 delegates, with a mighty " Aye," passed unanimously the following resolution:

> " That this Congress renews its greetings of friendship to Russian Co-operators and urges all sections of the Co-operative Movement to maintain and develop trading relations with the Russian Co-operative Movement, and to work for the full renewal of peaceable relations with that country."*

Another earnest of the sentiments of the Congress towards the Soviet Union and the British Government's policy towards that country was the prolonged outburst of cheers with which the Soviet Co-operative delegate was greeted when he was called on to deliver his fraternal address.

As regards the Liberal leaders—Sir Herbert Samuel, speaking at Edinburgh, referring to the Anglo-Soviet diplomatic rupture, said:

> " Apparently, the more hot-headed members of the Cabinet had overborne the more sober judgment of Sir Austen Chamberlain, who, in the matter of the Locarno Treaty had rendered great service to the peace of the world, and won confidence in a large degree. The same could not be said of Mr. Churchill, Lord Birkenhead and Sir William Joynson-Hicks."†

Mr. Lloyd George was more trenchant. At Perth, June 19, 1927, he declared:

> " When you are having a rupture with a country which has the second most powerful army in the world and a population of one hundred and forty millions, a people who can be terrible in war, you take some time to think it over, surely ? Will you believe it that the decision which precipitated the rupture with Russia—the breaking into Arcos—was never a subject of Cabinet decision at all ? The Cabinet was never consulted as to the preliminary steps which committed the British Empire to be the only civilised country in Europe which has broken with Russia."‡

Opposition to what the Government had done was not confined to politicians. The " National Council for the Prevention of War "

* *Daily Herald*, 9.vi.27. † *Daily Chronicle*, 18.vi.27.
‡ *Manchester Guardian*, 20.vi.27.

issued a statement over the names of distinguished economists, educationalists, men of letters, etc., declaring:

> "The severance of diplomatic relations with Russia is a grave check in the improvement of our international relations. Whatever may be the merits of the case which has been advanced against certain Soviet officials the obvious fact remains that our relations with Russia have grown seriously worse.
>
> So long as this break continues, satisfactory economic and political relations are impossible. Peace is in danger. We ask the Government to seize the earliest possible moment for negotiation and discussion, so that there may begin a new and better chapter in Anglo-Russian relations."*

From the Cabinet ranks dissentient voices emerged. Sir William Joynson-Hicks was bent on further trouble. Speaking, June 30, 1927, at the Constitutional Club, according to the *Times* (July 1) report, he declared:

> "The Government has been asked to get rid of Communism altogether. That was not quite so easy, but he thought that the time was approaching when many of the nations of the world would come to the conclusion that Communism in its extreme form was an enemy of mankind.
>
> He was not sure but that all nations in the world in the near future would have to combine to stamp out the form of belief and propaganda which was anti-Socialist, anti-civilisation, and anti-religious."

Sir William was probably well aware that this would be interpreted abroad as a *ballon d'essai* for a world diplomatic combination and subsequently for a world war against the U.S.S.R.

On the other hand, a few days later, Sir Austen Chamberlain, fresh back from Geneva, informed the House of Commons that although he had explained to the representatives of the Powers there his Government's reasons for severing diplomatic relations "no proposals were made by anyone for a joint conference with Russia or for any joint action in regard to Russia." In reply to the further question, "Did he take this opportunity of disabusing the minds of those other nations of the idea that we were attempting to form any sort of bloc against Russia?" he answered: "I did not find it necessary to use the opportunity to disabuse their minds of that impression because they did not entertain it."

Lord Birkenhead repeated in effect what he had averred on another occasion. Speaking at Shooters Hill, July 7, 1927, he announced:

* Ibid., 14.vi.27.

"We are not so foolish, however, as to declare a perpetual edict of hostility against any people in the world. . . . The whole hope of Western civilisation was to be found in a general readiness to let the dead past bury its dead."*

Which of the three speakers was expounding Cabinet policy or were the views held by the different members of that body, in so far as they were conflicting, capable of being fused into a definite policy? That question was never answered and during the Government's tenure of office they never made a serious attempt to come to terms with the U.S.S.R.

There was no doubt as to what people in Russia were thinking. The special correspondent of the *Daily Express*, Mr. H. J. Greenwall, after many conversations in Moscow, cabled:

> "Russian Government officials are convinced that Great Britain is not only moving her pieces on the international chess-board, but that the British Conservative Party is plotting and planning for Russia's downfall—not the Communist downfall, but Russia's downfall. If Anglo-Russian relations are to be improved and lifted out of the present *impasse* then a little plain speaking is necessary, because—realising fully the seriousness of the statement—I say that if no attempt is made to find a way out England and Russia will drift and drift until one day they will find themselves at war. Two things which in my opinion would remove all shadow of danger of a catastrophe are: (1) A resumption of trading relations between Great Britain and Russia, and (2) a definite statement by the British Government on its Russian policy."†

Mr. Greenwall no doubt found it impossible to deduce from Ministerial utterances at that time what British policy was.

Our Government, it will be recalled, contended that the Soviet Government must be held responsible for the activities of the Third International because several prominent members of the Russian Communist party were delegates to the former body. Yet strange to relate the British Conservative Government would not admit that the same logic applied to them. On July 15, 1927, a Tory rally was held in the Albert Hall to celebrate the Anglo-Soviet diplomatic rupture and according to the *Times* report the speakers included not only prominent Conservatives but also Maitre T. Aubert, President of the Entente against the Third International.‡

One can imagine with what indignation any Tory Prime Minister would reject the accusation that his Government must accept

* *Daily Telegraph*, 8.vii.27. † *Daily Express*, 9.vii.27.

‡See above, pp. 60, 306, 334.

responsibility for the utterances of the "Entente against the Third International."

Mr. Winston Churchill was apparently determined to confuse further the public mind at home and abroad as regards the Government's future Russian policy. Speaking in Devon, July 24, 1927, he exclaimed: "We have proclaimed them (the Soviet representatives) treacherous, incorrigible, and unfit for civilised intercourse."*

The mildest deduction one could draw from this essay in Billingsgate was that the Government had decided on "a permanent edict." It is impossible to reconcile the utterances of Birkenhead and Churchill, yet both claimed to be speaking for the Government! Four days later, in the course of a statement in the House of Commons, Sir Austen Chamberlain said:

> "There is no surer way to strengthen the Soviet Government and to rally the Russian people behind it than to take any action or to give countenance to any action which seems to the Russian people to threaten their national unity."†

The *Daily News* special correspondent present commented: "One had to rub one's eyes to make sure that the speaker of this admirable Liberal sentiment—delivered in tones of heart-deep conviction—was Sir Austen Chamberlain. But odder still—as Mr. Oswald Mosley pointed out—was the spectacle of Mr. Churchill warmly cheering the Foreign Secretary."

In reply to a question by Mr. R. C. Wallhead, M.P., as to whether the door was barred to an application from the Russian side, the Foreign Secretary replied:

> "Certainly not. If any application should come from their side I have no doubt they will state the conditions under which it is made, and we shall be prepared to discuss it. But there must be such a change of mind on the part of the Soviet that, if it is admitted, it will conform to ordinary diplomatic usages."

II. The Soviets declare themselves willing to open negotiations. Lord Birkenhead visits Berlin. The Soviet-Afghan treaty

After this speech by the Foreign Secretary, rumours appeared in the foreign press that tentative proposals had been put forward by London for a renewal of Anglo-Soviet relations. Both Sir Austen's speech and these rumours were brought to M. Chicherin's attention in Moscow, and on August 5, 1927, he commented in frank but conciliatory terms:

> "It should not be forgotten that the rupture of diplomatic relations and the Trade Agreement happened on the initiative

* *Manchester Guardian*, 25.vii.27. † *Daily News*, 29.vii.27.

of the British Government. I must declare that hitherto neither any official nor semi-official proposals about renewal of relations with the British Government have been received from anyone. It is evident that if the British Government did make an actual proposal for the renewal of diplomatic relations the Soviet Government would be willing at any moment to begin corresponding negotiations, insisting at the same time on guarantees for the future that no such inadmissible acts as the raid on Arcos, etc., should ever take place."*

The Soviet offer " to begin corresponding negotiations " which was obviously the only way to adjust existing differences and arrive at a settlement was ignored. Parliament was at this time in recess and the Ministers could not be questioned on the matter in the House.

Our Government, it will be recalled, had promised to grant every facility for trade, yet an announcement appeared in the press, August 23, 1927, that it had been decided to expel two of the directors of R.O.P., Ltd., without preferring any charges against them. The firm appealed against the expulsion order and at the same time declared that these directors had in no way violated their pledge to abstain from interference in the internal affairs of this country. The Home Office did not deny this claim, but it refused to cancel the expulsion order. The decision was hailed in those quarters which were opposed to all trading with the U.S.S.R. ; on the other hand, an English expert in trade and economics remarked to the *Daily Herald*:

> " Although the Home Office has been at considerable pains to emphasise that this latest blow at Russian trade in this country is not directed at the Russian Oil Products Company as such, it is significant that it comes at a time when R.O.P. petrol sales are soaring."†

The *Daily Mail* now made a discovery and had the temerity to indulge in a baseless prophecy. It announced editorially that the Soviets were " attempting to build up a huge air fleet," but it sought to console its readers and to deceive itself with the reflection that " it is no doubt easy enough to buy good aeroplanes. To keep them in thorough fighting order demands first-class fitters and mechanics. It is on this side that the Soviet forces are likely to be weak."‡

Yet less than ten years later many competent foreign air-experts affirmed that the U.S.S.R. had one of the most formidable air fleets in the world, built in its own factories by its own workers and maintained in order by its own mechanics.

* *Manchester Guardian*, 6.viii.27. † 24.viii.27.
‡ 1.ix.28.

Even a capable American business man, Mr. Irving T. Bush (to whom we owe Bush House in the Strand, London), after several visits to the U.S.S.R. summed up the future prospects of that country thus:

> " Russia had all the potential possibilities of the United States one hundred years ago. Great natural resources were there, largely undeveloped, as was the case with America. It needed the money and the brains of the world to help to develop American resources.
>
> We secured the help we needed by making money and brains feel safe under our laws. Russia can get similar help in the same way. Without the world's confidence Russia will not develop. It will stand an outcast among nations, exactly as an individual without the confidence of his fellow-men is an outcast in human society. The road to travel is simple and straight. The choice is this: whether they travel it to success or stand still in failure."*

Yet ten years later the Soviet Union had become the leading manufacturing country in Europe without the aid of foreign loans, whereas the U.S.A. remained a debtor country, paying a huge annual tribute to foreign investors up to the outbreak of the world war in 1914.

As the time approached for the annual Guildhall banquet and speech, it was hoped in some quarters that the Prime Minister, in his survey of foreign affairs would announce that the Government, without giving up any of its cards in advance, would agree to meet representatives of the U.S.S.R. in conference, which is the usual method of settling differences between Governments. These hopes were unfortunately doomed to disappointment. The Prime Minister declared:

> " Whenever the Russians are prepared to observe the ordinary decencies of international intercourse, to abstain from interference in British domestic affairs, and from a policy of intrigue and hostility elsewhere, they will find us ready to meet them with a spirit of liberality and goodwill."†

What did this statement mean? It was very general! The *Manchester Guardian* aptly commented: " Mr. Baldwin at the Guildhall made a reference to Russia which may mean nothing at all or may mean that he is really looking for a return to working relations with the Soviet Government."‡

* *Manchester Guardian*, 4.xi.27. † *Daily Herald*, 10.xi.27.
‡ *Manchester Guardian*, 11.xi.27.

When, even in the British press, there were different interpretations of this declaration, how could anyone expect that Moscow would understand what it meant? Only a face to face talk between plenipotentiaries could resolve the doubts, and Mr. Baldwin gave no hint that he was ready for this.

M. Litvinov, questioned at Geneva, December 2, 1927, respecting this declaration, replied:

> "Mr. Baldwin's speech at the Guildhall has been fully answered by the President of the Council of People's Commissars, who stated that the condition of mutual non-interference in internal affairs is accepted by the Soviet Government. Thus the assurances referred to by Mr. Baldwin have been given by the head of the Soviet Government in the same way as the references were made, namely, by way of public speeches, the only way, unfortunately, open to both countries for 'negotiations.'"*

Three days later M. Litvinov had an hour's conversation with Sir Austen Chamberlain, at the conclusion of which the following communiqué was issued:

> "M. Litvinov having asked Sir Austen Chamberlain for an interview, a meeting took place between them at the Hotel Beau Rivage this (Monday) afternoon. The meeting gave occasion for a frank exchange of views upon the relations between the Government of the U.S.S.R. and the British Government. It was not, however, found possible to reach any basis of agreement within the course of the interview.
>
> M. Litvinov and Sir Austen Chamberlain were in agreement on the text of this communiqué. Their interview lasted exactly an hour."†

What transpired at that meeting has never been officially disclosed, but the *Daily Herald's* correspondent at Geneva averred:

> "The discussion between the two statesmen was severely limited to Anglo-Russian relations, without, however, any reference being made to Tsarist debts or to the nationalisation of the property of British capitalists in Russia.
>
> On M. Litvinov's suggestion that they should discuss the obstacles in the way of a settlement, Sir Austen, as might have been expected, returned to the old theme of propaganda. M. Litvinov's reply—equally expected—was that the Soviet Government could not control a political organisation like the Communist International with branches in all countries.

* *Daily Herald*, 3.xii.27. † *Daily Telegraph*, 6.xii.27.

Then Sir Austen Chamberlain declared that the activities of Soviet agents must be stopped as a prelude to the resumption of relations.

Whereupon M. Litvinov ironically asked if the Soviet Government was expected to treat England as a friendly Power before the present state of potential hostility was ended by the resumption of diplomatic contact."*

The comments in the Tory press made it only too manifest that the British Government was not ready to restore relations except, of course, on terms of complete surrender on the part of the Soviets, terms which no sovereign State would accept. Thus:

"Soviet and pro-Soviet Press Agents have started a world campaign, designed to promote the myth or legend—for it is nothing else—that this interview was the first and promising link in the Anglo-Soviet negotiations now about to be resumed, the first arch in the bridge now being built between London and Moscow, etc. About this suggested bridge, the apt remark was made to me yesterday by a British diplomat that there was no fear of the present Government, with its accumulated knowledge of Soviet deceit and intrigue, ever being tempted to cross such a *pons asinorum*."†

"Opinion in London is sharply divided on the wisdom of the meeting between Sir Austen Chamberlain and M. Litvinov."‡

"That large part of the British public which cares for the honour and welfare of this country will breathe more freely at the news that Litvinov yesterday left Geneva for Moscow. It was a painful surprise that he should ever have been able to entangle the British Government in fresh negotiations."§

"M. Litvinov left Geneva this morning. M. Litvinov has been careful to observe the convention; he has neither given interviews indiscriminately nor indulged in any propaganda, and after his conversation with the British Foreign Secretary yesterday he was as punctilious as Sir Austen Chamberlain himself in not divulging what had passed between them.

Nevertheless, the departure of the last of the Soviet delegates has been hailed with relief."||

* *Daily Herald*, 6.xii.27.
† *Daily Telegraph*, 7.xii.27.
‡ *Morning Post*, 7.xii.27.
§ *Daily Mail*, 7.xii.27.
|| *Times*, 7.xii.27.

The British Foreign Secretary, December 9, 1927, gave an interview to the *Daily Herald's* representative, after which the latter cabled:

> "The Foreign Secretary very fully discussed with me the principal points of British foreign policy, in a very cordial and exceedingly frank conversation which lasted three hours. Sir Austen referred at some length to Anglo-Russian relations.
>
> He was inclined to regard the interview with M. Litvinov as premature, since neither Government had changed its position on the questions in dispute, and they had, therefore, made no progress.
>
> However, before coming to Geneva, he had informed his colleagues in the Cabinet that if M. Litvinov requested a meeting with him he would be received; and when M. Litvinov asked for an interview, Sir Austen, of course, acceded to his request.
>
> Sir Austen assured me in the strongest possible manner that he had done everything in his power to disabuse the Soviet representatives of their obsession that the British Government was planning an attack on them, overtly or covertly, or even to isolate them by a bloc of Continental Powers."*

Two days later Sir Austen was asked by Mr. C. J. Ketchum "What precisely were the conditions which the British Government laid down as a basis for re-opening the negotiations?" to which the Foreign Secretary replied: "All we require is that the abuses of which we complain shall cease. When we have sufficient proof that these abuses—and I refer to propaganda—have ceased, then we shall be happy to reopen conversations with the Soviet Government."†

Translated into simple terms, what Sir Austen's reply meant was that the Soviet Government should deny the right of asylum to the Communist International, although no such request had ever been made to the Governments of other countries in whose capitals the secretariats of other international organisations were domiciled, and to renounce all diplomatic means of retaliation, although at this time there was abundant evidence that the British diplomatic machine was working everywhere against Soviet interests. The British Government would never have approached any other Great Power on such lines.

At the end of December, 1927, the breach between Moscow and London was at least as wide as it had been when the Soviet diplomatic representatives walked up the gangway of the outgoing steamer at Dover on the previous June 3. Throughout all this period one London Conservative daily (the *Daily Express*) refused to be swayed by unreasoning passion and strongly urged sanity in our relations with the U.S.S.R. In February, 1928, it declared editorially:

* 10.xii.27. † *Daily Express*, 12.xii.27.

"Anglo-Russian relations have been too long the sport of the destructionists. The truth of the matter needs to be put with stark, staring simplicity:

1. Great Britain and Russia are the natural economic complements of each other.

2. Russia is emerging from a political nightmare, and is feeling her way towards normal and permanent associations with outside nations.

3. The economic situation between Great Britain and Russia, regardless of the rights or wrongs of their political differences, grows steadily worse.

4. Nothing is being done to remedy this situation, which reveals the leaders of both countries as gravely deficient in appraising the trend and the needs of the future.

The *Daily Express* urges the British Government to give earnest study to this question. The requirements of industry, the relentless logic of economics and the responsibility towards the world's peace demand statesmanlike action, not in reconstructing, but in constructing anew a firm, dignified, and workable relationship between the two countries."*

Unfortunately Whitehall was deaf to this and other reasonable appeals. Meanwhile, within the U.S.S.R. the rupture with Great Britain had the opposite effect to that which the Die-Hard elements confidently anticipated ; instead of weakening the Soviet Government and estranging Soviet citizens from it, it strengthened that Government and the people rallied around it more closely and enthusiastically than before the severance of relations. This enthusiasm expressed itself not only in verbal and written forms, but in more concrete terms. To quote just one example:

"Moscow, March 4, 1928.

A large and enthusiastic crowd of people, mostly ticket-holders, to-day witnessed a curious but brilliant ceremony at the Moscow aerodrome.

Fourteen battleplanes were, with much ceremony, presented to the Red Air Force, and the fuselage of each one bore the following inscription in big red letters:

'Our Answer to Chamberlain.'

These Russian built machines are, in fact, the first batch to be delivered out of 66 already built by public subscription to 'commemorate' the breach of relations with Great Britain."†

This general reaction to the hostility of the British Government

* *Daily Express*, 10.ii.28. † *Daily Herald*, 5.iii.28.

might have been anticipated by our Die-Hards had they realised the simple fact that human nature is much the same the world over.

The illogicality, or should we say, hypocrisy, of the Government's policy towards the Soviet Union because of the fact that a limited number of prominent Soviet citizens were delegates to the Communist International, was once more made manifest by the following news item:

> "An organisation known as 'The International Entente to Create a United Front Against Bolshevism' was described by M. Theodore Aubert, its founder and President, at a meeting at the Caxton Hall yesterday under the auspices of the Economic League and the Anti-Socialist Union.
>
> Lieutenant-Colonel Ashley, Minister of Transport, who presided, said that the Entente now had centres in 31 countries, and was represented in Great Britain by the Economic League."*

A British Cabinet Minister could be a delegate to an "International" without committing his Government, but a prominent Soviet citizen could not! Such, in fact, was the spurious reasoning of Whitehall!

Our Government next made a determined but futile attempt to persuade Germany to join in a general anti-Soviet bloc. A not very important dispute which arose between Berlin and Moscow gave Whitehall what they considered was a good opening. To quote the Diplomatic Correspondent of the *Daily Telegraph,* who usually reflected pretty accurately the views of the Foreign Office:

> "The keenest interest has been aroused in British circles by the controversy between Berlin and Moscow over the arrest of German engineers employed in the Donetz Basin by the Soviet authorities. Indeed, it is assumed in some diplomatic quarters that the Treaties of Rapallo (1922) and Berlin (1926), concluded in each case at a time when Germany believed that she was being cold-shouldered or maltreated by the Allies, are on the eve of interment; although this may be *too optimistic a reading of the European outlook.*"† (The italics are ours).

Further, Lord Birkenhead visited Berlin in the following month to do a little golfing for his health's sake and, at any rate in the opinion of some British press representatives in Berlin, to indulge in some recreations not conducive to the health of Europe.

For instance, the *Daily Express* of April 17, 1928, published the following cable from its Berlin Correspondent:

> "Lord Birkenhead was the guest of the Anglo-American Press

* *Morning Post*, 8.iii.28. † 15.iii.28.

Club here at luncheon to-day. In the course of the informal discussion after lunch, Lord Birkenhead gave it as his opinion that Germany was giving up her policy of holding the balance between the Western Powers and Russia in favour of a closer connection with England and France.

An interview of a non-political nature with Lord Birkenhead appears in to-day's *Berliner Zeitung Am Mittag*. The newspaper, commenting on Lord Birkenhead's presence in Berlin, declares his object in coming here 'is, of course, eminently political.'

'Lord Birkenhead,' it says, 'sees in Germany a future ally in the conflict which is bound sooner or later to develop with Soviet Russia. That he should come to Berlin at the present juncture and converse with Dr. Stresemann is not specially remarkable, in view of the fact that there are quite a number of problems waiting for discussion, such as, for instance, Mr. Kellogg's disarmament programme, the visit of King Amanullah to Moscow, and Anglo-Russian differences."

True, the Prime Minister, replying to a question in the House of Commons on April 16, 1928, said that Lord Birkenhead's visit to Berlin was a "purely private one," but the report of the *Daily Express* was supplemented by the representative of the *Daily Telegraph*, in the German capital:

"It is further asserted that no 'political discussions,' to say nothing of negotiations, took place between Lord Birkenhead and German official personages during his stay there, though it is admitted that in his private conversations he repeatedly expressed the opinion that Germany would do wisely to make common cause with the Western Powers against Russia.

This has been confirmed to me by a non-official personage who was present at several of the gatherings which took place in connection with the visit, as also that Lord Birkenhead's suggestions met with no encouragement in responsible German quarters.

It is not thought in leading circles here that Lord Birkenhead came to Berlin with an official commission. While it is considered possible that his real object here was not to play golf, but to take soundings as to the development of Germany's relationships to Russia, he is believed to have undertaken this investigation entirely on his own initiative."*

The usually well-informed Berlin Correspondent of the *New York Times* said quite categorically that Lord Birkenhead did propose the formation of an Anglo-Franco-German Coalition against Russia, but that Dr. Stresemann declined the proposals.

* *Daily Telegraph*, 27.iv.28.

The German Foreign Minister, in an interview with the *Koelnische Zeitung,* denied that Lord Birkenhead had discussed with him or with "any other responsible quarter" the formation of an Anglo-French-German agreement directed against Russia. This denial, while appearing to contradict the reports cabled to London by the representatives of the *Daily Express* and *Daily Telegraph,* in fact confirmed them. The report of the *Daily Express* stated that Lord Birkenhead had expressed his views in the course of an "informal discussion," and the report of the *Daily Telegraph* declared "in private conversation."

The correspondent of the *Daily Telegraph* commenting on the German Foreign Minister's disclaimer, cabled:

> "A very curious statement on the Earl of Birkenhead's visit to Berlin has been made by Dr. Stresemann, for publication in the *Koelnische Zeitung.* It is couched in exceedingly 'diplomatic' language, and, while appearing to deny, in reality it confirms much that has been said as to the importance of the British Minister's conversations here."*

It is scarcely necessary to add that Lord Birkenhead knew that any views which he expressed unofficially would be passed on to the appropriate official quarters.

The British Government's failure in a positive anti-Soviet policy did not discourage it from attempting an anti-Soviet negative policy. It made a vigorous attempt to exclude the U.S.S.R. from the circle of signatories of the Briand-Kellogg multi-lateral Pact.

Sir Austen Chamberlain, in the course of his reply, dated May 19, 1928, to the U.S.A., accepting the Pact, declared:

> "Universality would, in any case, be difficult of attainment, and might even be inconvenient, for there are some States whose Governments have not yet been universally recognised, and some which are scarcely in a position to ensure the maintenance of good order and security within their territories."

There can be no question that Soviet Russia was the State to which Sir Austen Chamberlain was obliquely referring.

The question of Russia being invited to sign the Pact was raised by the Labour Party in the House of Commons on July 30, 1928, when the following dialogue took place:

> "*Mr. Buxton:* If the United States Government propose that an invitation be given to the Russian Government, will the right hon. Gentleman support that proposal?

* *Daily Telegraph,* 3.v.28.

Sir A. Chamberlain: I shall not support it, neither shall I object to it."*

There are, however, more ways than one of opposing, and the press which supported the Government in this country persistently poured scorn on the proposal that the Soviet should be invited to be one of the original signatories of the multi-lateral Pact. For instance:

> "The idea of Mr. Kellogg standing side by side with Chicherin in the ceremonial hall at Versailles, with the Soviet sickle and hammer draped near the Stars and Stripes, has a humorous aspect."†

The oblique reference to Russia in the British Note of May 19, Sir Austen Chamberlain's reply in the House of Commons on July 30, together with the tendentious news in the Conservative press, could not but create the impression in Washington and Paris that the British Government would prefer the absence rather than the presence of M. Chicherin at the ceremonial signing of the Kellogg Pact on August 27, 1928, in Paris.

However, whilst the opposition of Whitehall prevented the U.S.S.R. from being one of the original signatories of the Pact, an invitation was eventually extended to the Soviet Union to become a signatory of this instrument, and it was signed at Moscow, September 6, 1928.

But the facets of Great Britain's hostility to the U.S.S.R. were many. It is axiomatic that the relations between Great Britain and Russia, be they friendly or hostile, are immediately reflected in the activities of the diplomacies of both Governments in Kabul. This is quite intelligible, because, on the one hand, the Indian Frontier tribes, a constant source of uneasiness to the Government of India, could be armed from Afghanistan, on the other hand, that country could be used as a convenient jumping off ground for an attack on Russia.

Under the terms of the Anglo-Russian Agreement of August 31, 1907, the Tsarist Government recognised British suzerainty in Afghanistan, and this treaty continued in force until the November Revolution (1917). On February 28, 1921, the Soviet Government signed an agreement with Afghanistan recognising the latter as a sovereign State. The British Foreign Office was so annoyed that, despite its long training in the practice of simulation, it gave open vent to its chagrin. In a Note to Moscow, dated March 16, 1921, it declared that "the Imperial Russian Government recognised that Afghanistan lay outside its sphere of influence."

The treaty of February, 1921, naturally enhanced enormously the

* *Hansard*, 30.vii.28, col. 1771. † *Daily Telegraph*, 9.viii.28.

prestige of the Soviet Government in Kabul, and much against its wishes the British Government was compelled to follow suit. On November 22, 1921, an Anglo-Afghan Treaty was signed in which the complete independence of Afghanistan was recognised. From that date onwards, in the opinion of the Soviet Government, British diplomacy strove incessantly to effect an estrangement between Kabul and Moscow. At any rate, certain facts are beyond question, viz., that during King Amanullah's visit to Great Britain in March, 1928, our authorities took every conceivable step to impress him with the power of Britain's naval and military forces, and no secret was made as to the moral which our Government hoped the Ruler of Afghanistan would draw. Thus:

> "Circumstances have arisen which may lead King Amanullah to abandon his proposed visit to Russia.
>
> It has been erroneously stated that the British Government do not desire that the King of Afghanistan should visit Russia. When his visit was first mooted it was regretted, but latterly opinion has veered round to regret at the possibility of the visit not taking place. The King and Queen of Afghanistan could not receive a welcome in Moscow approaching in any way that accorded them in London, and the King, with his quick intelligence would appreciate the difference between British rule and the present form of Russian Government."*

> "I am now in a position to state that, whatever doubts have been entertained on the subject in recent weeks, King Amanullah has definitely decided to return to Kabul by the overland route, as originally planned. This route will be via Warsaw and the Baltic capitals to Moscow, Angora, Teheran, Meshed and Herat.
>
> Some of the later stretches of this lengthy journey, which will have to be covered by road, may be somewhat trying to the royal travellers, but his Afghan Majesty is naturally anxious to show courtesy to his Russian and Persian neighbours, as well as to Turkey, a Moslem sister-State.
>
> These reasons are perfectly understood in British official circles. Indeed, the suggestion that the latter would view King Amanullah's visit to Moscow with any but feelings of perfect equanimity and serenity is wholly unwarranted. Great Britain has nothing to fear from a comparison between her conditions and those of Soviet Russia."†

Considerable attention was devoted by the British press, Liberal as

* *Daily Express* Diplomatic Correspondent, 16.iii.1928.

† *Daily Telegraph* Diplomatic Correspondent, 29.iii.28.

well as Tory, to King Amanullah's reception and stay in Russia. Thus, to quote a few of the headings:

> "Regal Show for Amanullah. National Anthem by Terrorist Band."*

> "King Amanullah and Moscow. Anti-British Ceremony Postponed."†

> "King Amanullah. Stay in Russia to be Cut Short."‡

> "Afghan King. Disillusioned by Visit to Russia."§

We do not think it is open to doubt that the press, taken as a whole, reflected the hopes and fears of the British Government, and that the aim of the latter was to convince the Afghan King that although the Soviet-Afghan Treaty of February, 1921, led to the international recognition of Afghanistan as a sovereign State, yet the military and naval might of the British Empire was greater than that of Soviet Russia.

III. The Submarine L55

It is with a sigh of relief that one turns for a moment from all this miserable intrigue to treat of an incident which although it recalled a series of events among the blackest in the history of British foreign policy, at the same time touched the deepest cords in the common humanity of both nations.

During the period of foreign intervention when the Government of this country had ordered some units of its naval forces to commit acts of piracy against the young struggling Workers' and Peasants' Republic, a British submarine, L55, when trying to force the defences of Kronstadt on June 4, 1919, had been sunk with all hands, and she lay at the bottom of the Baltic until she was raised by the Soviet authorities on August 9, 1928. The chief of the Soviet Naval Forces at once declared:

> "These men were our enemies, but Red Sailors nourish no enmity against them. The English sailors did the will of those who sent them and perished. We shall consider the wishes of the British Government concerning the burial. In any case, their remains will be interred with full martial honours."

What happened next is recounted in a message issued by the Official Tass Agency, August 22, 1928:

> "In the expectation that the British Government would wish

* *Daily News*, 4.v.28. † *Times*, 7.v.28.
‡ *Daily Telegraph*, 8.v.28. § *Daily Mail*, 12.v.28.

to transfer to the Motherland the bodies of the British seamen found in the submarine L55 raised from the Gulf of Finland by the Soviet Naval authorities, the U.S.S.R. from the very beginning took appropriate measures and was careful to preserve the personal belongings of the victims in order to hand them over to the relatives.

On August 18, the Norwegian Mission here was informed in this sense, and it was pointed out that the Soviet Government expected an urgent communication from the British Government on the question.

It was only on August 20 that the information was received through the Norwegian Mission that the British Government had made inquiries as to the possibility of sending a warship to transfer the remains of the crew to England.

The Norwegian Government was thereupon informed that the Soviet Government had no objection to the arrival of a warship belonging to a friendly nation such as Norway, or to that of a British merchant vessel, but it could not consent to a British warship entering Soviet territorial waters."

In the meantime, the bodies of the British sailors had been conveyed to Kronstadt and handled with all reverence. "Photographs received in England," wrote the *Daily Telegraph*, "show that apparently the Russians took every care of the remains and provided coffins for them."

Finally, arrangements were made that a British merchant steamer, the *Truro*, should convey the bodies from Kronstadt to Reval. What took place at Kronstadt on August 30 is thus recounted in a *Times* cable:

"At one o'clock, a Soviet naval representative, accompanied by the Norwegian Consul, went on board and shortly afterwards there came alongside the *Truro* a [Soviet] naval pinnace towing a barge, decorated with evergreens and crêpe, in which were 39 coffins, over which 20 Soviet sailors mounted guard with fixed bayonets. As the barge was nearing the *Truro*, the Soviet warships lowered their ensigns and the crews 'manned ship,' while the naval band in the barge played several funeral marches. As soon as the coffins had been transferred to the *Truro* she steamed out of the roadstead. The band in the warship *Aurora* played the *Dead March in Saul* as the *Truro* passed, a salute was fired from another of the warships lying in the roadstead, and all the merchantmen dipped their flags."*

* 1.ix.28.

The *Manchester Guardian* commented: "The reverence, tact and dignity shown by the Russians on this occasion are worthy of praise and gratitude."

The *Truro* reached Reval on the following morning, the coffins were transferred with full naval honours to H.M.S. *Champion* and the cruiser left the same evening for Portsmouth. The *Champion* reached Portsmouth, September 5, 1928, and arrangements were made by the Admiralty to give the dead sailors a public funeral with full naval honours two days later. The deepest feelings of the nation were touched by the whole episode and it is a pleasure to recall the moving tribute paid to the Soviet authorities by the *Daily Telegraph* editorially on the day preceding the funeral.

> "The public imagination has been stirred by all the circumstances of the discovery of the submarine, and the Admiralty has most happily satisfied the general sentiment in the arrangements which it has made for the obsequies of the crew who perished nine years ago. The care and thoroughness with which the Soviet Government prepared the remains for removal and collected the personal belongings which must mean so much to those who will ultimately cherish them have also provided matter for gratitude. Nothing, moreover, could have been more seemly and dignified than the ceremony at the transference of the remains to British custody a week ago at Kronstadt. The occasion is, indeed, one of mournful satisfaction. The amenities of civilisation have been satisfied in death, and to-morrow, as the coffins are carried proudly on gun-carriages to their resting-place in mother earth the nation will see in the ceremony that which unites the spirits of the dead crew with all those others whom death overtook in the stillness of ocean depths."*

Next day the officers and ratings were followed to their last resting place by an enormous crowd, including 500 officers and men from all branches of the Services. With full naval honours they were all, officers and men alike, buried in one huge grave in the Royal Naval Cemetery at Haslar, Portsmouth. It was said by many present that they had never seen a more affecting, impressive funeral in that great naval port.

It was fitting that that daily paper which had so unflinchingly fought against foreign intervention in Soviet Russia should on the morrow of the interment have reminded the nation that responsibility for the death of these sailors lay heavy on the occupants of high places in this country. The *Daily Herald* declared:

> "These men of the L55 were not, we must recall, killed in that

* 6.ix.28.

Great War which was to end war and save the world for democracy. They met their deaths many months after the Armistice in a deliberate attack, for which not they but their rulers were responsible, upon a people with whom we were not at war.

They had no quarrel, these sailormen, with those other sailormen whom they were sent to fight. They had no interest in destroying the newly-formed Workers' Republic, or in restoring the rule of Capitalism and Tsarism in Russia. Their lives were sacrificed for a cause which was in no conceivable way theirs.

There is a heavy burden of blood guilt upon the men who sent them to their deaths."*

The article ended with a much needed warning: "There are men in power in this land to-day who contemplate another endeavour to overthrow the Soviet régime. There are men who would welcome the opportunity again to order British warships to the waters where L55 met disaster. It is our duty to the dead to see that these men do not have their way."

When the House of Commons reassembled in the autumn of 1928, still another effort was made from the Labour Benches to induce Whitehall to apply itself seriously to restoring relations with Soviet Russia, but the effort met with the vague and stereotyped reply that "the Soviet Government should take the first step in this matter. Directly they show that they are prepared to observe the ordinary courtesies and decencies of international intercourse we shall be prepared to meet them." A diffuse statement of this character was liable to many and various interpretations and *Izvestia* at once replied:

"The Soviet Government has expressed a number of times its desire to receive from the British Government the concrete and exact conditions which, in the opinion of the Conservative Cabinet, might form a basis for the renewal of relations.

The British Government has declined systematically to lift the veil over its mysterious and wordy declarations; either because it could not formulate its desires clearly or because it was not desirous of so doing. The fact remains that the Soviet Government has never received concrete conditions."†

Our Government ignored the Russian request to express in concrete terms their conditions for a restoration of relations. The British Government, of course, recognised that sooner or later this country would have to come to terms with the Soviet Union, but wrongly they believed that time was working for them and that eventually the

* 8.ix.28. † *Daily Express*, 22.xi.28.

U.S.S.R. would be compelled by economic difficulties to accept their terms. Sir William Joynson-Hicks, in the course of a speech, December 11, 1928, said:

> "After ten years of the full operation of Socialism, the economic position of Russia was very bad. . . . On every point the economic and industrial position of Russia was going rapidly downhill."*

A few days after these "words of wisdom" had been cheered by a Tory gathering, the writers asked a prominent industrialist who, although a Conservative M.P., was completely at variance with his Party on the question of relations with the U.S.S.R., what he thought of Sir William's utterance. He replied:

> "Jix† reflects very accurately a big section of the party's mind; they believe that if they continue to hamper the U.S.S.R. commercially and diplomatically, they will compel her to offer terms acceptable to them; they have been entertaining similar hopes for the last four years; they are so blinded by prejudice that they refuse to see that the U.S.S.R. has become stronger and not weaker during this period."
>
> "But surely," we urged "the Government has many and varied sources of information. Jix can hardly believe what he says."
>
> "You never know," was the reply. "Judging from my own experience, I am not impressed with some of their sources of information. Jix and those for whom he speaks, swallow what the Russian emigrés tell them. He has probably convinced himself that his nonsense is the acme of wisdom."

The views expressed by our friend were considered by many competent observers at this time to be well founded.

Before the House of Commons rose for the Christmas recess a determined attempt was made to compel Sir Austen Chamberlain to state concretely the terms on which the Government would be prepared to renew relations with Russia, but his answers were so vapourous that they moved the *Daily Express* to comment that Sir Austen Chamberlain "under the fire of questions left many of his hearers in doubt about what he really wished to say—or to leave unsaid."‡

When at the end of 1928 the accountants totalled up the figures of Anglo-Soviet trade, the results fully justified those who had contended that the atmosphere of uncertainty created by Tory platform attacks

* *Times*, 12.xii.28.
† Sir William Joynson-Hicks was often called Jix at that time.
‡ 18.xii.28.

on the U.S.S.R. followed by the supreme blunder of the severance of diplomatic relations, would have a disastrous effect on trade between the two countries.

Soviet purchases and expenditure in Great Britain, which in 1925 amounted to £35,648,000, fell in 1926 to £17,773,000; in 1927 to £15,525,000, and in 1928 to £10,638,000. On the other hand, German and U.S.A. exports to the U.S.S.R. were higher in 1928 than in any previous year. As a rule a customer does not continue to patronise an establishment whose manager constantly hurls insults at him, especially if there are other tradesmen offering him better terms, coupled with civility.

CHAPTER XIII

RENEWAL OF DIPLOMATIC RELATIONS (1929)

I. ANGLO-RUSSIAN COMMITTEE SENDS AN INDUSTRIAL MISSION TO MOSCOW

FROM the dawn of 1929, the feeling steadily grew in volume that before the year closed, relations with the U.S.S.R. would be restored. This was no doubt partly due to the fact that a general election was in the offing, but it was by no means the only factor. Important business interests took certain decisions which greatly impressed public opinion.

The *Daily Telegraph*, January 10, 1929, announced that a syndicate entitled "Russian Softwoods Distributors Ltd." had been constituted by a large number of the leading timber importers in this country to market Russian timber; that they planned to purchase about 500,000 standards, valued at about £9,000,000, and that "an advance of £3,000,000 has been made against the contract."

On February 5, 1929, at a well-attended meeting of leading British manufacturers held in the Savoy Hotel, a decision was adopted "to take immediate action to institute a representative delegation to proceed to Russia not later than March 8." Commenting on this meeting and decision the *Financial News* declared:

> "From a practical point of view, the biggest step taken by Great Britain towards a resumption of unfettered trade with Russia has taken concrete form in the decision reached yesterday by important manufacturing interests to take prompt action for the extension of our export trade to Russia.
>
> A glance at the names detailed below will at once convince the British public as a whole, and more particularly those who have been lukewarm in their attitude towards the resumption of

business between the two countries, that something more than 'a gesture' is indicated."*

On the same day at the annual meeting of the Bradford Chamber of Commerce, the President, Mr. D. Hamilton, declared that "the time had now come when the peaceful commerical penetration of Russia might with advantage be speeded up. By that means, and not by a system of boycott, the Russian people could be brought back into the family of nations."

On the following day, commenting on this decision, Mr. A. W. Golightly (Chairman International Co-operative Wholesale Society) stated "that despite all difficulties the British Co-operative Wholesale Society had done £22,000,000 worth of trade with Russia in the last six years. The Soviet had honoured credits to the letter. I wish others were as prompt payers."

On March 12, 1929, a declaration was adopted at a joint conference of Employers' Organisations and the Trades Union Congress, in the course of which it was stated: "The subject of trade with Russia is recognised as one of first-class importance and it is agreed that improved trade with that country would have a very beneficial effect upon employment in this country."†

The Liberal Women's Conference at Torquay passed a resolution practically unanimously calling for the reopening of diplomatic relations with the Soviet Union.

The British Industrial Mission, referred to on a previous page, organised by the Anglo-Russian Committee,‡ left Victoria Station, March 25, 1929, by special train *en route* for Moscow. It consisted of 85 delegates representing 150 British firms. Its departure attracted considerable attention in business and political circles, both here and abroad.

> "It is claimed by the organisers that the delegation is the most comprehensive and influential combination of commercial interests that has ever left England on a similar mission. The object is to study conditions in Russia and to survey and investigate openings for British trade. The question of credits and of Russia's financial resources will form an important part of the inquiry. On the delegation's return a report will be drafted on which it is hoped an important extension of British trade in the Russian market will be rendered possible. The delegation represents a combined capital of not far short of £300,000,000."§

* 6.ii.29. † *Daily Herald*, 13.iii.29.

‡ This was an organisation of British business men and should not be confused with the Anglo-Russian Parliamentary Committee which was, and is, a purely Labour organisation.

§ *Manchester Guardian*, 26.iii.29.

The delegation reached Moscow on March 29, and were very cordially welcomed by the Soviet authorities. Subsequently many conferences were held between members of the delegation and the representatives of the various Soviet Trusts; the delegation also had a meeting with M. Litvinov at which there was an informal and frank discussion.

M. Maisky was then in Moscow on leave from his duties in Tokio and was appointed to assist the Mission. In addition to helping them in many ways he compiled for their guidance a book of facts and figures dealing with Soviet foreign trade actual and potential.

A Government Committee of the Soviet State Bank met the delegation on April 5. The Chairman of the former delivered a lengthy speech on the subject of the Soviet market. Here we can only quote a few extracts:

> "The Soviet Union's entire imports amount to 674,000,000 roubles in 1925-26; 624,000,000 roubles in 1926-27 and 820,000,000 roubles in 1927-28, the share of the three principal countries during those years being: Great Britain, 18.6 per cent. 15.5 per cent. and 5.5 per cent. respectively; Germany, 25.5 per cent. 25.2 per cent. and 29.5 per cent.; the United States, 17.7 per cent. 22.9 per cent. and 22.1 per cent. respectively. The U.S.S.R.'s import of machinery amounted to 147,000,000 roubles in 1926-27 and 222,000,000 roubles in 1927-28. At the same time the import of machinery from England declined from 16,000,000 to 10,000,000 roubles."

The speaker explained this tendency:

> "As long as our relations with England remain unregulated, the U.S.S.R. imports from England will be restricted to the most insignificant and absolutely necessary quantities, which it is impossible to account for beforehand. We shall place orders in England only from time to time. Orders and purchases in England will be made only to the extent that is convenient or advantageous for one consideration or another."

There was no reason why this process should not be reversed and subsequently much extended:

> "Should we succeed, however, in arriving at a mutually satisfactory agreement, and should we also succeed in working out a mutually satisfactory financial programme, we shall have no difficulty in placing in England industrial orders to the value of £150,000,000 sterling. Should in addition British capital agree to invest money in various concessions and contract operations,

our import programme could be raised to £200,000,000 and more."

There was one prerequisite:

> "All this requires a clear and definite fulfilment of one preliminary condition. Extensive economic co-operation between England and the developing trade of the U.S.S.R. is possible only if normal diplomatic relations are restored between our Governments. You will readily understand that serious economic or financial agreements between our countries are impossible without a corresponding legal basis. It is impossible to permit incidental factors of a non-economic order to disorganise or even disrupt such agreements. Such an elementary legal basis is the existence of normal diplomatic relations."*

The contentions of the President of the State Bank were only sound common sense, a fact which the delegation, as hard-headed business men, were quick to recognise, and on April 11, 1929, they passed a resolution stating:

> "The delegates emphatically confirm the conclusion that no economic development between the two countries is possible without the existence of normal diplomatic relations, and they undertake to make this fact generally appreciated by British public opinion. Also that from a practical business point of view it is not possible for the U.S.S.R. under the present conditions, when it lacks finance for the urgent requirements of the people, to undertake further liabilities in respect of claims unless a general economic situation is created by which both such requirements can be satisfied."†

A few days later, the members of the delegation began to drift home. Several gave immediate interviews to the press. A few were disappointed and critical, but the majority were agreed that the visit had been well worth while and that the Soviet Union offered a well-nigh unlimited market, provided suitable financial arrangements could be made. One member of the delegation, Mr. H. E. Metcalf, who had visited the Soviet Union on several previous occasions wrote: "In Russia everything is on an enormous scale, apart from the vastness of the country itself. They think in millions, and there are evidences that they will one day put even the United States of America in the shade. To keep pace with the rapid development that is going on in so many directions, very large foreign loans and credits are

* *Observer*, 7.iv.29. † *Daily Telegraph*, 20.iv.29.

needed, and will be forthcoming on our part as soon as a settlement of outstanding problems has been made."*

The statement of the President of the Soviet State Bank on April 5, was in itself a proposal for the restoration of diplomatic relations with Great Britain and the settlement of other issues afterwards, but when the question of this declaration was raised in the House of Commons, April 23, 1929, the Foreign Secretary gave his stereotyped reply: "If the Soviet Government at any time desires to make definite proposals to His Majesty's Government there are sources of communication."

Sir Austen expressed no willingness on the part of His Majesty's Government to retie the diplomatic cords between London and Moscow.

II. The General Election. The Second Labour Government. M. Dovgalevsky Visits London

From now onwards the three political parties were preparing for the general election. Parliament was prorogued on May 10, 1929, and shortly afterwards the three parties issued their election manifestos. The Conservative document contained no reference to the U.S.S.R., but made the amazing claim that "the promotion of peace and disarmament has been the prime object of our foreign policy, and that policy has proved successful over the *whole* field of foreign affairs."† (Our italics).

How peace and disarmament could be attained while no diplomatic relations existed between the British Empire (covering one-fourth of the world's surface) and the U.S.S.R. (covering one-sixth of the world's surface) was not explained.

The Labour Party's declaration stated: "Labour will re-establish diplomatic and commercial relations with Russia," and the Liberal Party's manifesto averred that the policy of the Party was "to re-establish normal political and economic relations with Russia at the earliest possible date, on the basis of the non-interference of each country in the domestic affairs of the other."

On the eve of the campaign, the Home Secretary, Sir William Joynson-Hicks, made an attempt to convince the electorate that the Government's policy had not been to hinder trade between the two countries. He declared: "I have never refused to issue a single permit to a Russian for the purpose of legitimate trade or commerce."‡

There is only one reply to that, i.e., from the date of the diplomatic rupture onwards, representatives of the Soviet trading organisations had the greatest difficulty in obtaining visas to visit this country, and

* *Manchester Guardian*, 22.iv.29.
† *Daily Telegraph*, 13.v.29.
‡ *Manchester Guardian*, 4.v.29.

technical experts who had to superintend the manufacture in this country of complicated machinery were unable to get visas for sufficiently long periods to enable them to carry out their duties.

Polling took place on May 30, 1929. The Labour and Liberal votes combined amounted to (about) 13,500,000 as compared with the Conservative 8,500,000. It may not have been without significance that Sir Austen Chamberlain only scraped home with the tiny majority of 43, in what was regarded as the Tory stronghold of West Birmingham.

The second Labour Government came into office on June 5, and it was generally expected that it would announce in the King's speech the immediate restoration of diplomatic relations with the U.S.S.R. Instead the speech contained the indefinite statement: "My Government are examining the conditions under which diplomatic relations with the Government of the U.S.S.R. may be resumed and are in communication with my Governments in the Dominions and the Government of India on the subject."

This was weak and disappointing. The late Mr. R. C. Wallhead, M.P., voiced a widespread apprehension when, in an interview with a lobby correspondent, he declared: "The reference to Russia is extremely vague in the light of the definite pledges made by every member of the Labour Party during the election."

There was still worse to come: in a debate on the King's speech, the Leader of the Opposition, Mr. Stanley Baldwin asked: "I should like to know whether the Prime Minister adheres to the statement of principle as to relations with Russia which he laid down in his Note on the 'Zinoviev Letter'?" To which the Prime Minister, Mr. J. Ramsay MacDonald replied:

> "Those conditions are laid down in a published despatch. Everyone who has read the despatch knows what they are. My colleagues know, my opponents know, and the representatives of Soviet Russia know. We stand by them; of course we do."

In view of the very abnormal conditions in which the Foreign Office Note in connection with the "Zinoviev Letter" was written, and that the conditions laid down in that Note were not and would not be accepted by the Soviet Government, the Prime Minister's reply created amazement, not to say consternation, among many followers of the Government. About an hour after the Prime Minister had made this extraordinary declaration, a member of his Cabinet remarked to the present writers: "Mac's statement was made impromptu; he did not stop to think, and now he has put his foot in it with a vengeance."

The member in question knew that if the conditions to which Mr. MacDonald had referred were adhered to there would be no renewal of relations with the U.S.S.R. The Prime Minister probably thought otherwise. He was timid to the core and his whole make-up prevented him from understanding the courageous men who constituted the Soviet Government.

Meanwhile, the Moscow press made it perfectly clear that the Soviet Government would not enter into a preliminary discussion of conditions for the renewal of relations. To quote *Izvestia*: "The Labour Government is deeply mistaken if it thinks the Soviet Union will enter a preliminary discussion on conditions. The settlement of disputed questions must come not before but after the unconditional restoration of normal diplomatic relations."

The *Daily Herald*, probably under official inspiration, commented:

> "The Soviet press is showing an undue and unwise sensitiveness on the question of 'conditions' for the resumption of diplomatic relations. They seem in Moscow to have jumped to the conclusion that something is to be demanded of them that is inconsistent with the dignity of the Union of Socialist Soviet Republics.
>
> Nothing is further from the minds of the British Government or of the British Labour Movement. Nothing could be more definite than the intention of that Government to resume diplomatic relations. But precisely because it wishes that resumption to be both full and friendly, it wishes at the very beginning to have an understanding on matters which, left on one side, might merely complicate and even endanger the treaty negotiations which must clearly follow the resumption of relations."*

However, despite this assurance the Prime Minister made another series of blunders which not unnaturally still further excited the suspicions of the Kremlin. The Government could have resumed diplomatic relations with the U.S.S.R. without submitting the matter to the House of Commons, because this was within the powers of the Executive, but the Prime Minister gave a pledge to the House, July 15, 1929, that relations would not be resumed until the House had had an opportunity of debating the matter. The following dialogue then ensued:

> "*Commander Locker-Lampson:* Are we likely to have a Debate before the House breaks up?
>
> *The Prime Minister:* Not at all likely.
>
> *Mr. Lloyd George:* Does that mean that, if the negotiations between His Majesty's Government and the Soviet are not concluded before we separate, the representatives of the Soviet

* 6.vii.29.

Government will not be admitted to this country until October or November ?

The Prime Minister: It means that any conclusion that His Majesty's Government may come to regarding recognition cannot become effective until it has been debated in this House."*

Shortly afterwards in one of the Lobbies, Mr. Lloyd George remarked to a fellow member that he was amazed at the Prime Minister's procrastination and that he (Mr. Lloyd George) was in favour of the immediate restoration of relations with Moscow. Had the Government there and then announced its decision to renew diplomatic relations, it would have been endorsed by a substantial majority in the House.

Regarding the discussion in the House on July 15, the Political Correspondent of the *Manchester Guardian* commented:

"Mr. Ramsay MacDonald's statement about resuming diplomatic relations with Russia, or, if one must be very exact, restoring the ordinary machinery of diplomatic relations by ambassadors, has proved thoroughly unsatisfactory to a large part of the Labour Party and to nearly all the Liberal Party. The attitude of the Liberal Party and of a large section of the Labour Party is that diplomatic relations should be simply restored, and that any discussions about propaganda or anything else should follow afterwards. It is probable that an attempt will be made from the Labour benches to bring in a motion to this effect. At least, such a motion will be put on the paper. If it came up for discussion I think there is no doubt that the Liberal Party would support it."†

Finally, on July 17, the Norwegian Embassy in Moscow delivered a Note to the Assistant-Commissar for Foreign Affairs, inviting the Soviet Government to send a representative to London for a preliminary discussion on the resumption of diplomatic relations between Great Britain and the U.S.S.R. The wording was unfortunate, because it lent itself to the interpretation that the British Government expected the Soviet Government to agree to certain terms, financial, etc., as the price for the restoration of relations. The Soviet reply, which was handed to the Norwegian Minister in Moscow, July 23, 1929, after welcoming the move of the British Government, continued:

"It being understood that the British Note has in view only the preliminary exchange of views exclusively upon questions of the procedure for the subsequent consideration of questions in dispute, but not of their substance; and so that these negotiations

* ***Hansard,* 15.vii.29, cols. 18/19.**

† 18.vii.29.

of procedure may be accomplished in the shortest time, the Soviet Government is instructing its plenipotentiary in France, M. Dovgalevsky, to depart for this purpose to London.

The Soviet Government will assume the rights and obligations of a State in a condition of diplomatic relations as soon as the British Government assumes those rights and obligations."

M. Dovgalevsky arrived in London on July 28, and had his first meeting with Mr. Arthur Henderson at the Foreign Office on the following day. At the close of the conversation the following official communiqué was issued by the Foreign Office:

"Mr. Henderson received the Soviet Ambassador in Paris, M. Dovgalevsky, at the Foreign Office this afternoon. The conversation lasted an hour and a half.

The present relationships between the two countries formed the subject of a friendly exchange of opinion and Mr. Henderson and M. Dovgalevsky explained the points of view of their two Governments.

The Ambassador intimated to Mr. Henderson that he would report to his Government, and hoped to be in a position to resume the conversation tomorrow or on Wednesday."

M. Dovgalevsky, after communicating with his Government met Mr. Henderson again at the Foreign Office on August 1, and handed him the following Note:

"The Government of the Union of Soviet Socialist Republics have done everything on their side to facilitate a *rapprochement* between the Union and Great Britain and the resumption of normal diplomatic relations between the two countries.

The fact, however, that the British Secretary of State for Foreign Affairs has stated to M. Dovgalevsky, the Soviet Ambassador to France, that it is impossible for the British Government to re-establish normal relations between the two countries before the solution of the questions outstanding between them, shows that the British Government do not desire or are unable to bring about the resumption of these relations.

If such were not the case, the British Government would not have proposed, as a preliminary condition for the re-establishment of normal relations, the solution of questions so complicated and contentious as the mutual claims and counter-claims. This new circumstance, which was not foreshadowed by the Note from the British Government addressed to the People's Commissariat for Foreign Affairs on July 17, requires a fresh examination of the question.

For that reason the People's Commissariat for Foreign Affairs finds itself compelled to ask for fresh instructions from the Præsidium of the Central Executive Committee of the Union, which will consider the new proposals of the British Government at its next plenary session."

Later the same day the following Note was issued by the Foreign Office:

"The conversations between Mr. Henderson and M. Dovgalevsky, which began on July 29, were resumed yesterday evening. M. Dovgalevsky returned to Paris this morning, and the conversations will not be continued for the present.

In his original invitation Mr. Henderson made it clear that it was the desire of His Majesty's Government to resume regular relations with the Government of the U.S.S.R. and that a responsible representative of the latter would be welcomed with a view to discussing the most expeditious procedure for the settlement of outstanding questions, including debts and propaganda.

Though the reply of the U.S.S.R. to this invitation was somewhat ambiguous, it was presumed that in offering to send M. Dovgalevsky to London, the U.S.S.R. had authorised him to discuss the procedure for settling outstanding questions on the lines proposed by Mr. Henderson.

In their first interview, Mr. Henderson explained to M. Dovgalevsky the lines on which His Majesty's Government wished to proceed, that he was anxious to avail himself of the present parliamentary recess in order to set up the necessary machinery for dealing with such outstanding questions as debts, claims, trade, etc.

He felt sure that, with good will on both sides, sufficient progress might be made to enable him on the reassembling of Parliament in October to report what had been achieved, that the principles on which a settlement could be worked out had been defined, and to request authority, even if complete settlements of all outstanding questions had not been reached, for the exchange of fully accredited Ambassadors between the two countries.

M. Dovgalevsky, on instructions from his Government, replied that in the view of his Government the best method of proceeding was the immediate exchange of Ambassadors, that the Government of the U.S.S.R. would not at present accept Mr. Henderson's proposals and would have to refer them to the next Session of the Præsidium of the Central Executive Committee.

His Majesty's Government adhere to their desire to resume normal relations with the U.S.S.R. and take note that the Government of the U.S.S.R. will consider the new proposals of His Majesty's Government at their next session."

What exactly did the British Note mean? It could certainly be interpreted as meaning that unless substantial progress was made on the questions of debts, etc., there would be no exchange of Ambassadors. Yet, according to the *Daily Herald,* which stood close to the Government, this was not its meaning. That journal commented:

> " It seems that either M. Dovgalevsky must have misunderstood Mr. Henderson or that the Moscow Foreign Office must have misunderstood M. Dovgalevsky. For in the Soviet Note it is declared that Mr. Henderson said that 'it is impossible for the British Government to re-establish normal relations between the two countries before the solution of the questions outstanding between them.'
>
> That is a complete—though we are bound to assume, an unintentional—misrepresentation of the situation. Mr. Henderson made no such statement, and the Government has no such intention.
>
> He suggested, not that a solution should be reached as a condition of the resumption of relations, but that during the recess the necessary machinery should be set up for dealing with the outstanding questions."*

Up to this date Anglo-Soviet trade had been excluded from the benefits of the Export Credits Guarantee Scheme, but the Labour Government decided that from August 1, 1929, this trade would receive the benefits of these Acts.

III. FULL DIPLOMATIC RELATIONS RESTORED. M. SOKOLNIKOV APPOINTED AMBASSADOR TO ST. JAMES'S

Negotiations for a restoration of relations remained in abeyance during August, but in an interview at Geneva, September 4, 1929, Mr. Arthur Henderson declared:

> " The actual resumption of relations cannot take place until a report has been made to Parliament.
>
> In the meantime, there is plenty of work to be done, and the interval between now and the opening of Parliament could still usefully be occupied in arranging the procedure and programme for the subsequent negotiations, which I hope will lead to the settlement of the outstanding questions between the two countries.
>
> The desire of the British Government is to re-establish relations as soon as possible on a friendly and stable basis, and the

* 2.viii.29.

invitation of the Government of the Union of Socialist Soviet Republics to send a responsible representative to London in order to discuss the most expeditious procedure still stands."*

On the following day the Trades Union Congress carried unanimously the following emergency resolution:

> "That the British Trades Union Congress, representing approximately 4,000,000 organised workers, views with anxiety the trade depression in the staple industries of the nation and, having regard to the vast potentialities for trade between this country and Russia, urges upon His Majesty's Government to take immediate steps to secure the resumption of diplomatic relations between Russia and this country, believing that such action would stimulate trade and thus secure the placing of orders in this country for the products of those industries, thereby alleviating unemployment; further, that the Trade Facilities Act should be re-enacted and extended to British-Russian trade."

The Soviet Government, on September 6, 1929, replied through the mouth of M. Litvinov to Mr. Henderson's statement. Moscow stated that it was willing to discuss all outstanding issues after diplomatic relations had been restored, and that if Mr. Henderson's statement was meant to be understood in that sense, the Soviet Government was agreeable to a meeting between representatives of both Governments. There was nothing new in this, it had always been the position of the Soviet Government; re-establishment of relations first and unconditionally and the discussion of all outstanding questions afterwards.

A few days later another Note was sent to Moscow asking the Soviet Government to send an envoy to London to discuss the resumption of diplomatic relations between the two countries. M. Litvinov at once replied:

> "The Soviet Government takes cognisance of the British Government's communication concerning inviting, on the basis of my statement of September 6, a Soviet Government representative to London by September 24 to consider with the Foreign Office questions of procedure. In accord with the above-mentioned statement and the Soviet Note of July 23, declaring that the Soviet Government is now ready to discuss exclusively questions concerning subsequent negotiations and not their substance, the Soviet Government agrees to send a representative to London by the date indicated with corresponding powers. The exact time and the British port at which the Soviet representative will arrive will be indicated later."†

* *Daily Herald*, 5.ix.29.

† *Manchester Guardian*, 14.ix.29.

Finally, M. Dovgalevsky again came to London, arriving on September 23, and met Mr. Arthur Henderson on the following day. The conversations continued until October 1, 1929, when an agreement was reached and signed. On the evening of that day the following statement was issued:

"Conversations between Mr. Arthur Henderson, the Secretary of State for Foreign Affairs and M. Dovgalevsky, the Russian envoy, continued this morning at the White Hart Hotel, Lewes. Agreement was reached in regard to the procedure to be followed on the resumption of full diplomatic relations, including the exchange of Ambassadors, for the settlement of the questions outstanding between the two Governments, as well as an agreement in regard to propaganda.

The outstanding questions include (1) definition of the attitude of both Governments towards the treaties of 1924; (2) commercial treaty and allied questions; (3) claims and counter-claims (inter-Governmental and private), debts, claims arising out of intervention and otherwise, financial questions connected with such claims and counter-claims; (4) fisheries; (5) the application of previous treaties and conventions.

The necessary document for submission to both Governments, which will be signed by Mr. Henderson on behalf of His Majesty's Government and by M. Dovgalevsky on behalf of the Soviet Government is now being prepared. It is hoped the document will be ready for signature before M. Dovgalevsky leaves for Paris on Friday. It is understood that before the agreement can become operative it must be submitted to and approved by the British Parliament."*

Speaking at Brighton the same evening, Mr. Arthur Henderson declared:

"We have completed an agreement whereby, when Parliament opens, we will ask for an exchange of Ambassadors, and, under the Ambassador a mission will come to London representative of the Russian people and the Russian Government. I venture to believe that the ultimate result of the whole thing will be that the relationship between these two great peoples will be established on a satisfactory and, I believe, a permanent basis."†

In the course of his speech on the Government's foreign policy to the Labour Party conference next day, Mr. Henderson said:

"I think it must be known to you and to all of our opponents

* *Times*, 2.x.29. † *Financial News*, 2.x.29.

that one of the things we did at the General Election was to make it unmistakably clear that if we formed a Government one of the first things we would do would be to bring about a resumption of diplomatic relations with Russia, and as soon as we had the opportunity it was decided by the Government that I should take the matter in hand, and should seek by conversations to lay down conditions on which a Treaty could be negotiated.

I am very happy to be able to report that as a result agreement has been reached on procedure that will be put into operation immediately on the exchange of ambassadors between the two countries.

When the House of Commons resumes it will be the business of the Government to make a report on the conversations that have taken place, and I shall be quite content to await the decision of the House of Commons and to await any attempt to prove that there has been any repudiation of pledges given either by myself or by Mr. MacDonald."*

On this part of Mr. Henderson's speech the *Daily Herald's* special correspondent commented:

"Naturally enough, one of the most applauded passages was the one in which he announced that his conversations with Mr. Dovgalevsky the day before, at Lewes, had been successful.

He prophesied that when Ambassadors had been exchanged, there would be such an agreement that it would bring the two countries together as they had not been for many years past.

The delighted delegates cheered to the echo."†

By a curious coincidence, the *Daily Telegraph*, on the following day, published some extracts from the Diary of Viscount d'Abernon, in the course of which he wrote:

"*Berlin, Aug. 30, 1922.* From the point of view of English policy, a big question presents itself—is a large Russia desirable? America is strongly for it, presumably as a counterpoise to Japan. English interests, I think, are much more certainly against it. As long as there is a strong Russia, India is, to a considerable extent, menaced. The Balkanisation of Central Europe is bad, but the Balkanisation of Central Asia would be an unquestionable relief to English policy.

Even as regards the Black Sea and the Mediterranean, a Russia divided into different States, whose commercial interests overpowered her political ambition, would make our position far more secure than in the event of the re-establishment of a power-

* *Daily Herald*, 3.x.29. † Ibid.

> ful Empire. A separatist policy for the Ukraine would unquestionably lead to a safer and more healthy position in the Black Sea, and would facilitate commercial control of the Straits, as opposed to political control."*

We quote this because it is a reflection of the mind of our governing class at that period. Subsequent events have shown how purblind these gentlemen were.

The agreement reached on October 1 was embodied in a Protocol and duly signed. It was issued by the Foreign Office to the press, October 4, 1929. On the evening before his departure from this country, M. Dovgalevsky issued the following statement:

> " Before leaving London I wish to express my satisfaction at the successful outcome of the negotiations between Mr. Henderson and myself embodied in the protocol relative to the procedure for the settlement of outstanding questions between the two Governments, which procedure will become operative immediately on the resumption of full diplomatic relations between the two States, including the exchange of ambassadors.
>
> This agreement has been concluded in the spirit of the first exchange of Notes between the two Governments on which the Soviet Government based themselves when accepting the invitation of the British Government to send a plenipotentiary to London. I have every hope that the agreement reached between Mr. Henderson and myself will be the beginning of the establishment at an early date of stable and lasting relations between Great Britain and the U.S.S.R. in the mutual interests of both countries."

Izvestia commenting on the outcome of the negotiations stated: " If the issue of the London Negotiations may be called a victory for Moscow, it is much more a victory for common sense."

We have referred in earlier pages to the delegation of the Anglo-Russian Committee which visited the U.S.S.R. early in 1929. Possibly with the object of not embarrassing the Tory party during the general election, the Committee's report was kept back until after that election and was only issued to the press on October 22, 1929. The report stated that the delegates visited many of the most important industries and that they were all impressed by:

> " 1. The extreme courtesy of all the officials with whom contact was made, their readiness to answer every enquiry, and their anxiety to supply the fullest information.

* *Daily Telegraph*, 3.x.29.

2. The high standard of ability that was generally displayed by both administrative and technical heads in all branches of industry.

3. The determination evinced by the administrators to develop every industry to the utmost extent possible upon the most modern lines."

Further the delegates found: "Every department of the Government appeared to be working with enthusiasm to elaborate plans to organise their section so as to enable it to contribute its full quota towards the successful carrying out of the five-year development plan of the Government. . . .

Generally speaking, they found that the directors in control of the factories were intelligent men, with a high standard of technical knowledge, but deficient in practical experience. (Very few chiefs of departments appeared to be over forty years of age, and since the Revolution they have inevitably suffered from their isolation.) The problem with which they were finding the greatest difficulty was the speeding-up of output, generally to be attributed to the great dearth of skilled, and particularly of the more highly skilled, types of workers; also to the more leisurely manner of working which has always characterised the Russian artisan."

As to the potentialities of the U.S.S.R. the Report stated: "Russia is potentially a very rich country, and her industrial re-organisation is being carried out to the limits of her financial capacity. The U.S.S.R., however, is without the capital necessary to develop fully her enormous natural resources, and financial facilities are only obtainable by the Government on most uneconomic terms, not only in regard to interest charges, but in regard to cost of purchases made in consideration of such facilities being granted to her. There is, therefore, every inducement for Russia to enter into trading operations on a large scale with British firms."

There were difficulties: "The barrier, however, against doing business with the U.S.S.R. on a large scale is Russia's lack of credit and liquid financial resources for her requirements, and the Government can only enter into obligations of an extensive character to meet the needs of the Russian people if long term credit can be obtained on reasonable terms.

"Further, for the proper development of her vast resources Russia requires capital to an extent that can apparently only be met by way of loans raised under equitable conditions, or, alternatively, by granting concessions to foreigners with capital to undertake such work of development. The establishment of a sound economic basis is, therefore, an essential consideration, but the U.S.S.R. is insistent on the renewal of diplomatic relations with His Majesty's Government as a precedent to a discussion of economic questions."

Finally, the report concluded:

> "The Committee is satisfied that there is a great volume of business available for Great Britain, subject to diplomatic recognition being afforded, and if arrangements be made for the financing of the business on long term credit or otherwise. The British Government has been informed of the views of the Anglo-Russian Committee and of its readiness to co-operate with the Government in all matters pertaining to the development of trading relations with Russia."

It cannot be doubted that had that report been published prior to the election it would have resulted in many more Tory casualties at the polls.

The subject of the renewal of diplomatic relations with the U.S.S.R. was debated in the Commons on November 5, 1929, when the Labour Party Motion, which was supported by all the Liberals and three Conservatives, was carried by 324 votes to 199, i.e., a Government majority of 125 votes.

During the course of the debate, Mr. Arthur Henderson, among other things, said:

> "I want to say very emphatically to the House that the Government do not intend to recommend Parliament to pledge the credit of the British taxpayer to any loan raised by the Soviet Government."

The only comment it is necessary to make on this statement at the moment is that it meant a considerable change of policy as compared with 1924, in effect it doomed the subsequent negotiations for a settlement of claims and counter-claims to futility. We shall return to this subject at the end of the next chapter.

The news of the House of Commons' decision was announced in Moscow on the following day which was the eve of the twelfth anniversary of the November Revolution and was naturally received with great satisfaction. The *Izvestia* comments are interesting and significant:

> "Confirmation of the protocol means in the nearest future the exchange of ambassadors with a simultaneous mutual confirmation of the obligation regarding propaganda, an obligation which also covers all anti-Soviet intrigues on the part of the British Government and its organs, which we have encountered everywhere in recent years. It means the immediate inauguration of negotiations for the regulation of disputed questions. If, as we

hope, the British Government approaches these negotiations with the desire to find a basis for a mutually advantageous solution it will meet with sincerity and goodwill on our side."

Sir Esmond Ovey was appointed British Ambassador to the U.S.S.R. and M. Sokolnikov was appointed Soviet Ambassador to the Court of St. James'.

The question of the renewal of diplomatic relations with the U.S.S.R. was debated in the House of Lords, December 4, 1929. From the Tory benches a resolution was moved that "the diplomatic recognition of the Soviet Government is at the moment undesirable." It is difficult to guess what was in the minds of those who moved the resolution, because they must have been aware that the Government would not be influenced on this matter by any decision of the Lords. The noble gentlemen took the matter so seriously that out of about 700 to 800 Tory Lords only 43 took the trouble to vote. The resolution was carried by 43 to 21 votes, but no one got excited about their decision. The *Morning Post* rather plaintively commented:

> "The Socialist Party, which does not believe in Second Chambers, is almost unrepresented in one wing in Westminster, and whether the flat disapproval of the Peers will influence their proceedings may be doubted."*

A more determined effort was made in another manner to prevent the application of the decision of the House of Commons. On December 6, 1929, the *Morning Post* with the aid of a number of probably well-meaning but badly-informed Churchmen, raised the bogus cry of religious persecution in the U.S.S.R., and argued that a condition for the restoration of diplomatic relations should be the cessation of such persecution. The aim of the agitation was to prevent an exchange of Ambassadors. But four days later the *Morning Post* in a leader felt moved to lament:

> "The departure of Sir Esmond Ovey, our new Ambassador to Russia, was recorded in our issue of yesterday, and it would indeed have been vain to imagine that any protest could undo an accomplished fact."

The agitation continued into the following year, but as we shall see in the next chapter, gradually it died a natural death, killed by the unfounded assertions of its sponsors.

The movement† started by the *Morning Post*, held a meeting in the Albert Hall on December 19,1929, to protest against the "persistent and cruel persecution of our fellow-worshippers in Russia." The speakers laboured hard to prove that the agitation was not a

* 5.xii.1929. † See Chapter XIV.

political stunt and, no doubt with the object of emphasising their disclaimer, they included in their list of orators that night Maitre Aubert, the President of the International Entente against the Third International.

In passing we would remark that a Tory Government at any rate at that time would certainly never have permitted the President of the Communist International to address a public meeting in this country. The attitude of Lord Brentford,* Major Sir Archibald Boyd-Carpenter and other prominent Tories who were on the platform that night towards the International Entente against the Communist International was in no way different from that of several prominent Soviet citizens towards the Communist International. Illogicalities, however, did not trouble these honourable gentlemen, and Christian virtues were hardly practised at the meeting, as the following day's press reports showed:

> "Opposition was first voiced during a speech by Prebendary A. W. Gough, and it continued when the Chief Rabbi (the Very Rev. J. H. Hertz) rose to speak. A man in the gallery started speaking in Yiddish, and cries of 'Put him out' were raised. The Earl of Glasgow, turning to stewards called, 'Take him out!' The interrupter was conducted out amid general cheering.
>
> After the meeting a man was found unconscious on the staircase. When he recovered he told the police that he had been attacked by several people. After treatment at St. George's Hospital he was allowed to go home."†

> "Another storm was aroused shortly afterwards, when a woman's shrill voice was heard from the back of the highest gallery. There were loud cries of 'Put her out!' and one man, rising excitedly in his seat, shouted 'Out! Out! Out!' A woman read a document demanding the release of all Irish prisoners, and cries of 'The unemployed want bread!' were heard."‡

Next day, December 20, 1929, the Ambassador and members of his staff were received by the Prince of Wales at St. James' Palace. The Ambassador presented his credentials which were accepted by the Prince of Wales, deputising for the King. The same evening the new Ambassador issued a statement to the press which was summarised as follows in the *Daily Herald*:

> "'The full renewal of diplomatic relations is a step undoubtedly based on sound economic and political necessities.
>
> The absence of normal relations between the two Governments rendered the international situation more acute and was a constant

* Formerly Sir W. Joynson-Hicks.
† *Daily News*, 20.xii.29.
‡ *Daily Telegraph*, 20.xii.29.

menace to the maintenance of peace, in which the working masses are vitally interested. On the other hand, under such conditions it was impossible to develop stable trading relations, founded on mutual confidence, and the well-known figures for the trade turnover between Great Britain and the U.S.S.R. confirm this.

I hope that the renewal of relations and their further consolidation, by taking into account the interests of both countries, will be followed in the coming year by favourable results, and will induce a movement of the trade turnover in an opposite direction. It is a favourable sign that already the orders of Soviet organisations in London amounted in October and November, 1929, to £3,687,000, as against £1,195,000 in the corresponding months of 1928.'

He referred to the extraordinary rapid progress which was being made in the industrialisation of the Soviet Union under the Five Years' Plan, and to the demand which this created for machinery and other products of British industry.

'Endeavouring to carry out more rapidly and successfully its plans of Socialist reconstruction, the Government of the U.S.S.R. on its side, will be ready to take steps towards a settlement of the financial claims which are being made upon it, taking into account our counter-claims.

But whatever step the Soviet Government may take for this purpose, it must be directly connected with the measures favourable to the further development and consolidation of the national economy of the U.S.S.R.

I hope that these questions will be investigated very thoroughly in the coming negotiations, and that every effort will be made to find a solution to the problems confronting us.

We have every intention of fulfilling loyally any obligations which we undertake, and at the same time rely on countries in friendly relations with us taking into account, on their side, the unalterable basis of our political and economic system.

'Under such circumstances,' the Ambassador concluded, 'it will be possible to consolidate the relations between the U.S.S.R. and Great Britain, founded, as they will be, on mutual benefit, and to lay the foundation of a lasting and peaceful co-operation between the peoples of the two countries.'"*

Two days later, Sir Esmond Ovey presented his credentials to M. Kalinin at the Kremlin. These two acts completed, diplomatic relations were formally restored, and for the first time since the November 1917 Revolution, the U.S.S.R. was represented by an Ambassador at the Court of St. James'.

* 21.xii.29.

CHAPTER XIV

PROTESTS AGAINST ALLEGED RELIGIOUS PERSECUTION AND SIGNATURE OF TRADE AGREEMENT (1930)

I. THE *MORNING POST* INITIATES THE ATTACK. THE "CHRISTIAN PROTEST MOVEMENT"

As we have seen in the previous chapter the resumption of relations with the U.S.S.R., however strenuously demanded by the British working class movement, the Liberal Party and large sections of the manufacturing and trading circles, was not at all to the taste of the majority of the Tory press and politicians who had engineered the rupture of Anglo-Soviet relations in 1927. Moreover, these elements no doubt imagined that as the notorious "Zinoviev Letter" had been employed to bring down the first Labour Government in 1924, so some anti-Soviet stunt or other might with advantage be used as a stick with which to beat and perhaps drive out the second Labour Government.

The attacks on the renewal of relations took a variety of forms—the most vigorous at first was that initiated by the *Morning Post* against what was termed religious persecution in the U.S.S.R. This protest movement, as was pointed out in the last chapter, no doubt, roped in a number of leaders and members of various churches who were honestly shocked at the stories of atrocities which it was alleged the Soviets had committed against priests and others simply and solely because they had dared to avow their faith in God—but this, however, cannot be said of many of its supporters, such as the notorious British and foreign reactionaries, the Russian monarchists and the "White" emigrés, many of whom were probably as little personally religious as the Bolsheviks themselves.

Actually, the stories of atrocities against priests in the U.S.S.R. proved for the most part to be a rehash of tales spread in the early years of the civil war and revolution and which neither at that nor any subsequent time were actually proved.

Many examples of religious persecution alleged to have been taken from the Soviet press of 1930 and no doubt supplied to the British protestors by their Russian "White" friends proved on examination to be distortions of what had actually appeared in the Soviet press. It was vehemently insisted by the *Morning Post* as well as by the ecclesiastics who joined the movement that the protests had nothing to do with politics. However, the columns of the *Morning Post* itself contradicted this assertion. There can be no doubt whatever that in the first place it was hoped by means of it to rouse such a wave of anti-Soviet feeling as would stave off an exchange of Ambassadors with the U.S.S.R. Thus the *Morning Post* on December 9, 1929, in the course of an article on the Christian Protest campaign said: "It is obvious that if this protest is to avail, no time must be lost in giving effect to it," and in the course of a leader said:

> "To resume relations with Soviet Russia and to give free entry here to her representatives and agents has always seemed to us a monstrous folly from a political point of view. There is, however, a consideration far stronger. Soviet Russia is the avowed and implacable enemy of the Christian faith. . . . These, then, are the people whom we are to receive and to welcome in England. It is, we believe, impossible for the Christian Churches of our land to acquiesce without indignant protest once the reality is understood."

A frenzied agitation was carried on during January and February, 1930 (after the exchange of Ambassadors), in the course of which the *Daily Mail*, the *Evening News*, and in a more guarded form, the *Daily Telegraph*, made strident demands for a severance of relations with the U.S.S.R. The *Daily Telegraph*, on February 13, 1930, in the course of a leader, said:

> "Dr. Lang foreshadows very plainly his intention of raising in Parliament, if the persecution continues, the question of the maintenance of diplomatic relations with the Soviet Government. That is a question that lies to-day on the conscience of multitudes who in politics have given support to the party now in office."

There is hardly need to quote anything from the *Daily Mail* and *Morning Post*; the language used by these journals in referring to the Soviet Government is well enough known—"Gang of thieves and assassins" (February 12, 1930); "The Red Devils of Moscow" (February 4, 1930) are just a few of the choice expressions employed by the *Morning Post*.

More significant than these fulminations were the words of the leader of the Unionist Party, Mr. Baldwin, at a luncheon on February 14, 1930, in Belfast, where he addressed the delegates to the annual meeting of the Ulster Unionist Council. Referring to the U.S.S.R., Mr. Baldwin said:

> "I cannot forbear from saying a word about our relations with Russia. The only dignified method is the method adopted by the United States of America, and put in clear words by Mr. Hughes, who frankly said they would not open relations with the Government of Russia—and I would not. It is inexplicable to me what the pull is that that Government seems to have with the Labour Party, and they will take anything from them. They have got

themselves into very deep water by once more admitting a Russian Ambassador to London, because our Government are finding out that the conscience of the whole country has been stirred, as it has not been stirred for a generation, by what we hear from that country of the persecution of the Christians.

This country has never regarded such treatment as is being meted out—I won't say only to Christians, but to all believers in a Supreme Being, whether Christians, Mohammedans, or Jews—we have never regarded it as a matter of indifference, or a matter which belongs solely to the competence of the Government of the country concerned. We have never failed to protest with all our strength. And to choose a moment like this, when you have had relations broken off, to enter into relations again is, to my mind, an intolerable humiliation for our country and is giving the lie to all that we have stood for for generations past."

It is interesting to observe that neither before nor since did Tories demand a rupture of relations with any country because of real or alleged religious persecution in that country. Mr. Cecil Wilson, M.P., a noted member of the Free Churches, after examining the Parliamentary records of the 40 years previous to 1930, dealing with the attitude of the British Government towards religious persecution in Tsarist Russia stated:

"On August 5, 1890, Mr. Atkinson (C., Boston) raised the case of Jews persecuted in the dominions of the Emperor of Russia. In reply Sir J. Fergusson (for the Under-Secretary for Foreign Affairs in Lord Salisbury's Unionist Government) said (Hansard, Col. 1897):

'These proceedings, which, if they are rightly reported to us, are deeply to be lamented, concern the internal affairs of the Russian Empire, and do not admit of any interference on the part of Her Majesty's Government.'

On February 15, 1892, when the same Unionist Government was in office, Mr. Cobb (L., Rugby) asked:

'Whether the attention of the Prime Minister has been called to the treatment by the Russian Government of the members of a very numerous Nonconformist sect in that country called the Stundists, the integrity and morality of whose lives are generally admitted;

Whether he is aware that, under the existing Russian law, it is a crime punishable by penal servitude for a Stundist to be found reading the New Testament or praying in company with his co-religionists;

Whether he is aware that thousands of men and women have

recently, for these offences and for refusing to conform to the orthodox religion, been transported without trial to Siberia, deprived of their children, ruined by heavy fines, flogged, and treated in some respects more harshly than the most depraved criminals;

And whether, in the interests of religious freedom, Her Majesty's Government, either alone or in conjunction with the Governments of civilised European nations, will without delay remonstrate with the Russian Government upon the course which they are taking?'

The reply of the Government spokesman (Mr. J. W. Lowther, afterwards Speaker of the House of Commons) was (Hansard, Col. 448):

'According to the *Novoe Vremya*, the main features of the law relating to Stundists are the prohibition to build chapels or schools, to hold prayer-meetings or assemblies, or to lease mills, manufactories or public-houses.

Her Majesty's Government do not propose to address remonstrances to the Russian Government on the subject of the administration of the laws affecting religious sects in cases where the persons affected are not British subjects.'

Twelve years passed and a Tory Government was still in power at Westminster.

On April 25, 1904, in the debate on the Aliens Bill, Sir C. Dilke (L., Forest of Dean) and Sir W. E. Evans-Gordon (C., Stepney) told the House about Jews, Stundists and Roman Catholics being persecuted in Russia for their religious beliefs, but the Tory Government of the day made no representations about the matter to the Tsarist Government.

The Tory Government went out and a Liberal Government came in; but there was no change in the policy of British Ministers with regard to religious persecution in Russia.

On June 20, 1906, Sir S. Samuel (L., Whitechapel) raised the question of a massacre of Jews; and Mr. Runciman (who still sits in the House of Commons as a Liberal) was the spokesman of the Liberal Government. He replied (Hansard, Col. 170):

'The impression which has been made, and the sympathy which has been aroused, not only in this country, but everywhere, by disturbances and loss of life in Russia, is well-known to the Russian Government, and these are not matters in which official diplomatic intervention is usual or desirable.'"*

As for quite recent times, we certainly do not recollect a single

* *Daily Herald*, 15.ii.30.

word from Lord Baldwin or anyone else demanding rupture of diplomatic relations with Nazi Germany, for instance, in spite of the well-authenticated atrocities against Jews, persecution of pastors, attempts to suppress Christianity and establish paganism in its stead.

It will perhaps be as well to give a brief outline of the actual attitude of the Soviet Government towards the churches and religion.

There is no need to stress the fact that in Tsarist Russia, the Orthodox Russian Church was a State Church of which the Tsar was the official head, who made and annulled all appointments. The principal ecclesiastical authority was the Holy Synod, the head of which, known as the Procurator, was a member of the Tsarist Government—the Council of Ministers. All the numerous dissenting sects, not to speak of the Jews, were severely repressed, both by the lay and ecclesiastical authorities. The Church was extremely rich; at the same time it largely depended for its income on the State and it actively supported the Tsarist Government in all its reactionary policies.

Mr. F. A. Mackenzie, for instance, although mostly critical of the Bolsheviks said in his *Russia before Dawn**:

> "The Russian Church was, even up to 1917, an instrument of the Government. Every village pope was, in effect, a policeman of the Tsar. The State paid for services received; it supported the church bountifully; it made it deplorably rich and woefully corrupt. The church was strong in ritual but weak in real religion. Many of the village clergy were as ignorant and as sottish as their parishioners. The innumerable monasteries were the homes of armies of idlers who adopted the religious life because it was the easiest they knew, and who often enough had not the decency to conceal their licentious lives. There were, of course, many good and faithful Christians, but the church as a whole had fallen very low.
>
> To readers outside of Russia this description may seem overdrawn. Few who knew Russia in the early years of this century will deny its accuracy. The church needed cleansing. But corrupt as the church was, it contained within itself forces which might well sweep Russia and hurl to destruction any who stood up against it.
>
> Then came the revolution. Most of the older clergy sympathised with the old Tsarism. This sympathy was deepened by the attitude of the Government towards the church. The union between State and church was dissolved, and the Russian Government became non-religious."

* Published 1923

At the May group of sessions of the Convocation of Canterbury at the Church House, Westminster, on May 1, 1923, the Archbishop of Canterbury, referring to the Orthodox Church in Russia, in pre-revolutionary days, "pointed out that . . . they must not forget the grievance which Liberalism had against the old régime and the silence of the Orthodox Church when the non-Orthodox creeds, especially the Jewish, were penalised or persecuted."*

As is well known, by the decree of January 23, 1918, the Soviet Government granted religious liberty to all religions and sects in Soviet Russia, at the same time the Church was separated from the State and the schools, and its secular property, like other private property, was nationalised.

The clergy resented this and almost from the first day of the revolution many of them, under guise of religious activities, carried on a vigorous counter-revolutionary propaganda.

It should be noted that for the first time in modern Russian history, complete religious liberty for all sects and religions was instituted under the Soviets. But all counter-revolutionary organisations having been dissolved, it was perhaps not unnatural that monarchists and reactionaries of all kinds who hated socialism and desired the overthrow of the Soviet system, should find their way into the various religious organisations, some of which (such as the dissenting sects, Catholics, etc.), had obtained freedom of organisation for the first time under the Soviets, and utilised them and particularly the authority of the priests and ministers over their congregations for anti-Soviet propaganda.

Similarly, cases were reported of priests, or *soi-disant* priests, travelling the countryside and, under guise of religious preaching, rousing the ignorant and superstitious peasantry to acts against the Soviet authorities whom they represented as anti-Christ.

The decree on religious communities issued April 8, 1929,† which

* *Times*, 2.v.23.

† The following is a summary of the most important provisions of this decree: All citizens as heretofore were entitled to freedom of conscience and religious worship Citizens of 18 years or upwards could form themselves into religious communities or groups on a purely voluntary basis which were required to register with the authorities. Such communities or groups and also religious conferences and the executive organisations elected by them were not recognised as juridicial persons.

By agreement with the authorities concerned, communities and groups could use churches for worship as well as the holy articles and properties required at their religious services, free of charge: this also applied to the living quarters of the church caretakers. A community or group might also rent ordinary premises as places of worship, but each religious community or group could only have the use of one building, and had to bear the cost of upkeep, insurance, local taxes, etc. The inspection of a building used as a place of worship could be carried out by the authorities at any time other than that during which it was being used for a religious ceremony.

Religious services were also permitted in premises not specially adapted for this purpose, but in this case notification had to be made to the authorities. Religious communities or groups as such were forbidden to form social or political organisations, mutual aid societies or circles of any kind, and in churches or premises used for religious services only books required for the direct purposes of such services might be kept.

gave a fillip to the whole agitation about "persecution of religion" in Russia was designed to strengthen the hands of the Government in dealing with counter-revolutionaries who disguised their activities under the cloak of religious organisations. Where this was the case, the Soviet Government had naturally not failed to take action and to prosecute and punish the guilty. But the decree was not aimed, nor was it used against, genuine religious beliefs or practices. There has been no instance of prosecution or punishment for genuine religious beliefs or activities.

The Soviet authorities were, and are, themselves scientific materialists. They may be right or wrong in this—but just as in other countries where the governing class professes Christianity the prevailing tone is based at any rate upon the Christianity of the organised church—so in the U.S.S.R., the prevailing tone, in harmony with the views of the governing class was, and is, atheistic. But whilst desiring that atheism or scientific materialism should spread, and giving full liberty to anti-religious propaganda, complete liberty of conscience and worship was granted by the Soviets for the first time in Russia to all citizens—Orthodox, Catholic, Jews, Protestant sects, etc., etc.

Members of religious communities and groups were empowered to make collections and receive voluntary donations in their churches and outside, but only from members of their own community, and only for purposes connected with the maintenance of their church, property and service, and for the support of their executive organs; all compulsory levies were strictly prohibited.

Religious instruction was not permitted in any State, public or private educational institution, but such instruction could be given to adult citizens (over 18 years of age) at special courses conducted by Soviet citizens; permission for the organisation of these courses had to be obtained from the authorities in each case.

Religious communities or groups could hold local, Republican, and All-Union congresses and conferences, but had to obtain permission from the authorities in each separate case.

Strict rules of procedure were laid down for cases of deprivation of a religious association of its church or premises in cases where an agreement with the State had been violated or where the local authorities demanded the use of such premises for national or local cultural needs.

The valuables of a church reverting to the authorities were taken over by the corresponding State Department (Commissariat for Education, Finance, etc.), but properties required for the religious ceremonies of the community were handed over to the congregation of believers for transference to their new place of worship. This also applied to stores of candles, wine, oil, coal, and money, providing the religious society had remained intact.

Providing sanitary and other conditions were observed permission could be granted to a religious community or group to erect new places of worship.

No religious ceremonies and no religious symbols of any kind were permitted in State, co-operative or private institutions and enterprises, but this regulation did not apply to religious rites and ceremonies at the request of dying or dangerously-ill persons in hospitals or prisons—such ceremonies were carried out in special rooms set aside for this purpose. Religious ceremonies could also be performed in cemeteries and crematoriums.

Religious parades and religious ceremonies in the open air might be held only with special permission from the authorities for every such performance. Permits were, however, unnecessary for religious ceremonies in connection with funerals.

No special permission or notification to the authorities was necessary for open-air religious parades or ceremonies round the place of religious worship where such ceremony was part of the religious service, provided they caused no street obstruction.

A great outcry was raised by the "Christian Protest Movement" about the closing of many churches and monasteries. Many had indeed been closed or converted into clubs, children's homes, museums, granaries, etc. It should, however, be borne in mind that the number of churches in the Russian Empire was enormous; thus Moscow was traditionally "the city of 40 times 40 churches." At the same time very many churches and synagogues were open and were functioning and a religious congregation could obtain a church free of charge providing they used it strictly for their religious observances. This still obtains at the present time.

It was characteristic of the methods pursued by the journals supporting the "Christian Protest Movement" that whilst stories of alleged atrocities, however wild, were published by them continuously, a Reuter's telegram in the opposite sense was for the most part ignored by them. This message read:

"MOSCOW, Sunday,
February 9, 1930.

With reference to the reports regarding the Soviet Government's attitude to the Church, a high official made the following statement to-day to a representative of the official Tass Agency:

'Russian counter-revolutionary priests abroad have evidently worked hard in exhuming atrocity stories from the war archives in the hope of terrifying the British public, but I believe that the British people are too wise to accept such trite stuff. Not even the invented names of would-be religious martyrs in the U.S.S.R. can lend colour to such incredible tales.

Remembering the oppressive rôle played by the Church under the Tsar, the people of the Soviet make no secret of their dislike for religion, but every visitor to the Soviet Union knows that we fight religion by education and propaganda and not by the methods of mediæval inquisition.

To this day tens of thousands of churches of all denominations function in the U.S.S.R., and priests who refrain from counter-revolutionary activities are allowed to conduct religious services unmolested. If churches in the U.S.S.R. are closed it only shows they are becoming less popular with the public. Even in England many churches have been closed as being superfluous.'"

In general, the Labour Government assumed a completely non-committal attitude in regard to the agitation. They steadily refused to take the propaganda at its face value, and in accordance with international etiquette and in spite of strenuous die-hard protests, the B.B.C., being a State corporation, refused to permit leaders of the "Christian Protest Movement" to broadcast their views, they also refused to broadcast the proceedings of their meetings. The B.B.C. made its position clear in the following reply to the Secretary of the "Christian Protest Movement":

> "Your letter of February 22 has received careful consideration here. While we accept your assurances that the aim of your Council is entirely non-political we cannot help feeling that a movement of this kind is almost bound to have political reactions, at least with respect to the present Government in Russia and possibly also the British Government, which recently re-established relations with them. It is contrary to the Corporation's character and licence to permit broadcasts of this nature.
>
> Another factor of importance in the attitude of the Corporation is that the B.B.C. is a member of the International Union of Broadcasting and that on more than one occasion that Union has had to use its influence to cause the cessation of contentious national propaganda. The policy of non-interference with the internal affairs of other countries is a vital principle of the International Union and it is therefore necessary for the B.B.C. as leaders in international wireless comity, to be exceedingly careful that they do not present even the appearance of violating this principle."*

When the British churches decided to hold intercessionary prayers for the "persecuted people of Russia," the Government forbade the reading of these services at the Army, Naval or Air Force services. This again roused a furious protest in the organs of the press which supported the "Protest Movement." The *Morning Post* went so far as to call it "the application of pure Soviet methods of Government in administration." The *Daily Telegraph* called it "an infringement of religious liberty." Did these gentry forget that, in the first place, the armed forces are official state organisations and that therefore it was in any case improper for a foreign Power with whom we were at peace to be attacked at any of its functions; secondly, that services in the armed forces are *compulsory* and that therefore soldiers, sailors and airmen who did not share the view of the "Christian Protest Movement" would be compelled to participate in prayers with which they might disagree? But, of course, this aspect was of no account to our Die-Hards; liberty of the individual has always meant for them liberty to impose their views on "the lower orders."

The Government decision had been announced to the forces in the following letter:

> "Sir—I am commanded by the Army Council to inform you

* *Manchester Guardian*, 28.ii.30.

that His Majesty's Government have decided, in view of the political character the controversy has assumed, that it is undesirable that intercessory prayers for Russian subjects should be read at religious services in the Army,—I am, Sir, your obedient servant,

H. J. CREEDY,

Permanent Under-Secretary for War."

The following comment by the Political Correspondent of the *Daily Telegraph* is interesting:

> "From a military point of view the most significant feature of the letter is the introductory wording. The customary opening formula of such letters from the War Office is similar, but it conveys the decision of the Army Council, and does not refer to a higher authority. In contrast, the wording of this letter appears to make the Army Council merely a forwarding agency, or 'post office' for the instructions of the Government.
>
> So unusual a formula in itself suggests an unwillingness on the part of the Army Council to bear the responsibility. It also suggests a considerable body of dissent within that body."*

At the same time an Admiralty Order stated that the arrangements made by the Archbishop of Canterbury for a Special Intercessory Service on March 16 "do not apply to His Majesty's ships or establishments."

Questions were raised in Parliament and the orders to the armed forces were finally somewhat modified so as to make it perfectly clear that it was only at *compulsory* services that the special prayers were not to be read.

But the Government did make one very important slip. When questioned in the House of Commons in regard to the alleged religious atrocities in the U.S.S.R., Mr. Henderson had, we think, very unwisely announced on February 13, 1930, that he was making enquiries through the British Ambassador in Moscow regarding the truth of the allegations against the Soviets. When later Sir Esmond Ovey's report was received, Mr. Henderson quite naturally and in accordance with diplomatic usuage refused to publish it—only issuing a translation of the decree on Religious Communities passed by the Soviet Government the previous April.

Every Government has its own sources of information, including its Embassy, in regard to affairs in other countries. The Government attitude towards religion and the position of the various Churches

* *Daily Telegraph*, 1.iii.30.

in any given country is, of course, a purely internal matter and to say the least it would have been a gross violation of diplomatic etiquette to have published the Ambassador's report. The Ambassador should not have been brought into the matter at all. As it was, however, the fact of the non-publication of the report was used as one more tap for the turning on of a stream of abuse both on the Soviet Government and the Labour Government and for tirades in Parliament and the press against normal relations between the two countries.

The report of the British Ambassador, as we have said, was not published, but on April 24, 1930, a correspondent in the *Manchester Guardian* gave what he claimed to be the general purport of it:

> "The gist of the report is that there is no religious persecution in Russia in the strict sense of the term. The Ambassador, his First Secretary and a number of agents made very wide inquiries in religious quarters. No case could be discovered of the punishment of a priest, or any other person, for the practice of the Christian or any other religion, or for the performance or observance of religious rites and services. Priests have been shot for counter-revolutionary crimes. Other foreign diplomatists have made similar inquiries with the same results. The people are free to worship and to be baptised, married and buried in Christian fashion, and there is similar liberty for Jews and Mohammedans. If, however, a Communist member of an otherwise Christian family dies, he is not allowed to be given a Christian burial and must have a Communist funeral. That is to say, a representative of the Communist party attends, and at the appointed time throws a handful of earth on to the coffin and then makes a speech on the merits of the departed and the advantages of the Revolution. As the profession of atheistic opinions is one of the necessary qualifications for membership of the Communist party, it is presumed that this is what the dead person himself would have wished. . . .
>
> The present rulers of Russia frankly avow that their aim is the eventual disappearance of religion in Russia, as the legislation published in the recent White Paper shows, and they hope to achieve this aim by detaching the young from religious influences. It is for this reason that it had been made illegal to give public or organised religious instruction to children under eighteen. Anybody over eighteen can be given religious instruction anywhere if he or she so desires.*

* Article 124 of the 1936 Constitution of the U.S.S.R. reads: "In order to ensure to citizens freedom of conscience, the church in the U.S.S.R. is separated from the state, and the school from the church. Freedm of religious worship and freedom of anti-religious propaganda is recognised for all citizens."

> Priests are automatically deprived of all civil rights* . . . The profession or practice of the Christian or any other religion does not in itself entail any disadvantage or restriction so far as the laity are concerned. The penalty for counter-revolutionary activity is the same for a priest as for anybody else. No doubt, by the very nature of his profession a priest is likely to feel constrained to preach against a Government whose declared aim is the extinction of religion and thus automatically to engage in counter-revolutionary activity.
>
> Churches have been destroyed or taken over for use as schools or clubs where they were not sufficiently used for worship. Otherwise the churches are open and the ceremonies are as magnificent as ever. Premises are given for the purposes of worship to religious groups if they number more than 20 persons. The number of churches required for religious purposes is, however, steadily diminishing on account of the rapid falling off in the practice of religion. Everywhere, and especially in the towns, the churches are growing emptier, and the majority of Christians in Russia to-day are over thirty."

Finally, the correspondent added: "The British Embassy in Moscow is, I understand, greatly concerned about the stream of falsehoods and inaccuracies that reaches the English press from Riga."

Towards the end of April, the agitation of the "Christian Protest Movement" became weaker and more sporadic. The last flicker of life was a meeting on July 14, 1930, at the Royal Albert Hall, when a resolution in a minor key was passed urging "the Soviet Government to give full liberty of religious teaching and worship to the people of Russia, and extending to all God-fearing people in that land its cordial greetings of sympathy and hope."

II. Fresh Outcry Against Soviet Propaganda. April 16, Anglo-Russian Commercial Agreement Signed. The Anglo-Soviet Debts and Claims Committee Set Up

A second line of attack on the renewal of relations was the question of propaganda. It will be recalled that when diplomatic relations between Great Britain and the U.S.S.R. were renewed in 1929, both sides undertook to "refrain and to restrain all persons under their direct or indirect control" from propaganda against and interference in one another's affairs. The Soviet Government, however, had always refused to assume any responsibility for the acts of the Communist International or as it was termed in short, the "Comintern." On the other hand, Mr. Henderson had stated in the House of Commons,

* By the Soviet Constitution of 1936, priests now enjoy full citizen rights, and may be elected as members of local Soviets and the Supreme Soviet, *i.e.*, the local councils and national parliament.

November 5, 1929, that in his view the pledge so far as the Soviet Government was concerned was clearly applicable to the propagandist activities of the Communist International which he regarded as "organically connected with the Soviet Government."

Izvestia, in a reply to Mr. Henderson, immediately repudiated this interpretation of the propaganda clause in the Anglo-Soviet Agreement and stated quite clearly once again that the Soviet Government could not undertake any responsibility for the actions of the Comintern.

Here then was a fruitful source of friction from the outset which those who were bent on bedevilling Anglo-Soviet relations would certainly not fail to utilise to the full and one could not help agreeing with the *Manchester Guardian* when it said in a leading article:

> "In one sense Mr. Henderson has only himself to blame. He was so far lacking in political realism as to repeat Mr. MacDonald's promise to treat the Communist International as 'an organ of Soviet Government.' He should have known the Communist (and Conservative) mentality better than to put the continuance of relations with Russia at the mercy of every chance manifesto and leaflet."*

As a matter of fact, an opportunity for a Tory outcry was not long in coming. On January 1, 1930, the Communist Party of Great Britain launched a new daily newspaper—*The Daily Worker*—in the first issue of which there appeared a message from the Comintern welcoming the appearance of the journal and hailing it as a powerful weapon to fight for communism in Great Britain. Immediately the cry went up that the propaganda pledge had been broken by the Soviet Government. The *Times,* the *Morning Post,* the *Daily Telegraph* and *Daily Mail,* all joined in the attack with gusto, linking it up with the alleged atrocities against Christians, the suppression of the kulaks† and the establishment of the collectives, etc.

The Labour and Liberal press on the other hand ridiculed the idea of making the Comintern message to the *Daily Worker* a cause for denouncing the Anglo-Soviet Agreement. Said the *Daily News* Foreign Affairs Correspondent:

> "In Whitehall, yesterday, there was no attempt to conceal that the attack, with its wild charges of 'Colonial brutalities,' 'preparation for another Imperialist war,' etc., had caused annoyance. On the other hand, it was pointed out that it contained nothing which might be characterised as subversive, and ungracious as the gesture might be, it was not likely to interrupt the relations so

* 4.i.30.

† Kulaks, literally tight-fists, rich peasants who employed other peasants on the arms for hire.

lately restored. It was doubted that any official representations would be made to Moscow on the subject."*

Mr. E. F. Wise, the Labour M.P. for Leicester, in a speech on January 30, put the matter in its proper perspective. He said:

"'The article dealing with propaganda in the treaty of 1924 and applying to Governments and to organisations under their control, or receiving financial assistance from them, was intended to cover the operations and activities of the Third International. It was argued that both the Comintern and the Soviet Government got their orders from the Communist party. It was essential, however, to understand the view of the other side, and the Soviet view was that, while the Russian Communist party was a very important element in the Comintern, it was not true that the Soviet Government could dictate policy to the Comintern.

I believe I am right in saying that some twenty countries are represented in the Comintern. There is a Communist party in every European country, and in some it is much stronger than the party here.'

Mr. Wise pointed out that it was not possible for Governments to restrict all propaganda carried on by their people in foreign countries. If China were to request our Government to restrain the activities of our missionaries in foreign countries it could not be done. The Vatican had recently interfered in affairs in Malta, but the Italian Government could not prevent its doing so. We must recognise some difficulties, if not impossibilities, in pressing that the present Russian Government should at this moment interfere in any direct and drastic way with the operations of the Comintern."†

Whatever view one might take of the relations between the Soviet Government and the Comintern or of the relations between other internationals on which members of various Governments were represented—one thing is surely clear, that if manifestos and appeals of these internationals were to be made the basis for a rupture of relations between countries it would be well-nigh impossible to maintain friendly relations between countries for very long at a stretch. As the *Daily Herald* rightly said in a leader on the subject:

"Sir Austen Chamberlain and his Tory satellites are devoting themselves enthusiastically to the task of attempting to wreck the newly-restored diplomatic relations with the Soviet Government. They search pertinaciously for causes of offence. They magnify every triviality. They delve diligently into the more grotesque

* 3.ii.30. † *Manchester Guardian*, 31.i.30.

> follies of Communist journalism. They seek day by day for reasons of quarrel. And they shout with indignation when the Foreign Secretary will not join in.
>
> Under such conditions as they demand, in such a temper as they display, no international relations could be maintained between any two countries ; nor would the peace of the world be safe for a moment."*

It was no doubt for this reason that in spite of the strong dislike of the Labour Government collectively and of Labour leaders individually for the Comintern, they refused to make a mountain of discord from the mole-hill of the Comintern New Year's manifesto, and in reply to the Tory campaign in the press and Parliament, Mr. Henderson contented himself with making enquiries or at most mild remonstrances on the subject to the Soviet authorities. In effect, the two Governments agreed to differ on their interpretation of the propaganda clause in so far as it concerned the Comintern.

The continuous sniping at Soviet " anti-British propaganda " did not, of course, cease. Almost every disturbance or unrest, every movement by workers or peasants to organise in order to improve their conditions in any part of the British Empire, was put down to " Moscow propaganda." Reading the Tory press of the years immediately following the resumption of British-Soviet diplomatic relations one might imagine that neither the British workers nor the natives of India and other parts of the British overseas possessions had anything whatever to complain of and had been living in blissful content until the wicked Bolsheviks came and stirred up trouble by persuading them that their really generous benevolent employers or masters were wicked.

In the case particularly of the Meerut Trial in India, the prosecution made a definite charge, without however giving any real facts or details, that the whole movement had been organised and financed by Moscow.

The Riga correspondent of the *Times,* not to speak of the *Daily Mail* and the *Morning Post,* gave a constant stream of misrepresentations of happenings in the U.S.S.R. The Anglo-Russian Parliamentary Committee, limiting itself to a few of the more flagrant examples, issued two pamphlets, one in 1930 and another in 1933, in which, giving chapter and verse, it was demonstrated how the real facts had been completely distorted.

The Soviet press in its turn used no unmeasured language in replying to many of these fulminations against the U.S.S.R. All this naturally did not conduce to the development of normal friendly diplomatic and trading relations. Nor did it facilitate the discussion between the

* 4.ii.30.

two Governments regarding a trade agreement which was proceeding in accordance with the Protocol of October 3, 1929, on the resumption of diplomatic relations.

In the meantime, unemployment in Great Britain was mounting, and Labour and many Liberal as well as some Tory members of Parliament pressed for a speedy conclusion of an Anglo-Soviet commercial agreement and a more liberal extension of the Exports Credits Scheme to Anglo-Soviet trade. When the subject was discussed in the House of Commons on February 5, 1930, on a motion by Miss Wilkinson, the Minister for Overseas Trade, Mr. G. M. Gillett, said that the Government had sent an investigator to Russia and was doing all it could to enter into such an agreement as the motion suggested, but if Russia desired credit, a settlement of the various debt questions was a fundamental necessity. And after referring to what had been done under the Export Credits Scheme he added significantly that "better results would follow from better feeling."

The Labour Government and the Labour Movement generally hoped to promote this better feeling by the conclusion of an Anglo-Soviet commercial agreement. Although the negotiations were unduly prolonged, nevertheless, a temporary Anglo-Russian commercial agreement was finally signed on April 16, 1930. This, as Mr. Dalton defined it in the House of Commons on April 14, was "to serve as a *modus vivendi* pending the conclusion of a full Treaty."

The Foreign Office on April 16, 1930, issued the following very adequate summary of the agreement:

> "By Article I the High Contracting Parties accord most-favoured nation treatment to the subjects, citizens, juridical persons, national produce and manufactures of each other with the following exceptions:
>
> I. Special provisions relating to trade contained in treaties between the Union of Soviet Socialist Republics and (*a*) those states whose entire territory in August, 1914, formed an integral part of the former Russian Empire; (*b*) continental border States in Asia.
>
> II. Rights accorded to any third country forming part of a customs union with the Union of Soviet Socialist Republics, and
>
> III. Privileges accorded by the Union of Soviet Socialist Republics to border States with respect to local trade between the inhabitants of frontier zones.
>
> By Article II His Majesty's Government agree, in view of the state monopoly of foreign trade in the Union of Soviet Socialist Republics, to accord to the Soviet Government the right to establish in Great Britain a Trade Delegation consisting of the

Trade Representative of the Union of Soviet Socialist Republics and his two deputies forming part of the Embassy of the Union of Soviet Socialist Republics.

These three persons are to be accorded all diplomatic privileges and immunities, and immunity shall attach to the offices occupied by the Trade Delegation and used exclusively for its commercial functions, which shall be to facilitate and encourage the development of trade between the two countries and to represent the interests of the Union of Soviet Socialist Republics in all that pertains to trade.

The Delegation shall be responsible for all transactions concluded by the Trade Representative and persons authorised by him, but not for the acts of State economic organisations except when such responsibility has been clearly accepted by the Trade Representative. The names of the Trade Representative and of the persons empowered to represent him shall be periodically published in the *Board of Trade Journal.* Any question arising from the commercial transactions entered into in this country by the Trade Delegation shall be settled by British Courts.

Article III accords national treatment to the vessels, cargoes and passengers of each country, and most favoured nation treatment as regards the coasting trade, subject to the reservation of the right of cabotage as regards trade between two ports on the same coast. Three notes annexed to this Article exclude from its provisions:

(*a*) Fishing rights;

(*b*) Immigrants, emigrants and pilgrims, and

(*c*) Ships, cargoes and passengers registered in His Majesty's self-governing Dominions.

By Article V the provisions of the agreement may also be extended, on condition of reciprocity, to any of His Majesty's Colonies, Possessions, Protectorates and Mandated Territories, if the Government of the Union of Soviet Socialist Republics are so notified by His Majesty's Ambassador at Moscow. In this event the Union of Soviet Socialist Republics' trading organisations may send thither agents acceptable to the Government concerned, to carry out commercial transactions. Such agents shall have no diplomatic or consular privileges or immunities.

Article VI provides that, if Union of Soviet Socialist Republics produce is accorded most-favoured-nation treatment in territories mentioned in Articles 4 and 5 which have nevertheless not adhered to the agreement, the Union of Soviet Socialist Republics will accord reciprocity reserving itself the right to denounce this article in respect of any Dominion or India.

Article VII provides that the agreement shall remain in force from the date of its signature till the entry into force of a commercial Treaty subject to the right of either Party to denounce the agreement or any arrangements entered into under Articles 4 or 5 at six months' notice.

The agreement is followed by a Protocol and an additional Protocol. In the former it is stated that the contracting Parties are animated by the intention to eliminate from their economic relations all form of discrimination, and that they will be guided only by commercial and financial considerations. They will adopt no legislative or administrative action as would place the trade of the other Party in a position of inferiority to that of any other foreign country.

In accordance with the above principle, trade between the United Kingdom and the Union of Soviet Socialist Republics shall be eligible for consideration on the same basis as trade between the United Kingdom and other foreign countries in connection with any legislative or administrative measures which are or may be taken by His Majesty's Government in the United Kingdom for the granting of credits to facilitate such trade. That is to say, that in considering the given transaction regard shall be had to financial and commercial considerations only.

The Additional Protocol lays down with reference to the relevant paragraph 2 that diplomatic privileges and immunities enjoyed by the trade delegation shall not be claimed in connection with any proceedings before the British Courts arising out of commercial transactions entered into by the trade delegation.

The signature of the agreement was accompanied by declarations by Mr. Henderson to the effect that the Union of South Africa and the Irish Free State were excluded from the operation of Articles 4 and 6, and by a declaration by the Soviet Ambassador reserving to his Government the right to hold vessels, military and merchant, of the former Russian fleet, which were either the property of the Russian Government or subject to nationalisation by Soviet law, and which escaped actual transference to Soviet Government organisations."

The Soviet Embassy in London issued the following statement the same evening:

> "The temporary commercial agreement between the United Kingdom and the U.S.S.R. signed to-day, is an instrument advantageous to both countries.
>
> It provides the necessary basis and proper machinery for the development of trade between Great Britain and the Soviet Union.

Every effort must now be made to use the possibilities which now exist beyond doubt for the development of trade between the two countries in order fully to consolidate the economic relations between Great Britain and the U.S.S.R.

Following upon the signing of this temporary agreement, negotiations for a permanent commercial treaty are to begin."*

The Ambassador of the U.S.S.R. in London stated to a *Daily Herald* correspondent that the Agreement:

"Would facilitate the conclusion of a permanent treaty, and would at the same time be to the immediate interest of the two countries.

It gives special advantages in the Soviet Union to British trade, and, by establishing a Soviet Trade Delegation in London, it will help forward a commercial rapprochement.

This Trade Delegation will be able to study the possibilities of the British market for supplying the needs of Soviet industry, and will also have full powers to place orders in Great Britain.

Another important point is that the two parties agree to base their economic relations on the principle of 'no discrimination'—that is, no political considerations of any kind can be invoked to the detriment of either in economic affairs.

So our economic relations will be determined exclusively by economic considerations.

Already the more favourable atmosphere created by the restoration of diplomatic relations has brought about a marked improvement in trade.

The new treaty, I hope, will be a powerful factor in further improving not only trade but also the general relations between the peoples of our two countries."†

The agreement was greeted with satisfaction not only in the U.S.S.R. but in Labour and Liberal circles, as well as by many Conservatives, but the Die-Hards, the Lord Brentfords (Joynson-Hicks), Locker-Lampsons, the Birkenheads, etc., supported by the *Morning Post* and *Daily Mail* opposed the treaty very bitterly.

The *Morning Post*, for instance, concluded a hostile leader with the words: "We shall, in fact, get little by this agreement but trouble. We shall import propaganda, of which we have already more than enough at home, and export 'credit facilities.'"

The *Times* and *Daily Telegraph* were somewhat more restrained in their language and more cautious in their condemnation, but they were none the less hostile.

* *Financial News*, 17.iv.30.

† 17.iv.30.

At all costs certain sections of Tories were determined to prevent the establishment of friendly relations between Great Britain and the U.S.S.R. and after the conclusion of the agreement they continued and, indeed, increased their campaign of misrepresentation and distortion of actual facts, with which we have dealt earlier.

In particular, they pursued a systematic propaganda against trade with the U.S.S.R., above all against Soviet exports to Great Britain, forgetting in their heat that if the U.S.S.R. like other countries were to place orders here, she could only pay for them by being permitted to export her own products. This indeed was even more true of the U.S.S.R. than of other countries, since she had no invisible exports, i.e., no shipping engaged in foreign trade and no foreign investments.

They pursued two lines of attack against Soviet exports. In the first place they appealed to our business instincts and accused the Soviet Government of systematic and deliberate dumping for the express purpose of upsetting the international and particularly the British market; secondly, they appealed to our instincts of humanity, alleging that the goods exported were produced by slave or terribly exploited labour and at the expense of the starvation of the Soviet workers and peasants.

Before proceeding to discuss the details of these attacks on Soviet exports, it will be as well to deal briefly with the negotiations on the question of British claims for pre-war debts and sequestrated properties and Soviet counter-claims. As mentioned in the last chapter, the then Foreign Secretary, Mr. Arthur Henderson, when announcing the restoration of diplomatic relations on November 5, 1929, added: "I want to say very emphatically to the House that the Government do not intend to recommend Parliament to pledge the credit of the British taxpayer to any loan raised by the Soviet Government," a statement of policy which doomed the subsequent negotiations to failure.

In the Protocol signed by Mr. Arthur Henderson and M. Dovgalevsky in October, 1929, on the occasion of the renewal of diplomatic relations, it was mutually agreed that the question of claims and counter-claims would be settled by negotiations, and in the absence of any disclaimer on the part of Mr. Henderson, the Soviet representatives naturally thought that the Labour Government would proceed on the basis of the Treaties of 1924, which included a guaranteed loan. Mr. Henderson's statement of November 5, 1929, therefore created an entirely new situation. However, the Soviet Government agreed to enter into negotiations on the disputed questions, although they could not have entertained any very serious hopes of their success.

A special committee consisting of representatives of both Governments was set up and held its first meeting in London, October 2, 1930, after which the following statement was issued by the Foreign Office:

> "The British and Russian members of the Anglo-Soviet Debts and Claims Committee were received by Mr. Henderson at the Foreign Office this morning. The Russian delegation were introduced by the Soviet Ambassador. Afterwards the British and Russian delegations withdrew in order to make arrangements for the date and place of future meetings.
>
> The Debts and Claims Committee is provided for in the Protocol signed by Mr. Henderson and M. Dovgalevsky on October 3, last year. According to the terms of the Protocol, a committee of experts was to meet in order to inquire into the whole question of claims and counter-claims as a necessary preliminary to a treaty in settlement of the question, which is eventually to be negotiated between the Secretary for Foreign Affairs and the Soviet Ambassador in London when the committee of experts has finished its work.
>
> The committee will meet again shortly to set up sub-committees for the purpose of dealing with the details of the questions under discussion."

We would underline the words "claims and counter-claims," because the Soviet Government had always adamantly maintained that by every canon of natural justice, their counter-claims were at the very least as justifiable as British claims. The sub-committees were duly appointed and had several meetings in the course of the next fifteen months. However, it soon became apparent that although the British Government pressed the claims of British nationals for pre-war debts and sequestrated properties, they emphatically refused to acknowledge the Soviet Government's counter-claims.

In the hope of breaking the deadlock, the Soviet representatives proposed the method of the 1924 Treaties, i.e., a guaranteed loan, but this was rejected with equal emphasis by the British side and finally the Soviet Ambassador in London proposed to the then British Foreign Secretary, Mr. Arthur Henderson, on July 24, 1931, that it would be better to postpone the negotiations until a more favourable atmosphere existed. That was how the matter stood when the Labour Government left office a month later—a subject dealt with in a subsequent chapter.

Sir John Simon (now Lord Simon) who became Foreign Secretary in the "National" Government, discussed the subject with the Soviet Ambassador on December 9, 1931, but no progress was made. Sir John reported the subject to his Government and the latter decided not to proceed with the negotiations for the time being. The British Foreign Secretary, in a long Note dated January 27, 1932, to the Soviet Ambassador, referring to the conversation of December 9, 1931, among other things stated:

> "You gave me to understand that the only proposal made by the Government of the Union of Soviet Socialist Republics was that His Majesty's Government should definitely accept the principle that a debt settlement must be associated with arrangements for a credit or a loan before any concrete progress could be made in the debts and claims negotiations. This is a principle which His Majesty's Government have refused to accept in the past, and they do not propose to alter their policy in the present circumstances. I assume, however, that it is still the intention of your Government, as it is that of His Majesty's Government, to abide by the terms of the Protocol signed by Mr. Henderson and Monsieur Dovgalevsky on October 3, 1929, and to settle by negotiation the question of Anglo-Soviet Debts and Claims. If this principle of maintaining the terms of the Protocol is admitted, then, since the only proposal so far made by your Government is based on a condition which is unacceptable to His Majesty's Government, I find myself reluctantly in agreement with the view expressed by Your Excellency to Mr. Henderson, that it would be better not to continue the negotiations at the present time."*

There the matter rested for the time being but the subject was opened again when another Trade Agreement was being negotiated in 1933 and 1934. We deal with this question in a subsequent chapter.

CHAPTER XV

AGITATION AGAINST SOVIET WHEAT AND TIMBER ON BRITISH MARKET (1930)

THE two chief commodities around which anti-Soviet agitation centred in 1930 and 1931 were wheat and timber. It will be recalled that pre-war Russia was a considerable exporter of both these products. Although the yield of grain per acre was very poor—one of the lowest in Europe indeed—nevertheless her aggregate harvest, owing to her huge size, was very high, and pre-war Russia was one of the main sources of the world's grain supply.

"One of the world's chief producers of grain in normal times,

* *Hansard*, 2.ii.32, cols. 24/25.

> Russia supplied 51 per cent. of the rye, 33 per cent. of the barley, 25 per cent. of the oats, and 22 per cent of the wheat grown."*

In the years 1909-13, Russia exported nearly as much wheat as the Argentine and Canada combined and more barley and oats than all the chief exporters of these grains, including Canada. Such exports were only possible because of the systematic underfeeding and exploitation of the masses of the Russian workers and peasants.

> "Even to-day, in estimating the margin available for export, the Central Statistical Committee of Petrograd takes the amount of corn required for home consumption at $5\frac{1}{2}$ cwt. per head of the population, an allowance far smaller than that of any civilised country, and just half the amount provided by the Russian Government itself for every Russian soldier."†

Nor did exports cease even in the worst famine years. At that time all this was considered quite natural and the *Times Book of Russia* (1916) stated that "in the famine year of 1897, Schwanebach estimated the exports at one-fourth of the entire harvest of the Empire."

Not a voice was raised at that time against Russian dumping or regarding the immorality of buying Russian grain whilst Russian peasants were starving. After the Revolution and up to 1924, Russia was out of the international grain market. Between 1924-26 Russian grain again entered the market, though on a much smaller scale than hitherto.

In the meantime, home consumption per head of the population in the U.S.S.R. had increased considerably and although the aggregate Soviet harvests were no less, there was a distinct falling off in Soviet grain exports in 1927-29. At the same time for a variety of reasons, other grain exporting countries considerably increased their acreage under wheat, with the result that world harvests and reserves of wheat increased in 1927-29, and in 1930 there was a very considerable fall in prices—no one then suggested or could suggest that the U.S.S.R. was in any way to blame for this drop in price. This was how the *Corn Trade Year Book*, 1930, described the position:

> "In the late summer of 1929, most of those engaged in the wheat trade were taking a bullish view of the market on expectations of heavily reduced crops in exporting countries. For many months the situation had been gloomy and depressed. The shadow of the record 1928 exporters' crops had been over every

* *Russian Almanac*, 1919, p. 77.

† *The Times Book of Russia*, 1916, pp. 161/162.

transaction. Confidence was weakened and business reduced to all but a retail basis. Now it seemed that the overburdening weight of supply was at last to be lifted. Canada was reporting severe drought damage in Saskatchewan and Alberta. The spring wheat production of the United States was being returned at 100 million bushels below that of the previous year. Argentina's and Australia's crops were still uncertain, but there appeared to be every likelihood of a considerable reduction in the output. Prices were put up sharply in North America and on the face of it there was ample justification for the advance. When the official crop estimates were published it was found that the wheat production of exporting countries fell below that of 1928 by no less than 80 million quarters. This represented an unprecedented seasonal variation in the world's surplus supply of new wheat."

However, the anticipated rise in prices did not follow. The report continued:

"And yet the eight months of the current season which we are now reviewing has been a time of unexampled depression in the wheat trade. It has been a period of crises, of heavily declining prices and serious financial difficulties. Despite the greatly reduced production in exporting countries, supplies have been constantly in excess of requirements. Both Canada and the United States have maintained their policy of the previous season and have held the greater part of their surplus wheat off the market. Yet even this extreme step, rendered possible by Government financial backing, has failed to prevent prices falling to new low records for post-war years.

The causes for the depression may be grouped under two headings:

1. The abundant crops secured by European importing countries in 1929.

2. Heavy carry-overs in exporting countries from the 1928 crops."

Between the beginning and the end of the 1929-30 season (i.e. August 1, 1929 to July 31, 1930) the price of wheat fell by nearly 50 per cent., but shipments of wheat from the U.S.S.R. for that season were less than one per cent. of the world total shipments.

In connection with the economic development of the U.S.S.R. under the First Five-Year Plan, Soviet agriculture was being reorganised by the establishment of large-scale collective farming, which made possible the application of machinery to agriculture on a big scale, with the result that in 1930, the U.S.S.R. had a bumper grain harvest. In accordance with her programme of industrialisation, the U.S.S.R. at that time also required to import large quantities of machinery and equipment for her heavy industries and as pointed out previously she could only pay for such imports by means of exporting as much of her own products as she could possibly afford. Accordingly, having obtained a good harvest, she again entered the world market with her wheat.

In August, 1930, the Soviet Union appeared on the British grain market as a seller, and her agents fought hard for the best possible prices, but the prices which they were compelled to accept finally were not fixed by them, but by the British market, which in turn reflected the state of the world market.

Unfortunately for the U.S.S.R.—although hardly unfortunately for the consumer—it was estimated that for the 1930-31 wheat year there would be a huge excess of supplies of wheat over the demand, with the result that prices rattled downwards. This was sufficient, and without stopping to analyse or even to look at the facts which they themselves had published, the whole blame for this fall in prices was put upon the U.S.S.R. For instance, the *Daily Express*, in a featured article on September 12, 1930, stated that the "bottom had been knocked out of the wheat market in Great Britain" by Russian exports, and yet in the same article we read: "The following table shows how wheat prices have fallen in recent years":

Year.	*A Quarter.*
1920	80s. 11d.
1922	47s. 10d.
1924	49s. 3d.
1926	53s. 3d.
1928	42s. 3d.
1929	42s. 3d.

No explanation was vouchsafed for the fall in prices between 1920 and 1922, or between 1926 and 1929. Had the *Daily Express* mentioned the notorious fact that Russia had exported little during these periods, the bottom would have been "knocked out" of their case more effectively than out of the wheat market.

On September 23, 1930, the *Morning Post*, in a prominently printed article headed "Serious Slump in Grain Prices," informed its readers that:

> "Grain prices yesterday reached new record low levels for the post-war period. The serious pressure of Russian dumping is forcing down wheat prices."

During October, 1930, prices continued to fall. Was the U.S.S.R., or were the grain-exporting countries of the southern hemisphere to blame? The *Financial News* supplied the answer:

> "All the latest cable advices emphasise the beneficial character of the soaking rains which have visited the Eastern States of Australia, and estimates of the out-turn now range from 170 to 200 million bushels, compared with 126 millions last year. Argentina also has had good rain, and it has come most opportunely for the standing crops. It is known that many traders are expecting very low wheat prices when Argentina and Australia are offering freely in competition with Canada and Russia, although it must be expected that stout resistance will be offered to declines below the present level."*
>
> "After keeping steady for most of the week, wheat turned weak on an increase of a million acres in the Argentine official estimate of sowings, good rains in Argentina, and lower offers of old and new crop; quotations are 3d. lower to 6d. per quarter higher on the week."†

Similar facts and figures appeared in a number of other journals—but this could not damp the ardour of the anti-Soviet die-hards. The matter was raised in Parliament when Dr. C. Addison, then Minister for Agriculture, gave the following reply:

> ". . . the fact is that the present slump in prices was foreseen and quite openly spoken about months before these Russian imports appeared in our ports at all. When I give the House the figures of the stocks they will understand why that is so.
>
> The corn trade estimated that the requirements of wheat importing countries this year will be 396,000,000 cwt., but the surplus estimated of the wheat exporting countries this year is 633,000,000 cwt. In other words, the surplus is not far short of twice as much as the requirements of the wheat importing countries. To that surplus of 633,000,000 cwt. the Russian contribution is expected to be 30,000,000. When the facts and figures are stated as they are, the case answers itself."‡

And a few days later, Mr. Graham, President of the Board of Trade, stated in the House of Commons, in reply to a question, that only 5 per cent. of the total wheat imported by Great Britain in the nine months ending September 30, 1930, had come from the U.S.S.R. Needless to say, the statements by Dr. Addison and Mr. Graham were

* *Financial News*, 20.x.30. † Ibid., 27.x.30.
‡ *Hansard*, 30.x.30, col. 266.

not given any prominence in the journals which attacked Soviet imports.

However, the agitation had one result which the opponents of trade with the Soviets by no means intended; as in the case of oil, the sustained free advertisement given to Russian wheat by this agitation, coupled with its good quality, led to a definite increase in imports, and in the year July 1, 1930 to June 30, 1931, out of a total of 108,000,000 cwts. of wheat imported into Great Britain, 26,000,000 or over 24 per cent. came from the U.S.S.R., as against only 5 per cent. in the first nine months of 1930.

At about the same time as the raging propaganda against Soviet wheat, a similar and indeed an even more vociferous outcry was raised against the importation of Soviet timber. Russia having the largest forest areas in the world, timber had always been an important article of her exports, and Great Britain had always been one of Russia's best customers for this article. Thus, in 1913, Russia had exported 7,597,500 tons of timber, 45 per cent, of which was shipped to Great Britain. In view of the agitation on the subject in 1930 and 1931, it is particularly important to bear in mind that in Tsarist Russia trade unionism was illegal and prison labour was used in the trade, but there were no protests on the part of the Tory press or any section of that Party just as there was no objection on the part of the Conservatives to the importation of products made by forced labour from the Colonial possessions of France, Holland, Italy, etc.

The world war and foreign armed intervention and blockade wrought ruin in the Russian timber industry as in most of her other industries, and up till about the end of 1921 Soviet Russia exported no timber. In the economic year, October, 1921, to September, 1922, the Soviet Government resumed exports of timber, but they amounted to less than 500,000 tons—about 7 per cent. of the pre-war Russian exports. In the meantime, Great Britain, unable to obtain Russian timber, had increased her purchases of timber from Sweden and Finland. The exporters of these countries took advantage of the absence of Russian timber on the world and British markets and raised their prices enormously.

"The average price for timber exported was, in 1913, 29.95 kr. per cubic metre, and in 1920, 110.32 kr. per cubic metre, i.e., an increase of only 268 per cent."* In other words, when in 1920 the cost of living was about 150 per cent. above pre-war, the Finnish and Swedish timber exporters were charging the timber consumers of Great Britain 268 per cent. above pre-war prices. However, the U.S.S.R. steadily increased her timber exports until by 1926 they amounted to 1,921,800

* In a pamphlet issued by "The Swedish Wood Exporters' Association and the Finnish Sawmill Owners' Association."

tons (still only some 25 per cent. of the pre-war Russian exports); at the same time prices fell very considerably—to about 37 per cent. of those in 1921.

So far from Soviet timber exports being attacked either as dumping or as slave produced, they and the consequent fall in price were welcomed. Naturally enough, the Swedish and Finnish timber exporters were not so enthusiastic about the re-entry of the U.S.S.R. on the timber market, and when the British Government severed relations with the U.S.S.R. in 1927, with the consequent unsettling of the Soviet timber trade, they were not slow in reaping an advantage. "U/S Redwood f.o.b. South Finland 3-in. by 9-in Deals rose from £13 10s. per standard in 1926 to £14 in 1927 and £16 in 1928."*

In spite of the Anglo-Soviet rupture in 1927, Soviet timber exports, as a result of the restoration and development of the Soviet timber industry after a short time again began to increase. British timber importers, as distinct from the Swedish and Finnish interests, welcomed this, the more so as Russian timber was admittedly of excellent quality. Already in August, 1928, three or four importing firms had combined to purchase the then available balance—about 80,000 standards—of Soviet whitewood, and so satisfactory was this transaction that on January 5, 1929, it was announced in the press that a syndicate of nineteen important British firms had been formed to purchase the whole of Russia's timber exports for 1929.

Prices as a result of the agreement fell somewhat. Thus "U/S Redwood f.o.b. South Finland 3-in. by 9-in. Deals fell from £16 per standard in the beginning of 1928 to £15 10s. in 1929, and to £15 in 1930."† It was, of course, not the Soviet timber organisations who demanded even this fall in price, but the British syndicate by buying in bulk were able in 1929 and in subsequent years to reduce the price charged by the Soviets as by other timber exporters.

British timber merchants visited the U.S.S.R. in July, 1929, and bore testimony to the prompt delivery by the Soviet organisations of the exact quality and quantity of timber stipulated. Throughout the whole of 1929, as far as we are aware, not a word of criticism was directed by any responsible person against the Anglo-Russian timber agreement, and no charges of "Soviet dumping" and "forced labour" were formulated.

However, in the spring of 1930, a raging campaign broke out against Soviet timber. The accusation of dumping of commodities such as wheat and timber, which could not in any case be raised in any large quantities in Great Britain, having fallen flat, a gallant attempt was made to convince the British public that Soviet timber should be taboo because it was produced by slave or at best serf or prison labour.

* Ibid. † Ibid.

The lie factories of Riga and Helsingfors worked at full pressure, producing the most harrowing tales of the woes of the Soviet peasants and workers generally and of the timber workers in particular. "Escaped Soviet prisoners" seemed to spring up like mushrooms in this and other countries, each producing a more hair-raising tale than the other. The Tory press lapped up these stories and spread them across their pages with gusto for over a year—till about the middle of 1931—after which they gradually died down, being renewed from time to time when negotiations were conducted for the purchase of Soviet timber by timber merchants in Britain.

A volume could be filled with the above-mentioned stories and their refutation. We shall limit ourselves here to but a few examples.

The *Times* of April 9, 1930, published a report from its "Riga correspondent" made up of a tissue of absurdities, amongst which it was stated:

> "The Soviet authorities have formally introduced a system of compulsory labour for the timber industry in the whole of the northern territory . . . the labourers in question will prepare timber for export and convoy it from the forests. . . . Now, *Izvestia* explains, it is necessary to authorise forced labour."

This was a most impudent invention. The *Izvestia* in question said nothing about forced labour; all it did was to draw attention to the shortage of labour in the timber industry and to the need to overhaul the personnel of some of the departments concerned with the enrolling of labour for this industry.

The subject of forced labour in the Soviet timber industry was also raised in the House of Commons and on November 25, 1930, Mr. Philip Snowden, in reply to a question said:

> "I made a statement on July 22 last, saying that, if there was any evidence at all that these imports fell within the Foreign Prison-made Goods Act, all that a person had to do was to submit his evidence to the Commissioners of Customs and Excise. Nearly six months have elapsed since that statement, and indeed, invitation, and not one representation has yet been made."*

Thus challenged, Sir Hilton Young, on December 11, 1930, sent a statutory declaration to the Prime Minister, signed by "three escaped Russian prisoners," together with a covering letter in which Sir Hilton stated that "the industry is apparently manned mainly by prisoners."

Since over two million men were engaged in the Soviet timber trade,

* *Hansard*, cols. 1087/1088.

and the work of felling, hauling and transporting was scattered over an enormous area, it is obvious that it would have required a large army to superintend the work of over two million convicts under such conditions.

The next " proof " came from a " former high Ogpu official," and was specially featured by the *Times*. In the course of his contribution this gentleman seriously asserted:

> " Every prisoner engaged in forest work has to fell and strip 35 timber logs a day. He must start out for the job early in the morning while it is dark, and is given a box of matches in order to be able to find the trees marked down for felling."*

So the convict would have to find his way through a dense forest in the depth of winter with four to six feet of snow on the ground with a box of matches!

But the next essay threw its predecessors completely in the shade. On this occasion we were regaled with a symposium of nine statutory declarations, which Commander Bellairs, M.P., sent to the Prime Minister.

The signatories of the declaration stated: that there were " 662,000 prisoners in the timber camps," that " the soil remains more or less frozen all the year round " ; that " in winter the work goes on uninterruptedly from five in the morning until eight in the evening " ; that " in winter every prisoner had to saw down 35 trees at soil level."†

Dr. Ferguson (who had been medical inspector of lumber camps in Northern Canada) in a letter to the *Manchester Guardian* of February 11, 1931, pointed out that " no trees could possibly grow in soil more or less frozen all the year round " ; that " as the sun rises in these regions in the winter time at 9 a.m. and sets at 4 p.m., the men must be working for eight hours in total darkness, and that in a dense forest " ; that it would be impossible to " cut down a tree at soil level . . . with six feet of snow on the ground and everything frozen solid."

Further, in the course of a letter to the authors of the present book, Dr. Ferguson stated:

> " An average of thirty fir trees, worth cutting, to the acre is considered a good average, so that each man clears an acre a day, and as there are 640 acres to the square mile and 662,000 prisoners at work, they would cut one thousand square miles a day. They would have to change camp on the run to keep up with the cut."

* 31.i.31. † *Times*, 9.ii.31.

On the basis of these statistics, in three months (which is the annual period of work in the forest area round Archangel) they would have cleared an area exceeding the total area of Great Britain, and would have cut about 70,000,000 standards of timber, which would be valued at approximately £1,200,000,000. Great Britain was probably the biggest importer of timber in the world, but even her imports were valued in 1930 at less than £43,000,000.

These affidavits did service for a time, but the more they were discussed, the more their absurdities became patent, till even a "White" Russian publication *The Anglo-Russian News,* stated editorially on March 14, 1931:

> "Offers of affidavits and sworn declarations from escaped Soviet prisoners are reaching this country from Finland, Poland and other countries. The majority of these affidavits are fictitious and British politicians and business men are warned against purchasing these 'documents.'
>
> The Editor of this Service has recently examined a number of these declarations and he has found them unreliable and misleading."

Later, even the *Times,* which sponsored one of these documents and featured all of them, fought shy of these affidavits. It published a series of articles on labour conditions in Russia, and commenting on their contents editorially on April 25, 1931, wrote: "No use has been made of affidavits from escaped prisoners."

The Soviet authorities denied absolutely that any forced labour was being used in the branches of the timber industry producing for export. Of course, convicts were, and are, employed in the U.S.S.R. as in other countries, on useful work for the State—road-making, hut building, etc.

In actual fact all the workers in the industry were, as in the case of other workers, engaged under terms negotiated between the competent Trade Union and the Soviet Timber Trust. The wages of the timber workers were in 1930-31 more than double those in pre-war days—not to speak of the various additional privileges enjoyed by the workers under the Soviets of which they never dreamt under Tsardom and which formed a substantial addition to their wages.

During the whole of the press and platform campaign against the import of Soviet timber, not the slightest reliable evidence was advanced to substantiate the charge that forced or prison labour was used in the felling, transporting, preparing or loading of timber for export.

Responsible British timber experts denied these stories. Thus, at the annual dinner of the Timber Trades Federation of the United

Kingdom, on March 18, 1931, the President of the Federation, Mr. E. P. Tetsall, in the course of a speech, said:

> "To suggest that a system of convict labour was in operation in the export timber trade of Russia was a serious misrepresentation which must operate to the prejudice of the British timber trade at the time when the opportunities for its expansion were favourable. It could be stated on authority that the accommodation was satisfactory, and food supplies in those Russian timber camps were better than in the towns. To the charge that they bought Russian timber only because it was cheap, they replied that *Douglas fir from Canada and the United States had been coming into this country for a long time at less money and was to-day being sold at lower prices than Russian timber.*"* (Our italics).

The only attempt to advance such evidence was the Report of the Anti-Slavery and Aborigines Protection Society, published June, 1931. The inquiry was carried out by Sir Alan Pim, K.C.I.E., C.I.S., and Mr. Edward Bateson, formerly a judge of the Egyptian Mixed Tribunals, no doubt quite honest, estimable men, but as their titles and positions would show, probably anti-Socialists and hardly the men to be impartial where the Soviets were concerned. The introduction to the report was written by Lord Buckmaster, G.C.V.O., and breathed hostility towards and ignorance of the Soviet system in almost every line.

When reviewing the general position with regard to "forced" and "slave" labour, the Report, as might be expected from the class position of the investigators, used these terms in the same sense as they are usually applied in capitalist countries.

It is hardly necessary to be a partisan of the Soviet system of Government and organisation of the national economy to see that such use of the terms "forced" and "slave" is wholly unjustified when applied to the U.S.S.R., the terms "slave" and "forced" labour necessarily imply slave owners and masters for whose benefit such labour is exploited.

Not even the worst enemies of the Soviet Government have ever contended that the Soviet leaders and members of the Soviet Government were exploiting the workers and peasants of the U.S.S.R. for their own personal gain. *No one was or is heaping up fortunes in that country*; the Soviet statesmen and public men live as simply as the masses of the people, and have always shared whatever hardships the country has had to go through. What the report designated as "forced" labour was really the *planned* organisation of the labour power of the country.

* *Times*, 19.iii.31.

When industry, agriculture, transport, etc., is nationalised and worked for the benefit of the whole people and an endeavour is being made to plan the various branches of the national economy so as to give the maximum results it is, so the Soviet authorities contend, unthinkable that such a state of affairs should be permitted to exist as would allow a large surplus of labour power to be idle in certain parts of the country when this labour was urgently required in other parts, or to allow some industrial enterprises to be overstaffed and others, no less if not more important for the country as a whole, to be hampered by a shortage of labour.

The compulsion here used is comparable rather to the compulsion applied to members of a family who persistently refuse to do their fair share of necessary work, thus making the labour more arduous for the rest and the whole life of the family less comfortable—but it certainly bears no resemblance to the labour of the Indian coolies who are forced to work for their English or Indian masters for a pittance not even sufficient to keep body and soul together,* nor to the slaves or serfs of the Belgian Congo, the Dutch East Indies, etc., etc.

The Soviet system is based on the principle of "he who does not work neither shall he eat," and endeavours to apply this principle to *all* its citizens. In other countries the principle is applied exclusively to the *working* population. We may prefer the capitalist organisation which leaves the worker "free" to choose, within certain limits, by which employer *he shall be exploited,* although it is a moot point as to how far our miners, for instance, unless they have a fair amount saved up, are "free" to go and work where they like. In any case, once an industry is organised nationally the distribution of labour available for it must be planned ; we may oppose such a system, but it is unfair to designate such labour as "forced" or "slave" labour.

The evidence given at the inquiry by the Russian "White" witnesses bristled with absurdities and contradictions. We cannot stop to analyse them here—suffice it to say that although, as indicated above, the report was definitely anti-Soviet and made the charge that convict labour had been used for loading timber, it nevertheless also stated that "Convict labour is not employed by the State Timber Trust for export production" and that "the conditions of voluntary labour are probably definitely superior to those existing in pre-war times."

Finally, the report stated that class (*a*), i.e. local inhabitants, for whom it is a customary seasonal occupation, "furnished the bulk of the labour required, and for this class *the conditions were certainly not worse than they were before the war.*"

It is, of course, possible that in isolated cases local officials may have

* See *Report on Labour Conditions in India,* by A. A. Purcell and J. Hallsworth; British Trades Union Congress Delegation to India, November, 1927, to March, 1928.

acted illegally and used convict labour for loading operations. Such practices were stopped immediately they were brought to the notice of the Central authorities and the report itself did not charge the Soviets with using forced labour for loading operations at the time the enquiry was being held.

Apart from the general hatred of the Tories for the Soviets which lay at the root of this agitation, as of other anti-Soviet campaigns, there can be no doubt that a powerful factor in this campaign were Scandinavian interests which stood to gain by a cessation or diminution of Soviet timber exports. This fact was referred to from time to time in the press and at public meetings.

For instance, during a discussion at the annual meeting of the Association of British Chambers of Commerce, on April 24, 1931, Mr. James Fiddles (the Aberdeen delegate) said that "a large part of the agitation relative to 'forced labour' was undoubtedly due to the operations of the agents of Scandinavian countries interested in timber."* Mr. Fiddles' charges were categorical and serious, yet so far as we know they were never challenged.

Again, the *Timber Trades Journal,* of March 13, 1931 (page 711), declared:

> "Scandinavian exporters have, moreover, been kept well informed of the campaign in this country against the use of Russian wood, on the ground that it is produced by slave or forced labour and, although they may very well despair of any British Government taking action to hamper the Russian export, they see the possibility, in certain quarters, of a *boycott sufficiently extensive to put a premium on Scandinavian wood.*" (Our italics).

And on page 767 the same journal stated:

> "The leading Finnish shippers seem inclined to stand firm for the present, possibly in the hope that the *intensive political campaign against Russian wood may bear fruit.*" (Our italics.)

But the most important reason for the intensification of the anti-Soviet campaigns in Great Britain and other countries was the economic position in the U.S.S.R. itself. The First Five-Year Plan which, when it was launched on October 1, 1928, had been derided and sneered at as a kind of megalomania on the part of the Soviet leaders, was now well under way so far as the actual constructions were concerned. Indeed, by the Spring of 1930 it was clearly evident that as a whole, the First Five-Year Plan would be completed in a little over four years. This in itself was hardly calculated to please those hostile to the Soviets.

* *Financial News*. 25.iv.31.

On the other hand, the rapid tempo of industrialisation, the shortage of a sufficient number of skilled workers and loyal experts to man the new enterprises efficiently, had created serious, albeit temporary, difficulties within the U.S.S.R.

Since the cessation of foreign armed intervention, the years 1930-31 were undoubtedly the most difficult years through which the U.S.S.R. had passed—on the one hand there were the heavy sacrifices required to carry out the great constructions of the Five-Year Plan and on the other, these new constructions, as well as the numerous newly-formed collective farms, were not yet able to yield a sufficiently increased output to satisfy the demands of the population.

These difficulties were increased by disloyal elements and wreckers who were doing their best at home to foster discontent among the workers and particularly among the more backward peasantry, not only by spreading all sorts of false rumours, but also by direct acts of sabotage and wrecking, both in industry and agriculture.* Abroad, too, the Russian " White " emigrés, as well as their foreign friends, were determined to exploit these difficulties to the full. They no doubt thought now, if ever, was the time to bring about the downfall of the Soviets by hindering the establishment of normal trading relations between the U.S.S.R. and other countries and by instigating hostility towards the Soviets, by the spread of all sorts of lies regarding forced labour in the timber and other Soviet industries, the unashamed misrepresentation of the organisation of collective farming as a reintroduction of serfdom, false accusations of dumping Soviet oil, grain, butter and other products, etc., etc.

The Russian " White " emigré press indeed made no secret of its object and hopes; as one example we may take a leading article in the Paris " White " emigré (Monarchist) Russian journal, *Vozrozhdenie,* April 12, 1930, which made daylight clear the source and object of all these stories about forced labour and dumped goods. This article deplored the fact that its prophecies of the coming terrible famine in the U.S.S.R. seemed to have fallen flat, but hoped that the heart of European public opinion might be touched by the description of the hard fate of the kulaks as a result of the Soviet policy of collectivisation, the more so as " cultured " opinion had been prepared for it by the " Christian Protest Campaign." At the same time, it was made clear that " reason " was also to be appealed to by stories of forced labour and cheap dumped goods. In this way, it concluded:

> " The hour for the fall of the Bolsheviks and the return of the emigrés to the Fatherland will be brought nigh."

These emigrés received the full backing of the anti-Soviet, and

* This was brought out subsequently in the Soviet State Trials of 1930, 1931, 1933, 1936, 1937, and 1938.

particularly of the Die-Hard Tory elements in Great Britain and other countries. Everything they could do to hinder the expansion of Anglo-Soviet trade and to stir up feeling against and false ideas about conditions in the U.S.S.R. was done by Tory political leaders within Parliament and outside and by various organs of the Tory press. For instance, the *Times*, November 1, 1930, published an article on "Inflation in Russia," which for a wholly erroneous conception, if indeed it was not deliberate misrepresentation, of what was actually happening in the U.S.S.R., it would be very hard to beat.

Starting out with the true statement that the currency in circulation had increased considerably, the writer came to the, for him, desirable conclusion that the "economic controllers of Soviet Russia lost control last April and the economic régime is speeding to a crisis."

To prove this he said:

> "There is one economic law that operates inflexibly in all countries, whether under Soviet or capitalist control, and that is that if the volume of currency in circulation increases more rapidly than the volume of consumable goods coming to market, prices will rise."

And since, according to the writer, "the volume of consumable goods coming to market" is not increasing but decreasing, therefore prices must have risen.

If the facts contradict this—so much the worse for the facts. Actually what the *Times* correspondent forgot was that there were then two markets in the U.S.S.R. The private market where neither prices nor supplies were regulated and where, therefore, capitalist economic law held good. Here it is quite true that the consumable commodities had not increased in comparison with the increase in currency and therefore prices had indeed risen enormously. But the trade done on the private market was only some five per cent. of the total home trade. On the other hand, on the State and co-operative market where both the supply of commodities and prices were regulated and where both manual and brain workers obtained their main supplies, prices had not increased; indeed, they had fallen slightly. Taking 1913 as one, the retail price index on the co-operative and State market on October 1, 1929, was 2.04 and on August 1, 1930, it was 2.03.

Actually, of course, the quantity of goods, both consumers' and producers' in the country as a whole, had increased and was increasing from year to year and from month to month, although it had not kept up with the demand.

The output of the light industries (mainly consumers' goods)

M*

although it had not increased as rapidly as that of the heavy industries, nevertheless did give an increase of over 11 per cent. in 1929-30 as compared with 1928-29. The grain harvest of 1930 was not only 22 per cent. in excess of 1929 but was actually above pre-war.

Seeing that in spite of all this, exports from the U.S.S.R. were still very much behind the pre-war volume, it is clear that the quantity of goods remaining at home was far greater than it was in pre-war days, when no one, least of all the *Times*, talked about the collapse of the régime, etc. What was happening was that the peasants kept more of their produce for themselves and they, as well as the town workers, fed better than they had done under Tsarism. Undoubtedly, the demand was greater than the supply, i.e., workers and peasants were demanding a higher and higher standard of living, which is as it should be, and was spurring the Soviet authorities to greater and greater effort in the production of goods.

The sting and real purpose of the article was in its last paragraph, in which it was affirmed that the internal currency collapse might affect " . . . the ability of the Soviet Government to honour the terms of credit arrangements entered into with foreign sellers."

This, by the way, was a neat dig at the growing demand for an extension of credit facilities for Anglo-Soviet trade and in particular for the re-enactment of the Trade Facilities Acts and their application to such trade. The Trade Facilities Acts, it may be added in parentheses, had lapsed in 1927 and had not been re-enacted, although they had been extremely useful for promoting foreign trade and employment at home, since they were applied for the carrying out of capital undertakings, and there was no statutory period for which guarantees were obtainable under those Acts, these having varied from one to fifty years.

The Overseas Trade Act, on the other hand, whilst also important for promoting foreign trade, was much more limited in scope.

Under the Overseas Trade Act no money was advanced by the British Government, but bills connected with " re-establishing trade, or any branch of trade between the United Kingdom and any country whatsoever " could be guaranteed.

Under the Trade Facilities Acts the interest, or principal, or both, on loans raised in the United Kingdom for the carrying out of capital undertakings could be guaranteed, providing that such were calculated to promote employment in the United Kingdom.

There was nothing in either of these Acts to exclude the U.S.S.R., but under the Tory Government, business with the U.S.S.R. was excluded by an Order of the President of the Board of Trade. The Labour Government, on the other hand, withdrew the embargo and instructed the " Advisory Committee " on the Overseas Trade Act that business with the Soviet Union should be considered on the same principles as with other countries.

Had the Trade Facilities Acts been re-enacted and applied to Anglo-Soviet trade, Great Britain would have obtained millions of pounds' worth of orders, she would have obtained a firm footing in the Soviet market for the supply of the capital goods then required by the U.S.S.R. and this would have meant that the latter in subsequent years would have looked to Great Britain for repeat orders of such goods for spare parts, etc.

As Mr. Lloyd George said in the course of his speech at the third session of the annual conference of the National Liberal Federation at Torquay on October 17, 1930:

> "We must also revive the Trade Facilities Act, which helped us so materially to reduce unemployment in 1922. We must revise and liberalise the conditions of our export credits so as to enable us to capture business like that which was available in Russia. Our timidity there was depriving us of millions a year of excellent business which would provide work more especially for our engineering trades."

However, the Trade Facilities Acts were not re-enacted.

CHAPTER XVI

ATTEMPTS TO ORGANISE AN INTERNATIONAL COALITION AGAINST THE U.S.S.R. AND THEIR FAILURE (1931)

I. The Commission of inquiry for European Union. The Rome Conference, March 26. The London Conference, May 18, and after

During the whole of 1930 and 1931 the anti-Soviet agitation raged unabated both in this country and abroad. Not only was the desirability of armed intervention in the U.S.S.R. openly discussed and advocated in the "White" emigré press published without let or hindrance in France, not only were military organisations of these emigrés permitted to organise military schools and courses, military exercises and parades in uniform in Paris, but what was far more important, French Government policy was at that time undoubtedly directed towards the formation of a bloc of European Powers against the U.S.S.R.

On May 17, 1930, the French Government sent a Memorandum, entitled "Memorandum on the Organisation of a system of European Federal Union," to the various European Governments, but excluded the Governments of the U.S.S.R., Turkey and Iceland.

The Memorandum, together with the replies thereto of the various Powers, were co-ordinated, published as a French White Paper and presented to the European States' Members of the League of Nations, on September 8, 1930, at Geneva.

M. Briand, the author of the scheme, addressed the League Assembly on the subject on September 11, 1930, and six days later the Assembly unanimously passed a resolution agreeing to the appointment of a Committee representative of all the States interested in the proposed federation, together with representatives of the League Secretariat, to study the project.

It is worthy of note that, less than three weeks later, to be precise, on October 3, 1930, a Council of Ministers was held in Paris to receive the reports of the French Delegation at Geneva, and on the same day the Council of Ministers ratified a decree which gave the French Government the right either to prohibit Soviet imports or else restrict them by a system of import licences.

The Government of the U.S.S.R. regarded this decree as a first step toward the organisation of an international commercial blockade against her, and retaliated by issuing a decree, on October 20, 1930, virtually closing the Russian market to France. Subsequent developments confirmed Moscow's suspicions.

The Committee for the proposed European Federal Union met in Geneva on January 16, 1931. Twenty-seven European nations were represented, twenty-two of them by their Prime Ministers or Foreign Ministers.

Seeing that the U.S.S.R. constitutes some 45 per cent. of the territory of Europe, it was preposterous that any European conference should have been held without her participation. The question of inviting her and also Turkey was discussed heatedly at a private meeting of the Commission. The Special Correspondent of the *Manchester Guardian* cabled his paper January 17, 1931, that the discussion had made " one thing at least very plain—namely, that *the French Government is at the head of the European combination against Soviet Russia*." (Our italics.)

Mr. Arthur Henderson proposed that the question should be referred to a sub-committee, which would examine, with special reference to economic questions, whether the co-operation of non-member States could and should be sought, and in what conditions.

This was finally agreed to and on January 20, 1931, the following resolution was adopted:

> " The Commission of Inquiry for European Union, having regard to the resolution of the Assembly of the League of Nations of September 17, 1930, decides to study the world economic crisis

in so far as it affects the European countries as a whole, and to invite through the Secretary-General the Governments of Iceland, Turkey and the Union of Soviet Republics to participate in this study."

This was a compromise between those who wished to invite the U.S.S.R. unreservedly and those who, like France and her then satellites—Poland, Rumania, etc.—desired her exclusion.

Although the Soviet Government naturally enough resented this vague and half-hearted invitation, they wisely refused to play the game of the French reactionaries of isolating the U.S.S.R. with a view to forming a bloc of European States against her. M. Briand, it must be stated, always denied that this was his aim, but the French reactionary press and statesmen like Poincaré quite openly advocated such a policy. In any case, whatever Briand may have said, it was his deeds which were important.

On February 5, 1931, the Secretary-General of the League of Nations, who had been appointed to act as Secretary to the Commission, at the request of M. Briand, who was appointed President, sent out invitations to a conference scheduled to meet in Paris on February 23, 1931. The aim of the conference was to consider means of disposing of the then grain surpluses in Eastern and Central Europe.

The Secretary-General also sent out invitations for a meeting in Paris on February 26, 1931, of the Committee set up by the European Union Commission to consider means of disposing of future harvest surpluses. This committee was composed of representatives of Austria, Belgium, Czechoslovakia, Estonia, France, Germany, Great Britain, Italy, Norway, Switzerland and Yugoslavia.

To neither of these conferences was the U.S.S.R. invited and this in defiance of the resolution of January 20, 1931, in defiance of the fact that the U.S.S.R. was the largest agricultural country in Eastern Europe, an exporter of grain and vitally interested both in the disposal of the then " present grain surplus " and " in the means of disposing of future surpluses."

The excuse given for this monstrous affront was that the Soviets were dumping wheat, to which the Paris correspondent of the *Manchester Guardian* very pertinently replied:

> ". . . one would have thought that if, as is alleged, Russia is responsible for the misfortunes of the Danubian countries, the latter would seize the opportunity to ask the Russian representative for explanations. The truth is that the organisers of the campaign against Russian dumping do not want explanations. *It would not be at all convenient if the Russian representatives pointed out at the Conference on February 23, that at the moment*

when the French decided to stop imports from Russia except by special licence, Rumanian wheat was cheaper than Russian wheat on the French market."* (Our italics).

The *Daily Herald* diplomatic correspondent also made some interesting comments on the discussions at the Conference. He said:

> "Fears as to the purpose of M. Briand's plans will be increased by a speech he made yesterday at the opening meeting of the European Agricultural Conference in Paris, in which he declared that the Conference was the first tangible result of the movement for European Federation.
>
> The agricultural conference was the outcome of the Commission of Inquiry for European Union, at which Great Britain, Germany and Italy were emphatic that there must be no suggestion that the movement was directed against Russia.
>
> But M. Briand, who sent out the invitations to the present conference, did not send one to Moscow. On his own responsibility he has excluded Russia from the Conference. And now, in his speech, he suggests that there are political questions involved, and that 'a European solidarity' is being prepared with Russia outside
>
> The immediate purpose of the conference is to consider how the *European* grain exporting countries can dispose of their surplus stocks.
>
> They want the exclusion from the European market not only of Russian but of all other non-European wheat.
>
> The campaign that is being launched in Paris under the banner of 'European unity' is an attack not only on Russia, but on Canada. And on Great Britain as well as Canada."†

However, the Conference closed February 25, 1931, without achieving any positive results and the same may be said of the second Conference referred to above which opened February 26, 1931.

The latter Conference appointed a sub-committee to examine the subject under discussion and to present a report to the Conference. This report was presented to the Conference on March 1, 1931, and was thus summarised by the *Times* Paris correspondent:

> "The Committee started from the point of view that the problem was not merely European but universal, and that a solution could only be found in an understanding between all the interested parties throughout the world. It had been discovered that while the area under grain in Europe was no larger than before the War, the yield was slightly higher. There

* 12.ii.31. † 24.ii.31.

was no over-production in Europe, but there was over-production in the world generally, and the conditions in which this over-production had come about, i.e. the appearance of Russian grain on the market, made it evident that the crisis would be settled only by patience and at the cost of much suffering. Opportunity for all the countries interested to proceed to an exchange of views would be afforded by the Conference arranged by the International Institute of Agriculture to take place in Rome on March 26."*

The U.S.S.R. participated in the Conference in Rome and her representatives made it clear that whilst the U.S.S.R. was prepared to discuss with other nations possible concrete measures for regulating the world wheat trade, such as exporting fair quotas, credit arrangements, etc., she was not prepared to agree to any reduction or limitation of her area of cultivation (since the ever growing demands of her increasing population made an extension of her area of cultivation essential) and that she would not be bound by any decisions taken anywhere without the participation of the Soviet Union.

The Rome Conference, amongst other things, decided to hold a conference of all the wheat exporting countries, including the U.S.A., in London, on May 18, 1931, for the purpose of organising the export of the 1931-32 wheat crop. The conference duly met, May 18-23, 1931, under the Chairmanship of Mr. Howard Ferguson, the Canadian High Commissioner. The U.S.A. delegation was of the opinion that too much wheat was being raised by the wheat-producing countries, and they suggested, as a remedy, the cutting down of the areas under wheat. The Soviet delegation, however, refused to agree to a reduction of the area under cultivation, but were in favour of regulating wheat exports by fixing definite export quotas, and their delegation made the following statement:

> "As far as our country is concerned, this suggested solution is unacceptable. In the conditions of our social system, with the extraordinary rate of development of our industries and the growth of the number of our industrial workers, as well as the raising of the standard of life of our working population, an increase in production is necessary first of all to meet the growing internal demands.
>
> At the same time it will no doubt lead also to a growth of grain surplus to meet our export requirements.
>
> It is manifest that one of the principal solutions for the regulation of wheat export is the fixing of definite export quotas.
>
> Such a proposal seems to us an acceptable basis if certain reservations and guarantees are provided.

* 2.iii.31.

At the Rome Conference the delegates of some countries, as well as the chairman of the Committee of Production and Distribution, in the summary of the activities of this Committee, recognised that the U.S.S.R. has naturally the right to occupy on the world's grain market the same place as was occupied by pre-war Russia.

There is no doubt that it would be correct if the quota for the U.S.S.R. were based on the quantity of wheat exported before the war.

At the same time, we think it necessary to emphasise that the establishment of a scheme based on quotas can be acceptable only in the case if the largest wheat exporting countries will participate in this proposed scheme."*

At the conclusion of the Conference the following official communiqué was issued:

"The Conference is convinced that among the underlying causes for the present position are:

1. The effects of economic depression throughout the world;
2. That there is more wheat produced than can be sold at a profit;
3. The absence of sufficiently adequate information regarding the movements of wheat, requirements of certain countries, and the quantities which are liable to be placed on the market;
4. The present uncertain state of the wheat market.

The Conference considers that where possible a reduction in the area devoted to wheat should be undertaken in whatever way each country considers to be most effective and practicable.

In view of certain reports that the attitude of the Soviet delegation created difficulties in the work of the Conference, the chairman (Mr. Ferguson, High Commissioner of Canada) wishes to state that these reports are unfounded and that the Soviet delegates showed a spirit of complete co-operation. The same may be said of all other delegations."†

In addition, the Conference decided "to recommend to the various Governments that a central organisation, somewhat in the nature of a clearing house of information and advice, should be established, and that all exporting countries should be parties to it and partners in it."

According to an official statement by the Soviet Delegation, "the position of the Soviet Delegation in regard to the scheme for regulating the market coincided in the main with the position of the overwhelming majority of the Delegations."

The Committee set up by the Conference held several plenary meet-

* *Financial News*, 22.v.31. † *Morning Post*, 25.v.31.

ings in London during July, 1931, at which official representatives from the following countries were present: United States of America, Argentine, Australia, Bulgaria, Canada, Hungary, India, Poland, Rumania and U.S.S.R.

The setting up of an International Wheat Information Service was recommended to the participating Governments. The duties of the service were to be informational and not advisory. It was to operate so far as possible through existing official and unofficial national and international agencies. Its scope was to be international. Its work was to be carried out in the interests of all countries. The objects of the service were defined as follows:

1. To foster collaboration between wheat exporting countries with a view to encouraging the effective distribution of wheat, and to facilitating the better understanding of the wheat problem.
2. To increase the scope, reliability and timeliness of wheat statistics and other relevant information, in order to assist the international trade in, and the effective distribution of, wheat.
3. To review and analyse all relevant information on the current international position and future outlook concerning the production, consumption, movement, and stocks of wheat and wheat products.
4. To promote, by investigation and education, the greater consumption and utilisation of wheat and wheat products.
5. To arrange for the timely distribution and publication of the information thus provided, utilising as far as possible existing governmental and international services and private publishing and distributing agencies.

It was proposed that each participating country should have a regular representative on the Standing Committee, and that each should also appoint one or more deputy members, who should, if possible, be resident in, or within easy reach of, London.

Although these Conferences demonstrated beyond a doubt that the Soviets were not only not guilty of the dumping of wheat but were prepared to participate in schemes to prevent dumping, and which might help to mitigate the effects of the European crisis, the outcry against the importation of Soviet wheat in the Die-Hard press did not cease.

In the meantime, whilst reactionaries in France were trying to form a bloc against the U.S.S.R. and their opposite numbers in Britain were doing their best to bedevil Anglo-Soviet relations, German and Italian business men were not idle—they brushed aside the wholly unfounded accusations of Soviet dumping, forced labour, the alleged economic danger to other countries of the successful carrying out of the Soviet Five-Year Plan, etc., and in April, 1931, Soviet-German and Soviet-Italian trading agreements were concluded, whereby the German and Italian Governments respectively agreed to give substantial guarantees on large orders for various manufactures placed by Soviet economic organisations in Germany and Italy.

The attitude of the Soviets to the question of trade with capitalist countries was well summarised in the following extract from a leader discussing the Soviet-German economic agreement in *Izvestia*, April 21, 1931:

> "In politics," said the *Izvestia*, "love and attachment do not play a great part; in politics one must be satisfied with mutual interests . . . we approve realism in politics and only wish that the industrialists of other countries would follow the German example, and having convinced themselves of the strength of the Soviet Union . . . they would direct their attention to the wide field for business deals opened up by the industrialisation of the Soviet Union.
>
> Industrialisation is not only a means for satisfying the needs of the given moment, but it awakens new needs for the satisfaction of which we shall require a long time still, economic connection with Western European and, in general, with world industry.
>
> Economic relations are closest between countries which are most highly developed industrially . . . there is no such thing as complete independence in this world, and the degree of independence to which our huge country can attain can but make us strong enough to defeat every effort of the capitalist countries to enslave (or exploit) us. But this will by no means preclude us from utilising the international division of labour power in our (mutual) interests."

On the other hand, the British Chamber of Commerce, in the course of a discussion on Anglo-Soviet trade on April 24, 1931, whilst rejecting a resolution which was not only offensive but constituted in effect a direct incitement to abrogate the temporary Anglo-Soviet Agreement of April, 1930, adopted the following resolution on the subject:

> "That the Executive Council be requested to study the effect on the trade and industries of this country through the exports from Russia to the United Kingdom and its important world markets; especially of manufactured goods which are steadily increasing as the 'Five-Year Plan' develops, and the offering of such goods for sale at prices which bear no relation to the true cost of production calculated on the regular commercial basis,

and to consider what, if any, steps can be taken in this country by the Government or the business world, jointly or separately, to counteract this entirely new method of marketing, which manifestly constitutes an organised and serious attack on the commercial system of the whole world."

This resolution adopted against the opposition of men like Mr. H. E. Metcalfe, who knew at first hand conditions of life and work in the U.S.S.R., certainly summed up the attitude of large sections of Tories whose intense dislike of socialism in general and the U.S.S.R. in particular seemed to blind them completely to the facts of the case.

Actually in 1930, the United Kingdom imported a total of £29,700,000 worth of goods (excluding precious metals) from the U.S.S.R., whilst total imports from all countries was £1,044,840,194, (excluding precious metals), i.e., imports from the U.S.S.R. only accounted for two per cent. of our total imports.

Secondly, over 73 per cent. of our imports from the U.S.S.R. were raw materials, nearly 23 per cent. foodstuffs and about 4 per cent. manufactured goods and finished articles.

The import of raw products and foodstuffs at competitive prices from whatever source, be it the Argentine, Sweden, China or the U.S.S.R., was and is an asset to this country, and if an important source of supply such as the Soviet Union had been eliminated, prices of essential raw materials would have soared and a serious blow would have been dealt to our industries.

In the absence of sufficient credits and having no invisible exports to pay for the imports she required in connection with the Five-Year Plan, the U.S.S.R. at that time exported large quantities of products which she would far rather have kept at home for her own population, and if she could have got better prices for her exports she would have been only too pleased, as it would have enabled her to keep for her own consumption some of the products she was compelled to export. Unfortunately, like other exporters, the prices of her goods were subject to the fluctuations of the world market.

Anyone conversant with the subject should have known that the general fall in prices the whole world over during these years was not brought about by Soviet exports. A fall in the price of grain, for instance, took place long before Russia had even entered the market as an exporter. Moreover, prices also fell in countries to which Russia did not export and, finally, the prices of articles which the U.S.S.R. did not export at all, such as rubber, copper, tin, wool, fell to an even greater extent than those articles which she did export.

The whole outcry against Soviet "dumping" was in reality only a mask for the organisation of a British and, if possible, international boycott of the U.S.S.R. There is a mass of evidence to support this. Thus, the *Sunday Times*, February 8, 1931, after pointing out " that a considerable measure of success seems likely to attend the Five-Year Plan," and that it is likely to " achieve very formidable results," went on to argue that " the idea of the Plan—is not merely economic, but political," that " deeds not words " are the " only effective means of protest," and continued:

> " What does protest by deeds imply ? It can only imply one thing, if it is to be effective, *and that thing is Boycott.* We can refuse to deal with Russia, diplomatically or economically. . . . There are many who hold that we should do so." (Our italics).

The *Sunday Times* itself recognised the danger inherent in such a policy and, on the whole, advised some moderation. Others like Lord Newton, however, had no use for such moderation ; he said roundly:

> " . . . the Five-Year Plan, of which we hear so much, and which is intended to transform Russia from an agricultural into an industrial country, is not really so much an internal question for Russia as a carefully thought-out scheme for forcing Communism upon Western Europe. Personally, I look upon it—I may be quite wrong—as a trial of strength between Communism and Western civilisation, in which the whole of Western Europe is threatened . . . if the League of Nations were a really practical body, which it is not, it would set to work to organise some kind of *combined defence by these nations against the danger with which they are threatened.*"* (Our italics).

Similarly, a Trade Defence Union, whose Chairman was Lord Brentford (popularly known at the time as " Jix "), was formed in February, 1931, and its principal objects were:

> " 1. To stop the British encouragement to prison labour by working with the Americans in placing an embargo on Soviet timber imports.
>
> 2. To bring home to our people that the Communists are using Russia for an economic war on the world in the hope that it may lead to world revolution, and that their efforts are particularly directed against the British Empire.
>
> 3. To explain to the people that the means by which the Communists hope to achieve their purpose is by the Five-Year Plan ; that this Plan is breaking down in finance ; and that its chief support is the buying by this country of 25 per cent. of their exports made by what is in effect slave labour. We can therefore wreck the plan by depriving the Communists of our free market.

* " House of Lords Report," 5.ii.31.

> 4. To bring about a common front at home of trade organisations and politicians, and to link up with organisations abroad so that the nations present one front in the economic war to the common enemy, Communism."*

The provisional committee of the Union comprised the Duke of Atholl, Commander Carlyon Bellairs, M.P., Sir Robert Horne, M.P., Major-General Sir A. Knox, M.P., Lord Melchett, Mr. E. Marjoribanks, M.P., Lord Sumner, Mr. H. G. Williams (secretary, Empire Economic Union) and Sir E. Hilton Young, M.P.

The extent to which this precious Union was concerned about "slave" or "forced" labour can be gauged not only by its leading membership, but by the following incident: an acquaintance of the authors of the present book was naïve enough to take its professions seriously and wrote informing them that she would be very glad to send a subscription for such a worthy end as stamping out forced labour, if they would make their appeal wider and advocate the exclusion of goods from the Dutch, French, Belgian and Portuguese colonies, where forced labour was to her knowledge very much in vogue. But our acquaintance drew a blank, for in a reply from the Union she was informed that "we cannot possibly think of approaching or taking any steps in regard to the countries you mention." Why this self-denial in a good cause? No explanation was vouchsafed.

Again, Mr. Winston Churchill, speaking in the House of Commons, on February 18, 1931, said:

> "The Government should take counsel betimes with friendly Powers for the international treatment of the problems of currency and trade and concert joint action against the uneconomic exportations which are in increasing measure to be apprehended from Russia."

Mr. Baldwin added his weighty voice; in the course of a speech in Newton Abbot, March 6, 1931, he declared:

> "On the subject of the home market I want to say a few words on a subject of the gravest importance—Russia. I am not going to abuse Russia. I am going to say nothing about Russia except to point out that at this moment she is to our economic development the greatest potential danger that exists to-day, and for these reasons. In Russia, they are working on what they call a Five-Year Plan. Very briefly that is a plan to industrialise Russia in five years, or in other words, to equip Russia with a vast potential power of manufacturing goods for export."

* *Times*, 12.ii.31.

After inveighing against giving credits to the U.S.S.R. and against Soviet dumping, he averred:

> "The credits she gets are being used to help the Five-Year Plan. In other words, we are helping to finance the very weapon which is going to run us through the vitals," and concluded: "So we want our tariffs to deal with this problem because the nations of the world are anxious on this matter—it has been discussed at the International Chamber of Commerce—and even if it is necessary to deal with it by the prohibition of Russian imports or even if it means the denouncing of the existing treaty."*

The sort of discussion which had taken place at the International Chamber of Commerce was made evident by a circular which was read at a meeting of the Russo-British Chamber of Commerce on March 10 by the Soviet representative. This circular, which was marked "private and confidential," had been sent to the Chambers of Commerce throughout the world, and contained the following questions:

> 1. Are you willing to supply detailed information concerning your imports from Russia?
> 2. Would your country agree to concerted international restriction of credit granted to Russia?
> 3. Are you willing to discuss in contact with other countries a joint international prohibition of imports from Russia? "†

Of course, it was subsequently denied that the action of the International Chamber of Commerce was in any way directed against the U.S.S.R.‡ However it is unnecessary to pursue this subject any further here.

II. Continuation of the anti-Soviet campaign. M. Litvinov at Geneva

The campaign against Soviet exports to this country and against the extension of credit guarantees to British manufacturers desirous of accepting Soviet orders continued unabated throughout 1931. In the first place much was made of the favourable trade balance which the Soviet Union had in her trade with Britain. This was for the most part made out to be far greater than it actually was by ignoring goods purchased from other countries (mostly from British Empire countries) on the London market, and the expenditure of the Soviets on their various trading organisations in Britain, on insurance, freights, etc.

* *Manchester Guardian*, 7.iii.31. † Ibid., 11.iii.31.
‡ Ibid., 12.iii.31.

To read the onslaughts on the Soviet favourable trade balance with Britain one might have thought that the U.S.S.R. was the only country which had a favourable balance in respect of trade with Britain. Actually, the Argentine, Belgium, Holland, Cuba, Canada and many other countries had large favourable trade balances against Great Britain, but no one suggested ceasing trade with them or limiting our purchases from them to their purchases from us.

Moreover, the critics ignored the fact that the trade of any two countries could not be considered as occurring in space independent of the rest of the world. Trade is, to put it simply, a triangular process. If one country, say, "A" sells more to another country "B" than she buys from her, but buys more from a third country "C" than she sells to the latter, then "C" can buy more from "B" with the money she has received from "A," and so on with other countries. Thus, although in some cases the trade balance is favourable, and in others adverse, the trade done between them works out finally to the advantage of all three or more countries trading with one another.

Further, it was also urged that it was unfair that we should grant credits to the U.S.S.R. on purchases from Britain while she sold her products to us for cash. To this again the reply was simple, the capital goods required by the fast developing U.S.S.R. for the construction of factories, of railways, new metallurgical, electrical and other works could not be expected to give a quick return. No country in the world has ever paid direct cash for such constructions. On the contrary, the credits or loans granted for such have always been for very long periods; ten, fifteen and twenty-five years and even longer. Unable to obtain such long-term credits or loans and having no invisible exports such as foreign investments, shipping, etc., the U.S.S.R. was compelled to export her raw products (for which cash was usually paid) in much larger quantities than she would naturally have desired, in order to pay for her essential imports.

These facts were taken into account to some extent at any rate, by the Labour Government, when on July 9, 1931, Mr. W. Graham, President of the Board of Trade, made the following announcement:

> "The Lord Privy Seal has been in touch with the Soviet Trade Representative with a view to the increase of British exports to the Soviet Union. It has been arranged that the Export Credits Advisory Committee, to whom the Government is very much indebted in this matter, will be prepared to consider sympathetically applications for guarantees in respect of orders for heavy engineering material to be placed in the near future, subject to agreement with exporters about prices, and provided that credits

up to thirty months from the date of the order, including the period of manufacture, could be arranged."

The guarantees covered 60 per cent. of the credits granted on Soviet orders. The insurance rates charged by the Advisory Committee were still extremely high and militated against the placing of many large orders. Moreover, shipbuilding was excluded from the new agreement, which was a great pity, as British shipbuilding was in a very depressed state at the time and the Soviets were anxious to place orders with British shipbuilders for ships designed largely for her own coastal trade. However, the agreement was a good beginning in the development of Anglo-Soviet trade ; as such it was warmly welcomed in Labour circles and Mr. T. Johnston, M.P. (the Lord Privy Seal), who, on the British side, had been largely instrumental in bringing about the agreement, was heartily congratulated on his success.

Although the agreement resulted in a very welcome increase in Soviet orders in Great Britain, providing work for many who would otherwise have been unemployed, Tory onslaughts on Soviet-British trade in general and the credits agreement in particular did not cease.

An attempt was made, particularly by the *Morning Post* and the *Daily Mail,* at a nation-wide boycott of Soviet goods by leading shops. A number of the latter gave, at any rate, their nominal adherence to such a boycott. They excluded, however, such luxury goods as caviare and Russian sables which they could not get from elsewhere. The poorer classes could do without cheap grain, butter, fruit, etc., but how could their wealthy customers be expected to do without their luxuries whatever the conditions under which they may have been produced ? In the net result this boycott met with no greater success than the earlier attempted boycott of Soviet oil, with which we have dealt in a former chapter.

After the Anglo-Soviet credits agreement the agitation against the U.S.S.R. became even more fierce ; to frighten traders, the Government and the banks, rumours were spread and repeated time after time that the U.S.S.R. was in financial difficulties, that she would be forced in the near future to repudiate her debts, etc. At the same time, although now and again prominent conservative leaders continued to predict the "considerable failure" of the Five-Year Plan, such a prophecy became more and more difficult as the undoubted success of the Plan became evident, hence attempts to demonstrate that the "whole object" of the Five-Year Plan was, in Mr. Cunliffe Lister's words in the House of Commons, July 22, 1931, "to launch an offensive on every market of the world."

Mr. Hacking,* during the same debate, mournfully declared: "The

*Former Parliamentary Secretary to Overseas Trade Department.

choice appears to be this: if, on the one hand, Russia does not go bankrupt, if she succeeds in her Five-Year Plan, partly on account of the fact that we are giving her these credits, she will undoubtedly play a great part in ruining this country by her competition. If, on the other hand, she goes bankrupt, we suffer a serious financial loss through non-payment of our exports. It is not a very happy ending, whichever view one takes, to our trade relationship with that country."*

On July 23, 1931, the "Anti-Soviet Persecution and Slave Labour League" held its first annual meeting (it had been founded January, 1931). The Chairman was Col. F. G. Poole, and Col. R. G. Pearse in his report of the activities of the League said:

> "It was the mission of the League to tell the people of England what the Russian menace really meant. The thing which underlay the new system of government in Russia was a definite denial of God and religion. A government of men had taken away the soul of a nation. On the economic side there was stark materialism.
>
> Dumping was part of a direct intention on the part of the Russian Government to undermine the system of the other countries of the world which did not subscribe to their creed."†

Such arguments showed, of course, that those who used them did not understand the elements of Soviet Socialist economics. Industry and the national economy generally being organised for the use of the people and not for profit, products were only exported in so far as it was necessary to pay for necessary imports. For the rest the object of the Five-Year Plan and the Soviet national economy generally was, on the one hand, to raise immeasurably and continuously the standard of living of the whole people, and on the other, whilst not out for autarchy, to make the U.S.S.R. if need be in times of crisis, as in the case of an attack upon her—military or economic—independent of other countries. Soviet citizens were ready for a time to tighten their belts in order to reach economic independence, but at the same time, as a result of the spread of education and culture among the masses of the people, their demands for all sorts of goods and the amenities of life were increasing by leaps and bounds and a moment's thought would have shown anyone not blinded by anti-Soviet prejudices that the most brilliant success of the Five-Year Plan would be hard put to it to satisfy these growing demands of the teeming Soviet millions for years to come.

However, in the ranks of the conservatives there were many who did

* *Hansard*, 22.vii.31, col. 1632. † *Times*, 24.vii.31.

see more clearly the future trend of events. For instance, Major Glyn, M.P., in the debate of July 22, in the House of Commons, pointed out:

> "A new generation is growing up in Russia which will know no other circumstances than those which exist to-day. You have an enormous country, composed of different races, who are attempting to work out one of the greatest experiments of modern times. It is a most colossal experiment, and if we do not supply the goods to meet their demands—you can not shut Russia out from the rest of the world—someone else will unquestionably supply those goods. I was in Russia before the War and during the War, and for a short time last year, and it is interesting to compare the Russia of to-day with the Russia of years ago. I am convinced that the most vitally important thing for us is to study the psychology of young Russia, the outlook of these young people, who one day will be the competitors of our children in world trade."*

Major Glyn, it is true, expressed the idea that if Britain would help Russia more the latter would "develop sanely politically along British lines," but in any case he strongly deprecated putting Russia "beyond the pale," and declared: "While I deplore the fact that Russia has not met her [Tsarist] debts, and that she has used political means of propaganda which are unfortunate, it will never stop until some other people stop political propaganda against her."†

Labour M.P.'s and also many Liberal M.P.'s, particularly business men and many manufacturers both inside and outside the House of Commons, urged the Government on the other hand to extend the facilities of the Export Credits Guarantee Department to much longer credit periods and to lower the cost of these credits.

In the meantime, on May 15, 1931, the Committee for the Study of European Union which was referred to above, met again in Geneva. The Secretary-General of the League of Nations had sent an invitation to the U.S.S.R. in a note which M. Litvinov characterised as one that "would be hard to beat" for sheer discourtesy to a Great Power (if it was not an intentional provocation to the U.S.S.R., Iceland and Turkey to refuse to participate in the work of the Council).

The League Note gave the following items of the preliminary agenda:

1. The report of the organisation sub-Commission on the organisation, constitution and methods of work of the Commission.
2. The proposal regarding the participation of the free Town of Danzig in certain parts of the work of the Commission.

* *Hansard*, 22.vii.1931, col. 1559. † Ibid., col. 1560.

3. Economic questions—the world economic crisis in so far as it concerns the European Powers as a whole.

Immediately following item three was added the remark that in accordance with the decision of the January session of the Commission the Governments of the U.S.S.R., Iceland and Turkey would be represented in the discussion of this item in the agenda. The Secretary-General added that, as certain Governments had reserved the right to propose alterations in the order of discussion of the various items on the agenda, he could give no indication as to when item three would be reached.

This meant that not only was a great Power excluded from expressing its view of the form of organisation, constitution and methods of the Commission in the work of which it was invited to participate, but whilst the Note informed these three Powers that they were only to participate in the discussion of the third point of the Agenda, it gave no indication as to when that point would be discussed.

In view of this, M. Litvinov in his reply naturally asked whether "their (U.S.S.R., Turkey and Iceland) delegations were to go to Geneva in order to find out for what date they were being invited there?" The *Izvestia* commented thus in the course of a leader:

> "It is time that an end be put to mere manœuvres and that some definite decision should be taken. Either it is impossible to decide questions relating to the organisation of Europe without the Soviet Union, and without Turkey—then these States should be given the opportunity to participate in the discussion of all questions, and then they must naturally participate in the discussion of the methods of work. Or 'Europe can be organised' without the Soviet Union, then is it necessary to delude oneself and others by issuing conditional invitations for an indefinite date to discuss a no-one-knows what agenda?"*

However, both the U.S.S.R. and Turkey accepted the invitation and at the session of the Commission on May 18, M. Litvinov made a speech which the Geneva correspondent of the *Manchester Guardian* characterised thus:

> "Those who insisted on the invitation to Soviet Russia to attend the Commission of Inquiry for European Union were justified this afternoon when the Commission listened to a remarkable speech from M. Litvinov, solid in substance, moderate in tone and extremely clever. *It was the most practical contribution to the discussion on the European crisis that we have yet heard*, and this is the general opinion this evening except among

* *Izvestia*, 27.iv.31.

those still under the influence of undying prejudice. The speech was, indeed, a change from the Geneva atmosphere that we know so well. *M. Litvinov was like a visitor from another world—a world where people at any rate face realities.*"* (Our italics).

M. Litvinov's speech contained, amongst other things, a reply to the accusations voiced in Britain and other countries against Soviet "dumping." He enumerated some of the causes of the economic crisis, their connection with the growth of armaments and of protection, the burden of reparations, the irregular distribution of the world gold reserve and stressed particularly the lowering in the purchasing power of the masses of the people. He also pointed to the absurdity of making the existence and policy of the U.S.S.R. responsible for the world crisis, and said:

> "The figures quoted in the report of the economic organisation of the League showed that not only the markets to which the Soviet Union exported but to a considerable extent also those in regard to which it was a consumer had been affected by the crisis.
>
> Did the fact that the Soviet Union was absorbing from 50 to 75 per cent. of the total export of certain branches of the machine industry in Germany, Austria, England and Poland, intensify or mitigate the world crisis? In 1930, 53.5 per cent. of the total tractor exports of the United States went to the Soviet Union, and in the same year the Soviet Union received about 12 per cent. of the textile machinery export of Great Britain, and from Germany 25 per cent. of the total export of agricultural machinery, 21 per cent. of the export of lathes, and over 11 per cent. of the total export of other machinery."

After ridiculing the accusation of dumping against the U.S.S.R. and giving some real examples of dumping by other countries, M. Litvinov proposed that the States represented on the Commission should adopt a joint declaration, subsequently to be converted into an international convention, making it compulsory to sell on the home market at prices not higher than on the foreign market. The Soviet Government, said Litvinov, was prepared to participate in such an international act.

M. Litvinov then turned to the alleged "diabolical plan" on the part of the Soviet Government to disorganise capitalist economy by selling its export goods below cost price, and said:

> "It would be difficult to imagine anything sillier than such a plan would be. It would not decide the fate of capitalism, but

* 19.v.31.

would, nevertheless, pin down export receipts and consequently reduce imports to the Soviet Union, thus delaying the socialist reconstruction."

Finally, M. Litvinov suggested a kind of economic non-aggression pact whereby each "European State should agree to establish identical treatment for all other States."

With the exception of the *Manchester Guardian* and *Daily Herald*, all the other papers which had given columns to anti-Soviet accusations of dumping, etc., gave only very short reports of M. Litvinov's speech. The *Morning Post* contented itself with a few facetious remarks, including the sneer: "The remedy he (M. Litvinov) suggested, naturally, was the abolition of the capitalist system."

Although at the session of the Commission there were some expressions of sympathy with Litvinov's proposals, they were not accepted, and the session of the Commission took no momentous decisions either on this or any other important subject. True, the Soviet proposal for an economic Non-Aggression Pact came up for discussion at subsequent sessions of the Commission for European Union. It always met with much hostility, although its importance could not but be recognised; thus, the Geneva correspondent of the *Sunday Times*, September 20, 1931, reported:

> "The Russian suggestion for an Economic Non-Aggression Pact, which was advanced recently by M. Litvinov, the Russian Foreign Minister, was recognised by the League of Nations' Second Committee (Technical Organisations) as of universal interest to-day.
>
> It was decided to request the League Council to instruct the Economic Committee to study the scheme and to invite Australia, India, the United States, Japan, China and Uruguay to participate in the elaboration of the Russian proposal."

The opposition to the Soviets also manifested itself when the Sub-Committee of the Co-ordination Committee, recommending preferential treatment for the cereal exports of the Eastern and South-Eastern European countries over a limited period, deliberately excluded the U.S.S.R.

Commenting on this amazing fact, M. Litvinov said:

> "The European Commission manifested geographical leanings and seemed to be desirous of changing the map of Europe. An attempt is being made to throw the U.S.S.R. out of Eastern Europe in order to discriminate against Soviet grain exports. . . ."

It may be as well to run on ahead here in order to finish with these attempts or apparent attempts at the establishment of a pan-European Union and the Soviet endeavour to bring about at least temporary economic peace among the nations.

The Soviet proposal for dealing with dumping, the essential part of which was:

> "The contracting parties once more solemnly confirm the principle proclaimed at the Economic World Conference of 1927* of the peaceful co-existence of the various countries irrespective of their social, political and economic systems; and the parties further undertake to forego in their mutual relations any discrimination whatever and to regard as incompatible with the principles of the present protocol the adoption by the respective countries of any special system directed against one or more of the countries signing the protocol or inapplicable to all the other countries,"

was tossed about from Committee to Committee and at the August-September session of the Commission of Inquiry for European Union, it was referred to a special sub-Committee. The latter met in Geneva, November 2, 1931, eighteen European and five Overseas States being represented.

The Soviet delegate, backed by the Italian delegate, who was in the chair, made a strong plea for a definite decision on the Soviet proposal, at the same time inviting additions and amendments which would make it an efficient instrument for the purpose in view.

In general, it may be said that, although all the delegates expressed themselves in favour of the principle of the Soviet Pact, the States which had established normal diplomatic and economic relations and were successfully developing trade with the U.S.S.R., such as Germany and Italy, defended the draft Pact, whereas those which had not renewed diplomatic relations or which were pursuing, in general, an anti-Soviet policy, such as Switzerland, Rumania, etc., in a more or less guarded manner, opposed the acceptance of, at any rate, the second part of the Pact. The question of dumping was only touched upon by the French and Spanish delegates, but was not developed or pressed, and no other delegate referred to it.

* At the World Economic Conference held in Geneva, May 4-23, 1927, a resolution was adopted dealing with the importance of the renewal of world trade. Amongst the most important commercial points recommended in the resolution was one concerning the abolition or reduction of export duties on raw materials, reduction of dumping, etc. The resolution also dealt with commercial agreements, customs, nomenclature, import and export restrictions and prohibitions, fiscal and legal equality of foreigners, etc.

The preamble to the resolution contained the following clause: "The Conference, recognising the importance of the renewal of the world's trade, and refraining absolutely from infringing upon political questions, regards the participation of all States, irrespective of their economic system, as a happy augury for the future co-operation of all nations."

Finally, after four days' deliberations of the Special Sub-Committee, the League Secretariat, on November 5, 1931, published the following communiqué:

> "The Special Sub-Committee endorses the general idea of a pact of non-aggression, *recognising the generous and profoundly humane elements in the proposal and the possibility of countries of different economic and social structure existing side by side.* It recommends that the economic relations between States should be guided solely by the necessities of economic life, and not by any consideration explicitly derived from differences in their political and social systems.
>
> Having regard to the different interpretations of economic aggression and discrimination, and in view of the fact that the Draft Pact does not seem likely to secure unanimous acceptance, or even acceptance by the majority of the members, *the Committee has decided to meet again before the meeting of the Commission of Inquiry for European Union next January to re-examine any amendments or further observations that the various Governments may send to the Secretary-General of the League.*" (Our italics).

So that whilst endorsing the *principle* of economic non-aggression, the adoption of concrete measures for putting it into practice was again, as usual, shelved.

The Soviet proposal was to have been discussed at the January, 1932, session of the Commission of Inquiry for European Union—but this session was postponed, and the proposal has remained in cold storage ever since.

However, although the Soviet proposals and indeed the whole Commission for the study of European Union came to naught, there was a distinct manifestation during its sessions of friendliness towards the Soviet Union by Mr. Arthur Henderson, the then British Foreign Secretary. The *Daily Herald* Geneva Correspondent, in the course of his report of the May 19 session, stated:

> "Speaking at the Commission for European Union to-day, Mr. Henderson held out a friendly hand to M. Litvinov, the Soviet Foreign Commissar, asking him to banish from his mind any thought that the members of the League were plotting war against his people.
>
> 'I assure him,' declared the British Minister, 'that we are hoping for increased peaceful intercourse and trade between his country and ours.
>
> And we shall welcome all the help that he can give us to secure

an atmosphere of confidence and trust based upon the mutual observation of our international obligations.' "*

Further, in view of the failure for a variety of reasons of the repeated plans by France to organise a European front against the U.S.S.R. and the increasing losses to French trade resulting from her hostility to the Soviets, the French Government already at the end of April, 1931, had taken the initiative in suggesting negotiations for a Franco-Soviet Pact of Non-Aggression and for the conclusion of a trade agreement. With a view evidently to furthering a Franco-Soviet *rapprochement*, M. Briand, who was a master of adroitness, took the opportunity of publicly welcoming M. Litvinov's proposal for an economic pact at the May, 1931, session of the Committee for the Federal Union of Europe as " a declaration of economic peace " (as though the Soviets had ever pursued an economic war!), and on June 3, 1931, the opening of Franco-Soviet commercial negotiations was announced in Paris.

On July 16, 1931, the *Journal Officiel* published a Presidential decree, countersigned by M. Rollin, Minister of Finance, M. Briand, Minister for Foreign Affairs, and M. Tardieu, Minister of Agriculture, rescinding the decree of October 3 last restricting imports into France from Soviet Russia. The rescinded decree prohibited imports from the U.S.S.R. except by special authorisation. Similarly, on the same date the *Izvestia* published an order rescinding all orders and instructions relating to the limitation of imports, etc., from France, in pursuance of the decree of the Council of People's Commissars, October 20, 1930.

Franco-Soviet business relations then began to develop apace. At subsequent sessions of the Commission for European Union, personal contact between M. Briand and M. Litvinov continued and it was reported that during the September, 1931, session of the Commission a Franco-Soviet non-aggression Pact had been drafted. Various circumstances stood in the way of its signature and such a Pact was only finally signed in November, 1932.

III. The Soviet Union and disarmament

It may be well to look back a few years at this point and give a very brief outline of the attitude of the Soviet Government towards the disarmament discussions at the League of Nations. On December 7, 1925, the Council of the League decided to establish a " Preparatory Disarmament Commission " to make arrangements for the summoning of a Disarmament Conference and amongst other non-Member States of the League the U.S.S.R. was invited to participate. The Soviet Government accepted the invitation but refused to send

* 20.V.31.

a delegation to Swiss territory until the Swiss Government had given satisfaction for the murder of Vorovsky at Lausanne in May, 1923.*

After some delay a Soviet-Swiss accord on this subject was reached and a Soviet delegation with M. Litvinov at its head participated in the fourth Session of the Preparatory Commission held towards the end of 1927. Up to this point the Preparatory Commission had not discussed a single concrete proposal for disarmament—but with the arrival of the Soviet delegation things began to hum. As Mr. Wilson Harris so well put it: "He (Litvinov) then entered on his main statement the essence of which was the revolutionary doctrine that the right way to bring about disarmament is to disarm."†

The Declaration of November 30, 1927, made by M. Litvinov on behalf of his Government recalled that the Soviet Government had always stood for disarmament. After giving a number of instances of this, the Declaration made the following bold concrete proposals:

"(*a*) The dissolution of all land, sea and air forces, and the non-admittance of their existence in any concealed form whatsoever.

(*b*) The destruction of all weapons, military supplies, means of chemical warfare, and all other forms of armament and means of destruction in the possession of troops, or military or general stores.

(*c*) The scrapping of all warships and military air vessels.

(*d*) The discontinuance of the calling up of citizens for military training, either in armies or public bodies.

(*e*) Legislation for the abolition of military service, either compulsory, voluntary, or recruited.

(*f*) Legislation prohibiting the calling up of trained reserves.

(*g*) The destruction of fortresses and naval and air bases.

(*h*) The scrapping of military plants, factories and war industry plants in general industrial works.

(*i*) The discontinuance of assigning funds for military purposes both in State budgets and those of public bodies.

(*j*) The abolition of military, naval and air Ministries, the dissolution of general staffs and all kinds of military administrations, departments and institutions.

(*k*) Legislative prohibition of military propaganda, military training of the population, and military education both by State and public bodies.

(*l*) Legislative prohibition of the patenting of all kinds of armaments and means of destruction, with a view to the removal of the incentive to the invention of same.

* See p. 110.

† *Daily News*, 1.xii.27.

(*m*) Legislation making the infringement of any of the above stipulations a grave crime against the State.

(*n*) The withdrawal or corresponding alteration of all legislative Acts, both of national and international scope, infringing the above stipulations."

The Declaration further proposed that the above programme of complete disarmament should be fulfilled "as soon as the respective Convention comes into force in order that all necessary measures for the destruction of military stores may be completed in a year's time." However, if other States were unwilling to proceed so rapidly, then the Soviets suggested the carrying out of the disarmament programme in gradual stages over a period of four years. At the same time they declared that the Soviet delegation was "ready to participate in any and every discussion on the question of the limitation of armaments, whenever practical measures really leading to disarmament are proposed." In his speech in support of the Soviet proposals, M. Litvinov stressed that however much certain political and industrial interests may be opposed to total disarmament "the problem of complete disarmament itself presents no difficulties and can be solved rapidly and completely. This programme at any rate is far more simple and demands far less time for detailed study than do those schemes which have up to the present been the basis of the work of the Preparatory Commission."

Finally he moved the following Resolution:

"Whereas the existence of armaments and their evident tendency to continuous growth by their very nature inevitably lead to armed conflicts between nations, diverting the workers and peasants from peaceful, productive labour and bringing in their train countless disasters, and whereas an armed force is a weapon in the hands of the Great Powers for the oppression of the peoples of small and colonial countries, and whereas the complete abolition of armaments is at present the only real means of guaranteeing security and affording a guarantee against the outbreak of war, this fourth session of the Preparatory Commission for Disarmament resolves:

1. To proceed immediately to the working out in detail of a draft convention for complete general disarmament on the principles proposed by the Soviet Union delegation, and

2. Proposes the convocation not later than March, 1928, of a Disarmament Conference for the discussion and confirmation of the proposals provided in Clause 1."

M. Litvinov then declared: "Since no serious points can be

urged against the essence of our programme, we foresee that certain groups of people will endeavour to describe our programme and resolution as mere propaganda. This time we are prepared to accept the accusation and we declare that this is indeed propaganda for peace. We are conducting such propaganda and shall continue to conduct it. If the Preparatory Commission on Disarmament is not the place for conducting this propaganda, then we can only conclude that we are here under a misapprehension. The Soviet Government is pursuing and always has pursued a policy of peace with all possible energy, not only in words but by deeds."

On the following day the Soviet delegation handed in a lengthy Memorandum which touched upon the origins and aims of the World War of 1914-18 and the nature of Liberal pacifism. The Memorandum then gave details of the losses—human and material—during this war, the rising danger of future wars, the growth of armies, armaments and military budgets as compared with 1913, the improvement in the machinery of human slaughter, etc.

The Preparatory Commission seemed stunned by the Soviet proposals and as M. Litvinov put it in his report to the XVth Congress of the Communist Party of the U.S.S.R. [December 14, 1927], the Soviet Declaration was "received as a sacrilege, as an attack at the very foundations of the Commission of the League of Nations, as a breach of all the proprieties."

As usual in the case of all knotty problems which came before the League of Nations, the serious discussion of the Soviet disarmament proposals was postponed. Although some individual Liberals in Britain supported the Soviet proposals, the Liberal and Tory press of December 1, 1927, denounced these proposals with a vehemence worthy of a better cause; here are a few of their choice expressions:

> "He [Litvinov] babbles for disarmament as babies for the moon."—*Morning Post.*

> "It may be that there are some people who will really be deceived by this clumsy and cynical farce; they cannot be many."—*Daily News.*

> "In the evident hope of putting decent and honest Governments in a false position, he [Litvinov] has put forward a scheme which can only be described at grotesque."—*Daily Mail.*

> "The Russians know just as well as does the rest of the world that apart from such States as are virtually disarmed already, there is not one which is ready even to consider such a proposal."
> —*Manchester Guardian.*

> "To say that precisely such a scheme might have been formulated by any schoolboys' debating club would be unfair to a rising generation whose minds are much less immature than those of its forerunners."—*Daily Telegraph.*

> "When the Soviet absurdities had been comfortably relegated to cold storage, the delegates took up the proper business of the meeting—namely, the constitution of a new Commission of Security."—*Times.*

On the other hand, the *Daily Herald* of the same date welcomed the Soviet proposals and declared:

> "The Russian plan cannot be lightly dismissed as Utopian. Nor would it be anything but a grave folly to denounce it as propaganda. It is a plan to which, if it is rejected, some effective alternative must be proposed, or the professions of the Governments, and the pledges of the peace treaties, be dishonoured. Mr. Litvinov, in fact, has done one of those simple things which are startling by their very simplicity. He has invited the Disarmament Commission to discuss—Disarmament! The reply of the other Governments should afford a significant revelation of their real intentions."

And on December 8, 1927, the National Joint Council, representing the Trades Union Congress and the Labour Party passed a Resolution also welcoming the Soviet proposals.

The British Government, however, soon showed their "real intentions." When on December 5, 1927, Mr. Tom Johnston, M.P., asked the Prime Minister "whether the Government is considering these proposals; and if, in view of their importance, he can give an assurance that the British delegates at Geneva will not be authorised to negative them without an opportunity having been afforded for their discussion in the House of Commons," Mr. Baldwin replied, "the Russian proposals do not appear to have been regarded by the Committee as a practical and helpful contribution to the problem and there would accordingly be no advantage in discussing them in this House."

On February 20, 1928, the Soviet delegation forwarded to the Secretary General of the League a detailed Draft Disarmament Convention based on the above-mentioned Soviet Disarmament Declaration.

The Preparatory Commission met again on March 16-24, 1928, and the Soviet proposals then came up for discussion. In the course of his speech [March 19] urging the importance of the subject, M. Litvinov said categorically:

> "The Soviet Government has declared and still declares through its Delegation in Geneva that it is ready to abolish all the military forces of the Union in accordance with its draft Convention as soon as a similar decision is passed and simultaneously carried out by the other States. The Soviet Government declares once more that it is ready for this, and asks the other Governments represented here if they also are ready?"

and in conclusion he put "the two main questions underlying" the Soviet proposals:

> (1) Does the Commission agree to base its further labours on the principle of complete disarmament during the periods proposed by us? and
>
> (2) Is it prepared so to carry out the first stage of disarmament as to make the conduct of war, if not an absolute impossibility, of extreme difficulty in a year's time?

For reasons of space we cannot, unfortunately, give an outline of the very instructive discussion which followed Litvinov's speech. Lord Cushendun* on behalf of Britain made a savage attack on the Soviet proposals, he ridiculed many of them and threw doubt on the sincerity of the Soviet Government. To these and other speeches, M. Litvinov replied in his own inimitable way; his speech was sharp as a poniard, witty and yet full of serious content.

A most interesting circumstance of the debate was the fact that only the German and Turkish representatives welcomed a discussion of the Soviet proposals—all the rest of the speeches were frankly hostile, and a number of representatives actually argued that the Soviet proposals were not in consonance with the constitution of the League of Nations—thus M. Politis (Greece) said: "The Soviet project is in complete contradiction to the fundamental principles of the League of Nations." M. Sato (Japan) declared that "the Soviet project contradicts the constitution of the League of Nations."

To the latter M. Litvinov made the fitting reply: "Although Article 8 of the League of Nations' Covenant only mentions the limitation of armaments, it appears to us that merely minimum obligations were intended, and this Article should by no means be allowed to serve as an obstacle to further and complete disarmament, should this be desired by members of the League. It seems to me that a better means for discrediting the League of Nations could scarcely be found than

* Formerly Mr. R. McNeill.

the assertion that it is a barrier to total disarmament. Man was not made for the Sabbath, but the Sabbath for man."

Finally, as might have been expected, the Soviet total disarmament proposals were rejected. Thereupon M. Litvinov, on behalf of the Soviet delegation, immediately proposed a Draft Convention for Partial Disarmament as "a first step to the carrying out of total disarmament." The discussion of the new Draft Convention was postponed to the next Session of the Preparatory Commission in spite of strenuous efforts made by M. Litvinov to ensure its immediate preliminary discussion. Expressing his keen disappointment at the closing session, M. Litvinov declared:

> "Voices have been heard—I recall the words of M. Politis—comparing the work of the Preparatory Commission to that of a scientist in his laboratory. It has been ironically remarked that the ignorant do not understand the necessity for slowness in such scientific research.
>
> I feel myself bound to declare that the Soviet Delegation does not regard the work of the Preparatory Commission as similar to the research work of an astronomer endeavouring to find a new star or planet. Great as are the services of astronomy, humanity can wait for the discovery of new stars.
>
> To agree to a similar slowness of work with regard to a question of such urgent practical politics as that of disarmament or reduction of armaments would be to ignore the true interests of humanity and the danger with which it is continually faced.
>
> May those who believe that they have indefinite time at their disposal for work in the Preparatory Commission not receive a rude shock one day. We, for our part, knowing something of international relations, see these dangers, and have tried to warn the Preparatory Commission to work speedily with a view to avoiding them."

The principle upon which the Draft Convention for the Reduction of Armaments was based was that the reduction should take place roughly in direct proportion to the existing armed forces of the various States. All countries were to be grouped in four classes (*a*) the most highly armed, which were to reduce their forces by one half; (*b*) the next powerfully armed by one-third; (*c*) the weakest by one-quarter and (*d*) the then practically disarmed States whose arms were to be fixed under special conditions. The Draft also proposed the complete destruction of the most aggressive types of armaments, including tanks and super-heavy, long-range, artillery, heavy bombing planes and other most noxious military aircraft. It also proposed the complete prohibition of air bombing, chemical warfare and preparation for this, etc.

The Preparatory Commission did not accept the Soviet Draft, but at its sessions in 1929, 1930, 1931, worked out its own Draft, which, to put it mildly, was very much less drastic and less logical and effective than that proposed by the Soviet delegation. The Soviet Government, however, reserved their right to present again their own proposals at the forthcoming Disarmament Conference which, after much delay and many attempts at further postponement, opened at Geneva, February 2, 1932.

The prospects for the success of the Conference were not too bright. Not only had it been demonstrated with extreme clarity at the sessions of the Disarmament Commission that none of the principal Members of the League had any intention of agreeing to any measures of real disarmament or effective reduction of armaments, but by this time the warnings given by Litvinov in his speeches at the Preparatory Commission of the imminent danger of the outbreak of fresh great wars, had already begun to be verified—the first step in the modern series of aggression which finally led to the outbreak of the present world war had been taken by Japan against China in September, 1931, by her attack on and subsequent invasion of Manchuria—a step the dire consequences of which were foreseen by few and to stop which no real concerted effort was made by the Powers. Indeed, Sir John Simon, speaking at the League as the representative of Great Britain, not only condoned Japan's aggression, but did it so well that his speech earned the gratitude of the Japanese representative who said that he himself could not have stated the case for Japan more effectively.

Although the policy of France since the end of April, 1931, was somewhat more friendly towards the U.S.S.R., that did not mean that bourgeois France had at last become really reconciled to the existence of a socialist Soviet régime in the U.S.S.R. Certainly they had no illusions on this subject in the Soviet Union and when France made her proposals at the Disarmament Conference, at which the U.S.S.R. was, of course, represented, the *Izvestia* characterised them as a frank and carefully prepared effort at preparing an attack upon the U.S.S.R., just as M. Briand's pan-European Plan was an effort to isolate the U.S.S.R. and to establish the hegemony of France in Europe.

Before proceeding further it is interesting to note here the attitude of the British press at the time of the Disarmament Conference. Although, as we have shown above, British journals, particularly the Conservative and also some of the Liberal papers, had derided the proposals for disarmament made repeatedly by the Soviet Government in years past, they now loudly welcomed the French proposals, although most of them conceded that, whatever their merit, they were certainly not calculated to bring about disarmament. Thus, the *Times,* February 8, 1932, devoted a long leader to the subject pointing out that the French proposal "makes no provision for the reduction or even limitation of national armaments." Again, the *Observer,* February 7, 1932, declared:

> "If M. Litvinov went too far in the right direction, he was safe enough because he knew that his proposal would not be accepted. If M. Tardieu goes too far in another direction, he probably feels a dual sense of security—both that his proposal will not receive assent, and that, if it did, *it would have no bearing whatsoever upon the question of disarmament.*" (Our italics).

Note the indirect attack upon M. Litvinov and the subtle assumption that however loud one might talk about disarmament at Geneva there was really no intention to disarm! At the same time the *Observer,* in the course of the same article, did, in effect, characterise the French proposals as an attempt to perpetuate by arms the Treaty of Versailles.

We cannot deal at length in this book with the proceedings of the Disarmament Conference; suffice it to say that on the whole the Soviet proposals and Litvinov's speeches throughout the sessions of the Disarmament Conference and of the Bureau of the Conference in 1932 and 1933 were greeted by the British press with much greater respect than hitherto, whilst the Labour and Liberal papers for the most part, welcomed them.

CHAPTER XVII

FROM THE FALL OF THE LABOUR GOVERNMENT TO THE OTTAWA CONFERENCE (1931—JULY, 1932)

I. THE NATIONAL GOVERNMENT RETURNED. REPORT OF THE SPECIAL COMMITTEE ON TRADE WITH RUSSIA

It was quite evident that towards the end of 1931, the French Government, although still vacillating, was ready on the whole to adopt a more reasonable attitude towards the U.S.S.R. It is very probable that had the British Labour Government continued in power, then despite the frenzied opposition of the Die-Hards, a new era of peace and friendship between the U.S.S.R., Great Britain and France might have been inaugurated. Moreover, since at that time the U.S.S.R. was maintaining good diplomatic and trading relations with Germany and

Italy, and was also improving her relations with other countries, this might well have meant the ushering in of a prolonged period of world peace and co-operation between nations.

It is outside the scope of this volume to discuss at any length the origin and results of the economic blizzard, unequalled in history, which raged over the world in the years 1929, 1930 and 1931, and which resulted in a phenomenal increase in unemployment and crushing poverty in the midst of overwhelming plenty.

Nature had been exceptionally bountiful and the productivity of labour had increased considerably. According to statistics compiled by the economic section of the League of Nations, between the years 1913 and 1928, population had increased by only 10 per cent., but the production of foodstuffs and raw materials had increased by 25 per cent. The prices of primary products fell disastrously and their producers had to cut down their purchases of manufactured goods. Factories, shipyards, etc., were either closed down or put on short time, unemployment leapt upwards. Production in the world's leading capitalist countries fell rapidly. The production indices for 1929 and for the second quarter of 1931 showed that the fall in the United Kingdom was from 106 to 87; in the U.S.A. from 107 to 79; in Germany from 102 to 75; and in France from 109 to 101.

The Board of Trade returns for the second quarter of 1931 showed that, compared with 1929, the exports of the twelve principal countries had dropped on the average by 42 per cent. and their imports on the average by 40 per cent.

There was one exception, that was the U.S.S.R., where the First Five-Year Plan was being carried through successfully and whose purchases on the London market—including exports and re-exports—had risen from £3,930,739 in the first nine months of 1928 to £11,760,290 in the corresponding period of 1931.

The unemployment figures in Great Britain rose from 1,188,000 in July, 1929, to 2,070,088 in July, 1930, and to 2,806,475 in July, 1931. In the latter month the number of unemployed in Great Britain, Germany and the U.S.A. combined was estimated at from 15,000,000 to 20,000,000.

In this country, France and the U.S.A., the majority of the bourgeois press, politicians, bankers and manufacturers argued that the only remedy for the desperate situation was to reduce wages and the social services where these existed. In May, 1931, the Austrian Credit Anstalt, the principal bank in Austria, failed, and on July 13, one of the most important German banks, the Darmstadter and National Bank, suspended payments. The effects were immediately felt in London, Paris and New York, because London financial houses had borrowed heavily in Paris and New York and lent to Austria, Germany and other Central European countries. Fears arose in Paris and New York as to the financial stability of London and there followed a considerable withdrawal of foreign balances from the British capital.

During the two weeks ending July 29, 1931, the Bank of England had to export gold to the value of £32,000,000. The bank rate was raised over two stages from 2½ per cent. to 4½ per cent., but even that did not stop the drain. The Federal Reserve Bank of the U.S.A. and the Bank of France each placed £25,000,000 at the disposal of the Bank of England to strengthen the Exchanges.

Let us say at once that there was no question as to Great Britain's financial stability, because the short term liabilities which caused the immediate trouble amounted to about £70,000,000, whereas British investments abroad at that date amounted to £4,000,000,000. Further, in 1930, Great Britain had a net credit balance on her foreign trade of £39,000,000.

The House of Commons rose on July 31, 1931, and on the same day the May Committee on National Expenditure issued their report which forecast a budget deficit of £120,000,000 for the next year, i.e., 1932-33. A Sub-Committee of the Cabinet consisting of the Prime Minister, Mr. J. Ramsay MacDonald ; the Chancellor of the Exchequer, Mr. Philip Snowden ; Mr. J. H. Thomas ; Mr. A. Henderson and Mr. W. Graham, met on August 12 and continued in session till August 23, 1931, to consider the situation.

In addition, the unusual step was taken by the Government of consulting the leaders of the Conservative and Liberal parties and acquainting them with the state of affairs. All were agreed that the budget must be balanced, but differences arose as to how. The Conservative and Liberal leaders urged the cutting down of unemployment pay and the lowering of the salaries and wages of Government employees, and declared that they would advocate and support such measures in the House of Commons.

During the twelve days, August 12 to 23, leading British dailies led by the *Times*, but excluding the *Daily Herald*, dinned into the ears of their readers that Britain was standing on the edge of a financial abyss, that if we left the gold standard the consequences would be catastrophic and that in order to balance the budget and to remain on the gold standard cuts in unemployment pay and in the wages and salaries of Government employees were essential. Their aim was clear: to frighten the Government into adopting such measures.

It is interesting to recall what Professor J. H. Jones wrote in the *Accountant*, August 22, 1931: " There is no new crisis in our financial affairs, but if a crisis could be produced by our press it would not be far distant. The recent weakness of sterling was not the result of our failure to balance income and expenditure, but if that failure does produce an exchange crisis we shall be able to thank our press for it."

The Trades Union Congress, in a statement pertinently declared:

> "The budgetary position and the May Report have been dragged in deliberately in order to force the adoption of a policy advocated in financial circles and by the National Confederation of Employers' Organisations and the Federation of British Industries, and given in evidence before the Royal Commission on Unemployment Insurance.
>
> Unemployment benefits are being attacked not merely for the money that can thereby be saved, but principally because the benefits are regarded as a protection to wage rates. Cuts in benefits are held to be a prelude to the much more important all-round cuts in wages that are deemed necessary."

Mr. J. Ramsay MacDonald, Mr. Philip Snowden and Mr. J. H. Thomas were apparently scared and succumbed to this agitation and to the pressure of the Conservative and Liberal leaders. Mr. Arthur Henderson and Mr. W. Graham affirmed that it was absurd to assert that the budget could not be balanced without the cuts proposed and they were supported by an overwhelming majority of the Labour Party, but all that had no effect on Mr. Ramsay MacDonald and his friends. The result was that the Government resigned and a "National" Government was formed on August 24, 1931, consisting of members of the Liberal and Conservative parties and in which Mr. MacDonald remained Prime Minister and Messrs. Snowden and Thomas held Cabinet positions.

An emergency budget was introduced including increased taxation and cuts in unemployment pay and in the wages and salaries of Government employees. Mr. Graham, on behalf of the Labour Party criticised in particular the reduction in unemployment pay, but on September 17, the Finance Bill was accepted by 297 to 238 votes.

Four days later, September 21, 1931, Great Britain went off the gold standard. Mr. Baldwin said we "slipped off," Sir Herbert Samuel said we were "thrown off" and Mr. Philip Snowden said we were "driven off." Anyhow we went off and next day the Conservative press, which had been scaring its readers with the calamitous results which would follow our leaving the gold standard, said that it was the best thing which had happened for British trade for years.

The Labour Party maintained that the cuts in the social services were made under pressure from the Banking Houses of London, New York and Paris. This was practically admitted by Mr. Neville Chamberlain when he said in the House of Commons, September 14, 1931:

> "It was the duty of the foreign bankers . . . to state under what conditions they thought it possible to raise the money.
>
> There was a widespread impression . . . that the root of the financial trouble in this country was the condition of the Unemployment Insurance Fund, and they (foreign bankers) were convinced that unless the Government of this country did intend to make the necessary reforms by putting it on a proper insurance basis, it was quite possible that confidence would not be restored."

However, there was no immediate change in policy of the "National" British Government in regard to Russia, the better credit facilities granted to British manufacturers accepting Soviet orders for machinery and equipment under the Export Credits Guarantee Scheme, were not immediately worsened by the "National" Government and the orders placed in Britain by the Soviet Government continued to increase during September and October providing work and wages for thousands of men who would otherwise have swelled the huge army of unemployed.

This, of course, did not prevent the continuation by the British Die-Hard press of its agitation against Soviet "dumping," although in regard to wheat this necessarily eased off in so far as the reports of harvest prospects in most of the wheat supplying countries were none too bright, and the *Financial News*, September 29, 1931, remarked in a leader:

> "The influences which have prevented prices from rising steadily during the summer are well known; first, there has been the large stock in the hands of the United States Federal Farm Board, whose intentions have always been in doubt; and, secondly, there have always been the rigorous import restrictions in European countries, which have resulted in home wheat of qualities normally used for cattle feed being substituted for the usual imports of the millers.
>
> "With two months of the wheat year past, the probabilities for the rest of the season can now be seen more clearly. They are distinctly encouraging. The weather over most of Northern Europe during August and September has been as bad as it could be for the harvest,"

—such is the topsy-turvey nature of our capitalist civilisation!

On October 8th the House of Commons was dissolved and a general election took place on October 27. As might have been expected, the Bolshevist bogey was then used at full blast by the "Nationals" as against their Labour opponents. In particular, it was sought to discredit the policy of the Labour Government in regard to credits for Soviet orders by more detailed and seemingly better substantiated reports of Soviet insolvency. The *Daily Express*, September 30, 1931, carried the following:

> "Reports reached Copenhagen yesterday from Helsingfors that Soviet Russia is about to suspend for a year all interest payments on foreign debts.
>
> The Soviet Embassy in Berlin has denied the reports.
>
> Rumours of this kind have circulated in the City for some time. It is known that Russia has been severely hit by two factors:
>
> 1. The depreciation of the pound sterling abroad.
> 2. The phenomenal fall in wholesale prices since 1929."

After showing how (1) had increased Soviet indebtedness to the U.S.A., as an instance, the report dealt with (2) and stated:

> "When Russia entered into credits with the world in 1929, prices were, in a number of cases, three times as high as those ruling to-day. Most of these credits were to run for two years, and will, therefore, be maturing about now.
>
> "In reliable quarters in the City it is stated that Russia has to find £110,000,000 by the end of this year.
>
> If prices had not fallen she might have been able to do so.
>
> One example is sufficient: in 1929 she based her credits on the fact that she was getting about 32s. a quarter for her wheat. To-day she is finding it difficult to sell at 17s. a quarter."

Which incidentally, although the *Daily Express* failed to draw the moral, proved how interested the U.S.S.R. was to get as high a price as possible for her exports.

The *Daily Mail* also published a similar report. This is only one example of many false stories on the question of Soviet default current at that time in organs of the British and foreign press. Soviet organisations immediately denied any intention on the part of the Soviet Government to default on any of their obligations. On the contrary, although as a result of Britain going off the gold standard a number of foreign grain firms which had made contracts for delivery of grain to this country, prior to September 20, intimated that they would not carry out their obligations under such contracts unless they were paid in gold sterling or other money on gold parity, the Soviet trading organisations did not follow suit as the following letter from the Russo-British Grain Export Company, to the London Corn Trade Association showed:

"September 29, 1931.

The Secretary,
The London Corn Trade Association,
40, St. Mary Axe, London, E. C. 3.

Dear Sir,—In the *Corn Trade News* of the 28th instant, a statement appears that certain foreign grain associations and (or) individual shippers have intimated to your Association that they consider all sales contracted before September 20, 1931, were made on the basis of gold sterling, and that all these contracts must be paid in gold sterling, or other money on gold parity.

As the sole Agents for the United Kingdom of Messrs. Exportkhleb, Limited, of Moscow, who have the monopoly of export of all cereals from the U.S.S.R., we would like to point out to you that no instructions affecting existing contracts have been received by us, and all contracts are being fulfilled without alteration, irrespective of the date they were made.

Yours faithfully,
(sd.) The Russo-British Grain Export Co. Ltd."

Later it was reported that "it was noticed in the wheat market that the Russians have ceased selling wheat on forward contracts. According to a further report the sterling price schedules of Russian exports, hitherto unchanged despite the event of September 20, have now been advanced."*

The *Izvestia* (October 1, 1931) characterised the rumour of Soviet default thus: "Vile though ridiculous in its clumsiness, the calumny evidently originates in circles which do not trade with the U.S.S.R., but which are anxious to frustrate this trade and to catch anti-Soviet fish in the troubled waters of the world crisis, bankruptcies and Bourse panic."

Had the Soviet Government not possessed a monopoly of the foreign trade of the U.S.S.R. there might indeed have been a default, for private merchants and manufacturers would have had difficulty in meeting the increasing obligations as a result of the depreciation of the pound sterling and the fall in prices. The Soviet Government, however, not only had and has the whole wealth of their huge country to back up their transactions with other countries, but because of their planned system of economy and their monopoly of foreign trade, could

* *Manchester Guardian*, 14.x.31.

readily cut their clothes according to their cloth, and when necessary restrict their imports in order to redress an adverse trade balance and to make available sufficient cash for essential imports.

It, of course, goes without saying, that the *Morning Post* and other Die-Hard journals pretended to see the "Hand of Moscow" very clearly in the street demonstrations of the unemployed and their restlessness under enforced idleness. The climax of these "reports" may be said to have been reached by the *Morning Post*, when after detailing Moscow plans and exact sums to be spent on instigating disorders, etc., during the British general election, the paper, although stating that it was impossible to obtain confirmation of these reports, added:

> "The above statement generally bears out the report published in the *Morning Post* yesterday, indicating that Moscow had given orders for a widespread campaign of hooliganism during the election, and urging, as a final demonstration, that raids should be made on polling booths with the object of destroying ballot papers."*

Evidently the *Morning Post* was trying to work up a kind of "Red Letter" case against Labour and frighten the country with the consequences in the event of the "National" Government being defeated. However, the elections went off without the predicted disturbances, bloodshed, destruction of ballot papers and other lurid events, which "Moscow agents" were supposed to have been preparing.

As a result of a rushed election in which the Tory and Liberal Party machines and all the anti-Labour forces of the country concentrated mainly on a wholly unprecedented campaign of misrepresentation of Labour's home policy, spreading such unscrupulous lies as the alleged depredations by the Labour Government on the Post Office Savings banks, etc., etc., the National Government won a resounding victory and although Labour still polled a total of 6,648,023 votes as compared with 8,389,512 in the 1929 election, the number of Labour M.P.'s elected was 52, compared with 287 in 1929.

With the return of the National Government, the Tory journals voiced a more and more strident demand for the adoption of full protection—a course which was ultimately adopted by the Government. In this connection it is interesting to observe that in an article in the *Morning Post* (November 5, 1931) by Sir Benjamin Morgan (Vice-Chairman of the Empire Economic Union) we find the following table of our adverse trade balance in the principal foreign markets for 1929:

* 21.x.31.

In £ millions

Country	*Retained Imports from*	*U.K. Produce exported to*	*Adverse Trade Balance*
Russia	23.1	3.7	19.4
Sweden	25.3	10.5	14.8
Denmark	55.8	10.6	45.2
Germany	66.3	36.9	29.4
Netherlands ...	41.3	21.8	19.5
Belgium	43.1	19.4	23.7
France	52.8	31.7	21.1
U.S.A.	183.9	45.5	138.4
Argentine	80.2	29	51.2

Figures given by the President of the Board of Trade in the House of Commons (*Hansard*, November 17, 1931, Cols. 649/50) showed a similar state of affairs in 1930.

It should be noted that in the table the item "Exports from the United Kingdom" does not include re-exports (goods imported into this country and later re-exported); it also does not include goods purchased on the London market and shipped direct to the purchasers from the country of origin. Such transactions, of course, provide the United Kingdom itself with considerable profits. Moreover, most of the re-exports to the U.S.S.R. and her purchases on the London market of goods directly exported from the country of origin, come from countries of the British Empire. Were all this taken into account the British adverse balance of trade with the U.S.S.R. would be seen to be much less than that shown in the table.

In any case, with the Soviet Union our adverse balance was one of the lowest, and yet she was the one country singled out for attack on that score, before, during and after 1929.

The first indication of a definite change in the credit policy of the Government towards the U.S.S.R. came with an announcement in the *Financial News*:

> "The *Financial News* understands that an alteration has come into force in the terms on which the Export Credits Guarantee Department will insure the risk on exporters' credits given to Russia.
>
> Hitherto credits given by British exporters to Russia have been guaranteed up to a limit of thirty months from the date of the order. For heavy goods this was roughly equivalent to twenty-four months from the date of shipment. The limit understood now to be in force is for twelve months from the date of shipment."*

* 7.xi.31.

The result of this policy was that whereas Soviet orders placed in this country increased from £3,900,000 in 1930 to £8,830,000 in 1931, towards the end of 1931 (when Soviet orders, following the better credit facilities which had been established by the Labour Government, were beginning to assume considerable proportions) a decline set in and orders which would have been placed in Britain went elsewhere.

This was made clear by Major Colville* (Secretary, Overseas Trade Department) when, in reply to a question in the House of Commons, December 7, 1931, he stated: "Most of these guarantees (November and December) were in respect of previous obligations. The amount of new business being guaranteed on a twelve-month basis is relatively small."

Manufacturers interested in booking Soviet orders were by no means pleased—many of them, however much they were opposed to the Soviet system took a more balanced and far saner view of what was happening in the U.S.S.R. than did our Die-Hard politicians. Thus Mr. Arthur Chamberlain, Chairman of the Tube Investments, Ltd., presenting his report at the annual meeting of the shareholders of that Company, December 2, 1931, said in regard to the U.S.S.R.;

> "Talking of Russia, has it struck you that one of the most extraordinary and interesting experiments ever undertaken for the betterment of mankind is going on to-day in Russia, and bears every indication of being ultimately crowned with success? Do you realise that some of their leaders prophesy that in ten years from now they will be producing as much wealth as is the U.S.A. to-day? They can fall far short of this in time and amount and yet be the largest new market ever suddenly opened to a hungry world, and their experiment the most enthralling attempt to improve the human lot that has ever been unfolded before the gaze of rival civilisations. It is not flattering to our intelligence or to our humanity that instead of watching this experiment with clear vision and some sympathy we are, and seem content to be, completely in the dark as to their aspirations and the progress being made towards their fulfilment.
>
> Nearly all the information published in this country is one-sided and unfriendly; nor is this surprising seeing that it nearly all comes not from Russia but from countries bordering on Russia, who are mightily afraid of her and who are her trade rivals for our markets. Do you think you would get a true picture of what was taking place in France if your French news was furnished from a correspondent in Berlin? It should be the

* Later Sir John Colville, Governor of Bombay.

rule and not the exception for our newspapers to get their news direct from their own correspondents in Russia, and these correspondents should be, if not sympathetic, at least able and impartial journalists, and should let us have the actual facts about Russia's aims, difficulties. I venture to say that a little of the cold impartial light of truth will make some of us ashamed of much that has been said and written here by people who ought to have known better.

I do not suggest there is nothing wrong with Russian methods, but I do say, and say 'most emphatic' that what they are doing is very interesting, absolutely sincere, certain to improve the lot of 180,000,000 people, quite likely to offer a safe alternative to capitalism and fully deserving of the intelligent attention and sympathy of all other people.

May I also remind you that trade is barter and you need not expect to send your goods to Russia unless you are prepared to accept theirs in exchange."*

Similarly, the *Machinery Publishing Co., Ltd.*, High Holborn, London, in its issue of December 10, 1931, page 344, stated:

"In addition to the support which the machine tool trade has received from the motor car industry, the large orders placed this year by the Soviet Union have greatly relieved the position. These contracts are valuable, and are looked upon as representing a reasonable trade risk, having regard to the guarantees of the Export Credits Guarantee Department. In due time, doubtless, some of these exported machines will be used in their turn to produce machine tools, but it will most probably be many years before Russia will be in a position to compete seriously in the world markets for machine tools. . . .

The value of exports to Russia in 1929 was more than doubled in 1930, and the figures for 1930 were in turn nearly trebled during the first nine months only of the present year."

The same journal in its issue dated December 17, 1931, page 382, declared:

"The singular position of the machine-tool trade is that a heavy loss in overseas markets generally has been made good by the rapid expansion of the Russian market . . . it seems that practically all the large increase of exports in November went to Russia. It may be assumed that Europe consists mainly of Russia at present for machine-tool market purposes."

* *Financial Times*, 3.xii.31.

The November figures of Soviet purchases were, of course, still dependent on the orders which had been placed in this country in earlier months as a result of the then better facilities.

We shall give here but one more example of the views of the more sane business world in regard to Anglo-Soviet trade. In an address to the Anglo-Russian Society on February 2, 1932, given by Mr. A. G. Marshall, a business man and engineer, who had lived in Russia before and during the revolution, and had visited the U.S.S.R. frequently since, he declared:

> "Finance was the key to the situation: credit insurance and short-term trade credits were certainly a most useful 'half-way house,' but what was undoubtedly needed for the solving of the problem of Russian trade with this country were long-term loans in place of short-term credits. If long-term loans were available the British manufacturer could receive cash against documents, prices would not be influenced by the cost of credits and this country could easily compete with the Continent and get the trade."

Particularly interesting was the report of the Special Committee on Trade with Russia (set up in April, 1931) adopted by the Association of British Chambers of Commerce and published December 8, 1931. The report pointed out that the general charge of dumping against the Soviets could not be maintained:

> "Except for wheat and petroleum the figures of 1913 and 1930 respectively do not show any signs of flooding our market. . . . With regard to timber, the importations have been largely increased, coming up to pre-war figures, and while a few years ago these importations were sold at cut prices and thus brought down the general market value, this does not appear to be the case to-day from evidence given by representatives of the import trade. With regard to butter and eggs, there does not seem from evidence by witnesses in the trade to be any marked tendency to dumping. Complaints have been received, however, with regard to fruit pulp."*

The report continued:

> "The representatives of the Russo-British Chamber of Commerce were most anxious to continue friendly trade relations with Russia and their only complaint seemed to be that the high cost of insurance in England under the export credits system handicapped them severely in the matter of competitive prices. They

* *Times*, 8.xii.31.

advocated a much more extended credit system and lower rates of insurance. They did, however, admit that a more balanced exchange of commodities would be of great benefit."

After referring to the Soviet monopoly of foreign trade, the report stated:

"From the economic point of view British manufacturers are anxious to do business upon favourable terms with Russia or with any other country. British manufacturers point out, however, that they have to face very serious obstacles in competition with other countries. In the first place the British Government (for reasons which may be quite sound) will not usually insure more than 60 per cent. of the value of the contracts, while other Governments go much farther. Then the British Government rate for this guarantee works out at nearly 11 per cent. in comparison with 5 per cent. or less in other countries. Again, other countries, especially America and Germany, have a large number of their technical men stationed in Russia assisting Russians to erect and maintain machinery, and naturally their influence tends to get orders placed in their own countries."

The report next referred to the balance of trade in favour of the U.S.S.R.:

"The balance of trade against Great Britain (excluding re-exports of foreign and colonial goods) rose from £18,860,117 in 1928 to £22,744,010 in 1929 and to £27,455,575 in 1930. During the first nine months of 1931 it amounted to £16,207,048. These figures do not take into account payments for services such as shipping freights, insurance, etc.,"

and continued:

"The great problem that the nations of the world have to face is their attitude towards Russia in the future. Russia is a country of enormous potential wealth which is fast being materialised by the efforts of the Soviet Government. It is impossible to cut her out of the community of nations whatever her politics may be. The Five-Year Plan may not be fulfilled up to 100 per cent. of the original scheme, but it appears to be making progress in production. There is no need to go into figures in order to grasp the position that with respect to such products as oil, coal, pig iron, steel, timber, chemicals, grain, sugar, furs, cotton and dairy produce, Russia may in a very few years be one of the greatest producers in the world, if not the greatest producer, and be in a position to undersell any other country if she is allowed to carry on her present export policy."

After referring to the Italian-Soviet and Franco-Soviet trade agreements the report concluded:

"We recommend that Great Britain should make some similar arrangement as in the case of Italy and France. Great Britain is Russia's best market and Russia would sacrifice a great deal to retain it. It is admittedly difficult for any two countries to arrange an exact balance of trade. To sum up—we require an arrangement with Russia to trade on a reciprocal basis, our trade with Russia being regulated to an amount approximately equal to the amount Russia buys from us plus the value of our invisible exports to Russia. If arrangements for payments could be made through a central clearing house or industrial bank, the question of insurance would not arise."

Obviously, although the report shows that the members of the Committee did have a sense of proportion and realism in their attitude towards the U.S.S.R., yet they did not really comprehend the true significance of the Soviet planned economy in general and the Five-Year Plan in particular.

More immediately important was the marked prejudice shown by the recommendation that the U.S.S.R. should be compelled to spend the entire proceeds of her sales on the British market on British visible and invisible exports. This would have been patent discrimination against the U.S.S.R., for other countries, as we have pointed out earlier, had far larger favourable trade balances in respect of their trade with Britain than the U.S.S.R., and yet no such proposal was made with regard to them. Moreover, had such a proposal been enforced it would have meant that the Soviet Union could not have used the proceeds of her sales in Britain on the purchase of consumers' goods in the British Empire, such as tea from India, wool from Australia, etc.

Side by side with the agitation in the Die-Hard press and also by such organisations as the "Society of British Creditors of Russia" for the curtailment of the facilities granted to Soviet-British trade under the Export Credits Guarantee Scheme, seemingly "scientific," certainly very ponderous, memoranda were published by the Bureau of Research of the Russian Department of the Birmingham University which sought to "prove" the fantastic character and inevitable failure of the U.S.S.R. Since later events have proved these efforts of the Research Bureau to have been indeed "fantastic," and utter "failures," it is unnecessary to say anything more about them here.

It will be instructive at this point to refer to the attitude of the British press towards the U.S.S.R. at the time of the Japanese attack and invasion of Manchuria in 1931-32. This Japanese adventure for a variety of reasons, into which we cannot enter here, was accompanied by severe tension between Japan and the U.S.S.R. and every effort was made by the Russian " White " emigrés living in Manchuria and elsewhere to increase this tension in the hope of provoking a Soviet-Japanese war. Such a war, they hoped, might so retard Soviet economic development as to lead to the downfall of the Soviets and then they (the emigrés) would come into their own.

The subjugation of Manchuria by Japan undoubtedly also threatened British interests and world peace but, as we have pointed out above, neither Britain nor the League of Nations did anything serious to prevent the Japanese aggression. On the contrary, time after time, the British Conservative press published all sorts of alarmist anti-Soviet " reports " from " Harbin," " Tokio " and " Riga," originating from Russian " White " emigrés and Japanese military sources. The object of the Japanese military in spreading anti-Soviet lies about Soviet action in the Far East was, of course, clear enough. Whatever difficulties Japan might encounter in her violation of Chinese sovereignty and of the interests of the other Powers in Shanghai, a war with the U.S.S.R. in the Far East, and one which could be represented as provoked by the Soviets, would, they hoped, prove not unwelcome to certain other Powers.

As for the British Conservative press, they were simply obsessed with an anti-Soviet bias which often blinded them not only to the real facts, but frequently even to the clear British imperial interests in the Far East ; just as later, in the case of the German and Italian aggression, and the renewed Japanese aggression in China, their fear of the triumph of the real democratic forces in China, Spain, etc., blinded them to the blows dealt by Fascism to British Imperialist interests. Or, more likely, they were not exactly blinded, they simply chose, both in 1931-32, as also in 1936-39, what to them was the less of two evils—they preferred Fascism to the popular movements in the various countries.

During the whole of 1931 and 1932, the Tory press continued their attacks on the Soviets for alleged anti-British propaganda. Every strike, every manifestation of discontent in Britain, India or elsewhere in the Empire (shades of the West Indies!) was systematically attributed to the machinations or instigations of the Soviet Government. The inconsistency of attributing this marvellous power of organisation and ubiquity to a Government which almost in the same breath was denounced as utterly incapable and as bringing their own country to ruin, never seemed to occur to these scribes.

In spite of the earlier refutations regarding the insolvency of the Soviets, rumours as to the probable default by the Soviet Government on their foreign obligations continued also after the General Election. Thus, under the heading "Soviet Trade Debts," "The City Anxious," the *Morning Post* published the following:

> "Increasing anxiety as to Russia's solvency on foreign trade account is being expressed in financial circles in the City which still have outstanding commitments. Most of the private firms which formerly advanced credits to the Soviets have already withdrawn them, and the Russians are finding it difficult to obtain renewals.
>
> It is understood that a large block of maturities fall due to-day, and though it is probable that they will all be met, eventual default is considered, in well-informed circles, to be not far-distant."*

It need scarcely be remarked that not only were all the maturities met, but that there was not the slightest danger then, as earlier, of any Soviet default, and it is interesting to observe that only four days later (December 23), the *Berliner Tageblatt,* commenting on a new Soviet-German trading agreement that had been concluded on December 22, declared:

> "Germany was particularly interested in these negotiations, the more so since, within their framework, it was possible to discuss Russia's ability to pay, which has excited considerable interest during the last two months. The German delegation came to the conclusion that there were no grounds whatever to fear that Russia would be unable to fulfil her obligations . . . It is also expressly emphasised that the idea of barter was never as much as discussed in the course of the negotiations."

Following the expiration on January 1, 1932, of the contract made by the Central Softwood Corporation with the Soviets for the purchase of the whole of the Soviet exports of softwood in 1931 up to a maximum of 600,000 standards (subsequently reduced at the request of the British importers to 507,500 standards), a group of important British timber importers, early in January, 1932, started negotiations with the Soviet Timber Trust for the importation into Britain of 450,000 standards of Soviet timber. At once all those opposed to trade with the Soviets raised a hue and cry. Some objected because this deal would hit the Swedish and Finnish timber interests, but most of the objectors relied on the more appealing argument that it would hit Empire interests.

* 19.xii.31.

The British importers were rumoured to have approached the Government asking for an assurance that the contract would not be interfered with by tariffs or preferences which were foreseen as one of the results of the forthcoming Imperial Economic Conference at Ottawa ; when this came to the notice of the Canadian High Commissioner in London, Mr. Ferguson, the latter at once took up the matter with the British Government through the Dominions Office. "The question of timber," said Mr. Ferguson, "will undoubtedly be an important factor in the negotiations for reciprocal trade relations at the forthcoming Imperial Conference, and I am greatly disturbed over the possibility of an arrangement such as this interfering with the success of that conference. My information is that Russian timber is being quoted at distress prices which render competition utterly impossible."* Actually it was subsequently denied both by the British Government and by the timber merchants that the British Government had been approached for any guarantee against the imposition of tariffs, etc.

The Die-Hards took up the cry against Soviet timber and indeed against other Soviet imports and the *Morning Post* again fulminated against "inhuman slave" labour, and demanded outright an embargo on Soviet timber as well as the immediate giving of the necessary six months' notice to terminate the existing Anglo-Russian Commercial Agreement.

The *Times,* albeit more cautiously, advocated a similar policy and in the course of a long leader, January 20, 1932, said:

> "The Government will be expected to deal firmly with this menace [dumping], and to seek the necessary powers if they do not already possess them.
>
> "Important as are the issues raised by the proposed timber contract, they are only part of a much larger question which the British Government, and other Governments as well, will have to face in the near future if our economic life is to be saved from a very serious danger. There are various opinions about the Five-Year Plan, and about the degree to which it is succeeding or failing. But on one point there is and can be no difference of opinion. The organisation of the whole production and commerce of Russia under the control of a single monopoly confronts the rest of the world with a problem of unparalleled magnitude,"

and it deplored the difficulty of organising international agreement:

> "No general agreement, it may be taken for granted, will be reached—possibly, indeed, no serious effort will be made to reach

* *Times,* 18.i.32.

one—until the threat to the trade of the rest of the world has become so clear and so menacing that every one will recognise the necessity of a common understanding to meet it."

In vain it was argued by experts in the timber trade that with the best will in the world to use Empire timbers, the latter could not possibly satisfy the British demand. For instance, Mr. Howard, who had been in the timber trade for some 50 years and had been endeavouring to develop a demand in Britain for Empire timber quoted facts and figures in the *Times*, January 20, 1932, proving that "it is impossible to expect to supply our requirements for softwoods solely from within the British Empire."

It was also useless to point out that at no time had Canadian timber imports into Britain exceeded 5 per cent. of the total imported, that Empire and Soviet timbers were of different textures and were scarcely competitive. Each had its use. For building and joinery purposes North European timber stood pre-eminent. Mr. Bamberger, a well-known timber merchant, stated in the course of a letter to the *Times*, January 26, 1932:

> "British Columbia's chief markets being the American Continent, the Orient and the Antipodes, the main specification she produces is strange to United Kingdom consumers. Admittedly a few of the English standard dimensions are produced, but they only touch on the fringe of this market's everyday requirements and even these few are very often unobtainable.
>
> With regard to Russia, Russian and Siberian softwoods are fine goods. The forests are old, the texture of the wood is mild, and admittedly much of the timber is of exceptional quality.
>
> There has recently been no dumping of Russian wood, because the trade has organised itself to defeat dumping, and the proportion of Russian imports to other European imports was approximately the same for 1930 as for 1912. With respect to stocks of European softwoods at present in this country, it should be remembered that at the beginning of the year stocks from ice-bound ports should necessarily represent from six to nine months' supply. . . .
>
> They (the timber merchants) will, I am convinced, continue to urge their clients to purchase Empire woods, as I and my firms are continuously doing, but until such time as the Empire is in a position to cater adequately for the United Kingdom demand in all its complexities they will, unfortunately have to look largely to other sources of supply."

These and other statements had, of course, little effect on those bent on bedevilling Anglo-Soviet relations and although the timber deal went through in the end in a somewhat modified form since the vast majority of timber merchants (170 out of a total of 175 British timber firms participated in the deal*) knew they could not do without Soviet timber, the agitation to close the British market to Soviet goods and to abrogate the existing commercial agreement continued with, if anything, greater bitterness with the coming change of the fiscal system in Britain and as the date of the opening of the Ottawa Conference drew near. The matter was raised in Parliament on February 8, in connection with the final breakdown of the Anglo-Soviet negotiations on pre-revolutionary Russian debts to Great Britain and the Soviet counter claims against losses suffered by Soviet Russia from British armed intervention in Russia.

Asked by Sir W. Davison, February 8, 1932, whether the Government did not consider it desirable after the failure of the negotiations to terminate the Anglo-Soviet Trade Agreement, Mr. Anthony Eden (Under-Secretary for Foreign Affairs) replied that the whole aspect of Anglo-Soviet relations was under consideration and that this was one of the aspects. In reply to another question, Major Colville, Secretary of the Department of Overseas Trade said that the question of trade with Russia was receiving careful and special consideration and an announcement would be made in due course.

Ten days later (February 18) a deputation from the Association of the British Chambers of Commerce was received by Major Colville and impressed upon the latter their view that the existing Anglo-Soviet Commercial Agreement was in practice disadvantageous to British trade interests. The British Empire Union went further and in a letter to the Prime Minister urged the "Government to give notice forthwith of the cancellation of the Trade Agreement with Russia, and to put into effect the full force of the Abnormal Importations Act against dumped Russian goods."†

II. Report of the Imperial Economic Committee. Anti-Soviet speeches in the House of Lords

At the same time a really staggering blow was given to the agitation against Russian wheat imports by the report on the wheat situation in 1931 issued by the Imperial Economic Committee, February 19, 1932. The report had been compiled in order to lay it before the Imperial Economic Conference which was to have met in Ottawa in 1931 and the report was almost completed when the Conference was postponed to 1932. In the section dealing with Russia the report said:

"Russia's inability to export between 1924 and 1930 was, how-

* *Times*, 17.ii.32. † Ibid. 18.ii.32.

ever, not wholly due to small crops or to the break-up of the large estates. It was partly the result of increased consumption at home due both to an increase in population and to an increase in the average consumption per head, and partly to resistance by the peasants to whom the State was unable to offer sufficient inducement to lead them to grow quantities adequate for the export programme. (p. 87).

In the past seven years, notwithstanding an addition of some thirty-four million acres to the area under wheat, Russia has only exported appreciable quantities on two occasions—1926-27 and in 1930-31—and in both cases she harvested exceptionally large crops on account of high yield per acre. Moreover, the whole of the increased production of 1930—383 million bushels—has not been pressed on the export markets." (p. 89).

So much for the accusation that it was at the expense of starving peasants that the Soviets exported grain. The report continued:

"The low price of wheat is perhaps as serious a matter for Russia as it is for other exporting countries. It may well be more serious. (p. 90).

. . . So far from regarding the low world price of wheat as a condition of affairs which the Soviet authorities have deliberately sought (as has been suggested), we think it is rather a condition from which they have every economic reason to desire to escape. (p. 91).

It would be an error to regard the re-entry of Russia into the international trade in wheat as merely incidental to her plans to expand her industrial equipment. It was but natural to expect that the time would come when she would seek to re-enter a trade in which she has played so large a part in the past and for competing in which she possessed such natural advantages. Her representatives at International Conferences have repeatedly stated that they hope in time to recover much of the trade they have lost." (p. 91).

Tables of wheat imports from the Empire, the U.S.S.R. and other countries proved conclusively that by no stretch of the imagination could it be said that Soviet wheat had ousted Empire wheat; it was mainly Argentine wheat which gained from a cessation of Soviet wheat exports in 1929 and it was the Argentine and the U.S.A. which lost from the increase in Soviet shipments in 1931. On the other hand, when Soviet Russia was completely out of the market it was again the U.S.A. and Argentine which took her place, and in the years 1924-27 when Russia was beginning to regain her position, our imports of

Empire wheat rose to above pre-war whilst the U.S.A. and Argentine wheat shipments decreased.

In 1929, when we imported no Soviet wheat, our imports of Empire wheat again fell below pre-war. In 1930 and 1931, on the other hand, when the U.S.S.R. again entered the British market on a large scale, our imports of Empire wheat (mainly Canadian and Australian) also increased.

This blow to the agitation against alleged Russian dumping, starvation of peasants, etc., was, however, warded off by the Die-Hard press by the simple expedient of almost completely ignoring it. This was, of course, quite natural. As the *New Statesman and Nation* so well put it:

> "The Tory Members of the House of Commons, encouraged by their protectionist successes, are now in full cry for the termination of our trade agreement with Russia. The Trade and Industry Committee in the House has passed a resolution urging the Government to bring it at once to an end. Yet presumably the coming of protection—wheat quota and all—has removed the principal arguments by which the anti-Russian fanatics used to buttress up their case. British farmers and importers of Empire timber are to be protected against the horrors of Russian 'dumping'; and there will even be power under the new measure to impose discriminating duties. What more can the most ardent protectionist want?
>
> What most of them do want, of course, is a boycott of Russia, not on economic, but on political grounds. They are frightened at the progress made with the Five-Year Plan, and quite prepared to damage British trade if therewith they can inflict damage on the country which is attempting to solve its economic problems on Socialist lines. Luckily, there are quite a number of British firms which can very ill afford to stop trading with the Soviet Union. It is to be hoped their influence will be strong enough to prevent a repetition of the folly of seven years ago."

Conservatives more nearly in touch with realities also took a sane view. Thus, in the course of a discussion in the House of Commons, March 3, 1932, in which Labour members urged the need to rectify our adverse balance of trade with Russia, not by limiting imports of Soviet goods which are required by Britain, but by stimulating British exports to the U.S.S.R. by a more liberal use of the Export Credits Guarantee Scheme, whilst certain conservative members opposed such a policy as though this would only benefit the U.S.S.R., Major Colville very justly pointed out that:

> "The Overseas Trade Acts, 1920-1930, authorised the Board

of Trade, with the consent of the Treasury and after consultation with an Advisory Committee composed of bankers and business men, to give guarantees in connection with the export of goods wholly or partly produced or manufactured in the United Kingdom. These guarantees do not extend to munitions of war. I say that in order that some points which have arisen at Question Time may be made plain. The Acts provide that the aggregate amount outstanding at any time shall not exceed £26,000,000. The House should note that the scheme exists, not for the benefit of Russia, as some people seem to imagine, or for the benefit of other foreign purchasers, but entirely for the benefit of United Kingdom exporters."*

After giving a short résumé of the application of the scheme since 1929, he made the comparatively welcome announcement that "after careful consideration of the position, the Government have decided, in the interests of trade and industry, that the Department's Advisory Committee should again be free, as in the past, to consider proposals involving credits of more than twelve months."†

Mr. C. M. Patrick (Unionist Member for Tavistock), whilst agreeing that caution should be exercised in extending credits and generally supporting the Government in their admitted intentions to revise the Anglo-Soviet Commercial Agreement, nevertheless declared:

> "I wish to touch only very shortly upon the question of Russian trade, because it so happens that perhaps I am the only Member in this House who has lived in Soviet Russia, and possibly I can make a few points upon the question as viewed from the other end, so to speak. I do not mean to say viewed through Russian eyes, but through the eyes of an Englishman in Moscow. In coming back to this country from Russia, it seems to me that there are two main objections to the principle of giving credits to that country. The first is, that there is a body of opinion here which holds that it is a mistake to facilitate in any way the progress of a country which, after all, is bound to be a commercial rival of ours in the future, if it is not so at present, and particularly to help such a rival in any way which involves us in serious obligations.
>
> That is a logical attitude to take up, but in this particular case it does not fit the facts. Even if we were to withdraw our credits from Russia and even to close our import market to her to some extent, it would not have the effect, in the long run, of diminishing her competitive power. The Five-Year Plan has progressed so far that they can more or less, if not entirely, do

* *Hansard* 3.iii.32, col. 1322. † Ibid., cols. 1323/24.

> without us. If we cut down our credits and restrict our market, I do not say that it would not cause a great deal of embarrassment to Soviet finances. I think that unquestionably it would, but the final result would be merely that such business as she does with us would be transferred to our commercial competitors probably in Germany and the United States. . . .
>
> There is a great deal of diversity of opinion about what our trade and other relations with Russia should be, but I think that there will be practically unanimous agreement upon one point, and that is, that it is highly desirable to increase our export trade with Russia. Whatever may be the precise figure of our adverse balance of trade with her, taking re-exports and invisible exports and so on, there is a very large margin in her favour as against us. I am convinced that if we use our potentialities for giving credit, and, furthermore, if we use the free right of unrestricted entry into our markets as a bargaining factor, we shall have no difficulty in coming to an arrangement with Russia. It would be something less one-sided and something which would be as much to the advantage of Russia as it would be to our advantage."*

The Die-Hards returned to the attack in the House of Commons when, on March 15, Commander O. Locker-Lampson introduced a Bill to prohibit the import of goods made by foreign forced labour. He made a vicious attack on the U.S.S.R. and, admitting that it would be very difficult "for the Government to withdraw recognition from Russia," he suggested that the Government should approach the League of Nations to take action in regard to Russia, that they should send a Commission of Investigation into Russia and that having carried his Bill, they should prohibit Soviet exports into Britain. However, the Bill never received a second reading.

Again, on March 24, 1932, on the motion for the adjournment, the Duchess of Atholl urged the Government to denounce the Anglo-Soviet Trade Agreement. In her speech she re-hashed all the old stories of forced labour in the U.S.S.R. It is interesting to note that the Duchess referred to the embargo placed by the United States on all products of forced or prison labour, but she omitted to state that not a single cargo of Soviet goods had been excluded from the U.S.A. Why? Because there were no proofs that forced or prison labour had been employed in their production.

As an illustration of the length to which misrepresentation of the Soviet position, not only by the notorious "Riga" and "Helsingfors" correspondents, went, it may be observed that Commander O. Locker-

* *Hansard*, 3.iii.32, cols. 1330 and 1332.

Lampson, in the course of the same session declared (on the authority of the Duchess of Atholl), that Stalin had stated in June, 1931, " he could offer very little hope of relief for the worker, and admits that the peasants can no longer be recruited voluntarily for industry." Needless to say, Stalin had made no such statement. The Duchess herself, in the course of her speech on March 24, said: " M. Stalin stated last June that the Five-Year Plan would have to be based on conscript labour—it could not be carried out otherwise."*

The Anglo-Russian Parliamentary Committee challenged the Duchess (or anyone else) to point out any such passage in Stalin's speech, a copy of which was in the possession of the Committee—but all that the Duchess was able to say in reply was that she had " paraphrased Mr. Stalin correctly."

On the other hand, another line of attack was to demand the termination of the Anglo-Soviet Trade Agreement as a reprisal for, as Sir Wm. Davison put it in the House of Commons, April 11, " the failure of the Russian Soviet Government to submit any proposals with reference to the money and property of British nationals appropriated without compensation." He also suggested that a duty should be clapped " on all Russian goods," the proceeds being used for the compensation of British creditors. The Government, however anti-Soviet, knew better than to follow this advice, but at the same time, they steadily refused to improve the conditions of the application of the Export Credits Guarantee Scheme, with the result that many valuable orders that might have been placed here went to Germany and other countries.

Sir Stanley Machin, an ex-President of the Association of British Chambers of Commerce and a member of the Executive Council, stated:

> " Anything may happen in Russia within the next 12 months. Business men in Britain have a feeling that the Soviet régime is getting near the end of its tether.
>
> Certain sections of the trading community have been putting pressure on the British Government to assist them in giving Russia long term credits. The Government wisely refuses to respond.
>
> Quite frankly, I feel that the less we have to do with the Soviet the better."†

The *Daily Express* tried to make the British public's flesh creep by throwing all realities and facts to the wind and screeching:

> " The wheat gamble has failed. The oil gamble has failed. The gamble of the Five-Year Plan has failed.

* *Hansard*, 24.iii.32, col. 1247. † *Sunday Graphic*, 17.iv.32.

Russia is finding it more and more difficult to obtain foreign credits. The demoralisation of markets which was to bring a Soviet triumph has brought a Russian catastrophe."*

Can it be that they had some inkling of the wrecking game which some treacherous Soviet officials in high places (only unmasked in 1934-1938) were carrying on in the U.S.S.R. and that the British Die-Hards were hoping for the success of these plots?

In the House of Lords on April 20, Lords Lloyd, Phillimore, Lovat, Newton, Mount Temple and Banbury, made violent attacks on the U.S.S.R. in reply to which Lord Snowden (then Lord Privy Seal) said that all the allegations of Soviet anti-British agitation were "at least five years old" and that comparatively little of such agitation had been carried on for the last few years ; he also pointed out once again that:

> "there was no guarantee to the Government of Russia in regard to any trade concession. On that point the whole of the debate had been carried on under a misapprehension. Credits were given not to Russia, but to British traders in order to finance the orders given to them in their transactions with Russia."†

Lord Snowden stressed the value of this trade to British industry, but pointed out that he was very dissatisfied with the British balance on Anglo-Soviet trade and that "it had been decided not to give guarantees for further credits with Russia for more than twelve months without attaching more stringent conditions than in the past,"‡ but the whole question was now under consideration.

Although the Die-Hard press took up the cry of the reactionary noble Lords with alacrity, adding suppositions obtained heaven knows where, that the Soviets would soon be unable to meet their financial obligations, certain wiser counsels also made themselves heard. Lord Revelstoke (Director of Messrs. Baring Bros.), in a letter to the *Times*, April 27, 1932, referring to the Debate in the House of Lords, made a strong appeal for the cessation of abuse. He hoped that commercial intercourse might lead Russia away from collectivisation and urged the justice of the Soviet demand that a settlement of the Tsarist debts could only be contemplated in the event of a long-term loan being granted them, enabling a more rapid development of their national economy and declared:

> "The Russians have been criticised, perhaps somewhat unfairly, for demanding what would be a perfectly natural and indeed a necessary concomitant of a settlement of their debt—a reconstruction loan." He urged in conclusion "would it not

* *Daily Express*, 18.iv.32. † *Daily Telegraph*, 21.iv.32. ‡ Ibid.

be well for us in this country, seeing the magnitude of the issue at stake, to forbear from doing or saying things which will make that day more distant than it need be? Instead of antagonising Russia by hard words, and forging one more link in the iron chain of restrictions which is dragging the European nations step by step along the road which leads to Collectivism; instead of refusing to buy something which we need, for the fancied satisfaction of depriving Russia of a resource, would it not be well, whenever we get the chance, to allow the softening influences of commercial intercourse to do their work in establishing common ground between us and a people with whom, in spite of all, we still share the bond of brotherhood?"

This letter was warmly welcomed by responsible journals, such as the *Spectator*, *New Statesman and Nation*, and others.

A little later, May 23, 1932, Major Colville announced in Parliament that "as a result of the negotiations with the Soviet Trade Representative, it has been agreed that further credits for the sale to Russia of goods manufactured in this country may be granted, with the Export Credits Guarantee, up to a total amount of £1,600,000. The terms will be fixed by the Advisory Committee in each case, but the maximum period of credit will be 18 months and a substantial portion will be at 12 months." This step the *Morning Post* roundly denounced, stating in the course of a leader:

"The National Government are gambling with the taxpayers' money, and the folly of the whole proceeding is that the net result is to bolster up a Five-Year Plan which is already tottering."*

Reynolds', on the other hand, made a plea for extended credits to the U.S.S.R. and declared in the course of a leading article:

"Millions of pounds of Russian trade are available. Our business men want it. Our workpeople need it. But the Government refuse to follow the lead of Germany and America and finance it.

In 1925, British exports and re-exports to Russia were £19,000,000, exceeding both German-Russian and American-Russian trade. Three years later, following the stupid Tory attack on the Soviets, our trade fell by two-thirds, while the trade of our German and American competitors increased considerably.

The suggestion that the Russians might default has been exploded times without number. Indeed, the startling truth is that *German-Russian trade is being financed mainly by the City of*

* *Morning Post*, 24.v.32.

> *London and that the Soviets are paying Germany, which is not repaying Britain!*
>
> The argument that the Russian request for credit up to three and five years for large machinery orders is unreasonable is equally false. Under the Trade Facilities Act, the British Government guaranteed the principal and interest on millions of pounds of money to Mexico, Greece, Bulgaria, Turkey and other countries (many of which have defaulted) up to 25 years. Take one example. The Hungarian Electrical Scheme was financed to the extent of £1,200,000 for 25 years."*

And in spite of all the prophecies of Soviet defaults and failure of the Five-Year Plan, etc., by learned and non-learned scribes, the Soviet Government obstinately refused to fall in with these prophecies; thus, in reply to a question, Major Colville stated in the House of Commons:

> "Exports to Russia were included within the scope of the export credits guarantee scheme from August 1, 1929, and from that date until May 31, 1932, the total credits which the Department had contracted to guarantee in connection with exports to Russia amounted to £15,380,000. There has been no failure to date to pay off punctually the very substantial proportion of these credits which have already matured."†

But anti-Soviet prejudice continued unabated. This is well illustrated by a debate in the House of Lords, June 22. At this session Lord Marley (who had just returned from a visit to the U.S.S.R.) said:

> "We all know that in your Lordships' House the subject of Russia is one which destroys the balance of thought among many noble Lords. Yet it is a fact that while you have unemployment amounting in this country to nearly 3,000,000, in France to 3,000,000, in Germany to 6,000,000, and in the United States to 12,000,000 or 13,000,000, in Russia to-day there is no unemployment, and Russia is a country with growing wealth, whose people are looking forward year by year to the gradual increase in the standard of life which they are actually receiving, and who have a constructive plan giving hope and belief to millions—a hope and belief which is completely absent from the minds of the masses of the workers of Great Britain and other countries to-day."‡

Later, replying to some remarks of the Marquess of Reading, Lord Marley said:

> "I had very much in view the comparison between the two

* 5.vi.32. † *Hansard*, 13.vi.32, col. 13.
‡ *House of Lords Official Report*, 22.vi.32, col. 75.

countries and I had the remembrance that whereas the standard of life in this country has been far higher than in Russia and is falling, the standard of living in Russia has been far lower and is rising. I would remind him that in this country we have a movement for an increase in hours of work despite the fact that there are millions and millions of unemployed, while in Russia the hours of work are being reduced and now stand at an average of seven hours per day."*

The noble Lords were outraged and Viscount Snowden (Lord Privy Seal) allowed his spleen to get the better of his judgment when, replying to Lord Marley, he said:

> "The noble Lord said that there are no unemployed in Russia. I do not think he would find any unemployed in Dartmoor gaol. Russia is under a system of industrial conscription. Russia has confiscated all the capital, repudiated all public debts, and yet, starting without any capital liability at all, Russia has ever since been coming to the capitalist countries of the world, cap in hand, begging them for export trade and loans—to this country which has repudiated its liabilities!"†

Really, Lord Snowden had surpassed himself. He compared the U.S.S.R. to Dartmoor gaol! So a country which had got rid of its capitalists and landlords and which, on the ruins left by Tsardom, the world war and foreign intervention and blockade, had built up in record time a successful large-scale State industry and collective agriculture; a country which in less than five years had carried out work which took Europe more than a century; a country which in the short space of fourteen years was fast stamping out illiteracy and had opened wide the gates of knowledge and culture to the workers and peasants; a country in which, even according to a bitter enemy of the Soviets, the nation is imbued "with an incredibly intense, never flagging, enthusiasm born of unflinching optimism," and where, according to this hostile critic of the Soviets:

> "The system is maintained in vigour by the rising generation, whose thoughts and feelings are Soviet, and who, hitherto, have shown all the enthusiasm necessary for the government to hope to reach its goal by their aid."‡

—such a country was nothing but a "Dartmoor gaol!"

We would have liked to see Lord Snowden and his colleagues try to build up a successful industry and agriculture by the Dartmoor gaol

* Ibid., col. 83. † Ibid., 29.vi.32, col. 347.

‡ *Lloyds Bank Limited Monthly Review*, June, 1932.

system. How many inmates or visitors to Dartmoor gaol or any other penal settlement would testify to the support of the system by the inmates of the gaol or settlement and to their " unflagging enthusiasm " and " unflinching optimism " regarding the work of the authorities of that gaol ?

The truth is—and Lord Snowden (who at one time had called himself a socialist) of all people might have been expected to know this—that a planned system of the national economy involving, of course, also the planned organisation of labour, is as poles asunder from the organisation of a penal settlement.

It was, of course, also absurd to speak of Russia " going cap in hand, begging for export trade and loans." True, the Soviet Government desired credits for the purchase of machinery and equipment for the construction of its factories, the development of transport, roads, etc., but how many of the British Dominions and other developing countries have financed such undertakings which, by their very nature, require the lapse of some time for their construction and before they can yield returns, except by way of loans and long-term credits ?

The U.S.S.R., like other countries, naturally went for its purchases where the terms were most accommodating. At the same time, to pay for her imports, the Soviet Government naturally demanded access to foreign markets for her exports. Which country did not aim at this?

However, anti-Soviet speeches in the House of Lords were not in themselves important—we quote them here more as examples of the prejudices and modes of thought of that class of people and as curiosities in face of subsequent developments in the U.S.S.R. than because of their intrinsic interest.

What, however, was important, was the pressure of the Canadian Government at the Inter-Imperial Conference which opened in Ottawa on July 21, 1932. We deal with this subject in the next chapter.

CHAPTER XVIII

THE OTTAWA CONFERENCE AND THE DENUNCIATION OF THE ANGLO-SOVIET COMMERCIAL AGREEMENT (JULY-DECEMBER, 1932)

I. RUSSIAN " DUMPING " DISCUSSED. EFFECTS OF THE OTTAWA AGREEMENT

EVEN before the opening of the Ottawa Conference it had been rumoured that the Canadian Government wished the question of Soviet competition to be made a subject of discussion. They were not successful in the attempt to place the matter definitely upon the agenda, but from the opening to the closing day, the subject hung like a cloud over the Conference Hall.

Mr. Bennett sounded a veiled anti-Soviet note in his opening speech when he declared:

> " They must safeguard their established standards of living and be active to defend the free institutions of the Empire when they found them menaced by organised economic hostility operating through State-controlled standards of living, State-controlled labour and State-aided dumping dictated by high State policy."*

As might have been expected, this was eagerly seized on by the British " Die-Hard " press. On July 23, 1932, the editor of the *Morning Post,* who represented his paper in Ottawa during the Conference, in the course of his report of Mr. Bennett's speech, wrote:

> ". . . no scheme of inter-Empire trading is possible if Russia is not prevented from lowering prices by artificial and political methods.
>
> This is the first fence to be cleared, and cleared quickly. If not, the Conference may fail."

Similarly, the *Daily Mail* Ottawa correspondent cabled:

> " It is pointed out that the preferences would be ineffective if Russia were allowed to continue dumping.
>
> Mr. Bennett, the Canadian Prime Minister, supported by Mr. Bruce, head of the Australian delegation, will therefore urge that definite steps be taken to prohibit or control Russian exports to the British Empire."†

And as the days passed the negotiations with Canada were more and more centred around the demand that Britain should close her market to the Soviets.

The *Manchester Guardian,* in a leading article on August 19, 1932, put the position very aptly thus:

> " So pervading is the sentiment of common sacrifice and goodwill that a section of the Canadian Cabinet, their friends the Canadian textile manufacturers, and some of our most zealous Protectionists were ready to risk the break-up of the Conference on this crude demand that Britain must surrender her Russian trade or receive no benefits from Canada. The British delegates . . . were faced with something like a conspiracy which would have turned the Conference into a political engine to fight ' Bolshevism,' instead of a co-operative undertaking for the

* *Times,* 22.vii.32. † 25.vii.32.

removal of trade barriers and the cultivation of world trade. . . . A new campaign is already beginning, and we may expect that Ottawa agreements, whatever they may be, will be described as frustrate because (in the words of the *Morning Post*) when the 'choice was presented of Empire or Soviets the latter was chosen.' For mischievous perversion this appeal to irrelevant non-rational prejudice would be hard to beat."

The British delegation certainly could not be suspected of pro-Soviet leanings; nevertheless, it had a sufficient conception of realities to understand the folly of, at any rate, the open policy of discrimination against the U.S.S.R., demanded by Canada. As the Ottawa correspondent of the *Daily Telegraph* put it: "It is generally accepted that it would be undesirable to seek to put Russia out of business. This would have disturbing effects over a wide area."

But the British delegates or some of them would seem to have been not averse to action of some kind against the Soviets, for as the *Daily Telegraph* also reported:

> "The British Government is prepared to take powers to prevent, by prohibition or special duties, the marketing in Britain of foreign goods, sold at cut prices. In the case of Russia this step would involve the renunciation of the trade agreement, which is terminable at six months' notice.
>
> It is gathered that British Ministers are unanimously agreed on this course. They believe that with their hands thus freed, and successful long-term agreements settled here designed to promote a general advance in commodity prices, the prospects of leading other countries along the same path at the coming World Conference will be rosy."*

Ostensibly, it was Russian cut prices, Russian dumping, Russian flooding of the market which was disturbing the peace of mind of Mr. Bennett and Mr. Bruce and the British "Die-Hards."

It is a well-known fact that whilst one can see the mote in another's eye one fails to detect the beam in one's own eye, and it is probably for this reason that our imperialists overlooked such facts as the following:

> "In Canada, wheat farms in high cost areas have been kept in production by a mistaken attempt at price maintenance and extended credit under Government guarantee. A prominent cause of the fall in price of mutton and lamb has been the enormous increase in shipments from Australia and New Zealand, those shipments rising from 7,400,000 carcases in 1929 to 11,350,000 carcases in 1931.

* 27.vii.32

> In Australia, under the Paterson Scheme, butter has been sold in the home market at exorbitant prices, while the surplus has been dumped abroad."*
>
> " One of the difficulties of the situation is that the Dominions have been largely responsible for such flooding of the British market with meat imports as has taken place and for the consequent depression of prices."†

The two chief commodities about which Canada was concerned were wheat and timber. We have already dealt with these subjects, but it may not be out of place to point out here that in regard to wheat, for instance, it seemed to be not so much Canadian interests as anti-Soviet prejudice and hostility which actuated the demands of Mr. Bennett; the grain growers of Canada themselves were by no means clamouring for preferences in the British market for, as the *Morning Post* Special Correspondent cabled from Ottawa, they said:

> " Even were there to be not a bushel of foreign wheat consumed within the bounds of the Empire, the wheat-producing Dominions, after fully supplying the Empire market, would still have some two hundred million bushels to sell in foreign markets.
>
> Some wheat producers, therefore, feel that a preferential tariff would, by diverting more foreign wheat to non-Empire markets, intensify competition in those markets, and that the advantages which they gained through preference in British markets would be outweighed by the increased difficulties in marketing the rest of their crop.
>
> They have, therefore, withdrawn their demands for the Preference."‡

As for timber, we would only add here the view of the *Financial News* timber trade correspondent (who was " a member of a well-known firm of British timber merchants "). Writing in the *Financial News* (Supplement), June 6, 1932, he said:

> " The rapid advance by which Russia has, by 1931, regained for herself 40 per cent. of our market has only been achieved in the last four years. It should be observed that the advance has not been secured at the expense of the North American shipments; and that, since Canada's true market is in the U.S.A., and the Pacific countries of Asia, the timber exports of Russia are of little concern to the Dominion. Canada's contribution to British timber imports is only about 3 per cent."

* *Financial News*, 26.vii.32. † *Times*, 18.viii.32.
‡ *Morning Post*, 28.vii.32.

Also the view of the *Timber and Plywood Journal*, which on August 20, 1932, declared:

> "We are all agreed on the desirability of widely expanding the inter-Empire trading bond, and we are even prepared to make sacrifices for that ideal. *There is a limit, however, to the burden that British backs can bear;* the time has come when additional weight must be measured by single straws, for the imposition of extra bales is no longer possible.
>
> Before agreeing to exclude Russian timber, this country must have definite guarantees against the exploitation of the British market by those who stand to gain by that move. Sweden and Finland are protesting loudly against low prices; but to-day's figures savour somewhat of retribution, *for our pockets were ruthlessly tapped ten years ago when Russian wood was not available.*" (Our italics).

The Soviets on their side not only denied the accusation of dumping, but as we have shown in earlier pages, made repeated efforts to come to world agreements which would have made dumping on the part of any country practically impossible. Dealing with the accusation of dumping against the Soviets, the Chairman of the U.S.S.R. Trade Delegation in London, in a speech at the Sixteenth Annual General Meeting of the Russo-British Chamber of Commerce on July 12, 1932, said:

> "The foreign trade of the Soviet Union occupies a comparatively small space in the fabric of its national economy. The value of the total exports from the U.S.S.R. is not more than 4 per cent. of the aggregate national income of that country. There exists a still less proportion if the comparison is drawn between our exports and world trade turnover.
>
> For some reason our exports have become a very attractive target for many biassed critics. The continual fall in price level which has taken place since the beginning of the present world economic slump has been, in one way or another, attributed to our export activities.
>
> It is no fault of ours that the prices for commodities have been falling; to substantiate my point, I should like to take a few examples, viz.:
>
> *Timber.*—Certain people are endeavouring to create the impression that the exportation of timber into Great Britain from the U.S.S.R. is something entirely new and without precedence. There is no truth in it whatever. Russian timber has always occupied the principal place on the British market. At present,

our exports of timber to the United Kingdom are still below pre-war figures. *We do not lower our prices deliberately.* They depend mainly upon those quoted by our competitors.

Wheat.—The price for grain began to fall before we entered the wheat market, and continues to do so at present when we are not selling but purchasing wheat.

Then, again, such goods as rubber, copper, wool, cotton, tin, tea, coffee and others were affected by the fall in price level perhaps more than any other commodities, although in respect of these goods we are only buyers and not sellers. *It is apparent, therefore, that the fall in prices has been due to causes other than those for which we are responsible.*" (Our italics.)

After protracted and anxious negotiations at the Ottawa Conference, the British delegation agreed to a tax on foreign grain of 2s. per quarter and to a variety of other taxes on foods imported into the United Kingdom (all these articles were to enter free of duty into the United Kingdom from Canada), in return for preferences for the import of certain British goods into Canada. The following formula, constituting Article 21 of the British-Canadian Agreement, was adopted on August 20, 1932, for the regulation of foreign imports:

" This Agreement is made on the express condition that, if either Government is satisfied that any preferences hereby granted in respect of any particular class of commodities are likely to be frustrated in whole or in part by reason of the creation or maintenance directly or indirectly of prices for such class of commodities through State action on the part of any foreign country, that Government hereby declares that it will exercise the powers which it now has or will hereafter take to prohibit the entry from such foreign country directly or indirectly of such commodities into its country for such time as may be necessary to make effective and to maintain the preferences hereby granted by it."

It will be seen that this was a general formula applying to all foreign countries, the U.S.S.R. not being specifically mentioned.

But it was clear enough that it was the U.S.S.R. which the formula had in mind; the *Daily Herald* Ottawa correspondent reported:

" Mr. Bennett fought hard to make this clause include a specific mention of Russia.

The attitude of the British Ministers was clearly against taking any risk which might lead to another break with the Soviet, but, pushed by Canada and the ' Die-Hards ' at home, a serious situation may arise."

On the other hand, the *Daily Mail* Ottawa correspondent declared:

> "I understand that the British delegation has given a definite undertaking to Canada to serve Russia with a six-months' notice that she intends to seek a revision of the present Anglo-Russian trade agreement,"*

and the *Daily Express* correspondent was equally clear:

> "The formula agreed is to the effect that Great Britain shall take all legislative and administrative steps to control uneconomic competition from State controlled products.
>
> There is no specific mention of Russia, but it is a gentleman's agreement that action shall be taken against Russian dumping."†

The Canadian anti-Soviet attitude at the Ottawa Conference was shown up in its true light all the more by the fact that where Canadian interests were directly concerned Mr. Bennett was prepared after all to "sup with the devil." The Canadian Government on February 28, 1931, passed an Order-in-Council prohibiting all imports from the Soviet Union of coal, woodpulp, lumber, timber of all kinds, asbestos and furs. Canadian traders were by no means unanimously in favour; the only interests which applauded whole-heartedly were lumber merchants.

Moscow replied to Ottawa by placing an embargo on all Canadian products, instructing its representatives abroad not to purchase any Canadian goods. This policy was no doubt harmful to both countries and could not be continued indefinitely, but it is interesting and important to note that Mr. Bennett's Government was the first to climb down.

On December 16, 1931, it was reported in the British press that "in deference to pressure from Canadian furriers, the Government has amended the Order-in-Council which last February placed an embargo upon furs and other commodities from Russia, and, while dressed or manufactured furs are still excluded, the amendment permits the importation of raw furs."

Similarly, it was later reported in the *Daily Telegraph* that whilst the Ottawa Conference was actually in session, negotiations were proceeding between the Aluminium Company of Canada and representatives of the Soviet, the result of which was reported in the *Daily Telegraph*, September 17, 1932:

> "A huge direct barter deal has been arranged by a Canadian firm with Soviet Russia.

* 20.viii.32. † 20.viii.32.

The Aluminium Company of Canada will exchange £250,000 worth of aluminium wire for oil of an equivalent value."

——no word here of "forced labour."

Discussing this deal with a correspondent of the *Daily Telegraph* (September 19, 1932), Mr. Bennett was stated to have said:

> "This deal gives temporary employment to over 200 men in Toronto, and *is therefore useful now*.
>
> Oil is not included in the list of commodities which the Government has been empowered by Parliament to place an embargo upon, and so long as it is offered here at *a fair competitive price*, it is difficult to see what preventive action we can take without fresh legislative sanction." (Our italics).

The Ottawa Conference as such is, of course, outside the province of this book, except in so far as it affected Anglo-Soviet relations; we shall not, therefore, stop to deal with the general agreements and results of the Conference, except to point out that discussing the subject later, the *Manchester Guardian*, in the course of a leader, declared with justice:

> "Why, one may wonder, is it necessary to denounce the Commercial Agreement at all? Everyone knows that the allegations about Russian 'dumping' are largely nonsense and only another way of saying that, after some years' absence from the world markets, Russian exports have returned and, because of the already demoralised conditions, have helped to force weak prices lower. Everyone knows also that the motives which led to the drafting of the Ottawa formula were crude and mercenary in the last degree. It was admitted during the Conference by British Conservative newspapers (which are above the suspicion of prejudice) that Mr. Bennett's anti-Russian drive was forced on by three sections—Canadian industrialists aggrieved at the tariff settlement and hoping to wreck any agreement with Britain; certain high Protectionist 'British elements' who were fishing in troubled waters; and the Canadian lumbermen, who, having lost their market in the United States, are desperate to unload their stocks on this country and wish to keep out the cheaper Russian timber which British merchants prefer to buy."*

However, after the conclusion of the Ottawa Agreement, the spate of lies and distortions in a number of British journals of events in the U.S.S.R. generally and the "failure" of the Five-Year Plan in particular, assumed wider proportions than ever.

* 8.x.32.

At the same time there was a general outcry by both British manufacturer and working-class organisations against the policy of the Export Credits Guarantee Department in limiting the guarantees to credits for a period generally not exceeding twelve months, and its restriction of their total guarantee of bills on Soviet orders to the sum of £1,600,000. The latter sum was very soon exhausted, and many Soviet orders which would have gone to Britain went to Germany. So insistent was the demand for better credit facilities that at last the Government, to the disgust of the Die-Hard press, made a timid move early in September, 1932, and again extended the credit guarantees to eighteen months. There seemed to be some hope too that the amount to be guaranteed by the Department would also be raised somewhat.

After this, things began to look up in regard to Anglo-Soviet trade, but in the meantime the Cabinet was considering its line of action in regard to the Anglo-Soviet Commercial Agreement. It soon became evident that the earlier supposition that at Ottawa the British delegates had undertaken to give the necessary notice to denounce this Agreement was a fact. This was stated definitely by Sir H. Samuel and Lord Snowden when they announced their resignation from the Government at the end of September, 1932, and a little later Mr. Bennett, the Canadian Premier, was quite explicit as to the real meaning of Article 21* of the British-Canadian Agreement. Speaking in the Canadian House of Commons on October 12, 1932, he said:

> " With regard to Soviet competition, the conference agreements involved the safeguarding of the countries of the Empire against unfair competition from any economically State-controlled country *whose standards of living and State-aided dumping rejected the theory and practice of the free institutions of the British Empire*."† (Our italics).

So one result of the Ottawa Conference was to be a valiant battle against any country which rejected " the theory and practice of the free institutions of the British Empire! "

All this, of course, had an extremely unsettling effect on the normal development of Anglo-Soviet trade, and although people like " A.A.B." in the *Evening Standard* continued to inveigh against doing anything to further such a development and could still continue to write such nonsense as: " The Germans know, and the Americans are beginning to know, that the Soviets are on their last legs; that the Five-Year Plan, while it has achieved wonderful results in the enslavement and brutalisation of human beings, is economically a dead failure; and that another Russian revolution is only a question of time,"‡ big

* See p. 435. † *Morning Post*, 13.x.32. ‡ 4.x.32.

industrialists, particularly those in the engineering trades and labour leaders generally, uttered warning after warning against the denunciation of the Anglo-Soviet Commercial Agreement. It was argued, not without reason, that even if in accordance with the Ottawa agreement or for any other reasons some change in Anglo-Soviet trade relations must be made, negotiations for such a change could be started without denouncing the 1930 agreement until a new one had been negotiated; the more so since the 1930 Anglo-Russian agreement had from the first been regarded as a temporary arrangement and envisaged the subsequent conclusion of a full commercial treaty.

The anxiety in the business world may be illustrated by a report in the *Manchester Guardian*:

> "Inquiries from engineering firms in the Manchester district on the possibility of the Russian trade agreement's being terminated because of the undertakings given to Canada at Ottawa (discussed in our London Correspondence yesterday) revealed a disinclination to believe that this would happen. It would probably be not unfair to state that the disinclination is based rather in a faint hope that the statement is not true than in any belief that the British delegates could not conceivably have done anything so damaging to the engineering industry, important sections of which have subsisted for some time past almost entirely upon Russian orders.
>
> Inquiries made yesterday of a number of representative men in the industry established that there has lately been much eagerness locally to secure new Russian business and that, until sinister leakages about Ottawa decisions were circulated, there was an impression that the Government was taking serious note of strong representations from this area about the folly of limiting credits or otherwise putting new difficulties in the way of Anglo-Russian trade."*

There were numerous appeals against the abrogation of the Treaty and for the furthering of Anglo-Soviet trade, by Labour leaders and Trade Union officials: thus, Mr. R. Moss, Manchester District Secretary of the Amalgamated Engineering Union, in the course of an interview, referring to the uneasiness about Ottawa said:

> "If it is true that Russian orders are to stop, it will be a terrible blow to the Manchester district—a tragedy, nothing less. On the mere suspicion that it may be true the numbers of unemployed in the engineering and allied trades are already increasing seriously. In Manchester and Salford there are about 14,000 men in these

* 8.x.32.

trades on the 'live register' of unemployed. In the whole Manchester area of the A.E.U., including Warrington, Ashton, Broadheath, Oldham and similar centres, where the allied trade unions have about 50,000 members, this union has about 15,000 unemployed. The majority of the 50,000 would soon be out of work if there are no more orders from Russia."*

At the Conference of the Labour Party at Leicester, the following resolution was adopted unanimously on October 3, 1932:

"The Conference enters its emphatic protest against the proposal to abrogate the Anglo-Russian Commercial Agreement of 1930. Further, in view of the widespread unemployment in this country and in view of the fact that the Soviet trading organisations have meticulously honoured every commercial bill bearing their endorsement, this Conference emphatically protests against the Government's policy of refusing adequate credits to finance British exports to Russia, and calls upon the Government to reverse this policy without delay.

Therefore, this Conference instructs the Executive Committee to bring this resolution to the notice of the Prime Minister at their earliest convenience."

The timber traders on their part once again protested against regarding Soviet timber as dumped. In the course of editorial notes *Timber and Plywood*, September 3, 1932, said:

"Indeed, in the last two seasons the Russians made contracts with buyers in this country far more favourable to themselves than did the shippers in Sweden and Finland, and last year the Russian sellers gave a substantial reduction in their contract prices with the Central Softwood Buying Corporation owing to the inability of the latter to market the wood at the prices which were originally paid to the Russians.

We often hear in the daily press that the Russians dump their timber into this country at ruinous figures, but an intimate knowledge of market conditions shows that this is scarcely correct. The usual acceptance of the term dumping is the sending over of unsold goods to be disposed of in the country to which they are exported at the best possible prices.

On the acceptation of the word, *Russia is the only country which during the last couple of years, has not dumped timber into Great Britain.* She has contracted each year for a certain maximum quantity which she has sold to a British corporation or company, while at the same time *both Swedish and Finnish*

* *Manchester Guardian*, 8.x.32.

exporters have despatched or dumped many cargoes of wood into Great Britain, chiefly into London, and much of this wood has had to be sold at public auction for what it would fetch." (Our italics).

On the other hand, the Conference of the National Union of Conservative and Unionist Associations at its session in Blackpool, October 7, 1932, carried a resolution moved by Commander Oliver Locker-Lampson "urging the Government to take action against the continued importation of goods from Russia 'which could never have been dumped at depreciated prices but for the conditions of labour which prevail nowhere in Europe outside the Soviet.'" He declared:

"I asked the Government to stand firm about Russia, India and Ireland. Let Mr. Gandhi starve on his goat's milk; let us refuse to take our marching orders from that mountebank, Mr. de Valera, or from that gang of crooks and cranks who terrorise Russia to-day."*

II. Termination of the Anglo-Soviet Commercial Agreement, October 17. The "Jesus Christ Safety Match" story

And it was this policy which won. Mr. J. H. Thomas (then Secretary of State for the Dominions) announced in October that in accordance with our obligations under the Ottawa Agreement, a Note had been sent on the previous day to the U.S.S.R. representative, terminating the temporary Anglo-Russian Commercial Agreement. The text of the Note was as follows:

"Sir,—I have the honour to inform you that His Majesty's Government in the United Kingdom of Great Britain and Northern Ireland have decided to terminate the temporary commercial agreement signed at London on April 16, 1930, in accordance with the provisions of the first paragraph of Article 7 thereof.

The agreement will accordingly cease to be in force six months from the date of the present Note—that is, from April 17, 1933.

I take this opportunity at the same time to inform you that His Majesty's Government in the United Kingdom remain anxious for the furtherance of trade between the two countries and are prepared with this object to enter into discussions upon the situation created by the denunciation of the temporary commercial agreement at the earliest moment convenient to the Government of the Soviet Union.

I have, etc.,

JOHN SIMON."

* *Daily Telegraph*, 8.x.32.

The Government, on October 18, 1932, in reply to questions regarding their announcement that the above Note had been sent, made it clear that no previous investigations of alleged unfair trading methods, dumping, etc., on the part of the U.S.S.R. had been undertaken, nor did they make any such direct accusations. As regards future action, Mr. Thomas, in reply to further questions, stated that "before any action is taken investigation, examination and proof will be necessary. All I am announcing to-day is that we are taking the necessary power to act if after investigation we find it necessary."*

At the same time it is significant that no such action was taken in regard to other countries which from time to time had been accused (true, in much more restrained terms) of dumping, etc. The Governments of these countries—Denmark, Sweden, Norway, the Argentine—were merely invited to open conversations on tariff matters with Britain.

Curiously enough, on the very day when the Government made the announcement of the denunciation of the Anglo-Soviet Commercial Agreement, Sir A. Steel-Maitland (Minister of Labour in the former Conservative Government), who had just returned from a visit to the U.S.S.R., declared in the course of a speech at Edinburgh:

> "Russia is faced at the moment with two great temporary difficulties—the need for capital and the present agrarian difficulty. But if these are surmounted, I have no doubt as to the success of the Russian scheme of industrialisation. It could not have succeeded in a country like our own. Success will probably be longer in coming than the ardent desire or the sanguine imagine. It is not a question of a five-year plan. But fifteen or twenty years will probably see an industrialised Russia. If this view of the future of Russia is a true one—and I believe it to be so—the question of the attitude of this country towards Russia is of great importance.
>
> I went to Russia with a strong dislike of the way in which the Bolshevik régime was started. I have that dislike still. I am, from the point of view of the immediate future, in favour of increasing trade with Russia as much as possible. In this country capital is lying idle. In Russia it is urgently needed. Why should not the supply meet the demand? Of course, security would have to be forthcoming, and this should not be impossible."†

The *Spectator*, October 22, 1932, commenting on the situation, remarked:

> "The denunciation of the Russian Trade Agreement, as part

* *Hansard*, 18.x.32, col. 12. † *Manchester Guardian*, 19.x.32.

of the bargain exacted by Canada at Ottawa is profoundly unfortunate. Curiously enough, while Mr. Thomas was announcing it in the House of Commons on Tuesday, Sir Arthur Steel-Maitland, Minister of Labour in the Conservative Government of 1924-29, who has just visited Russia and come back, not at all converted to Bolshevism but deeply impressed with realities, was talking extremely sound sense at Edinburgh about the desirability of extending our trade with Russia. Her purchases from us have risen steadily in the last two years—of no other country can that be said—and Germany and America are eager enough to snatch Russian orders that might be keeping British workmen employed. It is true that denunciation of the agreement only leaves us free to interfere with Russian trade if the process controversially termed dumping (several countries complain of dumped British coal) is held to have taken place, but Tuesday's announcement introduces more uncertainty and mistrust into a world half-ruined by those evils already. The action taken was promised at Ottawa, but it is from every point of view pernicious."

However, the Conservative press as a whole and the Die-Hard press in particular, loudly hailed the denunciation of the Anglo-Soviet Commercial Agreement. The Labour, Co-operative and Liberal press, many business men and Trade Union leaders as vehemently denounced this action by the Government. In the U.S.S.R. they were naturally furious at the action of the British Government. The *Izvestia,* October 21, 1932, in the course of an article on the denunciation of the Agreement, quoted the resolution on this subject passed by the Labour Party Conference at Leicester* as the resolution "of an organisation representing millions of the British workers." It referred to the increase of British exports to the U.S.S.R. in 1931, and continued:

"It is the business of the British Government to decide whether it can sacrifice economic interests to illusory political aims. It will be the affair of the Soviet Government to decide what means to adopt to convince the British 'Die-Hards' that Soviet trade is no current coin in British world policy, that the development of trade with a great country with a population of 160,000,000 is valuable and deserves to be considered. But already to-day we must protest most energetically against the reasons given by Mr. Thomas for the step taken by the British Government."

[This refers to the insinuations contained in Mr. Thomas' statement, and taken up by the Die-Hard press, of Soviet "dumping" and "sweating."]

* See p. 440.

Pravda, October 21, 1932, also devoted a leader to this subject, and amongst other things said:

> "The denunciation by the British Government of the Anglo-Soviet Temporary Commercial Agreement destroys the basis of Anglo-Soviet trade.
>
> Apart from the fact that this will inevitably lead to a limitation of Soviet orders and purchases on the British market, it will also tend to a rise in the cost of the raw products of British industry and of the basic foods. This will be a blow, in the first instance, to the wide masses of the workers and the petty bourgeoisie."

The Chief of the Foreign Department of the Commissariat of Heavy Industries, in an interview granted to the department's newspaper, was reported to have said:

> "We are absolutely unable to lay a firm foundation for Anglo-Soviet business relations in the face of the periodical blows which we have received during the past five years. . . .
>
> We took steps to strengthen the share of British production in our machine imports; but the way the Conservative Party in England is treating business relations with the U.S.S.R. is forcing us now to reconsider the opportunities which we have recently offered to British industrialists.
>
> When a group of big British business men visited the U.S.S.R. the other day they made the interesting discovery that Americans, Germans, Frenchmen and Italians are participating in the construction of the great hydro-electric power works of the Dnieprostroi. The British were absent. The construction of a big plant upon British design and with British equipment was suggested, but the prospects of doing useful business have again become doubtful. . . ."*

The question was discussed in the House of Commons repeatedly in the ensuing days, Ministers giving various explanations of the true meaning of their act, but it was Mr. Neville Chamberlain, we consider, who gave the real explanation. Speaking in the House of Commons on October 21, 1932, he said:

> "The hon. Member talked about a hypothetical case where the Russian Government might find that they were able to produce wheat at a cheaper price than anybody else. I daresay they could but how are you to estimate what the cost is in Russia? How are you to compare the costs where there are no overhead charges in the shape of interest on capital, investments in land,

* *Manchester Guardian*, 24.x.32.

etc., *as in ordinary trading? Obviously you cannot do it. It is possible under the Russian system to ignore various items of expense which must be taken into account by ordinary traders.* Therefore, it is perfectly obvious that the Russian Government have it in their power, without being fairly accused of selling under cost, to destroy utterly the market in which ordinary traders are engaged by the simple process of always quoting under the ordinary market price."* (Our italics).

Here was an open and unashamed confession that *the object of the National Government was to take economic measures against the U.S.S.R., because it had eliminated financiers, landlords' royalties and parasitic private owners and middlemen.* In other words, to take but one example, the British worker was not to be provided with cheap houses because the builder is to be compelled to buy timber at high prices from Canada in order to provide royalties for Canadian landlords and fat dividends for Canadian capitalists and financiers! This indeed, had already happened in the case of the London County Council housing schemes.

Thus, Sir P. Harris, M.P., for many years a member of the Housing Committee of the London County Council, stated in the House of Commons:

> "We are building houses on a large scale, and one of our greatest difficulties is to produce houses at such a figure that we can let them at a reasonable rent.
>
> They (the L.C.C.) have a large preference for Dominion timber, and they are importing the greater part of it now from Canada and refusing to take Russian timber. Already, however, there have been complaints from the Master Builders' Association that, owing to the insistence on preference for Canadian timber for municipal houses, there has been a large increase in the price of that timber of something like 20 or 30 per cent. So serious has the matter become that the First Commissioner of Works informed us that he was keeping a close watch on the operation of the Canadian timber organisation. If under pressure from Canada the Board of Trade suddenly, without any inquiry or consultation with this particular Committee, sweeps down and prohibits the importation of foreign timber from Russia and elsewhere, we may find ourselves at the mercy of the Canadian timber producers."†

As a résumé of the whole episode as it affected the British commercial world, we cannot perhaps do better than give a few quotations

* *Hansard*, 21.x.32, col. 532. † Ibid., cols. 548/9.

from a letter by Sir A. Herbert, President, Machine Tool Trades Association, in the *Manchester Guardian*, October 28, 1932:

> "No opportunity is lost to ask questions in the House with the object of disparaging Russian affairs and Russian business. Every report which is critical of Russian progress or Russian conditions is published under flaming headlines, but no space is available for articles which attempt to deal with the subject dispassionately and fairly.
>
> The main criticism against Russian trade with this country is that Russia buys too little from us in proportion to what she sells to us, but the very effect of the unfair criticism and misrepresentation which is so liberally employed is to throw every possible obstacle in the way of improvement in the balance of Russian trade.
>
> The raid on Arcos and the temporary rupture of trade relations which followed was the first serious blow. Whatever motive inspired this action, its effect was to bring about an immediate and most grave reduction in the flow of Russian orders, which had reached a very high level.
>
> In due course the unwisdom of this rupture was realised; trade relations were resumed, a commercial agreement negotiated, and insurance facilities made available through the Export Credits Insurance Department. But the insurance scheme was limited in its scope and subject to continual interruptions and uncertainties. In the early part of this year, for instance, at the very moment when Russia was prepared to place a much larger volume of orders, it was completely suspended and everything thrown into the melting-pot.
>
> Russian orders were held up for some time in the hope that insurance would shortly be resumed, but this hope was disappointed, and as the orders were urgently required they were diverted to Berlin.
>
> After these orders were lost insurance was again made available in September and there was every prospect of new contracts being placed, but now the whole situation is again thrown into a confusion by the announcement that the British Government has given notice to terminate the commercial agreement with Russia.
>
> Russia is the only country in the world which is engaged on a wide scheme of industrialisation, and consequently it is from Russia alone that large-scale orders for industrial plant are available. The importance of her orders can be gauged by the fact that for a considerable period she has taken 80 per cent. of the total exports of British machine tools, and this in spite of the fact

that she is still buying on an enormously greater scale in Germany and to some extent America, while Canada, by contrast, has been taking a minute fraction of the remaining 20 per cent."

When the final estimates for the first Five-Year Plan* were being prepared and allocations of important orders to be placed abroad were being considered by the Soviet Government, the stupendous folly of the Arcos raid and rupture of diplomatic relations put an effectual obstacle in the path of Anglo-Soviet trade and prevented us from getting a normal share of these orders.

At this time, when the second Five-Year Plan was being drafted and important orders for machinery, etc., being allocated, it seemed that the "National" Government was again determined that British industry should get as few of these orders as possible.

During the debates in Parliament, the Government refused to accept amendments providing for inquiry before prohibiting imports and to make prohibition applicable to all sweated goods from any foreign country.

Both Mr. Baldwin and Mr. Chamberlain, however, insisted that the Government was not animated by any hostility to the U.S.S.R. and was anxious to foster Anglo-Soviet trade, whilst at the same time safeguarding Canadian interests.

The Anglo-Soviet Commercial Agreement having been denounced, the great need was to start negotiations for a new agreement and to do everything possible to promote as friendly an atmosphere as possible between the two countries. But this was the last thing in the world desired by the Die-Hards and the lie factories began to work at double pressure, spreading rumours of food riots and other disorders in the Soviet Union, the use of Moscow gold in fomenting unemployed marches and protests against the means test in Great Britain, etc.

The growing army of unemployed in Britain and the hardships entailed upon vast numbers of our people by the Means Test and its harsh application demanded by the authorities had inevitably led to a growing resentment by the chief sufferers which had expressed itself in hunger marches and similar manifestations by the unemployed. The attempt to cut down wages of already low paid workers in the textile and other industries had inevitably led to strikes and resentment on the part of the workers.

Stalin was accused of fomenting discords abroad because reports of strikes and hunger marches in Britain had been printed in the Soviet press (as in the foreign press generally) and questions were solemnly asked and answered on the subject in Parliament.

* The first Five-Year Plan was completed December 31, 1932, and the second Five-Year Plan was being drafted at the time under review here.

The fulminations against Stalin and other Soviet leaders were all the more striking when they are compared with the treatment meted out by the same press to the recognised Dictator of Italy.

On October 23, 1932, Mussolini stated in the course of a speech in Turin:

> "In those countries where the currency has been watered down the conditions of the people have not in any way improved and, it is true, at this very moment while we are meeting in this square, from many points of Great Britain growing bands of unemployed are marching towards London."*

Speaking in Milan on October 25, 1932, Mussolini said:

> "This will be the century of Fascism and during it Italy will be again the leader of Roman civilisation. Within ten years Europe will be changed. Injustices have been perpetrated, particularly towards Italy. . . . Within ten years Europe will be either Fascist or Fascicised. The antithesis must go, New York can be overcome only by the doctrines and practice of Rome."†

On October 27, 1932, the *Daily Telegraph* published an article by Mussolini in which he said:

> "Already other nations are beginning to turn their gaze towards us. All over the world peoples are asking: What have you accomplished? Even the spirit of Fascism of these days has permeated beyond the frontiers of Italy, and has found life in the soil of other lands."

There was no single adverse criticism of these statements by the Die-Hard press, no questions on the subject were asked in the House of Commons, no report on the matter was requested by Sir John Simon from the British Minister in Rome, nor was Mussolini accused of Fascist propaganda abroad, etc., etc., although the last quoted statement was actually written for a British paper!

Of the hundreds of sensational "news" stories spread about the wicked Soviets at this time we choose just one as an illustration because it is perhaps the most amusing and curious—it became known subsequently as the "Jesus Christ Safety Match" story.

On October 23, 1932, Mr. R. Simpson, a correspondent of the *Sunday Chronicle*, informed its readers:

> "I am able to reveal through the *Sunday Chronicle* to-day the crowning outrage which Moscow has perpetrated.
>
> People in this country, and indeed the rest of the civilised world, will be shocked to learn that, as part of its fanatical anti-

* *Times*, 24.x.32. † Ibid. 26.x.32.

God campaign, the Soviet Government is now making mockery of the figure of Christ as a trademark on a match-box.

These match-boxes are being sold openly in London, and in various parts of the provinces.

One came into my possession yesterday. On the lid is a picture of Christ crucified on the Cross. Above it are the words: 'Jesus Christ Safety Matches.'

On behalf of the *Sunday Chronicle* I handed this box of matches to the Home Office yesterday, and I was assured that it would be considered with a view to possible action. . . .

This time the 'Reds' have gone too far. This match-box with its offensive picture and wording, is the ultimate insult. . . .

I understand that thousands of these boxes have been smuggled into the country in foreign-made coffins."

Thus, there was everything here: Soviet blasphemy, dishonest smuggling, sinister and above all "foreign" coffins!

The *Morning Post* (October 26, 1923) also reported the "smuggling" of "Jesus Christ Safety Matches" under the title "Soviet's Latest Infamy."

Mr. A. Denville, M.P., solemnly asked a question on the subject in the House of Commons and Sir J. Gilmour (Home Secretary) promised to make inquiries. This incident in the House of Commons was reported in the *Morning Post* (October 27, 1923) under the heading "Sacrilege from Russia" and a special correspondent of the *Daily Mirror* (October 26, 1932) gave an account of an interview with Mr. Denville in which the latter is reported as characterising the match-box incident as "part and parcel of a deliberate campaign of blasphemous poison gas from Moscow," etc.

Arcos denied that any such match-boxes had been exported from the U.S.S.R. It was also denied in Moscow. Subsequently the real facts of the case were disclosed by *Reynolds' Illustrated News*. Said this journal in its issue, November 20, 1932:

"Recently, a person returned from India bringing with him a match-box which he had bought in one of the native bazaars. It bore an ordinary crucifix on the label, and the crude inscription: 'Jesus Christ Safety Matches.'

These matches can, or until recently could, be bought all over India. They are, as a rule, imported from Sweden without Labels. The Indian merchants put their own labels on, and a favourite series consist of the pictures of the leaders of the various religions of the East. 'Buddha Safety Matches,' for example, have been sold in large quantities among the more simple-minded Buddhists, who are very fond of carrying emblems of the Buddha.

The 'Jesus Christ Safety Matches' were marketed for the especial benefit of native converts to the Christian religion. They are the reverse of blasphemous, for, as will be seen from the accompanying illustration, they are not even a caricature of the figure of the Christ."

Reynolds added:

"Actually we are in a position to challenge the editor of the *Sunday Chronicle* and Mr. Denville for proof that they have seen, during the period in question, more than two of the 'blasphemous match-boxes,' or that there was more than one in the possession of the newspaper at the time the great crusade was set on foot."

Similarly, the Marquess of Donegall, writing in the *Sunday Dispatch,* November 20, 1932, said:

"There was, if you remember, a question asked in the House of Commons about a brand of matches. It was stated that they bore a picture of Christ on the label and came from Russia. . . . *The matches in question did not come from Russia but from Southern India.* Nor were the labels designed in any spirit of irreverence, for the offending label formed one of a series of 'founders of great religions.'"

Subsequently, the *Sunday Chronicle,* November 27, 1932, admitted in effect that its "discovery" was a mare's nest and stated:

"The *Sunday Chronicle* has since discovered that the matches were made in India, and in taking this early opportunity of throwing fresh light on the situation it is satisfied that the charge against the Russian Government in this instance cannot be upheld.

A cable from the British United Press correspondent at Madras states that the matches were ordered by Indian Christians from the Krishna match factory at Gattur in the Ramnad district.

The proprietor of the factory affirms that the labels bearing the words: 'Jesus Christ Safety Matches' were prepared at the express request of certain Indian Christians in Tuticorn, a port at the southern extremity of India. The labels were printed at the Nadar Press at Sivakara."

A very grudging admission and not the apology which the Soviets surely had every right to expect.

Although the *Morning Post* published the Arcos denial on October 28, neither this paper nor most of the other journals concerned in spreading the story had the decency to give the real facts.

CHAPTER XIX

NEGOTIATIONS FOR A NEW AGREEMENT—A DIFFICULT START (1932-1933)

I. M. Maisky appointed Ambassador to the Court of St. James. Negotiations opened

M. Jean Maisky arrived in this country on October 27, 1932, as Soviet Ambassador to the Court of St. James. It was a very happy choice for many reasons. M. Maisky was no stranger to this country and had many personal friends here. Almost exactly twenty years earlier he had landed on our shores as a political refugee and from that date until shortly after the March (1917) Revolution, he had lived in this country, mastering its language and studying its customs, history and literature. He returned to London in 1925 as Counsellor to the Embassy and remained here until the rupture of diplomatic relations in 1927, during which period one of his main duties was dealing with the press.

The sixteen months following October, 1932—during which the new Trade Agreement was being negotiated—were certainly hectic ones and witnessed not a few dramatic episodes. M. Maisky had not long to wait after his arrival to realise the frigidity towards his Government of influential circles in this country. He presented his credentials to His Majesty King George V on November 8, and was duly invited to the Guildhall banquet on the following day. The difference in the ovations accorded to the Japanese and Soviet Ambassadors by the Lord Mayor's guests could not have been more marked. The Japanese Ambassador was duly announced by the Toast Master, and as he walked between the row of guests on either side to the dais where the Lord Mayor stood, he was warmly applauded—whether the object of the guests was to congratulate the Japanese Ambassador on his Government's successful annexation of Manchuria and its contemptuous defiance of the League of Nations we cannot say.

M. Maisky was next announced, but the very mention of the name of the representative of Soviet Russia seemed to have suddenly transformed the two rows of guests into penguins, and he passed down to the Lord Mayor's dais in frigid silence. However, boorish behaviour of that kind usually defeats its own ends, and the quiet dignity and poise with which M. Maisky bore himself was freely acknowledged later by many of those present.

The British Government, of course, understood too well the need for some good-will between countries if trade was to be fostered to satisfy completely the Die-Hard, one might well say, "disturbers of the peace." Accordingly, when the late Lord Mount Temple moved a resolution in the House of Lords, November 1, 1932, "that in the opinion of this House no export credits should be provided for Russian trade, nor any further commercial agreement, temporary or otherwise, concluded between His Majesty's Government in the United Kingdom and Northern Ireland and the Government of the Soviet Union, till that Union has taken some steps to liquidate its debts to the British Government and British nationals," Lord Templemore, speaking for the Government, rejected the motion.

Whilst declaring that he regarded "with the utmost loathing the present régime in Russia," and that the "problem of past debts is one which continues to engage the very anxious consideration of the Government, and they will take any opportunity which may come their way to secure a settlement of this very difficult and most unfortunate problem," nevertheless, he made it clear that the Government "held that the question of debts and the question of current trade and of such credits as may be necessary to enable that trade to be carried on are questions which must be considered separately on their merits."

"It is because we feel," concluded Lord Templemore, "that the proposal of my noble friend will increase unemployment without in any way benefitting those whom he wishes to help that the Government cannot support this Motion." Lord Londonderry, Secretary of State for Air, was equally, if not more, emphatic. He declared:

> "If we took the line the noble Lord suggests, and cut off trade with Russia, as I think he said, if Russia does not pay something on account, we should find not only that we should add to unemployment in this country, but we should also receive universal condemnation from the trades affected by the loss of Russian trade.
>
> Whilst the relations we have now with Russia are condemned by many people, and whilst it cannot be said that we look on Russian policy with any favour in this country, one does feel that a breach of relations with that country at this time would lead to further difficulties in Europe than exist at present, and I feel that on the eve of the World Economic Conference we should do everything we can to help deliberations aimed at making the streams of commerce flow into great rivers throughout all the countries of the world. If we begin by cutting ourselves adrift from the commercial relations we have with Russia at present I think we should do real disservice to that cause of economic reconstruction which we all have at heart. If we consider the other point—that of preventing trade with Russia altogether—I venture to ask whether we should help ourselves or help those

Russians with whom we may and do sympathise in the cruel and remorseless tyranny under which they are now living, I say in that way we do not help them at all and we certainly do not give any assistance to the traders of this country."

Turning to the difficulties through which the country was passing, Lord Londonderry said:

"We have passed through a very difficult time, and we have found that the Russian Government have given us no assistance at all. In fact, in the past we have attributed much of the troubles of this country to the machinations of the Russian Government, but I am not sure that we are not inclined to attribute our own difficulties a great deal too much to Russian propaganda, and to the activities which Russian Governments have continued in this country. I think it is wise that we should consider this problem as a whole, and realise that it is of the highest importance that as time goes on Russia should take its place among the nations of the world. I have already referred to the World Economic Conference, and one must feel that no successful result can come from that Conference if a whole population of 180,000,000 people is left out."

Finally, Lord Mount Temple was induced to withdraw his motion.

British business interests clamoured for a speedy conclusion of a new agreement; thus, at a meeting of the directors of the Manchester Chamber of Commerce on November 14, 1932, a resolution, from which the following is an extract, was adopted:

"The Board of Directors of the Manchester Chamber of Commerce earnestly hope that the British Government and the Russian Government will lose no time in arranging a new Anglo-Russian trade agreement to replace that which will shortly lapse in consequence of the notice to that effect given by the British Government.

The Chamber expresses no views regarding the past agreement, being more concerned with the future trade relations between the two countries . The potential importance of these trade relations renders it highly undesirable that they should remain unregulated by any mutual agreement or that there should exist doubts as to what the future position will be.

The Chamber conceives that notwithstanding certain obvious limitations to which both parties are subject, an agreement could be arrived at which would be in every way preferable to a state of confusion and uncertainty."*

* *Manchester Guardian*, 15.xi.32.

Similarly, Sir Felix Pole, chairman of Associated Electrical Industries, Ltd., speaking at Rugby, November 18, 1932, declared:

> "I hope our Government will speedily conclude a reciprocal trade agreement with Russia, and that the time is not far distant when the two countries will have resumed normal banking and financial intercourse. If we do not do this, I believe that in ten years' time we shall greatly regret the omission."*

The Amalgamated Engineering Union wrote to the Prime Minister, November 18, 1932, pointing out the serious position in regard to unemployment in the engineering industry, and concluded: "Our object in again† addressing you is with a view to urging that every effort should be put forward to foster trade with Russia in respect to British engineering products, and by so doing assist in alleviating the acute distress which has been prevalent in the engineering centres of this country over a long period of years."‡ Other trade union and labour bodies also voiced the demands of organised labour for an extension, not a curtailment, of trade with the U.S.S.R.

At about this time joint discussions were proceeding between the Trades Union Congress and the Federation of British Industries, in the course of which the subject of Anglo-Soviet trade was dealt with as a means of providing employment, and on December 1, the T.U.C. published the following statement:

> "The broad purpose of the discussion, on which there is general agreement between the two bodies, is to secure the maximum amount of trade with Russia, not only with the object of increasing employment in this country immediately, but to obtain a fair share of the expanding Russian markets in the future. Although certain industries have obtained substantial orders from Russia, these orders have not restored the balance of trade between the two countries and Russia has bought more from other countries than from us.
>
> To promote better results the two bodies have been discussing the extension of British Government credit guarantees to all classes of goods and commodities ordered by Russia; and also the question of the length of the period for which such credits may be given and the conditions upon which credits may be granted."§

* *Daily Herald*, 19.xi.32.

† The Union had written to the Prime Minister, August 10, 1932, pointing out the adverse effect in respect "to the unemployment of our members with a Manchester firm, arising out of the failure of the Government to grant the necessary export credits on Soviet orders to British industry."

‡ *A.E.U. Monthly Journal*, Jan. 1933.

§ *Times*, 1.xii.32.

Things did not move too quickly. The Soviet Government, no doubt angry at the summary way in which it had been treated, and not knowing exactly what it was that the British Government had in mind with respect to the U.S.S.R., was in no hurry to reply to the British note of October 17, evidently waiting for further clarification. At last, on November 11, 1932, Sir John Simon (Secretary of State for Foreign Affairs), in the course of a conversation with M. Maisky, intimated that the British Government were anxious not to injure Anglo-Soviet trade and desired to secure its development "on proper terms" and to conclude a new commercial agreement with the Soviet Government.

The Soviet Government in its turn was again in no hurry to reply and the matter became further complicated when *Izvestia*, November 13, 1932, published a statement from its London correspondent that:

> "According to reliable sources, the British Intelligence Service, in order to substantiate questions in Parliament directed against the Soviet Government, commissioned its Riga agents at the beginning of November to fabricate documents and materials dealing with the organisation of the Comintern, under the personal direction of Comrade Stalin, of the unemployed movement in England, as well as with preparation of civil war in India. . . .
>
> Relying on a message from Riga in the *Times* (of November 8) . . . the Foreign Office has asked the British agents in Moscow to send any documents, real or bogus, which might, however remotely, bear out the documents forged by the Intelligence Service about the direction of the Comintern and its organisations by the Soviet Power, and about the identity of the Comintern with the Soviet Government."

In the course of a leader in the same issue, *Izvestia* referred to this message and to the many known anti-Soviet forgeries and lies concocted and spread by Russian "White" emigrés and their friends and by the "Riga Correspondents" of various foreign journals, and continued:

> "We shall not attempt here to expose the futility of charging the Soviet Government and Comrade Stalin with the leadership of unemployed movements in England or with the preparation of civil war in India. The only truth in this absurdity is this: England is suffering from a degree of want lately described by Fenner Brockway in his book *Hungry England*, which is driving the unemployed into a movement the like of which England has not seen since Chartism. . . . It is also a fact, which we shall

not deny, that Comrade Stalin is not only the leader of the Soviet proletariat, but is looked upon as their head by tens of millions of workers and peasants throughout the world. But does that mean that for that reason Comrade Stalin should be made responsible for the shutting down of Fords' factories or the bankruptcy of Insull, or for the exclusion of the English textile industry from the Indian market by Japanese competitors? Such a syllogism shows the ravings which the English Intelligence Service can offer the Foreign Office, relying on its interested confidence.

The Foreign Office is presided over by Sir John Simon, who . . . has shown that he knows how to make subtle legal distinctions. Sir John Simon, as a lawyer, must surely understand that the Soviet Government cannot be made responsible for the doings of the English Communist Party. Sir John Simon must also know that it is one thing to be recognised as the intellectual leader of the international proletariat and another to be made responsible for the action of every Communist group and party in every part of the world. If our correspondent is right in asserting that a responsible organ of the British Government has ordered the British agents in Moscow to send it with all speed documents relating to the Soviet Government's participation in unemployed movements in England, or in the preparation of civil war in India, that would only prove that even ex-Liberal Ministers . . . are ready to do everything asked of them by their present friends.

But the whole world knows that the Die-Hards are afraid of a change in the relations between the U.S.S.R. and the U.S.A., that they are angry at the improvement in the relations between France and the U.S.S.R., as expressed in the Soviet-French negotiations for a Non-Aggression Pact ; that they, along with the Secret Service and Sir Henry Deterding's friends, are trying to prevent the conclusion of a pact between the U.S.S.R. and Rumania, and that they are constantly at work endeavouring to make worse the relations of the U.S.S.R. with Germany and other countries."

The above statement by the London Correspondent of *Izvestia*, as well as paragraphs from the *Izvestia* leader, were widely quoted in the British press.

Replying to questions in the House of Commons on December 7, 1932, in regard to alleged Soviet propaganda in India and to allegations in the *Izvestia* report that " the Foreign Office had instructed their agents to furnish documents, real or bogus, establishing connection between the Soviet Government and the Communist International," Mr. Eden (Under-Secretary for Foreign Affairs) stated that on November 28, 1932, Sir John Simon had informed the Soviet Ambassador that if the Soviet Government desired that matters of trade and other subjects should "be discussed in the usual manner as between Governments in friendly relations they must apologise for the language of the *Izvestia* article and also take steps to ensure that no further statements of the kind referred to in . . . the question should be made in future. It was emphasised to M. Maisky that future indulgence in these tactics would only confuse the issue between commercial negotiations and propaganda and render the former, which should be treated on their merits, impossible of conclusion. My right hon. friend added that, as previous assurances given on behalf of H.M. Government had been ignored, he would repeat finally and categorically that the policy of His Majesty's Government is to promote trade relations on a permanent and stable basis, and that they expect the Soviet Government to state clearly in their reply to these representations what is their policy towards this country."*

The Soviet Government declined to assume responsibility for everything which appeared in *Izvestia.* However, the whole matter, so far as it affected the two Governments, was finally disposed of when Mr. Eden made the following statement in the House of Commons, December 13, 1932:

> "On December 5, during the absence of the Foreign Secretary at Geneva, the Soviet Ambassador called on the Permanent Under-Secretary for Foreign Affairs and made an oral communication to the effect that, while the Soviet Government only took responsibility for official communications in the *Izvestia,* they desired to state that, with regard to this particular incident, they did not entertain, and had not at any time entertained, the suspicions of the Foreign Secretary and of the Foreign Office which were expressed therein. On the contrary, they dissociated themselves from such statements.
>
> M. Maisky repeated this declaration to Sir Robert Vansittart on December 9, and added that he himself had communicated with the editor of the *Izvestia,* who had now replied that he had been misled by one of his correspondents; that he recognised that the statements in question were inaccurate, and that he wished to express his regret for having published them.
>
> In these circumstances, H.M. Government regard the matter as closed."

* *Hansard,* 7.xii.32, col. 1597.

At the same time, on December 9, 1932, M. Maisky sent a note to the British Government to the effect that he and the Trade Representative in Great Britain of the Soviet Union had been appointed to conduct the negotiations.

The decks were now cleared, at any rate officially, for the opening of negotiations, and a preliminary discussion took place on December 15, between the Soviet delegates and the British representatives, Mr. W. Runciman (President of the Board of Trade) and Col. Colville. On the same day, at a reception given by the Society for Cultural Relations between the peoples of the British Commonwealth and the U.S.S.R., M. Maisky made a strong plea for more friendly relations and cultural intercourse between the two countries, and after referring to the negotiations for a trade agreement which were starting, he remarked that:

> "Great Britain and the Soviet Union, politically and economically, represented two different worlds—two different lines of thought, of art, and of culture. The forces hostile to progress and to friendship between nations were speculating constantly upon this difference in order to maintain a great wall of mutual ignorance, misunderstanding, and suspicion between the peoples of the Soviet and the peoples of the British Commonwealth. Such a state of things constituted the gravest danger to the cause of peace. One of the best methods of combating this danger was to develop cultural relations between both countries and in that way to bring both peoples nearer together.
>
> 'Our policy,' said M. Maisky, 'is and has always been to select critically from bourgeois culture all that is good and valuable from the point of view of the toiling classes and to incorporate this in the cultural life of Soviet society. On the strength of this we are ready to take your technique, your science, your art and literature, your Stephenson, your Darwin, your Shakespeare, your Shaw. We are actually taking them because we think they can greatly enrich our cultural life. . . .'
>
> For 15 years some extremely powerful forces in this country had engaged in a continuous campaign of deliberate misrepresentation as to what was going on in Soviet Russia. He thought that in this respect the Society for Cultural Relations could be of great help, not only to the Soviet but still more to Great Britain. On the Soviet side they expected them to give the people the plain truth and only the truth about the Soviet Union, about its manifold activities in science, in art, in literature, in sport and cultural development. That would be a great service

to both countries, and again, in its turn, to the cause of international peace."*

On the previous day, Mr. Arthur Chamberlain, Chairman of Tube Investments, Ltd. (speaking at the Queen's Hotel, Birmingham, on the occasion of the Thirteenth Ordinary General Meeting of the Company), like many other business men, also made a strong plea for common sense in the relations between the two Governments when he said:

"We are starving for want of consumption. Here in the industrialisation of Russia is a vast and practically untapped reservoir of consumption. Is it not common sense to try to tap it? Is it too much to ask the ants in both countries to keep silence for 12 months? May I not rightly urge the Government to turn their attention to the making of a new trade treaty with Russia, and that they should enter on this task with as much verve and determination to achieve something really good as they did at Ottawa? I count the gain to the world of friendly and increased commercial relations between this country and Russia as no whit less important than its most ardent protagonist makes out for Ottawa."†

The view held in the U.S.S.R. regarding the abrogation of the Commercial Agreement and negotiations for a new one, was expressed by M. Molotov, Chairman of the Council of People's Commissars in a speech on January 23, 1933, at the session of the Central Executive of the U.S.S.R., in the course of which he declared:

"We are still in the dark as to the object of this denunciation. We can only guess it. If the purpose was to frighten the Soviet Union, then this is childish. We never were, and are not afraid of such things.

If, however, it was meant to cause us loss, then this, too, was a miscalculation. Probably those in Great Britain who require Soviet orders will understand this well enough. We know one thing—that those countries which have maintained normal diplomatic and trade relations with us have gained as compared with others; the more so, since the Soviet Union—as distinct from some capitalist countries—has always fulfilled punctually its financial obligations. . . .

We, of course, note the declaration of the British Government that it continues to be interested in the development of trade between the two countries."

* *Manchester Guardian*, 16.xii.32.

† *Times*, 15.xii.32.

In the meantime British timber merchants who had benefited greatly by the 1932 agreement for the bulk buying of Soviet timber, opened new negotiations in good time for the 1933 Soviet timber supplies. With the denunciation of the Anglo-Soviet Commerical Agreement, the timber negotiations had been suspended owing to the uncertainty as to what discrimination against Soviet imports the British Government might insist on in the proposed new Anglo-Soviet agreement. However, the deal could not be put off indefinitely and negotiations were resumed between the British Company "Timber Distributors Ltd." and the Russian White Sea Timber Trust, and an agreement was signed December 30, 1932, for the supply of 395,000 to 435,000 standards of Soviet timber in 1933. If the Board of Trade did not actually bless this agreement as was reported in some quarters at the time, it does not at any rate seem to have opposed it. Another important Anglo-Soviet deal was that announced on January 13, 1933, for the supply of a large quantity of tea to the U.S.S.R., by the Indian Tea Association (London).

On the other hand, on January 14, 1933, the Executive Committee of the Association of British Chambers of Commerce, published a report giving its views as to the considerations which the Government should bear in mind in its negotiations for a new trading agreement. The following were the suggestions made in this report:

"1. Any new arrangement should be of a temporary character only, and intended to serve as a *modus vivendi* pending the conclusion at some future date of a formal treaty of commerce and navigation.

2. In view of the U.S.S.R. Government's monopoly of foreign trade, our relations with other countries should not be taken into consideration in the preparation of the new agreement.

3. The new agreement should aim at placing the trade between the two countries on a reciprocal basis, and provide not only for the protection of British industries and agriculture, but for the protection of Dominion industries and agriculture as well, in conformity with the principle laid down in Article 21 of the Agreement with the Canadian Government adopted at Ottawa in August, 1932.

In arranging for such protection as is referred to above, prices and standards of labour in this country and in the Dominions, as compared with Russia should be taken into consideration. It is believed that such protection as we suggest might be obtained by a system of licences and/or quotas and/or prohibition.

4. The Association considers it is essential that in any new agreement Russian shipping should be given no advantage over

British shipping. The present unfair working of the Soviet monopoly of foreign trade should be altered. At least one-half of the freights, insurance, etc., in connection with the shipping services should be British.

Article 3 of the existing agreement, which deals with the rights, privileges, and facilities of British vessels and their cargoes and passengers, should be revised.

5. As it is contemplated that on the termination of the Five-Years Plan the demand for machinery and tools will largely cease, exports from this country to Russia may in future be much reduced. To provide against this contingency Russia should give access to its immense markets for consumers' goods. It should be borne in mind that it may be considered advisable to appoint a trade delegation in the near future for the purpose of organising our trade with Russia, and with that in view our exports as a whole should receive consideration at this stage, and not the existing exports of particular goods. It is considered that the agreement should provide for the granting of facilities to any such trade delegation as may be found necessary. There should be adequate consular representation of Great Britain in Russia.

6. The U.S.S.R. should, under any new arrangement, accept responsibility for the acts of all economic organisations such as the co-operative societies.

7. Diplomatic immunity should not extend to the buildings occupied by the Russian Trade Delegation.

8. The Committee is opposed to the extension of the system of export credits for the promotion of trade with Russia and believes that if trade between the two countries is arranged on a reciprocal basis it should prove unnecessary. In the event, however, of it being necessary to grant credits to promote trade with Russia, the security for such credits might take the form of a lien on exported goods, or some other concession.

9. In negotiating any new agreement, temporary or otherwise, His Majesty's Government should stipulate for the recognition of old debts contracted by Russian subjects and for the payment of compensation for British property confiscated in Russia."*

It will be seen that from the first to the last point the Association asked for definite discrimination against the U.S.S.R. For instance, the Association urged that in framing the new Treaty our imports from Russia should be regulated "by a system of licences and/or quotas and/or prohibition," and that "standards of labour in this

* *Times*, 14.i.33.

country and in the Dominions as compared with Russia should be taken into account." But the Association did not suggest that " standards of labour in this country and in the Dominions as compared with " Germany, France, Czechoslovakia, Italy and Poland, and particularly Japan, where wages were very low and whose goods were often in direct competition with ours, " should be taken into consideration," not to mention the " standards of labour " in British India. In this connection it is relevant to recall that a short time previously the representative of the Association voted on the National Wages Board in favour of the proposed reduction of ten per cent. in British railwaymen's wages.

Again, the Association declared that it " is opposed to the extension of the system of export credits for the promotion of trade with Russia." Surely this was a case of hopeless and invincible mental blindness. The extension of the Export Credits Guarantee Scheme to British-Russian trade reduced our adverse trade balance with Russia, enabled British firms to give employment to thousands of workmen, brought a handsome profit to the competent Government Department and, on the authority of the Minister in charge of the Acts, every Russian bill had so far been punctually met.

Or take point (2), the Association proposed that:

> " In view of the U.S.S.R. Government's monopoly of foreign trade, our relations with other countries should not be taken into consideration in the preparation of the new agreement."

Why on earth should the fact that the U.S.S.R. had established a monopoly of foreign trade subject her to discrimination as compared with other countries ? Since when had we set up to dictate the organisation of foreign trade or other institutions in foreign countries under pain of our discrimination against them ? The organisation of the monopoly of foreign trade in the U.S.S.R. was as much its own internal affair as was, say, the setting up of industrial and trading cartels in France, Germany and other countries, or the regulation of foreign trade in various countries by different State restrictions, quotas, etc., the affair of these countries.

It was surely too late in the day to treat a great Power like the U.S.S.R. with a Government which, whether we liked it or not, had " made good," as though it was an inferior and a pariah among the nations.

And so we might go on from point to point. Whatever the intentions of its authors, the effect of it was not to promote trade between Great Britain and the U.S.S.R., but to place every possible obstacle in the way of its development.

This was the view not only of labour circles, but of many industrialists and others interested in trade with the U.S.S.R. The *Manchester Guardian,* in the course of its report from "Our London Staff," said:

"It (the report) is interesting, however, for what seems to be its underlying hostility to any trade agreement at all. One of the conditions stipulated is 'the recognition of old debts contracted by Russian subjects, and the payment of compensation for British property, confiscated in Russia.' This may seem fair enough, but to make it a condition of a trade agreement would mean in practice to complicate and probably bring the whole trade negotiations to a standstill. The debts and compensation question has been discussed for ten years, without any settlement being reached, and to be of value the trade agreement must be got quickly.

In paragraph 8 of the 'suggestions' it is stated that the extension of the system of credits is opposed. It seems to have little point, since the export credits guarantee department looks at all the credits from a business point of view, unless it is framed in hostility to trade with Russia altogether.

The seventh paragraph suggests that diplomatic immunity should not extend to the buildings occupied by the Russian Trade Delegation. It seems trivial to raise this question after recognising the diplomatic immunity of the Russian trade representatives for twelve years. It is partly a question of facilitating trade and partly a question of the status of the Russian representatives, because foreign trade in Russia is a function of the State. The immunity is granted only to the chairman of the trade delegation and his two deputies under the terms of the present treaty.

There is also a demand that 'in view of the U.S.S.R. Government's monopoly of foreign trade, our relations with other countries should not be taken into consideration in the preparation of the new agreement.' This rather cryptic demand suggests that the association do not wish to give 'most-favoured nation treatment' in the agreement. This point would not be accepted by the Russian Government. They would regard it as a discrimination against Russian trade."*

The report of the Association was discussed at the Coventry Chamber of Commerce on February 20, 1933, when the following resolution was adopted:

"The Coventry Chamber of Commerce should inform the Association that while agreeing that some of the proposals, on

* *Manchester Guardian,* 18.i.33.

the subject of the memorandum relating to trade with Russia, would be beneficial, the Chamber was strongly of the opinion that *the clause relating to export credits was unworkable and that the withdrawal of these credits would seriously affect British trade.*"

In introducing the subject, Mr. D. M. Gimson (of Messrs. Alfred Herbert Ltd.) said that:

> "He felt the Association of British Chambers of Commerce had made a mistake in issuing the memorandum, which had the intention of restricting trade with Russia."

In the course of the discussion, Mr. Bernard Powell-Brett said:

> "The subject was a very important one to manufacturers of this country. He would like to see everything possible done to encourage trade with Russia. Last year the total production of machine-tool makers was four million odd pounds, of which more than half went to Russia. If that trade were stopped it would be a very serious thing. The Chamber should encourage and help trade with Russia and not place any obstacle in the way. *He had not heard of a single case where Russia had not met her bills.* He had every confidence in that country's ability to pay. The proportion of British equipment in Russian factories, he was told, was five per cent., the rest coming from other countries. That was a very serious matter for this country."

Many other similar examples might be cited. Numerous trades councils and other working class organisations urged the Government to conclude a new agreement as speedily as possible and to extend credit facilities so as to encourage the placing of Soviet orders in this country.

II. The Diplomatic Corps and misuse of currency in the U.S.S.R. Dispute about the Lena Goldfields Concession

Whilst the negotiations for the new Commercial Agreement were proceeding slowly, the Die-Hard press continued to do its best to stimulate hostility to the U.S.S.R., both in its leading articles and particularly in the "reports" of its notorious Riga correspondents.

On every possible occasion the subject of Anglo-Soviet relations and conditions in the U.S.S.R. was raised in the form of hostile questions in Parliament and often the impression left was wholly at variance with the real facts. It will suffice to give here but two examples of this.

On March 6, 1933, in reply to questions in the House of Commons regarding diplomatic privileges in Russia in the matter of purchasing foodstuffs and other articles, Sir John Simon said:

> "On October 24 last, the Soviet authorities issued an order to the effect that foreign diplomats in Moscow would not, in future, be permitted to purchase foodstuffs and other necessities of daily life at the State shop for roubles, but only for foreign currency; and an intimation was subsequently given to His Majesty's Ambassador at Moscow that the privilege of free importation of such foodstuffs and necessities, previously enjoyed by them, might be withdrawn.
>
> A somewhat similar situation has also arisen in connection with the purchase of railway tickets in the Soviet Union, instructions having been issued by *Intourist*, the Soviet travel organisation for foreign nationals, that in future all their tickets must be paid for in foreign currency. Representations by the Doyen of the diplomatic body have produced an assurance that diplomatists, consuls and diplomatic couriers will continue to receive tickets and sleeping-car berths in exchange for roubles for all journeys in the Soviet Union or to any place in the countries bordering the Union and in Germany, Austria and Czechoslovakia; but the continuance of similar facilities has not yet been assured in the case of journeys to this country."*

Sir John Simon added that representations on these matters had been and were being made to the Soviet Government by the British Ambassador at Moscow.

The impression left by Sir J. Simon's statement was not in consonance with the real state of affairs. It may be recalled that towards the end of 1930 a system of rationing of foodstuffs had been instituted for the whole of the population of Moscow. By this system every citizen holding a ration card could obtain a fixed monthly quantity of various foods at low prices in accordance with the category to which he belonged. Thus a factory worker was entitled to purchase more than an office worker. Similarly, the more responsible workers could obtain somewhat larger supplies than workers in less responsible positions.

It should be noted that heads of departments and even members of the Soviet Government could obtain nothing beyond their definite ration of foodstuffs. Only one exception to this rule was made, namely, the Diplomatic Corps. Special shops known as "Insnab" (Supplies for Foreigners) were opened for the latter where they could purchase for Soviet roubles unlimited quantities of foodstuffs at fixed low prices.

* *Hansard*, 6.iii.33, cols. 794/5.

However, it soon became apparent that certain diplomats or members of their staffs abused this privilege. In the first place they changed their *valuta* (foreign money) on the " black exchange," i.e., illegally, and thus obtained a far larger number of roubles than that authorised by the Government exchange rates ; in other cases roubles were bought in foreign countries and smuggled into the U.S.S.R. through the diplomatic post. It should be noted that the export and import into the U.S.S.R. of Soviet currency had been prohibited since 1926. They then used these roubles for the purchase of enormous quantities of foodstuffs over and above their own requirements. The surplus, so the Soviet authorities averred, these diplomats or members of their staffs then distributed or even sold at high prices to individuals who had no diplomatic privileges.

It was pointed out, for instance, that in the course of one month, one diplomat purchased at the " Insnab " half a ton of sugar, another diplomat purchased three-quarters of a ton of butter and so on.

This quite naturally caused public discontent and in order to put a stop to such abuses the authorities closed the " Insnab " shops at the end of October, 1932, and the diplomatic corps were informed that they could purchase supplies in the free market for roubles or at the " Torgsin " shops—the special shops where foods and other articles could be purchased at prices below those prevalent in the now closed " Insnab " shops. In the " Torgsin " shops unlimited quantities could be obtained, but only for foreign currency.

This arrangement was quite fair. Diplomats undoubtedly obtained their salaries, etc., in their own currency ; it was, therefore, no hardship for them to purchase their supplies with such currency. If, on the other hand, they obtained illegally high rates for their currency by utilising the " black bourse," then it was only fair that they should pay correspondingly high prices for their supplies. As before, diplomats retained the right to import supplies for their own needs from abroad.

After the Commissariat for Foreign Affairs had explained the position to the Doyen of the diplomatic corps at Moscow, the foreign diplomats, with very few exceptions, no longer protested against the new arrangement.

As regards the purchase of railway tickets, there was no question here of the abrogation of any diplomatic privileges or any discrimination against Great Britain or any other country.

In view of the fact that the Soviet Government required as much foreign *valuta* as possible to pay for her foreign purchases, the Soviet authorities made a regulation whereby tickets for foreign countries bought in Moscow had to be paid for, as a general rule, in foreign currency. But tickets for countries which had a railway convention with the U.S.S.R., namely, Germany, Italy, Austria, Czechoslovakia, Poland, the Baltic States, etc., could, in accordance with such convention, be paid for in roubles.

Great Britain and France, however, had no such railway convention with the U.S.S.R., and, consequently, it was not possible to purchase for roubles a direct ticket from Moscow to London or to Paris. A passenger to London could purchase for roubles a ticket as far as, say, Germany, but for the rest of the journey to London foreign currency had to be paid.

The other example we would give concerns the Lena Goldfields dispute. In reply to a question in the House of Commons, March 13, 1933, Mr. Baldwin reviewed briefly the intervention of the Foreign Office in the dispute arising from the annulment by the Soviet Government of the Lena Goldfields Concession. Mr. Baldwin stated that after negotiations between the Chief Concessions Committee and the Lena Goldfields Company had broken down in September, 1931, the latter had applied to His Majesty's Government. Mr. Baldwin continued:

> " Representations were accordingly made to the Soviet Government both through the Soviet Ambassador in London and through His Majesty's Ambassador at Moscow. The Soviet Government, however, still maintained that the matter was one for direct settlement between the company and the Chief Concessions Committee; and though they were warned that His Majesty's Government could not accept this point of view, and would be obliged, if no settlement were reached by other means, to claim from them the full amount of the arbitral award, it was nevertheless felt desirable, in order to explore every possibility of effecting an amicable settlement, to authorise His Majesty's Ambassador at Moscow to discuss unofficially with the President of the Chief Concessions Committee, the prospects of a settlement at a sum of £3,500,000, representing approximately the proved capital losses of the company after taking into account all the counter-claims put forward on behalf of the Committee."*

Mr. Baldwin further pointed out that the Chief Concessions Committee having refused to settle at the latter figure and the Soviet Government failing to offer " an early and satisfactory settlement,"

> " . . . the situation necessarily reverts to that reached prior to the direct conversations between the company and the Chief Concessions Committee and the subsequent negotiations for a settlement without reference to the award: and the payment to

* *Hansard*, 13.iii.33, col. 1600.

P*

be claimed is the full amount specified in the award, namely, £12,965,000."*

But before ever the arbitration court had met, the Soviet Chief Concessions Committee had maintained that:

"Considering that the concession agreement has been dissolved by the one-sided action of the Lena Goldfields, in obvious disregard of the definite meaning of par. 96, according to which the 'concession can only be dissolved before the expiration of the term by decision of an Arbitration Court,' the lawful basis for the Arbitration Court which was appointed for the settlement of differences arising in connection with the carrying out of the concession agreement has thus disappeared." (From a letter, dated May 8, 1930, signed by the Chairman of the Chief Concessions Committee.)

The Chief Concessions Committee accordingly withdrew their representatives and declared that they could not recognise any decision of this court which now only represented one side of the dispute. Consequently, the Soviet side was by no means bound by the award of the fantastic sum of nearly £13,000,000 by the so-called Arbitration Court.†

Further, by what system of logic or equity could the Foreign Office now insist on the payment by the Soviet Government of nearly £13,000,000 when, according to the admission of His Majesty's Government "the proved capital losses of the company after taking into account all counter-claims put forward on behalf of the Committee" was "approximately £3,500,000"?

* Ibid., col. 1601.

† The Lena Goldfields concession whereby a British Company was empowered to work the Lena Goldfields on certain terms had worked satisfactorily at first, but, so the Soviet Government contended, the concessionaire had failed to carry out many of its obligations and, in accordance with the provisions of the Concession Agreement, the Chief Concessions Committee of the U.S.S.R. had made repeated protests to the Company in 1929.

It was finally agreed that the questions under dispute should be submitted to an Arbitration Court, again in accordance with the provisions of the Agreement, but on the eve of the first meeting of the Arbitration Court, the Company decided to wind up the concession, withdrawing its engineers, etc.

This one-sided action was not in accordance with the Concession Agreement and since the Arbitration Court had been summoned to adjudicate on the disputes of the two parties on questions concerning the *working* of the agreement and *not its winding up* (for the latter object the Soviet Government contended different experts would have been required than those actually appointed), the Soviet Government refused now to recognise the validity of the Arbitration Court, but suggested that by mutual goodwill the questions under dispute could be settled by direct negotiations between the Lena Goldfields Company and the Soviet Chief Concessions Committee, and if no agreement could be reached, a new Arbitration Court could be appointed for adjudicating on the matters in dispute. The Company, however refused to fall in with the Soviet suggestion and insisted on proceeding with the Arbitration Court, even in the absence of the Soviet representatives.

The Arbitration Court duly sat without the participation of the Soviet side.

In the course of his reply, Mr. Baldwin also said:

> "One last opportunity of settling the case seemed to have arrived when the Soviet Ambassador in London represented last month that it would be unfortunate if public agitation on this question were to revive during the continuance of the present Anglo-Soviet commercial negotiations. My Right Hon. Friend then informed His Excellency that it lay with the Soviet Government to prevent that danger by offering an early and satisfactory settlement, which would effectively contribute to that spirit of confidence in the relations between the two countries which it is the object of the negotiations to promote, and requested him to warn them that in default of an offer of such a statement, he would be obliged to make a public statement on the lines of that which I am now making."*

The "last opportunity" referred to the following. On December 21, 1932, Mr. Eden, Under Secretary of State for Foreign Affairs, in reply to a question which sought to obtain an assurance from the Government that they would make the conclusion of a new Anglo-Soviet Agreement dependent upon the settlement of the dispute over the Lena Goldfields Concession, stated that:

> "In the past few days this matter has been under consideration by my Right Hon. Friend. . . . When the House next meets, he will, I trust, be in a position to announce such action as has been taken in the meantime."†

In view of Mr. Eden's statement, the Soviet Ambassador quite naturally made known his opinion that the moment was not a favourable one for the settlement of the Lena Goldfields dispute. The latter could only be settled amicably by direct negotiation between the Lena Goldfields Company and the Soviet Chief Concessions Committee.

Naturally a settlement would have been attained more speedily if more friendly relations existed between the two countries—but in any case it was surely monstrous that a dispute over the Lena Goldfields concession should be permitted to stand in the way of the conclusion of a satisfactory Anglo-Soviet Commercial Agreement.

In general, however, British business circles interested in Anglo-Soviet trade as well as all sections of the Labour Movement, were waiting impatiently for the outcome of negotiations for a new trading agreement, which it was hoped would stimulate Anglo-Soviet trade, but on March 12, an event occurred which threw the whole subject of Anglo-Soviet relations into the melting-pot and seemed at the time to

* *Hansard*, 13.iii.33, col. 1600. † Ibid., 21.xii.32, col. 1054.

endanger the very existence of Anglo-Soviet trading and diplomatic relations—we refer to the arrest in Moscow of employees of Metropolitan Vickers Ltd., on charges of wrecking and espionage. The treatment of this case by the British Government and press threw a vivid light on the fundamental bitter hostility of large sections of the British governing class to the Soviet Government. In view of its importance we deal with the whole episode of these arrests and the trial which followed in a separate chapter.

CHAPTER XX

THE METRO-VICKERS TRIAL, MOSCOW, APRIL, 1933, AND THE AFTERMATH

ON Sunday, March 12, 1933, the following British subjects were arrested in the U.S.S.R. on charges of espionage and sabotage: Mr. Allan Monkhouse, Mr. Leslie Thornton, Mr. William MacDonald, Mr. John Cushny, Mr. Charles Nordwall, Mr. A. W. Gregory.

First, it will be relevant to quote here once again* the definition given by Canning regarding the legal position of strangers residing in or visiting a foreign country:

> "It is one of the most important principles of the Law of Nations that a stranger visiting a foreign country, virtually binds himself to a temporary and qualified allegiance to its laws and submits to their observance, however unwise such laws may appear to be to him, however harsh and oppressive they really are, and however they may be at variance with his own notions of political liberty or with the impressions of a happier experience. Such an individual has no right to complain of the operation of the laws of a foreign state upon himself if they are executed impartially and in the same manner in which they would operate among native subjects. The fundamental principle is this: an Englishman going into a foreign country accepts the authority of its legislation, abdicates for a time the benefits of British jurisprudence and subjects himself to all the consequent inconveniences."

But to come more up-to-date, the same principle was expounded by Sir Austen Chamberlain (then Secretary of State for Foreign Affairs) on December 12, 1924:

> "British subjects who go to a foreign country are subject to

* See p. 75

the local law as they find it, and the fact that something may constitute an offence in one country and not in another affords no ground for protesting against the conviction of a British subject in the former case."

Presumably the position as thus authoritatively explained was known to His Majesty's Ambassador in Moscow, Sir Esmond Ovey. However, that gentleman on March 12, 1933, before he had any knowledge of the charges, before he had even seen any representative of the Commissariat for Foreign Affairs, cabled our Foreign Office:

> "It is inconceivable that the Soviet Government can produce credible evidence of any criminal malpractice on the part of the company. There may conceivably be, of course, some minor question of insignificant douceurs, tipping or presents which might consequently be distorted into 'bribery.'
>
> On the assumption that the Soviet Government do not at once liberate prisoners I am inclined to suggest at the risk of His Majesty's Government incurring an accusation of participation in prejudging an issue of which legal remedies have not been exhausted, that the Soviet Ambassador, London, should be frankly warned that if his Government wish to continue to entertain friendly relations with His Majesty's Government they must refrain from being drawn by an excessive zeal on the part of the police into permitting the trumping up of frivolous and fantastic accusations against a friendly and reputable British company. Otherwise it will obviously become impossible for any British subject to conduct business in Russia, and conclusion of trade agreement will be pointless."*

This dispatch, we repeat, was sent on March 12, 1933, the day on which the arrests were made.

It seems hardly credible that a man with an ordinary understanding of human nature, let alone a trained diplomat, could fail to realise that the effect of such a policy on any foreign Government would be to stiffen their backs, that it could not possibly help the accused and that it was calculated to precipitate a crisis between the two Governments.

It is necessary to interpolate here that for some time prior to this episode Sir Esmond had been sending very pessimistic reports to his Government respecting conditions in the U.S.S.R. It is true that the winter of 1932-33 had been a difficult one for the Soviet peoples. They had been keeping the equivalent of huge armies in the field in the construction of capital enterprises and had to tighten their belts in order to obtain foreign valuta for the purchase of machinery from abroad.

* "White Paper," *Cmd.* 4286, 1933.

Things were difficult but in no way catastrophic. However, Sir Esmond went so far as to state that the Soviet régime, owing to the difficulties created by the carrying through of the first Five-Year Plan and the initial work on the second, was facing famine at home and bankruptcy abroad. Subsequent events show that he was a bad analyst and a worse prophet. In 1933, the Soviet Union had a record harvest and every foreign bill was met promptly ; there was never any default.

It was bad enough to prejudge the issue privately, but to prejudge it publicly was infinitely worse, yet this was precisely what Mr. Baldwin did. In reply to questions in the House of Commons on March 15, 1933, after enumerating the individuals arrested and stating that " their health appears to be generally satisfactory and permission to exercise has been promised," he went on to say:

> " Immediately on receipt of news of the arrests His Majesty's Ambassador at Moscow made urgent representations to the Commissariat for Foreign Affairs, requiring to know, among other points, exactly on what charge the arrests had been made, and what facilities for their defence would be granted them. As he has received no categorical or satisfactory answer on these matters, he has been instructed to press for the fullest possible information from the Commissar for Foreign Affairs, M. Litvinov.
>
> Moreover, as His Majesty's Government are convinced that there can be no justification for the charge on which the arrests were made, Sir Esmond Ovey has been instructed to represent in strong terms the grave view which they take of these proceedings against British subjects of high standing engaged in normal commercial pursuits to the benefit of both countries, and the unfortunate consequences to Anglo-Soviet relations which may follow unless it is rectified."*

While it was quite right and proper for the British Government to request information regarding the charges to be preferred against their nationals and to take steps to afford them every assistance for their defence consistent with Soviet laws and sovereignty in the U.S.S.R., nevertheless, how could His Majesty's Government be " convinced that there can be no justification for the charge " until they knew what this charge was and what the facts were upon which such charge was based ?

Mr. J. H. Thomas, M.P. (Dominions Secretary), apparently in an endeavour to live up to the unenviable reputation which he had deservedly earned in connection with the British-Irish negotiations, decided to make bad worse.

* *Hansard*, 15.iii.33, col. 1949.

In the course of a speech at a meeting in Swansea, March 17, 1933, he said:

> "I know nothing that has stirred British public opinion more than the arrests of a number of our fellow-citizens in Russia.
>
> Public opinion in this country is satisfied that the men who have been arrested are respectable and harmless British subjects engaged in their normal commercial vocations. It seems absurd to suggest that such men should lend themselves to any measures calculated to destroy their own livelihood. It is not understood here what motive underlies these arbitrary proceedings, but on one thing I think the whole country will agree, and that is that British subjects must not be made the subject of any shortcomings in official projects.
>
> Heresy hunting is not countenanced here. I do not know what is the object of this apparently foolish act on the part of Russia. I do know that in past times Governments, in order to divert attention from home affairs, get embroiled in foreign difficulties, and if that is the real object of Russia in this matter, I have no hesitation in saying that no one in this country will be deceived. Commercial relations must always be to the benefit of both parties, and if these are to be facilitated these subjects must not be exposed to unwarrantable hindrances and hardships in the pursuit of them.
>
> We have already given abundant evidence of our anxiety not to interfere with Russia, however much we may disagree with her political aims, but clearly it would be a profound mistake to assume that the relationship of a commercial and diplomatic character which is essential between two nations could be continued if our people were subject to the petty tyranny and punishment and indeed agonising mental strain that these men are now undergoing."*

The *Referee*, March 19, 1933, referring to this statement, rightly commented:

> "It seems that Mr. J. H. Thomas cannot—to use a vulgarism—open his mouth without putting his foot in it.
>
> It is the duty of our Ambassador in Moscow to do what he can to assist the men in the matter of obtaining justice, while at the same time maintaining good diplomatic relations.
>
> But Mr. Thomas's blundering reference to the motives of the Moscow Government are not likely to do anybody any good. It may be true that the Soviet is staging the trial in order to cover

* *Times*, 18.iii.33.

its domestic troubles ; that remains to be seen. But publicly to threaten Moscow with a breach of diplomatic and commercial relations over a case which is still *sub judice* is folly bordering on impertinence."

Similarly the *Manchester Guardian,* March 18, 1933, said:

". . . If it is true that we have demanded withdrawal of the accusations by the Russian Government we may doubt whether we are going the best way about achieving our purpose. We may have our own opinion about the merits of the Russian Government, about the tyranny of the O.G.P.U., about the methods and the motives of trials for sabotage and counter-revolution ; but the reaction of the Moscow Government to a demand from a foreign Government for the repudiation of an official act is likely to be much the same as the reaction of any other Government to a similar demand from Moscow. . . .

It is unfortunate that on any difficult and delicate question Mr. Thomas should be allowed to speak."

The joint efforts of Sir Esmond Ovey, Mr. Baldwin and Mr. J. H. Thomas produced the results which anyone could have foreseen. M. Litvinov, Soviet Commissar for Foreign Affairs, replied on March 17, 1933, to the threats of our Government as follows:

"No pressure and no threats can cause the Soviet Government to relax the law in favour of British citizens. If the British Government and the British Embassy are so certain of the innocence of the arrested men, the alarm they have expressed over their fate is incomprehensible.

Concretely and practically the claims of the Ambassador in this case reduce themselves to a proposal for the exemption from Soviet jurisdiction of all British subjects, granting them immunity for any crime or delinquency and providing that in the event of any Englishman being accused of a crime the proceedings against him shall be stopped immediately, in spite of the available data and proofs, even the accused's own depositions, as soon as his Government expresses a conviction of his innocence.

It is sufficient to formulate such proposals to make it obvious to the Government of an independent country that they are unacceptable and cannot be discussed.

In the event of the existence of data and proofs that a crime was being committed by a certain person the authorities responsible for the observance of the law and the safety of the country are obliged to take measures to prevent the crime and verify the data and proofs ; only in this way can they establish the guilt or innocence of the arrested party or establish the motives of the crime. Such is the inevitable procedure in all countries.

The arrests of foreigners happen not only in the U.S.S.R. Quite recently there have happened abroad such cases of the arrests and sentencing of people occupying prominent posts, including the representatives of important banks. Such cases cannot be avoided and should not be allowed to influence international relations determined by more important and profound considerations than the interests of individual citizens or firms.

In the U.S.S.R. are living hundreds and thousands of Germans, Americans and citizens of other countries who suffer no persecution. Hundreds of Englishmen have arrived in the U.S.S.R., lived here and left without one of them being arrested. Finally, the representatives of Metro-Vickers themselves have lived in Russia for nearly ten years, and hitherto nothing has happened to them.

Such measure as arrest and prosecution have been adopted by the Soviet authorities only in the face of serious causes and in the interests of the safety of State property. It would be wrong if such episodes affected political and economical relations between the U.S.S.R. and Great Britain which were equally profitable to both countries."

At the same time our "Die-Hard" press was backing the Government's efforts to stir up public panic and anti-Soviet feeling.

With one accord the Conservative press spoke of the charges (about which they demanded information) as "ridiculous," "monstrous," etc.

The *Morning Post*, March 16, 1933, in a leader approving Mr. Baldwin's statement, finished a violent anti-Soviet tirade thus:

> "It will be necessary to break off diplomatic relations altogether with a Government that shows itself so patently indifferent to the comity of nations. On the strength of its communistic basis Soviet Russia claims large privileges and exemptions in its intercourse with the outside world. But it cannot be allowed a complete dispensation from civilised practice and international law."

The *Daily Telegraph*, March 16, 1933, spoke of "Trumped up allegations against British subjects."

The *Daily Express* said that the Prime Minister, Mr. MacDonald, should immediately return to London and—

> " . . . Teach the Russians that we will not submit to the maltreatment of our nationals on Soviet territory.
>
> He should place a ban on all Russian trading, detain Russian

imports at the Customs, withhold Government credits for British exports here.

The British Government, through the mouth of its head, should say to Moscow: 'Until you have explained, and justified if you can, your outrageous conduct, you shall enjoy none of the privileges accorded by this country to a civilised nation.'"*

The *Daily Mail* accused the Soviet Government of seeking a way to repudiate its indebtedness to Metropolitan-Vickers, and added:

"... failing an explanation there is bound to be a rupture of diplomatic relations between the two countries. The British Government really take a serious view of the present incident."†

While the following appeared in the *Evening News*:

"Having secured the release of these men, the next thing for the British Government to do is to notify the Soviet Government that its antics are intolerable and its judicial methods uncivilised, and that the bed-rock price of any further dealing between the two countries must be the setting up in Moscow of extra-territorial courts, such as are now maintained in the far more civilised countries of Egypt and China"!‡

In spite of much and convincing evidence to the contrary, wild charges were made in the Conservative press of the application of third-degree methods, torture, etc., to the accused.

Fortunately for the honour of British commonsense, some powerful voices were raised in opposition to these ravings. Thus, in an interview with the *Daily Herald*, March 18, 1933, Mr. G. Lansbury said:

"The Labour Party will be as determined as anyone else that justice shall be done, but it cannot take the line taken by the Government—that of prejudging the questions at issue before the case has been heard.

Speaking on behalf of myself and my friends, I will rely on the Russian Government acting as honourably and as impartially as would the British Government under similar circumstances. Before passing any judgment on the matter the Labour Party will await the trial."

Similarly, Mr. W. M. Citrine,§ General Secretary, Trades Union Congress, stated:

"I share with other people the anxiety attendant on these men's arrest.

* 16.iii.33. † 17.iii.33. ‡ 16.iii.33.

§ Now Sir Walter Citrine.

None the less, I cannot conceive that any good will be done by uttering threats to break off trading or diplomatic relations with Russia.

One feels confident that no one appreciates the gravity of the situation more than the Russian Government itself. We must all guard against any hasty step which will prejudge the issue."

The *Daily Sketch,* in an article entirely anti-Soviet and affirming its conviction of the innocence of the accused, nevertheless declared:

"Whichever be the true explanation, our Government must use every effort to secure a fair trial. And one would add that those efforts are not assisted by any attempt to make political capital out of the plight of these Britons or by the language of insult and violence into which some newspapers have allowed themselves to be betrayed by their indignation."*

During this time, M. Maisky, contrary to all diplomatic usage, was subjected to personal annoyance and some press attacks. A certain well-known publicist hired two private detectives to dog his footsteps in the hope no doubt of discovering some action which would be unseemly for a diplomat. The investment, it is hardly necessary to add, paid no dividends.

As to the press attacks, the *Daily Express* was a bad offender. A somewhat ambiguous phrase in Mr. Baldwin's House of Commons' statement, March 15, 1933, from which we have already quoted, gave that journal an opening for one of its attacks. Mr. Baldwin stated "similar language will be held to the Soviet Ambassador in London to-morrow, as His Excellency has been unable to come to the Foreign Office to-day."†

The Foreign Office naturally understood the words to mean that the Ambassador was awaiting information from his Government and the words, of course, cast no personal reflection on M. Maisky. Next day, the *Daily Express* came out with a front page feature article headed "Soviet Diplomat Flouts Whitehall"; "Ambassador Off to the Pictures"; "His Excellency is Too Busy To-day"; "Invitation to Foreign Office Ignored."

The paper explained that it had sent a representative to the Embassy to find out why the Ambassador had not been to the Foreign Office but without success. The story concluded: "Three hours later, M. Maisky, the Soviet Ambassador, arrived at the Adelphi Theatre with his wife to witness the performance of a musical comedy film. They occupied seats which had been specially booked for them

* 18.iii.33. † *Hansard*, 15.iii.33, col. 1949.

at their own request."* The paper also contained a photograph of M. and Mme. Maisky in the Picture House with the caption: "The Russian Ambassador, who was too busy yesterday to go to the Foreign Office, taking his seat at the premier presentation† of the new film, 'The Kid from Spain,' last night." Apparently they had been trailed to the cinema and as though by some arrangement with the management the lights were specially switched on so that the picture could be taken inside.

On the same evening, the *Evening News* commented: "It should also be made clear to the Soviet Ambassador in London that the British Government is not going to stand about twiddling its thumbs while he goes to the pictures."

On the same day as that on which this "news" appeared, M. Maisky, having in the meantime heard from Moscow, visited the Foreign Office, but the *Daily Express* was not satisfied and returned to the attack on another score:

> "The Russian Ambassador, looking as bland as ever, called at the Foreign Office yesterday. He was told by Sir Robert Vansittart, the Permanent Under-Secretary of State, of the Government's serious view of the arrest and incarceration of the British subjects in Moscow.
>
> He returned to the Embassy looking as satisfied with himself as ever.
>
> His attitude reflected the expression of his Government's present feelings towards this country."‡

Whether that journal expected M. Maisky to leave the Foreign Office with a hang-dog look on his face was not explained.

Three days later, March 20, the *Daily Express* published another feature article on its front page headed "Soviet Ambassador Recalled," and underneath the readers were informed:

> "The *Daily Express* understands that M. Maisky, the Soviet Ambassador in London, has been recalled to Moscow, and is to be replaced by M. Dovgalevsky, at present Ambassador in France.
>
> M. Maisky, it is held, failed to interpret sufficiently strongly to our Foreign Office the Russian Government's view of the legality of the Metropolitan-Vickers' arrests."

* *Daily Express*, 16.iii.33.

† The Diplomatic Corps which, of course, included M. Maisky, had been invited some weeks earlier to attend this premier presentation.

‡ 17.iii.33.

Needless to say this "report" had no foundation in fact.

Now to turn for a moment to the six men arrested, two, Mr. Monkhouse and Mr. Nordwall, were released after having been detained for forty-eight hours. Mr. Monkhouse stated that:

> "I have no criticism to make of the way they treated me. I had a comfortable, roomy cell and fine meals brought in from outside with caviare and soup. They gave me smokes, but no drinks."*

The Moscow Correspondent of the *News Chronicle* (March 15, 1933) reported:

> "Mr. Nordwall also said he was treated 'extraordinarily nicely,' and I have since been officially assured that the four other Englishmen still held are treated equally well."

Mr. Monkhouse is also stated to have said:

> "My examiners seemed first-rate technical men who knew their job. They were extraordinarily nice to me and exceedingly reasonable in their questioning.
>
> The G.P.U. prison is the last word in efficiency, entirely clean, orderly and well-organised. This is the first time I have ever been arrested, but I have visited English prisons and can attest that the G.P.U. quarters are much superior."†

Finally, it was reported in the *News Chronicle*, March 20, 1933:

> "The British Consul in Moscow, Mr. T. Rapp, and the acting Third Secretary of the Embassy, Mr. G. Walton, saw all four of the prisoners this evening.
>
> They indicated that they are being well treated and sent messages to their families, assuring them that they are as comfortable as possible, considering the situation. All four appeared in good health, although somewhat tired."

As to the release of these four prisoners; it is necessary to deal with the matter somewhat at length.

On March 19, 1933, Sir Esmond Ovey had a discussion on the subject with M. Litvinov, who made the following offer:

> "I was ready as soon as the Prosecutor had studied the case and had questioned the prisoners, to ask the Prosecutor whether or not it would be possible to modify the measures of detention in the case of some of the prisoners and to release them on bail which the firm would no doubt readily offer. I was ready to use

* *News Chronicle*, 15.iii.33. † *Daily Herald*, 15.iii.33.

all my influence to obtain the Prosecutor's consent to this, but I could count on success only under the circumstances that the British Government would not hamper my efforts by further public declarations of their intention to exert pressure.

In reply to his query about the amount of bail required, I explained that there was as yet no decision whatever about bail, that I had still to arrange this and in the event of the Prosecutor agreeing to the principle, I could then find out the sum, which would probably not be identical for all the arrested men."

One would have imagined that in view of M. Litvinov's efforts, and the obvious failure of the "big stick" policy, the British Government would by this time have learned wisdom. Such was not the case: they surrendered completely to the "Die-Hards." On March 20, 1933, Mr. Eden (Under-Secretary of State for Foreign Affairs) announced in the House of Commons that as a result of the arrests the negotiations for a new Anglo-Soviet Commercial Agreement had been suspended.

On this subject the *News Chronicle* (March 21, 1933) rightly said:

"The suspension of the commercial negotiations, announced by Mr. Eden yesterday, may do some harm in Russia; it will undeniably also do harm to this country's trade; and it must provoke an acute ill-feeling between the two countries which may have the gravest consequences, and which must at least complicate the efforts for a stable European settlement.

We see nothing in the facts so far as they are known to justify so enormous a hazard. We have the gravest doubts whether either Mr. Baldwin or Mr. Eden really know what the real charges against these men are or what evidence can be brought in support of them. It is the duty of the British Government to watch carefully what is happening in Moscow. But it is no less its duty not to allow itself to be swept by prejudice into hasty action which it may have heavy cause to repent."

But the British Government seemed to have had no intention of considering the matter coolly. On the contrary, from the Soviet *Red Paper* we learn that on March 28, Sir Esmond Ovey called on M. Litvinov and informed him that:

". . . he had been entrusted to tell me [Litvinov] the contents of the Bill which his Government proposed to place before Parliament."

In reply to this M. Litvinov said:

"I expressed surprise that the British Government was polite enough to consider it necessary to inform me as to its Bills before placing them before Parliament. Drawing out a paper, Sir Esmond said that he had instructions from his Government 'to give me the following information should he not receive from me a satisfactory answer about the stopping of the trial.' He then began to read the paper to me.

I stopped him, saying: I could save his time and could state right away that, according to the opinion of the Prosecutor, the trial would take place and that the trial could under no circumstances be stopped, irrespective of what the British Ambassador might tell me. If what Sir Esmond wanted to read to me had for its purpose to influence the Prosecutor's decision, then I could see no reason for listening to this information, since it would have no influence whatever on the decision."

After further conversation, Sir Esmond Ovey made another attempt to frighten M. Litvinov with the consequences, but the latter interrupted and said:

> "Permit me, Sir Esmond, to tell you that even if such methods of diplomacy might perhaps be successful, let us say, in Mexico,* they are doomed in advance to complete failure in the U.S.S.R. and the sooner you realise this the better it will be for all. We do not bargain with our independence."

Again to return to the case of the prisoners still in custody. For some reason which has never been explained the British Government did not take advantage of M. Litvinov's offer with regard to releasing the prisoners on bail. In fact, the next step was taken by the Soviet Government. On March 23, 1933, the Soviet Embassy informed Sir Felix Pole (Chairman of Metro-Vickers) that the Moscow authorities were prepared to release on bail (25,000 roubles on account of Mr. Thornton and 15,000 roubles each for Mr. Gregory and Mr. Cushny) three of the four Britishers. As regards the fourth man (Mr. MacDonald) it was considered that the preliminary investigation of his case had not been completed, but probably he too would eventually be released on bail.

In reply to this offer the Metropolitan-Vickers Co., on March 24, 1933, sent the following amazing message to their representative, Mr. A. Monkhouse, in Moscow:

> "The Company has had under consideration the Russian Public Prosecutor's offer, through the Soviet Embassy in London, to release Messrs. Thornton, Cushny and Gregory on bail.

* Sir Esmond Ovey had been British Ambassador to Mexico before he went to Moscow.

Please see the Public Prosecutor immediately, and thank him for the offer.

But point out that the company do not think it just to make a bargain covering only three Englishmen, and leaving MacDonald and the Russian staff in prison, as they are confident that all accused, of both nationalities, are equally innocent.

We hereby authorise you to accept a reasonable bail for all our employees, English and Russian, on the understanding that this does not imply approval of trial."

If the object of the company had been to stiffen the backs of the Soviet authorities, to increase their suspicions and to prevent the possibility of lenient treatment for their employees, they went exactly the right way to achieve such a result.

How on earth could the London office of the company be absolutely sure that all their employees, both British and Russian, were innocent until the evidence against them had been sifted? In any case, when bail is granted to an accused it by no means signifies that the authorities or even that the one who stands surety is convinced of his innocence before the trial has taken place.

We could understand and even applaud the company in wishing to help, and offering bail for all their employees, both British and Russian, but in every country it is the judicial authority which decides whether bail can or cannot be granted in any given case.

But to accompany a request for bail by a declaration of their conviction of the innocence of all the accused and by an expression of disapproval of the impending trial was, to say the very least, a most improper proceeding and certainly not calculated to help the accused.

The result of this extraordinary message was, as might have been expected, a blank refusal by the Soviet Public Prosecutor to consider it on the grounds that the cable contained "unacceptable and unwarranted expressions of opinion regarding the innocence of the accused, as well as an unwarranted expression of disapproval of the trial."

Commenting on the Metropolitan-Vickers message to Mr. Monkhouse, the *Izvestia,* March 27, 1933, declared:

"The wire from the British firm to their representative in Moscow is a splendid illustration of the mental condition of certain representatives of the British bourgeoisie and of the way they cannot comprehend the most simple things.

The Soviet judicial authorities expressed their readiness to liberate on bail a number of British citizens who are accused of a serious crime. The British firm considers it necessary to declare that if it agrees to offer this bail then 'this does not imply approval of the trial.' Who has asked you, Gentlemen, for your approval, and what need have the Soviet courts for such an approval?

In addition, the firm considers it necessary to declare that it does not approve the liberation of only some of the accused on bail and that it considers it just that all should be liberated. We again ask, do these gentlemen understand that they are dealing with a court of an independent country, and that to express to this court the views of the British business men as to what they consider just or unjust is, to say the least, uncalled for?

The attempt to speak to the Soviet Union as one would to a dependent colony has failed before although it cost British Imperialism a cool £100,000,000. One might have thought that experience bought so dearly would not have been in vain, but it is evident that deep-rooted ideas are difficult to eradicate. However, the sooner representatives of the British bourgeoisie will give up such ideas, the better for themselves."

Messrs. Metropolitan-Vickers seemed to have forgotten that in Great Britain groups of arrested persons are not released on bail as groups. The Court decides which of the accused, if any, shall be released and the amount of bail to be administered in each individual case and whether some of the accused should be retained in custody and bail refused.

Finally, on April 4, 1933, Mr. Thornton, Mr. Gregory and Mr. Cushny were released on bail, but Mr. MacDonald was kept in custody.

On April 3, 1933, Mr. J. Ramsay MacDonald, Prime Minister, announced that the Government would present a Bill to the House of Commons on April 5, 1933, empowering the Government to place an embargo on Soviet exports to this country after April 17, 1933, when the Anglo-Soviet Commercial Agreement would have expired as a result of its denunciation by the British Government on October 17, 1932.

Next day, April 4, 1933, the *Daily Telegraph* stated in a leader:

> "It will certainly be said in Russia that the British Government is taking these enabling powers as a means of putting pressure upon the Soviet Court."

And the *Financial News*, in the course of its leader, April 5, 1933, said:

> "Out of small beginnings, the Anglo-Soviet disagreement has grown to the proportions of a serious diplomatic crisis, and to the ordinary man it seems strange that the situation should have

been allowed to get out of hand as it has done. The Metro-Vickers employees had scarcely been arrested when protests began in the most violent form and threats of an embargo on Russian goods started to be broadcast with complete abandon. . . .

The Russians, as we shall see later, have everything to lose and very little to gain from a commercial rupture with this country ; and if the object was to repudiate debts owing to British firms, it would have been an unthinkably clumsy method of going to work, since no plausible repudiation could possibly be undertaken except on account of a commercial rupture as the immediate excuse. As it is, a temporary rupture at least seems inevitable. The trial could not be called off, after the attitude the British Government has taken, by any self-respecting Government."

And as regards the financial effects of the proposed embargo, the *Financial News,* in the same issue, declared:

"The main danger, however, is financial. Russia owes this country probably around £13,000,000 for goods supplied, of which, according to an official announcement a month ago, about £10,000,000 is represented by credits guaranteed under the Trade Facilities Act. The Government's liability on this £10,000,000 is about £7,000,000. And, in the event of an embargo, we could count this as dead loss.

As regards Germany, outstanding credits to Russia are estimated at about $250,000,000, and we should remember that credits given by foreign banks to Germany have been to no small extent used ultimately for the financing of Russian business. Under the last Standstill Agreement, again, a plan was concluded for the loan of blocked Reichmarks (of an amount reported to be Rm. 35,000,000) by English banks to Russian importers from Germany, the credits to be secured on timber shipments from Russia to this country. Such transactions have now, it may be noted, ceased completely."

However, despite these warnings, Sir John Simon, on behalf of the Government, introduced the Embargo Bill on April 5.

As to Sir John Simon's speech, we cannot do better than quote here the comments of the *New Statesman and Nation* of April 8, 1933:

"The debate on the Russian Embargo Bill showed the House of Commons at its worst. The sympathy and anxiety for the prisoners in Moscow which everybody feels, was overwhelmed in an orgy of prejudice and passion, and to this the Foreign Secretary pandered disastrously. His only object, and the object of the Bill, he insisted, was to help the accused men ; but it would be difficult to conceive anything more harmful to their interests than the manner and much of the matter of his speech, and the furious cheers with which his supporters greeted it.

In the early stages of the affair the British Government behaved with an insolence to the Russians which it would never have dreamed of in the case of any other country ; it continues, despite the obvious effects in Moscow, to treat them as irredeemable knaves and fools. Sir John Simon and other members of the Government profess that they do not want a complete breach with Russia ; but a large section of their party would obviously welcome it, and for these infatuated anti-Bolsheviks it seems that peace, trade and even the safety of the arrested engineers, are bagatelles as compared with the chance of venting their spite."

Moving the Labour Party amendment to the Embargo Bill, Sir Stafford Cripps made a crushing reply to Sir John Simon and a powerful exposure of the untenable position taken up by the Government. We can only quote a few of the more pertinent passages of his speech:

"The House is being asked to grant powers to the Government as against a particular foreign nation, powers which, as far as I know, are unprecedented in any recent years in the history of this country."*

"Every country which is recognised by this country as an equal in status, internationally, is, by that very recognition, acknowledged to have the right to be treated fully in accordance with the comity of nations. At the present time, as has been the case for some years past, Russia is so treated by this country. The mutual exchange of Ambassadors is the outward sign of that recognition. Therefore, apart from any special circumstances which may be urged—and the Foreign Secretary has urged none to-day—Russia is in the same international position *vis-à-vis* this country as Germany, the United States, or any other great nation in the world. If that be so, it behoves the House to inquire what are the necessary conditions precedent to the interference by one country in the internal affairs of another and to the taking of reprisals if that interference is not successful."†

Sir Stafford then quoted historical precedents for his contention that "until a decision has been given by the local court, it is not in accordance with the comity of nations that any interference should be

* *Hansard*, 5.iv.33, col. 1781. † Ibid., col. 1782.

embarked upon by a foreign State."* Turning to the arrests, Sir Stafford said:

> "It will be noticed that the proceedings started in a perfectly regular way, just as they might in this country, with a search warrant which was issued for the searching of these offices. Certain documents were taken, and receipts were given for the documents by the police who conducted the search, and as a result of the search, apparently two or more of the members of the staff were put under arrest."†

After analysing a number of the despatches in the White Paper, Sir Stafford came to the conclusion that:

> "1. There was no undue delay in replying to our Ambassador's questions.‡
>
> 2. There was no suggestion of any sort throughout the White Paper that anything has been done as regards any of these persons other than would be done to any other accused person in Russia. That, after all, is the absolutely fundamental basis of any interference, namely, that we must before interfering establish the position that something unusual, unfair and improper has been done to our nationals which would not be done to the ordinary person who has submitted himself to the jurisdiction of the Russian courts.§
>
> 3. There does not seem to me to be anything in the White Paper which could entitle a Minister of the Crown to get up in this House and say that His Majesty's Government were convinced that there could be no justification for the charges."||

After pointing out that the U.S.S.R. was not the only country in which considerable delay sometimes occurs in the formulation of charges, Sir Stafford rightly said:

> "I venture to suggest to the right hon. Gentleman that, if that demand had been made by the Ambassador of the United States as regards a national of the United States in this country, he would have been the first person to resent it. There is no way out of that argument except by saying that we ought not to acknowledge Russia as an equal in the comity of nations."**

He concluded by a warning that this sort of emergency legislation was jeopardising both future relations with the U.S.S.R. and the fate of the arrested Britishers, and appealed for a more reasonable attitude

* Ibid., col. 1784. † Ibid., col. 1786. ‡ Ibid., col. 1789.
§ Ibid., col. 1790. || Ibid. ** Ibid., col. 1792.

and even a gesture of good-will on the part of the Government in order to minimise this danger.

It is worthy of note that not only did the Prime Minister (April 3, 1933), when announcing that the Enabling Bill would be introduced, state that it was meant primarily to deal with the situation which would arise as a result of the lapsing of the Anglo-Soviet Commercial Agreement, but when the Bill was being discussed (April 5, 1933) other members of the Government avoided giving a clear pledge that this Bill would not be used also as a measure for dealing with the regulation of our trade relations with the U.S.S.R.

It was only after persistent pressure by the Labour and Liberal members and after a plea by Sir Austen Chamberlain, that Mr. Runciman (President, Board of Trade) gave a pledge that the Bill would not be used for any other purpose than that of helping the arrested Britishers, when, on April 6, 1933, in the course of the debate, he said:

> "I will at once, therefore, give an undertaking on behalf of the Government, that we shall not use these powers for any other purpose."*

The Attorney-General and Sir John Simon later repeated this pledge. The way in which such a pledge had to be almost extorted from the Government is an indication of the fact that there was something other than concern for the safety of our fellow-countrymen behind the "sabre rattling" of the British Government in their dealings with the U.S.S.R.

However, it is not surprising in view of the then composition of the House of Commons that the Bill was passed by an overwhelming majority.

Meanwhile the investigation of the case against the accused had been taking place, and we think it advisable, before proceeding further, to treat briefly of the legal system of the U.S.S.R.

The well-known K.C., Mr. D. N. Pritt, M.P., after a careful study of the system, wrote:

> "Investigations into serious criminal charges are in the hands, in their earlier stages, of investigating officers, who are neither judges nor policemen, but are civil servants working under the Commissariat of Justice, or in some cases the G.P.U. Such investigation may, of course, begin before any particular person is suspected, but so soon as the evidence casts suspicion on any individual, he may be arrested and questioned; he cannot at this stage have the assistance of an advocate, but is entitled to refuse to answer questions, and has a right of appeal to the Procurator

* *Hansard*, 6.iv.33, cols. 1949/50.

against any decision of the investigating officer. No formal charge can be made against him until the investigation has proceeded far enough to provide justification for an accusation of a definite offence."

As regards the help of an advocate, Mr. Pritt continued:

"When the charge is made and the investigation is concluded, the accused is entitled to be represented by an advocate, whether he can afford to pay or not, and he and his advocate have full access to the whole dossier of the case; in the preparation of the dossier, moreover, it is the duty of the investigating officers to search for and to incorporate statements and other material which tend in favour of acquittal as fully as those which tend to show guilt. After the charge is made, release on parole or on bail is granted, on the whole more freely in Russia than in England."

Regarding the functions of the Procurator, he wrote:

"Even if the investigators regard the case as sufficiently strong to go to trial, it cannot proceed unless the Procurator, on independent examination, makes up his mind that there is a proper case for trial. The Procurator is a somewhat remarkable official. Whilst, on the one hand, he is the public prosecutor, and will have to present the case for the prosecution in court if it goes on trial, he has also a general controlling power not only over officials of the Commissariat of Justice, but over most other Government organs, including the G.P.U. itself, checking any abuse of their powers and generally 'keeping them in their places.'"

As regards the trial itself, Mr. Pritt stated:

"The trial court consists of one professional judge and two lay assessors, who all sit together and decide questions both of law and of fact. The hearing itself is remarkable for ease and simplicity, the court does not dominate either the accused or the advocates. The foreign observer gets the impression of an informal, friendly and even easy-going trial, conducted without heat and with the real co-operation of all concerned, and with a real desire to arrive at the truth."

As regards the fairness of the Soviet trials, he concluded:

"The only true standard by which to form an estimate of the Russian, as of any other legal system, is the homely one as to whether it gives what the ordinary sane citizen regards as a fair trial. Nobody can complain that the law is framed to protect the social system; the real test of merit is this: when any individual is accused of anti-social activities against that system, does he have an adequate opportunity of knowing the charge against him, proper assistance in meeting it, and an impartial consideration from the court which tries him? On all these points, it is not in human nature that any country should be perfect, but in my considered judgment Soviet Russia is better than most countries, and not far short of the best."

Now to return to the trial of the Metro-Vickers engineers. The investigation having been completed, the trial began at 12 noon, April 12, 1933. The accused were charged with collecting secret information of work in military shops and of the capacity of munition shops ; organising failures and delays in production ; wrecking plants ; damaging motors ; undermining military industries ; collecting State war secrets ; working out plans of wrecking in the event of war ; damaging turbines ; hiding defects in equipment supplied by Metro-Vickers ; bribing Russian engineers to assist and carry out all these activities, etc., etc.

According to the indictment, the accused, Mr. William MacDonald, in the preliminary examination, acknowledged the

> "Intelligence activity carried out in the U.S.S.R., under cover of the firm of Metro-Vickers, guided by Thornton. Monkhouse, head of Metro-Vickers' office in Moscow, also participated in this illegal activity of Thornton. Travelling assistant of Thornton and participator in espionage was Engineer Cushny. This main group of intelligence agents engaged in espionage in the U.S.S.R."

Also, according to the indictment, the accused Mr. Leslie Charles Thornton had stated in the preliminary examination that:

> "According to Richards' proposals, through Metropolitan-Vickers' employees living in different parts of the country, data was collected concerning the political situation inside the country and transmitted verbally to Richards by Monkhouse or myself. Espionage activity in U.S.S.R. territory was headed by me and Monkhouse."

Further it was stated in the indictment that the prosecuting magistracy organised an Expert Commission consisting of engineers: Brailo, heating engineer ; Golubtzov, turbine engineer ; Smirnov, technological engineer ; Snedkov, Novikov and Ulakov, turbine experts, to check technical evaluation of all documents available in the case. The Commission came to the conclusion that the basis of all investigated cases of failures was either due to criminal negligence or direct wrecking.

After the reading of the indictment at the first session of the court, each of the accused was asked individually whether he pleaded guilty. All the Russians and Mr. MacDonald pleaded guilty. Mr. Thornton, who had pleaded guilty in the preliminary examination, now withdrew that plea.

As regards the trial—as several books have been written on it,* it is not necessary to deal with it at length here, except to quote a few short excerpts from the proceedings.

One of the Russian accused, Gussev, enumerated a number of wrecking acts committed by himself or by others (particularly the accused Sokolov who, said Gussev, had been mentioned to him by Mr. MacDonald as useful for the work of causing breakdowns) on his instructions, including damage of a number of boilers, freezing one boiler, disarrangement of 1,400-h.p. motor upon which depended the entire work of munition plants, etc.

The above confessions by Gussev were confirmed by Sokolov, Assistant Chief at Zlatoust Electric Power Station, when questioned by the Prosecutor.

M. Vyshinsky, the Public Prosecutor, then turned to Mr. MacDonald and asked: "Do you corroborate this part of Gussev's testimony?"; to which Mr. MacDonald replied, "I do."

Gussev further stated that being a non-family man and receiving 500 to 600 roubles salary monthly, he had no pecuniary interests in the 3,000 roubles which he alleged Mr. MacDonald gave him for committing wrecking acts. His wrecking activities were chiefly prompted by ideological motives, namely, hostility towards the Soviet Power.

The following dialogue then took place:

Vyshinsky: Accused MacDonald, do you corroborate Gussev's testimony in this part, or not?
MacDonald: I gave him money.
Vyshinsky: How much?
MacDonald: About 3,500 roubles.
Vyshinsky: Where did you get it?
MacDonald: From the firm. From the Moscow office.
Vyshinsky: From whom personally?
MacDonald: Through Chief Engineer Thornton.

Before the court, Mr. Thornton withdrew some depositions which he had made in the preliminary examinations. On this matter the following dialogue took place between M. Vyshinsky and Mr. Thornton:

* "The Moscow Trial," by A. J. Cummings. Published by Gollancz, 1933. "The Moscow Trial," by W. P. and Z. K. Coates. Published by the Anglo-Russian Parliamentary Committee, 1933.

Vyshinsky: You said this voluntarily?
Thornton: Voluntarily.
Vyshinsky: Perhaps some special methods were applied to you?
Thornton: No.
Vyshinsky: Were you tortured?
Thornton: No.
Vyshinsky: Third degree?
Thornton: No.
Vyshinsky: Thornton stated on March 19:

"These testimonies were given by me wholly of my own free will without outside influence or pressure. The testimonies were given by me in the English language and were written in my own handwriting.

The protocols of interrogations first in Gussev's, mine, and each other's presence, and then in Kutuzova's, mine, and each other's presence, that were shown to me during this interrogation and in which I confess facts about my spying activities and my connections with other persons I have read. I can make no additional remarks about the records of these protocols. The protocols are taken down correctly and are confirmed by my signature.

This protocol was read by me and I confirm its accuracy.

(Signed) LESLIE C. THORNTON.

March 19, 1933."

Do you confirm this?

Thornton: No, it was written, and I signed it.

Vyshinsky: Do you confirm that you made it voluntarily without being influenced, without any pressure?

Thornton: Yes.

Vyshinsky: Everything that you read?

Thornton: Yes.

Vyshinsky: Then you signed?

Thornton: Yes, and now the Court will examine it.

The President: But why did you give such information?

Thornton: I did it because, as I have said, I was frightened.

The President: How were you frightened? By whom were you frightened? Where and when were you frightened?

Thornton: I was not frightened by arrest and by the consequences, but simply this way.

The President: No, you give a straight reply, so that it will be clear and plain to everybody who frightened you, when did they frighten you, in what room?

Thornton: I want to speak through the interpreter.

The President: When you find it difficult to reply, you always resort to the aid of the interpreter. But very well, you may.

Thornton: No, I will speak in Russian. I was simply afraid, but of what I do not know myself.

Member of the Court, Martens (reads the following deposition written and signed by Thornton):

> "All our spying operations on the U.S.S.R. territory are directed by the British Intelligence Service, through their agent, C. S. Richards, who occupies the position of managing director of the Metropolitan-Vickers Electrical Export Company, Ltd.
>
> Spying operations on U.S.S.R. territory were directed by myself and Monkhouse, representatives of the above-mentioned British firm, who are contractors, by official agreements, to the Soviet Government, for the supply of turbines and electrical equipment and the furnishing of technical aid agreements. On the instruction of C. S. Richards, given to me to this end, British personnel were gradually drawn into the spying organisation after their arrival on U.S.S.R. territory and instructed as to the information required. During the whole period of our presence on U.S.S.R. territory, from the total of British staff employed, twenty-seven men were engaged in spying operations. Of the above, fifteen men, which included:
>
> | | |
> |---|---|
> | Monkhouse | Annis A. |
> | Cox | Annis H. |
> | Thornton | Shipley |
> | Teasle | Pollitt |
> | Shutters | Waters |
> | Burke | Nordwall |
> | Riddle | Clark |
> | MacDonald | |
>
> were engaged in economic and political spying, also in the investigation of the defence and offence possibilities of the Soviet Union.
>
> The remaining twelve men, who included the following:
>
> | | |
> |---|---|
> | Jule | Gregory |
> | Jolley | Smith A. |
> | Cornell | Fallows |
> | MacCracken | Noel |
> | Richards C. G. | Charnock |
> | Cushny | Whatmough |
>
> were engaged in political and economic spying.

On March 11, 1933, the following men were engaged in spying operations:

Nordwall—economic, political, defence and offence investigation.

Gregory—economic and political.

Pollitt—economic, political, defence and offence investigation.

Whatmough—economic and political.

Riddle—economic, political, defence and offence investigation.

Thornton—economic, political, defence and offence investigation.

Monkhouse—economic, political, defence and offence investigation.

Cushny—economic and political.

Facts above (about?) the spying activities of the above-mentioned men who were under my direction I shall give in a further protocol.

(Signed) LESLIE C. THORNTON.

March 13, 1933."

Mr. Thornton admitted that he had written the above confession, but he now denied the accuracy of the document, declaring that he had written it while excited. The Prosecutor analysed the document point by point, and contended that Thornton was not as excited when writing as he now claimed; the Prosecutor pointed out that Thornton had remembered at that time the exact number of employees of Metro-Vickers concerned, namely, twenty-seven, and that of these twenty-seven, according to his written testimony, fifteen were engaged in collecting information as to the facilities of the U.S.S.R. for defence and attack, and twelve in political economic espionage.

The following dialogue then occurred:

Vyshinsky: And what was your object in doing that? I ask—for what purpose?

Thornton: I simply don't know, but I was asked to confess.

Vyshinsky: And you have gratified that request?

Thornton: Yes, I gratified that request.

We have quoted these few extracts because they are of special significance. All the accused were defended by Soviet counsel and as in all Soviet trials the prisoners were granted the last word. These defences were no mere formalities as may be judged from the following statement by Mr. Cushny when he was called on to make his last plea: "After hearing the very able defence put up by my Counsel to-day, there is really very little left for me to say. He has torn to shreds the flimsy fabric put up by the Public Prosecutor."

The trial ended and the sentences were pronounced on April 18, 1933, at 11.30 p.m. British time. Mr. Gregory was acquitted; Messrs. Monkhouse, Nordwall and Cushny were sentenced to deportation from the U.S.S.R., Mr. MacDonald to two years' and Mr. Thornton to three years' imprisonment.

The news was at once cabled to Great Britain and the general comment was surprise at the mildness of the sentences. But even these were not final because the accused had still the right of appeal.

Yet at 9.30 a.m. on April 19, 1933, the British Government, *without waiting for the result of the appeal to the Central Executive Committee*—which it had been decided to make on behalf of the two men sentenced to imprisonment—without even waiting for an official report from our Embassy of the proceedings of the trial and of the sentences, issued a Proclamation prohibiting as from April 26 the importation of about 80 per cent. of the Soviet commodities that this country had latterly imported.

Moreover, it was reported in the *Daily Herald*, April 19, 1933, that: "Within an hour of the announcement of the sentences the decision was taken in Downing Street." Commenting on the imposition of the embargo, the *Manchester Guardian* declared:

> "The Government's object now, one would think, should be to secure the commutation of the sentences of Mr. Thornton and Mr. MacDonald and their early release. If this is what the Government had in mind—as it properly should have—it is making it as difficult as possible for the Russian Government to do the right thing. It must have occurred to everyone that the only realistic interpretation of the sentences is that the Russians are extremely anxious not to break with this country, and that there was at least a strong probability that as a final gesture the two imprisoned men would be sent home. That probability will not be strengthened by a blundering threat which makes any concession by the Soviet Government appear as extorted by force and under humiliation.
>
> It is not too much to say that the Government is gambling with the liberty of Thornton and MacDonald."*

Further, the *Daily Herald* (April 20, 1933) stated that when our Government took their decision to place the embargo on Soviet goods coming into this country: "It was, when it took the step, already in possession of information that any sentences of imprisonment passed by the Court would probably be commuted by the Soviet Government."

The *Daily Herald* also reported that on April 19, 1933, directly Sir John Simon returned from Windsor, where the King had signed the

* 20.iv.33.

Embargo Proclamation, he received M. Maisky at the Foreign Office and that the Ambassador " expressed to Sir John Simon his deep regret at the precipitate action that had been taken. He warned Sir John that the issue of the proclamation would make it far more difficult for the Soviet Government to exercise a clemency that would now be widely interpreted as a surrender to intimidation. If, he said, the sentences were not commuted, if Mr. MacDonald and Mr. Thornton had to serve their sentences, the responsibility, in his view, would lie with the Foreign Secretary."

And the *Daily Herald* (April 20, 1933) explained the action of the British Government as follows:

> " Had its only care been for the lives and liberty of the sentenced men, had it genuinely desired to avoid forcing a dangerous crisis, it had only to wait forty-eight hours.
>
> But in that case the commutation would have appeared plainly to the world as an act of clemency. The Soviet Government would have gained credit for it. The British Government would, indeed, look a little ridiculous.
>
> If, on the other hand, it launched its proclamation before the Soviet Government could act, its action could be represented as a surrender by Moscow to the firm diplomacy of Sir John Simon."

If this was indeed the explanation, then this " Gambler's Throw," as the *Daily Herald* well called it, was petty and cruel beyond words. And indeed it was reported that:

> " Foreign opinion in Moscow is to-day inclining to the fear that the trade embargo proclaimed by the British Government will influence the Central Executive Committee of the Soviet Union, to whom the petition must be made, against remitting the sentences."*

The *Financial News* (April 20, 1933), in the course of a leading article, said:

> " It would, admittedly, be absurd to presume that the matter could have been settled quietly if the original British protests had been less precipitate and violent; but there must have been a chance of it; for there are strong grounds for believing that the seeds of the case were sown in a blunder on the part of the O.G.P.U. It is, however, certain that the British attitude made it impossible for Russia, where spectacular trials of this kind are 90 per cent. political, to call off the trial, to acquit all the prisoners, or even to limit itself to deportation.

* *Daily Telegraph*, 21.iv.33.

No country would dare to give the appearance of grovelling to that extent. And now, when far milder sentences have been announced than were generally anticipated and there should be some hope of securing the exit from Russia of the two men sentenced to imprisonment, the British Government has repeated its initial error; for the Communist bosses must be much less likely to be accommodating when they are being threatened. As before, the British Government seems to be suffering from an unusual inability to wait a week. Just as it acted unwisely before in officially asserting the Britons' innocence and demanding their release before they had heard a word about the charges, so its case would be much stronger now if it had waited for full details of the trial."

The *News Chronicle* (April 19, 1933) declared:

"The relative mildness of the sentences suggests that, properly approached, the Soviet Government may be induced without too much difficulty to commute the sentences passed on Thornton and MacDonald. Everything, no doubt, depends on the form of approach. Threats are useless for the purpose. The embargo is worse than useless. But it seems clear that the Soviets are not looking for trouble; and if the British Government will in this one respect emulate their example, it should be possible to secure the return of these unfortunate men to this country and to close the entrance to a quarrel between two countries from which both parties have much to lose and neither anything to gain."

The *Spectator* (April 21, 1933) argued:

"To declare the defendants innocent in advance and then threaten an embargo was to demand a complete acquittal under menace. It is, of course, arguable that the Embargo Bill was responsible for the lightness of the sentences, but it is equally arguable that without it they would have been lighter still. The actual imposition of an embargo now makes it next to impossible for the Soviet Government to revise the sentences. For what the Cabinet's action amounts to is a confident assertion that Thornton and MacDonald are completely innocent, and a claim to dictate the verdict of a foreign court. That is an impossible attitude for any Government to adopt."

So much for the efficacy of the embargo in helping the two imprisoned Britishers. But in one matter the embargo was extremely efficacious, i.e. in injuring Soviet-British trade.

As regard our exports to the U.S.S.R., the expected happened. The

Soviet Government retaliated in kind, and as a reply to the British embargo on the entry of her goods into this country it issued decrees whereby:

1. All Soviet trading organisations were forbidden to place orders with or make purchases from Britain.
2. Soviet citizens were forbidden to charter ships flying the British flag.
3. Measures to limit to the utmost the transportation of British products through Soviet territory were promulgated.
4. The use of British ports or sea bases by Soviet export organisations were limited.

Simultaneously the Commissariat for Water Transport ordered the imposition of higher dues and taxes on British ships in Soviet waters instead of the reduced rates hitherto in force under the old Trade Agreement.

The embargo had been imposed. What next ? The Soviet Government, as every well-informed student of foreign affairs expected, stood firm. The leaders of the new Russia were not cowards, an oft-demonstrated fact, but one which Mr. J. Ramsay MacDonald and his Cabinet colleagues seemed quite unable to grasp. Informed circles of public opinion immediately realised that the embargo was sheer lunacy, and could not but defeat its own ostensible object.

The Cardiff City Council, May 8, 1933, appealed to the Government to raise the embargo on Russian goods. The Federation of Engineering and Shipbuilding Trades, May 15, passed a resolution condemning the embargo on trade with the U.S.S.R. and calling for its immediate removal.

The Women's National Liberal Federation, May 16, 1933, adopted unanimously a resolution calling for the immediate removal of the embargo on Soviet imports on the grounds that "it causes dislocation of trade and unemployment at home, plays directly into the hands of the Soviet by providing a cause for grievance, is an unjustifiable assumption by the Government of the right to dictate under threat of force the verdict of a foreign court, and must harm the cause of the prisoners themselves."*

The National Conference of Labour Women, May 25, 1933, carried a resolution condemning the embargo on Russian imports and calling for its immediate removal. Miss Annie Loughlin (member General Council, Trades Union Congress), moving the resolution, declared: "The embargo meant that 60,000 to 70,000 men were or would be thrown out of employment, apart from transport workers who might be handling goods in process of exchange. Since the imposition of the

* *Manchester Guardian*, 17.v.33.

embargo every other country in the world, even Germany under Hitler, had been trying to secure the trade that this country had rejected."*

Mr. A. J. Cummings, who was present in Moscow during the trial on behalf of the *News Chronicle,* in a public appeal to the British Government to make "a friendly gesture," declared: "One lesson to be learnt in this country by statesmen and public alike is that the Soviet régime is as firmly established as any in the world to-day; and that the only practicable alternative to a war of intervention which is as physically impossible as it would be inconceivably stupid, is a policy of co-operation based on political goodwill."†

Mr. Ramsay Muir, in the *Westminster Newsletter,* stated: "The Government has definitely failed to secure their release, which was the declared object of their policy. Everybody who has any knowledge of Russian affairs is agreed that they would almost certainly have been released long ago but for the way in which the embargo on Russian trade was imposed, before there had been any time to consider the proceedings at the trial and without waiting for the result of the appeal which had been made on their behalf. In short, the Government has succeeded triumphantly (*a*) in prolonging the imprisonment of the two Englishmen, and (*b*) in putting a stop to trade between this country and Russia, and thus increasing unemployment. If these were the objects of their policy, they have been brilliantly attained. But do we want a Government which does such things?"

The Co-operative Congress, June 7, 1933, carried unanimously a resolution declaring:

> "That this Congress places on record its profound regret that the British Government should have singled out for denunciation the Anglo-Russian Commercial Agreement of 1930.
>
> It considers that the nation's export trade to the Soviet Union should be developed to the fullest possible extent in the general interests of both countries, particularly in the interests of the unemployed workers of Great Britain.
>
> With these aims in view, the Congress calls on the Government: (*a*) to remove forthwith the embargo on Russian trade into this country imposed by the British Government, and (*b*) to conclude a new commercial treaty with the Soviet Union and to guarantee to the Soviet Union adequate long-term credits on favourable terms for the purpose of facilitating the development of Anglo-Russian trade."

The National Committee of the Amalgamated Engineering Union, June 9, 1933, in a resolution "carried unanimously, protested against

* *Manchester Guardian,* 26.v.33. † *News Chronicle,* 31.v.33.

the termination of the trading agreement with Russia and the embargo on Russian goods, and demanded that continued influence should be brought to bear on the Government through the Trades Union Congress to promote a new agreement on lines likely to bring, not only increased trade, but a closer bond of unity between the two countries."*

Meanwhile, the excited atmosphere of the trial days had passed, and people had begun to study the proceedings of that episode with cooler heads. The *Aeroplane*, April 26, 1933, editorially commented:

> "Now, from some forty years' business experience, I think I can say without much fear of contradiction that industrial espionage in one form or another is an established business in all countries. Any man who does not try to find out what his competitors are doing and how they do it is not fit to hold his job. Espionage of this sort may range from the head of one firm standing an elaborate dinner to the head of another firm in the hope of getting him to talk and let out trade secrets, all the way down to petty bribery by a minor official of one company who wants to find out how a competing company does a certain job, so that he can acquire merit by presenting that information to his superiors."

That was definite enough, but there was something much more specific to come:

> "I have in this office practically a complete list of all the Russian aircraft factories and aero-engine factories, with a fairly reliable description of what each makes, and the amount of its output, and the number of people it employs. It came to me more or less by accident, just as all sorts of other highly confidential and secret information come to me by accident. But those figures were got by some form of enquiry for which the persons responsible might reasonably be shot if they were caught, just as I would be liable to be shot, and should certainly be imprisoned, if I were caught asking questions about exactly what is being made at Woolwich Arsenal, or Devonport Dockyard, or let us say, at Porton, or even at Farnborough."

Mr. A. J. Cummings cabled from Moscow, April 30, 1933:

> "For my part I was frankly surprised at the judicial decencies which were observed in the conduct of the trial; at the absence of crude methods of trickery; at the latitude allowed the prisoners. . . .

* *Daily Herald*, 10.vi.33.

> The interrogators do not appear to have employed exceptionally severe methods—according to their own standards of practice—or even to have approached the third-degree methods familiar in the United States of America."*

The Political Correspondent of the *People* (April 30, 1933), aptly reminded its readers that:

> "The Chancellor of the Exchequer has set aside £180,000 to be spent on the British Secret Service this year.
>
> The Secret Service is divided into two main wings. There are the secret agents who work at home—under the Special Branch of Scotland Yard. And there are those who scour the continents of Europe and Asia, under the control of Sir Robert Vansittart, the cool, masterly head of the Foreign Office."

Becoming more specific, the correspondent said:

> "Connected with most of the British Embassies in foreign capitals there is a woman who can be relied upon to ferret out secrets from the agents of foreign Powers whenever these are needed. . . .
>
> But apart from the regular full-time members of the Service, there are a number of part-time agents. These are engaged, most of their time, in their professional capacities as bankers, financiers, heads of industry or members of the armed forces."

Sir Stafford Cripps, K.C., M.P., speaking at Bristol, May 6, 1933, said that "he had read through part of the verbatim report shorthand notes of the trial of the engineers in Russia and his view and the view of many lawyers with whom he had discussed the matter was that it was impossible to say through reading the notes that the men were not guilty. Clearly, he proceeded, there was no possible justification for taking political action against the Russian Government on the strength of the trial."†

And the Dockers' K.C., Mr. Ernest Bevin,‡ wrote:

> "There are British spies just as there are Russian spies and German spies and French spies. There is not a nation which has a clean record in this respect. In this year's estimates you will find £180,000 for 'secret service.' Nobody is allowed to know how it is spent, or where it goes. Parliament may not discuss it; the Auditor-General may not ask about it. It is for espionage and any other 'dirty work' which governments dare not openly avow."§

* *News Chronicle*, 2.v.33.
† *Morning Post*, 8.v.33.
‡ Now the Rt. Hon. Ernest Bevin, M.P.
§ *Daily Herald*, 8.v.33.

Subterfuge is, of course, resorted to. Mr. Bevin continued:

> "There are Civil Service posts which people 'in the know' know quite well to be just camouflage for men whose real job is 'Intelligence.' But I suppose that to mention any of them would be to bring down all the terrors of the Official Secrets Act on one's head—like Compton Mackenzie."

The British Government is not lenient when spies are caught. Mr. Bevin proceeded:

> "There is in some English prison now a German lad of 29. He is half-way through a ten-year term. 'A hireling of mischief,' the Lord Chief Justice called him in sentencing him. Ten years' penal servitude for a lad of 24! And five years for the German caught the other day at Chambèry! Governments are not apt to be lenient in these matters."

The Foreign Office, instead of using every opportunity to keep in friendly contact with the Soviet Embassy, seized on an event which took place on May 3 to snub the Soviet Ambassador. On that date, Sir John Simon, the Foreign Minister, gave a reception to the retiring French Ambassador, M. de Fleurian. The entire Diplomatic Corps was invited except M. Maisky, a discourtesy which was widely and adversely commented on in diplomatic and political circles at that time. The Soviet Government, which was not in the habit of turning the other cheek to the smiter, replied in kind. At the end of May a diplomatic reception was given in Moscow, but no invitation was sent to the British Embassy.

No complaint was made as to the treatment which the two prisoners were receiving in Moscow. An *Exchange Telegram*, dated Moscow, May 14, stated that Mr. Thornton and Mr. MacDonald "were visited in prison this morning by Mr. Watton of the British Embassy, who found them in good health. Their quarters have been changed, and they now occupy a smaller room, which is comfortable. They are not working. They receive newspapers and magazines from England and continue to be allowed to receive additional food. Both are hopefully awaiting an early release."*

Notwithstanding the embargo which would have justified the Soviets in suspending payments temporarily, all Soviet bills were duly met. Sir Walter Preston, M.P., Chairman of Platt Bros. & Co., at the annual general meeting of the company, June 15, 1933, declared:

> "Sundry debtors and bills receivable at £405,836 3s. 4d. compares with £642,496 6s. 2d. for last year, and indicates that these

* *Manchester Guardian*, 15.v.33.

debts are being collected in a satisfactory manner. As last year, a large proportion of the total is represented by Russian bills, and the comment I made last year about the promptitude with which those bills are paid still holds good."*

By this date it was apparently evident even to the least imaginative member of the Government that neither threats, cajolery nor press diatribes would frighten the Soviet Government or induce it to barter away the tiniest fraction of its sovereignty. Foreign nationals who violated its laws on its territory would be dealt with according to its jurisprudence, irrespective of their nationality. Sir John Simon was now anxious for a way of escape; an opportunity offered at the World Economic Conference which opened in London, June 12, 1933, and with which we deal in the next chapter. M. Litvinov headed the Soviet delegation, and was present at the Garden Party given by His Majesty, June 18; on the afternoon of June 23, the news was circulated that "M. Litvinov had been entertained to luncheon at 10, Downing Street, by the Prime Minister, Mr. Ramsay MacDonald, and Miss Ishbel MacDonald."

Later in the day, the Press Association sent out the following message: "The Press Association understands that M. Litvinov has agreed to a meeting with the Foreign Secretary, and that the meeting will take place at the Foreign Office on Monday."

"The phraseology of this announcement," wrote the Political Correspondent of the *Morning Post*, "caused even greater surprise. It was taken as a clear indication that the initiative had been assumed by Sir John Simon."

The *Morning Post* was right. What actually happened was as follows. When M. Litvinov arrived in this country for the Conference the Foreign Office assumed that he would call there and ask for an interview with the British Foreign Secretary, Sir John Simon. Instead the Foreign Commissar simply sent his cards. Shortly after the Conference opened M. Litvinov was stopped in one of the corridors by someone evidently instructed, who indicated that Sir John Simon would like to make contact with him. The Foreign Commissar replied that the British Foreign Secretary could easily do that if he so desired without the aid of intermediaries, as they were both attending the Conference. Finally, Sir John Simon stopped M. Litvinov in one of the corridors and invited him to come and see him at the Foreign Office.

The two Foreign Ministers duly met and afterwards the following agreed statement was issued:

> "An exchange of views took place this morning at the Foreign Office between M. Litvinov and the Secretary of State for

* *Times*, 16.vi.33.

Foreign Affairs, in which they made clear to one another the position of their respective Governments on the present obstacles to the renewal of Anglo-Soviet trade negotiations. Colonel Colville,* Secretary of the Department of Overseas Trade, was also present.

It was arranged to have another meeting within the next few days for the continuation of these conversations."†

Commenting on the course of the discussions, the Lobby Correspondent of the *News Chronicle* wrote:

"It was soon obvious that neither Minister had power to take or promise decisive action. The conversations were accordingly adjourned until to-morrow or Thursday.

In the meantime, M. Litvinov will communicate with the Soviet Government, and Sir John will consult the Cabinet.

The difficulty appears still to be who shall make the first move. The British attitude is that Messrs. Thornton and MacDonald must be released before the embargo on Russian goods is lifted. The Russian demand is the precise opposite.

In British circles I find optimism about the outcome of the talks. Soviet spokesmen are less hopeful."‡

Another interview took place between the two sides, June 28, 1933, after which the agreed communiqué stated: "M. Litvinov called at the Foreign Office this morning and had a further interview with the Secretary of State and Colonel Colville. The conversations opened on Monday last are being carried on, and it is intended to have another meeting this week."§

"The talk lasted for an hour and twenty minutes," wrote the Lobby Correspondent of the *News Chronicle*. "Another meeting is to be held. A certain amount of progress was made. The question of who shall make the first move is proving a stumbling-block, but in political circles it is believed that this difficulty will be overcome. The conversations so far seem to have been conducted in an entirely friendly atmosphere."||

Another meeting was held between Sir John Simon and M. Litvinov at the Foreign Office, June 30, 1933. The interview lasted an hour and a half and at the close the agreed statement read: "A further meeting between M. Litvinov, Sir John Simon and Colonel Colville took place at the Foreign Office to-day. While progress is being made, the matter is not yet complete, and a further meeting is expected at an early date."**

* Previously Major Colville. † *Manchester Guardian*, 27.vi.33.
‡ 27.vi.33. § *Times*, 29.vi.33. || 29.vi.33.
** *Times*, 1.vii.33.

"This is the first occasion," pointed out the Parliamentary Correspondent of the *Times,* "on which the official statement has recorded progress, and last night there were high hopes that a way would quickly be found out of the deadlock caused by the imprisonment of the British engineers and the consequent interruption of trade between Great Britain and Soviet Russia."

A final meeting of the two Foreign Ministers took place on July 1, and late in the evening of that day the following official statement was issued in London:

> "The Soviet Embassy has informed the Secretary of State for Foreign Affairs that the petitions of Messrs. Thornton and MacDonald, who were sentenced in April last to terms of imprisonment of three years and two years respectively, came before the Præsidium of the Executive Committee of the Soviets to-day (Saturday) and that the sentences have been commuted so that both men are to leave Soviet territory immediately. They are being liberated this evening. At the same time the Commissar for Trade has cancelled the counter-embargo against British imports.
>
> A supplement to the *London Gazette,* published this evening, contains a proclamation made by the King in Council to-day revoking the embargo which was declared by the previous proclamation of April 19 made under Section 1 of the Russian Goods (Import Prohibition) Act, 1933.
>
> Arrangements will now promptly be made to resume the Anglo-Soviet trade negotiations at the point where they were interrupted in consequence of the arrest of the Metropolitan-Vickers engineers."

The statement issued in Moscow on the same day read:

> "On July 1, the British Government removed the embargo and the Commissariat for Foreign Trade took steps the same day. In the evening a meeting of the Central Committee granted an amnesty for Mr. Thornton and Mr. MacDonald, who are to be deported.
>
> Both were freed to-day, and must leave immediately. Upon the suggestion of the British Government, the negotiations for a trade treaty which were interrupted are to recommence on July 3." (*Exchange Telegraph*).

Mr. Thornton and Mr. MacDonald were released from the Sokolniki prison at 11.8 p.m. and were then taken to the British Embassy. "When I went to congratulate them at midnight," cabled the Moscow correspondent of the *Daily Telegraph,* "I found them dazed by captivity, and still more by the release, which came as a complete surprise. Mr. Thornton I had met already during the terrible days of the trial, but I had only seen Mr. MacDonald 'across the footlights.' They both looked better than during that ordeal, a fact not difficult to understand, and both have put on weight, especially Mr. MacDonald, but it is 'prison fat.' Mr. MacDonald has shaved off his beard."*

The press and public gave a general sigh of relief that the unhappy state of tension between the two Governments was at an end, and the *Times* (July 3, 1933) commented: "The incident, therefore, is now closed and the way is clear for putting trade relations between the two countries on a more satisfactory and permanent basis."

The Chairman of Metropolitan-Vickers, Sir Felix Pole, when informed of the agreement, replied:

> "I am very pleased and very relieved to hear the news. No orders have been placed with us by the Russians during the embargo. Now, of course, if they resume trade with us, as I hope they will, we shall be ready to work for Russia and I hope to get orders."†

On the other hand, *Izvestia* commented: "The British Government acted very reasonably in deciding to end a struggle which could bring material loss to both sides, but could never end in a victory for England. Colonial methods are inapplicable to the Soviet Union."

It is perhaps of little moment to discuss as to which side gave way, but in the interests of historic accuracy it must be placed on record that the British embargo was withdrawn in the morning, although it was not and could not be issued in the *London Gazette* until the evening, whereas the prisoners were not released until the evening.

In conclusion, we would only make a few comments on this episode. The Soviet Government was denounced by its enemies and reproached by some of its friends because of its whole attitude respecting the arrests, trial and imprisonments. For our part we are convinced that had the Soviet Government been less firm, had it succumbed to the threats of the British Government, their pusillanimity would have been equivalent to giving *carte blanche* to every foreign national visiting or working in the U.S.S.R., including the German and Japanese spies and wreckers. As a matter of indisputable fact, the subsequent course of events have justified to the hilt the attitude then taken up by the Soviet Government. Although foreign nationals have since been arrested in the U.S.S.R., as in other countries, no Government has made demands even remotely resembling those presented by the British Government in connection with the trial of the Metro-Vickers' engineers.

* 3.vii.33. † *Observer*, 2.vii.33.

CHAPTER XXI

THE WORLD ECONOMIC CONFERENCE (1933)

THE year 1933 was a year of profound economic and financial depression. World production of raw materials in 1932 had declined by about 30 per cent. as compared with 1929 ; international trade had been reduced during the same period by more than 25 per cent. in volume and by about 50 per cent. in value. National incomes had fallen seriously in all the capitalist countries, in some by as much as 40 and 50 per cent. World unemployment had reached the enormous figure of 30,000,000.

There were no prospects of recovery in 1933, indeed the economic crisis had deepened as 1933 advanced. The economic crisis was, of course, no sudden thing. Fundamentally it was inherent in the capitalist system itself, which even in normal times is accompanied by periodic economic crises of greater or less severity, but in this case there was superadded in the first instance the tremendous general increase in productive powers during the comparatively short period of the war years ; then there were the terms of the Versailles " peace " with its reparation exactions, etc., the financial dislocations resulting from the breakdown of the gold standard, the additional high tariff barriers set up in many countries, the drastic fall in prices and in wages, etc., etc.

Under such circumstances it was decided that something really must be done to bring order into the world economic chaos—although what precisely, neither the convenors nor most of the subsequent participators in the World Economic Conference seemed to have any inkling.

The formal initiative for calling the Conference was taken at the Lausanne Conference on Reparations held in June-July, 1932, when a resolution was passed inviting the League to call a World Conference on monetary and economic questions. Subsequently, the League Council set up a Preparatory Commission of Experts to draw up a Draft Annotated Agenda for the World Economic Conference, and this Commission suggested that the deliberations of the Conference should be organised under the following six items:

1. Monetary and credit policy.
2. Prices.
3. Resumption of the movement of capital.
4. Restrictions on international trade.
5. Tariff and treaty policy.
6. Organisation of production and trade.

The question of war debts was omitted in order not to offend the susceptibilities of the U.S.A. The U.S.S.R., U.S.A. and other non-League members took part in the World Economic Conference, but the Soviet Union did not participate (she had not been invited to participate) in the drafting of the Agenda.

The Conference was opened in London on June 12, 1933, by King George V, who, in the course of his speech, declared:

> " It cannot be beyond the power of man so to use the vast resources of the world as to ensure the material progress of civilisation. No diminution in those resources has taken place. On the contrary, discovery, invention and organisation have multiplied their possibilities to such an extent that abundance of production has itself created new problems. And together with this amazing material progress, there has come a new recognition of the interdependence of nations and of the value of collaboration between them. Now is the opportunity to harness this new consciousness of common interests to the service of mankind."*

However, although we entirely agree that it is not beyond the wit of man to utilise the good things of this earth for " the material progress of civilisation " and for the good of all, it certainly was quite " beyond the wit " of the World Economic Conference to do so.

We cannot deal here with the general proceedings of the Conference except to note that practically every solution, however inadequate and partial, suggested by any of the delegates for any one of the problems facing the Conference, was objected to by other delegates as being contrary to their national interests and finally fell through. Only the Soviet delegation, headed by M. Litvinov, attempted to place really concrete radical proposals before the Congress.

In the first place, since many of the immediate economic difficulties confronting the world were due to the surplus stocks which could find no markets, M. Litvinov gave a comprehensive survey of what quantities of such goods the U.S.S.R. could absorb in the very near future, providing suitable credit terms could be arranged, and he suggested that other countries should state their import potentialities with " the same frankness and precision," and he remarked:

> " This Conference has set itself the task of finding measures for putting an end to, or at least mitigating, the crisis. As far as may be judged from the Agenda drawn up by experts for the Conference, attention is to be concentrated upon questions regarding limitations of output, tariffs, methods of credit-policy and of raising prices.
>
> Not wishing to go into a theoretical discussion on these points,

* *Times*, 13.vi.33.

the Soviet delegation ventures to express a doubt of the adequacy of such methods for fighting the crisis. In the opinion of the Soviet delegation it would be better to concentrate upon the potential absorption of the stocks which are exercising pressure upon the markets, and upon attempts to enable the industries making the means of production to increase the use of their capacity."

Further, it will be as well to note that in the report of the Preparatory Commission of Experts it had been declared that:

"In essence, the necessary programme is one of economic disarmament. *In the movement towards economic reconciliation the Armistice was signed at Lausanne; the London Conference must draw up the Treaty of Peace.* Failure in this critical undertaking threatens a world-wide adoption of ideals of national self-sufficiency which cut unmistakably athwart the lines of economic development. Such a choice would shake the whole system of international finance to its foundations; standards of living would be lowered, and the social system as we know it could hardly survive. These developments, if they occur, will be the result not of any inevitable natural law, but of the failure of human will and intelligence to devise the necessary guarantees of political and economic international order. The responsibility of Governments is clear and inescapable."* (Our italics).

Accordingly, M. Litvinov reminded the Conference of the previous Soviet proposal for the conclusion of a Pact of Economic Non-Aggression in 1931 at the Commission of Inquiry for European Union. "Unfortunately," pointed out M. Litvinov, "this proposal was itself the victim of aggression, taken prisoner and thrown into a dungeon—one of the League of Nations Commissions," and he suggested that this proposal should now be taken out of its dungeon and given a new lease of life.

Finally, at the session of the Conference, June 21, 1933, M. Litvinov, on behalf of the Soviet delegation, formally proposed a draft protocol of a Pact of Economic Non-Aggression whereby the Governments of the countries enumerated below:

"Recognising the cessation of economic aggression to be the most important condition for the peaceful co-operation of all States in the economic field irrespective of their politico-economic systems.

Considering that the cessation of economic aggression would help to dispel the existing atmosphere of mistrust and alarm.

* *Times*, 20.i.33.

Considering that the improvement of the present difficult economic position requires that all countries in addition to the renunciation of war as a means of the solution of international conflicts should renounce completely all avowed and concealed forms of economic aggression, agree on the following:

1. The contracting parties declare that they will in their economic policy adhere to the principle laid down at the International Economic Conference of 1927 and confirmed by the special committee of the Commission of Inquiry for European Union in 1931, of the peaceful co-existence of all countries irrespective of their social, political and economic systems.

2. The contracting parties will abstain in their mutual relations from all forms of discrimination. In accordance with this the parties will consider as inconsistent with the principles of this protocol the adoption and application in their countries of a special system directed against any one country and putting this country in a worse position as regards its foreign trade than all other countries.

3. In accordance with the principles proclaimed in Clauses 1 and 2 of this protocol, the contracting parties solemnly undertake to refrain in the future from the application, on any grounds whatsoever, as a means of their economic policy, of special discriminatory Customs duties, established for one country only, or special conditions for such imports and exports, special railway tariffs, special charges on merchant vessels, special conditions for admission to their territory of economic organisations, and, finally, any kind of boycott established in relation to the trade of any one country by legal or administrative measures.

4. All measures of discrimination in force in the countries signing this protocol to be withdrawn from the moment of the protocol coming into force in the respective countries.

5. This protocol to be ratified and come into force in the countries notifying ratification. . . ."

Discussing the Soviet protocol for Economic Non-Aggression, the *Daily Telegraph's* Diplomatic Correspondent (June 21, 1933) spoke of it as "an attempt to embarrass the British Government" and apparently in order to warn off possible supporters of the proposed Pact, he stated: "I gather that M. Litvinov is relying on the support for his *strange* protocol of certain Central European States. In such a case Britain will know what to think of certain professions of friendship and appeals for co-operation—meaning assistance." (Our italics).

It is wonderful how history repeats itself. When at the Disarmament Conference the Soviet delegation proposed a real measure of disarmament the whole Tory press was up in arms against it and M. Litvinov was roundly abused.

Secondly, any scheme of even slight, partial disarmament presented to the Conference was immediately torn to pieces by each country objecting to that part of the scheme which affected most of its own favourite branch of arms.

So, in 1933, not only was M. Litvinov abused for his pains, but because the Soviet proposal would also incidentally have put an end to the British embargo on Soviet goods the British delegation to the World Conference was up in arms against it and Mr. Runciman proposed an amendment to exclude from the proposed Soviet Pact "measures of discrimination taken on political grounds"—thus virtually killing the Pact at the start.

Moreover, since it would have been indeed embarrassing for some Powers to have to discuss in the open the positive Soviet proposals for easing the then world economic crisis, an attempt was made to shelve the question by relegating it to the Sub-Committee on Commercial Policy. The *News Chronicle*, June 22, 1933, reported this as follows:

> "Litvinov's proposal for a pact of economic non-aggression was sent by the Economic Commission to its Sub-Commitee on Commercial Policy for examination. *By this move there will be no public debate on the proposed Pact, as the Sub-Committee meets in private.* Many delegates expressed the view that this was the first step towards shelving the proposal." (Our italics).

The Pact of Economic Non-Aggression would, of course, have applied to the British embargo on Soviet goods and the Soviet counter-embargo on British goods, nevertheless, it was ridiculous to represent the Soviet proposal as an endeavour to "embarrass the British Government."

The sessions of the Conference dragged on, desultory discussions took place in the various committees, but no definite, still less binding, proposals were adopted which could in any way ease the difficult world economic conditions.

On July 13, when the Soviet proposals were discussed, the latter were supported only by Poland, Turkey and the Irish Free State.

At last, on July 14, steps were taken to bring the already practically moribund conference to an end and as the *Daily Express* put it: "To-day the date of the official funeral of the Kensington Conference is announced. The conference was born on June 12 and died very soon afterwards. July 27 is the Day of Disposal: chief mourner James Ramsay MacDonald."*

* *Daily Express*, 15.vii.33.

The World Economic Conference adjourned *sine die*, July 27, 1933, and as the *Bulletin of International News* (August 3, 1933) so aptly put it: "Not even its funeral orators at the final session attempted to gloss over the fact that it had failed."

M. Maisky, dealing with the matter less laconically, in his speech at the concluding session of the Conference, summed up the results of the latter thus:

> "The Soviet delegation put forward two proposals at the Conference; the Pact of Economic Non-Aggression and the question of extending the import possibilities of various countries. It would have appeared that a conference whose main task, according to its draft Annotated Agenda, consisted in the conclusion of a universal 'treaty of peace,' ought to have voted without reservation for the Soviet proposal. Matters proved otherwise.
>
> With the exception of Turkey, Poland and the Irish Free State, to whose representatives I deem it my duty to express our sincere gratitude, no one supported the Soviet Pact of Economic Non-Aggression; and the Pact itself once again, as at the Commission for European Union in 1931, was relegated to one of our Conference's numerous sub-committees, where to all appearances it has to remain quite a considerable time in a state of suspended animation.
>
> The second Soviet proposal—for the expansion of import possibilities—met with even less sympathy at the World Economic Conference, notwithstanding the fact that its purpose was to secure the absorption of world commodity surpluses, the existence of which is regarded by most delegations as one of the principal reasons for the disastrous fall in world prices. Our second proposal was finally likewise buried in one of the commissions of the Conference.
>
> I should, however, record the fact, in the interests of objectivity, that the Conference has not accorded such severe treatment only to the Soviet's proposals, which many delegations were inclined to regard as unwanted step-children. Scarcely better, as it has turned out, has been the fate of the Conference's own cherished offspring—those proposals which were drawn up and laid before the Conference by the experts of 17 States, such as, for instance, the stabilisation of world currencies, the abolition of financial and currency barriers, the raising of prices, the lowering of tariffs, the development of public works, etc. What has the World Economic Conference done on all these questions? Precisely nothing. The discussion and decision on all these questions I

have enumerated have been remitted to the appropriate commissions and adjourned to a more auspicious future.

During the second half of the Conference, when its organisers finally realised that the discussion of the main problems of the Conference must for various reasons be put into cold storage, pride of place was granted to questions of the co-ordination of production and marketing. In this field of the Conference's work many delegations anticipated results which, perhaps, might not be so sensational, but at all events would be more concrete and positive. But what has actually happened?

Let us take timber, for example: the discussion of this question has been postponed to the beginning of October. Or coal: the question has been remitted to the Council of the League of Nations. Or wine: this has been remitted to the International Wine Office; tin—to the International Tin Commission, etc. As for wheat, the question has been excluded from the official programme of the Conference altogether. And so on, and so forth. I could easily add to these examples, but I think it is hardly necessary.

The whole work of the Conference, all the work of its numerous commissions and sub-commissions during these six weeks, has been deeply penetrated by one fundamental mood, one aspiration; 'adjournment'—to adjourn the serious discussion of problems, to adjourn the adoption of any serious and binding decisions on those problems. Finally, our whole Conference in its entirety has also decided to 'adjourn' itself, apparently in the hope that the future will prove kinder to it than the present has been.

And so if we compare the tasks formulated in the Draft Annotated Agenda with the materials which have been circulated to us in the last few days by the Secretariat, one has no need to launch upon polemical exaggerations, one need only keep rigidly to the facts—the simple actual facts—to arrive at one inevitable conclusion. *The practical results of the first session of the World Economic Conference have turned out to be something like zero.*" (Our italics).

Nevertheless, the Conference could count two successes, but these were achieved outside it. First was the fact that the presence of M. Litvinov and the Foreign Secretaries or other important representatives of the States bordering on the U.S.S.R., facilitated the conclusion on July 3-5, 1933, of Pacts for the definition of an aggressor between all these States. The *Daily Telegraph*, on July 29, 1933, admitted that "The one outstanding success achieved during the London

Conference was achieved outside it, when Russia and a group of her neighbours attested in Conventions of Non-Aggression their common purpose of avoiding war among themselves, and did Europe the service of eliminating one of its danger zones."

The second important result was, as we pointed out in Chapter XX, that the presence of M. Litvinov in London and his meetings with Sir John Simon, the Foreign Secretary, facilitated the settlement of the Anglo-Soviet dispute, arising out of the trial in Moscow of the Metro-Vickers engineers, the removal of the British and Soviet trade embargoes and the resumption of the Anglo-Soviet negotiations for a new Commercial Agreement.

The conclusion of the Pacts for the definition of an aggressor and the removal of the British and Soviet embargoes on Anglo-Soviet trade were undoubtedly outstanding by-products of the Conference.

CHAPTER XXII

THE NEW TRADE AGREEMENT AND THE ENTRY OF THE U.S.S.R. INTO THE LEAGUE OF NATIONS (1933-34)

I. THE AGREEMENT SIGNED, FEBRUARY 16, 1934. REACTIONS OF THE TIMBER TRADE

IT is not an exaggeration to say that the liquidation of the Metro-Vickers trial dispute ended the stage of abnormally strained Anglo-Soviet relations. From that time onward relations between London and Moscow may be said to have been, if not quite normal, nearly so. Disputes there have been, but not unlike those which take place between Governments in normal friendly relations.

There were a number of weighty grounds for this turning point in Anglo-Soviet relations. The two main reasons were: firstly, the growing economic strength of the U.S.S.R. By the end of 1932, the first Five-Year Plan had been in the main successfully completed in four and a quarter years. In view of the fact that when first launched the plan had been derided as "fantastic," "Utopian," "impracticable," etc., this success could not but make a profound impression on many influential circles in Britain. The foundation for the building up of a strong industrial economy as well as for a large-scale collective agriculture had been well and truly laid, and it began to dawn on many who had formerly shut their eyes to this fact that the U.S.S.R. was becoming a mighty world Power and would henceforth, whether they liked it or not, have to be treated as such. Secondly, at the beginning of 1933, Hitler had come to power in Germany.

True, there were many among the governing classes in Britain who so far from being alarmed, even welcomed the rise of a black reactionary barbarism in Germany, but on the other hand Hitlerism was recognised for the filthy evil thing it was not only by the leaders and wide masses of the organised British working-class, but also by most of the leaders and many members of the Liberal Party, and a number of the more far-seeing Conservatives.

With the rise of Nazidom, war became an imminent possibility and the need to cultivate friendship with the Soviet Union was obvious.

Thus, although there were still many hurdles to be overcome, the difficulties which had arisen as a result of the Metro-Vickers trial had been liquidated, and there was a growing volume of opinion in Britain which stood for a *rapprochement* with the U.S.S.R.

There were three matters under negotiation between the two Governments during the next eighteen months: (1) the Trade Agreement; (2) Soviet timber exports to Great Britain and (3) the Lena Goldfields Claim. The three subjects were unrelated and had they been treated throughout as separate matters, as they finally were, solutions would have been arrived at much more quickly. We shall deal with these questions in the order given above, but before doing so it is necessary to recall some matters which impinged on them.

The Ottawa Agreement between Canada and the United Kingdom contained, among others, the famous Article 21, referred to in a previous chapter, which read:

> "This Agreement is made on the express condition that, if either Government is satisfied that any preferences hereby granted in respect of any particular class of commodities are likely to be frustrated in whole or in part by reason of the creation or maintenance directly or indirectly of prices for such class of commodities through State action on the part of any foreign country, that Government hereby declares that it will exercise the powers which it now has or will hereafter take to prohibit the entry from such foreign country directly or indirectly of such commodities into its country for such time as may be necessary to make effective and to maintain the preferences hereby granted by it."

In simple language, the aim of the article was to prevent the preferences (in the case of timber, 10 per cent.) being frustrated as a result of dumping or subsidies by any foreign State.

The Lena Goldfields Company had been working in the Soviet Union on a concession basis and the dispute concerning it which arose towards the end of 1929 is dealt with briefly in Chapter XIX.

As regards the Trade Agreement, it is perfectly true that the British Government had to take cognisance of Article 21 of the Ottawa Agreement, but this should have applied equally to the Treaties with all other countries whose exports competed with those of Canada on the British market.

Probably under Canadian and Die-Hard pressure, the British negotiators wanted to include in the Anglo-Soviet Agreement a clause giving them power to impose an embargo on Soviet timber exports if there was reason to suspect that the Soviets were by State action frustrating Article 21 of the Ottawa Treaty. On this issue a deadlock arose in September, 1933. The *Daily Herald* explained:

> "The British side insists on inserting in the treaty an article declaring its right at any time to impose an embargo on any class of Russian goods.
>
> This, the British negotiators say, is necessary because they are bound by Article 21 of the Ottawa Agreement in Canada, which provides that an embargo shall be placed on any class of goods from any foreign country when 'through State action' on the part of that country, the Ottawa preferences are being 'frustrated' with regard to that class of goods.
>
> The Russians refuse to agree to such a clause on two grounds.
>
> First, they object to something which they regard as discrimination against Russia. They point out that no effort has been made to insert such a provision in any other Trade Treaty.
>
> State action in countries other than Russia affects, or may at any moment affect, the price of commodities.
>
> There are, for example, currency measures, subsidies to industries and to shipping, export bounties.
>
> Yet neither in the German, Argentine or the Scandinavian trade agreements—all 'post-Ottawa'—is there any such embargo clause.
>
> Secondly, the Russians object on practical business grounds.
>
> They point out that the effect of such a clause must inevitably have a paralysing effect on Anglo-Russian trade.
>
> With the menace of an embargo hanging over their heads British importers will be nervous about giving orders to Russia for delivery any appreciable time ahead."*

Finally, this obstacle was overcome by the adoption of clauses under which, in the event of a complaint being preferred against either party, the party against which the complaint was made should be given at least three months' time: to settle the matter by negotiations, to furnish an explanation, or to remedy the fault.

When this obstacle was removed, another arose: the Lena Goldfields claim. The Soviet representatives argued that this case constituted a dispute between a Soviet Trust and a group of private British investors,

* 18.ix.33.

that it was a civic and not a diplomatic affair. They further stressed that if matters which affect the law courts of any country are to be dragged into trade negotiations by another country, negotiation becomes impossible. This is obvious because in all trade negotiations there is naturally fine balancing of advantages and disadvantages, and the introduction of an extraneous matter as a condition of a settlement would naturally upset this delicate balancing. It was an open secret in December, 1933, that the action of the British Government in bringing forward the Lena Goldfields case had resulted in the continuation of the deadlock. The *Daily Herald* rightly declared:

> "The Draft Agreement is there, awaiting only the signatures. Yet signature is still postponed.
>
> It is postponed because the British Government refuses to sign unless the Soviet Government will agree to something which is quite extraneous to the Trade Agreement and its purposes.
>
> British trade and British industry, as well as Russian trade and Russian industry, are being held to ransom in the hope of compelling the Soviet Government to pay £3,500,000 instead of £1,000,000 to a band of international investors.
>
> No more stupid policy could be conceived. Quite plainly the Russian Government will refuse—as any government must do —to yield to such pressure.
>
> What then? Will this Government dare to scrap the Agreement, to declare that it places the protection of the interests of the shareholders (British and foreign) in the Lena Goldfields Corporation before the protection of the interests of British trade?
>
> Hardly. Yet if it is not going to do this mad thing, it had better extricate itself quickly from the false position into which it has been put by its own stupidity.
>
> And for the sake of both countries it had better sign that Trade Agreement right away."*

The Soviet negotiators, much though they desired a settlement, considered that their attitude was reasonable and they refused to give way; shortly afterwards it was rumoured that "the negotiations for the settlement of this claim are likely to be left to the company and will take place after the trade agreement has been signed."

Private and public representations were made to the Government to expedite the conclusion of the negotiations, and Mr. J. L. Garvin joined in the appeals. He declared editorially: "We hope the Lena Goldfields case will no longer delay the Anglo-Russian trade negotiations."†

* 13.xii.33. † *Observer*, 31.xii.33.

Three weeks later Mr. Garvin repeated his admonition, if anything in stronger terms. He wrote:

> "Let the National Government be as resolute as President Roosevelt in its decision to make a big settlement with Soviet Russia. By comparison with the new world issues which have arisen, all minor disputes like that concerning the Lena Goldfields should be swept out of the main business. They should be the subject of separate and subordinate negotiation."*

The *Daily Herald* and Mr. Garvin were right as far as they went, but it was not the whole story. The British side also raised the questions of the Tsarist debts, sequestrated properties and the prices charged in "Torgsin" where British and other diplomats made their purchases; they wanted to make a settlement of these issues a condition for the conclusion of the Trade Agreement.

Mr. A. J. Cummings, in the course of a strong appeal to expedite the signature of the Agreement, in the *News Chronicle*, February 2, 1934, asked whether the conclusion of the Agreement was to be wrecked "unless the British Embassy in Moscow can be guaranteed for all time against a rise of a penny a pound in the price of potatoes."

The Soviet representatives argued that these matters were separate and distinct from the proposed Trade Agreement and emphatically rejected the British extraneous stipulations, and finally Whitehall agreed to leave these issues in abeyance for the time being.

At last the terms of the Treaty were agreed and the signature was scheduled for noon, February 16, 1934. However, at the eleventh hour a new difficulty was created by the British side. On the evening of February 15, the Foreign Office informed the Soviet Embassy by letter that the British Foreign Secretary would append to the Treaty a declaration to the effect that the British Government maintained its former attitude respecting pre-war claims. The Soviet Ambassador countered by sending to the Foreign Office on the following morning a declaration to the effect that the Soviet Government maintained its former attitude respecting their own counter-claims.

When the Soviet representatives presented themselves at the Foreign Office next day they were kept waiting some time while hasty discussions took place between Sir John Simon and his advisers. At length M. Maisky sent a message through a Foreign Office official to the Foreign Secretary stating that if the British side was not ready perhaps it would be better to postpone the signature. An official then presented himself and proposed on behalf of Sir John a "compromise," viz., that both declarations should be dropped. This was accepted by

* *Observer*, 21.i.34.

the Soviet representatives and the instrument was duly signed on February 16, 1934.

Under its terms mutual most-favoured-nation treatment was granted; reasonable time was provided for the settlement of any disputes that might arise out of the Ottawa Agreements ; a schedule for an approximate equalisation of Soviet sales and purchases was accepted ; Anglo-Soviet trade was to enjoy the full benefits of any Government guaranteed export scheme ; diplomatic privileges were granted to the Soviet trade representative and his two deputies; and mutual most-favoured-nation treatment was accorded in the ports and territorial waters of both countries. The Soviet press whole-heartedly welcomed the Agreement, both as an instrument for the expansion of Anglo-Soviet trade and also because its conclusion implied the establishment of friendlier relations between the two countries. *Izvestia,* February 17, 1934, in the course of a leader, said:

> "There is every possibility for a considerable extension of Soviet-British economic relations. This is clear from an elementary analysis of the structure of Soviet and British foreign trade.
>
> "The U.S.S.R. exports large quantities of such products as timber, oil, wheat, which are the main items of British imports. On the other hand, Great Britain is a world exporter of equipment and semi-manufactures which were the main articles of Soviet imports during the first Five-Year Plan and which will continue to play a certain rôle in Soviet imports during the second Five-Year Plan. In addition, the U.S.S.R. purchases the so-called colonial raw products, such as rubber, jute, non-ferrous metals, etc., through the intermediary of the British market. Further, the British merchant fleet derives no little profit from Soviet charterings."

Then, after discussing proofs of these contentions and the obstacles in the way of the development of Anglo-Soviet trade, *Izvestia* pointed out that, unlike the position of affairs in Tsarist days, at the present time the economic interests of Great Britain nowhere come into conflict with those of the U.S.S.R. and concluded thus:

> "The signing of the Anglo-Soviet Commercial Agreement will undoubtedly be welcomed by wide circles of public opinion in the U.S.S.R. and no doubt also in Great Britain. We should like to hope that this Agreement will not only restore a basis for the stable and normal development of Soviet-British trade, but that it will form a stabilising point for the improvement of Soviet-British relations as a whole.
>
> This is certainly the clearly-expressed desire of the Soviet

Government. The People's Commissar for Foreign Affairs, Comrade Litvinov, expressed this when he said: 'In so far as it depends on us, we are ready and should like to have as good relations with Great Britain as with other countries.' It is now the turn of the British Government."

Pravda, February 17, 1934, in a leader, analysed the cause of the lack of stability in Anglo-Soviet relations and insisted on the growing strength and power of the U.S.S.R. In the course of the article *Pravda* stated:

"The signature in London on February 16, 1934, of the Anglo-Soviet Commercial Agreement is undoubtedly an important fact and forms a considerable success in the policy of both countries.

This Agreement which will form an essential basis for the development of normal economic relations between the U.S.S.R. and Great Britain, could, at the same time, form a starting point for the improvement of relations between the proletarian State and one of the most important capitalist States in the world and serve as an additional factor to assist the consolidation of peace."

The Agreement was published as a White Paper on February 19, 1934, and naturally attracted widespread attention. The press comments next day were significant of the change of attitude towards the Soviet Union which had taken place since 1932.

The *Times* welcomed the Agreement and stated:

"But it is impossible to keep a great country like Russia in an isolation ward. A boycott would only be effective if it could be made general, which is impossible. Even if it could be made effective it would hardly achieve any useful purpose,"

and speaking of Article 2 (safeguarding the effectiveness of preferences granted to the Dominions) the journal continued:

"It is more likely to prove effective since Russia must be anxious as are other producers not to depress prices to uneconomic levels. With these main difficulties overcome there is a real possibility, given good will and good faith on both sides, that the trading relations between the two countries may be developed to their mutual benefit, and that this development may make a substantial contribution to the general revival of trade and to the economic recovery which must follow a revival of trade."*

The *Daily Telegraph,* in the course of a leader, commented:

"However deep-seated the dislike of each country for the

* 20.ii.34.

> economic and political system of the other, there is no reason why Great Britain and Russia should not trade freely with one another. Their products are of the complementary kind which renders exchange eminently desirable. We can supply Russia with almost all the capital goods she requires ; and any expansion of British export trade so necessary to provide employment in these difficult times is heartily to be welcomed.
>
> To help in financing these increased exports, Russian trade will enjoy equal advantages with other foreign trade in the matter of credits. The best justification for this is that hitherto no loss has been incurred on Soviet credits amounting to over £12,000,000."*

The " Die-Hard " element threatened that they would vigorously denounce the Agreement when it was submitted to the House of Commons for ratification, yet when it was brought before the Commons on March 1, 1934, it was accepted without a division, a very significant fact which the Parliamentary Correspondent of the *News Chronicle* emphasised:

> " A warm welcome was given to the new Russian trade agreement in the House of Commons last night, when Mr. Runciman (President of the Board of Trade) explained its provisions.
>
> There was scarcely any opposition to it—a change from a few years ago when the mere mention of Russia was enough to cause uproar on the Tory benches.
>
> It was left to Die-Hards such as the Duchess of Atholl and Sir William Davison to criticise the agreement.
>
> The Duchess regretted that there was no clause to protect us from the dangers of Russian wireless propaganda, and Sir William was, of course, indignant at the agreement being signed before any settlement of the Russian debt and the Lena Goldfields dispute had been arrived at.
>
> Not long ago their attitude would have been uproariously cheered. Last night it caused only laughter."†

Simultaneously with the negotiations for the Trade Agreement, the question of Russian timber exports into this country, in particular in competition with Canadian timber, was also discussed.

The Canadian Government, despite the preferences which it received under the Ottawa Agreement, was not satisfied. It invoked Article No. 21 of that instrument with the result that Mr. Runciman (President of the Board of Trade) on July 20, 1933, wrote to the

* 20.ii.34. † 2.iii.34.

Chairman of the Import Duties Advisory Committee advising him of the Canadian Government's action and asking him if his Committee was willing to undertake the necessary investigation. Among other things, Mr. Runciman wrote:

> "I am asking Mr. Bennett to arrange for the Canadian timber interests to formulate a detailed statement of their case, setting out as fully as possible the grounds on which they contend that action under Article 21 is called for in relation to Russian timber products. This statement, when received, would be forwarded at once to the Committee, and would provide the starting point for the inquiry."*

The Chairman replied that his Committee was willing to carry out the enquiry. At this time, Mr. R. B. Bennett, Prime Minister of Canada, was in London for the World Economic Conference, and he had many conversations with Mr. Walter Runciman, President of the Board of Trade. What the former urged can, we think, be gauged from well-informed press reports: "It would come as no surprise if Mr. Bennett should prove to have made proposals to the Imperial Government for a very drastic cut in the quantity of timber that Russia shall be allowed to send to this country in future."† "It would cause little surprise if the Canadian Government should invite the Government of the United Kingdom to examine the import of timber from Soviet Russia in the light of Article 21."‡

The Timber Trade Federation was following these proceedings with unconcealed anxiety and the Executive Council of that body met in London, September 7, 1933, to consider the situation. Next day, the *Manchester Guardian* reported:

> "I understand that the meeting expressed resentment at the interference of Canadian politicians in our domestic affairs, and it was decided to send a strong protest to the Government and to request that the evidence of the Federation should be heard before any steps were taken to discriminate between the imports of Russian and Canadian timber.
>
> The Federation thought it unfortunate that they had not been consulted before the arrangements with Sweden and Finland were arrived at during the period of the embargo on all imports from Russia. I am told by a large importer in this country that Canada cannot supply enough suitable wood for domestic purposes and also that she cannot approach within reasonable distance of the prices asked for the same quality woods by the Russians."

* *Times*, 9.ix.33. † Ibid., 24.viii.33. ‡ Ibid., 25.viii.33.

On November 1, it was revealed in the press that a document submitted to the British Government by the Canadian Government on the question of Russian timber had been sent to Moscow with the approval of Ottawa for the comments of the Soviet Government.

Meanwhile, the important group of British timber merchants who dealt in Russian timber were negotiating a new timber contract with the Soviets. For purely business reasons they were on sound grounds, because as the *Morning Post* was compelled reluctantly to admit: "There is no doubt a great profit in Russian timber, and none would dream of denying either its excellence or its cheapness."*

Representatives of the Canadian timber trade protested against the unrestricted import of Russian timber to Britain. They argued that Russian timber exports to this country were increasing at the expense of all other competitors including Canada, and that Russia's combination of low prices, bulk sale and the "fall clause"† were frustrating the preference granted to Canada at Ottawa. The reply of Timber Distributors Ltd., was devastating. They pointed out: (*a*) that during the previous six seasons the Soviets obtained on the average a better price for their timber than their competitors; (*b*) that even if the "fall clause" operated to the full, Russian prices would still remain higher than Canadian.

Early in January, 1934, it was reported that a tentative agreement had been made between Timber Distributors Ltd., and the Soviet selling organisations, under which 435,000 standards of Russian timber would be imported into this country during the 1934 season, but it was also rumoured that this Agreement might "be over-ruled by action on the part of the British Government."‡

Action was taken, but not as drastic as the *Morning Post* apparently anticipated. Timber Distributors, Ltd., issued a statement on January 22, 1934, declaring that at the request of the Government, they had decided to limit imports of Russian timber during the current year to 350,000 standards and that in future contracts the "fall clause would be dropped." Officials of Timber Distributors, Ltd., in reply to enquiries, said that the Board of Trade had not issued a definite instruction respecting the reduction of the import, but it had clearly indicated that a reduction was very desirable, with the object of giving "an adequate opportunity to the Canadian exporters."

Paradoxically, it was Great Britain and not the Soviet Union which suffered from this reduction. As the *Financial News* aptly stressed: "If we cut Russian imports by £1,000,000—roughly the equivalent of the reduction from the 435,000 standards originally contemplated—

* 17.xi.33.

† Under this clause the Soviets guaranteed a rebate to Timber Distributors Ltd should competitors reduce their price below that charged by the Soviets.

‡ *Morning Post*, 9.i.34.

the engineering and metal trades lose £1,000,000 of business during 1934. Russia is confident she can sell the rest of the timber in other European markets."*

Timber imports from Russia were cut down, the total Anglo-Soviet trade turnover was reduced, but would this help Canada? The article continued:

> "The Scandinavian countries will fill the gap next year, and perhaps, in return, buy more British coal or textiles. The one thing certain in this game of General Post, however, is that Canada will not sell more timber against Scandinavian competition. Still, the British Government has made its gesture to Mr. Bennett. The Import Duties Advisory Committee can now bring its report on the Canadian timber problem out of its pigeon-hole; and if that should prove not wholly to have accepted Mr. Bennett's arguments, no great harm will be done, as Canada's demands for a restriction on Russian imports have been satisfied in advance."†

In addition, this restriction sent up the price of timber in Great Britain. A special correspondent of the *Daily Telegraph* wrote: "I am informed that the greater opportunity offered to Canada since the Russian restriction plan was adopted is already costing the consumer in the United Kingdom in the neighbourhood of 10 per cent. more for his wood."‡

The other outstanding issue was the Lena Goldfields claim. After prolonged negotiations an agreement was signed in Moscow on November 4, 1934, under which the Soviets agreed to pay £3,000,000 over a period of years to the Company. In passing, we would observe that although the non-settlement of this claim was allowed for a time to delay the conclusion of the Anglo-Soviet Commercial Agreement, the Company's biggest creditor was the Deutsche Bank and the settlement reached between the Company and the Soviet Trust could not be accepted by the Company until the German creditors had given their consent:

> "Power of ratification was given by the agreement to the company's Ordinary shareholders. The latter, at their meeting in December, delegated this power to the directors. *The directors decided to exercise the power as soon as acceptance of the offer made to them was received from certain German creditors. This acceptance reached London on Thursday.*"§ (Our italics).

British interests for a time were subordinated to German by a Government loud in its claim to be patriotic.

* 23.i.34. † *Financial News*, 23.i.34.
‡ 26.v.34. § *Financial News*, 12.i.35.

II. The League of Nations and the U.S.S.R. The Eastern Pact of Mutual Guarantee

About this time a still greater change began to take place in the attitude of many well-known politicians and publicists in this country towards the Soviet Union. The causes were many, but the two principal ones were (*a*) the stability and rapidly growing strength of the U.S.S.R.; (*b*) the re-armament and openly proclaimed aggressive aims of Nazi Germany.

Many public men here and abroad now realised that the sooner the U.S.S.R. joined the League of Nations the better it would be for all, and that it was due to the dignity and power of the U.S.S.R. that a special invitation be sent to Moscow inviting the Government of that country to join the League.

As usual the driving force in this country was the Labour Movement. The National Joint Council representing the industrial and political wings of the Movement passed a resolution April 25, 1934, appealing to the British Government to do all in its power to make easy the entrance of the U.S.S.R. into the League of Nations. The Joint Council sent a representative deputation to the Government on May 14, 1934, and presented the following resolution to the Prime Minister, Mr. Stanley Baldwin, and the Foreign Secretary, Sir John Simon:

> "The National Joint Council urges the Government to take all possible steps to bring Soviet Russia and the United States of America into closer association with the League upon the basis of the Pact of Paris, to join with them in a Pact devised to define and prevent aggression, and to work wholeheartedly with a view to strengthening the League of Nations.
>
> The National Joint Council would warmly welcome an indication that Soviet Russia is willing to become a member of the League of Nations. If Soviet Russia were to join the League, the foundations of peace, and therefore of civilisation, would be strengthened. The National Joint Council appeals to the British Government to do all in its power to facilitate the entry of Soviet Russia to the League by the offer of an invitation of a permanent seat on the Council to which her power, influence and dignity entitle her."*

The Foreign Secretary, in reply, welcomed the proposal coldly. He said, to quote the *Times* (May 16, 1934), that, "as regards Soviet Russia it had been the practice that Governments wishing to join the League should themselves make application. The Soviet Government had not so applied, but they knew that if they did so that would be welcomed by the British Government, as he himself had stated in the House of Commons." Replying to the question whether the British

* *Daily Herald*, 16.v.34.

Government would take any initiative in the matter, Sir John Simon said he would keep the question clearly in mind.

Had the great Power been any other than Soviet Russia, Sir John Simon would have tumbled over himself in taking the initiative, and he knew quite well that a great State like the U.S.S.R. owed it to herself not to apply for membership of the League until she knew that she would be accepted and given a permanent seat on the Council.

What was the Soviet's attitude towards the League of Nations at this time? She had been in the past, not without good reason, suspicious of that institution. She had not forgotten that when Poland made an unprovoked attack on her in the Spring of 1920 the League never moved a finger in her defence, that some League members without any protest from the League itself aided Poland, and that when it looked as though the Soviet forces would occupy Warsaw, Britain and France, both League members, threatened to come to the aid of Poland with all their forces, if the Soviet Union insisted on peace terms unacceptable to these Powers.

But since then the U.S.S.R. had become a strong world Power and the anti-Soviet intrigues of France and other Powers within the League of Nations had practically ceased. On the other hand, by 1934 the immediate aggressive aims of Nazi Germany and Japan had become absolutely clear, and since their aggression was contrary to the interests of the Powers—both great and small—within the League, Germany and Japan had withdrawn from the League. Under such circumstances the attitude of the Soviet Government towards the League underwent a change. This change was first indicated by M. Stalin in an interview with Mr. Duranty, December 25, 1933, in the course of which the following passage occurred:

> "*Duranty:* Is your position in regard to the League of Nations always a negative one?
>
> *Stalin:* No, not always and not under all circumstances. You perhaps do not quite understand our point of view. Notwithstanding the withdrawal of Germany and Japan from the League of Nations—or perhaps just because of this—the League may become something of a brake to retard the outbreak of military actions or to hinder them.
>
> If this is so and if the League could prove to be somewhat of an obstruction that could, even to a certain extent, hinder the business of war and help in any degree to further the cause of peace, then we are not against the League.
>
> Yes, if historical events follow such a course then it is not impossible that we should support the League of Nations in spite of its colossal defects."

A few days later, December 28, 1933, M. Molotov, Chairman of the Council of People's Commissars, speaking at the opening session of the Central Executive Committee of the U.S.S.R., gave a similar indication of the changed Soviet attitude towards the League. M. Molotov declared:

> "That the danger of new wars has become particularly imminent this year is quite clear if only from the following fact. This year, Germany and Japan have announced their decision to withdraw from the League of Nations. Germany has done this evidently in order to untie her hands for rearming, considering her participation in the League of Nations as a hindrance thereto. On the other hand, Japan announced her exit from the League of Nations in connection with her desire to have a completely free hand for her intervention in China. It has thus happened that even the League of Nations has, to a certain extent, stood in the way of the 'liberty' of the interventionists.
>
> In connection with all this it must be recognised that the League of Nations has exerted a certain restraining influence upon those forces which are preparing for war."

Similarly, M. Litvinov, the People's Commissar for Foreign Affairs, in his report to the Central Executive Committee, December 29, 1933, stated:

> "One may, however, concede that the tendencies which are interested in the preservation of peace would seem to be gaining the upper hand in the League of Nations and probably this is the explanation of the deep changes noticeable in the composition of the League."

The Soviet Ambassador in London, M. Maisky, in an address to the National Peace Congress, Birmingham, June 25, 1934, said:

> "We people of the Soviets do not believe that war is inevitable or inexorable.
>
> We consider that war is not the product of some organic quality of human nature, but is a result of the defective organisation of human society.
>
> We are firmly convinced that the Socialist organisation of human society at which we are working so hard in our country will finally destroy at their roots the reasons which produce war, and will ensure a stable and permanent peace between the peoples.
>
> Peace is the most important principle of the Soviet foreign policy. It could not be otherwise.
>
> A country which draws inspiration in its life and efforts from

the ideals of Socialism—a country engaged in Socialist reconstruction on a scale never seen before in history ; a country which has within its frontiers from the Baltic to the Pacific immeasurable resources cannot and in reality does not harbour any aggressive intentions.

The Soviet Union wants peace, only peace—prolonged, permanent and unlimited peace.

This is the point of view from which the Soviet Government approaches every problem of international policy.

From this point of view it approaches the question of the League of Nations.

Recently some European Governments have been inviting the U.S.S.R. to join the League of Nations.

The Soviet Government will make its decision as to entry or non-entry into the League of Nations solely and exclusively according to the measure in which the League of Nations in present conditions can play the part of a real factor in reinforcing peace."*

M. Maisky's speech, which was warmly greeted and punctuated with applause, made a profound impression on the Congress. Four days later the General Council of the League of Nations Union, meeting at Bournemouth, passed a resolution calling on the Government to facilitate the entrance of the U.S.S.R. into the League with a permanent seat on the Council. There can be no doubt that by this time there was a strong demand in the country in favour of our Government facilitating the entry of the Soviet Union into the League and this demand made itself felt at Westminster when a debate on foreign affairs took place, July 13, 1934. In the course of the discussion, Mr. Attlee, Leader of the Opposition, declared that the Labour Party "trusts that His Majesty's Government will forthwith declare their readiness to vote for the admission of Russia to the League of Nations, and for the grant of a permanent seat on the Council of the League to Russia."†

Sir John Simon, the Foreign Secretary, replying, said:

"Certainly we are prepared to welcome Russia warmly to the League of Nations if Russia makes that application. We are satisfied that it would be a contribution to the peace of the world if that result came about. It is necessarily a matter for Russia to decide whether she makes that application or not, but His Majesty's Government would welcome that result if that result were obtained. . . ."‡

* *News Chronicle*, 26.vi.34. † *Hansard*, 13.vii.34, col. 690.

‡ Ibid., col. 697.

We have made no sort of secret of our view as to the desirability and importance of bringing Russia within the circle of the League of Nations, and we welcome this opportunity of promoting that object."*

The terms used by Sir John Simon on this occasion were certainly much warmer than those he employed in reply to the Joint Labour Delegation eight weeks earlier. That was satisfactory, but not unexpected. The surprise of the debate was Mr. Winston Churchill. There was no hesitating here. He boldly declared: "I believe that the statement which the Right Hon. Gentleman has made as to the welcome which would be extended to Soviet Russia in the League of Nations is one about which there will be no dispute in this country, even among those who have the greatest prejudices against the political and social philosophy and system of government which the Russian people have, I will not say chosen for themselves, but have found it necessary to adopt."†

In the course of the same debate the attitude of Great Britain towards the "Eastern Pact of Mutual Guarantee" was discussed.

The proposal to conclude such a Pact, also referred to as an Eastern Locarno, was first made in the Spring of 1934 after prolonged conversations between M. Litvinov and M. Barthou. In view of the professed aims of the Nazis to win for Germany *lebensraum* in Eastern Europe, at the expense, amongst others, of the Baltic States, there was at that time throughout Europe a very real feeling of uncertainty, of uneasiness that peace might be violated at any moment.

All attempts to reach an agreement on universal disarmament or even serious general reduction of armaments had failed, the Kellogg Pact, not to speak of the Covenant of the League of Nations which sought in words to outlaw war, had been violated with impunity. Non-Aggression Pacts between neighbours which might ensure peace between them, could not secure the general peace, since an unscrupulous Power such as Nazi Germany could use them merely as a means of assuring for herself non-intervention in case of her launching an attack on another neighbouring State. Consequently, to ensure security in Eastern Europe, the "Eastern Locarno Pact" had the aim of procuring immediate mutual assistance of the various countries in Eastern Europe should any of them be attacked by one or more countries. Put concisely the instrument envisaged:

A Pact of Mutual Assistance between the Baltic States, Soviet Russia, Poland, Czechoslovakia and Germany;

A guarantee by Russia to France and Germany in the event

* Ibid., col. 699. † Ibid., col. 734.

of conditions arising which would bring the original Locarno Pact into operation ; and

Reciprocal assurances by France in respect of the boundaries of Russia and the Eastern boundaries of Germany.

M. Barthou, the French Foreign Minister, who had been very active in supporting this pact had discussed the subject very exhaustively with Sir John Simon a few days earlier. Mr. Attlee emphatically supported the proposed pact. He stated: "The Labour Party urgently hopes that His Majesty's Government will give their cordial approval to these proposals, will co-operate in pressing Germany and Poland to participate in the Eastern Pact, and will agree to Russia becoming a guarantor of the Locarno Pacts of 1925."*

Sir John Simon, after giving a detailed analysis of this proposed pact, declared that His Majesty's Government was convinced "that an Eastern pact of mutual guarantee, based on the strictest principles of reciprocity and conceived with the genuine purpose of strengthening the foundations of peace in the world—by creating a further basis for reciprocal guarantees, is well deserving the support of the British Government and of the British people."†

Mr. Churchill was more downright. He apparently fully understood the deep significance of the U.S.S.R. being a signatory of this proposed instrument. He stated:

> "It involves the reassociation of Soviet Russia with the Western European system. Remember that it is an historic event."

On this occasion there was a measure of agreement seldom seen in the Commons. The *News Chronicle* was justified in commenting: "The House of Commons yesterday supported, with a warmth and a real unanimity which it has not shown for many a long year, the policy which Sir John Simon expounded with a frank directness that has become almost equally rare in the pronouncements of our Foreign Office."‡

We have referred in the opening paragraphs of this chapter to a turning point in Anglo-Soviet relations. Here it is right and essential also to mention the part played by Sir Robert Vansittart (now Lord Vansittart), then Permanent Under-Secretary of State for Foreign Affairs, in paving the way for a *rapprochement*. Sir Robert—who was fully alive to the world-dominating aims of the Nazi Government—had in the first week of July, 1934, a full and frank talk with M. Maisky on the subjects of the Nazi menace, the Soviet's attitude thereto and Anglo-Soviet relations. This was the first heart-to-heart talk which had taken place up to that date between the permanent

* *Hansard*, 13.vii.34, cols. 689/90. † Ibid., col. 700. ‡ 14.vii.34.

head of the Foreign Office and the Soviet Ambassador to Great Britain. The two diplomats soon discovered that there were no conflicting interests between their two countries and that they were in hearty accord regarding the Nazi menace.

M. Maisky reported the conversation to Moscow where it was very well received and Sir Robert Vansittart was equally impressed. The atmosphere had been much cleared and the path made easier for an improvement in relations.

The attitude now taken up by the British Government was warmly welcomed, albeit without illusions, in Moscow. *Pravda* declared:

> "As a result of the London talks, a realistic basis has been created for the conclusion of regional security pacts. . . . Italy also now views the prospect of an Eastern Locarno favourably. . . .
>
> The speech of Sir John Simon and of British statesmen so well-known in our country, such as Sir A. Chamberlain and Mr. Winston Churchill, proves that Great Britain has decided to support France . . . all these statesmen supported the idea of an Eastern European Pact. . . . From the tribune of the House of Commons, from the lips of some of the most important British statesmen it has now been recognised . . . 'that the U.S.S.R. is undoubtedly interested in the preservation of peace.' All this witnesses a certain swing in the direction of peace which cannot but be welcomed."

The journal went on to stress the importance of the proposed pact for the consolidation of peace in Eastern Europe and pointed out that such a pact would also play a very great rôle in strengthening peace in other parts of the world, and continued: "All the signatories of the proposed pact would guarantee the inviolability of one another's frontiers. At the same time the projected pact assumes that for its complete realisation it will be necessary for the U.S.S.R. to enter into the League of Nations. As is well known, both France and Great Britain have expressed themselves in favour of this."

Shortly after this debate in the House of Commons, the Soviet Embassy gave a reception to the Diplomatic Corps, etc., and the large and representative attendance was a reflection of the improved relations between London and Moscow. The *Manchester Guardian* correspondent present recorded his impressions thus:

> "The Diplomatic Corps, as it happened, were gathered together to-day as the news was coming in of the Vienna events.* It was

* The Vienna events referred to here were the attempted Putsch and the murder of Dolfuss, July 25, 1934, by Austrian Nazis instigated and aided by Berlin, as became apparent later.

in the pleasant garden of the Russian Embassy where the Ambassador and Mme. Maisky were giving their summer party. The French Ambassador came early, the German Ambassador last. The Japanese Ambassador and M. Maisky seemed to be having a very cordial conversation. The Polish Ambassador, who is soon leaving, was saying some of his farewells. Altogether it was the most distinguished and biggest gathering of diplomatists that one can remember at these parties. . . .

The most striking figures were the Ministers of the Eastern States, Iraq, Ethiopia, Afghanistan and Saudi Arabia in their robes. There was a strong gathering from the Foreign Office, headed by the Foreign Minister."*

In passing, we may observe that the U.S.S.R. was admitted to the League of Nations and given a permanent seat on the Council on September 18, 1934. When the Labour Party Conference met on October 1, 1934, the U.S.S.R.'s entry into the League was enthusiastically hailed by the assembled delegates. The Chairman, in his presidential address, to the accompaniment of loud cheers, declared: "The initiative which the Soviet Government has taken to promote the conclusion of the proposed Eastern Pact of Mutual Assistance is evidence, too, of her growing recognition that the best guarantee for peace and security lies in the Collective System. We welcome as an event of historic importance Russia's entry into the League of Nations, and her election to a permanent seat on the League Council."

Next day, the following resolution was submitted to the Conference:

"This Conference expresses its deep satisfaction at the entry of the Union of Soviet Socialist Republics into the League of Nations, with a Permanent Seat on the Council of the League, believing that this historic event will greatly strengthen the League, improve the relationship between neighbour States, render the Collective Peace System more effective, hasten a world agreement for progressive disarmament, thereby creating new opportunities for effective international co-operation both in economic questions and in other fields, and assist in a general advance of the peoples of the world towards a Co-operative World Commonwealth."

Mr. Arthur Henderson, M.P., proposing the resolution, said:

"In submitting that resolution I am quite sure this Conference will be so unanimous that there is no need to occupy a great deal of time upon it. . . .

As the resolution says, the fact that Soviet Russia is now a

* 26.vii.34.

member is really a historic and I would say a significant event. I think it would be impossible to exaggerate the possible advantages that must come to the nations of the world as the result of this entry into the League. . . .

We believe that Russia ought to be right at the very forefront of the League of Nations, and it would have been adding insult to injury if she had not been given a seat on the Council and come into the League as a co-equal with any other Power."

The resolution, needless to add, was carried unanimously, and with loud and continued applause.

The political stability and rapidly growing industrial power, and the promptness with which all Soviet bills had been met had made a deep and favourable impression on British business men. The country was not therefore astonished when, at the General Meeting of Tube Investments, Ltd., the Chairman, Mr. Arthur Chamberlain, declared: "I should say that to-day money could be lent to Russia with greater security and greater ensuing benefit than to any other country in Europe."*

This declaration, which evoked hearty echoes in influential business circles, constituted a public recognition of the stability and rapidly growing strength of the U.S.S.R.

CHAPTER XXIII

THE SHADOW OF NAZIDOM (1935-1937)

I. IMPROVEMENT IN ANGLO-SOVIET RELATIONS. MR. EDEN IN MOSCOW

THE year 1935 was memorable in the annals of Anglo-Soviet relations. Whilst it would perhaps be an exaggeration to say that Moscow and London drew much closer together, it is no exaggeration to say that relations between the two capitals lost much of their customary coldness and suspicion; this, as already mentioned, was due in no small degree to the rising menace of Nazi Germany.

Undoubtedly an equally important factor was the progress registered within the U.S.S.R. itself. On January 1, 1935, the rationing system of bread, flour and cereals which had been introduced during the period of the first Five-Year Plan, was abolished. This was made possible by the fact that the State at the beginning of 1935 had at its disposal two-and-a-half times as much grain as it had in October, 1928. However, many other products—although they were much

* *Times*, 6.xii.34.

more abundant than they had been during the previous eight years—were still retained on the rationing list.

As usual, the question of timber imports from the U.S.S.R. came up for discussion and decision early in January, and on February 6, 1935, despite opposition from Canadian quarters, a contract was signed between Timber Distributors, Ltd., and the Soviets for the purchase of 400,000 standards of timber during the coming season.

This contract, which was valued at about £6,000,000, exceeded the previous year's contract by 50,000 standards and the British Customs, under the new tariffs, collected about £600,000 on the transaction. The famous "fall clause" (which had been struck out in the previous year's contract) was inserted in the 1935 contract "at the request of British importers after considerable discussion."

Meanwhile, the question of how to establish firm peace throughout all Europe had been exercising the minds of the British and French Governments. After a three days' discussion, an Anglo-French agreement was signed in London on February 3, 1935. Under this instrument the other Locarno Powers—Germany, Italy and Belgium—were invited to discuss with Great Britain and France the conclusion of an Air Convention which would guarantee mutual assistance if their Air Forces became the victim of aerial aggression by any of the contracting parties. That was not all. The agreement envisaged the secure establishment of peace throughout Europe by means of Regional Pacts of non-aggression and mutual assistance. The relevant clause read:

> "Great Britain and France were agreed that nothing would contribute more to the restoration of confidence and the prospects of peace among nations than a general settlement freely negotiated between Germany and the other Powers.
>
> This general settlement would make provision for the organisation of security in Europe, particularly by means of the conclusion of pacts freely negotiated between all the interested parties, and ensuring mutual assistance in Eastern Europe and the system foreshadowed in the Rome *procés-verbal* for Central Europe.
>
> "Simultaneously and in conformity with the terms of the declaration of December 11, 1932, regarding equality of rights in a system of security this settlement would establish agreements regarding armaments generally which, in the case of Germany, would replace the provisions of Part V of the Treaty of Versailles at present limiting the arms and armed forces of Germany."*

The authors of the declaration had, of course, in mind the Eastern European Pact of Mutual Guarantee (later referred to as the "Eastern Locarno") which, as explained in the preceding chapter, had been

* *Manchester Guardian*, 4.ii.35.

proposed in July, 1934, by France and the U.S.S.R. This pact, which was to have included the U.S.S.R., Poland, the Baltic States, Czechoslovakia and Germany, was intended to do for Eastern Europe what the Locarno Pact envisaged for Western Europe. Further, under the proposed Agreement the U.S.S.R. was to offer guarantees to both France and Germany "in the event of conditions arising which bring the provisions of the Locarno Treaty into operation"; France was to offer an assurance respecting "the boundaries of Russia" and also the frontiers of the Reich "on Germany's Eastern side." So far the scheme had been hanging in the air. Germany had expressed strong opposition to the proposed pact and Poland had meekly followed in her trail.

Moscow lost little time in declaring herself respecting the London Pact of February 3, 1935. In identical notes handed to the British and French Foreign Offices on February 20, 1935, it warmly welcomed the agreement provided that it meant that Europe was to be covered with a network of pacts to secure peace. The Note declared:

> "In the establishment of a unified scheme embracing various parts of Europe the Soviet Government is inclined to see a recognition of mutual dependence in the preservation of peace in all these parts, a recognition ensuing from the impossibility, under present circumstances, of localising a war started at any point in Europe.
>
> It therefore considers that the objective of the London conversations is the organisation of security in Europe. This can only be reached by the realisation of all the regional pacts and agreements mentioned in the London communiqué, and that the disregarding of this, or that, of these agreements, far from 'strengthening prospects of peace' could be rather considered as an open encouragement of a breach of peace in the region concerned."

Next the Note drew attention to some facts of the highest importance which are all too often forgotten. It continued:

> "After the London agreement it is possible to state that the idea of the necessity of adopting the most prompt and effective measures to counteract military aggression through pacts of mutual assistance is actively supported by four of the largest States of Europe, namely, the U.S.S.R., France, Britain and Italy, as well as the countries of the Little and Balkan Ententes, having jointly a population of 365,000,000 or 70 per cent. of the population of the whole of Europe.
>
> It cannot be doubted that the overwhelming majority of the

other countries of Europe also regard sympathetically all that can be undertaken for the strengthening of peace, and that thus the existing 'tendency to aggravate the danger of war' is represented by a comparatively small number of adherents."

The Soviet reply was cordially welcomed in Britain and was scarcely opposed even by our Die-Hard organs. The Diplomatic Correspondent of the *Daily Telegraph* stressed that the readiness of the Soviets to co-operate was "regarded in London as a helpful factor" and suggested that a British Minister might visit Berlin, Moscow and Warsaw. Mr. J. L. Garvin welcomed and supported in most enthusiastic terms the Soviet Note and thesis. Among other things he declared: "It is idle to think that you can segregate 'Western' and 'Eastern' questions into different compartments by any kind of diplomatic bulkheads which would be strong enough to prevent an explosion in either from shattering the other." He concluded: "As M. Litvinov said, and as was repeated by M. Maisky, the Russian Ambassador to London, in his admirable speech the other day, 'Peace is indivisible.' That is no mere phrase. It is the most fundamental of facts."*

Even the *Morning Post*, which lost no opportunity of trying to bedevil the relations between London and Moscow, admitted that: "It is practically certain that the Foreign Secretary will visit Moscow and probably Warsaw and Prague as well. The reason for going to Moscow as well as to Berlin is the obvious one that no general settlement is possible in Europe without Russia."†

The subject was raised in the House of Commons, February 25, 1935, when Sir John Simon, the Foreign Secretary, said he hoped to visit Berlin shortly and that visits to Moscow and other European capitals were under consideration.

Berlin was bitterly opposed to the proposed Eastern Locarno and heard with very bad grace that a British Cabinet Minister was likely to visit the U.S.S.R. The Diplomatic Correspondent of the *Manchester Guardian* stated:

> "The principal effort of German diplomacy at the moment (and, no doubt will be for some time to come) is to keep the problems of Eastern and Western security apart. The thesis that 'peace is indivisible' is not accepted by the German Government, and there can be no doubt that in the coming discussions at Berlin the German attitude will be that while the Western problem is ripe for discussion the Eastern problem is not.
>
> German polemics against Russia continue, and altogether a chasm between Russia and the rest of Europe is being created by

* *Observer*, 24.ii.35. † *Morning Post*, 26.ii.35.

> the present policy of the German Government. That chasm can be closed by the suggested visit to Moscow, a visit that will have a far more than merely formal importance. That it will find no favour in Berlin is, perhaps, regrettable, but it will help towards the removal of misunderstandings that are more regrettable still."*

Meanwhile, although Moscow had intimated in the usual way that a visit of a British Minister would be welcome, the British Government were apparently hesitating for fear of displeasing Berlin, an attitude which naturally was deeply resented in the Soviet capital.

A writer in *Izvestia* declared: " We wish to believe that the trip of the British Secretary of State for Foreign Affairs to Berlin has the aim to strengthen the cause of peace. Tactics which consist in hanging on Germany's lips and even reading in her eyes what she really desires, can only increase tension in Eastern Europe and this may lead to dire results. The first such result might be to place the Baltic States at the mercy of German Fascism deprived of all effective defence and assistance, and this is precisely the objective significance of the compromises suggested by Sir John Simon. In general, British tactics provide an evil lesson to Europe, because everybody is going to ask: ' Whence comes this extreme kindness? ' The answer is clear. This kindness is the result of German rearmament. No sooner had Germany provided herself with a few hundred bombers than certain people no longer dared say to her firmly and openly: ' Hands off the frontiers of other countries.' "†

However, despite the frowns of Berlin, Sir John Simon informed the House of Commons, March 7, 1935, that Mr. Eden, the Lord Privy Seal, would visit Moscow.‡ Two days later, M. Maisky, the Soviet Ambassador, expressed to the Foreign Office his Government's warm gratification at the prospect of Mr. Eden's visit to Moscow. Meanwhile, evidence accumulated that the Soviet thesis that " Peace is indivisible " found greater and greater favour in Whitehall. For instance, the Parliamentary Correspondent of the *Times,* after pointing out that in the Berlin talks the Air Pact of the Locarno Powers, the Eastern Pact, a Central European Pact and the Arms Convention, would be discussed, continued:

> " British Ministers feel that all the four subjects ought to be examined simultaneously, for they all form parts of one logical whole. They do not view with favour any suggestion for pacts of non-aggression on the part of two particular nations as they feel strongly that the problem of the peace of Europe is one and indivisible.

* *Manchester Guardian,* 1.iii.35. † *Izvestia,* 3.iii.35.

‡ Sir Robert Vansittart did much to bring about this visit.

It is expected that the date for Mr. Eden's visit to Moscow will be announced within the next day or two. The British Cabinet regard the visit to Moscow as one of first-class importance and not in any way an appendage to the Berlin conversations."*

Meanwhile, certain timber interests which objected to the Anglo-Soviet Timber Contract signed on February 6, 1935, had not been idle. Although the Board of Trade was cognisant of all the details of that agreement when it was concluded, some five weeks later it notified the Soviet Government that it objected to the "fall clause," and the 200 members of Timber Distributors Ltd., were informed of this fact on March 12, 1935. This, coming particularly at that time, was a rather ungracious act. There was no justification for it on the grounds of unfair competition because as the *Daily Telegraph* (March 14, 1935) admitted, Russian prices were higher than Canadian. The sequel was instructive. A new agreement was concluded about a week later without the "fall clause" and Timber Distributors Ltd., in a letter to their shareholders, wrote that as a consequence of the dropping of this clause (with its contingent risk) there would be a reduction in the schedule of prices. The *Morning Post* commented:

> "It seems, what has been lost by the compulsory omission of the obnoxious 'Fall' clause (which provides for repayment to British importers when market prices fall below contract prices) has, to a large extent, been regained by straightforward reduction of prices.
>
> The Canadians, having secured with great difficulty the British Government's ban on this clause, are now faced with an immediate reduction of their competitors' prices, instead of merely a contingent, though larger reduction, as provided for by the 'Fall' clause."†

As a matter of fact, to quote the same journal five days later, there was "an average reduction on each standard of about 11/3d.," whilst under the "Fall" clause, the Soviets were liable "to refund up to 22/6d. a standard."

The moral of all this, for reasons which are notorious, is that Canadian timber cannot compete with Russian. The trade prefers the latter. Russian timber continued to fetch higher prices than Canadian.

Now to turn to political matters again. It was feared in some quarters that the fact that the Lord Privy Seal (who was not then of Cabinet rank) was to visit Moscow, and that the Lord Privy Seal and

* 14.iii.35. † 22.iii.35.

the Foreign Secretary (Sir John Simon) were to visit Berlin together, might give offence to the Soviets and might be interpreted on the Continent as derogatory to the Kremlin. The Government, however, sought to put an end to such speculations. Sir John Simon, at a demonstration, March 15, 1935, stated emphatically:

> "The visit which I shall be paying to Berlin, upon which the Lord Privy Seal will accompany me, is, of course, quite independent in origin from that which my colleague will pay subsequently to Russia and to Poland. Let me make it clear, however, that His Majesty's Government attach no less significance to the visit as of exceptional importance and welcome most sincerely the opportunity which will thus be afforded in three great capitals of Europe to promote that international understanding which is the Government's chief concern."*

On the day following this speech the German Government, in flagrant defiance of the Versailles Treaty, reintroduced conscription, a fact which increased the value of the Moscow visit in the eyes of Whitehall. The Diplomatic Correspondent of the *Manchester Guardian* nine days later wrote:

> "There would seem to be a slight change in the attitude taken towards Eastern security here in London. While the Eastern Pact was formerly regarded with a certain scepticism, or even indifference, the conviction has begun to grow that Eastern security has become a more urgent matter than it seemed by reason of the rapid rearmament of Germany and the tenacity with which Hitler and his advisers cling to their Eastern plans."†

This correspondent's conclusions were underlined on the same day in Moscow in an interview, published by *Pravda*, with Sir Austen Chamberlain, in the course of which the latter said: "There is no doubt about the necessity of the co-operation of Soviet Russia in any complete system of European security. Peace is the common concern of every member of the League of Nations. If war breaks out anywhere it is impossible to predict how far it may spread. Security in Eastern and Central Europe is no less essential than security in Western Europe."‡

This statement, coming from the gentleman who was Foreign Secretary at the time of the Arcos raid, was a good overture to Mr. Eden's visit as exemplifying the change *vis-à-vis* the Soviet Union which had taken place in influential political circles in this country. Next day, the Lord Privy Seal, who was joined by M. Maisky in Berlin, crossed the Soviet frontier—accompanied by Viscount Cran-

* *Times*, 16.iii.35. † 26.iii.35. ‡ *Morning Post*, 27.iii.35.

borne (his Parliamentary Private Secretary) and a large number of special correspondents—and reached Moscow on the morning of March 28 1935. Mr. Eden was welcomed on the platform by M. Litvinov (Commissar for Foreign Affairs), and Lord Chilston, the British Ambassador.

In the afternoon, Mr. Eden and M. Litvinov had lengthy conversations, and in the evening the British guests were entertained at a reception. M. Litvinov, speaking at this gathering, heartily welcomed Mr. Eden and declared:

> " Mr. Eden's visit here marks an important milestone in the history of the relations between Soviet Russia and Great Britain. While, during the last fourteen years, economic and cultural relations between our countries have been showing normal and satisfactory development, the visit of Mr. Eden follows on what must be described as a distinct improvement on the political side of these relations also.
>
> We, in this country, have long been aware of what people are beginning to realise in your country, Mr. Eden—that as Sir Austen Chamberlain said the other day: 'There is nothing that should hinder the development of the most friendly relations between the U.S.S.R. and Great Britain and that such relations are essential for the preservation of peace,' and what constitutes the basis of international life and the basis of peace if not a steady improvement of relations between States and an increase in their mutual understanding and confidence. . . .
>
> In conclusion, I will take the liberty of expressing my personal satisfaction at seeing Mr. Eden here, for, having worked side by side with him at the table of the League of Nations on the solution of international problems, I have had many opportunities of appreciating his personal gifts and high qualities.
>
> I raise my glass to the health of His Majesty the King of England, to the prosperity and happiness of the British people and to your very good health, sir."*

Replying to the toast, the Lord Privy Seal, after explaining that he was not empowered to negotiate, but only to explore, said that his visit to the Soviet capital nevertheless marked a notable and hopeful landmark in the relations between the two countries:

> " British foreign policy " (continued Mr. Eden) " was based on the League, and the essence of the League was universality. It should indeed be a world-wide League. Clearly, therefore, it was a great gain when a great nation, covering one-sixth of

* *Manchester Guardian*, 29.iii.35.

the world's surface and numbering 170,000,000 inhabitants, took its place at Geneva. The main object of the League was peace and the betterment of relations between countries. Peace was also the prime object of the policy of the United Kingdom. He was confident that this was also the foreign policy of the Soviet Union. M. Litvinov had mentioned the anxious position now existing in Europe. In his firm belief this position could only be improved by a frank exchange of views between the representatives of the great nations."*

The *Times* special correspondent, who accompanied Mr. Eden, cabled, March 28, 1935:

"In the Soviet view it is on the British attitude that peace or war may ultimately rest. All competent observers here share one conviction—namely, that Russia to-day is anxious for peace, and that its people are alarmed about Germany's intentions. In Soviet opinion, Germany's aggressive intentions towards Russia have been repeatedly revealed in, for instance, Herr Hitler's book, the utterances of Herr Rosenberg, and the Hugenberg memorandum, and were not unequivocally disclaimed during the Berlin conversations. This Russian conviction could be removed by German participation in a pact for automatic mutual assistance against an aggressor. The German arguments against this proposal are held to be patently insincere, and to be equally applicable to the Locarno Treaty."

Next morning, the Lord Privy Seal and the Soviet Commissar continued their talks. Respecting this conversation the *Daily Telegraph's* correspondent cabled:

"Mr. Eden, it seems, is making a special point of removing Soviet fears that British policy is deliberately calculated to countenance, and even encourage, the rapid growth of German armed strength.

It is obvious here that the Soviet has been for a long time entertaining suspicions that British policy is framed on lines hostile to Russia, because Britain is unsympathetic to a Communist régime. . . .

It is already clear that Mr. Eden has gone far to remove Soviet suspicions to which I have referred.

The result is that the Soviet is more ready to recognise that good relations with Britain in all parts of the world are of larger importance than the pursuit of an academic political policy—a policy once actively directed in an anti-British sense."†

* *Times*, 29.iii.35. † 30.iii.35.

In the afternoon of the same day, Mr. Eden had a conversation with M. Stalin in the Kremlin. The Lord Privy Seal was accompanied by Lord Chilston and Mr. Strang, whilst M. Stalin was accompanied by M. Litvinov, M. Molotov and M. Maisky.

In the evening of that day a special ballet was given in honour of the British visitors:

> "Thousands stood in silence in the great Moscow Opera House last night while 'God Save the King' was played on the arrival of Mr. Eden and the British delegates to witness a special ballet.
>
> A thunder of cheers, lasting several minutes, followed, as faces were turned towards the former Royal box, where Mr. Eden was seated.
>
> Semenova, Russia's greatest ballerina, was brought back specially from Turkey in honour of the British visitors. This brilliant scene rounded off a memorable day in Anglo-Russian relations."*

Next day, March 30, 1935, was in the main devoted to social functions. In the morning, Mr. Eden visited the Museum of Western Art and later drove to M. Litvinov's country house for lunch. M. Litvinov's chef excelled himself that day. As usual, he served an appetising meal, but when the butter was placed on the table it bore the Foreign Commissar's famous slogan, "Peace is indivisible." So delighted were all present that they felt it would be a sacrilege to cut the butter and so destroy the lettering. In the evening a reception was held for the diplomatic corps. "Next morning" (so wired Mr. A. J. Cummings, from Moscow) "in company with Mr. Eden, M. Litvinov and a number of Embassy and Soviet officials, I had a trip on Moscow's new underground railway which is to be opened on May 1. The subway is a model of skill and artistry. The stations are lofty, spacious, beautifully designed, well-arranged and imposing, with their strong marble pillars and tessellated sides. Pictures of Stalin and industrial scenes adorn the walls. The layout is in all respects superior to the London and New York underground railways, although the Moscow line is only a little less noisy than the Hampstead Tube."†

Next followed a tour of an aeroplane construction factory and another visit to the Grand Opera House. On the evening of March 31, the following official communiqué was issued:

> "Conversations have taken place in Moscow in the last few days between Mr. Eden, Lord Privy Seal, and M. Litvinov,

* *Daily Telegraph*, 30.iii.35. † *News Chronicle*, 1.iv.35.

People's Commissar for Foreign Affairs, upon the principal elements of the present international situation, including the proposed Eastern Pact and the other questions set forth in the Anglo-French communiqué of February 3, as well as regards the future development and improvement of Anglo-Soviet relations.

During his visit, Mr. Eden was received by M. Stalin and M. Molotov and was able to exchange views with them on the same subject.

In the course of the conversations, which were conducted throughout in an atmosphere of complete friendliness and frankness, Mr. Eden informed M. Litvinov of the recent talks between the British Ministers and the head of the German Government. It was agreed that these talks had helped to clarify the European situation.

Mr. Eden, M. Stalin, M. Molotov and M. Litvinov were of the opinion that in the present international situation it was more than ever necessary to pursue endeavours to promote the building-up of a system of collective security in Europe, as contemplated in the Anglo-French communiqué of February 3, and in conformity with the principles of the League of Nations.

It was emphasised in the conversations by MM. Stalin, Molotov and Litvinov that the organisation of security in Eastern Europe and the proposed pact of mutual assistance do not aim at the isolation or the encirclement of any State, but at the creation of equal security for all participants, and that the participation in the pact of Germany and Poland would, therefore, be welcome, as affording the best solution of the problem.

The representatives of the two Governments were happy to note, as a result of a full and frank exchange of views, that there is at present no conflict of interest between the two Governments on any of the main issues of international policy, and that this fact provides a firm foundation for the development of fruitful collaboration between them in the cause of peace.

They are confident that both countries, recognising that the integrity and prosperity of each is to the advantage of the other, will govern their mutual relations in that spirit of collaboration and loyalty to obligations assumed by them which is inherent in their common membership of the League of Nations.

In the light of these considerations, Mr. Eden and M. Stalin, M. Molotov and M. Litvinov are confirmed in the opinion that the friendly co-operation of the two countries in the general work for the collective organisation of peace and security is of primary importance for the furtherance of international efforts to this end."

The finale of this historic visit came some hours later when Mr. Eden left Moscow for Warsaw. Before he boarded his train, speaking into a radio-microphone, he said: "I am happy to thank the Soviet and M. Litvinov for the hospitality shown me in my visit to Moscow"; to which M. Litvinov replied: "I wish you success. Your success will be our success—now."*

"M. Litvinov was beaming" (so wired Reuter). "Everyone, indeed, was smiling, and the general impression was that the visit had been a success, both politically and socially."

On all hands it was recognised as of major importance. "The visit to Moscow," declared the *Daily Telegraph* (April 2, 1935), "had an importance which attaches to no visit to another capital, since it bridged the gulf of mistrust which has existed since 1917."

The *Times* of the same date was equally emphatic: "Mr. Eden's visit to Moscow has indeed been both important and successful. It has renewed or established personal contacts. It has been very valuable in opening up a fresh line of communication between Western Europe and Russia, so long held back from ordinary political contact with the outside world."

The Soviet press and people were equally pleased and attached great importance to the significance of Mr. Eden's visit and its outcome. However, Germany, in view of her expansionist aims in Eastern Europe, was strongly hostile to the Eastern Pact and Warsaw took its orders from Berlin, with the result, now a matter of history, that the Eastern Pact was never completed.

One of the British journalists who accompanied Mr. Eden to Moscow, as already mentioned, was Mr. A. J. Cummings. He remained behind and travelled the country to collect information regarding the mood of the people towards Great Britain and the attitude both of leading officials and ordinary citizens towards world affairs. His conclusions are extremely interesting because they embody prophecy and warnings which events have largely justified. Respecting the feelings towards Great Britain, he wrote:

> "The rapid growth of pro-English sentiment has astonished me. Everybody and everything English seems to be regarded with special favour. Scores of thousands of Russians are learning the English language.
>
> There are English study circles in every factory and every club, and large numbers are studying English privately.
>
> It will be a great misfortune if Great Britain does not take

* *Daily Express*, 1.iv.35.

advantage, in the best sense of the word, of this unexampled movement towards rapprochement between Bourgeois and Bolshevik States."

As regards the attitude towards world affairs, he wrote:

> "There is a profound conviction that the peace of Europe rests primarily on British statesmanship. In some quarters it is feared that Britain will hestitate too long before coming to a decision to join and actively to encourage a great European peace bloc. . . .
>
> The Soviet Government probably has better information than any in the world of the nature of Germany's military preparations and of the extent in detail of her existing military strength in men, munitions and the entire paraphernalia of war.
>
> Men of sober judgment are absolutely convinced that unless Europe establishes in the near future a system of security which will make it impossible for a single Power to dare to break peace there will be another great European war within three years from now."*

The opportunity of a century was lost, the serious admonition was ignored by our Government which, of course, "has sources of information not available to the average citizen."

As already mentioned, the proposed Eastern Pact never materialised and Paris and Moscow were reluctantly driven to the conclusion that the only course left to them was to conclude a Franco-Soviet Pact of non-aggression and mutual assistance, which was duly signed, May 2, 1935, by M. Laval, then French Foreign Minister, and M. Potemkin, then Soviet Ambassador to France.

II. Anglo-German Naval Agreement. Death of King George V. M. Litvinov attends the Funeral

Meanwhile, the Anglo-German Naval Agreement, under which (broadly speaking) the naval forces of Germany were restricted to 35 per cent. of those of Great Britain, had been signed. London wanted to complete this agreement, among other ways, by the conclusion of an Anglo-Soviet naval treaty. The first talks on this subject took place in Moscow, June 21, 1935. "Lord Chilston, the British Ambassador, to-day visited M. Litvinov, the Commissar for Foreign Affairs," wired the *Daily Telegraph's* correspondent, "and informed him that the British Government was anxious to discuss the question of naval armaments with the Soviet Government."†

According to the same report, the British Ambassador informed

* *News Chronicle*, 20.iv.35.

† *Daily Telegraph*, 22.vi.35.

M. Litvinov of the contents of the Anglo-German Naval Agreement, and of the fact that Great Britain was negotiating with France and Italy respecting naval armaments. The cable concluded:

> "It is to be hoped that Lord Chilston's talk with M. Litvinov will check the severe strictures on British policy in the Soviet press. England is accused of evading her obligations for collective action, assumed under the Franco-British joint declaration of February 3, and of showing weakness towards Germany over the naval armament in the hope of reducing the threat to her of the Nazi air force."

The Soviet Government apparently did not find the explanation satisfactory, because the next issue of *Pravda* repeated its previous criticism of British policy. However, the negotiations between the two Governments were continued.

The question of British trade with the U.S.S.R., which was never quite absent from the pages of our press or the minds of British manufacturers, was now again ventilated. However, British and other exporters were no longer in a position to drive exacting bargains.

> "The Soviet Government's foreign trade position," wrote the Moscow correspondent of the *Manchester Guardian*, "is stronger than ever in its history. It has achieved substantial favourable balances of trade for the past two years, it has increased its gold production startlingly in two years, and the rate of increase is being accelerated and it has extracted unsuspected reserves of gold and foreign currencies from the population through the special '*foreign valuta*' shops of Torgsin. Its trading organisations are now able to enter foreign markets as cash buyers and they are prepared to insist on gaining all the advantages of this position."*

Up to this date, however, British banks were slow to face up to the changed situation. British manufacturers, on the other hand, had no delusions on this matter. For instance, Mr. Reincke, the Chairman of Messrs. Beardmore & Co. Ltd., at the annual meeting of the company, June 28, 1935, declared:

> "We, in common with other British manufacturers, have done, or are doing, considerable business with Soviet Russia, and the scope of this business could, in my view, be greatly extended if ways and means could be found in this country of extending credit facilities to Russia, commensurate with what is done by other European countries and the United States of America, and

* *Manchester Guardian*, 24.vi.35.

which take account of the fact that our respective resources can be rendered mutually complementary if the value of British co-operation is estimated correctly on the Russian side."*

This and similar statements, which were in part at least appeals to the Government to assist with guaranteed credits, although they did not pass unheeded, were not taken up as promptly as they should have been. It was generally accepted by this time that the Soviet's financial position was very different from two years earlier, but many even well-informed observers must have been amazed when they read an article by the Soviet Commissar for Foreign Trade. After pointing out that the Soviet's favourable balance of foreign trade for the three years 1933, 1934 and 1935, was estimated at 450 million gold roubles, he continued:

"In addition to this favourable trade balance, the U.S.S.R. has sharply increased her output of gold. This has placed the U.S.S.R. second in the world output of gold, the first place being held by the Union of South Africa. With the constant favourable nature of the trade balance and the growth in gold production, the U.S.S.R. has been able to meet a large part of its foreign indebtedness and to create certain reserves of gold and foreign exchanges.

At the end of 1931 the foreign trade indebtedness of the U.S.S.R. reached its highest point—1.4 milliard roubles (£140,000,000 at par). By October 1, 1935, this had been reduced to 139 million roubles (£13,900,000 at par) and it is further anticipated that by the end of this year it will be further cut down to between 100 and 120 million roubles (£10,000,000 to £12,000,000 at par)."†

As to the condition on which the Soviet's trade with the outside world would be conducted in future, the Commissar for Foreign Trade continued:

"The strong interest of the capitalist countries in the Soviet market and their interest in the development of economic relations with the U.S.S.R. have been factors strengthening the conviction that the only means of extending their economic connections with the U.S.S.R. on a large scale lies in the granting of long-term financial credits or in loans to the U.S.S.R. It is not amiss to point out in this connection that capitalist countries are perhaps more interested in this than the Soviet Union itself.

The credit agreements with Germany and Czechoslovakia concluded in 1935 were the first attempts at a reconstruction of trade

* *Times*, 29.vi.35. † *Pravda* 7.xi.35.

relations with the U.S.S.R., which took into consideration the tremendously increased economic power of the U.S.S.R. We may note in particular the bond form of credits received by us in Czechoslovakia. Various projects granting the U.S.S.R. long-term loans under normal conditions are beginning to be discussed in the pages of the foreign press. Similar projects are being received by Soviet trade organisations also."

This speech attracted considerable attention in business circles in this country, not only because it re-emphasised the strong financial position of the U.S.S.R., but also because it revealed the folly of the policy pursued by our banking houses in previous years in financing Germany and cold-shouldering the U.S.S.R. This was well brought out in a letter to the *Times* by Mr. Robert Boothby, M.P.

". . . During the period of 1924-30 we declined to give Russia the short and medium-term credits of which she stood in so much need. We gave them to Germany instead—where, for the most part, they lie frozen to-day. But Germany used them to build up a huge credit position between herself and Russia, which formed the basis of a huge volume of trade. It is no exaggeration to say that Germany owes the entire modern structure of her industries, and therefore her present capacity for armament production, to her export trade with Russia during these critical years. A trade which we literally threw away. After the crisis of 1931, Germany defaulted widely on her foreign commitments. Russia, on the other hand, has repaid in full—a remarkable achievement, for the figures of her short-term foreign indebtedness in 1930 were astronomic."*

In conclusion, Mr. Boothby advocated " a long-term loan " which, in his opinion, would have done " more for the distressed areas than all Mr. Lloyd George's schemes put together."

The late Lord Allen of Hurtwood, went further. He advocated not only economic, but also close political co-operation between the two countries. Speaking at the " Congress of Peace and Friendship with the U.S.S.R." he said, among other things, that:

" There was probably no single development which would be more far-reaching in its influence than for Britain and Russia to draw closer together. This must not, of course, take the form of an alliance of Powers to protect their exclusive interest against other nations ; it should mean an ' alliance of initiative ' to press forward policies to strengthen the League. . . .

* *Times*, 20.xi.35.

Our two countries needed each other for economic reasons. British export trade would gain; Russian development could be helped forward. Britain had lost millions of her capital by taking financial risks in many remote parts of the world. The risks of financing trade with Russia were far less. The Soviet Government had never dishonoured any obligation voluntarily entered into.

He concluded: If our two nations tried the experiment of spontaneous and genuine friendliness instead of grudging contacts, the League of Nations would be in a stronger position to restrain the disorders and dangers that threatened Europe."*

Nevertheless, it can hardly be said that the British Government acted on Lord Allen's advice, and as regards trade, the most hopeful rumour as 1935 drew to its close was that "reports of Anglo-Russian credit conversations show that the possibilities of the Russian market are not overlooked in this country." Further, the correspondent wrote:

"Improved short-term credit facilities on a basis similar to that granted by Germany and by other Continental countries should, therefore, go a good way to improving our trade relations with Russia."†

It seems incredible to-day that at the end of 1935 both the British Government and our banking houses should have been approaching this question so gingerly.

The next meeting between British and Soviet statesmen was occasioned by a very sad event, the death of His Majesty, the late King George V. As soon as the news reached Moscow, M. Kalinin (then President of the Central Executive Committee of the U.S.S.R.) cabled to Queen Mary: "I beg your Majesty to accept my profound condolences and the expression of sincere sympathy on the occasion of the heavy loss that has befallen the Royal Family and Great Britain."‡ And M. Molotov (Chairman of the Council of People's Commissars) cabled the Prime Minister, Mr. Baldwin: "I beg you and the Cabinet to accept the expression of sincere condolence on the death of his Majesty King George V on behalf of myself and of the Government of the U.S.S.R."§

Among the innumerable wreaths sent to Windsor Castle, there was "A chaplet with a black and red ribbon bearing the words: 'From the Central Executive Committee of the Union of Soviet Socialist Republics.'"||

On the night before the funeral, M. Litvinov, in company with representatives from several States, dined with the new Monarch.

* *Times*, 9.xii.35. † *Financial News*, 11.xii.35. ‡ *Times*, 22.i.36.
§ Ibid. || *Daily Telegraph*, 27.i.36.

"Five Kings sat down to dinner with King Edward," reported the *News Chronicle* (January 28, 1936), "at Buckingham Palace last night, the King being the host to brother monarchs for the first time. It was an historic scene as the six monarchs, with the President of the French Republic and all the other royal guests and heads of foreign missions, including M. Litvinov, Russian Commissar for Foreign Affairs, assembled in the white and gold State dining room on the first floor."

Commenting on this and other episodes, the Diplomatic Correspondent of the *Morning Post* wrote:

> "M. Litvinov is the first Soviet Minister to come to London in an official capacity and the first to be received at Buckingham Palace. He was among the foreign statesmen with whom King Edward conversed at the reception at the Palace on Monday night, and he was among those who were given a private audience by His Majesty yesterday.
>
> M. Litvinov has also profited by his visit to have conversations with members of the Cabinet. He lunched with Mr. Eden yesterday, and afterwards called on Mr. Baldwin."*

Although nothing concrete emerged from these conversations, they were by no means without effect. The Diplomatic Correspondent of the *Manchester Guardian* commented that although "nothing new was discussed . . . the cordiality with which M. Litvinov was received . . . may perhaps be regarded as marking a new period in the relations between this country and Russia."

M. Litvinov again visited London less than two months later when he came here to attend a meeting of the League Council which opened at St. James' Palace, March 16, 1936. The special subjects then under discussion were the German re-occupation of the demilitarised Rhineland zone, and her denunciation of the Locarno Treaty. Although the Soviet Union was not directly interested and although the "plaintiffs" were France and Belgium, the Soviet representative gave his wholehearted support to the Western Powers.

Speaking at a public session of the Council, March 17, 1936, M. Litvinov pointed out that this was the third occasion within the short period of eighteen months, that the Council had had to deal with the infringement of international obligations. He declared:

> "We cannot preserve the League of Nations if we turn a blind eye to breaches of those treaties or confine ourselves to verbal protests. We cannot preserve the League of Nations if it does not carry out its own decisions, but, on the contrary, accustoms

* 30.i.36.

the aggressor to ignore its recommendations, its admonitions or its warnings."*

Referring to Germany's policy *vis-à-vis* France, he quoted from Hitler's *Mein Kampf* the pertinent passage:

> "Never permit two Continental powers to arise in Europe. In every attempt to organise a second military power on the German frontier, even though it be by the formation of a State capable of becoming a military power, you must see an attack on Germany.
>
> You must consider it not only your right, but your duty, to prevent such a State coming into existence by all possible means; including the force of arms. If such a State has already come into being, it must once again be shattered."

M. Litvinov then solemnly warned the Council: "The remilitarisation of the Rhineland zone bordering on France is a question of setting up the domination of Germany over the whole European continent. I ask you, must and shall the League of Nations condone the promotion of this objective?" After pointing out that his Government was passionately attached to real peace, but had no illusions about a sham peace, he added: "We are for the creation of security for all the nations of Europe, and against a half-peace, which is not peace at all, but war."

He concluded:

> "But at whatever new international agreements we might desire to arrive, we must first of all ensure their loyal fulfilment by all those who participate in them. The Council of the League must declare its attitude towards unilateral infringements of such agreements, and how it intends and is able to react against them.
>
> From this standpoint, the greatest possible satisfaction of the complaint made by the French and Belgian Governments becomes of exceptional importance. *I declare in the name of my Government its readiness to take part in all measures which may be proposed to the Council of the League by the Locarno Powers and are acceptable to the other members of the Council.*"† (Our italics).

The probabilities are that the assembled delegates knew that the Soviet representative had read the Nazi mind and intentions accurately. To quote the Special Correspondent of the *Daily Telegraph*:

> "After reading the relevant quotation from *My Struggle*, M.

* *Daily Telegraph*, 18.iii.36. † Ibid.

> Litvinov faced his colleagues at the Council table, and with a dramatic movement of the hand said: 'These, gentlemen, are the purposes for which Germany requires the remilitarisation of the Rhineland zone bordering on France.' At this thrust there was some embarrassment. M. Avenol, Secretary-General of the League, gazed wide-eyed at the Soviet Minister's admonishing finger. Mr. Eden examined his finger tips, and M. Titulescu, leaning back, gazed at the high ceiling with an expression which seemed to denote expectation of further out-spokenness."*

How different would have been the subsequent history of Europe had the Soviet Union's warning and offer of help been seriously heeded and acted upon!

Nazis in Germany and their sympathisers in Britain continued to assert that the Franco-Soviet Pact was directed against the Reich. This absurdity was refuted again and again by Soviet representatives. M. Maisky, speaking in London, March 19, 1936, declared:

> "This pact is open, even now, for Germany to enter, and if Germany were to care to say 'Yes,' there would be no greater pleasure anywhere than in Moscow and Paris. If Berlin really thinks that the Franco-Soviet Pact is an instrument for the encirclement of Germany why does it not wish to remove the sting from this diplomatic document in the simplest possible way, by joining the Franco-Soviet agreement."†

There was no advance from Berlin, but that did not prevent the Soviets from continuing to put forward their plans for maintaining peace in Europe and from leaving the door open to Germany. M. Maisky, speaking in London, May 15, 1936, said:

> "We think that the best method would be to apply the system of regional and group pacts of mutual assistance, not to replace the Covenant of the League, but to *underpin it*. When I say 'regional pacts,' I have in mind such pacts as, for example, Locarno, and the Eastern Pact of Mutual Assistance which the Soviet Government has been advocating since 1934. To make myself clear I should like to remind you that this Eastern Pact, according to the wishes of the Soviet Government, should embrace the U.S.S.R., Germany, Poland, Czechoslovakia and the three Baltic States. Germany was invited from the very beginning to join this pact on equal terms with the other countries, but unfortunately, she has so far persistently refused to accept the invitation.

* *Daily Telegraph*, 18.iii.36. † *Manchester Guardian*, 20.iii.36.

You will see that the regional pacts which the Soviet Government have in mind *have nothing in common with the old-fashioned closed alliances, but on the contrary, represent the new form of collective security* adapted to the particular circumstances of the present situation. Bear in mind that regional pacts in no way relieve the League States as a whole from their duties under the Covenant. Such regional pacts are designed to effect the more rapid concentration of neighbouring forces to oppose the first attack by the aggressor and to secure the necessary breathing space for mobilising the general forces of the League. Remember in modern war you have to move quickly! "

III. The Montreux Conference

Later in the year, considerable differences arose between London and Moscow. The Montreux Conference in June-July, 1936, was called to consider Turkey's appeal for the abrogation of the Treaty of Lausanne (1922) and permission to re-fortify the Dardanelles. The conference opened on June 22, and the new Treaty was signed July 20, 1936.

Turkey's claim respecting the re-fortification of the Straits was regarded by all the participating delegations as eminently reasonable and was speedily conceded, but a battle royal was fought out on another matter between, on the one hand, Great Britain, and on the other hand, France, the U.S.S.R. and Rumania. Briefly, the issue was that the three last named proposed that in the event of a war, Turkey being neutral, the Straits should be freely open to Powers acting under regional pacts of mutual assistance concluded within the framework of the League—such as the Franco-Soviet pact. In other words, that there should be unfettered egress and entrance to Powers applying a League policy. But the British delegates opposed. They wanted to hold the scales even as between, on the one hand, an aggressive Reich, and on the other, France, the U.S.S.R. and Rumania resisting a German attack. Fantastic though this sounds to-day, it is the sober truth.

The *Times* correspondent cabled from Montreux:

> " The main issues in dispute at Montreux have narrowed down to two, in both of which the thought of Germany can be discerned: the Soviet insistence on freedom of the Straits for Russian warships, and the Soviet-Franco-Rumanian demand that the Straits shall not be closed to warships bent on rendering aid under treaties which have been juridically dovetailed into the Covenant of the League."*

* 13.vii.36.

This was amplified next day in a leader:

> "M. Litvinov has proposed, and the French and Rumanian Governments have supported his proposal, that the Straits should not be closed in wartime (Turkey being neutral) to warships coming from outside in the fulfilment of agreements 'supplementary to the Covenant' concluded or 'hereafter to be concluded' between the signatories of the Convention. It is clear that the Franco-Soviet Pact, that *bête-noire* of the German Reich, falls under the head of these supplementary agreements, and that French and Rumanian support has been given to the Russian proposal in order to enable the French Government to assist these Powers, in the event of German aggression, without infringing the Covenant at the expense of a neutral Turkey."

The *Manchester Guardian's* special correspondent cabled:

> "What has particularly disturbed several delegations has been the apparent defence by the British delegation of the German point of view. They have been surprised to hear British delegates using against the Franco-Soviet Pact the very argument used by Hitler to justify the repudiation of the Treaty of Locarno—namely, that by the terms of the pact France and Russia agree to act in advance of a decision of the League Council. This is not in fact the case. The pact merely authorises France and Russia to act if the League Council cannot arrive at a unanimous decision. This is explicitly authorised by Article 15 of the Covenant."*

M. Litvinov, supported by the French and Rumanian delegates, refused to give way, and finally the British delegates beat a retreat. "After more inter-delegation lobbying and telephone calls to London," cabled the *Times* correspondent, "the British delegation were able to accept the French and Russian proposals for the passage of the Straits by belligerent warships in wartime when Turkey is neutral, and with this the last serious obstacle to agreement was overcome."†

The much disputed Article (19) in its final form read that in time of war:

> "Vessels of war belonging to belligerent Powers shall not, however, pass through the Straits except in cases arising out of the application of Article 25 of the present Convention, and in cases of assistance rendered to a State victim of aggression in virtue of a treaty of mutual assistance binding Turkey, concluded within the framework of the Covenant of the League of Nations,

* 13.vii.36. † 16.vii.36.

and registered and published in accordance with the provisions of Article 18 of the Covenant."

Article 25 here referred to declared that:

"Nothing in the present Convention shall prejudice the rights and obligations of Turkey, or of any of the other High Contracting Parties members of the League of Nations, arising out of the Covenant of the League of Nations."

After the signature of the new Convention the *Times* wrote editorially: "The British Government made most concessions, but M. Litvinov was not opposed to a bargain."

Whilst these negotiations were proceeding at Montreux direct Anglo-Soviet talks were taking place in London on two other important subjects. The President of the Board of Trade, Mr. Walter Runciman, informed the House of Commons, July 30, 1936, that an Agreement had been concluded between the Export Credits Guarantee Department and the Soviet trade representative in London, under which the Department would give guarantees for orders placed in this country by the representatives of the Soviet Government up to ten million pounds. Further details were: "The orders are to be for goods the manufacture of which will give rise to a substantial amount of employment in this country. They are not to include any munitions of war. The Export Credits Guarantee Department has agreed to make arrangements which will enable the Soviet Government to pay cash for all these orders. From time to time, the Soviet Government will issue Notes carrying interest at 5½ per cent. per annum and payable in five years.

"Whenever the Soviet require money to pay British manufacturers, they will go to the Department with a sufficient number of notes for the transaction. The notes, which the Department guarantees, will probably be sold through banks and will not be negotiable on the Stock Exchange.

"The resulting money will be paid for the Soviet Government into a special account at Lloyds Bank in this country, the money in this account being used only to pay for goods manufactured in the United Kingdom. The notes, which are guaranteed 100 per cent. by the Department, will probably be used for purchases of machinery and equipment."*

There was no doubt as to how the City viewed this agreement. "There is likely to be a scramble," wrote the *Financial News* (July 31, 1936), "for the Five-Year Sterling Notes that are to be issued as a result of the Anglo-Soviet export credits agreements. . . . The Notes should make a welcome addition to the scanty array of available

* *Daily Telegraph*, 31.vii.36.

'shorts.' They will be keenly competed for by banks and discount houses."

The agreement was universally hailed as a sound and desirable business transaction. A lone Die-Hard in the *Morning Post* bewailed that "what the Conservative Party violently opposed in 1924" was considered to be "good business and policy in 1936."

On the same day, July 30, 1936, it was officially announced that the U.S.S.R. had agreed to adhere to the Three-Power Naval Treaty—between Britain, France and the U.S.A.—concluded some four months earlier in London. This Treaty concerned the size of warships and the advance exchange of information between the signatory Powers. We cannot go into the whole history of this instrument here, only to explain that representatives of Great Britain, the U.S.A., France, Japan and Italy met in London in December, 1935, with the aim of concluding a Naval Agreement. Japan withdrew in January, 1936, but the other Powers decided to continue without her. Agreement was reached in March, 1936. Italy at the time did not associate herself with the instrument. It was, of course, realised that the Treaty would be of little value without the adherence of Germany and the U.S.S.R., and the signatory Powers agreed that Great Britain should open up negotiations with these two Powers, with the object of concluding bilateral Anglo-German and Anglo-Soviet agreements similar to the London Treaty. Hence the Anglo-Soviet negotiations. Commenting on their successful termination the *Times* declared:

> "The terms of the understanding have not yet been made public; but they are understood to be such as to give ground for hope that they will facilitate the adherence of Germany to the desired agreement, and will also smooth the way towards concord in the Far East. If that hope proves well founded the Government may fairly be congratulated upon having achieved a material advance towards the elimination of naval competition throughout the world and towards some alleviation of the burden of armaments."*

Organised Labour in Britain was fully alive to the dangers of Nazi aggression and clear-sighted in its policy for dealing with this threat. The Chairman of the Trades Union Congress in his presidential address to the annual Congress, September 7, 1936, declared:

> "If the Soviet Union, France and ourselves formed a pact of non-aggression and mutual assistance based on the League Covenant and open to all, it would unquestionably preserve peace both in Europe and Asia. Such a pact would without doubt gain the adherence of the Scandinavian States, the Baltic States, the

* 31.vii.36.

Little Entente and Turkey. It should be open to all, including Germany. But if Germany, because of her aggressive policy, refused to enter, we should make it clear that our policy was to go on without Germany's co-operation to develop the system of mutual guarantee within the framework of the League and in conformity with the principles of collective security."

We think it will be generally accepted that had this commonsense advice been acted upon by the Government of the day, the second world war, with all its horrors, might never have broken out.

It is of interest to recall here that on March 4, 1936, a film record of the Red Army manœuvres at Kiev in September, 1935, was shown at the Soviet Embassy in London. The guests included the Diplomatic Corps, British Ministers and many other M.P.'s, representatives of all the British Services, as well as many other publicists and the press.

This film, for the first time in the history of the screen, demonstrated the important part which parachute troops could and would play in modern war. Unfortunately, many who saw it were little impressed at the time.

Next day, the *Times* ridiculed the film as " pervaded by artificiality." The Military Correspondent of the *Morning Post* was little impressed ; on the other hand, the *Daily Express* and the *Daily Herald* representatives realised the portent of the scenes filmed.

The *Daily Express* special representative wrote:

" A sensational film of the Soviet army manœuvres at Kiev last autumn was shown privately by the Russian Ambassador at the Soviet Embassy last night.

A series of scenes never before attempted in war—or on the screen—succeeded each other with breath-taking rapidity.

The rattle of anti-aircraft guns, the hum of giant airplanes, the scream of gas syrens and the hiss of falling bombs accompanied the scenes.

I have never seen such a striking ' shot ' as the surprise transportation by air of a whole division behind the enemy lines.

Hundreds of men jumped simultaneously from reconnaissance airplanes landing by parachute to cover the descent of the rest.

Superb photography showed machine guns and light artillery pieces dismantled and wrapped in waterproof circling through the air by parachute.

Squadron after squadron of bombers followed, landing not only thousands of troops, but also lorries, artillery, and tanks clutched to the fuselage between the landing wheels.

Within a few minutes the whole division—Lewis gunners,

> machine gunners, mechanised troops, artillery and tanks—rushed into action, attacking the enemy in the rear.
>
> The fondness of the Russian commander, Marshal Voroshilov, for Cossack cavalry struck the only old-fashioned note in a super modern panorama of war."*

At the conclusion, Mr. Hannen Swaffer, who was much impressed, asked M. Maisky, "Why do you show this? Other nations do not show official proof of their armed power." The Soviet Ambassador replied: "Why shouldn't we? We have no intention of attacking anybody. On the other hand, we show that, if we are attacked, we are ready."

How the representatives of the Services as a whole were impressed we cannot say, but next day in the Members' smoke room of the House of Commons, one soldier-politician who had been present at the Embassy and who claimed to have some knowledge of Russia entertained a large group of members by ridiculing the Red Army manœuvres in general and the whole idea of parachute troops playing any important part in actual warfare. He summed up his impression by asserting that the film had convinced him that the Russians were as unpractical as ever.

However, this film could not but be recalled after the German invasion of the Low Countries and the enemy occupation of Crete

When the Soviet army manœuvres took place in the second week of September, 1936, near Minsk, Great Britain was represented by Major-General A. P. Wavell, C.B., C.M.G., M.C. (then Commander of the 2nd Division at Aldershot) and a small staff. At the conclusion of the manœuvres "the Chairman of the Council of People's Commissars of White Russia gave a dinner to the Soviet leaders and the foreign delegates, at which the Czechoslovak and British representatives spoke in Russian. Major-General A. P. Wavell said he hoped in the near future to greet delegates of the Red Army in England."†

Not a big thing in itself but indicative of the friendlier feelings existing between London and Moscow. Some six weeks later it was announced that "the King has been pleased to approve the appointment of Commander (Acting Captain) H. Clanchy, R.N. as Naval Attaché to His Majesty's Embassy in the U.S.S.R., and to his Majesty's Legations in Rumania and Bulgaria, with headquarters at Moscow."‡

Commenting on this appointment the same journal added: "This is the first time that a naval attaché has been appointed to the Embassy in Soviet Russia."

That the Soviet Government was only too anxious to support Great Britain whenever the latter, albeit primarily in her own interests, faced

* 5.iii.36. † *Times*, 14.ix.36. ‡ Ibid., 22.x.36.

up to the fact that war in any part of the world, and that Fascist aggression in Spain, were vital concerns of all the peace-loving powers, was evidenced by the comments of the Soviet press on certain passages in a speech which attracted world attention at that time, delivered by the British Foreign Secretary, Mr. Eden.* The latter declared.

> "The world has now become so small—and every day with the march of science it becomes smaller—that a spark in some sphere comparatively remote from our own interests may become a conflagration sweeping a continent or hemisphere. We must, therefore, be watchful at all times and in all places. We cannot disinterest ourselves from this or that part of the world in a vague hope that happenings in that area will not affect us. We must neither mislead others nor be misled ourselves by any of those comfortable doctrines that we can live secure in a Western European glasshouse. It is for this reason that I have again and again insisted that the foreign policy of our country, with its many and comprehensive interests, must work for a comprehensive settlement. Nothing short of that will give us the peace and the confidence that we so ardently desire."†

Later in the same speech, Mr. Eden said:

> "Once again, however, the Spanish tragedy is creating grave international anxieties. Why is this? It is because the nations are not observing in the letter and in the spirit the agreement to which they came last August. . . .
>
> Let us be clear about this, if we, the nations of Europe, cannot collaborate to deal with the Spanish problem, then we shall be moving into deeper and more dangerous waters."

Izvestia commented that Mr. Eden was:

> "serving the cause of peace by dispelling the illusion that England can live in safety by hiding 'in a West European glasshouse.' He is all the more right, since by their intervention in Spain, Italy and Germany are busy laying beneath the glasshouse a mine of enormous destructive power. Even Conservative British journalists who have visited Spain have been constrained to admit that were it not for the Italian and German aid to the Franco bands, the Spanish Government would long ago have put an end to the rebellion. When the landing of German and Italian troops on Spanish soil began England evidently became anxious.

* Mr. Eden had become Secretary of State for Foreign Affairs in December, 1935.
† *Times*, 15.xii.36.

It became clear long ago that Berlin and Rome were endeavouring to transform Spain into a vassal of their own, and that this was obviously a menace to the vital interests of Britain in the Mediterranean Sea and formed an equal menace to France. And if Mr. Eden twice in his speech emphasises 'the profound interest' of Britain in the preservation 'of the integrity of Spain and Spanish possessions' then he evidently has in mind the aggressive policy of conquest pursued by Germany and Italy in Spain. Mr. Eden warns Berlin and Rome against this policy.

For a number of years leading political circles in Britain carried out a policy which in fact signified that the best means of safeguarding the inviolability of the fire-proof safe was—to give the key of it to the safe-breaker. Obviously at the present moment, as a result of the pressure of events, they are beginning to realise that such methods are hardly of any advantage. In the meantime we must wait and see what concrete and practical deductions will be made by Britain from this, indeed belated, but nevertheless still valuable recognition."*

These remarks were not only comments, they constituted an offer to Britain of closer collaboration for the maintenance of world peace, but there was no response from London. The Soviet Government, as so often in the past, stretched out its hand, but the hand was left hanging in the air.

IV. The Spanish Civil War and Non-Intervention

It will be as well to pause here to consider very briefly the struggle in Spain, 1936-1939, and the proceedings of the Committee for so-called Non-Intervention in Spain, the more so since it forms a typical example of the perfidy of the Fascist Powers and the short-sightedness, weakness and complacency, if not worse, of the then British and French Governments.

It will be recalled that in February, 1936, a Radical Republican Government had been formed after elections in which the Popular Front parties (Republicans, Socialists and Communists) had obtained a majority. The Fascists, however, were not prepared to accept the verdict of the electorate and after careful preparation, on July 18, 1936, staged a military revolt in a number of garrison towns in Spain and in Spanish Morocco. (The command of the army it should be observed had been left by the Republican Government in the hands of the old Generals and officers.) At that time the Spanish people wholeheartedly supported the Republican Government, but the latter was desperately short of arms and it is to the undying shame of the

* *Izvestia*, 16.xii.36.

French Popular Front Government that on July 25, 1936, it decided to prohibit the export of arms to the legal Government of Spain, thus breaking an existing agreement whereby France had undertaken to supply war materials to Spain.

On the other hand there was no doubt at all, even at that time, that Germany and Italy were freely supplying the rebels with arms. The French Government, however, were naturally not anxious for a Fascist victory in Spain ; accordingly on their initiative and after much delay caused by the tactics of Italy, Germany and Portugal, an agreement was reached at the end of August, 1936, whereby Britain, France, U.S.S.R., Germany, Italy and Portugal agreed to prohibit the export of arms to either side in Spain. It is this August agreement to which Mr. Eden refers in the above quotation from his speech. Later, other States also adhered to this agreement and a Committee was formed for the application of the Non-Intervention agreement.

Although an agreement to withhold arms from both sides was obviously unfair to the Spanish Government, since by international law they had the right to purchase arms abroad, whereas rebels had no such right, nevertheless, in view of the then nature of the Governments of the various Powers, there was something to be said for the advisability of such an agreement since its loyal acceptance and execution by all Governments would have avoided the danger of international complications and would have left the Spanish people to find their own solution of their difficulties.

However, Germany and Italy (as well as Portugal) had no intention of letting down their friend Franco and his Fascist followers. Whilst the Non-Intervention Committee engaged in interminable discussions and France and Britain meticulously carried out the pledge to prohibit the export of arms to Spain, the Fascist Powers not only did everything possible to impede the work of the Committee, but continued without pause to send planes, munitions and men to Franco.

At length the Soviet delegates to the Committee lost patience and on October 7, 1936, announced that unless the Committee did something effective to stop intervention by Italy, Germany and Portugal, the U.S.S.R. would leave the Committee and resume complete freedom of action, and M. Kagan, who in the absence of M. Maisky headed the Soviet delegation, after drawing attention to the numerous cases of violation of the Non-Intervention Agreement by the Fascist Powers declared:

> " The Soviet Government can under no circumstances agree to convert the Non-Intervention Agreement into a screen covering military aid to the insurgents from certain participants of the agreement, against the lawful Spanish Government. The Soviet

Government is, therefore, obliged to declare that unless the violations of the Non-Intervention Agreement are immediately discontinued it will consider itself free from the obligations arising out of the agreement."

Two days later, M. Kagan proposed: "That an impartial committee shall be sent to the Spanish-Portuguese frontier to ascertain the true state of affairs there; and that, after reporting, the committee shall leave on the frontier a permanent sub-committee to keep watch."

Further, at a later date, the Soviet representative made an urgent appeal to the Chairman of the Committee, Lord Plymouth, to convene it without delay in order that an effective control might be established over the ports through which arms were imported into Spain.

The reaction of the Committee was characteristic; all it did was to request the remarks of Italy, Germany and Portugal on the Soviet allegations. The *Daily Herald* demanded that the British Government should support the Soviet proposals, but other journals, notably the *Times* attacked the proposals on the ground that they might alienate Portugal from taking part in the proceedings of the Committee!

It goes without saying that the German, Italian and Portuguese Governments hotly denied the accusations against them and in spite of a masterly analysis by M. Maisky proving how baseless and illogical were these denials, the Committee acepted them and Franco continued to receive enormous quantities of planes, tanks, guns and other ammunition. Finally, at the session of the Committee on October 28, 1936, M. Maisky, on behalf of his Government, declared:

"The Soviet Government adhered to the declaration regarding non-intervention presuming equal obligations for all the participants of the Agreement. The violation of the obligations even by one of the participants of the Agreement relieves also the other participants of the obligations.

The Soviet Government, as probably the whole world, is firmly convinced that even after the Agreement came into effect the Governments sympathising with the objects and aims of the Spanish rebel generals continued abundantly to supply them with military aeroplanes, tanks, artillery, machine-guns, rifles, munitions and other war materials.

The proceedings of the Committee have convinced the Soviet Government that at present there are no guarantees against further supplies to the rebel generals of war materials. In these circumstances the Soviet Government is of the opinion that until such guarantees are created, and an effective control over the strict fulfilment of the obligations regarding non-intervention established, those Governments who consider supplying the legitimate Spanish Government as conforming to international law, international order and international justice are morally entitled not to consider themselves more bound by the Agreement than those Governments who supply the rebels in contravention of the Agreement."

M. Maisky stressed the need to discuss immediately proposals for establishing control on the Spanish land frontiers and ports and concluded:

"My Government earnestly desires to effect the real enforcement of the Non-Intervention Agreement and the best proof of this is our agreement to the establishment of complete control over the importation of arms and munitions into Spain. Only by framing and enforcing adequate measures to carry out such effective control can this Committee justify its existence."

The sessions of the Committee dragged on until at last, on November 12, 1936, it drafted a tentative agreement for a measure of supervision to secure the application of the Agreement on Non-Intervention.

Italy, Germany and Portugal did everything possible to delay the definite application of the decision and in the meantime, on November 18, Italy and Germany gave *de jure* recognition to Franco as the legal Government of Spain! Britain did not go so far, but the British Government refused to recognise either side as belligerents and Mr. Eden stated that Britain would regard any search of British ships outside the three-mile limit as an act of piracy—this, of course, signified that within Spanish waters British ships could be bombed and sunk with impunity and Franco, using German and Italian planes, took full advantage of this hint. Moreover, in their eagerness to appease the Fascists, the British Government, again without laying down any conditions, hastened to announce their continued neutrality, irrespective of the policy pursued by the Fascist Powers, and early in December, 1936, a Bill was passed making illegal the carrying of arms to Spain.

Of one thing the British and French Governments were not quite so sparing—gestures which did nothing to impede the Fascists and rendered no benefit to the Spanish Government. Thus, in December, 1936, as if sublimely unconscious that one-sided intervention was already a fact, the French and British Governments made an appeal to Germany, Italy, Portugal and the U.S.S.R., to renounce all action which might lead to foreign intervention in Spain! They also suggested co-operation in offering mediation to the two sides. This suggestion came to nothing as Germany and Italy made it perfectly clear that they would have nothing to do with any Spanish Government other than the Franco Government.

Very characteristic too was the way the question of volunteers was dealt with. At the outbreak of the Spanish rebellion, genuine volunteers from France, Britain and other countries had rallied to the Spanish Republican Government. On the other hand, Italy and Germany sent not driblets, but thousands upon thousands of conscripted soldiers to aid Franco. By the end of December, 1936, the flow of men to Franco Spain was such that it could no longer be passed over. The Non-Intervention Committee discussed the subject, but before any decision had been made, the British Government already took steps (January 10, 1937) to prevent the departure of volunteers to Spain from Britain.

The Committee itself after much haggling passed a resolution providing for the prohibition of recruitment and departure of volunteers for Spain as from February 20 and for the coming into force of a system of supervision by March 6, 1937. Actually, the observers who were to carry out the supervision did not start their duties till the second half of April. Not that this mattered a great deal, for not only were the observers given no right of search or detention, but the control left so many gaps that both supplies and men for the rebels continued to pour into Spain. But Germany and Italy regarded even this emasculated control as irksome, and using as a pretext the alleged firing of torpedoes by a Spanish Government submarine on a German cruiser (which by the way was not even hit) off Oran, the German Government, amongst other things, demanded the impounding in a neutral port of all the Spanish Government submarines and a joint naval demonstration by Germany, Italy, Britain and France, and when the Governments of the two latter refused these monstrous demands, Germany and Italy withdrew from the International Naval Patrol.

France and Britain, with the support of the U.S.S.R. and other Governments, proposed to take over the zones vacated by the two Fascist Powers, but Germany and Italy opposed and there ensued interminable discussions in the Non-Intervention Committee as to new systems of control, the withdrawal of volunteers, the granting of belligerent rights to both sides in Spain, etc., etc. The latter point was particularly stressed by the Italian, German and Portuguese representatives and was accepted conditionally by the British Government who suggested a plan, the substance of which was that instead of the Naval Patrol system, international observers should be placed in Spanish ports to carry out the duties previously performed by the Naval Patrol system ; that a Commission be sent to Spain to supervise the withdrawal of volunteers; and that belligerent rights be granted to both parties when "the Non-Intervention Committee place on record their opinion that the arrangements for the withdrawal of foreign nationals are working satisfactorily and that this withdrawal has in fact made substantial progress."

Labour leaders in the House of Commons and in the country denounced the proposal to grant belligerent rights to mutinous officers as "outrageous." M. Maisky on the Non-Intervention Committee also insisted that it would be contrary to tradition and law to grant belligerent rights to the Spanish insurgents, and on August 6, 1937, he put the following pertinent question to the representatives of Germany, Italy and Portugal: "Were they prepared to state that their Governments agreed unconditionally to the withdrawal of all volunteers from Spain? Volunteers are the heart of the British Plan, and it is a question to which I must have an answer." But, of course, there was no answer.

Having got away with it so far, the Fascists took another step forward—their submarines, disguising their identity, began early in August, 1937, to attack merchant vessels in the Mediterranean indiscriminately without warning, even when bound for non-Spanish ports. This was too much; even the *Daily Mail* which was certainly no friend of the Spanish Republican Government, demanded that steps be taken to "unveil the identity of these marauding submarines" and to "track them down,"* and the Diplomatic Correspondent of the *Daily Telegraph*, on the following day, declared: "There is no doubt in the minds of Ministers regarding the situation in the Mediterranean. Signor Mussolini's declaration that he 'will not tolerate Bolshevism or anything like it' on the shores of the Mediterranean may perhaps be followed by an Anglo-French resolve not to tolerate piracy or anything like it upon Mediterranean waters."

Accordingly it was decided to hold a Conference at Nyon to devise ways and means for combating the submarine menace in the Mediterranean. This Conference acted with commendable speed, the reason for this being the absence from it of Italy and Germany. All the Mediterranean Powers except Spain and all the Black Sea Powers, as well as Germany, had been invited. The exclusion of Spain which was the Power most interested in the subject and the invitation to Germany, which was neither a Mediterranean nor Black Sea Power, was strongly condemned by the U.S.S.R. But anyway, Italy and Germany refused the invitation, no doubt imagining that without them the Conference would not be held or might be postponed indefinitely —the pretext for their abstention was a strong note of protest which the Soviet Government had sent to Italy.

* 2.ix.37.

Brushing aside the make believe " mysterious " nature of the submarines, the Soviet Government roundly accused Italy of these acts of piracy. The obstructionist Powers being absent, the Nyon Conference met on September 10, 1937, and by the evening of September 11, an " Arrangement " (as the agreement was officially designated) was concluded, which made clear that no belligerent rights were conceded to either side in Spain and provided that the naval forces of the participating Powers would counteract, and if possible, destroy, any submarine which attacked (contrary to the rules of international law as laid down by the London Naval Treaty of 1930) merchant ships not belonging to either party of the Spanish conflict, as well as for the policing of the high seas of the Mediterranean by the British and French fleets.

In his closing speech at the Nyon Conference, M. Litvinov, drawing attention to some of the weak points of the Arrangement said:

> " I am particularly glad that the Conference took our observations into account and registered in the agreement, in a form permitting of no misinterpretation, the refusal to recognise that any one enjoys belligerent rights and consequently the right to stop commercial vessels on the high seas, still less to sink them. We desire, it is true, that all such illegalities should be immediately penalized, even though the regulations laid down by international conventions intended for war-time might be observed. The reply made to me was that there could not be the same punishment for a thief and a murderer—that, as a matter of fact, the sinking of commercial vessels by submarines was in practice impossible if these rules were observed, and that if, nevertheless, piracy did not cease in spite of the present agreement, further measures would be discussd.
>
> I am prepared to be satisfied by this reply for the moment. I regret that in spite of our opposition the commercial vessels of the Spanish Government have been excluded from the scope of the protection scheme because, as it was explained to me, such protection might be interpreted as intervention in the Spanish conflict.
>
> In order not to complicate the work of the Conference I abstained from comparing this scrupulousness with the methods of non-intervention practised by other States not represented here."

He concluded: " At a time when aggression, international lawlessness, adventurist impudence have been accustomed to success, any action combating these phenomena which takes the form not merely of discussion, protests, and declarations but of practical steps must be particularly welcomed, while to-day we have before us an international agreement with very material backing."

Later Italy tried to hold up the Arrangement by expressing her desire to discuss participation in the scheme. But once again the other Powers adopted a take it or leave it attitude which paid. The scheme was put into force immediately, the submarine attacks in the Mediterranean ceased and subsequently Italy participated in the patrolling of the Mediterranean trade routes.

Unfortunately, on every other question appeasement of the Fascist Powers was the order of the day—interminable discussion took place on withdrawal of volunteers, the patrol of Spanish ports and the granting of belligerent rights to both sides in Spain. Plan followed plan, but it was as clear as day that the Italian and German Governments were merely using the Non-Intervention Committee to cover up their own active intervention on behalf of Franco. As M. Maisky said during the session of the Committee, October 16, 1937:

> "Non-intervention was from the very beginning violated by certain Powers, but lately, especially during the last six or seven months, it has become a complete farce. Violations of non-intervention have finally reached such dimensions and have acquired such a flagrant nature that they have become an international scandal of the first magnitude."

At session after session the Soviet delegates protested against the obstructionist tactics of the German and Italian Governments and demanded positive acts to stop the one-sided intervention—but it was in vain. Let us give but two examples. When the question of the withdrawal of volunteers was raised, the Soviet Government had insisted that this should take place by categories and that the Italians and Germans should be precluded from withdrawing their infantry which was least valuable to Franco and leaving intact their aviation, artillery, tank and similar forces. This proposal was at first adopted unanimously by the Committee but subsequently the Italian and German Governments raised objections and at the session of the Non-Intervention Committee, March 31, 1938, the Chairman, Lord Plymouth, on behalf of Britain agreed to a "compromise," viz., that withdrawal should not be necessarily by categories!

Again, when early in 1938, Franco's, or rather Italian and German, planes repeatedly bombed British ships carrying food and other *non*-military supplies to Republican Spain, the British Government abstained from action. Mr. Chamberlain, in the House of Commons, declared with fatuous innocence:

> "It is not a nice thing to hear of British ships being attacked

in port. As far as I know there is no foundation for any suggestion that these ships have been carrying arms or munitions. They have, of course, been carrying food, coal, oil and other stores which are of value in carrying on the war, and no doubt that is the reason why they are being attacked. We do not admit the right of General Franco or anybody else to attack these ships. What we say is that we do not believe any practical means of preventing it, without adopting a policy which would be completely at variance with that which we believe to be in the true interests of this country, has been found."*

British public opinion was incensed but there can be little doubt that in Italy and Germany the Governments heaved a sigh of relief. Thus, referring to this and later statements by Mr. Chamberlain in the House of Commons on the same subject, the *Times* Rome correspondent stated:

> "The impression one has here is that Signor Mussolini is anxious that General Franco should use to the full the advantage which his superiority in the air confers on him; that he had a moment of doubt whether British public opinion might not compel Mr. Chamberlain to take active measures to protect British ships from bombardment in Spanish territorial waters, but *now that that doubt is removed, Signor Mussolini intends that the advantage shall be pressed to the utmost.*"† (Our italics).

The activities or rather the futilities of the Non-Intervention Committee were very well summed up by the Soviet delegate in his speech at the meeting of the Sub-Committee, June 28, 1938:

> "Scarcely any important decisions of the Committee survived and were not changed or annulled at the insistence of the interventionist Powers. . . .
>
> What was the fate of the comprehensive sea and land control scheme which was brought into force on April 9, 1937? Hardly a few months had elapsed before the interventionist Powers, by deliberate action, created a situation calculated to explode the sea part of the observation scheme, and the Committee, instead of frustrating this attempt acquiesced, and by abolishing the naval patrol rendered the sea observation scheme absolutely worthless, thus creating the circumstances desired by the interventionist Powers which they have exploited to the full to supply General Franco with vast quantities of arms and troops.
>
> What was the fate of the British Plan which was unanimously adopted by all the participating Governments on November 4,

* *Hansard*, 21.vi.38, col. 941. † 28.vi.38.

1937? Hardly a few weeks passed when, under pressure of the interventionist Powers, one after another of the major component parts of the Plan began to be changed and emasculated: the proposal about observers in Spanish ports to replace the naval patrol was completely dropped and an innocuous paragraph inserted, very convenient for the interventionist Powers from the point of view of continuing or even increasing their intervention in Spain; the decision about the date of restoration of land control was, under pressure of the interventionist Powers, completely changed and advanced to suit their designs; the decision about the counting and evacuation of the 'volunteers' by categories was not to the liking of the interventionist Powers and the Committee, with a speed deserving a better cause, hastened to suggest the abolition of categories. . . ."

And in a speech at Leningrad, June 25, M. Litvinov put the Soviet position on the subject thus:

"From the very outset we did not have excessive faith in the signatures of the Fascist countries which openly mock at paper obligations and treaties, and hence we introduced into the Committee a proposal to guarantee effective control with the help of the French and British navies. I am convinced that the adoption of our proposal would not only have put an end to the war in Spain, without arousing any international complications, but would have brought a shattering defeat to the given aggression and to aggression in general.

Unfortunately, those States whose interests, as I have pointed out before, are most threatened by the Italo-German intervention in Spain, preferred the tactics of conniving with the aggressors, and took the course of endless concessions to them. The aggressors do not wish such a control, then such a control is cancelled; they propose another system of control more advantageous to them, and this system is adopted. They demand the rights of a belligerent for Franco, and these rights are promised to him.

Under such conditions the Committee not only did not in the slightest degree succeed in ensuring non-intervention but it is listing more and more to Franco's side. Our rôle in the Committee now resolves itself to attempts to straightening out this list to the best of our ability and as far as possible, and at least to prevent the intervention of the Committee itself in Spanish affairs on Franco's behalf."

The Spanish Republican Government also raised the question of the cessation of intervention in Spain at the League of Nations—but so far as practical results were concerned they fared no better. Speaking at the session of the Political Committee of the League, September 29, 1938, M. Litvinov, *inter alia*, said:

> "If the Non-Intervention Committee had anything to boast of, it was that it had genuinely interfered with the supplies for the legitimate Republican army and with the provision of food for the civil population in the territory occupied by the latter. The sea routes to rebel territory were controlled by no one, and the rebels and interventionists could and did receive all that they required by those and other routes, whereas most of the sea routes to Republican Spain were blockaded and the solitary land frontier was closed. The London Committee had throughout displayed an inclination to meet every possible demand of the rebels and the States which supported them, ignoring the interests of the Republicans, and how far might it not have gone along that road if the Soviet brake had not been applied in the Committee?"

With every day of the existence of the Non-Intervention Committee two things became more and more clear:

(1), that the Italian and German Governments were bent on using it as a blind for covering their active intervention in Spain on behalf of the insurgents. True, this was always hotly denied by their representatives on the Committee, but the Italian press frequently boasted of Italian help to Franco. Thus, the *Popolo d'Italia*, June 26, 1937, said: "In this great fight, which has brought face to face two types of civilization and two conceptions of the world, Fascist Italy has not been neutral, but has fought, and victory will also be hers." And when Santander fell, August 26, 1937, the Italian press and Mussolini himself hailed it openly as an Italian victory.

The Italian press published the names of the ten Italian Generals who directed the fighting before Santander, and Mussolini in reply to a wire sent to him by Franco, declared: "I am particularly proud that the Italian Legionaries have, during ten days of hard fighting, contributed mightily to the splendid victory of Santander, and that their contribution receives coveted recognition in your telegram."*

Finally, when as a result of Italian and German might of arms the Spanish Republican Government fell and Franco, on February 21, 1939, staged a triumphant review of his army in Barcelona, pride of place was given to the Italian Commander, General Gamberra, who, with his Italian Legionary Army Corps, was at the head of the parade.

(2), that the British and French Governments steadily refused to

* *Times*, 28.viii.37.

align themselves with the U.S.S.R. against the Fascist Powers. And that the British Government did so with their eyes open, that they knew and understood Italy's game, was made unequivocally clear by a statement made by Lord Halifax:

> "It has never been true, and it is not true to-day, that the Anglo-Italian Agreement had the lever value that some think to make Italy desist from supporting General Franco and his fortunes. *Signor Mussolini has always made it plain from the time of the first conversations between His Majesty's Government and the Italian Government that, for reasons known to us all—he was not prepared to see General Franco defeated.*"* (Our italics).

It should be stated here that an Anglo-Italian Agreement, the origin of which we discuss in the next Chapter, had been concluded early in 1938, but its ratification by Britain was made dependent on a settlement of the Spanish question. However, without waiting for any real settlement and relying on various promises by Mussolini, the Agreement was actually ratified by the Chamberlain Government, November 16, 1938.

To sum up the whole subject we would quote what we ourselves wrote in 1939 after analysing the work of the Non-Intervention Committee: "Throughout the whole sorry business of 'non-intervention,' the U.S.S.R. fought hard for fair play for the Spanish Republican Government. Unfortunately for the most part they found very few supporters in the Committee. It may be asked, why did the U.S.S.R. join in the farce of the Non-Intervention Committee? The reason is clear enough. In the first place, had she kept out the whole blame for the failure of the policy of non-intervention would have been thrown on the refusal of the Soviet Government to co-operate. Secondly, by her presence on the Committee, she did assure that the Spanish Government had one friendly voice to speak for it, she made the task of the direct interventionists at least somewhat more difficult, and was able to secure greater publicity for the nefarious acts and the condonation of these acts by other Powers."†

In conclusion we would add that the policy pursued by the British Government in the Non-Intervention Committee left a strong suspicion in the minds of the Soviet Government that the Chamberlain Government was pro-Fascist at heart, a suspicion which made itself felt during the Anglo-French-Soviet negotiations of 1939.

But to return to our narrative.

* *House of Lords Report*, 3.xi.38, col. 1628.

† "World Affairs and the U.S.S.R." by W. P. and Zelda K. Coates. Lawrence& Wishart, Ltd., London.

V. 1937—January–May. Coronation of George VI. Naval Agreement signed. Scottish Congress of Peace and Friendship with the U.S.S.R.

Although when the year 1937 dawned, Anglo-Soviet relations were normal, that is to say, no one ever even mooted the idea of severing diplomatic relations, nevertheless, certain small groups existed in this country who endeavoured to prevent relations between the two capitals from becoming cordial. For instance, the Archbishop of Canterbury, in a broadcast discussion, denounced the "aggressive atheism" of Moscow, and its "anti-Christian doctrine" of class struggle. However, the Archbishop added that there was a "more insidious menace" in the Reich and Italy where "even in the name of religion the idols of Race and State are usurping the supremacy of Christ."

Sir Arthur Page went one further: In the columns of the *Times* he wrote:

> "On September 17, 1934, the British Government 'cordially welcomed' the admission of the Soviet Union to the League of Nations. Is it fortuitous or a mere inconsequence that since the declaration of friendship our foreign relations have become progressively unstable and involved? There are some offences that a Christian nation is not at liberty to condone.
>
> I state at once a fundamental and a platitude when I protest that Christians and anti-Christ go ill together; and if they join hands which of the two will suffer? To thoughful men there can be but one answer. 'Is it nothing to you all ye that pass by.'"*

Sir Arthur's absurdities were subjected to a devastating analysis and crushing attack by Mr. A. J. Cummings. He wrote:

> "If he (Sir Arthur Page) could lift his gaze for a moment from the repulsive spectacle of godless Russia and look a good deal closer home he might discover a much more real and obvious explanation of the deplorable breakdown of our foreign policy.
>
> It is a sufficient commentary on his distorted vision that the nation from which he recoils in horror is one of the few great Powers, if not the only one, which, in these last two or three perilous years, has pursued steadfastly the cause of peace and collective security through the League—the cause to which eleven million British Christians (of whom, I hope, Sir Arthur Page was one) pledged their names a year ago.
>
> It was not 'godless' Russia but Christian Italy which broke its solemn word and murdered a helpless fellow member of the League.

* 6.i.37.

It is not 'godless' Russia, but a still normally Christian Germany which threatens the peace of Europe to-day.

And it is the money of the priests, supported by the Christian Governments of Berlin and Rome, which has helped to inspire and prolong the bloody rebellion in Spain against the people's Government."*

An obscure body, the Anti-Socialist Union, opened an Anti-Communist Exhibition in the Dorland Hall, London, February 2, 1937, which apparently was aimed mainly at the U.S.S.R. The absurdities to which the promoters went were aptly described by a representative of the *News Chronicle*, who visited this exhibition. He wrote:

"Prominent among the arch-Communists mentioned are my colleague, A. J. Cummings, and Miss Eleanor Rathbone, M.P.!

It would seem that anyone who by any chance wrote a word for a non-Tory paper or spoke from a 'suspect' platform is qualified for appearance in the All-Red Gallery.

Spanish atrocities are specially on view—all done by the Government, of course: Franco and his Moors never appear. Half of the exhibition is devoted to Red sacrilege.

The whole thing is so fantastic and palpably ludicrous that none save the Die-Hard will be moved. The Communists will 'laff and laff and laff' and possibly make converts.

Intelligent people will look on sadly and wonder that such things could be in 1937."†

The *News Chronicle's* strictures were not too severe; subsequently the venture was scarcely mentioned even in the press of the extreme Right, and a few weeks later "it folded its tent like the Arab and silently crept away."

Other quarters pursued their vendetta against the U.S.S.R. by trying to prevent the truth about that country being broadcast. For instance, Professor John Hilton, in a wireless talk to British school children, February 9, 1937, told them some well authenticated truths about the U.S.S.R. He declared that in the Soviet Union unemployment had been abolished, that every citizen had the right to work, leisure and education. That women have the same rights as men, and that no one can be ill-treated because of his race. The *Daily Mail* was furious. In a column headed "Schools Hear Soviet Praised," it accused the B.B.C. of "Left-bias" and of "spreading Soviet propaganda through its curriculum to schools."

When the matter was raised in the House of Commons, the Postmaster-General had no difficulty in convincing the members that the

* *News Chronicle*, 9.i.37. † 2.ii.37.

B.B.C. in this matter "maintained a fair balance between conflicting points of view."

Another attempt was made by the Soviet Government to warn and rally peace-loving Powers against the growing Nazi menace. A "prominent Soviet personality," in an informal talk in Moscow, March 11, 1937, declared:

> "Britain holds the key to Europe's peace. Nothing can stop Hitler except collective action, and that depends primarily on Britain.
>
> Recent declarations and moves by Roosevelt—the Neutrality Bill, for instance—were only encouraging Hitler because they were based on individual action.
>
> 'It is high time a peace conference was called,' he added. 'In a year or two it may be too late.'"*

Turning to possible Soviet aid for France, he added:

> "Should the Spanish events be re-enacted in France, and German troops crossed the French border to help the Fascists, the Red Army would go to the assistance of France without hesitation."

Unfortunately, this warning and offer of co-operation, like so many others, was passed unheeded by the Chancelleries to which it was addressed.

Whilst endeavouring to strengthen the policy of Collective Security abroad, the Soviet Government was also applying its energies to strengthening its frontiers at home.

Meanwhile, certain developments within the frontiers of the U.S.S.R. attracted attention abroad. Sir Josiah Stamp, speaking at Leeds, April 7, 1937, stated:

> "One of the most far-reaching, economic changes in the world was the emergence of Russia into a really prominent position as a gold producer.
>
> Since the weird psychology of the world was still ready to regard gold as its most precious thing, Russia now had something which enabled her to dispense largely with intense export methods, for she could buy nearly all she wanted with her own gold."†

A few days later, the *Daily Telegraph* reported:

> "Negotiations between the London bullion market and the Soviet have been successfully concluded by which Russian gold bars will now be accepted in London as good delivery. This

* *News Chronicle*, 12.iii.37. † *Daily Telegraph*, 9.iv.37.

arrangement is of some importance, for among other implications it means that gold coming from Russia need not be shipped to the U.S.A., since it will accord with the specifications required in London. . . .

It is one of the conditions of dealing in gold that the buyer cannot stipulate for any particular type of bars. Now Russian gold bars with their mint mark can circulate from hand to hand."*

The Soviet Union was attaining equal success in the sphere of culture. The *Times*, April 14, 1937, recorded:

"An international contest in violin playing, organised in memory of Ysaye, has recently been held in Brussels. Of seven awards, five went to Russians. These five young people, four of them still in their teens, played to a private gathering at the Russian Embassy on Monday night. It was immediately apparent that all are remarkably gifted, and all should, with reasonable luck, make their mark in the world. All played on first-rate instruments, and all commanded a splendid tone, though naturally of varying types. It seemed impossible for them to play out of tune even, either in the most far-fetched double-stops or in the technical intricacies contrived by virtuoso composers."

Soviet musicians have also won honours at other international contests.

The imaginary uncouth, unwashed, long-bearded Bolshevik incapable of appreciating the fine arts, had now been banished to the dusty files of old newspapers.

The Soviet Commissar for Foreign Affairs, M. Litvinov, arrived in London, May 9, 1937, as leader of the Soviet delegation attending the coronation of His Majesty, King George VI, and a few days later it was reported:

"History repeated itself last night when, for the first time for 26 years, a King and Queen were entertained at an official banquet by the Foreign Secretary in the Foreign Office.

Glittering decorations, the gleaming jewels of princesses and duchesses, the blaze of colour of the uniforms of a score of countries, were much the same as were seen in 1911, when King George V and Queen Mary were entertained by Sir Edward Grey after their coronation.

But many of the 120 guests at last night's function, at which, in accordance with tradition, Mr. and Mrs. Anthony Eden were host and hostess, represented a very different order.

* *Daily Telegraph*, 15.iv.37.

> Four places away from the Queen, in the seat which, in 1911 was occupied by a member of the Imperial House of Russia, sat M. Maxim Litvinov, People's Commissar for Foreign Affairs of the Union of Soviet Socialist Republics."*

And the Soviet Navy was naturally represented at the review at Spithead. The "Naval Correspondent" of the *Manchester Guardian* describing the event, wrote:

> "The King's passage along the line of foreign ships on his way back to the eastern end of Spithead was particularly interesting because of the differences in the way each nation greeted him. All played the British National Anthem, of course. Some were content with one verse, as is our custom; some went solemnly through it three times. Some played it before they cheered, some afterwards.
>
> The cheering differed but slightly from our own methods. The Japanese, for example, shouted 'Hurrah!' three times and did not shout 'Banzai!' The roar from the *Graf Spee* might have been either 'Hoch' or 'Hurrah!' One could not tell.
>
> The most noticeable of all the cheers came from the Russian ship. It was not given in three roars but in a continuous ripple, as though the cheers were taken up by division after division from the bow to the stern and then started again in the bows. It was curiously effective as it swept across the water. The American *New York* gave the 'Ra, ra, ra' of the American universities."†

However, that was not the only episode in connection with the Soviet battleship *Marat*, which attracted favourable comment:

> "The Russian battleship which attended the Coronation Review of 1911, took 15 hours to get into position and anchor—to the vast amusement of other navies.
>
> The *Marat* anchored in 53 minutes, which is considered by naval authorities 'good going.'"‡

To complete the picture, we would add that during the stay of the Soviet sailors in this country not a single one was apprehended for drunkenness or any other form of unseemly conduct.

During 1937, there was much talk of an ideological war, and it is very instructive that even the *Times*, whose practice not so long ago had always been to place home and foreign affairs of the U.S.S.R. in the most unfavourable light, admitted that: "The desire to line

* *Daily Herald*, 15.v.37. † *Manchester Guardian*, 21.v.37.
‡ *News Chronicle*, 24.v.37.

up against one another the conflicting ideologies of contemporary Europe, belongs entirely to Herr Hitler, not to M. Stalin."*

Meanwhile, negotiations which presented considerable difficulties had been proceeding in London between representatives of Great Britain and the U.S.S.R., and Great Britain and Germany, for naval limitation agreements. The instruments which were finally signed, July 17, 1937, were based on the London Naval Agreement of 1936, but with some important modifications. These were explained by the "Naval Correspondent" of the *Manchester Guardian* thus:

> "The Soviet Government reserves to itself complete freedom of action with regard to its Far Eastern forces so long as Japan is not a signatory to limitation treaties. Thus Russia is not bound under the new agreement to disclose what ships she is building in Far Eastern yards for use in those waters, nor need she disclose particulars of their design. But if any of those ships is transferred to European waters, then Russia must inform the British Government of the details of the design.
>
> Moreover, Russia can build ships in the Far East that do not conform to the 1936 treaty limitations without giving any particulars of the design, though she must inform Britain that she is doing so, and such ships may only be retained in the Far East and cannot be sent to other waters."†

As regards the size of guns, the correspondent continued:

> "It became known some time ago that in preparing the new agreements, a difficulty had arisen about the size of the guns to be mounted in the Russian cruisers. Russian armament makers could not supply a 6-in. gun; their pattern was 7.1 in., and vessels ordered for the Soviet navy were designed for guns of that calibre. Treaty requirements were for nothing bigger than 6 in., and Germany was disinclined to agree to any deviation."

However, the deadlock was surmounted:

> "The difficulty has been overcome with some ingenuity. Russia is allowed her 7.1-in. guns and Germany is given the right, if she desires to exercise it, to lay down two more 8-in. gun cruisers, though for the present, in order not to disturb the cruiser holiday among the big Powers, she does not propose to do so. This means, in effect, that if Germany does bring her total of 8-in. gun cruisers up from three to five, no one can say that she has broken the 'holiday' and endangered all the agreements."‡

* 7.vii.37. † 19.vii.37. ‡ *Manchester Guardian*, 19.vii.37.

Two functions, among others, held in the winter of 1937, testified to a better understanding in this country of the U.S.S.R. and its importance as a great world Power. The first was the Scottish Congress of Peace and Friendship with the U.S.S.R. held in Edinburgh, November 6 and 7, 1937, and attended by "274 delegates representing 121 organisations, of which 12 included the Scottish Trades Union Congress and Town Councils, and the others represented over 497,000 people."* The speakers included the Duchess of Atholl, M.P., Mr. J. Westwood, M.P., Mr. Neil Maclean, M.P., Professor Talbot Rice, Sir Robert Greig, etc., etc. Of the many excellent speeches delivered, the one which attracted most attention came from the former stern critic of the Soviets, the Duchess of Atholl. Her Grace declared:

> "Anyone, therefore, trying to be impartial and trying to examine the facts, was obliged to admit that Russia had given definite and substantial proofs of her desire for peace, and of her readiness to co-operate with other countries to that end. . . .
>
> It was a great mistake to imagine that under a system of collective defence we should only give help and receive none. No one could minimise the great weight which could be thrown into such a system by a country with the vast man-power and natural resources of Russia—more especially in the case of a war of any duration.
>
> The path of honour with Russia is the only path to lead up to ultimate safety. Only by keeping the word we have plighted to Russia can we have any solid hope of being able to preserve that peace which we all so much desire, or if that peace be broken, of preserving the liberties which are more dear to us than peace."†

The second event was a dinner organised in London, November 24, 1937, under the joint auspices of the Anglo-Russian Parliamentary Committee and the London Trades Council. The *Daily Herald* reported:

> "Representatives of the Labour Party and the T.U.C., and scores of trade-union leaders and co-operators celebrated the twentieth birthday of the U.S.S.R. at a great London dinner last night when M. Maisky, the Soviet Ambassador, was their guest of honour."‡

Proposing the toast "The U.S.S.R. and World Peace," the Right Hon. Clement Attlee, M.P. (the then Leader of the Opposition), declared:

> "We look back and we recall our feelings when Tsardom was overthrown and instead there was a people's Government.

* *Scotsman*, 8.xi.37. † Ibid. ‡ 26.xi.37.

The remarkable thing is that the Russian Revolution should have endured. It is a miracle.

Out of chaos the Russians are building a new society based on social justice. And world peace cannot endure unless it is built on social justice.

Enemies of the Soviet Union dislike it not because they are afraid it will attack them, not because it is 'godless,' but because they are afraid lest a State should go forward based on the principle of social justice."*

Mr. H. H. Elvin, Chairman of the T.U.C. General Council, supporting the toast said:

"The Soviet Republics have done a marvellous work. They have passed from the stage of experiment to the stage of achievement. And they are playing a tremendous part in the struggle for world peace."†

Replying to the toast, M. Maisky said:

"Between the U.S.S.R. and Great Britain there is no fundamental difference of interest in any part of the world. They have one common interest—to maintain universal peace.

Let the other nations fall into line and strengthen the great Peace front.

If Tsarist Russia existed to-day, there would be a bloc of Fascist States from the Far East to the Western Mediterranean. A reign of terror would emerge triumphant over all the earth."‡

The big and representative attendance at this dinner was an added proof that organised Labour in Great Britain realised all that the success of the U.S.S.R. meant to democracy, to the working class movement, to human progress and to world peace.

CHAPTER XXIV

ANGLO-SOVIET RELATIONS IN 1938

I. Chamberlain and Appeasement. Resignation of Mr. Eden. Lord Halifax appointed Foreign Secretary

The year 1938 was a fateful and tragic year for Europe. It witnessed in March the betrayal of Austria by the League Powers and her annexation by Germany. It witnessed Mr. Neville Chamberlain's

* Ibid. † Ibid. ‡ Ibid.

meetings with Hitler at Berchtesgaden on September 15, and at Godesberg on September 22 and 23. It witnessed the meeting of Chamberlain and Daladier with Hitler and Mussolini on September 29 and 30, at Munich, where the betrayal of Czechoslovakia was consummated. All this set a series of events in motion which led inevitably to the present European war.

Although Anglo-Soviet relations were not marked by any serious direct disputes in 1938, nevertheless they were far from happy. The reason for the latter was not far to seek. As we have seen in the preceding and earlier chapters, the Chamberlain Government and a very strong section of the ruling classes in Britain, even before Mr. Chamberlain became Prime Minister, were extremely compliant towards, and some even welcomed, the rise of Fascism and Nazidom in Italy, Germany and Japan. Both within the League of Nations and outside, the British Government for the most part resolutely rejected the proposals made by the Soviet Government to organise a system of collective security which would have made aggression by the Fascist Powers a non-paying proposition.

Mr. Chamberlain himself, who had become Prime Minister and First Lord of the Treasury in May, 1937, was an appeaser of the Fascist Powers *par excellence*. He was very much influenced by certain powerful financial interests which desired close collaboration with the Fascist Powers. He detested the U.S.S.R. and all it stood for, he could not understand that a country with a constitution and Government so different from the British and other capitalist countries could possibly expect to be treated as an equal. On the other hand, he undoubtedly ardently desired to maintain peace, or if this was impossible, at least to keep Britain from being involved.

He himself had been a successful business man and found in that sphere that much could be done by personal contact, and without understanding the fundamental difference distinguishing relations between private business firms and relations between countries, he sought with a sublime confidence born of ignorance of the subject to conduct foreign affairs in the same way as he had conducted his private business affairs. Now personal contacts and a certain amount of give and take between statesmen undoubtedly have their place in foreign relations—but this is not a substitute for understanding of historical and world affairs and it was this understanding which Mr. Neville Chamberlain entirely lacked. He thought by making concessions he could appease the hungry wolves of Fascism, or if their appetites should continue to grow in spite of all the chunks thrown to them—Manchuria, militarisation of the Rhineland, Austria, Albania, Abyssinia, Spain, Czechoslovakia, etc.—then out of gratitude to Britain and France the wolves would turn East and devour the U.S.S.R. which in any case he would regard as a good riddance, whilst Britain would enjoy all the blessings of peace. And it was to this end that Chamberlain and his anti-Soviet and pro-Fascist supporters both within and outside the Government bent all their energies in the sphere of foreign affairs.

In this policy he was opposed by the Labour Movement, the vast majority of the Liberal Party and by his own Foreign Secretary, Mr. Eden, who had a wide following among the younger and more progressive Conservatives. Mr. Eden, whilst perhaps lacking that strength of character and firm insistence on his own line which would have made him a really great Secretary of State for Foreign Affairs, nevertheless did have a real grasp of the realities of world affairs in which he was keenly interested. After having served as Under-Secretary of State for Foreign Affairs between August, 1931, and December, 1933, he became Lord Privy Seal in January, 1934, and in June, 1935, was appointed Minister without Portfolio for League of Nations Affairs. In December, 1935, he became Secretary of State for Foreign Affairs. He had been keenly interested in League of Nations affairs for a long time, and since 1934, and particularly since his visit to the U.S.S.R. in March, 1935 (with which we have dealt in an earlier chapter), he had realised to the full that, whether one liked it or not, the U.S.S.R. had become a mighty Power, and that she could act as an important bulwark against the steadily growing aggression of the Fascists. Agreeing as he did with M. Litvinov that " peace was indivisible," he became a firm advocate of an understanding with the U.S.S.R.

Although when he became Prime Minister in May, 1937, Mr. Chamberlain retained Mr. Eden as his Foreign Secretary, he sought to dominate the conduct of foreign affairs and to minimise Mr. Eden's influence as far as possible. Things came to a crisis early in 1938. Italy had conquered Abyssinia and Republican Spain had been betrayed, but not yet subdued ; under such circumstances Mr. Chamberlain and his supporters were anxious to come to an understanding with Italy, whereby British capital might participate in the exploitation of Abyssinia. As for Spain, a Franco victory, to say the least, did not frighten them, for there again would be a Fascist Government in need of money and capital which British financial interests—so they hoped—could supply at a good profit.

Mr. Eden, however, had other views ; he was ready enough to come to an understanding on terms with Italy, and in his conversations with the Italian Ambassador he had insisted, amongst other things, that as a preliminary to the start of negotiations for the conclusion of an agreement, Italy should cease intervention in Spain by withdrawing therefrom her men and materials and that there should be an end to the Italian anti-British propaganda campaign. But Mussolini knew his Chamberlain; the reply was not only in the negative but a hue and cry was raised in the Italian press that "Eden must go." At this point Mr. Chamberlain stepped in and in a subsequent meeting with the Italian Ambassador on February 18, 1938, in the presence of Mr. Eden, he swept aside all the conditions laid down by the latter and offered to enter into immediate negotiations for an Anglo-Italian Agreement conceding practically everything demanded by the Italians. There was only one thing left for Mr. Eden—to resign, and on February 20 his resignation was officially announced. Lord Cranborne, the Under-Secretary of State for Foreign Affairs, also resigned, but other supporters of Eden's policy in the Cabinet (and there were a number), retained their posts.

Thus Mr. Chamberlain attained his great desire for an agreement with Mussolini, sacrificing the most popular Minister in his Cabinet and driving another nail into the coffin of collective security and world peace.

The Labour and Liberal press roundly condemned the sacrifice of Mr. Eden. The Conservative press was on the whole non-committal, and only the *Daily Mail*, and to a slightly less extent the *Daily Express*, were enthusiastic. The two opposite views taken in Britain on the subject are well illustrated in the following brief quotations from leading articles:

> "The real significance of Mr. Eden's departure is that a turning-point has been reached in our foreign policy. The break with the theories of Geneva has come at last, and the nation looks forward to a new era of sound achievement in high politics."*

> "Throughout the world the resignation of the Foreign Secretary will be regarded as a signal victory for the dictators, and a humiliating defeat for the leading democracy. It will be rightly said that Britain concedes to force what she would not concede to reason. From Berlin to Tokio every swashbuckler who believes that might is greater than right will take new heart from this event, and men and women who had fixed their hopes on a new order in human affairs will be correspondingly cast down."†

Mr. Lloyd George and Mr. Churchill came out strongly in favour of Mr. Eden's policy and protested against his being forced out of office. The joy-bells at Eden's forced resignation were muffled in Britain, but in the Fascist countries they rang out loud and clear. The *Financial News*, in the course of a leader, summed up the position thus:

> "So the flags are out and there is general rejoicing in Berlin

* *Daily Mail*, 22.ii.38. † *Star*, 21.ii.38.

and Rome. 'It is another big victory for the Duce.' 'Mr. Eden's resignation is welcome—the appointment of Lord Halifax would be appreciated.' In fact, the Fascist Powers seem to have found London almost as easy a task as Vienna. The spectacle of a capitulation to Italy, involving the sacrifice of the Foreign Minister who was primarily responsible for the Government's refusal to be intimidated by the back-door attacks made on this country, on the very same day as a bitter rhetorical attack on Britain was made by Hitler, is by no means pleasant. No sane person will be convinced by the suggestions made in some quarters that Mr. Eden resigned on an issue of impracticable idealism. He resigned on a supremely practical issue—a refusal to associate himself with overtures to a country which, so far from giving any earnest of even being willing to live at peace with ourselves, has continued unofficial aggression against British interests in every way that is open to her. That would not, in itself, have justified Mr. Eden in failing to make the maximum of effort to avoid resignation at the present juncture. Whatever the disagreements, it was obviously the duty of the Cabinet as a whole to make every conceivable effort to prevent them from coming to a head at this moment; and all sections of the Cabinet must share some blame for the humiliating fiasco which has occurred. We cannot delude ourselves for a moment into thinking that it is regarded abroad as anything but surrender, publicly confessed, to intimidation from the 'Berlin-Rome axis.' As such, unfortunately, it is regarded in both France and America, and we have earned the mistrust of the countries which are our friends just as we have earned the pleased contempt of the countries which have worked incessantly against us."*

And Rome and Berlin had their second wish too—Lord Halifax did indeed succeed Mr. Eden as Secretary of State for Foreign Affairs. The *Manchester Guardian's* political correspondent thus summed up Lord Halifax on his appointment:

"He [Lord Halifax] has been working in pretty close intimacy with Mr. Chamberlain ever since he became Prime Minister, and has obviously been moving within the orbit of Mr. Chamberlain's ideas on foreign policy and obeying his wishes by taking over the Foreign Office when Mr. Eden was away, and by going to Germany when Mr. Chamberlain wanted him. He will continue to be Mr. Chamberlain's faithful coadjutor, and will devotedly accept his foreign policy from his chief."†

* 22.ii.38. † 25.ii.38.

The appointment of Lord Halifax on February 25, 1938, was a clear indication that so long as Mr. Chamberlain remained in office, the orders of the day would be appeasement of the Fascist Powers and a worsening of relations with the U.S.S.R.

On the other hand, competent observers and well-informed publicists in the course of 1938 advocated, as never before, close collaboration between London and Moscow and the inclusion of the U.S.S.R. in all negotiations and conferences affecting European and world peace. Not only was there a very marked distinction between the policy of the Government and its Labour and Liberal political opponents *vis-à-vis* the Soviet Union, but within the ranks of its own party also, the policy of the Government met with much criticism.

II. Dispute on Consulates. March 17, Soviet offer of collective action rejected

We now turn to the questions directly at issue between the two countries, dealing with them in chronological order. Early in the year, a dispute arose over the question of Consulates in both countries. "On January 11, His Majesty's Ambassador at Moscow," said Sir John Simon,* "was informed of the decision of the Soviet Government to apply within two months a principle of 'parity' to all foreign consular representations in the Soviet Union—that is, that no State would be permitted to maintain there more consular establishments than were maintained in its territory by the Soviet Union. The Soviet Government interpreted this principle as requiring the closure of His Majesty's Consulate-General at Leningrad."†

"His Excellency has pointed out," continued Sir John, "on my instructions, that the so-called principle of parity, which has never been previously invoked in this connection, is contrary to the accepted basis for consular representation—the protection of a country's nationals and interests abroad wherever they may need it, and that His Majesty's Government cannot but regard the demand for the enforced closure of their Consulate-General at Leningrad as a discourteous act, lacking any basis of justification."

Finally, said Sir John, "he has pointed out to the Soviet Government that they are free to open a Consulate in this country, in addition to the Consular Department of their Embassy in London, at any place where their interests may require one. The Soviet Government, however, have maintained their demand, and since in these circumstances no useful purpose would be served by further discussion, they have now been informed that the Consulate-General at Leningrad

* Then Deputy Leader of the House of Commons.

† *Hansard*, 21.ii.38, col. 16.

will be closed as soon as the work entailed by its closure can be completed. His Majesty's Government will then be without any Consular representation in the Soviet Union."

The Soviets had a Consulate-General in London ; this was the only Consulate which they had in this country, and all they asked was that a British Consulate-General should be established in Moscow and that that Consulate should be the only one in the U.S.S.R.

What impelled the Soviets to make this request ? No official explanation was given and none is issued in such cases. We have only the press reports to guide us. " There is every reason to suppose." wrote the Diplomatic Correspondent of the *Times,* " that in fact the request was made on political grounds. The British Government, however, maintain that Consulates are opened or closed, not for political reasons, but where the interests of British residents and commerce demand them ; and the request for the abolition of the Leningrad office is held to be extremely discourteous."*

" The real reason,' declared the *Daily Herald,* " was understood to be Moscow's desire to clear all foreigners from Leningrad, rapidly being converted into a naval base."†

The latter journal was probably correct. Leningrad was being converted into a great naval base and the Soviet Government no doubt had good reasons for wishing that no foreign Consulates—because this decision applied to all countries—should exist in that great and vitally important port. There was nothing exceptional in the Soviet Government deciding to exclude foreigners from a particular area. In this case the district happened to be a port much used by British shipping, but that did not affect the principle.

The result of this dispute was that between the date of Sir John Simon's reply in the House of Commons and June 22, 1941, visas for Great Britain to Soviet citizens were not issued in Moscow, and conversely, visas for the U.S.S.R. to British citizens were not issued in London. Such visas had to be obtained in neutral capitals.

As already mentioned, serious students of foreign affairs, in the course of this year, continued to stress the imperative importance of close collaboration with the U.S.S.R. Professor Seton Watson, addressing the members of the London Lyceum Club, March 3, 1938, said that " the British Empire was in real danger. It was for the younger generation to decide whether it was worth fighting for and also whether we could escape by ' throwing things over the back of the sledge.' " He continued: " an ideal thing would be a real, lasting understanding between France, Britain and Germany, not at the expense of anyone else, but that would be difficult to attain. Strategically, Britain needed Russia. If the other Powers eliminated Russia from

* 18.ii.38. † 24.iii.38.

Europe, Britain and France combined would be on the defensive and in a very dangerous position. That was the aim of some Powers."*

The British Government a few weeks later was given an exceptionally favourable opportunity of coming to an understanding with the U.S.S.R. On March 17, 1938, after Austria had been annexed by Germany, and Czechoslovakia had been openly marked down by Herr Hitler for destruction, a statement to representatives of the press was made by M. Litvinov in Moscow. In this statement which, together with a covering letter was delivered in London, Paris, Prague and Washington, M. Litvinov declared that:

> "The present international situation puts before the peace-loving countries, and, in particular, before the big Powers, the question of their responsibility for the future fate of the peoples of Europe and elsewhere.
>
> The Soviet Government is conscious of the obligations devolving on it from the Covenant of the League, the Briand-Kellogg Pact and its treaties of mutual assistance concluded with France and Czechoslovakia.
>
> I am, therefore, in a position to state on its behalf that it is prepared, as hitherto, to participate in collective action, the scope of which should have as its aim the stopping of the further development of aggression and the elimination of the increased danger of a new world slaughter.
>
> The Soviet Government is prepared to begin immediately, together with other States in the League of Nations or outside it, the consideration of practical measures called for by the present circumstances.
>
> Tomorrow it may be too late, but to-day the time has not yet passed if all the States, and especially the Great Powers, will adopt a firm and unequivocal stand in regard to the problems of the collective saving of peace."†

The official organ of the British Labour Movement, the *Daily Herald*, strongly urged the Government to reply affirmatively to the Soviet Note:

> "A proposal is made by the Government of the Soviet Union that leading members of the League, together with the United States, should take counsel together on the present international situation.
>
> Their purpose should be to combine their forces in defence of peace, so that further aggression may be deterred and the tragedy of war averted.

* *Manchester Guardian*, 4.iii.38.

† *Daily Telegraph*, 18.iii.38.

This is precisely the kind of practical lead which millions of British people have been hoping for years would come from their own Government. It has come from another Government.

It does not matter from where it has come. The only thing that matters is that it has come and that it should not be allowed to decline into fruitlessness for want of welcome and support."*

Unfortunately, the British Government decided to reject the proposal. When the subject was raised in the House of Commons, March 24, 1938, the Prime Minister vaguely replied that the Soviet proposition "would appear to involve less a consultation with a view to settlement than a concerting of action against an eventuality that has not yet arisen. Its object would appear to be to negotiate such mutual undertakings in advance to resist aggression, as I have referred to, which, for the reasons I have already given, His Majesty's Government for their part are unwilling to accept."†

Apropos this reply a former Tory Cabinet Minister was heard to remark: "Neville is determined to go down to history as the Premier who always missed the bus."

Meanwhile, within the Soviet Union they were acting on their own warnings to other countries. On May 1, 1938, Marshal Voroshilov, Commissar for Defence, in a message, declared that the nation must be maintained in a "state of mobilisation." The warning continued:

> "We cannot fail to realise that at present the world is transformed into an armed camp. The flames of war are blazing in two continents, while our numerous enemies, attempting in every way to undermine our constructive work from within, prepare open war against us. . . . With ten-fold energy, without wasting an hour, we must work insistently on further perfecting the fighting capacity of the Red Army as well as on raising its political consciousness and technical level."‡

And *Izvestia* in a leading article said:

> "The Fascist aggressors threaten to violate peace. With the compliance of the bourgeois Governments, the hordes of Fascism have broken into Spain and China endeavouring to deprive these countries of their national independence. Austria has ceased to exist. . . . Czechoslovakia is threatened—all this is in the nature of a prelude to 'a big war' for a new re-division of the world, as a preparation for the realisation of the deeply laid Fascist plan for a counter-revolutionary war against the U.S.S.R . . . the workers of our Motherland are well aware that in the case

* *Daily Herald*, 18.iii.38. † *Hansard*, 24.iii.38, col. 1408.

‡ *Izvestia*, 1.v.38.

of an armed attack the Soviet Union must rely first of all on her own forces. . . . The Red Army and Navy are trustworthy defenders of Soviet freedom and independence."*

Moscow certainly used the only language which present-day Berlin, Rome and Tokio understands, and, what is still more important, respects. Mr. Winston Churchill, addressing a crowded demonstration in the Free Trade Hall, Manchester, under the joint auspices of the Defence of Freedom and Peace League and the League of Nations Union, among other things, declared:

> "We must recognise the service which Russia is rendering in the Far East. Russia, without firing a shot, is holding the best troops of Japan close-gripped upon the Siberian front, and the rest of the Japanese armies may not in the end be found capable of subjugating the Chinese."

Again, referring to the importance of the U.S.S.R., he stated:

> "To the east of Europe lies the enormous Power of Russia, a country whose form of government I detest, but which at any rate seeks no military aggression upon its neighbours; a country profoundly menaced by Nazi hostility. We should certainly not go cap in hand to Soviet Russia or count in any definite manner upon Russian action. But how improvidently foolish we should be when dangers are so great to put needless barriers in the way of the general association of the great Russian mass with the resistance to an act of Nazi aggression."†

It is possible that Mr. Churchill himself was surprised to hear these references to the U.S.S.R. more warmly applauded by the vast audience than any other part of his lengthy speech. Mr. Churchill's powerful plea against the exclusion of the U.S.S.R. was strongly supported by another Tory, who, as our readers are aware, had been in the past, a bitter opponent of the Soviet Union. Commander Locker-Lampson, M.P., speaking at Leeds, June 12, 1938, declared: "Do not forget Russia has an air force superior to anything in Europe. If there is to be another war the side that has Russia as an ally will win."‡

Why was the U.S.S.R. being cold-shouldered by the Chamberlainites? We think that Lord Listowel gave the correct explanation when he wrote: "The real root of the trouble is the class prejudice of the wealthy coterie that controls the machinery of government."§

The policy of this blinded "wealthy coterie" was all the more

* *Izvestia*, 1.v.38. † *Manchester Guardian*, 10.v.38.

‡ Ibid., 13.vi.38. § Ibid., 15.vi.38.

amazing because internally the Soviet Government was marching steadily from strength to strength, or perhaps it would be more correct to say that it was this fact which caused their blindness. Sir Alexander Roger, after a visit to the U.S.S.R., told a *Financial News* reporter that he

> " was astounded by the progress that had been made towards the perfection of the new system that has replaced the old, which was razed to the ground twenty years ago. Industry is absorbing 1,500,000 additional people annually, and the output of cars of all types, except, of course, luxury classes, is in the neighbourhood of 225,000 a year." He also said that " though a generation was growing up that had no knowledge of conditions under the old régime, they had, nevertheless, great belief in the general lines along which the authorities were working."*

Regarding the capital city of the country, Sir Alexander said:

> " In Moscow, industry is being decentralised and all factories are being equipped with complete cultural amenities. The city is being completely rebuilt with huge blocks of workers' flats and wide thoroughfares. In this, of course, the authorities are helped by the fact that the ground and buildings belong to the State, so that the compensation element, which is the great deterrent to any replanning of London, does not enter into the cost factor. Moreover, the general plan is being developed in every other city and town in Russia."†

These facts were, of course, well-known to the members of the Chamberlain Government, but blinded by class prejudice, they preferred to imitate Nelson at Copenhagen. Their action, however, unlike that of the famous sailor, if persisted in, could not but lead to defeat not victory.

Again the Government was given sound advice. At the Trades Union Congress on September 8, 1938, a statement was overwhelmingly adopted calling on the Government to " leave no doubt in the mind of the German Government that it will unite with the French and Soviet Governments to resist any attack on Czechoslovakia." The statement declared that Hitler had " demanded that Czechoslovakia yield its democracy to force and admit a totalitarian system within its boundaries. British Labour emphatically repudiates the right of the British or any other Government to use diplomatic or other pressure to compel acceptance of such a humiliation."‡

A former Labour Cabinet Minister present at the Congress told the writers that a member of the then Tory Cabinet had said to him that

* *Financial News*, 13.vii.38. † Ibid. ‡ *Daily Herald*, 9.ix.38.

Soviet help would be an absolute necessity to Britain and France if war broke out. The former asked: "Then why do you keep Moscow at arm's length? Why do you spurn all their advances?" The Tory, shrugging his shoulders, replied: "We have our wild men to deal with." An ex-member of the British diplomatic service, Captain Harold Grenfell, R.N. (former British Naval Attaché to the Tsarist and Provisional Governments), in effect, underlined this estimate of the situation. He wrote:

> "An open declaration, now, of solidarity with the French and Russian Governments, would, of course, immediately stop the German sabre-rattling. But it is wasted time demanding, or imploring, that Mr. Chamberlain shall make it.
>
> The *raison d'être* of our 'National' Government was, and remains, the hostility of British plutocracy (the actual ruling political power in twentieth century England) to Moscow and all that 'Moscow' represents. That now, or ever, the 'National' Government will publicly take up a position committing it to enter a general European war as ally of Soviet Russia is simply unthinkable, besides being a complete reversal of its present policy, which is to betray the Czech democracy (as it already has the Spanish) in expectation that this will lead to the rupture, first, of the Czech, and next the French Alliance with U.S.S.R."*

Also in Moscow, there were no illusions as to the British Prime Minister's real aims. Dealing with events in Czechoslovakia, the failure of the Runciman Mission to bring about the capitulation of the Czechoslovak Government, the impression made by the Henlein (Sudeten leader) putsch, etc., and Mr. Chamberlain's meeting with Hitler at Berchtesgaden, September 15, *Pravda* wrote:

> "Mr. Chamberlain's idea of foreign policy is well-known—he stubbornly advocates an accord and deal with the aggressor. There can be no doubt that if Mr. Chamberlain wanted to declare on behalf of his Government that Britain, acting jointly with the other peace-loving countries, will not allow the violation of the independence and integrity of the Czecho-Slovak Republic, there was no necessity for the 'dramatic gesture' to which the British Premier resorted. It was perfectly clear that the purpose of his German visit was a bargain for which Czechoslovakia would be forced to pay. . . ."†

Would this bring peace? *Pravda* continued: "The British Government has refused to adopt the path of collective security against the aggressor." After referring to the reports that Mr. Chamberlain

* *News Chronicle*, 15.ix.38. † *Pravda*, 17.ix.38.

intended to try and organise a conference of the four Powers—Britain, France, Germany and Italy—to discuss the Czechoslovak and other European problems, the article proceeded:

> "The British Conservative press and quarters supporting Mr. Chamberlain want to make political capital by claiming that an accord with Fascist Germany and new concessions to Hitler would save Europe from war. There is no greater falsehood than this assertion. The policy of an agreement with the aggressor does not postpone but accelerates the advent of war."

Finally, the article pointed out that the annexation of the Sudetenland by Germany could not but put an end to Czechoslovakian independence, and declared:

> "It would only pave the way for Fascist Germany to establish her domination over Central and South-Eastern Europe. This would signify that having secured her rear and obtained sources of raw material Fascist Germany could increase her intervention in Spain. This would signify in effect the encirclement of France. . . ."*

III. Munich and after

A meeting of the Assembly of the League of Nations at Geneva provided the Soviet Government with another opportunity to make its position crystal clear respecting the German threat to Czechoslovakia and also for contact between British and Soviet Ministers.

M. Litvinov, speaking on behalf of his Government, before a plenary meeting on September 21, 1938, *inter alia*, declared:

> "When, a few days before I left for Geneva, the French Government for the first time enquired as to our attitude in the event of an attack on Czechoslovakia, I gave in the name of my Government the following perfectly clear and unambiguous reply.
> 'We intend to fulfil our obligations under the pact, and, together with France, to afford assistance to Czechoslovakia by the ways open to us. Our War Department is ready immediately to participate in a conference with representatives of the French and Czechoslovak War Departments, in order to discuss the measures appropriate to the moment. Independently of this, we should consider desirable that the question be raised at the League of Nations if only as yet under Article II, with the object, first of mobilising public opinion and, secondly, of ascertaining the position of certain other States, whose passive aid might be extremely valuable. It was necessary, however, to exhaust all

* Ibid.

means of averting an armed conflict, and we considered one such method to be an immediate consultation between the Great Powers of Europe and other interested States, in order if possible to decide on the terms of a collective *démarche*.'

This is how our reply was framed. It was only two days ago that the Czechoslovak Government addressed a formal enquiry to my Government as to whether the Soviet Union is prepared, in accordance with the Soviet-Czech pact, to render Czechoslovakia immediate and effective aid if France, loyal to her obligations, will render similar assistance, to which my Government gave a clear answer in the affirmative."*

Two days later, September 23, M. Litvinov and M. Maisky had a long conversation with the British representatives, Earl de la Warr, the Lord Privy Seal and Mr. R. A. Butler, the Under-Secretary of State for Foreign Affairs. The Soviet representatives again urged an immediate meeting of the Great Powers of Europe and other interested States to decide on ways and means of maintaining the sovereignty and territorial integrity of Czechoslovakia. M. Litvinov was asked by the British side if he would agree to London as the *venue* of the proposed conference and he immediately replied in the affirmative. Thereupon Earl de la Warr said he would at once cable his Government and that as soon as he received a reply he would again communicate with M. Litvinov. Whitehall did not reply and the proposed Conference was never held.

However, when in the last week of September, 1938, after the indeterminate meeting between Mr. Neville Chamberlain and Hitler at Godesberg, September 22 and 23, the storm seemed to be on the point of bursting, the British Government performed an apparent *volte-face*. An inspired statement was issued from Whitehall, September 26, 1938, declaring:

"If in spite of all efforts made by the British Prime Minister, a German attack is made upon Czechoslovakia, the immediate result must be that France will be bound to come to her assistance and Great Britain and Russia will certainly stand by France. It is not too late to stop the tragedy and for the people of all nations to insist on settlement by free negotiation."†

The *Daily Mirror*, in an editorial, commented:

"'And Russia.'

Please note the reference to the enormously powerful ally hitherto hardly mentioned in these days of acute anxiety.

* *Verbatim Record of the* 19*th Ordinary Session of the Assembly of the League of Nations*, pp. 12/13.

† *News Chronicle*, 27.ix.38.

It hasn't hitherto been considered 'quite nice'—so it seemed—to mention Russia. But Russian aeroplanes can be useful in a crisis even if Russia isn't considered quite respectable by the best people in the most exclusive circles."*

On the same date, September 26, the Soviet Government again explained to its own people the policy to which they were pledged *vis-à-vis* Czechoslovakia. The *News Chronicle* correspondent cabled from Moscow:

"All Russia was told officially for the first time to-day of the Soviet warning to Poland—that if the latter attacked Czechoslovakia, Moscow would denounce the Soviet-Polish Non-Aggression Pact.

The official view, as expressed in *Izvestia*, is that Poland's statement, that military measures on the Czech frontier are 'purely defensive,' suggests that 'Warsaw's understanding of defence may be like that of Japan, who defends herself by invading foreign soil.'

At the same time is made public here the text of the Soviet-Czechoslovak treaty and Russia's obligation to assist Czechoslovakia if attacked is emphasised."†

On September 28, Mr. Chamberlain made his speech to the House of Commons, which ended with the dramatic announcement that Herr Hitler had graciously agreed to meet him together with M. Daladier and Signor Mussolini in Munich on the following day. During the whole course of his report, the Prime Minister never once mentioned the U.S.S.R. However, it is pleasant to record that a Tory newspaper, the *Daily Mirror*, protested against this base ingratitude. Editorially, it declared:

"What of Russia? Complete silence. Do we snub and ignore this mighty nation whose support was so welcome but twenty-four hours ago? They cannot even wait at table."‡

And in its news columns, it added:

"A warning from the German Military Chiefs that war against Britain, France and Russia would be most 'unpopular' in the army, led Hitler to accept Mr. Chamberlain's 'last, last appeal' for a further talk and to issue an invitation to a peace conference at Munich to-day, which will be attended by M. Daladier and also Signor Mussolini."

After the "Munich Settlement," the German Government only allowed two days to elapse before revealing in effect that the Soviet

* 27.ix.38. † 27.ix.38. ‡ 29.ix.38.

analysis of the Chamberlain policy, noted on a previous page, was correct. Dr. Halfeld, the well-known Nazi journalist, in the *Hamburger Fremdenblatt*, summing up the results of Munich, wrote:

> " The historical aspect of Munich lies in the fact that the firm determination of Adolf Hitler and the political far-sightedness of the Duce succeeded in eliminating Soviet Russia from the concert of the European Great Powers.
>
> The Soviet Foreign Commissar, Litvinov-Finkelstein, has hardly been heard at all in the diplomatic negotiations of the last few weeks. His words no longer have any weight because responsible leaders in Paris and London were not ideological agitators, but the delegates of the desire for peace of their peoples.
>
> Those in the Council of Four replace the Council of Geneva, which has long shrunk to a mere shadow of its former importance. The League of Nations is dead—long live the European Council of the civilised great Powers! "*

Was that all? Was the Reich now satisfied? Quite the contrary. Dr. Helfeld continued:

> " England, with her feelings for honour, will be the first to realise that a proud and mighty nation of 80,000,000 people cannot tolerate the thought that it has been deprived of its colonial mission through a verdict imposed by violence.
>
> The method which Adolf Hitler and Neville Chamberlain have mutually promised to adopt with regard to future questions opens the possibility that new goals may be approached as a result of the fresh start made at Munich."

As a result of the cold shouldering of the U.S.S.R., and the ignoring of the League, the German Government quite naturally felt that it was in a more favourable position to stake out its claim for Colonies.

Arrangements had been made that the House of Commons should devote four days, October 3-6, to discussing the " Munich Settlement " and the Government's foreign policy. Mr. Neville Chamberlain opened his apologia, October 3, 1938, and for the second time never once mentioned the U.S.S.R., an omission (to use no stronger word) for which he was strongly and effectively attacked from the Opposition benches. Next day, the *Daily Herald* editorially commented:

> " Throughout the whole of his two speeches in Parliament and throughout the whole of the correspondence published in the White Paper, there is no mention by Mr. Chamberlain of Russia, whose co-operation is so essential in maintaining peace. He tells of future action for peace—but he does not mention Russia.

* *Daily Telegraph*, 3.x.38.

Labour has no love for Fascism, but it is ready to co-operate with the Fascist Powers in securing peace if they genuinely wish to secure peace. But the Government is not ready to co-operate with Russia.

Why? Does it set ideological differences above peace? If it does, then let it have the courage to say so and accept the verdict of public opinion."*

In the House of Commons, the attack was maintained against the Treasury Bench, with the result that the Government was compelled to make amends. The most definite statement from the Ministerial side was made by Sir John Simon. He declared: "It is our hope that Russia will be willing to join in the guarantee of Czechoslovakia. It is most important that she should do so. The Government have no intention whatever of excluding Russia or trying to exclude Russia from any future settlement of Europe. If outstanding differences are to be resolved it must be on the basis of free consultation with all European Powers."†

However, when the Prime Minister wound up the debate, October 6, 1938, he again omitted any reference to the Soviet Union.

By this date, the reports from Czechoslovakia and Germany coupled with the searching criticism of the four days' debate in Parliament, had removed the last traces of gilt from the Munich gingerbread and the Government looked round for scapegoats.

Mirabile dictu, they fixed their attention on the U.S.S.R.! Lord Winterton, Chancellor of the Duchy of Lancaster, in the course of a speech at Shoreham, October 10, 1938, stated that the Soviet Union did not offer help in the Czechoslovakian crisis, but "only made vague promises owing to her military weakness."‡

This statement naturally caused considerable amazement and as one would expect, the Soviet Ambassador, M. Maisky, next day made a strong protest to Lord Halifax at the Foreign Office. The same day, the Soviet Embassy issued a statement which is so important that we quote it in full:

"This morning's newspapers reported the speech of Lord Winterton, Chancellor of the Duchy of Lancaster, made at a meeting held at Shoreham last night, wherein it is alleged Lord Winterton said that Russia did not offer help in the Czechoslovak crisis, but 'only made very vague promises owing to her military weakness.'

This statement of Lord Winterton's is a complete perversion of the actual position of the U.S.S.R., which was explicitly, and without leaving any room for misunderstanding, stated by the

* 4.x.38. † *Hansard*, 5.x.38, col. 346. ‡ *Daily Herald*, 11.x.38.

People's Commissar for Foreign Affairs, M. Litvinov, in his speech at Geneva on September 21.

In this speech, M. Litvinov recapitulated his conversation with the French Chargé d'Affaires in Moscow on September 2, in which, on behalf of the Soviet Government, he declared that the U.S.S.R. intended to fulfil all her obligations under the Soviet-Czech pact, and, together with France, would afford assistance to Czechoslovakia by the ways open to the U.S.S.R. He added that the Soviet War Department was ready to start immediate staff talks with the representatives of the French and Czechoslovakian War Departments in order to discuss the measures appropriate to the moment. Independently of this, M. Litvinov suggested the raising of the Czechoslovakian question at the League of Nations under Article 11 and immediate consultation between the Great Powers of Europe and other interested States to decide the terms of the collective démarche.

It is not the fault of the U.S.S.R. if these proposals—made nearly four weeks before the Munich Agreement—brought no response."*

Instead of apologising, as was generally expected, Lord Winterton, at another meeting on the evening of October 12, 1938, stated: "The Russian Embassy in London objects to my statement that Russia made no precise promise of military assistance, only vague promises because of her military weakness. This statement is nevertheless completely accurate."†

Several newspapers were quick to point out that Lord Winterton's declaration was in contradiction with the inspired statement‡ issued from Whitehall, September 26, 1938.

Next day, October 13, the Soviet Embassy issued a sharp rejoinder:

"In connection with the second statement on the position of the U.S.S.R. in the Czechoslovak crisis, made by Lord Winterton, Chancellor of the Duchy of Lancaster, at Horsham last (Wednesday) night, the Soviet Embassy can only say that it is useless to argue with a man who deliberately shuts his eyes to the real facts. In any case, the Soviet Embassy is convinced that no amount of effort on the part of Lord Winterton can turn an original falsehood into a truth."§

Behind the scenes, Lord Halifax endeavoured to act as a mediator and to make amends, with the result that the Prime Minister, November 3, 1938, informed the House of Commons that:

"On October 11, the Soviet Ambassador called the attention

* *Manchester Guardian*, 12.x.38. † Ibid., 13.x.38.

‡ See p. 591. § *Times*, 14.x.38.

of my Noble Friend, the Secretary of State for Foreign Affairs, to the remarks of my Right Hon. Friend, the Chancellor of the Duchy of Lancaster, and I understand that the latter has since had an opportunity of discussing the matter in person with M. Maisky. I hope that any misunderstandings that may have arisen have now been cleared up."*

The matter was settled privately but not publicly. Many M.P.'s felt that a full explanation was due to Parliament, and Mr. Arthur Henderson|| raised the matter on the motion for the adjournment, November 14, 1938. After referring to Lord Winterton's speeches, the Soviet protests and the Prime Minister's answer to the House of Commons, November 3, he continued:

"That reply is wholly insufficient, because it gives no indication whatsoever of the view that is taken by His Majesty's Government in relation to the statement of the Chancellor of the Duchy of Lancaster."†

The Prime Minister made an amazing reply. He accused Mr. Henderson of trying to make bad blood between the Governments of the two countries, he ignored Mr. Henderson's very apt question; he admitted, however, that Lord Winterton "had an interview with M. Maisky in which he said frankly to him that he had, upon a public platform, commented upon the action of a friendly Government. But he added that he wanted to make it plain that he himself, in common with all members of the Government, desired to preserve the most friendly relations with Russia."‡

Mr. Hugh Dalton rose at once and pointed out that the Prime Minister had "not dealt very adequately with the question raised" and continued:

"The Right Hon. Gentleman, whatever he may have said privately to M. Maisky—which, if I may say so, is not evidence in this House—has hitherto failed to retract the statement which he made, and which, we submit, is in conflict with the facts."§

To this Lord Winterton replied:

"I am indebted to the Prime Minister, who has given a complete and exact account of the interview between the Russian Ambassador and myself, which I believed, and I have reason to think the Russian Ambassador believed, was an end of this question. The Russian Ambassador was good enough to say

* *Hansard*, 3.xi.38, col. 378. † Ibid., 14.xi.38, col. 649.
‡ Ibid., col. 651. § Ibid., col. 652.
|| Son of the late Rt. Hon. Arthur Henderson.

> that the incident was closed, and I cannot think it would be in the public interest to add anything or subtract anything from the statement I made on that occasion."*

It was evident to all present in the Chamber during this altercation that the Prime Minister was very irritable and uncomfortable, as he well might be. After this public apology the incident was regarded as closed.

However, Lord Winterton did not stand alone at that time in endeavouring to belittle the U.S.S.R. Colonel Lindbergh, the noted American flyer, for reasons best known to himself, took a hand. He arrived in Moscow, August 17, 1938, was present at an air display next day, and later visited other countries. So far no full account has been published as to whom he saw in Great Britain and exactly what he said. We are compelled to rely on obviously incomplete press reports. In the Londoner's Diary of the *Evening Standard*, September 30, it was stated: "I hear a strange story . . . that incontrovertible evidence has been brought out of Russia that while the Soviet warplanes are splendid, the flying personnel has been impaired by the recent purges. The loss of the best pilots and engineers has 'grounded' the massive Soviet squadron . . . This news was imparted to Dr. Benes . . . I am assured that the man who brought it was Colonel Lindbergh, who is beginning to rival Colonel Lawrence in political mystery."

Giving more details as to what Lindbergh did and said in London before the "Munich settlement," Miss Ellen Wilkinson, M.P., wrote:

> "Col. Lindbergh was taken to a lunch at which various eminent men—editors, publicists and M.P.'s—were present. He made a speech, the general line of which might have been dictated by General Goering. I am sure it wasn't, but the effect was the same. Germany was top in the air—could take on Russia, France and Britain, even if Italy did not come in. The Russian air force was not effective—it had shot its best men."

There was something very mysterious about this "hush-hush" lunch. Miss Wilkinson continued:

> "A few days after this famous lunch—and what a scared attempt was made to swear everyone to secrecy when it was fortunately too late—Colonel Lindbergh having completed whatever was his mission in England, returned to Germany."†

News of what Lindbergh was saying reached Moscow. There was a prompt reply. *Pravda*, October 10, 1938, published a letter signed

* Ibid., cols. 652/3. † *Sunday Referee*, 23.x.38.

by eleven of the Soviet Union's most famous airmen, in the course of which they said:

> "Not long ago, Lindbergh came to the Soviet Union again. Incidentally, no one had invited him. And if he was permitted to come, it was at the request of Americans. Taking advantage of the permission to visit the country, Lindbergh attended the celebration of Aviation Day, and now, on returning to London, he has utilised his sojourn in the U.S.S.R. for the purpose of casting slanderous and villifying statements upon the Soviet Union."

The letter continued:

> "Lindbergh declared in London that Germany possesses an air force strong enough to defeat the air forces of Britain, France, the U.S.S.R. and Czechoslovakia. What grounds had he for such an assertion? Allah alone knows. . . .
>
> His second statement outdistanced the first. He said that while in Moscow he had been offered the post of Chief of the Soviet Civil Air Fleet."

After comparing Lindbergh's claim with the empty boasts of a Gogol character, the airmen continued:

> "Lindbergh in the role of chief of our Civil Air Fleet! What a joke. We would not permit such an 'airman'—and a had-been airman at that—to command even the most humble operation.
>
> Then followed another thumping lie. 'The Soviet Air Force,' said Lindbergh, 'is left without leadership and is in a state of chaos. . . .'"
>
> "Evidently, this is the reason for the brilliant Soviet air achievements. And the latest flight of Kokkinaki and that of the heroic women flyers—Grizodubova, Osipenko and Raskova—are also striking evidence of the condition of Soviet aviation.
>
> The Soviet land has hundreds and thousands of splendid flyers who are able not only to fly, but who can be utilised as excellent organisers and leaders at any time."

Additional proof that Lindbergh did say what was attributed to him came from the next issue of the *Spectator*. It stated: "How news travels from a London luncheon-table to Moscow I have no means of knowing, and no special desire to know. But in the case of Colonel Lindbergh's remarks on the relative air-strengths of European Powers, it seems to have travelled accurately. Now that

Moscow has seen fit to mention it there is not much point in concealing the fact that Colonel Lindbergh did say in London that not only had Germany a stronger air force than Britain, France or Russia, but that she was as strong as all the three put together."*

At this time, Colonel Lindbergh was in Western Europe, but as far as the writers know he made no public reply to the letter of the eleven Soviet aviators. However, an interesting episode was reported from Germany shortly afterwards:

> " Berlin, October 19.
>
> At an informal dinner party, which was held here at the house of the American Ambassador last night, Colonel Lindbergh, who is paying a visit to Germany, was invested by Field-Marshal Goering, on behalf of the Fuhrer, with the Order of the German Eagle with star. This is the highest rank of the order and also the highest honour which Herr Hitler can bestow."†

Perhaps some day the whole of the facts will be revealed. In the meantime, we must leave our readers to draw their own conclusions.

The attempts to belittle the fighting forces of the U.S.S.R. no doubt helped to spread an impression that the U.S.S.R. was militarily weak and was of little value as an ally. However, in the last months of 1938, well-informed students of foreign affairs continued to stress the importance of collaboration with the Soviet Union. For instance, Sir Norman Angell told Cambridge undergraduates, October 13, that the choice before this country was surrender to Germany or co-operation between the Western States and the U.S.S.R. " Here we are not concerned with likes or dislikes," continued Sir Norman, " but with the bayonets which we are going to accept if they happen to stand on the side of law."‡

The Duchess of Atholl, at a League of Nations' demonstration, Manchester, November 11, declared: " It is the aim of Germany to divide France and Russia and also France and Britain, but that will be more difficult. I am told that what has happened has already increased the Russian tendency to isolation, and however much we may dislike certain things about the Soviet régime, we must endeavour to keep Russia in the League of Nations."§ It is significant that this was the most loudly cheered sentence of the Duchess's speech.

The Dean of Canterbury, Dr, Hewlett Johnson, at an anti-Fascist demonstration, December 4, 1938, at Leeds, said that:

> " Russia was doing the things about which Christians had been talking for centuries . . . that within a generation Russia would be producing more than the whole of the rest of the world.

* 14.x.38. † *Times*, 20.x.38. ‡ *Daily Herald*, 14.x.38.

§ *Manchester Guardian*, 12.xi.38.

> Russia ought to have been at Munich, and Russia must, by the determination of the British people, be beside us in the great coming fight against capitalism which was being driven into its last ditch."*

Professor Seton-Watson, in an address to the Liberal Party Organisation at Caxton Hall, December 15, 1938, after stating that he thought "friendship with the Soviet Union essential," continued: "We have common interests with Russia in the sphere of foreign policy, no territorial designs on each other's territorial integrity. I understand that this view is widely held in the United States, which in this day must try to strengthen its relations with Russia in the Pacific."

CHAPTER XXV

THE ANGLO-FRENCH-SOVIET NEGOTIATIONS, 1939

I. January to August 21, 1939

It is no exaggeration to say that when the fateful year of 1939 dawned, the Chamberlain Government had learned nothing from the results of their disastrous policy of the previous year. Apparently they had decided to continue the line of currying favour with the Nazi and Fascist Powers and keeping the powerful U.S.S.R. at arm's length; thus creating suspicion of their intentions in Moscow.

Mr. Neville Chamberlain, the Prime Minister, and Lord Halifax, the Foreign Secretary, arrived in Rome on January 11, 1939, on a three days' visit to the Italian Government, and at a banquet given by the latter on the same day in their honour, the British Prime Minister raised his glass to "H.M. King of Italy and *Emperor of Abyssinia*." "This was a public confirmation," wrote the *Daily Telegraph's* Rome Correspondent, "of Great Britain's recognition of the new Italian Empire, which caused great satisfaction here."

If the British Government expected gratitude from Rome they were soon disillusioned, because immediately after the British statesmen returned to London the Italian press resumed its violent and abusive campaign against Great Britain's closest ally, France, and on January 26, 1939, at the conclusion of a mass meeting addressed by Mussolini, the worked-up crowd yelled "To Paris! To Paris!"

As for Germany, a month later the tone of her press continued to grow more minatory and on February 26, 1939, Dr. Goebbels published an article in the *Völkischer Beobachter* headed "War in

* *Daily Telegraph*, 5.xii.38.

Sight," in which he sneered at the democracies for failing to hinder the German successes of the previous two years "as they did not rightly estimate the power of the authoritarian states."

Next day, as if to earn further contempt from the "authoritarian states," the British Government announced their decision to recognise the Government of General Franco as the Government of Spain, despite the freely admitted fact that the legally elected Republican Government of Spain was then still in control of one-third of the territory of the latter, and that Franco was upheld to a considerable extent by Italian and German bayonets.

After Mr. Neville Chamberlain's visit to Germany and Italy, he could hardly refuse an invitation to the Soviet Embassy in London and on March 1, 1939, he attended a reception given by M. and Mme. Maisky. He went no doubt in deference to public opinion but throughout he seemed unable to shake off an air of martyrdom. We can well understand his discomfort at this forced support, even only in appearance, of the side opposed to the one he was in reality backing.

The rumblings of the coming volcanic outburst were distinctly audible to all who took an intelligent interest in international affairs and the question was naturally much canvassed "What will the Soviet Union do?"

The answer to this all-important question was discussed in a now famous speech by M. Stalin on March 10, 1939, in the course of which he denounced the policy of trying to buy off the Nazi and Fascist Powers by sacrificing Abyssinia; accused "certain American and European politicians and pressmen of inciting Germany to attack the U.S.S.R."; said that if attacked the Soviet Union would answer with a double blow; stated that the U.S.S.R. stood for the support of nations which were the victims of aggression and were fighting for their independence; declared that one of the Soviet tasks in the field of foreign policy was "to be cautious and not allow our country to be drawn into conflicts by warmongers who are accustomed to have others pull the chestnuts out of the fire for them."

The meaning of this speech ought to have been, and probably was, quite clear to the Chancelleries of London and Paris, viz., that the U.S.S.R. was supremely interested in and would enter into business-like relations for the maintenance of genuine peace, but that she was fully conscious of her position as a Great Power and would not agree to be treated as less.

However, in Great Britain, the Government, despite all their sources of information were still drugging themselves and the country with doses of wishful thinking. A glaring example of this was the speech made by Sir Samuel Hoare, the Home Secretary, on the same day as that on which M. Stalin spoke. Had the two speeches been printed side by side a suitable heading would have been "Realism versus Star Gazing." Sir Samuel Hoare said:

> "Suppose that political confidence could be restored to Europe; suppose that there was a five-year plan immensely greater than any five-year plan that this or that particular country has attempted in recent times, and that for a space of five years there were neither wars nor rumours of wars. Suppose that the peoples of Europe were able to free themselves from a nightmare that haunts them and from an expenditure upon armaments that beggars them. Could we not then devote the almost incredible inventions and discoveries of our time to the creation of a golden age in which poverty could be reduced to insignificance and the standard of living raised to heights that we have never been able to attempt before?
>
> Here indeed is the greatest opportunity that has ever been offered to the leaders of the world. Five men in Europe, the three dictators and the Prime Ministers for England and France, if they worked with a singleness of purpose and a unity of action to this end, might in an incredibly short space of time transform the whole history of the world. These five men, working together in Europe and blessed in their efforts by the President of the United States of America, might make themselves the eternal benefactors of the human race.
>
> Our own Prime Minister has shown his determination to work heart and soul to such an end. I cannot believe that the other leaders of Europe will not join him in the high endeavour upon which he is engaged."*

Five days later, March 15, 1939, German troops occupied and annexed Bohemia and Moravia and Hungarian troops followed suit in Ruthenia. The Czechoslovak Republic ceased to exist. This tragic event, though not unexpected by competent observers, stunned the world. The policy of "appeasement" had not only proved a complete failure but a failure which enormously strengthened the aggressor nations for their next move. Contemptuously the Berlin wireless commented "the day of the Western democracies is over."

On the evening of this tragic day the Soviet Ambassador in London, M. Maisky, in the course of a public speech, declared:

> "The foreign policy of the Soviet Government has always been a policy of universal peace. Not a peace at any price, but peace based on law and order in international affairs. . . .
>
> By reason of her geographical position the U.S.S.R. is most

* *Manchester Guardian*, 11.iii.39.

particularly interested in the preservation of peace in Europe and Asia. Had not the British Empire the same interest?

Our two countries do not always see eye to eye as to the best methods for securing peace, but it is equally true—and the fact is of paramount importance—that at present there is no conflict of interest between the U.S.S.R. and the British Empire in any part of the world.

You will find that in the last resort the fate of peace or war in our time depends on the kind of relations which exist between London and Moscow."*

The speeches of MM. Stalin and Maisky left no doubt as to the foreign policy of the U.S.S.R. Had the hand then stretched out by Moscow been firmly grasped, the world war, even at that late hour, might have been prevented. Unfortunately, the outstretched hand was ignored and the Chamberlain Government continued to treat the mighty U.S.S.R. as a third-rate Power.

Naturally, the German occupation of Czechoslovakia created consternation in London and the adjournment of the House of Commons was moved at 3.46 p.m. to allow the Prime Minister to make a statement. Mr. Neville Chamberlain gave an "account of the facts as they" were known to him, but added, *inter alia*, some comments which revealed his amazing state of mind: "I have so often heard charges of breach of faith bandied about which did not seem to me to be founded upon sufficient premises, that I do not wish to associate myself to-day with any charges of that character."†

However, if the Prime Minister was not awake the country was and two days later, March 17, Mr. Neville Chamberlain, speaking at Birmingham, was constrained to say that we must ask ourselves whether the subjugation of Czechoslovakia was "the last attack upon a small State" or whether it was "in fact a step in the direction of an attempt to dominate the world."

On March 20, 1939, the British press carried large headlines announcing that Great Britain had approached the Soviet Union to join in a pact to resist further aggression. The announcement which appeared in the *Daily Mail* was typical of the press as a whole:

"The British Government have formally invited Soviet Russia to consider joining in a pact with Britain and France, and any other Powers willing to co-operate, to resist German aggression.

The request was conveyed by Viscount Halifax through M. Maisky, the Soviet Ambassador, when they met at the Foreign Office yesterday.

* *Daily Telegraph* and *Daily Herald*, 16.iii.39.

† *Hansard*, 15.iii.39, col. .

The significant step is the first stage in the revision of British foreign policy indicated by the Prime Minister in his speech at Birmingham on Friday.

It follows Herr Hitler's annexation of Czechoslovakia, and reports that the independence of other States, notably Rumania, in South-Eastern Europe is threatened."

The text of the British Note has never been published, but an official communiqué issued in Moscow, March 21, 1939, stated:

"Poland and Rumania did not apply to the Soviet Government for help, nor did they inform that Government of any danger threatening them. What actually happened was that on March 18 (Saturday), the British Government informed the Soviet Government of the existence of weighty reasons to fear an act of violence over Rumania and inquired about the possible position of the Soviet Government in such an eventuality.

In reply to this inquiry the Soviet Government put forward a proposal for the calling of a Conference of representatives of the States most closely interested—namely, Great Britain, France, Poland, Rumania, Turkey and the Soviet Union.

In the opinion of the Soviet Government such a conference would give the maximum possibilities for the elucidation of the real situation and the position of all the participants at the conference. *The British Government, however, found this proposal premature.*"*

The *Manchester Guardian's* Moscow Correspondent aptly commented:

"The proposal is almost identical with that made by the Soviet Union last year after Herr Hitler's seizure of Austria and is in line with the Government's consistent advocacy of collective action against aggression.

Apparently the British Government is still unwilling to accept this policy, but the reason given—that it is premature—is held to be unconvincing in the light of the British Government's assertion of the imminent danger towards Rumania.

The Soviet Union does not intend that the Western Powers shall manœuvre her into bearing alone the main brunt of resistance to Herr Hitler. It is believed that any efforts to commit Russia alone will only convince Russia that British policy still seeks to involve the Soviet Union in a mutually ruinous war with Germany."†

The Soviet Note clearly shows that there was a profound difference

* *Manchester Guardian*, 22.iii.39. (Our italics.)

† 22.iii.39.

of opinion between London and Moscow as to the manner in which the danger should be confronted. The British Government wanted vague and ambiguous declarations, the Soviet Government urged a firm and clear understanding, coupled with definite plans worked out by the States resisting aggression. The British Government, as just mentioned, characterised the Soviet proposal as " premature " and in its turn asked whether the U.S.S.R. would join with Poland, France and Great Britain in a declaration denouncing aggression and contemplating an immediate meeting of the Four Powers in the event of further aggression. The Soviet Government replied that this proposal was extremely vague and therefore far from satisfactory, but agreed to it and, in order to strengthen the declaration, proposed that it should be signed not only by the Foreign Secretary of each country but also by the Prime Minister. However, Poland refused to sign a declaration jointly with the U.S.S.R. and the proposal was dropped. London did not approach Moscow again until April 15. On March 22, 1939, Germany annexed Memel, contemptuously ignoring the guaranteeing Powers, among them Great Britain and France, and it was generally feared that Germany would next seize Danzig, for which preparations had been and were in full blast.

Government circles in London became more alarmed and on March 31, 1939, the Prime Minister, Mr. Neville Chamberlain, announced in the House of Commons that His Majesty's Government had given a guarantee to the Polish Government:

> " As the House is aware, certain consultations are now proceeding with other Governments. In order to make perfectly clear the position of His Majesty's Government in the meantime, before those consultations are concluded, I now have to inform the House that during that period, in the event of any action which clearly threatened Polish independence and which the Polish Government accordingly considered it vital to resist with their national forces, His Majesty's Government would feel themselves bound at once to lend the Polish Government all support in their power. They have given the Polish Government an assurance to this effect.
>
> I may add that the French Government have authorised me to make it plain that they stand in the same position in this matter as do His Majesty's Government."

To give this guarantee to Poland without a prior agreement with the U.S.S.R. was stark madness, and went a long way towards condemning the subsequent Anglo-French-Soviet negotiations to futility.*

* The Prime Minister admitted in the House of Commons, May 10, 1939, that the British-Polish Agreement was concluded without prior agreement with the Soviet Government.

The British Government could not claim that they had acted in ignorance of the Polish Government's views for on March 24, 1939: "Lord Halifax received the Polish Ambassador, who was understood to have stated that his Government were reluctant to join with Britain, France and Russia in an open declaration of united resistance to aggression; they did not see how their interests, or the interests of others, could be served by such publicity."

Meanwhile the aggressor powers continued their advance and on April 7, 1939, Italy annexed Albania.

Increasingly threatening though the international situation had become, and despite the fact that the British Government had made a hesitant approach to the Soviet Government, Mr. Neville Chamberlain continued to manifest his aversion to the U.S.S.R. For instance, on April 13, 1939, when he spoke in the House of Commons on the "European situation" and announced a British guarantee to Rumania and Greece, without consulting the Soviet Government, he was on the point of sitting down without having made any reference to the Soviet Union, when a number of members from both sides of the House shouted, "What about Russia?" He lamely added: "It is a little difficult, perhaps, to avoid the exhibition of strong feelings, but I hope that hon. Members will not assume that, if I have not mentioned Russia in what I have said this afternoon, that means that we are not keeping in the closest touch with the representatives of that country." However, it was not until April 15, 1939, that Sir William Seeds, the British Ambassador to Moscow, approached the Soviet Government requesting the latter to make a unilateral declaration guaranteeing Poland and Rumania, already guaranteed by Great Britain and France.

The talks thus begun continued until August 26, 1939, but as no *Blue Book* or other official Government publication has been issued on the course of these conversations, we have been compelled to piece the story together from a careful study of the British and Soviet press and from statements in the House of Commons. There may be gaps in our narrative but we do not think that anything essential is missing.

The Soviet Government, on April 17, in reply to the British proposal, presented an 8-point programme, the essentials of which were: A Triple Defensive Alliance of France, Britain and the U.S.S.R.; a Military Convention and the guaranteeing of all States situated between the Baltic and Black Seas.

It seems difficult to believe to-day, but it is a sober fact that the Soviet reply was left unanswered for more than three weeks. In the interim, to be precise on April 26, the Reich Government denounced the Anglo-German Naval Treaty and the German-Polish Non-

Aggression Pact, a fact which caused additional disquiet in London But still the Soviet Government was kept waiting for a reply. And that was not all. The Prime Minister, Mr. Neville Chamberlain, went out of his way to hurl a frigid and calculated insult at the Soviet Government. We quote from *Hansard*, May 5, 1939:

> " *Mr. Gallacher:* In view of the statement made by Stalin that the Soviet Union is very anxious indeed to provide assistance for any country that is attacked by an aggressor, will not the right hon. Gentleman consider making personal contact in order to get Stalin's own view?
>
> *The Prime Minister:* Perhaps the hon. Member would suggest with whom I should make personal contact, because personalities change rather rapidly."*

We repeat that this was a " frigid and calculated " insult because up to that date the U.S.S.R. had had only one President and three Foreign Secretaries. There had been far fewer comparable Government changes in the Soviet Union than in Great Britain.

Then, on May 9, 1939, the British Government replied reiterating its request of April 15, but with some slight modifications. The reply ignored the Soviet Union's proposal for a triple pact and suggested that the U.S.S.R. should give a simple guarantee to Poland and Rumania, but in such a form that the British Government would decide when the guarantee should come into operation, in other words, the British Government would decide when and where, for and against whom the Soviet forces should march. The British Cabinet Committee handling the negotiations must have known that the Soviet Government would not accept their proposal. On May 14, the Soviet Government replied to the British Note of May 9, reiterating its programme of April 17, but in a more simplified form. The reply stressed that if it were seriously intended to resist aggression then it was absolutely essential to have (*a*) a three-power pact to resist a direct attack; (*b*) a military convention side by side with the political agreement; (*c*) a joint guarantee for all the States bordering on the Soviet Union between the Baltic Sea and the Black Sea. It is necessary to record here that on May 12, 1939, Mr. Neville Chamberlain had announced in the House of Commons that the British Government had concluded a Pact of Mutual Assistance on certain conditions with Turkey, so that by this date Great Britain had given guarantees to Poland, Rumania, Greece and Turkey.

Whilst the Anglo-French-Soviet negotiations were taking place in Moscow, the British Foreign Office was also in touch with M. Maisky

* Col. 2224.

in London; all our daily papers, on May 18, 1939, carried reports of these London conversations. To quote only a typical one, from the diplomatic correspondent of the *Daily Telegraph*:

> "M. Maisky, the Soviet Ambassador, called twice at the Foreign Office yesterday. At the request of Viscount Halifax it is understood he had long talks with Sir Robert Vansittart, chief diplomatic adviser to the Foreign Secretary. . . .
>
> Pending the outcome of the discussion it had been decided not to send fresh instructions to Sir William Seeds, British Ambassador in Moscow. Presumably these will be considered to-day by the Cabinet Foreign Affairs Sub-committee.
>
> The British Government wished to convince the Soviet that a declaration of Russian willingness to help Poland and Rumania would assure mutual assistance between Britain and Russia. The Soviet insists that, if this be the case, there can be no valid objection to a definite Anglo-French-Soviet mutual assistance agreement.
>
> While Britain adduces various reasons for wanting to avoid this direct engagement, the Soviet undoubtedly suspects the British Government's good faith in the matter. It was still maintained in Soviet circles last night that the 'principle of reciprocity' had not been accepted by the British Government."*

This report casts a flood of light on the differences between the Soviet and Anglo-French points of view. The former wanted a solid agreement, the latter a vague "declaration" which could mean anything or nothing.

Meanwhile the Axis Powers had not been idle: on May 22, 1939, a German-Italian Treaty of Political and Military Alliance "without mental or other reservations" was signed in Berlin. On the eve of the completion of this instrument, Mussolini declared that a *bloc* of 150 million people had been formed and that "this *bloc*, formidable both in men and arms, wants peace, but it is ready to impose it if the great conservative and reactionary democracies should try to stop our irresistible march."

One would have thought that after the conclusion of this ominous instrument, the Chamberlain Government would have wanted a comprehensive and water-tight military alliance with the U.S.S.R., but this was not so. The British Ambassador in Moscow on May 27 replied to the Soviet Note of May 14, agreeing to discuss the conclusion of a Pact of Mutual Assistance and a Military Convention, but *mirabile dictu* restricting the guarantee to Poland and Rumania. This counter-proposal was trifling with the subject because the question of

* 18.v.39.

guaranteeing the Baltic States in which the U.S.S.R. was vitally interested was left open.

M. Molotov,* in the course of a speech before the Supreme Council of the U.S.S.R. on May 31, 1939, explained the last-mentioned British proposal thus:

> " Apart from a number of points in the British draft which are not sufficiently straightforward and definite we would draw particular attention to the fact that whilst the proposals provide for immediate help to Poland, Rumania, Turkey and Greece, they give no guarantee of help for the other States on the borders of the U.S.S.R.—Latvia, Estonia, Finland—unless these countries ask for such help. This is surely, to say the least, extremely dangerous. It is almost a direct invitation to Germany to leave Poland and other countries alone for the time being and to attack instead the other States on the Soviet borders by the time-honoured Nazi methods of the instigation and financing of internal disturbances and revolts and then marching in on the ' invitation ' of a puppet Government.
>
> Weak countries such as Latvia or Estonia, of course, would not dare to offend Germany by asking the help of the Democracies, for whilst the latter were still conferring and deciding as to whether the given aggression ' is aggression within the meaning of the act ' their independence would be trampled under foot by the German armies and their women and children killed by the Nazi aerial bombs.
>
> So far as the Soviet Government is concerned it is not a question of bargaining about the concession of this or that point of interest to itself but of the conclusion of an agreement which should be a real bar to further aggression."

In passing, we may note (on the authority of the French Yellow Book), that on June 1, the French Ambassador in Berlin informed his Government that if the British-French-Soviet negotiations were successful, Hitler would not make war.

The Soviet Government, on June 2, replied to the British Note of May 27 (1) reiterating its request for the inclusion of the Baltic States in the Pact; (2) proposing that eight States should have full equality in the Provisions of the Pact, viz., Latvia, Estonia, Finland, Rumania, Poland, Greece, Turkey and Belgium; (3) that the Triple Pact of Mutual Assistance and the Military Convention should come into force simultaneously.

* On May 3, 1939, M. Molotov had been appointed People's Commissar for Foreign Affairs, M. Litvinov being released from this post by his own request. At the same time M. Molotov retained the post of Chairman of People's Commissars until May 6, 1941, when M. Stalin took his place. (See p. 665).

Competent observers, alarmed at the leisurely way in which the negotiations were being conducted on the British side, raised warning voices. Mr. Winston Churchill, in the course of a speech, June 3, 1939, stated: " All hoped that nothing would prevent the conclusion of a triple alliance of Britain, France and Soviet Russia. A great French soldier told me the other day: ' Without Russia, there can be no eastern front. Without an eastern front all the weight will fall upon the west; but with a strong eastern front war may be averted altogether.' "*

And on the question of the Baltic States, Mr. Winston Churchill wrote:

> " Nor should there be any serious difficulty in guaranteeing the Baltic States and Finland. The Russian claim that these should be included in the triple guarantee is well-founded. There is no sense in having a crack in the peace diving-bell.
>
> People say, ' What if they do not wish to be guaranteed? ' It is certain, however, that if Lithuania, Latvia and Estonia were invaded by the Nazis or subverted to the Nazi system by propaganda and intrigue from within, the whole of Europe would be dragged into war. The independence of the Baltic States is of the highest consequence to Poland. The closest relations, political and military, have been established between them, severally and jointly, and Poland. If their independence or integrity is compromised by Nazidom, Poland must fight. Great Britain and France must fight. Why not then concert in good time, publicly and courageously, the measures which may render such a fight unnecessary? "†

M. Titulescu, the well-known former Rumanian Minister, after pointing out that continuous staff talks had been taking place between Germany and Italy, whereas " little or nothing of the kind " had taken place between Great Britain and France on the one hand, and the countries which they had guaranteed in Eastern Europe on the other, continued: " When the agreement with Russia is signed—for I hope it will be—a great deal will have to be done in the military sense to make it a live thing. But shall we be given enough time for all this? Let us hope so, but it is not easy to believe."‡

British public opinion was by this time also very uneasy at the slowness of the negotiations and to appease these apprehensions the Government decided to send someone to Moscow to speed up the talks. One would have thought that in view of the Chamberlain-Hitler-Mussolini negotiations of 1938 they would have sent the Prime

* *Times*, 5.vi.39. † *Daily Telegraph*, 8.vi.39.
‡ *Manchester Guardian*, 8.vi.39.

Minister and the Chief of the Imperial General Staff. However, instead they sent an unknown Foreign Office official, Mr. William Strang. He was no doubt an efficient official in his Department, but at that particular juncture his appointment was like saying to Moscow: "You must not expect us to pay you anything approaching the same courtesy as we have paid to Berlin and Rome."

Mr. Strang left for Moscow on June 12, 1939, arriving in that city on June 14, and on the former date, Lord Halifax, the Foreign Secretary, was invited by M. Maisky, the Soviet Ambassador, to visit Moscow. Here was another opportunity to speed up the negotiations, but all that His Lordship replied was that he would bear the invitation in mind and he never returned a definite answer. Naturally, this episode strengthened the suspicion in the Soviet capital that the British Government was not seriously bent on bringing the negotiations to a successful conclusion.

On June 15, the first meeting took place in Moscow between Sir William Seeds (the British Ambassador), Mr. Strang, M. Naggiar (the French Ambassador) and M. Molotov, the Peoples' Commissar for Foreign Affairs. The British-French side put forward certain suggestions to overcome existing differences, but these were regarded as unsatisfactory by the Soviet side.

On the following day, the Soviet Government proposed that as the British and French Governments were not prepared to accept satisfactory proposals *vis-à-vis* the Baltic States, the British, French and Soviet Governments, as a first step, should conclude a Triple Defensive Alliance to come to one another's assistance only in the event of direct aggression. Five days later the British-French representatives, ignoring the Soviet proposal of June 16, submitted another formula respecting the Baltic States which was regarded as unacceptable by the Soviet representatives.

Impatience both outside and inside the Soviet Union at the slowness of the negotiations was being increasingly and authoritatively expressed. Mr. Winston Churchill, speaking at the City Carlton Club, June 28, said (to quote the *Times*): "It seemed to him that a full and solid alliance should be made with Russia without further delay. The Russian claim that we should stand together in resisting an act of aggression upon the Baltic States was just and reasonable, and he trusted we would meet it in the fullest manner."

Mr. Vernon Bartlett, after referring to the reluctance or professed reluctance of the Baltic States to accept a guarantee, pointed out that "the Monroe Doctrine guaranteed a considerable number of Latin American States against their will and that, as one consequence, peace has been maintained in that part of the world."*

* *News Chronicle*, 29.vi.39.

On June 29, M. Zhdanov, a member of the Political Bureau of the Communist Party and President of the Foreign Affairs Committee of the Soviet Union, in the course of a frank article in *Pravda*, speaking for himself and not committing his Government, explained why the negotiations had reached a deadlock. After pointing out that the conversations had been going on for 75 days, of which the Soviet Government had taken 16 to return its answers, whilst the Anglo-French side had taken 59 days, he continued: " It seems to me that the British and French Governments are not out for a real agreement acceptable to the U.S.S.R., but only for talks about an agreement in order to demonstrate before the public opinion of their own countries the alleged unyielding attitude of the U.S.S.R., and thus facilitate the conclusion of an agreement with the aggressors. The next few days will show whether this is so or not."

He argued that Great Britain and France had created an " artificial stumbling block " by not accepting the Soviet proposals respecting the Baltic States, and added that " when Great Britain is interested in guaranteeing a country she finds the necessary way, without waiting for these countries to ask for guarantees." M. Zhdanov continued:

> " The *Sunday Times*, of June 4, 1939, said: ' Poland has, for her part, agreed that if Britain was involved in war on account of an invasion of Holland, she would come to Britain's assistance, while Great Britain has agreed that if Poland was involved in war on account of an invasion of Danzig or Lithuania, she would come to Poland's assistance.'*
>
> It is thus clear that Poland and Great Britain guarantee both Lithuania and Holland simultaneously. I do not know whether Lithuania and Holland were consulted as to whether they desired this two-sided agreement. In any case, nothing has been reported by the press in regard to such a consultation. Moreover, both Holland and Lithuania, so far as I know, deny the fact of such a guarantee. Nevertheless, the Pact for a two-sided guarantee of these countries has in the main already been concluded, as the *Sunday Times* reports, and it is no secret that the report of the *Sunday Times* has not been denied."

M. Zhdanov's article was a grave warning to the Chancelleries of London and Paris and its timeliness was forcibly emphasised by the fact that on the very day that it appeared, the Chief of the German General Staff arrived in Helsinki to return the visit to Berlin of the Finnish Commander-in-Chief.

Further, four days earlier, Dr. Goebbels, speaking at Essen declared: " If the British try to threaten us that does not matter to us,

* This article was written by the Diplomatic Correspondent of the *Sunday Times*.

for we know that there is no force behind their threats. Take, for example, China, where the Japanese strip them naked, and the British can do nothing. Great Britain remains stupid, and cannot cope with our might. . . ."

On July 1, the British-French side proposed a formula regarding the Baltic States which the Soviet Government found acceptable—no guaranteed country would be mentioned in the Principal Treaty, but the names would appear in a special annexe—but they at once nullified this advance by proposing the inclusion in the list of guaranteed countries, Holland and Switzerland, two countries which consistently had refused to *recognise* the U.S.S.R.

The Soviet Government replied two days later, July 3, agreeing to the formula respecting the Baltic States, but adding that as the inclusion of Holland and Switzerland—the negotiations to date had been conducted on the basis of guaranteeing eight countries, viz., Belgium, Greece, Turkey, Poland, Rumania, Latvia, Estonia and Finland—would mean additional obligations for the U.S.S.R., the latter felt that she should have some additional guarantees in the form of Mutual Assistance Pacts with Poland and Turkey.

The British-French negotiators were not ready for further talks until July 8, but on that date and the next, two long meetings were held. Three main difficulties emerged: (1) Britain and France insisted on the guarantee for Holland and Switzerland irrespective of the conclusion of a Mutual Assistance Pact between the U.S.S.R., on the one hand, and Poland and Turkey on the other. This the Soviet side could not accept. (2) Neither side would agree to the other's definition as to what constituted " indirect aggression " on the Sudeten or Danzig model and which would justify the application of the Triple Pact. (3) The Soviet representatives insisted and the British-French side demurred to the coming into operation simultaneously of the Triple Pact and the Military Convention.

Meanwhile, in Great Britain some people who regarded the negotiations with the Soviet Union as a disagreeable necessity began to ask, still in superior tones, " Does the Soviet Union want an Agreement? " but others stressed that some influential circles definitely did not want an Alliance with the U.S.S.R. Mr. A. J. Cummings wrote:

> " Does the British Government know that Moscow knows that less than three weeks ago the hope was expressed in high British quarters that the Anglo-Soviet Pact could be ' avoided '?
>
> That knowledge is the chief stumbling block in these mysterious delays; and it provides the answer to cunning hints now emanating from Whitehall that Russia ' does not want the pact.' "*

* *News Chronicle*, 13.vii.39.

Another meeting took place in Moscow on July 17. The British-French delegation dropped for the time being the question of Holland and Switzerland, but there still remained unresolved two vital issues: (*a*) what constituted "indirect aggression"; (*b*) the simultaneous coming into force of the Triple Pact and the Military Convention.

Meanwhile, General Ironside, who had been in Poland, left Warsaw for London by plane on July 21. It was circumstantially rumoured in the British, French and Polish capitals that the Polish Government had convinced Ironside that Germany would open hostilities at the end of August, and naturally he must have reported this to the British Government.

Mr. Lloyd George, who had from the beginning followed the course of these events very closely, told his countrymen on July 23 what he thought of the British Government's policy:

> "Chamberlain guaranteed Poland, Rumania and Greece against the huge army of Germany.
>
> It looked magnificent, but men who had some knowledge of the problems pointed out to him that it was not war. I was the first to call attention to that obvious fact in the House of Commons. I denounced it as sheer madness to give such a pledge in the absence of military support from Russia.
>
> Russian troops could alone hope to reach the battlefield in time to save the Polish Army from being crushed by an overwhelming German superiority in men, and especially in equipment.
>
> The Chief of our General Staff was abroad in France when this harebrained pledge was given. I have good reason to believe that on his return he and his advisers pointed out that we did not possess the means to redeem it."*

Then, after denouncing the British Government's handling of the negotiations with the Soviet Union, he concluded:

> "Lord Halifax visited Hitler and Goering. Chamberlain flew into the Führer's arms three times in succession. He went specially to Rome to embrace Mussolini, to present him with the official recognition of the conquest of Abyssinia, and practically to tell him that we would not bother him about his invasion of Spain.
>
> Why send only a Foreign Office bureaucrat to represent us in an infinitely more powerful country which was offering to come to our aid?
>
> There is only one answer. Mr. Neville Chamberlain, Lord Halifax and Sir John Simon do not want any association with Russia.

* *Sunday Express*, 23.vii.39

If they do not, they ought not to have dallied with her, and above all, they ought not to have insulted her with the glaring contrast between the standing of the emissaries we despatch to transact business with her and those we had already despatched to confer with Hitler and Mussolini.

We may drive her into a hostility which would suit the Dictators but would be fatal to the Empires of France and Britain."*

On the day when this article appeared another Conference was held in Moscow at which the Soviet representatives again insisted that the Triple Pact and the Military Convention should come into force simultaneously. They proposed that staff talks should start immediately and intimated that if the Military Convention were concluded the remaining difficulty, viz., a formula covering "indirect aggression" could easily be solved. Two days later, the British Government agreed to the proposals for immediate staff talks and decided to send a Military Mission to Moscow. The French Government followed suit. After announcing this decision to the House of Commons, July 31, 1939, the Prime Minister added: "The British delegation will be headed by Admiral the Hon. Sir Reginald Plunkett Ernle-Erle-Drax, and will include Air-Marshal Sir Charles Burnett and Major-General Heywood."† Replying to pointed complaints from the Liberal and Labour benches about the dilatoriness of the negotiations, he innocently declared: "The Anglo-Japanese Alliance, which was a bi-lateral arrangement, took six months to negotiate. The Anglo-French Entente of 1904 took nine months. The Anglo-Russian Convention of 1907 took 15 months."‡

Did not the Prime Minister realise that even when the last-mentioned of these instruments was concluded, the conquest of the air was still in its infancy, the internal combustion engine was still in its early stages and tanks had not yet been invented? Was he aware that in the intervening years methods of warfare had been completely revolutionised? to say nothing of the far greater urgency of the international situation in 1939.

Immediately after Mr. Chamberlain's announcement there were many enquiries and comments in the lobbies of the House of Commons respecting the personnel of the Mission. It was quickly realised that few, if any, members of the House of Commons had ever heard of any of the members of the Mission before, and later it transpired that the Mission had no plenipotentiary powers. In fact, the sending of this Mission was just a sop to quieten public uneasiness. What the British and French Governments should have done was clear.

* Ibid. † *Hansard*, 31.vii.39, col. 1929.

‡ Ibid., col. 2023.

They ought to have sent Lord Gort and General Gamelin with full powers to conclude a comprehensive military alliance. Such action, even at that late hour, might have saved the peace.

The sands in the hourglass of fate were rapidly running out. It was July 31, and Hitler was expected to strike at the end of August, but the Governments of Britain and France made no haste. In fact, the immediate sequel was astounding. The Soviet Embassy which had to advise its Government as to the time of arrival of the Mission, naturally asked how the Mission would travel. " By air? " " No, that would be difficult because the Mission consisted of twenty persons and their luggage." " By a fast cruiser? " " That would be inconvenient, it would mean turning twenty officers out of their cabins." " By a fast steamer? " " Don't know. That is left to the Board of Trade."

Finally the Mission left on August 5, 1939, travelling by a slow boat and arrived in Moscow on August 11, 1939. They could, of course, have flown to that city in 24 hours. Naturally, the impression left in Moscow was exceedingly bad. There they could not but come to the conclusion that the sending of the Mission did not mean serious business.

Both sides met in Conference on August 12, and the negotiations continued up to and including August 17. The main difficulty emerged immediately. It was Poland. The British and French representatives asked the Soviet delegation what the U.S.S.R. was able and willing to do to aid Poland in the event of a German attack. Marshal Voroshilov replied that the Polish Army single-handed could not possibly withstand an attack by the powerful mechanised army of Germany; that the Red Army was willing and able to co-operate with the Polish Army in defence of Poland, but in order to do so the Red Army would have to cross Polish territory and, jointly with the Polish Army, face the German Army on the Polish-German frontier.

The British and French delegations, through the usual channels, made the necessary enquiries in Warsaw and then came with their reply. The essence of their astounding answer was that the Polish Government did not require armed help from the U.S.S.R. in fighting Germany, provided that Great Britain and France gave effective assistance; that in no circumstances would the Polish Government allow Soviet forces to enter its territory, but that they would welcome help in the form of Soviet military supplies; that the Polish Government was adamant in its attitude and that nothing more could be done. After an interval of three days, conversations were resumed on the morning of August 21, but no progress was made. The deadlock was complete.

II. The Soviet-German Non-Aggression Pact

In these circumstances the Soviet Government was reluctantly driven to the conclusion that an Anglo-French-Soviet Pact with a comprehensive Military Alliance, which even at this last minute might have preserved peace, was unobtainable. Meanwhile, the whole world, including particularly the German Government, had been closely following the negotiations. On several occasions the German Foreign Office strongly hinted that Germany would be willing to conclude a Non-Aggression Pact with the U.S.S.R. The Soviet Government, as many in Britain knew at the time,* refused to listen until they realised beyond a doubt that there was no possibility of concluding with Great Britain and France a Three-Power Pact coupled with a Military Convention.

Then and only then, with their eyes fully open, the Soviet Government concluded a Pact of Non-Aggression with Germany. The decision was announced in the late hours of August 21, and the Pact was signed in Moscow on August 23, 1939. This instrument was not an Alliance but only a Pact of Non-Aggression, and there was nothing in the Soviet-German Pact which precluded the Soviet Government from concluding a similar Pact with Great Britain and France. However, the Governments of the two latter were not interested in such a Pact and the joint Mission left Moscow on August 26, 1939.

During the whole of the Anglo-French-Soviet negotiations in 1939, there were very powerful influences in Britain which were seeking an understanding not with the U.S.S.R., but with Nazi Germany. The mild manner in which Mr. Chamberlain at first treated Hitler's disruption of the precious Munich Agreement by his brutal march into Prague† was one pointer. There were many others. During the very days on which the destruction of the Czechoslovakian Republic was taking place, British and German industrialists had been getting together. A delegation representing the Federation of British Industries left London on March 13, 1939, to meet their opposite numbers of the Reichsgruppe Industrie—the German equivalent of the Federation of British Industries. A convention of both sides was held at Dusseldorf on March 15 and 16, followed by a joint declaration which appeared in the press on March 22, 1939, and which, after dealing at length with the necessity for collaboration between the two sides concluded:

> "The ultimate objective must be to increase world prosperity. The Reichsgruppe Industrie and the Federation of British Industries believe that the result of their discussions has been to lay

* See e.g. the statement of Sir Stafford Cripps, p. 699.

† See *World Affairs and the U.S.S.R.*, by W. P. and Zelda Coates, 1939, p. 211.

a sound foundation upon which the individual industries can usefully begin with mutual advantage. In order to ensure the success of this policy it has been agreed between the Reichsgruppe Industrie and the Federation of British Industries to form a standing committee of the two organisations which will meet regularly to review progress. The F.B.I. have invited the German members of this joint committee to pay a visit to England in June for this purpose, and this invitation has been accepted by their German colleagues."

More illuminating still was the fact that although as a result of public indignation, Mr. Chamberlain on March 17 had taken a stronger line than at first regarding Hitler's march into Czechoslovakia, it was revealed later that the Chamberlain Government still did not exclude the possibility of an *alliance* with Germany. Sir Nevile Henderson, British Ambassador to Germany, who incidentally revealed in his Memoirs his admiration for Hitler, described in a Note to Viscount Halifax how in an interview on August 28, 1939, he had urged on Hitler that if his demands on Poland were *reasonable*, he could have British friendship—in other words (although, of course, Sir Nevile did not put it thus), Britain was prepared to do a Munich on Poland—but it must be done gently so that British public opinion would not be alarmed. Sir Nevile continued:

> " At the end Herr von Ribbentrop asked me whether I could guarantee that the Prime Minister could carry the country with him in a policy of friendship with Germany. I said there was no possible doubt whatever that he could and would, provided Germany co-operated with him. Herr Hitler asked whether England would be willing to accept an alliance with Germany. I said, speaking personally, I did not exclude such a possibility provided the developments of events justified it."*

One more instance. In July, 1939, Lord Kemsley—a man with powerful political connections, the proprietor of the *Daily Sketch*, *Sunday Times*, and of a number of other influential Sunday, daily and evening newspapers, as well as of six provincial weeklies—discussed with Dr. Dietrich, Official Head of the German Press, the question of an exchange of articles in which the German point of view would be stated in articles to be published in the British press, whilst articles in the German press would give the British case.†

Further, on the invitation of Dr. Dietrich, Lord Kemsley visited Germany, arriving at Bayreuth, July 27, 1939, where he had talks with Hitler, Rosenberg, Dietrich and others. Nothing definite

* Cmd. 6106, 1939, p. 130.

† Related by Lord Kemsley himself, *Sunday Times*, 3.iii.40.

materialised and in a letter on August 1, 1939, Lord Kemsley, after pointing out the state of public opinion in Britain, emphasised his own faith in the Munich policy. He said: " Nevertheless, if opinion here could be convinced that confidence could be re-established, i.e., if the fundamental basis of the Declaration which the Führer and Mr. Chamberlain signed the day after the Munich Conference could be accepted afresh by both sides, there would be much better hope of useful discussion," and he expressed his sincere desire for an understanding.

Perhaps the most revealing point of all was the following passage in Lord Kemsley's article of March 3, 1940:

> " But on August 21 there was announced from Berlin the fact that the Soviet-German Pact had been successfully negotiated; as the official record shows, it was signed on August 23 by Ribbentrop and Molotov. As this document established and finally decided a complete re-orientation of Germany's traditional anti-Communist policy, and foreshadowed the coming of an aggressive alliance between Germany and Russia against the Allies, it made any hope of agreement by discussion very improbable. This was my view at the time, and *I was supported in that view by some of the highest political authorities in this country*." (Our italics).

Why, if an understanding with Germany was in itself desirable, should it have become undesirable after the conclusion of an understanding between Germany and the U.S.S.R.? Obviously because the understanding with Germany was intended as an understanding *against* the U.S.S.R.

CHAPTER XXVI

ANGLO-SOVIET RELATIONS AFTER THE OUTBREAK OF THE WAR, 1939-1940

I. The U.S.S.R., Poland and the Baltic States. Anglo-Soviet Agreement October 11, 1939

With the outbreak of the war, bitterness against the U.S.S.R. naturally did not decrease and after the obstructive policy pursued by the British and French Governments during the negotiations with the Chamberlain and Daladier Governments, the tone of the Soviet press was decidedly anti-British and anti-French—although it was certainly not pro-German. There followed measures taken by the British Government—measures which under war conditions may have been unavoidable, but which dealt fresh blows to the interests of the U.S.S.R.

Early in September, 1939, the export from Britain of machinery, machine tools, rubber, cocoa, etc., which had been ordered previously by the Soviet Trade Commissariat was prohibited. The Soviet Government on their side, September 9, empowered the Foreign Trade Commissariat to restrict or prohibit the export of goods to countries in which legislative or other measures or the establishment of foreign exchange restrictions created conditions unfavourable for Soviet trade. It was also empowered to prevent the shipment of goods abroad unless paid for in advance. This was followed on September 14 by a Soviet Government Order recalling Soviet merchant ships on their way to Britain.

Nevertheless, the importance of not antagonising the U.S.S.R. further was recognised by some in Britain. Mr. Lloyd George and others deplored the loss of the U.S.S.R. as an ally and urged strongly the need to take steps to renew contact with the Soviet Government and to come to a friendly understanding.

With the outbreak of war the realistic Soviet leaders knew perfectly well that the danger to themselves had not ultimately decreased, although their agreement with Germany secured them for the time being from the menace of a German attack. But this possibility remained a constant danger, and accordingly the Soviet Government immediately took steps to strengthen their country in every possible way.

The first act was an announcement on September 5 that an additional 1½ million men would be called to the colours, whilst the Red Army of the 1937 class (due to retire towards the end of September) serving in the Baltic, Polish and Ukraine frontier districts were to have their term of service extended for an extra month. A few days later more reservists were called up, the mobilisation being confined to the West, " in order," as the official statement said, " to strengthen further the defences of the country in view of the German-Polish war, which is acquiring an ever wider and more threatening character." This was intended as a purely precautionary measure, for the Soviet Government could in no way be certain as to how long the Poles could resist Germany, nor could they rely on Hitler to respect the Soviet-German agreement should it suit him to violate it.

But Polish resistance broke down far more quickly than had been anticipated, for reasons into which we need not enter here. Within a fortnight of the opening of hostilities the resistance of the armed forces of Poland had been broken and the Polish Government was in flight.

In such circumstances the U.S.S.R. had three courses of action open to her: (1) to do nothing; (2) to throw in her lot with the Allies against Germany; (3) to march into Poland herself. She chose (3).

Why? Because had she done nothing, then the whole of Poland would undoubtedly have been overrun by the Nazi jackboot—this would have signified that their own bloodbrothers—the Byelorussians and Ukrainians of Western Poland would have been subjected to Nazi brutality, and, Treaty or no Treaty, would the Nazis have stopped at the Soviet frontiers?—the rich cornfields and mineral wealth of the Ukraine would undoubtedly have been too great a lure and Stalin and his comrades had read *Mein Kampf*.

Had they chosen course (2) and thrown in their lot with the Allies against Germany, the immediate results so far as Western Poland and the U.S.S.R. were concerned, would have been exactly the same, and in view of their experiences during the Anglo-French-Soviet negotiations and in their long previous fight for collective security, they had every reason to expect that Britain and France would look on passively whilst Germany and the U.S.S.R. were at death grips. Further, it was well known that powerful circles in Britain and still more influential sections in France were still trying to switch the war from Germany on to the U.S.S.R. Accordingly the Soviet Government chose the third course.

On September 17, 1939, the Red Army marched into Eastern Poland and on the same morning M. Molotov handed a note to the Polish Ambassador in Moscow, advising him of the step taken by the Soviet armed forces and declaring that in view of the collapse of organised Government in Poland the "Polish State and its Government had virtually ceased to exist; the treaties concluded between the U.S.S.R. and Poland have thereby ceased to operate." The state of affairs in that country, said the Note, was a menace to Soviet interests, whilst the Byelorussians and Ukrainians in Eastern Poland had been left without protection.

The Polish Ambassador refused to accept the Note, but agreed to inform his Government of its contents. The same day a copy of the Note to the Polish Ambassador was transmitted to all the Diplomatic representatives in Moscow, together with a Note declaring that "the U.S.S.R. will pursue a policy of neutrality in the relations between the U.S.S.R. and your country."

By her march into Poland the U.S.S.R. for the time being saved millions of Ukrainians, Byelorussians and Jews from the Nazi bestialities, increased the distance between Germany and the old Soviet frontier and gained additional time to strengthen her defences against an attack from the Nazis which the Soviet Government knew it could expect sooner or later.

"Our troops entered the territory of Poland," M. Molotov later told the Supreme Soviet of the U.S.S.R.* "only after the Polish State

* 31.x.39.

had collapsed and had actually ceased to exist. Naturally we could not remain neutral towards these facts, since as a result of these events we were confronted with urgent problems concerning the security of our State. Furthermore, the Soviet Government could not but reckon with the exceptional situation created for our brothers in Western Ukraine and Western Byelorussia, who had been abandoned to their fate as a result of the collapse of Poland."

But in Britain hostility to the U.S.S.R. received a new fillip. In the British press of the time there was a great outcry. The *Daily Herald*, *Yorkshire Post*, *Evening Standard*, *Evening News*, and some other journals characterised the Soviet action as "cowardly," "murder," "dastardly," "imperialist," "hyenas," "stab in the back," etc.

Apart from the Communists and a comparative handful of Labour and Socialist adherents, British "Left" circles were more whole-hearted, certainly more vocal, in their denunciation than the Right. Many members of the Labour and Socialist parties had very fixed ideas of what was meant by "imperialism," by "aggression" and never related these terms to time, place or epoch. The march of one country into another was "imperialism," "aggression," irrespective of circumstances, and so even though it meant that the defence of the Socialist State would be facilitated and even though it meant the liberation of millions of human beings from being ground down by the Nazis—the crossing of the Soviet frontier by the Red Army implied for them that Stalin was as much an imperialist as Hitler!

The Conservative attitude, although in general very bitterly anti-Soviet, may be summed up in the following quotations from the British press, September 18, 1939:

The *Daily Express* Political Correspondent declared:

> "The Russians' invasion of Poland caused no surprise in London diplomatic quarters yesterday. Some such step had been anticipated for some time.
>
> It should not be assumed that the new move is necessarily to the disadvantage of the Allied cause.
>
> If, as is expected, the Russians advance until they have a common frontier with the Germans in Polish territory, it will be necessary for Hitler to maintain considerable forces there as 'a precautionary measure.'
>
> He will thus be forced to have an army in the East big enough to keep down the Poles and to ensure that Russia does not advance further."

In the *Daily Mail*, Mr. G. Ward Price wrote:

> "Russia resented the incorporation of 3,000,000 Ukrainians in Poland. Her entry of Polish territory can be considered as

intended to ensure that these former Russians do not now fall under German sway.

There is no need to assume that the co-operation of the Soviet Government with Germany will go further than the protection of their own interests under the Russo-German Pact."

The *Daily Telegraph* stated:

"Reading between the lines, it is plain enough that the Russian Government is alarmed at the rapidity of the German advance and the threat it offers to Russia's western frontier. The new Russo-German Non-Aggression Pact is worth no more and no less than Herr Hitler's agreements with Austria, Czechoslovakia and Poland, and Stalin cannot watch the German steam-roller crashing over prostrate Poland without an uneasy suspicion that the driver may forget to stop. Stalin has presumably read *Mein Kampf*. If so, he has no doubt noted Herr Hitler's conviction that Germany's true field of expansion is to the eastward; that what he covets most in Europe is the granary of the Ukraine. Like most monomaniacs, Herr Hitler has been true to himself if nothing else; and there is point in M. Molotov's insistence that Poland's White Russians and Ukrainians are under Red protection. . . .

Whatever the future may hold, two things are certain. The presence of a powerful Russian army on his eastern frontier will immobilise a large part of Herr Hitler's forces at a time when they are needed in the west; and Poland, brutally stricken to the earth, will rise again."

The Liberal press was also loud enough in denouncing the Soviet march into Poland, but was not altogether blinded by it to the real significance of the move. Thus the *News Chronicle* declared:

"Soviet intervention in Poland has no doubt been hastened by the speed of the German advance. It may be that Moscow had begun to fear lest the impetus of Hitler's drive might carry him further than was convenient to Stalin and find him establishing himself on or dangerously near the existing Russian frontier. Immediate Russian action to occupy a slice of East Poland and, more especially, to safeguard the Polish Ukraine from German penetration before it became too late would be an obvious reaction to such a fear."

And the *Star*, whilst also denouncing Russian "crocodile tears," etc., nevertheless declared:

"No realist can be surprised that Russia should have decided that it could not stay out of the Polish cockpit. The temptation

> was in any case great. Large Russian minorities lie along the eastern parts of Poland, and the frontier is no more than an arbitrary line. . . .
>
> Russia could not stand still with her enormous army and see the German war mechanism advancing to her very frontier without the gravest misgivings. As firmly fixed as Hitler's desire to advance to the East is Russia's permanent policy of preventing Germany from sharing a common frontier."*

On September 18, an official statement was issued from Downing Street declaring that the Soviet action in Poland " could not be justified by the arguments put forward by the Soviet Government " but that its " full implications were not yet apparent " and these sentiments were repeated by Mr. Winston Churchill (First Lord of the Admiralty) two days later in the House of Commons. On the whole, though there were many bitter things said about the Soviet Government, there was general agreement that a cautious attitude must be maintained and that there could be no question of breaking off diplomatic relations —a course of action which had actually been hinted at in some sections of the press.

As the days passed, passions cooled, and this was the case in particular when the terms of the Treaty of Amity and on the Frontier between the U.S.S.R. and Germany, September 28, 1939, were published. It was then seen that the U.S.S.R. had only demanded and obtained those parts of Poland which were ethnologically, geographically and historically part of the Soviet Ukraine and Byelorussia and that the frontier line agreed on followed closely the " Curzon Line " (laid down as a just frontier between Poland and Russia by the Supreme Council of the Allies in 1919).

Mr. Lloyd George came out strongly against those who recklessly demanded stern action against the U.S.S.R. The following extracts from a letter he sent to the Polish Ambassador on September 28, 1939, are interesting:

> " It is a notorious fact that the Polish peasants are living in great poverty owing to the operation of the worst feudal system in Europe. That aristocracy has been practically in power for years. All the promises of concessions made from time to time to the peasants have been thwarted by its influence on recent Polish Governments. That is why the advancing Russian troops are being hailed by the peasants as deliverers.
>
> The German invasion is designed to annex to the Reich provinces where the decided majority of the population is Polish by race, language and tradition. On the other hand, the Russian

* 18.ix.39.

armies marched into territories which are not Polish, and which were forcibly annexed by Poland after the Great War, in spite of the fierce protests and the armed resistance of the inhabitants. The inhabitants of Polish Ukraine are of the same race and language as their neighbours in the Ukrainian Republic of the Soviet Union.

I felt it was a matter of primary importance to call attention at once to these salient considerations lest we commit ourselves rashly to war against Russia under the impression that her intervention was identical with that of Germany. The distinction between the two cases is increasingly acknowledged by British and French opinion. In these circumstances it would be an act of criminal folly to place the Russian advance in the same category as that of the Germans, although it would suit Herr Hitler's designs that we should do so. I am delighted that our Government have shown no indication of committing this country to such an attitude or enterprise."

Similarly, Mr. Churchill, in the course of a broadcast, October 1, 1939, in effect *welcomed the Russian action in Poland.* He said:

" What is the second event of this first month? It is, of course, the assertion of the power of Russia. Russia has pursued a cold policy of self-interest. We could have wished that the Russian armies should be standing on their present line as the friends and allies of Poland, instead of as invaders. But that the Russian armies should stand on this line was clearly necessary for the safety of Russia against the Nazi menace. At any rate the line is there, and an Eastern Front has been created which Nazi Germany does not dare assail.

When Herr von Ribbentrop was summoned to Moscow last week it was to learn the fact, and to accept the fact, that the Nazi designs upon the Baltic States and upon the Ukraine must come to a dead stop."*

At the same time a declaration accompanying the Soviet-German Treaty made suggestions for peace negotiations between Germany on the one hand and Britain and France on the other. Britain was at that time decidedly not prepared for peace with Hitler, who, flushed with triumph, could hardly have been expected to make anything but a robber's peace offer. Why did the Soviet Government agree to this suggestion? To us it seems that the reason was two-fold; in the first place, it was a concession to Hitler which, if nothing came of

* *Times,* 2.x.39.

the offer, would cost them nothing; secondly, should Britain and France accept, then in a Conference the U.S.S.R. could make its voice heard as an equal, insisting on terms which they considered fair and assuring general peace (the Soviet press made it clear that all they asked was that the terms offered by Hitler should be considered calmly and judicially). In Britain, too, there were a number of people—notably Mr. Lloyd George—who were strongly against rejecting the peace offer out of hand.

In the *News Chronicle*, Mr. Cummings, after pointing out the decisive importance of Russia both in regard to a possible peace conference and if the war continued, urged that Britain and France might well use the "occasion to declare their war aims in more specific terms. Mr. Chamberlain apparently doesn't think it necessary. The neutrals, especially the Americans, think otherwise."*

On the previous day, Mr. Chamberlain had said in the House of Commons that this was not the time "for the French and British Governments to state their war aims in more specific form."

As we have pointed out, the Soviet-German Treaty of August 23, 1939, did not in any way preclude normal trading relations between the U.S.S.R. and Britain or the conclusion of a Soviet-British Non-Aggression Treaty. Many people in Britain saw the need of encouraging trade between the two countries, and the Soviets were always perfectly willing to maintain friendly political and trading relations with Britain.

On September 23, for the first time since the conclusion of the Soviet-German Non-Aggression Pact, M. Maisky had an audience with Lord Halifax—the latter put certain questions to the Soviet Ambassador and four days later, September 27, M. Maisky again called on Lord Halifax and informed him that the Soviet Government intended to maintain neutrality and were prepared to accept the proposals to open the trade negotiations envisaged when Mr. Hudson visited Moscow.†

Towards the end of September, trade negotiations between the British Government and the Soviet Trade Delegation in London proceeded with the object of securing the release by Britain of commodities which the U.S.S.R. desired to purchase in exchange for the release of Soviet timber consignments to Britain, and on October 11, 1939, it was announced that "an agreement for the exchange of Russian timber for certain quantities of rubber and tin was to-day concluded between the Soviet Trade Delegation in London and the Ministry of Supply."

Although the Mutual Assistance Pacts concluded by the U.S.S.R. with the Baltic States—Estonia (September 28, 1939), Latvia (Octo-

* 10.x.39. † Mr. Hudson had visited Moscow in March, 1939.

ber 5, 1939) and Lithuania (October 10, 1939)—led to much abuse and many cynical references in the British press regarding the Soviet Government, nevertheless, on the whole, the voices raised in favour of a better understanding with the U.S.S.R. became more numerous and louder as time went on. It was also realised by many that the safeguarding of Soviet strategic interests in the Baltic by no means favoured the German war effort.

The Anglo-Soviet Agreement of October 11 was certainly welcomed and hopes were expressed in many quarters that this would be but the first of a number of similar agreements. Lord Halifax, the Foreign Secretary, in his speeches in the House of Lords on October 4 and October 26, was more conciliatory towards the U.S.S.R. than might perhaps have been expected from him.

Good economic relations with the U.S.S.R. were, of course, of the utmost importance, on the one hand in order to enable Britain to obtain many essential products, thereby reducing their sale to Germany, and on the other, in order to hinder the establishment of closer economic relations between the U.S.S.R. and Germany. And this was precisely the line taken by many of the more far-seeing in Britain—the more so since the German Government was doing everything possible to extend trade with the U.S.S.R. The Soviet Government on their side made it clear time and again that they intended to maintain strict neutrality and were prepared to do trade on that basis with Britain and France in the same way as with Germany.

Negotiations, or rather conversations—trade and diplomatic—continued, but against formidable obstacles: on the one hand, the ingrained hostility towards the U.S.S.R. of the Munichites in the British Government and their supporters; on the other, the not unreasonable suspicions entertained by the Soviet leaders towards the Munichites.

Pleading for a more realistic British approach to the U.S.S.R., the *News Chronicle* rightly said:

> " She [Russia] knows that it has long been the hope of some quite influential people in Britain that sooner or later Russia and Germany could be egged on to destroy each other while we held the ring and pocketed the stakes.
>
> And after Munich, when Russia was cold-shouldered out of the conference room and the four Western Powers pledged each other to life-long friendship, the die-hards openly talked of the desirability of giving Germany a free hand in the East. Germany was to be a mobile bulwark against Bolshevism, and we were to aid and abet. 'I was at a loss to understand,' wrote Lord Londonderry last year, 'why we could not make common ground

in some form or other with Germany in opposition to Communism.' . . .

Our die-hards are still toying with the idea of setting Russia and Germany at each other's throats to our own advantage. Talk of making peace with a Conservative German Government and then joining with it to fight the 'Red Menace' isn't calculated to increase Anglo-Soviet cordiality. And such talk is prevalent."*

The writer (John Bouverie) concluded: "I predict that she will go on being difficult just as long as we provide grounds for her suspicions."

However, in spite of these difficulties and also those inevitably arising as a result of British action in regard to contraband, and Soviet protests in defence of its interests as a neutral, there might have been grounds for improved Anglo-Soviet relations had not the Soviet-Finnish conflict given full scope to those bent on bedevilling these relations.

II. The Soviet-Finnish Campaign

The Soviet-Finnish campaign (December, 1939-March, 1940) was dictated by the strategic interests of the U.S.S.R.; it was essential that Finland should not be used as a jumping-off ground for an attack on the U.S.S.R. Summing up the causes of this war, M. Molotov, People's Commissar for Foreign Affairs, afterwards stated that the issues between Finland and the U.S.S.R. could have been settled without war but for "foreign influences" and the incitements of "certain third States":

"All through October and November of last year the Soviet Government discussed with the Finnish Government proposals which, in view of the existing international situation—a situation that was growing more and more inflammable—we considered absolutely essential and urgent for safeguarding the security of our country, and especially of Leningrad. Nothing came of these negotiations because of the unfriendly attitude adopted by the Finnish representatives. The decision of the issue passed to the field of war.

It may safely be said that had Finland not been subjected to foreign influences, had Finland been less incited by certain third States to adopt a hostile policy towards the U.S.S.R., the Soviet Union and Finland would have arrived at a peaceful understanding last autumn, and matters would have been settled without war. But in spite of the fact that the Soviet Government

* 25.x.39.

reduced its request to a minimum, a settlement could not be reached by diplomatic means. . . .

Incontrovertible facts have shown that the hostile policy which we encountered on the part of Finland last autumn was no fortuitous thing. Forces hostile to the Soviet Union had prepared in Finland such a *place d'armes* against our country and in the first place against Leningrad, which, should a foreign situation arise unfavourable to the U.S.S.R., was to play its part in the plans of the anti-Soviet forces of the imperialists and their allies in Finland. Not only has the Red Army smashed the Mannerheim Line and thereby covered itself with glory as the first army to force its way under most difficult conditions through a deep, powerful zone of perfectly modern military fortifications, not only has the Red Army together with the Red Fleet destroyed the Finnish *place d'armes* which had been made ready for an attack on Leningrad, but it has also put an end to certain anti-Soviet plans which some third countries had been hatching during the past few years."*

The chorus of protests and cries of indignation in Britain which followed the outbreak of Soviet-Finnish hostilities was deafening. All but the Communists and a handful of leaders and adherents of the Labour and other parties joined in the sport. Mannerheim, the former Tsarist courtier who used to be known as "butcher Mannerheim" because of his atrocities against the Finnish workers, suddenly became the perfect gentleman and the hero and leader of "democratic" Finland.

During the period of the "phoney" war between Germany and Britain and France, war correspondents had had little opportunity of exercising their art and they took that provided by the Soviet-Finnish war with both hands; there followed an orgy of sensational reports of the "gallant, skilful fight of the Finns" compared with the alleged ineptitude, wretched equipment and brutalities, etc., of the Russians which could not but fan the anti-Soviet agitation.†

Actually, whatever mistakes may have been made by the Red Army in the early stages of the Soviet-Finnish war, these were rapidly corrected and the conduct of the campaign was in general a brilliant piece of work in which the underlying strategy later pursued by the Red Army in the war against Germany can already be discerned, viz., first to weaken the enemy by drawing off his forces from the main position by a series of feint attacks at other points, in the meantime

* Report to the Supreme Soviet, 29.iii.40.

† This and other aspects of the Soviet-Finnish campaign are dealt with more fully in *The Soviet-Finnish Campaign*, 1939-1940: *Military and Political*, by W. P. and Zelda K. Coates. Published by Eldon Press, Ltd.

accumulating the necessary material for the main attack, and then to strike the main target with all possible strength.

The main military target which the Red Army set itself in the Finnish campaign was the Mannerheim Line—a modern system of fortifications erected under the guidance of British military experts assisted by Swedish and German specialists—sometimes called the Mannerheim-Kirke Line after Baron Mannerheim and General Sir Walter Kirke who had directed its construction. This was a fortified zone including a number of improvements over both the French Maginot Line and the German Siegfried Line, and as is well known, neither of the two latter were stormed; the Maginot Line was not pierced by the Germans but outflanked.

In order to gain the time required in the difficult geographical and meteorological conditions to bring up the troops and huge military supplies necessary, the Soviet Command engaged in a series of feint attacks on what is known as the waist-line of Finland, giving the impression that their main object was the cutting of Finland in two.

> "These attacks (on the waist-line) were to draw off as many Finnish reserves as possible and to keep them occupied, and also to deceive the enemy as to the direction of the main offensive. If the deception was carried out properly the Finns would have great difficulty in relieving the exhausted front line on the Karelian Isthmus when the big and continuous attack was opened there.
>
> The further the Finns were drawn from their railheads in the northern regions, the harder it would be for them to extricate themselves from the fighting. But the key of the plan was that these attacks must appear so real and the threat so imminent that the deception could be kept up for two months.
>
> Two immediate preliminary actions were needed to operate this plan. The first was to take the forward zone of the Mannerheim Line in order to remove the artillery and air threat against the Soviet base at Leningrad and to provide space for the amassing of the forces for the great attack. The second was to take Petsamo, the only port the Finns possessed in the Arctic north, to prevent the possibility of intervention by a naval power."*

After carrying out these two preliminary actions within less than a week after the outbreak of hostilities, the Soviet forces made repeated thrusts in the direction of the waist-line, as well as in the Far North, whilst also continuously probing the Mannerheim Line for weak spots; at the beginning of February the attack on the Mannerheim Line began in full force and made steady progress from February 8 onwards, becoming ever more intense, until by March 2, Viborg Station

* *The Soviet-Finnish Campaign*, by Major A. S. Hooper, 1940.

was occupied and by March 11, 1940, the ring round Viborg was closed.

The Mannerheim Line had been stormed by direct assault within about a month—the first and only break through of this kind in modern military history. The remarkable nature of this feat is even more astounding when one recalls the appalling weather conditions—30, 40, sometimes even 50 and more degrees below zero, and the fact that the network of railroads in central and southern Finland gave the Finnish army the great advantage of operating along good inner lines of communication, whilst the Soviet Union had only the Murmansk railroad, running 700 miles along the Finnish border, for the supply of her entire western front. For the Isthmus front, i.e., for the supply of the troops on the Mannerheim front, there was only the Leningrad bottleneck with but one bridge across the River Neva.

> " General Meretskov's plan, well conceived and boldly executed, was on a scale worthy of the past great masters of the art of war. In contrast to the days of Tsarism, he had the advantage of superior weapons, but for all that he could never have brought the campaign to its decisive conclusion had it not been for the fighting qualities of the rank and file of the Red Army. . . .
>
> In Finland, the Red Army, in a race against time, achieved what no other modern army has yet dared to attempt, that is, it attacked and broke a modern defensive system of fortifications by frontal assault . . . As a feat of arms it stands out in all history as unique. Only military ignorance or political prejudice would dare to deny it."*

By " the race against time " the author refers to the fact that the Soviet Command considered it essential to storm the Mannerheim Line by the end of March before the thaw had set in.

Later on the real facts about the war began to be recognised more and more but during the campaign they were completely swamped by the flood of sensational lies and distortions let loose in the press concerning the campaign.

One of the favourite lines of attack on the Soviet Union was the imputation of all sorts of imperialist motives—the total conquest of Finland, of Scandinavia, and so on. Many well-known men—political and military leaders—actually called for direct war on Russia, advocating fantastic schemes of sending naval squadrons to Leningrad and Petsamo, blockading Murmansk, etc., and there were carefree discussions in some British and French journals of waging war against Russia and Germany combined! Others demanded full

* Major A. S. Hooper, *op. cit.*

military aid to Finland, irrespective of whether that might or might not lead to war with the U.S.S.R.

However, some of the leaders of the Labour Movement did preserve a certain amount of sanity. Although their denunciation of Soviet " blatant imperialism " in speeches, manifestos and pamphlets were as vehement, often even more so, than that of the other political parties, and although they advocated sending all help to Finland, some of them did definitely condemn any idea of making war against the U.S.S.R. and still more of switching the war against Germany to one against the U.S.S.R. Thus, to give only two examples of many, at a meeting in London on December 4, 1939, Mr. Herbert Morrison, M.P., in an unmeasured denunciation of the Soviet Government and Stalin, declared: " If British reactionaries and Herr Hitler made any move towards a Nazi-British alliance against Russia, Labour would oppose it," whilst Mr. W. Lawther, President of the Mineworkers' Federation, declared that " while we agree that this action (" Russia's act of aggression against Finland ") is entirely wrong, the Mineworkers' Federation does not associate itself with the general anti-Soviet or Fascist declarations."

Short of the disastrous step of actually making war on the U.S.S.R., no effort was spared to antagonise her. There were urgings and boastings in Parliament and in the press of the help rendered or about to be given to Finland.

Although in spite of the continuous aggression of Japan, Germany and Italy since 1931 onwards, Britain had never suggested their expulsion from the League of Nations, and although the League had been practically moribund since 1937, Britain now actively helped in resuscitating this corpse and giving it a brief semblance of vitality in order that the U.S.S.R. might be expelled therefrom. For once the League acted, in the approving words of the *Daily Telegraph*, " with promptitude and unflinching firmness."

The actual expulsion took place on December 14, 1939. The whole proceedings were regarded by many correspondents at Geneva as a farce. The *Daily Express* correspondent, Mr. Sefton Delmer, cabled: " Certainly, this has been the best rush job I have ever seen the League perform. All time-wasting has been quashed with almost totalitarian severity."

In the course of December, 1939, and in January, 1940, influential voices were raised in Great Britain in favour of severing diplomatic relations with the Soviet Union. In the former month British subjects in the U.S.S.R. were warned to be ready to leave that country at a moment's notice.

On January 2, 1940, Sir William Seeds—British Ambassador—left Moscow on holiday and it was emphasised that this did not signify any intention to break with the U.S.S.R., although there was much speculation on this point in the British press, and the Diplomatic Correspondent of the *Yorkshire Post** declared that " France, I am told, would not at all mind a diplomatic break with Moscow. Britain, I gather, is disinclined to initiate a breach, but would not be greatly put out if Russia made the first move " ; the *Manchester Guardian* of the same date declared that " whether relations between Russia and the Western Allies can remain normal indefinitely is not at all sure," whilst the *News Chronicle*† gave it as their view that " so long as Russia remains a potential source of supply to the Nazis, Finland must be counted an anti-Hitler front."

On the other hand, Mr. A. J. Cummings, in the *News Chronicle* of the following day, although also condemning Soviet action in Finland, declared:

> " It would be criminal folly on their part deliberately to provoke a war with Germany and Russia combined, and I agree with Lord Strabolgi that such a development would end any hope of another change of policy in Russia favourable to our interests before the present war is over."

About this time the suggestion was made in the *Daily Express*, and in other quarters which opposed direct war on the U.S.S.R., that Britain should pursue in Finland the policy of " non-intervention " so successfully pursued in Spain by Germany and Italy, the policy which had enabled Franco to win the war against Spanish democracy ; in other words, give all aid to Finland and call it " non-intervention ! "

Actually, the British Government adopted a more frank policy—they openly proclaimed that they were giving and were going to give all the aid in their power to Finland. The assistance rendered by the British Government was made known by Mr. Chamberlain —the then Prime Minister—in the House of Commons on March 19, 1940.

Mr. Chamberlain declared that " no appeal that was made to us by the Finnish Government remained unanswered " and he gave the following list of things asked for by the Finns and those actually sent:

> " Aeroplanes promised, 152 ; actually sent, 101. Guns of all kinds promised, 223 ; sent, 114. Shells promised, 297,000 ; actually sent, 185,000. Vickers guns promised, 100 ; all sent. Marine mines promised, 500 ; sent, 400. Hand-grenades promised, 50,000 ; all sent. Aircraft bombs promised, 20,700 ; sent, 15,700. Signalling equipment promised, 1,300 sets ; sent, 800. Anti-tank rifles promised, 200 ; all sent. Respirators promised,

* 2.i.40. † 3.i.40.

> 60,000 ; all sent. Greatcoats promised, 100,000 ; all sent. Battle-dress suits promised, 100,000 ; all sent. Anti-tank mines promised, 20,000 ; sent, 10,000. Ambulances promised, 48 ; all sent.
>
> The list includes many minor items such as medical stores, tents, equipment, sandbags, steel helmets, sand, etc., and also large quantities of small arms ammunition, and I may add, in fact, that arrangements were made here for the manufacture of very large supplies of ammunition and ammunition cases."*

"Everything was done," he added, "to despatch these articles with the minimum of delay."

But it was not materials alone which Britain was ready to furnish to Finland. In the same speech, Mr. Chamberlain also announced that:

> "In the middle of January our representative was informed by Field-Marshal Mannerheim that he did not then require men, as his resources in man-power were sufficient, in his opinion, to last until the thaw came. He did, however, say that he would be very glad to have some 30,000 men in May, but he stipulated that they should be trained soldiers. I may ask the House to bear in mind these two facts—30,000 men, to arrive in Finland in May."†

Mr. Chamberlain stated that plans had been made in accordance with the Finnish requests and that 100,000 "heavily armed and equipped" men were ready to sail at the beginning of March. Reinforcements would be sent later if required.

In December, 1939, the British Government promised to issue a White Paper on the Anglo-French-Soviet negotiations. It was widely rumoured at that time that the aim of the publication would be to pave the way for a severance of diplomatic relations. However, wiser counsels prevailed and on March 6, 1940, the Prime Minister informed the House of Commons that after further consideration, the Government had decided not to issue the publication.

Unlike a number of highly-placed and other individuals, the British Government as a whole did not quite lose its sense of proportion. Thus, although on February 14, 1940, the Government announced in the House of Commons that, contrary to the provisions of the 1870 Foreign Enlistment Act, British subjects would be permitted to fight for Finland, and two days later, Col. Colville, Secretary of State for Scotland, stated in Edinburgh that "Russia is a possible enemy of the British people and Empire," and although Mr. Chamberlain himself on more than one occasion sneered at and belittled the U.S.S.R., he studiously refrained from pledging himself to break off relations with her.

* *Hansard*, 19.iii.40, cols. 1840–41. † Ibid., col. 1841.

The constant flow of abuse against the U.S.S.R. in press, radio, meetings and Parliament during the Soviet-Finnish war was, naturally enough, answered by the Soviet press in the same coin, perhaps even with interest, and relations between the two countries were further embittered.

On February 22, 1940, a unique opportunity occurred for the inauguration of more friendly relations, when M. Maisky, the Soviet Ambassador, informed the British Government of proposed Soviet-Finnish peace talks (in response to a Finnish request) and suggested that Britain should act as intermediary. But on the plea that the terms appeared unduly harsh, the British Government declined the Soviet offer, thus letting the opportunity slip without in any way helping their friends, the "White" Finns.

Peace between the U.S.S.R. and Finland was concluded on March 12, 1940. In his report to the Supreme Soviet on March 29, M. Molotov dwelt on the aid given to Finland by Britain, France, the U.S.A., Sweden and Italy, and on the efforts of the British and French Governments to prevent the termination of the Soviet-Finnish conflict; with regard to the Soviet-Finnish Peace Treaty he stressed that contrary to the "downright falsehoods" published in the British and foreign press, the U.S.S.R. had respected the independence of Finland, and added:

> "The British and French press also wrote that the Soviet Union wants to convert Finland into a mere Baltic State. That, too, is absurd, of course. It is sufficient to point to the fact that after having occupied during the war the region of Petsamo on the Arctic coast, the U.S.S.R. voluntarily restored this region to Finland, considering it necessary to let Finland have an ice-free ocean port. From this it follows that we regard Finland also as a northern and not merely a Baltic country. There is no truth in these fabrications of the British and French newspapers which are old hands in the art of forgery in their anti-Soviet propaganda. The truth lies elsewhere; it is that the Soviet Union, having smashed the Finnish army, and having every opportunity of occupying the whole of Finland, did not do so and did not demand any indemnities for her war expenditure as any other Power would have done, but confined her demands to a minimum and displayed magnanimity towards Finland. . . .
>
> We pursued no other object in the Peace Treaty than that of safeguarding the security of Leningrad, Murmansk, and the Murmansk railway. But we considered it necessary to settle this problem on a reliable and enduring basis. The Peace Treaty is based on the recognition of the principle that Finland is an in-

dependent State, recognition of the independence of her home and foreign policy, and at the same time, on the necessity of safeguarding the security of Leningrad and the north-western frontiers of the Soviet Union."

The peace terms granted by the U.S.S.R. which then had Finland at her mercy, had shown how false were the accusations of Soviet imperialist aims, etc., and as the real truth of the strength and ability of the Soviet armed forces gradually became better known the voices raised in Britain for an improvement in Soviet-British relations became gradually more insistent and suggestions began to be made that a British Minister—preferably Mr. Eden—should be sent to Moscow to initiate more friendly Anglo-Soviet relations. Of course, much denunciation of Soviet action in Finland as a " crime " and a " blunder " continued.

III. Trade Questions. Mr. Churchill, Prime Minister. Burma Road. The Baltic States. Anti-Comintern Pact.

During the whole of the Soviet-Finnish campaign both Anglo-Soviet trade and diplomatic talks were suspended, but on March 27, M. Maisky called on Lord Halifax, the chief subject of conversation being the detention in the Pacific of two Soviet cargo ships containing tin, antimony, wolfram, copper and other metals and bound for Vladivostok, on suspicion, so it was reported, that the goods might ultimately be destined for Germany.

The Soviet view was that their ships being State-owned should be immune from the contraband control. The British argued that State-owned ships, such as warships, were indeed immune from such examination, but not commercial ships, even though they be State-owned. No settlement was reached.

In his report to the Supreme Soviet,* M. Molotov insisted that the U.S.S.R. intended to maintain strict neutrality as she had done from the beginning of the war and made it clear that whilst Soviet-German economic relations were developing satisfactorily, there was no reason whatever why similarly good relations should not be established with Britain and France. The only obstacle was the hostility of the " ruling circles " of the two latter countries to the U.S.S.R. He referred to the detention of the Soviet ships, the refusal to fulfil old Soviet orders for machinery placed by them in Britain before the war, etc., and declared:

> " Attempts have been made to justify these hostile acts towards our foreign trade on the ground that by trading with Germany we are helping her in her war against Britain and France. It

* 29.iii.40.

does not take much to see that these arguments are not worth a brass farthing. One has only to compare the U.S.S.R., say with Rumania. It is known that Rumania's trade with Germany constitutes half her total foreign trade and that, moreover, the proportion of Rumania's national production borne by her exports to Germany of such basic commodities, for example, as oil products and grain, far exceeds the proportion of the Soviet national production borne by the exports of the U.S.S.R. to Germany. Nevertheless, the Governments of Britain and France do not resort to hostile acts against Rumania, nor do they think it feasible to demand that Rumania should cease her trade with Germany."

The general tone of the speech though not friendly towards Britain and France, was not cordial towards Germany either. It was perfectly clear, both from this speech and from reports coming from the U.S.S.R., that the Soviet Government were willing to restart the trade negotiations and would welcome a *rapprochement* with Britain, but although many British publicists recognised the advisability of meeting them half-way, this was by no means universal—the *Daily Herald* being among the most hostile of the press, and official British quarters treated the Soviet overtures very coldly. Bitter attacks on the U.S.S.R. continued to be made by, for instance, Sir Paul Dukes, at meetings under the auspices of the Ministry of Information. The warmest official comment came from Mr. Churchill, and this was cold enough. In a broadcast (March 30) he made a violent attack on the U.S.S.R., but definitely stated that "it is not part of our policy to seek a war with Russia . . . our affair is with Hitler and the Nazi-German power."

The real hope of small but influential circles of the British governing classes was vividly illustrated in an editorial article in the *Nineteenth Century and After*, April, 1940:

> "Hard blows alone will dissolve the German-Russian partnership and *promote a Russian political order that will let the Allies send their managers and experts to recondition Russian industry and enable them, instead of Germany, to draw on Russia's exportable surplus,* and perhaps threaten an isolated and fully blockaded Germany with armed risings in her eastern border regions." (Our italics).

On April 9, 1940, the "phoney" period of the war with Germany was brought to an end by the German invasion of Norway and Denmark. It was clear that now more than ever it was essential to come to a friendly understanding with the U.S.S.R., and on April 19, 1940, Lord Halifax informed M. Maisky that the British Government was prepared to discuss " in an exploratory manner, whether a basis can be found for reaching a trade agreement between the two countries, taking into account the existing war situation."*

The announcement of this news was accompanied by an explanation from the diplomatic correspondent of the *Daily Herald* (and in less peremptory tones from those of other papers) that any agreement with the U.S.S.R. " would have to contain reliable guarantees that the commodities delivered to Russia shall not be sent on to Germany, and that Russian exports of contraband materials to Germany shall be regulated and restricted."†

Within ten days, on April 29, the Soviet Government sent their reply. Without disclosing the exact terms of the note, most of the daily papers hastened to explain that the reply was " unsatisfactory " and, said the diplomatic correspondent of the *Daily Telegraph*, " there appears little prospect of negotiations being opened "—Was the wish father to the thought?

What was the Russian position? Briefly it was (1) a denial that the U.S.S.R. was supplying Germany with foreign goods imported by the former ; Soviet imports were exclusively for her own use. The increased importation of metals from the U.S.A. and other countries via Vladivostok was due to the fact that before the war these were purchased on the British market and imported via European ports, which had now, of course, become impossible, and to the increased Soviet need for these metals. (2) The Soviet Government was prepared to discuss guarantees that British products imported into the U.S.S.R. would not go to Germany. (3) They were also prepared to discuss Soviet trade with neutrals. (4) They absolutely refused any discussion as to what they would or would not do with their own products. Why if there was a real desire to come to an understanding this reply should have been considered " unsatisfactory " as a basis for negotiations is a mystery, and all this was in striking contrast with the British attitude towards other neutrals—Italy, Japan, Rumania and other smaller countries. However, desultory discussions between the Governments on the *basis* for negotiations continued.

On May 3, 1940, after hard fighting, the British troops which had been sent to Norway were forced to withdraw. With the disasters suffered in Norway the strong public dissatisfaction with Mr. Chamberlain's whole policy—which had been growing more and more intense—came to a head and, after a two days' Parliamentary debate on the withdrawal from Norway, the Prime Minister's majority on a vote of confidence (May 8) was down to 81—a virtual defeat.

Two days later, Mr. Chamberlain resigned and on May 10, Mr. Winston Churchill became Prime Minister. Early the same day the

* *Daily Telegraph*, 22.iv.40. † *Daily Herald*, 22.iv.40.

Germans invaded Holland, Belgium and Luxemburg. Great Britain was undoubtedly in a tight spot. On May 13, Mr. Churchill, addressing the House of Commons for the first time as Premier, declared:

> "I would say to the House, as I said to those who have joined this Government: 'I have nothing to offer but blood, toil, tears and sweat.' We have before us an ordeal of the most grievous kind."*

Turning to the question as to the aim of his Government he said:

> "You ask, what is our aim? I can answer in one word: It is victory, victory at all costs, victory in spite of all terror, victory, however long and hard the road may be; for without victory, there is no survival. Let that be realised; *no survival for the British Empire*, no survival for all that the British Empire has stood for, no survival for the urge and impulse of the ages, that mankind will move forward towards its goal." (Our italics).

And at the same session of the House, Mr. Lloyd George, welcoming the appointment of Mr. Churchill, spoke of this "very critical and terrible moment" and also declared: "He is exercising his supreme responsibility at a graver moment and in times of greater jeopardy than have ever confronted a British Minister for all time."†

For Anglo-Soviet relations, the appointment of Mr. Churchill as Prime Minister was a promising step, since though Mr. Churchill had been bitterly anti-Soviet in the past, he stood out, nevertheless, as a leading anti-Munichite, as one who had always warned the country against the menace of Nazi aggression and had been in favour of a *rapprochement* with the U.S.S.R. for this purpose since 1934. The coming to power of Churchill would lessen Soviet distrust of the British Government and improve the chances of an agreement, it was felt. At various Trade Union Conferences the need for establishing friendly relations with the U.S.S.R. was voiced time and again, and many publicists pressed for a British-Soviet *rapprochement* and for the sending of an influential representative to Moscow.

The tone of the Soviet press also became rather more friendly towards Britain, but the Soviet Government insisted that although they desired the establishment of good relations with Britain and the conclusion of a trading agreement on a reciprocal basis, they were not prepared to relinquish their strict neutrality or to permit any interference in their internal affairs by any country. The Russians also insisted that as a first step, the detained Soviet vessels should be released. But so far from that being done another vessel carrying

* *Hansard*, col. 1504. † Ibid., 1512.

Soviet cargo had been detained about the middle of May and taken to a Canadian port.

On May 23, in the House of Commons, Mr. Butler (Under-Secretary of State for Foreign Affairs) declared that steps were being taken to improve relations with Moscow, and soon after it was announced that the British Government had decided to send Sir Stafford Cripps to Moscow as special envoy to explore the possibilities of trade relations. This declaration of policy was welcomed both by Parliament and the press who now realised the necessity of improving relations with the U.S.S.R., but the announcement had been made without any prior consultation with the Soviet Government. Moscow replied on May 26, declining the appointment of a special envoy for which there was no need, but stating that they would be willing to receive Sir Stafford as Ambassador. Finally, after some haggling, Sir Stafford was appointed Ambassador to the U.S.S.R. on June 5, 1940, arriving in Moscow on June 12 ; on June 21, the British Foreign Office at length telegraphed his credentials as Ambassador.

By this date a number of new catastrophic events had occurred in Europe. On May 10, 1940, Germany invaded Belgium, Holland and Luxembourg, practically the whole of the latter country being occupied the same day. On May 15, the Dutch Army was forced to capitulate and on May 27, the Belgian King and Army did the same. On May 30, the first news of the evacuation of the British Expeditionary Force from Dunkirk was announced by the Ministry of Information. With the aid of the Navy and screened by the R.A.F., the evacuation continued day and night on that date and on the following day. On June 4, Mr. Winston Churchill, the Prime Minister, announced in the House of Commons that in all 335,000 men, British and French, had been evacuated. He said that it was a " miracle of deliverance," but added that we had suffered a " colossal military disaster " and had lost enormous quantities of war material. On June 10, with France ridden by Fifth Columnists and traitors and now on her last legs, Italy, looking for easy spoils, declared war on France and Britain. On June 11, the French Government left Paris, and less than a week later (June 17), Petain in a broadcast announced that he had applied to the enemy for their conditions for concluding peace and complete capitulation followed on June 21, 1940, with the signing of the armistice terms.

The reaction of the U.S.S.R. to Hitler's meteoric successes was an intensified effort (begun indeed as we have seen on the morrow of the Soviet-German Pact of August, 1939) to strengthen further her position at home and abroad.

Already the 1940 budget adopted by the Supreme Soviet of the U.S.S.R. at the beginning of April, 1940, had shown an increased expenditure on defence which now amounted to 57,000,000,000 roubles out of a total budget of a little over 179,913,000,000 roubles. Armaments production was speeded up. In June, 1940, the hours of labour were increased to eight hours for workers with a 7-hour day and to seven hours for those with a 6-hour day, except in injurious trades where the 6-hour day remained; office workers' hours were raised from six to eight hours. The 7-day week, i.e., 6 days work and the seventh as a day of rest, was substituted for the 6-day week (i.e., 5 days work and one day rest) customary hitherto.

Later, steps were taken to increase the flow of trained and skilled labour to industry.

The U.S.S.R. was also strengthened at this time both in population and on her frontiers. The settlement on June 28, 1940, of a dispute with Rumania which had lasted for twenty-two years and the liberation of the Bessarabian people from the hated Rumanian yoke was effected by the restoration to the U.S.S.R. of Bessarabia, which Rumania had seized at a time when Soviet Russia was too weak to withstand the robbery. At the same time Northern Bukovina, of great strategic importance, and whose population are mainly the blood brothers of the Soviet Moldavians and Ukrainians, was also ceded by Rumania to the U.S.S.R.

In the Baltic States: between June 17-21, 1940, the Fascist or semi-Fascist Governments in Estonia, Latvia and Lithuania fell and Left-wing Governments were set up. Elections by secret ballot held in these States, July 14, 1940, in which 81.6 to 95.5 per cent. of the electorates voted, resulted in the formation of new Governments which decided to set up Socialist Soviet Republics, and on July 21, 1940, the Parliaments of these three Republics applied for incorporation into the U.S.S.R. as Constituent Republics of the Union, and were accepted by the latter in August.

These changes which strengthened the U.S.S.R. led British public opinion to desire more strongly the establishment of more friendly Anglo-Soviet relations. The transfer of Bessarabia and Northern Bukovina was, on the whole, welcomed by the British press and even greeted as a typical example of Soviet realism, although the same cannot be said of the attitude towards the incorporation of the Baltic States within the Soviet Union.

Contacts between Sir Stafford Cripps and the Soviet Foreign Office became more frequent and it was announced on July 3, 1940, that the two Soviet ships detained by the British had been released, although the cargoes were not allowed to go to the U.S.S.R., being purchased by the French authorities.

But relations continued to be on the whole pretty frigid, with the press of both countries, although somewhat less hostile to one another than hitherto, every now and again abusing the other side. Statements made by British Ministers from time to time seemed to imply a desire for establishing better Anglo-Soviet relations—one such statement may be worth quoting here as it throws a flood of light on the whole subject. On July 11, 1940, Mr. Neil Maclean put a question regarding the allegations made in a German White Book published a few weeks earlier, that Britain had been preparing for an attack on the Baku oil fields; to this Mr. Butler (Under-Secretary of State for Foreign Affairs) in a written reply said:

> "The policy of His Majesty's Government has been and remains to improve and strengthen the relations between this country and the Union of Soviet Socialist Republics. Success in this policy has appeared more likely since March of this year when the Union of Soviet Socialist Republics made a friendly approach to His Majesty's Government and proposed the resumption of trade negotiations. This move on their part constituted a welcome departure from the unfriendly attitude which the Soviet Government had adopted ever since the breakdown of the political negotiations in August of last year. His Majesty's Government at once responded to this approach by the Soviet Government, and it is to be hoped that the discussions on which His Majesty's Ambassador in Moscow is at present engaged may finally remove any danger which may have been apprehended that the Soviet Government would work either economically or militarily against Great Britain in the interests of Germany.
>
> Ever since the outbreak of war, His Majesty's Government have had to guard against this danger when making their military plans. It was natural, therefore, that the Staffs, who in a totalitarian war have to consider all future hypotheses, should consider how to counter Russian assistance to Germany. Apart from actual military assistance one of the most valuable forms of help which the Soviet Government were in a position to give Germany was to supply her with oil from the Caucasus. It was thus the duty of the General Staffs to examine whether in certain eventualities it would be possible to interfere with the output of oil from the Caucasian wells.
>
> I might add that no attempt was made at any time to enlist the co-operation or acquiescence of either Turkey or Iran in these hypothetical plans. I trust that this statement will dispel any false and mischievous impressions which German propaganda has sought to create."*

* *Hansard*, 11.vii.40, col. 1359.

Mr. Butler's statement by no means corresponded with the facts; actually the Soviet-German agreement had never been a military alliance and there had never been the slightest danger that the U.S.S.R. would join Germany in the war against Britain and France. From the first, the Soviet Government proclaimed their strict neutrality and expressed a desire to come to a friendly understanding with Britain on a reciprocal basis which would respect Soviet neutrality.

Without dwelling on the earlier constant rebuffs to the U.S.S.R. when the latter strove to organise a united front against aggression, we may recall that it was Britain who was the first to stop imports to the U.S.S.R. after the outbreak of the war with Germany. However sharply Soviet leaders and the Soviet press might criticise British foreign policy, they never once called for war against Britain or her Empire, whereas sections of the British press and various British public men did frequently call for war against the U.S.S.R. It was the British Government who proclaimed their intention to help the Finns, i.e., refused to behave as a neutral in a war which did not directly concern them. It was the British Government who recalled their Ambassador from Moscow and left the British Embassy there vacant for months.

Unfortunately, soon after Mr. Butler's statement an excellent opportunity for improving relations with the U.S.S.R. was again missed by the British Government. For some time there had been Anglo-Japanese negotiations on the demand of Japan that the Burma Road across which China received most of her supplies from the U.S.A. and the U.S.S.R. should be closed. This was, of course, a question which vitally concerned the Soviet Union and the U.S.A. To appease Japan the British Government finally agreed to the Japanese demand, and on July 17, 1940, it was announced that the Burma Road would be closed to the transit of arms and ammunition, as well as petrol, trucks and railway materials to China for three months as from July 18.

This was done without any previous consultation with the U.S.S.R. which had done so much to aid the Chinese in their struggle against Japanese imperialism and which had vital interests in the Far East. Mr. Churchill himself announced in Parliament that the British Government had taken "into full *consideration* the attitude of the two very important Great Powers" (U.S.S.R. and U.S.A.). (Our italics.)

This action had a deplorable effect both in the U.S.A. and in the U.S.S.R. Here was an opportunity for reaching a friendly understanding with the U.S.S.R. which might have had most important consequences subsequently not only in the Far East but also on British fortunes in the West. A friendly understanding with the U.S.S.R. was surely at least as important as the few months' respite obtained from Japan's demands.

Another event which embittered Anglo-Soviet relations was the hostile attitude of the British Government towards the incorporation of the three Baltic States in the Soviet Union. The former Legations of the Baltic States continued to be recognised and instructions issued by the Central banks of Estonia, Latvia and Lithuania on July 13, 1940, for the transfer of their balances in British banks to the London branches of the Soviet banks were ignored in London—their assets by decision of the British Government, being "frozen." Also, about 30 ships of the Baltic States lying in British ports were not permitted to pass into Soviet possession.

Sir Stafford Cripps had a number of audiences with members of the Soviet Government and was also received by M. Stalin, whilst M. Maisky from time to time saw Lord Halifax or Mr. Butler and was also received by Mr. Churchill, but there was no real amelioration in Anglo-Soviet relations.

Small wonder then that under such circumstances M. Molotov's speech delivered at the Seventh Session of the Supreme Soviet on August 1, 1940, after stating that Soviet-German relations remained friendly as hitherto and that there had also been some improvement in Soviet-Italian relations, made the following non-committal statement regarding Soviet-British relations:

> "As regards Soviet-British relations, no essential changes have lately occurred. It should be recognised that after all the hostile acts committed by Britain against the U.S.S.R., of which we have had occasion to speak more than once at the Supreme Soviet, it was difficult to expect that Soviet-British relations would develop favourably, although the appointment of Sir Stafford Cripps as Ambassador to the U.S.S.R. does, possibly, reflect a desire on the part of Britain to improve relations with the Soviet Union."

He finished his speech on a note of warning that the war might expand and that they must be on the alert so that no untoward event would catch the U.S.S.R. unawares.

Commenting on this speech, the *Times*' Moscow Correspondent said: "His remarks about England, although cool, reflected an improvement in the atmosphere since the Commissar last spoke to the Supreme Council in March, in spite of the fact that the Soviet Government feel they have received a new cause of annoyance through the British blocking of the gold and credits of the Baltic States."*

Although, according to Mr. Vernon Bartlett, the final verdict of "diplomatic London" was that M. Molotov's speech might have been worse, the diplomatic correspondents generally expressed bitterness and disappointment at Molotov's speech, which for the *Daily Herald*

* *Times*, 3.viii.40.

diplomatic correspondent confirmed "the belief that Soviet Russia and Nazi Germany have done a new deal in Eastern Europe. . . . The speech is clear evidence that German influence in Moscow is stronger than ever. The Soviet Government is very, very anxious to please and placate Hitler."* Some of the papers were rather more realistic. "If any confirmation was needed," said the *Times*,† "of the resolve of the Kremlin to remain strictly neutral, the speech provided it." This admission was made in an article distinctly unfriendly towards the U.S.S.R.

The *Evening Standard*,‡ after remarking that the diplomatic correspondents had evidently expected Molotov to denounce Germany and sing "God Save the King," concluded:

> "The diplomatic correspondents were disappointed. It is a strange phenomenon, since these were the same who assured us at the beginning of the war that Russia would march where Germany marched, that the only course of salvation for Britain was to send troops and munitions from the West to fight a new enemy in the Arctic or the Black Sea.
>
> Instead of plunging from side to side, it is better to understand the design of Soviet policy revealed in the words of Soviet statesmen, and the facts of history and geography. Stalin said in March, 1939, that he was not going to pull other people's chestnuts out of the fire. Since then the Russians have avoided what they most feared; single-handed combat with Germany against Poland. They have gained a more defensible frontier. Molotov repeats the policy to-day. It is still the Soviet plan to keep out of war while strengthening their position to repel aggression. That does not mean they have overlooked the permanent facts of geography and history which dictate that a finally triumphant Germany is a menace to Russia.
>
> Molotov is not Mr. Moto or the Man in the Iron Mask. He is the miller of Dee, and he sings:
>
> 'I care for nobody, no, not I,
> If nobody cares for me.'
>
> The Miller was almost enticed to believe that somebody did care for him before this war. But that is another story which has a moral for the future."

Mr. Churchill himself seemed to realise the rôle—albeit passive—that the U.S.S.R. was playing in the war, when in a speech in the House of Commons, August 20, 1940, referring to Hitler's air attack on Britain, he said: "We may be sure therefore, that he will continue

* 2.viii.40. † 3.viii.40. ‡ 3.viii.40.

as long as he has the strength to do so, and as long as any preoccupations he may have in respect of the Russian Air Force allow him to do so."*

On September 27, 1940, Germany, Italy and Japan signed a ten-year Tripartite Pact whereby the signatories undertook to "assist one another with all political, economic, and military means, if one of the high contracting parties should be attacked by a Power not at present involved in the European war or in the Sino-Japanese conflict." Article 1 stated that "Japan recognises and respects the leadership of Germany and Italy in the establishment of a new order in Europe" and Article 2, that Germany and Italy adopted the same attitude towards Japan. Article 4 provided for the meeting without delay of joint technical commissions, and Article 5 stated that the three Powers "affirm that the aforesaid terms do not in any way affect the political status which exists at present as between each of the three contracting parties and Soviet Russia."

The British press wavered between fear that the U.S.S.R. would throw in their lot now with the Axis Powers (and the latter undoubtedly wished this) and the hope that the Soviet Government would consider the Tripartite Pact as directed mainly against the U.S.S.R. and that the latter would therefore declare open hostility towards the Axis. But the U.S.S.R. remained calm; just as when the Anti-Comintern Pact was first signed† the Soviet press had insisted that whatever its name, and whatever the pretence, in actual effect this Pact would be directed more against Britain, France and the U.S.A. than against the U.S.S.R. so now it looked upon the transformation of the Pact into a Military Alliance as directed against Britain and the U.S.A. Needless to say the Soviet Government refused any adherence whatever to the Tripartite Pact.

In press and public speeches the U.S.S.R. affirmed once again her adherence to strict neutrality, whilst Marshal Timoshenko, Commissar for Defence, in a message to graduates of a Military Academy, said the flames of the second Imperialist war were enveloping West and East. The Soviet Union stood outside its orbit, but "this does not mean that we are safe from any provocations that may threaten our borders. . . . We must be ready for any emergency and further strengthen the Red Army's fighting capacity."

This attitude of maintaining strict neutrality whilst preparing economically and militarily for any eventuality was repeated time after time by the Soviet leaders. On the whole, the Soviet press was becoming more friendly towards Britain. Articles in the Soviet press

* *Hansard*, 20.viii.40, cols. 1165–6.

† The Anti-Comintern Pact was concluded on November 25, 1936, between Germany and Japan. Italy joined the Pact November 6, 1937.

made it perfectly clear that the Soviet leaders were in no wise elated by the German successes or disposed to give them exaggerated importance. More and more frequently articles were published highly appreciative of the British Air Force, Navy, etc.

However, the Anglo-Soviet negotiations did not seem to be leading to tangible results. Although a number of politicians in Britain including some leading members of the Labour Party sought to put the blame for the failure of the negotiations on the Soviet Government, this was by no means the view of large sections of the organised British workers, nor was it the view of many Labour M.P.'s and Trade Union leaders.

An incident which occurred on October 11, during the period of the Battle of Britain showed on the one hand the feeling of at any rate a large section of the ordinary folk in London and on the other the attitude of the Soviet Ambassador towards this country. M. Maisky accompanied by Mme. Maisky and Admiral Sir Edward Evans toured East End Air Raid Shelters. When the crowd learned the identity of their visitors there were tremendous cheers and calls for a speech.

> " M. Maisky, Soviet Ambassador, replying to cheers from 4,000 people in a shelter at Stepney, E., last night declared:
>
> ' Your warm greetings are very welcome to me and my wife, but are more welcome still to my country.' "*

A few days later, Mr. Shinwell, M.P., speaking in County Durham, urged the British Government to make a serious effort to come to an understanding with the U.S.S.R., and declared:

> " I am convinced, because of what I know, that the Russian Government is anxious for a friendly understanding with this country.
>
> If we had as Foreign Minister, instead of Lord Halifax, someone who would set aside all the errors of the past and seek to reach a friendly understanding with Soviet Russia, there would be a response that would gratify those throughout the world who desire to preserve our freedom."†

Mr. A. J. Cummings, in the *News Chronicle*, gave evidence of the change in the mentality of even some of the higher-ups in Britain:

> " Some Blimpish acquaintances of mine are now bitterly regretting that Chamberlain did not bring off the original deal with Stalin and are confessing (a little sheepishly) that they would rather work in peace-time with the Communists of Moscow than with the Nazis of Berlin! Well, we shall see. Unless, sooner or

* *Daily Mail*, 12.x.40. † *Daily Herald*, 14.x.40.

later, we work with Moscow there will never be any peace worth having."*

In the House of Commons questions were asked continually, particularly by Labour members, as to why there was such a delay in coming to an understanding with the U.S.S.R., and the Ministers concerned invariably replied that the Government wanted an agreement and would do everything possible to attain it. Unfortunately, as we have seen, the actual acts of the Government *vis-à-vis* the U.S.S.R. were not, generally speaking, of a nature to further these aims.

It will be recalled that when the Baltic States were incorporated at their own request in the U.S.S.R., the British Government had refused to recognise this step and had detained both Baltic assets in British banks and Baltic ships in British ports. The Russians, throughout the talks, both in Moscow and London, urged that as a preliminary to good understanding the British Government should recognise the Soviet right to the assets and ships of the three Baltic States.

About the middle of October it was apparent that some compromise had been reached on the question of the Baltic ships in British ports and the Baltic assets in British banks and Sir Stafford Cripps was reported to have declared " Now we have got somewhere." However, at this point the Ministry of Shipping high-handedly requisitioned ten of the Baltic ships ; in reply to Soviet protests, the British Government explained that this was an unfortunate inter-departmental error and that the matter would be put right at once. Instead, a further 13 ships were seized. Could the Russians be blamed for thinking that this was deliberate sabotage of an Anglo-Soviet understanding? In retaliation the Soviet Government refused to remit to London the instalments due in connection with the Lena Goldfields Settlement. Hitherto these payments had been made regularly and punctually.

IV. The Balkans and the Danubian Question

New difficulties were created by the British Government's attitude to the Danubian question. Early in September, 1940, reports were published that a Conference of " experts on international questions regarding the Danube " was to be convened by Germany at Vienna ; no German official notification of the proposed Conference was made to the U.S.S.R., and the Soviet Government at once protested against this slight, declaring that as a State bordering on the Danube, the Soviet Union was vitally interested in all matters concerning that river and insisted on participation in all discussions and decisions on the question. When this protest (made on September 12, 1940) was pub-

* 17.x.40.

lished in the British press, it was generally conceded that Russia was within her rights in demanding a voice in any settlement of the Danubian question. Germany wasted no time in haggling, and on October 26, 1940, it was announced in Moscow and Berlin that:

> " As the result of negotiations between the Soviet and German Governments and with the consent of the Italian Government, it was considered necessary to liquidate both the international Danube Commission and the European Danube Commission, creating instead of them an amalgamated Danube Commission consisting of representatives of the U.S.S.R., Germany, Italy, Rumania, Bulgaria, Hungary, Slovakia and Yugoslavia.
>
> The amalgamated Danube Commission is called to regulate questions of shipping along the Danube, from its mouth to Bratislava (Slovakia).
>
> In conformity with the agreement reached on the above-mentioned question, negotiations between experts—delegates of the U.S.S.R., Germany, Rumania and Italy—on the regulation of a temporary international régime on the Maritime Danube from its mouth to Braila was to commence on October 28, 1940, in Bucharest."

Under the Treaty of Paris, of 1856, a European Commission was formed to regulate questions concerning traffic on the Danube from Braila in Rumania to Sulina, at the mouth of the Danube, Great Britain, France, Germany, Russia, Austria-Hungary, Italy, Rumania and Turkey being represented on it. At the end of the 1914-18 war the Commission was reconstituted and representatives of countries other than Great Britain, France, Italy and Rumania were excluded, but in 1939 Germany was admitted.

Another Commission—the International Danube Commission—was formed under the Treaty of Versailles to control traffic from Ulm to Braila. On this commission there served representatives of Britain, France, Italy, Rumania, Austria, Bulgaria, Czechoslovakia, Hungary, Wurthemburg and Yugoslavia. Soviet Russia, although the greatest Black Sea Power, was excluded from both Commissions and being at that time powerless to insist on her rights, was forced to accept this humiliation. But now times had changed.

When the success of the Soviet protests against Germany's high-handed action was first published, it was on the whole welcomed in the British press. But on October 29, 1940, Sir Stafford Cripps, on behalf of the British Government, lodged a protest with M. Molotov " against the decision taken by the Government of the U.S.S.R. concerning the necessity for organising a new (united) Danube Commission and the participation of the representatives of the U.S.S.R., in the negotiations with the representatives of Germany, Italy and Rumania in Bucharest." The British Government also declared that they regarded the action of the Soviet Government as a violation of neutrality and that they would refuse to recognise any agreement which violated existing Treaties.

The Soviet Government replied on November 2, declaring that they considered as "incorrect the assertion of the British Government to the effect that the recognition by the Soviet Government of the necessity for the formation of the new Danube Commission and the participation of the U.S.S.R. in the Bucharest negotiations constitute a violation of neutrality." The Soviet Note further declared that the formation of the Danube Commission and the participation of the U.S.S.R. was only the restoration of justice towards the U.S.S.R. violated by the Treaty of Versailles and continued:

> "The Danube Commission must naturally be composed of representatives of the States situated on the Danube or closely connected with the Danube and using the Danube as a trade channel—for instance, Italy.
>
> It is clear that Great Britain, being removed thousands of kilometres from the Danube, cannot be classed as such a State.
>
> It is also clear that the question of the composition of the Danube Commission has no relation whatever to the question of neutrality."

If the British Government really desired an understanding with the U.S.S.R. then the reason for this protest was certainly a mystery. No one ever explained how the U.S.S.R. compromised her neutrality by maintaining her right as a Riparian State to participate in questions concerning traffic on the Danube. No protest was sent by Britain to Hungary, Rumania and Yugoslavia, who were at that time also neutrals. If the object of the protest was to make clear that Britain reserved her ultimate right to a say in the question, why could not the Foreign Office have stated this and left it there? The more so since at that time Britain could not make her protest effective and was only further obstructing the course of the Anglo-Soviet trade negotiations.

There were comparatively few comments in the British press, but the *Evening News* and the *Evening Standard* as well as some of the weeklies expressed strong disapproval of the British Foreign Office action. Many M.P.'s too were at a loss to understand the *raison d'être* of the British protest.

On the whole question of the Balkans and the steady encroachments made by Germany on these States, the British press again varied between imputing agreement on the German steps between Germany and the U.S.S.R., and assurances that the position of the latter was becoming more and more insecure and that she would no doubt very soon throw in her lot with Britain, and indeed calling upon her to do so.

That the Soviet Government was fully alive to the danger of the conquests made by Germany in Europe there can be little doubt. But they were anxious not to do anything to provoke a German attack on the U.S.S.R., the more so since the attitude of the British Government both before and after the outbreak of the war could not inspire them with very much faith in the professed desire of the British Government to establish really friendly relations with them. Accordingly they steered a course of strict neutrality, at the same time doing everything possible to strengthen their economic, military and strategic positions.

To return to the Anglo-Soviet talks in Moscow. On October 22, after the requisitioning of the Baltic ships, Sir Stafford Cripps presented a three-point British proposal:

> " *De facto* recognition of the incorporation of the Baltic States in the Soviet Union;
>
> A guarantee that Russia would be a participant in any peace settlement which might be concluded after the war, and
>
> An assurance that Britain would not be associated in any attack against Russia."*

In return the U.S.S.R. was requested to observe neutrality in the war and to undertake that no anti-British propaganda would be conducted in British territory. Point 1 made no difference whatever to the existing state of affairs, and there was no suggestion that the gold and ships of the Baltic States would be handed over. As for Point 2—could anyone envisage a European peace conference settling anything without Russian participation? In regard to this point, the Diplomatic Correspondent of the *Times*, November 18, 1940, declared that the British Government " were prepared to invite the Soviet Union to share as an equal partner in the peace conference—when, among many problems to be settled, there would be the formal status of the Baltic States." Thus emphasising that the incorporation of the Baltic States would remain open for the *peace conference* to adjudicate.

Point 3 might have been important if the British Foreign Office had manifested some real change of heart towards the U.S.S.R. of which the attitude regarding the Baltic States and the Danubian question gave little promise. As to the question of Soviet neutrality, the Soviet Government could say with justice that it was neutral; as for propaganda, M. Vyshinsky, Soviet Vice-Commissar for Foreign Affairs, was reported to have said that it must be a mutual undertaking—to

* *Daily Telegraph*, 16.xi.40.

which Sir Stafford Cripps had replied that the British Government would agree.

The Soviet Government now allowed a little time to elapse and about ten days after the receipt of the British Note concerning the Danubian Commission, Molotov accepted a long-standing invitation to visit Berlin. So far, in spite of the fact that Ribbentrop had visited the U.S.S.R. twice since the August, 1939, Agreement, the Soviet Government had refused to accept the invitation of the German Government to send the Soviet Foreign Minister on a visit to Berlin, but on November 9, 1940, it was announced in Moscow that " On the invitation of the German Government, and in reply to last year's visit to Moscow of the German Foreign Minister, Herr von Ribbentrop, the Chairman of the Council of People's Commissars and People's Commissar for Foreign Affairs will in the immediate future visit Berlin in order to continue and deepen the friendly relations existing between the two countries by a resumption of personal contact and by an exchange of views on foreign problems." The following evening, Molotov, accompanied by many high economic Soviet officials, left Moscow for Berlin.

The British press hummed with prophecies as to the Soviet-German talks. According to these, the U.S.S.R., apart from an economic agreement, was to be invited (1) to put pressure on Turkey to remain neutral in the event of a German march on Greece via Bulgaria ; (2) to assist in one form or another in an attack on Iran, Afghanistan and even India, in return for a share of the spoils ; (3) to allow Japan a free hand in China ; (4) to join with the Tripartite Powers to build the new World Order. Undoubtedly, the Nazi Government intended to put some such plans before Molotov. Whilst the Soviet press and radio insisted that the visit envisaged the discussion of economic questions only, the Nazi press dwelt mainly on political aspects and there can be little doubt that the realisation of the above-named projects was very much desired by Hitler. But the amazing part was that the British journals, Labour, Liberal and Tory, should have imagined that the Soviet Government would for one moment consider any such plans. The *Daily Herald* went so far as to print a cartoon depicting Molotov as A Red Riding Hood about to enter the bedchamber of Hitler, the wolf. Did they really know so little of the calibre of Molotov and the Soviet statesmen generally? The various diplomatic correspondents and leader writers gave varying degrees of credence to the possibility of the Soviet Government agreeing to the German plans, but even in the course of a comparatively sensible and sober estimate of the position, the diplomatic correspondent of the *Times* declared:

" An economic and industrial agreement, probably on a large

scale, possibly even allowing German technicians into Soviet factories, would come as no surprise from the meeting. The constitution of the Soviet mission, with its Deputy Commissars of smelting industries and aircraft plants, suggests that such an agreement is under way. Declarations of solidarity in reconstructing the world, in harmony with the Japanese and the Italians, may also emerge. Beyond that point the issue of the meeting has to be awaited."*

The Soviet-German talks lasted for only two days and, as became known later, they were a deep disappointment to the Nazis. Not only did Molotov refuse any part in the fashioning of the "new world order," or to interest himself in any of the other Nazi political and strategic schemes, but there was also, of course, no agreement "to allow German technicians into Soviet factories."

In the meantime, the Anglo-Soviet talks hung fire, but renewed hope came when on December 22, 1940, Mr. Eden replaced Lord Halifax as Secretary of State for Foreign Affairs. Lord Halifax had always been known as deeply hostile to the U.S.S.R. Although he had visited Berlin and Rome he had, as already mentioned, refused an invitation to visit Moscow, and he had been one of the pillars of the "Munich policy." Eden, on the other hand, was looked upon as having a far more progressive foreign policy ; he had been to Moscow (page 538) and was well liked there, it was accordingly hoped that under his guidance the Foreign Office might pursue a more definite policy for attaining an Anglo-Soviet understanding.

In concluding this Chapter there is another important fact that we must stress, viz., the contrast in the attitudes of the British and Soviet press to differences between the two Governments from October, 1939, to the end of 1940. There was a marked tendency on the part of a large section of the British press to exaggerate questions at issue, although it is true that after the collapse of France, the British press followed the Government's lead and somewhat modified its attitude. But the Soviet press *throughout the entire period* stressed that all the questions, given good will on the British side, could be settled to the mutual advantage of both countries.

* *Times*, 12.xi.40.

CHAPTER XXVII

ON THE EVE OF THE GERMAN ATTACK ON THE U.S.S.R.

I. Soviet-German Economic Agreement. The Balkans

When Mr. Eden took over the Foreign Office, relations between the latter and the Soviet Embassy in London certainly became more friendly. M. Maisky had many talks with Mr. Eden and gave a lunch in his honour on February 12, 1941, and at a reception given by the Soviet Military Attaché on February 25, Mr. Butler, Under-Secretary of State for Foreign Affairs, Capt. H. H. Balfour, Under-Secretary of State for Air, Sir Edward Grigg, Joint Parliamentary Under-Secretary of State for the War Office, as well as many high representatives of the British fighting services, were present. In Moscow, Sir Stafford Cripps had interviews with M. Mikoyan, People's Commissar for Foreign Trade, and M. Vyshinsky, Assistant Commissar for Foreign Affairs—but all this did not seem to have any effect on the course of the negotiations. The British Government continued to refuse both to recognise the incorporation into the U.S.S.R. of the Baltic States and to release the ships and gold of the latter.

On the other hand, Soviet-German negotiations, which had been proceeding since October, 1940, resulted in the conclusion of a Soviet-German Economic Agreement, whereby the Soviet Union undertook to deliver to Germany, industrial raw materials, oil products, and foodstuffs, especially cereals. Germany was to deliver to the U.S.S.R. industrial equipment. At the same time Agreements were concluded on Soviet-German mutual property claims concerning the Baltic States and the migration of populations therefrom, as well as one for the delimitation of the Soviet-German frontier from the River Igorka to the Black Sea.*

The conclusion of these agreements sent a flutter of speculation throughout the British press. The comments varied—from a tendency to belittle to a complete over-estimation of their significance—but there was a general undertone of resentment, an allegation that the U.S.S.R. had done something which belied her neutrality. Yet no such resentment and accusations were voiced against Turkey when she concluded a Trade Agreement with Germany in July, 1940.

The German press made the most of the agreements, hailed them as a great German diplomatic success and declared that " the pact will be a great shock to Churchill! " We imagine that Mr. Churchill's nerves were sufficiently strong to survive the " shock." On the other hand, the mental shock suffered by some press correspondents certainly

* All these agreements were concluded January 10, 1941.

seems to have been shattering, judging from the following expression of opinion in the *Observer*:

> "The diplomatic result of the agreement, at a moment when the United States is preparing to give greater help to China against Japan, will be to place Russia as a virtual supporter of Germany and therefore antagonistic to Britain and the United States on the one side, and on the other side the supporter of the United States and Britain against Germany's ally Japan.
>
> Russia is supplying petrol, railway material, etc., to China. Russia is therefore blowing hot and cold in a supposed spirit of impartiality, by being on both sides at once: a new type of neutrality which in the nature of things cannot continue indefinitely."*

The U.S.S.R. had consistently traded with China and had rejected all Japan's demands and protests on that score and if belatedly the U.S.A. were preparing to help China—this had nothing whatever to do with the attitude of the U.S.S.R. towards China. Whilst not refusing to conclude trading and other agreements with Japan, the U.S.S.R. did not conceal her sympathy with China and actually as though to emphasise her willingness and intention to conclude agreements with all countries willing to do so, the conclusion of a barter agreement with China was announced on January 13, 1941.

There was, of course, nothing in the Soviet-German Treaty which would have prevented the conclusion of a similar agreement with Britain, and *Izvestia*† remarked:

> "Attempts made by the Press hostile to the Soviet Union to prove that any Agreement concluded between the U.S.S.R. and Germany is directed against third Powers cannot stand even the slightest criticism, since in the course of 1940 the Soviet Union has concluded and intends to conclude in 1941 economic treaties and agreements with other States, both belligerent and non-belligerent. It is time it was understood that the Soviet Union as a non-belligerent Power follows its own independent policy, and will continue to follow it regardless of what statesmen of the eastern and western hemispheres may think of this."

Pravda of the same date declared that: "The U.S.S.R. is consistently pursuing its policy of peace and friendship towards Germany as towards all States willing to pursue a like policy towards the U.S.S.R."

The only thing which prevented the conclusion of an Anglo-Soviet trading agreement and the establishment of friendly relations was the persistent unwillingness on the part of the British Government and

* *Observer*, diplomatic correspondent, 12.i.41. † 11.i.41.

influential circles in Britain to look realities in the face and to treat the U.S.S.R. as a powerful neutral country. It was as if they said to themselves—"The U.S.S.R.? After all she is only a workers' country—she can't expect from us the respect, tolerance, understanding and friendship we have consistently shown towards Turkey, Spain, Japan and even Italy, before she entered the war."

Instead of drawing the lesson from the Soviet-German Agreement that Britain must make a more determined effort to come to an understanding with the U.S.S.R., the British Government continued its policy of pin-pricks and the British press inveighed continuously against Soviet exports to Germany; on January 28, 1941, in reply to a question in the House of Commons, Mr. Dalton (Minister for Economic Warfare) said:

> "I have little evidence that United States exports to the Soviet Union reach Germany directly, but ample evidence that the Soviets are exporting Russian goods to Germany and replacing these goods by imports from the U.S.A. United States exports of cotton to the Soviet Union, which are normally negligible, amounted during the last quarter of 1940 to 30,000 tons, considerably more than recent annual imports into the Soviet Union from all sources. Large quantities of cotton are now being exported from the Soviet Union to Germany.
>
> In regard to other important commodities, exports of copper and brass from the U.S.A. to the Soviet Union rose from small quantities before the war to 57,000 tons, and exports of wheat from negligible quantities to 100,000 tons in 1940. Both wheat and petroleum are commodities of which the Soviet Government have undertaken to supply large quantities to Germany under their recent trade agreements. The value of exports of oil-drilling machinery from the U.S.A. to the Soviet Union during the first eight months of 1940 was nearly double that of the exports during the whole of 1938 and there were considerable further shipments during the last four months of the year."

This statement was wholly misleading. As to copper, it was true that the quantities imported by the U.S.S.R. from the U.S.A. before the war were small, but in 1937 the quantity of copper and copper-products re-exported from the United Kingdom to the U.S.S.R. was 77,752 tons, and in 1938 it was 85,713 tons, i.e., 30,000 tons in excess of that obtained by the U.S.S.R. in the U.S.A. in 1940. Seeing that the markets for the purchase of copper represented by the re-exports from the United Kingdom were closed to the U.S.S.R., the quantity bought in the U.S.A. barely supplied Soviet needs of this commodity and could have no reference at all to her exports to Germany. As for cotton, wheat and oil, the amounts imported by the U.S.S.R. were only fractions of the amounts produced in that country. The cotton imported was one per cent. and the wheat only 0.1 per cent. of that raised in the U.S.S.R., whilst the amount of oil imported was less than .03 per cent. of that produced in the U.S.S.R. in 1940, and was actually less than that imported in 1937, and not very much more than in 1938.

As a matter of fact, the U.S.S.R. had always imported cotton, wheat and oil via Vladivostok for her Eastern districts and exported far larger quantities of these commodities via her European ports, because it was cheaper to do this than to transport these products over the huge land distances between the various parts of the U.S.S.R. Nor was there any substance in the complaint against the imports of oil machinery from the U.S.A. There was an ever growing demand for oil by the rapidly developing branches of Soviet national economy, as well as for building up military reserves. To meet this demand the Soviet authorities not only introduced modern methods of working in the well-known Baku, Grozny and Emba oilfields, but Soviet oil experts and geologists had done an enormous amount of prospecting work since 1938 and new oilfields had been discovered and exploited. Particularly important in this connection was the "Second Baku," an oil-bearing area covering over a million square kilometres, i.e., more than double the area of France.

In March, 1939, some six months before the outbreak of the war, a decision was adopted by the 18th Congress of the Communist Party of the U.S.S.R. to develop the "Second Baku" as quickly as possible and to raise the output of oil in these areas to about 6,400,000 tons by the end of the Third Five-Year Plan, i.e., by 1942. It was for this reason that the importation of drilling machinery in 1940 and subsequently was so much higher than in 1938. It was not Germany's needs, but Soviet needs which caused the U.S.S.R. to develop her oil production.

The Soviet Government insisted that all their imports were exclusively for home use and the facts undoubtedly bore them out. Had there been any real wish to come to a friendly understanding with the U.S.S.R. no such trivial accusations would have been made in Parliament. What was even more reprehensible and could not but cause concern in Soviet quarters was Mr. Dalton's statement in a reply to a supplementary question:

> "We have made it quite clear to both countries concerned what are our feelings in regard to this matter. I hope that, as a result of conversations now taking place in Washington, it may be possible to take some steps to reduce this practice."

This—if it meant anything—was a clear intimation that the British Government would seek to put a spoke in Soviet-American trading relations.

For the rest, the U.S.S.R. was pursuing a definitely independent foreign policy and refusing to permit Germany to influence her in any way. This was strikingly illustrated when on January 13, 1941—only two days following the publication of the texts of the above-mentioned Soviet-German Treaties, Tass, the Soviet News Agency, issued a strong denial of the report in the foreign press that the U.S.S.R. had been consulted, and had agreed to, the dispatch of German troops to Bulgaria:

> "Tass is authorised to state that: First, if German troops are really present in Bulgaria and if the further dispatch of German troops to Bulgaria is really taking place, then all this has occurred and is occurring without the knowledge and consent of the U.S.S.R., since the German side has never raised before the U.S.S.R. the question of the presence or dispatch of German troops to Bulgaria. Second, in particular, the Bulgarian Government has never approached the U.S.S.R. with an inquiry regarding the passage of German troops to Bulgaria, and consequently could not receive any reply from the U.S.S.R."

Although at the time, and indeed earlier and also on various occasions subsequently, the Bulgarian Government professed to be neutral, about seven weeks later, on March 2, it was announced that Bulgaria had adhered to the Axis Tripartite Pact and that German troops in agreement with the Bulgarian Government had crossed the German frontier.

Moscow lost no time in replying to this move. On March 3 and on the two following days, an official statement of the Soviet Government was broadcast over the radio in Russian, Bulgarian, French and German, declaring that in response to the note of the Bulgarian Government on March 1, informing them of the German-Bulgarian understanding, the Soviet Government had replied as follows:

> "In reply to the communication of March 1 from the representative of the Bulgarian Foreign Office to the official representative of the Soviet Government in Bulgaria, to the effect that the Bulgarian Government had agreed to the entry of German troops into Bulgaria, and that this action had the purpose of preserving peace in the Balkans, the Soviet Government deem it necessary to say:
>
> 1. The Soviet Government cannot share the view of the Bulgarian Government as to the correctness of her attitude in

this question, as this attitude, independently of whether the Bulgarian Government wishes it, leads not to the consolidation of peace, but to an extension of the sphere of war and the involving of Bulgaria in war ;

2. The Soviet Government, true to its peace policy, is not in a position to render any support whatever to the Bulgarian Government in the execution of her present policy.

The Soviet Government finds it necessary to make this statement, particularly in view of unhindered rumours spread in the Bulgarian press which fundamentally misrepresent the real attitude of the Soviet Government."

Both after the publication of the first Soviet statement, January 13, regarding the entry of German troops into Bulgaria and particularly after the second statement on March 3, the British press, although welcoming the Soviet moves as encouragement to both Turkey and Yugoslavia to stand firm against Axis threats and bribes, was nevertheless somewhat ironical, stressing the view that the U.S.S.R. would limit herself to words, to moral support, but would refuse to help the Balkan States to defend themselves against Germany by force of arms. Yet in November, 1940, the Soviet Government had offered to conclude a mutual assistance pact with Bulgaria—a pact which would undoubtedly have been welcomed by the Bulgarian masses of the peasantry and workers, who have always been pro-Russian. Had the Bulgarian Government accepted this offer it is possible that Yugoslavia and Turkey, perhaps also Greece, would have adhered to it, thus presenting a solid block against Germany which the latter might have thought long before attacking, and if she did so the small Balkan countries would have received assistance from their powerful Eastern neighbour—the Soviet Union.

But the Bulgarian Government preferred Nazi domination to Soviet co-operation. What under the circumstances were the Soviet Government to do? Were they to stand up for Bulgarian independence against Germany and the Bulgarian Government combined—with the Bulgarian army as reported at the time officered by Germans—and without any certainty as to what British reaction would be if the U.S.S.R. were embroiled in armed conflict with Germany? It was sound Soviet policy to maintain strict neutrality, to strengthen their country in every possible way, to pursue an independent policy, but to prevent the war from spreading as long as possible and so far as it lay in their power to provide Germany with no excuse for an attack on the U.S.S.R.

Having, in effect, subjugated Bulgaria, the German Government pursued their war of nerves against Turkey, Yugoslavia and Greece. From time to time there had been insinuations that should Turkey be involved in war with Germany, the U.S.S.R. would take the opportunity of stabbing the former in the back and that it was this fear of the Soviet attitude which caused Turkey to hesitate to put up a firm resistance to German pressure. Accordingly at a period when this pressure was becoming most acute, M. Vyshinsky, Vice-Commissar for Foreign Affairs, on March 15, 1941, suggested an exchange of views on the subject between the two Governments and gave the Turkish Ambassador to Moscow a written assurance that the U.S.S.R. had no designs whatever on Turkish territory and the Dardanelles; the talks finally resulted in the issue on March 24 of a communiqué simultaneously in Moscow and Istanbul:

> "After news had appeared in the foreign press to the effect that, if Turkey were involved in war, the Soviet Union would take advantage of the difficulties she [Turkey] would have to face to attack her in turn, the Soviet Government have informed Turkey in this connection:
>
> 1. Such news does not in any way coincide with the attitude of the Soviet Government;
>
> 2. In case Turkey should resist aggression and should find herself forced into war for the defence of her territory, Turkey could then, in accordance with the Non-Aggression Pact* existing between her and the U.S.S.R. count on the complete understanding and neutrality of the U.S.S.R.
>
> The Turkish Government has expressed to the Soviet Government its most sincere thanks for that declaration and has let it be known that, should the U.S.S.R. find itself in a similar situation, it could count on the complete understanding and neutrality of Turkey."

Although, generally speaking, the communiqué was welcomed in Britain, and the *Times* Angora correspondent said that the Soviet-Turkish declaration was "regarded as one of the most important of this war," the *Manchester Guardian*† thought the terms of the declaration too vague:

> "If Turkey fights outside her own frontiers, does the undertaking hold? Russia's motives are the desire for security and fear of Germany. She might, had her diplomacy been astute, have ranged the Near Eastern Powers together in a block to resist Germany. She has preferred to see them fall to Germany one by one until only Turkey, apart from Greece, has the spirit

* Concluded in 1925 and subsequently revised in 1929 and 1931.

† 26.iii.41.

> to resist. But if Greece were to be beaten, and Turkey to yield, might not Russia, isolated, herself be in danger? It looks as though Russia does not want to make it easy for Turkey to go to war alongside Greece and Britain lest that should bring war to the Straits and so endanger Russia. Only if Germany, contrary to Russia's hopes, attacks Turkey directly—and no doubt Germany will for the time give 'assurance'—will Russia smooth Turkey's road of self-defence."

This was more or less the attitude taken by many organs of the British press. Yet apart from the fact that there had been nothing in the attitude of the British Government to suggest that if the U.S.S.R. became involved in hostilities with Germany she could count on British support, we have seen that when the Soviet Government nevertheless offered a Mutual Assistance Pact to Bulgaria (whose population had long been regarded as the most favourably disposed towards the U.S.S.R.) the Bulgarian Government refused it. Was it likely that Prince Paul, Regent of Yugoslavia would have been more ready than King Boris to co-operate with the U.S.S.R.?

German pressure on the Yugoslav Government was as successful as it had been on the Bulgarian Government, and on March 25, 1941, in spite of strong public disapproval, the Government adhered to the Tripartite Pact, thus surrendering Yugoslav independence and opening their country to Nazi domination. On the occasion of the signature of the Pact, Hitler and Prince Paul exchanged telegrams: Prince Paul sent Hitler his "most cordial felicitations and sincerest wishes for the further prosperity and success of the great German people."

But the Yugoslav people refused to accept this betrayal of their country. Widespread disorders greeted the return of the Ministers who had signed away their country's independence. At these demonstrations British and Russian flags were carried and cries of "Long Live Britain" and "Long Live Russia" mingled with shouts of "Down with Hitler," "Down with Mussolini." On March 27, 1941, young King Peter assumed power, the Regency Council was dissolved. Its head, Prince Paul, was stopped in an attempt to reach the German frontier, members of the Government were arrested and General Simovich, a former Chief of the General Staff, formed a new national Government.

In the U.S.S.R., as in other countries, the events in Yugoslavia were followed with great interest and in denying a report that the Soviet Government had sent congratulations to the new Yugoslav Government, *Pravda* declared that "there would have been nothing extraordinary if the congratulations had actually been sent. If such congratulations were not sent, it was perhaps an omission on the part of the Soviet Government—perhaps they just didn't think of sending them. The Yugoslav nation has undoubtedly a glorious past; its people are worthy of that past and deserve congratulations."*

On April 5, only eight days after the establishment of the new national government, a Soviet-Yugoslav Treaty was concluded whereby " the two contracting parties pledged themselves to abstain from any aggression towards the other and to respect the independence, sovereign rights and territorial integrity of each other. Should one of the contracting parties be subjected to aggression by a third State the other contracting party pledged itself to preserve its policy of friendship."

The following day Germany attacked Yugoslavia. The conclusion of the Soviet-Yugoslav Treaty was a clear intimation of the Soviet attitude towards Nazi aggression even though for the reasons explained earlier, the U.S.S.R. was not prepared under the circumstances to join the armed struggle against Germany.

The Soviet and Yugoslav press greeted the Treaty enthusiastically and in German " political circles " it was reported to have made a " great sensation "—which we can well believe. The British press, although for the most part annoyed that the Soviet Union was unwilling to adopt the tactics of the fool-hardy knight-errant, nevertheless appreciated the significance of the Agreement. The *Times* commented:

> " At the very hour of the Nazi invasion, Soviet Russia has signed with Yugoslavia a pact of non-aggression and friendship which, though it may have no practical sequel, is a significant gesture of goodwill in a moment of crisis. Recent events have shown that Stalin is an astute, if detached, observer of the international scene. His swift reaction to Hitler's latest aggression will make its impression throughout the Near East."†

The *Daily Telegraph* of the same date declared:

> " The ' honest broker ' in Berlin may not be much disturbed yet by the pact of friendship with Yugoslavia which Russia announced an hour or two before Germany's declaration of war. Yugoslavia obtains no material assistance under the pact, but Moscow clearly meant it to be a hint to Nazism that the Soviet must not be quite disregarded. Germany's haunting fear of a war on two fronts is already a stark reality."

On April 12, M. Vyshinsky, Deputy Commissar for Foreign Affairs, issued a stern rebuke to Hungary on the seizure of Yugoslav territory

* *Times*, 2.iv.41. † 7.iv.41.

north of Belgrade. On the following day a Soviet-Japanese Pact of Neutrality was signed in Moscow.

It was characteristic of the growing tension between the U.S.S.R. and Germany that in commenting on the Soviet-Japanese Agreement, *Pravda,* whilst resolutely denying statements which had appeared in the British and American press that it was directed against Germany, or alternatively, that it was concluded under German pressure, also disclosed the fact that in November, 1940, the German Government had suggested to the Soviet Government that they should join the Axis by adhering to the Tripartite Pact—making it a Four-Power Pact—but that the Soviet Government had, of course, refused. German diplomatic circles were reported as being very angry at this disclosure and it was grandiloquently declared that by this action the U.S.S.R. had now lost the opportunity of participating in the creation of the "New Order"!

From about the beginning of April, 1941, persistent rumours circulated in Britain and other countries that the Germans were massing troops on or near the Soviet-German frontier. Mr. Churchill, on April 9, 1941, stated in the House of Commons that:

> "At the present moment he (Hitler) is driving south and south-east through the Balkans, and at any moment he may turn upon Turkey. But there are many signs which point to a Nazi attempt to secure the granary of the Ukraine and the oilfields of the Caucasus as a German means of gaining the resources wherewith to wear down the English-speaking world."*

It was also reported that the German Government was encouraging the formation and strengthening of Russian "White" organisations in Germany. Other reports spoke of the arrival of German troops on the Finnish border and in Finland. At the end of April, *Pravda* itself stated that 12,000 German troops fully equipped and with tanks and artillery, had arrived in Finland. It was further reported that for the first time since August, 1939, the official German Army Journal, *Wehrmacht*, had told its readers that they "must never forget that Hitler was the first to take up the fight against the Bolshevik terror régime. . . ."

There were also numerous rumours that Hitler was making far-reaching demands on the Soviet Government, and in connection with these rumours, opinions were freely expressed as to the poor chance the U.S.S.R. would stand against a German attack. Thus, to give here but two examples, the foreign editor of the *Daily Express* declared:

> "Against the reformed panzer divisions from the rest of

* *Hansard*, 9.iv.41, col. 1598.

> Europe few military authorities would allow the massed Russian Army more than three months before capitulation if they fought alone."*

The Military Correspondent of the *Evening Standard* wrote:

> "I do not hold a high opinion of the Red Army's power myself. Its mechanisation is immense, but its supply and repair services are poor. . . . The political condition of Russia is even more tempting to an aggressor of Hitler's calibre. The Stalinist dictatorship is rigid, but brittle. I hold that the grip of the régime on the country has weakened since the present war began."†

The Soviet Government denied that Germany was making any demands on them and *publicly*, at any rate, they gave no credence to the reports of the massing of German troops on the "East Wall," i.e., the Soviet-German frontier for the purpose of attacking the U.S.S.R. But there can be no doubt that the shadows were deepening over the Soviet peace sky and the Soviet Government took a number of precautions. On April 29, the transit of foreign-owned military goods across the U.S.S.R. was forbidden. The Government continued more energetically than ever to perfect their military preparedness and, in the words of Marshal Timoshenko, Commissar for Defence, set about "the task of reorganising the entire system of military training of the Red Army in the light of the experience and requirements of modern warfare."

In his speech on May Day, 1941, Marshal Timoshenko, whilst stressing the Soviet policy of keeping the U.S.S.R. out of the war, declared that "the international situation is very tense and fraught with all kinds of surprises. Therefore the entire Soviet people, the Red Army and Navy, must be in a state of fighting preparedness. . . . The Red Army and Navy are steadily improving the methods of their military training, and are perfecting their training by the experience of the present war."

And a few days later, M. Stalin, addressing officer graduates from military schools, declared that: "The Red Army has been reorganised and re-equipped in the light of the experience of the present war," and he stressed the need of intensive study of modern military weapons and tactics. Similar ideas formed the theme of many articles in *Pravda*, *Red Star* and other Soviet papers. "In the present complicated situation," said one such article in *Pravda*, "we must be ready for all sorts of surprises."

On May 6, 1941, M. Stalin, who had hitherto held no official post

* 1.v.41. † 3.v.41.

in the Soviet Government, was appointed Chairman of the Council of People's Commissars, i.e., Prime Minister of the U.S.S.R. in place of M. Molotov, who, however, retained his post as People's Commissar for Foreign Affairs. The reason for this step was quite clear; in the first place the dual office of Premier and Foreign Secretary was too onerous for one person to carry for long, particularly in those trying times; secondly, the international position was undoubtedly becoming more and more strained, at any time a quick decision on an important question might be essential and it was obviously convenient that the strongest and most popular and universally trusted Soviet leader should be at the head of affairs.

In the main this was the interpretation put upon the appointment of Stalin as Premier in the British press—although article after article discoursed at length on the "*inner*" meaning of it all. The diplomatic correspondent of the *Observer* suggested, amongst other alternatives, that Stalin had in mind to stave off a German attack by "a spectacular deal with Germany possibly even involving a personal meeting with Hitler."*

A coming meeting with Hitler as a reason for Stalin's assumption of office was mooted in many papers, whilst the diplomatic correspondent of the *Sunday Times*† declared that "the Axis Powers seriously hope that Russia will in one form or another join the Axis."

On May 9, 1941, the Soviet Foreign Commissariat notified the Norwegian, Belgian and Yugoslav Legations in Moscow that the U.S.S.R. no longer recognised their status since their countries had lost their sovereignty. This step was probably calculated to ease somewhat the strained relations between Germany and the U.S.S.R.; at the same time it was only giving as it were a *de jure* status to the *de facto* situation and in no way weakened either the U.S.S.R. herself or the States concerned.

However, the Soviet Government was freely accused of pursuing an "appeasement" policy and the *Daily Express* Political Correspondent even declared that: "The Soviet and German Governments are believed to be beginning negotiations for a complete military alliance. Stalin is reported to want such an alliance as a means of staving off the threat to his country's interests which he sees in the German conquest of Europe."‡ Logic was evidently not the strong point here, for this meant—if it meant anything—that Stalin would actually help Hitler to obtain the position which he feared, just because he feared it. The *Daily Mail* diplomatic correspondent roundly stated on the same day that: "Negotiations for a full alliance between Germany and Soviet Russia are taking place." The diplomatic correspondent of the *Times* said: "While evidence as to the

* 11.v.41. † 11.v.41. ‡ 21.v.41.

progress of Russo-German negotiations for a new treaty, perhaps of alliance, is still scanty, there is good reason to believe that the German Government recently opened conversations with the U.S.S.R. on various economic matters and on some sort of agreement at the expense of either Turkey or Iran or both."* The political correspondent of the *Daily Express* next stated that:

> " Hitler and Stalin plan to spring their new all-in agreement on the world soon, and the two dictators are expected to meet—probably in Poland—to shake hands on the alliance.
>
> When the terms of the pact are announced the British Government will consider the future of its diplomatic relations with Stalin's Government."†

The *Manchester Guardian*‡ diplomatic correspondent decided that there was a possibility of a political and military alliance between Germany and the U.S.S.R. but was not prepared to give odds either way.

All these stories may have been spread by Nazi agents with a view on the one hand of playing a war of nerves on the U.S.S.R. and on the other of frightening Turkey to accede to Axis demands by holding up the bogey of a Soviet-German agreement at her expense, and as such they were dismissed by the diplomatic correspondents of the *Daily Herald* and the *Daily Telegraph*. True, on May 24, 1941, the German Government officially denied that they had made any territorial promises to the U.S.S.R. in return for closer Soviet-German political co-operation and *Reynolds News* announced on May 25 that " so far the Soviet has agreed only to trade discussions " which was certainly true.

Rumours of German preparations for an attack on the U.S.S.R., of her far-reaching economic and political demands and of negotiations for a military alliance, Soviet or joint Soviet-German claims on or action against Iran, Turkey, etc., continued to circulate throughout the world. From all the welter of speculation two things stood out as certainly true. First, that Berlin was disappointed with Soviet exports to Germany—particularly of oil and wheat—the Soviet Government refused to export large quantities of these products on credit, they demanded machinery and other goods in return, and Germany was unable to comply with these conditions ; Soviet industry and agriculture demanded large quantities of oil, and exports had to be limited in any case. Secondly, there can be no doubt at all that Germany was massing troops on the Soviet-German frontier and in its immediate vicinity, and we can hardly imagine that the Soviet leaders were not aware of the fact.

* 22.v.41. † 22.v.41. ‡ 24.v.41.

But the Soviet Government desired not to provoke an attack and to avoid war for as long as possible. Moreover they were far from certain as to the attitude of Britain in case of a German onslaught. Accordingly they made no outward sign. And it was, of course, by no means certain that these concentrations implied an imminent German attack—they might possibly signify bluff or blackmail against the Soviet Union. On June 13, 1941, Moscow radio broadcast an official statement which, after enumerating the rumours about German demands and troop concentrations, and Soviet counter-measures, declared categorically:

> " 1. Germany did not present any claims to the U.S.S.R. and does not propose any new, closer agreement in view of which no negotiations on this subject could have taken place;
>
> 2. According to the information at the disposal of the U.S.S.R., Germany abides by the provisions of the Soviet-German Pact of non-aggression as unswervingly as the Soviet Union, in view of which in the opinion of Soviet quarters the rumours of Germany's intention to disrupt the Pact and undertake an attack on the U.S.S.R. are devoid of any ground, whereas the dispatching of German troops relieved from operations in the Balkans to the Eastern and North-Eastern districts of Germany which is now taking place is connected, it should be assumed, with other motives having no bearing on Soviet-German relations.
>
> 3. The U.S.S.R., as follows from its peace policy, abided and intends to abide by the provisions of the Soviet-German Non-Aggression Pact in view of which rumours to the effect that the U.S.S.R. is preparing for war with Germany are false.
>
> 4. The summer camp drills of the Red Army reservists held at present, and the forthcoming manœuvres have no other purpose than training of reservists and checking of work of railroad organisation. They are carried out, as is known, every year, in view of which, to present these measures of the Red Army as inimical to Germany is, to say the least, absurd."

It will be seen that whilst this statement denied that Germany had made demands on the U.S.S.R. it did not deny the presence of German troops on her frontier, but put a different interpretation on this fact no doubt in order not to give any pretext for a German attack.

At the same time reports also multiplied that the Germans were sending an ever increasing number of troops into Finland.

Reports and speculations continued regarding alleged concessions made or about to be made by Stalin to Hitler, but the general view was that Hitler was either playing a gigantic game of bluff or that his troop concentrations were meant merely as a threat to enforce the granting of far-reaching demands he had made or was about to make. According to the diplomatic correspondent of the *Times*:

> "The British Government by no means assume that Hitler is definitely planning to attack the Soviet Union. It is far better to recognise that Hitler, by concentrating his forces in the East, is trying to put pressure automatically on Moscow in the hope of securing political and economic gains by agreement, or at any rate without fighting, and that the concentrations may act as a screen for sudden military operations elsewhere."*

The diplomatic correspondent of the *Daily Herald* voiced a general feeling when he said: "It is a rash prophet who will either forecast a Russo-German agreement or forecast a Russo-German war as the outcome."† The General Secretary of the National Union of Railwaymen declared: "He [Hitler] will not, in my opinion, drive things so far as to get into war with the U.S.S.R."‡ On the other hand, the *Daily Mail*§ expressed the belief that Hitler would certainly attack the U.S.S.R.

However, there was one man in Great Britain, Mr. R. H. Naylor, an astrologist, in whose mind, at any rate on the eve of June, 1941, no doubt existed as to the possibility of war between Germany and the Soviet Union. In his "Naylor's Monthly Forecast" for June, 1941, he prophesied:

> "The cheerful idiots who possess wishbones in the place of backbones, the other people who see world events in distorting mirrors have assured us, ever since the outbreak of this fantastic war, that the link-up between Stalin and Hitler was a temporary affair.
>
> It would soon snap, they chanted; Hitler would soon fall out with Stalin, or there would be a combined attack upon Russia, or something else miraculous would happen to our advantage.
>
> Nothing of the kind has happened. The stars foretold that nothing of the kind would, or could happen, for they are linked together by destiny, these two. I have said that time and time again, thereby making myself a target for many bitter criticisms."

And on June 22, after the readers of the *Sunday Express* had learned from the radio that the German armies were marching into Soviet territory, on turning to Mr. Naylor's usual article, they read: "Zero hour near in Eastern Mediterranean. Don't count upon opera-

* 16.vi.41. † 17.vi.41.
‡ *Railway Review*, 20.vi.41. § 18.vi.41.

tions there being held up because of differences between Stalin and Hitler. I still hold to my forecast that they won't quarrel yet."

As two months earlier* so now on the very eve of the German attack, the chances that the U.S.S.R. would be able to stand up to Hitler's forces were by many considered to be very slim. "A Student of War," in the *Daily Telegraph* thus summed up these chances:

> "Russia could probably place in the field double the number of German divisions. She has a number of armoured divisions and a numerically vast air force. The tanks and aeroplanes I have seen appear to be modern and good.
>
> But I cannot believe that even Stalin has any confidence in his armed forces. Their showing against Finland was lamentable. Pruning is not as good when applied to the officer class of an army as when applied to trees. Their aeroplanes might damage Germany, but it is in the perfect discipline and liaison of all its parts that the German army is formidable, and, never characteristics of the Russian army, these are completely lacking at present.
>
> Somehow, I imagine, Stalin will find a formula which will save his face and his dubiously efficient army. Otherwise he will probably receive short shrift. Germany would have to undertake an occupation, but that need not be too onerous if the Russians are treated as Hitler has treated the Poles."†

It was well known that many military experts considered that the German Panzers would go through the Red Forces "like a knife through butter." Sir Bernard Pares, however, although he declared that "No one can suppose that the Red Army in efficiency is the equal of the German," pointed out that it was now [1941] a far more efficient force than it was in 1914."‡ The General Secretary of the N.U.R. also expressed confidence that if Hitler did attack, the armies of the U.S.S.R. would not collapse and added:

> "There is respectable expert testimony to the strength, efficiency, inventiveness and foresight of Soviet Russia's defence organisation. Not a few of the Nazi methods of making war were innovations developed in the training of the Red armies and air force. In the technique of industrial production the great Soviet factories do not lag behind, and the Soviet centres of production are located well out of the normal range of Nazi raiders. The Soviet fleets are stronger and strategically better dispersed

* See pages 663-4.

† *Daily Telegraph*, 16.vi.41.

‡ *Manchester Guardian*, 21.vi.41.

than many people appreciate when they discuss the possibilities of a Nazi-Soviet war."*

The military correspondent of *Reynolds*, whilst taking a non-committal attitude, declared that "Stalin's army may surprise Hitler."†

Turning now to the relations between the British and Soviet Governments themselves during the first six months of 1941 we can note that although there had been no fundamental move towards an Anglo-Soviet understanding, relations were becoming somewhat less cold. Thus when Mr. Eden visited Turkey, Sir Stafford Cripps travelled from Moscow (February 27) to meet him there by Soviet aeroplane and with Soviet assistance. It was reported that Mr. Eden not only had long talks with Sir Stafford, but also several interviews with the Soviet Ambassador in Turkey, and British sources in Ankara expressed "gratification over the harmony of the talks, adding that Mr. Eden found that the Soviets were near the British viewpoint throughout the talks with Cripps and the Russian envoy."‡

In general the British and Soviet press mutually became less hostile, although the U.S.S.R. was still spoken of by, for instance, Mr. A. J. Cummings, of the *News Chronicle*, as a "near Ally" of Germany—which the Soviet Union was not and never had been—and the policy of publicly pillorying the U.S.S.R. for her trade with Germany had continued.

In Trade Union, co-operative and working-class circles generally impatience at the delay in coming to an understanding with the U.S.S.R. had been growing. At the Co-operative Conference in York (April, 1941) a resolution was adopted "regretting the failure of the Government to come to an amicable understanding with the Soviet Union and instructing Co-operative M.P.'s to urge a more friendly attitude towards Russia as a means by which the war could be ended more quickly," and at the Annual Conference of the Scottish Trades Union Congress a resolution was carried declaring "the policy of friendship with the Soviet Union calls for full support of all affiliated Unions and Trades Councils."

However, on April 24, Mr. Butler, Under-Secretary of State for Foreign Affairs, in reply to a question in the House of Commons, stated that there had been no progress in the negotiations for a Trade Agreement and general settlement with the Soviet Union. The main stumbling block which prevented such an agreement was, of course, the steady British refusal to recognise the incorporation of the Baltic States in the U.S.S.R. and to release the detained gold and ships of these States.

* *Railway Review*, 20.vi.41. † 22.vi.41. ‡ *News Chronicle*, 1.iii.41.

"Russia's real interests," wrote Sir Bernard Pares in May, "are manifestly the same as our own. There was never a time when our co-operation was more needed and some understanding more desirable";* and again:

> "In my view our co-operation would have averted this war. It might have saved Yugoslavia, for Bulgaria would hardly then have refused Moscow's direct offer (not of non-aggression but of mutual assistance). Anyhow, the Yugoslavs, who are 100 per cent. pro-British and pro-Russian, thought so, for on the overthrow of the 'appeaser' Tsvetkovich they carried the British and Soviet flags side by side through the streets of Belgrade.
>
> Since our glorious repulse of direct invasion, it is the British Empire that is threatened, and that has brought Hitler to the gates of Russia. And now the menace travels farther—to British oil and to Russian Central Asia. Is it in our interest or in theirs that we should be content to stand scowling at each other? '*Cui bono?*'—which, if correctly translated, means 'Who gains by it?' Need we ask?"†

II. Arrival of Rudolf Hess

On May 10, 1941, there occurred the sensational flight and landing in Scotland of Rudolf Hess, Hitler's official deputy. The real purpose of his flight was presumably disclosed by Hess to the British Government representatives who interviewed him, but it was not disclosed by the Government to the British public.

M. Stalin gave the Soviet interpretation of the Hess incident in his speech on November 6, 1941, when, after referring to the Nazi Government's attempt to form a "general coalition" against the U.S.S.R. by playing on the fears of the spectre of revolution among ruling circles in various countries, and to the desired result of this policy in France, he declared:

> "The German Fascist strategists thought that the same would occur in Great Britain and the U.S.A. The notorious Hess, properly speaking, was despatched to Britain for that very purpose by the German Fascists in order to persuade British politicians to join in a general crusade against the U.S.S.R. . . .
>
> The Germans miscalculated. Great Britain and the U.S.A. despite the efforts of Hess, not only did not join in the campaign of the German Fascist aggressors against the U.S.S.R., but, on the contrary, allied themselves with the U.S.S.R. against Hitlerite Germany."

The British Government neither confirmed nor denied M. Stalin's

* *Manchester Guardian*, 10.v.41. † *Manchester Guardian*, 17.v.14.

version of the Hess affair, but Mr. Churchill seemed to lift just a corner of the veil which enshrouded the mystery when, speaking in the House of Commons on November 12, 1941, he said:

> "In the various remarks which the Deputy Fuehrer, Herr Hess, has let fall from time to time during his sojourn in our midst, nothing has been more clear than that Hitler relied upon the starvation attack more than upon invasion to bring us to our knees."*

A year later, early in October, 1942, the Swedish Nazi newspaper announced that Hess' flight "was part of Hitler's well considered policy always directed towards an alliance with Britain."†

To protect himself Hitler had agreed in advance to repudiate all knowledge of the plan in the event of the failure of the enterprise. The Nazi paper further explained that the Hess mission was to offer Britain "a profitable agreement in the form of an alliance to make war on Russia as the result of which Germany was to receive the Ukraine and the Caucasus oil regions, Japan was to receive Siberia, and the rest of Russia was to be split into separate homogeneous States. Britain's positive share, which was to be guaranteed by Germany, was the retention of the mandated territories, especially in the Middle East, but Germany was to receive back her former Colonies."‡

If this was indeed the proposal made by Hess—and it is not impossible—then it illustrated once again the far-sightedness of Mr. Churchill in seeing through the Nazi wiles—for he certainly rejected Hitler's offer, whatever it may have been. Why the statement or offer made by Hess should not have been published we are at a loss to understand, unless it was (we give this interpretation as a purely personal one with all diffidence) that Mr. Churchill and others of the British Government in the know were afraid of the pressure that might be exerted to accept the Hess plan by some influential anti-Soviet circles, which would dearly have liked to switch the war to one against the U.S.S.R. By keeping the offer secret but rejecting it, he was thus freed from embarrassing opposition, just as later, by his immediate bold public acceptance of the U.S.S.R. as an Ally in the war against Germany, he put an effective stop to any public opposition to his policy by these sinister circles.

On June 7, 1941, it was announced that Sir Stafford Cripps had been requested by the British Foreign Office to return home for a short time for consultation; by the time he arrived in London (June 11) the reports of German concentrations on the Soviet border had become very explicit—and with them went rumours of German

* *Hansard*, 12.xi.41, col. 31. † *Times*, 5.x.42. ‡ Ibid.

demands on the U.S.S.R. regarding which the *Daily Mail* expressed the following view:

> " If Stalin fought, could he hold Hitler until winter arrived to close the campaign? If he could, the whole course of the war would be altered. Britain will be much stronger by next spring, and American war production will be rising to its peak. . . .
>
> We hope the Government will give Sir Stafford Cripps a free hand in negotiations with Russia. No interests must be allowed to stand in the way of a possible agreement. On Stalin's decision may hang our chances of victory and his own chances of survival."*

But so far as official relations between the two countries were concerned, no change occurred, though leading publicists and others alive to the situation, whilst doubting the probability of a German attack on the U.S.S.R., urged that, should such an attack materialise no anti-Soviet prejudices should prevent full co-operation with the U.S.S.R.

> " Russian submission would be perilous for us. Russian defeat would be calamitous for us . . . there have been many moments during the war when it would have suited Russian interest to establish closer contact with us. Here often a Russian illusion blocked the path ; Moscow believed that Britain had ambitions against her, or at least that we would relax our war effort against Germany if the Germans went eastward. In the past, we must admit there had been some ground for this belief. Just over a year ago most newspapers in this country were clamouring for war against Russia.
>
> Can such illusions be removed? This much at least might be publicly stated: Even if Hitler moves eastward Britain's war against Germany will be maintained with mounting ferocity. All assistance in our power will be given to the Russians."†

And again on the following day:

> " Russian and British interests interlock. Hitler knows it and has always known it. After the long sad story of relations between the two countries, Britain and Russia should be able to understand now.
>
> If Germany goes to war with Russia, we should recognise our interest in sustaining Russia's resistance. We should attempt to make our friends the Americans understand too. For the rest we shall not forget the biggest fact of all. Whether he fights

* *Daily Mail*, 13.vi.41. † *Evening Standard*, 19.vi.41.

Russia or treats with Russia, his aim will be the same—to secure the best circumstances for the early invasion and conquest of this Island."

The diplomatic correspondent of the *News Chronicle*, after discussing what sort of help we could render to the U.S.S.R., declared:

"It must be said, however, that there is little indication as yet in London of any appreciation of the tremendous political repercussions which a clash between Germany and Russia—which for many people personify the political creeds of Fascism and Communism—would cause throughout the world, and particularly in those countries and among those sections of opinion, in which hatred of Communism on religious or social grounds is even more fervent than dislike of Fascism."*

The *Daily Express* declared:

"Whatever one's views may be of Bolsheviks, they at least did not trample down the world under insolent jackboots . . . if Stalin's army decides to fight, with or without permission, we must be ready to support it in whatever way is possible."†

On Sunday, June 22, 1941, the day when Hitler opened his attack on the U.S.S.R., the Sunday press was still uncertain as to the outcome of the Soviet-German tension.

The *Sunday Times* declared:

"Of what we would do were Russia to be attacked, either on a small scale or (what is less likely) on a large scale, little can be said at present. But our recent nightly raids on the Ruhr clearly show that we should batter Germany as hard as we could."

This journal warned Britain against assuming that Germany would attack Russia and not Britain.

The *Sunday Dispatch* gave a similar warning:

"Those in this country who dream of Germany being diverted towards Russia—and therefore away from us—would be repeating in war the cardinal mistake they made during the years before the war. If Hitler goes East it is only to be in a materially stronger position to come West."

The Editor of *Reynolds* declared:

"Great Britain, to-day, has an opportunity to open a new chapter in her diplomatic relations with Russia; an opportunity

* 20.vi.41. † 21.vi.41.

which, grasped firmly and exploited fully might result in a smashing defeat for the Axis. . . . A new opportunity is here. Let us seize it. In 1939, Hitler stole a Russian-German agreement from under the noses of our negotiators in Moscow. Let us be as daring and realistic now. We do not go to Moscow as suppliants. We are a great people, prepared to aid Russia and to be aided by Russia on honest terms; prepared also, if need be, to fight and win the battle against Hitlerism alone."

But though during the weeks immediately preceding June 22, 1941, the air was thick with reports of German demands on and even of an ultimatum to the U.S.S.R., Moscow remained calm. Actually, the Nazi Government presented neither demands nor an ultimatum before Germany treacherously attacked the U.S.S.R. Perhaps Hitler knew that what he coveted from that country—control of her oil and wheat and German *Lebensraum* at the expense of the Ukraine, Byelorussia and other parts of the Soviet Union—would never be granted by Stalin and his comrades; a stab in the dark might therefore be more effective than to give warning of it by the time-honoured method of an ultimatum—a method long ago discarded by Hitler and his fellow thugs.

CHAPTER XXVIII

GERMANY AND THE U.S.S.R. AT WAR. GREAT BRITAIN AND THE U.S.S.R. ALLIES, 1941

I. Mr. Churchill's Speech

At 4 a.m., on June 22, 1941, German forces, without giving any reason, invaded the territory of the U.S.S.R. and the Luftwaffe coming from many directions including German-occupied Poland, Finland and Rumania raided Zhitomir, Kiev, Sevastopol, Kaunas, and several other towns. An hour and a half later the German Ambassador handed a Note to M. Molotov, the Soviet Foreign Commissar, declaring that Germany had decided to "proceed against" the Soviet Union. It was a case of stark unprovoked aggression.

At 5 a.m., on the same day, Goebbels read Hitler's proclamation to the German people, the essence of which was that the Soviet Union in agreement with Great Britain and the U.S.A. was preparing to attack Germany and that he had struck first. Among other things he said:

"While our soldiers from May 10, 1940, onwards had been breaking the power of France and Britain in the west, the Russian

> military deployment on our eastern frontier was being continued to a more and more menacing extent.
>
> From August, 1940, onwards, I therefore considered it to be in the interests of the Reich no longer to permit our eastern provinces, which moreover had already been so often laid waste, to remain unprotected in the face of this tremendous concentration of Bolshevik divisions.
>
> Thus came about the result intended by the British and Soviet Russian co-operation, namely, the tying-up of such powerful German forces in the east that the radical conclusion of the war in the west, particularly as regards aircraft, could no longer be vouched for by the German High Command.
>
> This, however, was in line with the object, not only of British but of Soviet Russian policy."*

At 11.15 a.m., M. Molotov, in a broadcast to the Soviet peoples, explained what had happened, reminded them that Napoleon had doomed himself when he invaded Russia, that Hitler would suffer a similar fate, and concluded:

> "All our people must be united and steadfast as never before. Everyone of us must demand from himself and from others discipline, organisation, and a self-sacrifice worthy of the true Soviet patriot."

The British Government acted quickly. Mr. Eden, the Foreign Secretary, invited M. Maisky to meet him at noon at the Foreign Office and they soon found a firm basis for agreement. The B.B.C. announced early in the day that the Prime Minister, Mr. Winston Churchill, would speak at 9 p.m. The world throughout that day eagerly awaited this speech. "Would he seize the opportunity which history had presented to him? Would his speech sound the tocsin of ultimate Nazi-Fascist defeat?" These questions were canvassed in every corner of the globe on that eventful day. Fortunately for Great Britain, the U.S.S.R. and civilisation, the hour had brought the man.

At 9 p.m., Mr. Churchill began to speak. One could sense the intense hush with which his words were followed from the Arctic to the Antarctic, from the Atlantic to the Pacific, and it soon became evident that he was equal in stature to the occasion.

He opened thus:

> "I have taken occasion to speak to you to-night because we have reached one of the climacterics of the war. In the first of these intense turning points a year ago France fell prostrate

* *Daily Telegraph*, 23.vi.41.

under the German hammer and we had to face the storm alone.

The second was when the Royal Air Force beat the Hun raiders out of the daylight air and thus warded off the Nazi invasion of our islands while we were still ill-armed and ill-prepared.

The third turning point was when the President and Congress of the United States passed the Lease and Lend Enactment devoting nearly 2,000,000,000 sterling of the wealth of the New World to help us defend our liberties and their own.

Those were the three climacterics. The fourth is now upon us. At 4 o'clock this morning Hitler attacked and invaded Russia. All his usual formalities of perfidy were observed with scrupulous technique."

After denouncing Nazi perfidy and crimes in trenchant terms the Prime Minister continued: "All we know at present is that the Russian people are defending their native soil, and that their leaders have called upon them to resist to the utmost." There was more than Russia, huge and important though that was, at stake. He went on:

"But even the carnage and ruin which his victory—should he gain it, and he has not gained it yet—will bring upon the Russian people will be only a stepping-stone to an attempt to plunge the 400,000,000 or 500,000,000 people in China and the 350,000,000 who live in India into that bottomless pit of human degradation over which the diabolical emblem of the swastika flaunts itself.

It is not too much to say here this summer evening that the lives and happiness of 1,000,000,000 additional human beings are now menaced with brutal Nazi violence.

It is enough to make us hold our breath, but presently I shall show you something else that lies behind it, and touches very nearly the life of Great Britain and the United States."

"No one," stated Mr. Churchill, "has been a more persistent opponent of Communism than I have been for the last 25 years. I will unsay no word that I have spoken about it, but all this fades away before the spectacle which is now unfolding."

"The past, with its crimes, its follies and its tragedies, flashes away. I see the Russian soldiers standing on the threshold of their native land, guarding the fields which their fathers had tilled from time immemorial, and I see them guarding their homes where mothers and wives pray—ah, yes, for there are times when all pray for the safety of their loved ones, for the return of the breadwinner, of the champion, of their protector—I see the 10,000 villages of Russia, where the means of existence was wrung so hardly from the soil, but where there are still primordial human joys, where maidens laugh and children play."

Then, pausing as if to draw special attention to what was to follow, he said: "But now I have to declare the decision of His Majesty's Government, and I feel sure it is a decision in which the great Dominions will in due course concur. But we must speak out now at once, without a day's delay. I have to make a declaration. Can you doubt what our policy will be?" Answering his own question, the Prime Minister added: "We have offered to the Government of Soviet Russia any technical or economic assistance which is in our power and which is likely to be of service to them."

If Hitler still had any delusions about effecting divisions in the ranks of the Allies they were quickly shattered:

> "This is no class war. This is a war in which the whole British Empire and Commonwealth of Nations is engaged without distinction of race, creed, or party. It is not for me to speak of the action of the United States of America, but this I will say. If Hitler imagines that his attack on Soviet Russia will cause the slightest division of aim or slackening of effort in the great democracies which are resolved upon his doom, he is woefully mistaken. On the contrary, we shall be fortified and encouraged in our efforts to rescue mankind from his tyrannies. We shall be strengthened, and not weakened, in our determination and our resources."

In concluding his historic speech, Mr. Churchill stressed that if Hitler succeeded in defeating the Soviet Forces he would next turn all his military strength on Great Britain, and added:

> "The Russian danger is therefore our danger, and the danger of the United States, just as the cause of any Russian fighting for his hearth and home is the cause of free men and free peoples in every quarter of the globe. Let us learn the lessons already taught by such cruel experience. Let us redouble our exertions and strike with united strength while life and power remain."*

Progressive humanity throughout the five Continents, and nowhere more so than in Great Britain, emitted a tremendous sigh of relief, and it is not difficult to imagine the feelings of Hitler as the speech was being translated to him. The course of history had been changed in thirty minutes.

* *Times*,. 23.vi.41.

Naturally, the most discussed question in next day's press, Monday, June 23, was the German attack on the U.S.S.R. The leader-writers and military correspondents did not directly ask and answer the question: "How long will the Russian front hold?" They asked and answered it by implication, and in doing so they drew on the "dope"—the word was a hundred per cent. accurate on this occasion —which Whitehall had been ladling out during the previous weeks. Here are a few of the extracts:

> "The Poles . . . fought for 18 days. Stalin can do better than this." (Military Correspondent, *Evening Standard,* 23.vi.41.)

> "For the next few months, perhaps only weeks, most of the Nazi energy and war effort must be expended Eastwards. Undoubtedly we shall gain thereby, during this phase, provided we take full advantage of the interval." (Military Correspondent, *Evening News,* 23.vi.41.)

> "The Fuhrer at any rate believes that he can smash the Red Army and Air Force by midsummer. Then, having seized all the corn, oil and other stocks he can lay his hands on, he would swiftly turn right about and throw the entire weight of his land, air and sea forces against this country.
>
> We may have to pay for the comparative peace of these early summer days by greatly increased risks of invasion in the autumn." (Ward Price, *Daily Mail,* 23.vi.41.)

> "The Germans' assault is due to a desperate shortage of oil and grain. If these can be denied her for four months, or even less, till the Panzers stay in harbour and the Luftwaffe is ground-bound for lack of oil, and the German armies, perhaps, lie encompassed by snow, then Hitler will have lost his last and greatest stake. Germany will be beaten." (Military Correspondent, *News Chronicle,* 23.vi.41.)

> "Nobody in this country will yield to the temptation of congratulating himself to the momentary diversion of Hitler's forces towards the East." (*Times* Leader, 23.vi.41.)

> "The Red Army may, or may not, prove that it can fight. It had a real value to us as a threat.
>
> If Hitler removes that threat once and for all he will face us in a few weeks in more terrible guise than he did last autumn. We must work now as never before." (*Daily Express* Leader, 23.vi.41.)

> "But the prize he may win is almost sufficient justification for

any risk. He may hope to seize a useful navy which would assist his plans against Britain. He may have cast his eyes upon the Russian Air Force, the capture of which would wipe out the reinforcement that America has so far been able to send us. He will at least hope to secure the wheat and oil he so much needs; and there is a mineral wealth in Russia which must also figure in his desires at the present time." (*Daily Telegraph,* A Student of War, 23.vi.41.)

"Russian military power is a riddle to which the only clue yet afforded was the war against Finland. And the Russian performance in that war was strikingly unimpressive." (*Daily Herald* Leader, 23.vi.41.)

As we have pointed out earlier, by this time, military experts, after analysing the campaign, had come to the conclusion that the Soviet campaign in Finland had shown the remarkable strategic and fighting ability of the Red Forces.

There was nothing to choose between the views published in the press on June 23, and those expressed privately in the corridors of the House of Commons when the members reassembled on June 24. One member in conversation with the authors summed up the judgment of the majority of his colleagues thus: "The Red Army at most will last three months."

It is perfectly true that there were men and women in Whitehall, Fleet Street and in all parties in the House of Commons who had accurate ideas of the prowess of the Soviet Forces, but they were in a minority. The majority were blinded by prejudice, political and social. For years they had conducted an anti-Soviet propaganda based on a distorted—to use the very mildest term—assessment of conditions in the U.S.S.R., and finally became the victims of their own propaganda.

On June 24, Mr. Eden, the Foreign Secretary, informed Parliament that the Soviet Government had accepted the British offer to send economic and military missions to Moscow and that collaboration would be on a mutual and reciprocal basis.

Prime Minister Stalin, on July 3, 1941, in the course of a stirring appeal to the Soviet people to defeat the Nazi invaders said:

"In this connection the historic utterance of the British Prime Minister, Mr. Churchill, regarding aid to the Soviet Union, and the declaration of the United States Government signifying readiness to render aid to our country, which can only evoke a feeling of gratitude in the hearts of the people of the Soviet Union, are fully comprehensible and symptomatic."

On July 12, an Anglo-Soviet Agreement was signed in Moscow by Sir Stafford Cripps on behalf of Great Britain and by M. Molotov on behalf of the U.S.S.R. Its provisions were:

> " 1. The two Governments mutually undertake to render each other assistance and support of all kinds in the present war against Hitlerite Germany.
>
> 2. They further undertake that during this war they will neither negotiate nor conclude an armistice or treaty of peace except by mutual agreement."

Mr. Churchill, in announcing the conclusion of this Agreement to Parliament on July 15, said: " It carried with it the full assent of the Great Dominions of the Crown," and concluded: " It is, of course. an alliance, and the Russian people are now our allies."

Up to the time of this declaration, despite the Prime Minister's historic speech of June 22, and the fact that the Soviet Union was an ally, a real fighting ally, in deeds and not in words, old prejudices and habits of thought prevailed to such an extent that she was not recognised as such.

" I read, in an official document circulated in Whitehall on Friday," wrote Mr. Hannen Swaffer in the *Daily Herald*, Monday, July 7, 1941, " that Russia was ' our associate, but not an ally.' . . . Even to-day, I doubt the wholeheartedness of Whitehall's support of Russia. . . . The sneering at Russia which is still heard in Whitehall must stop immediately."

Further, for some time prior to Sunday, July 6, 1941, all the National Anthems of the Allies were played by the B.B.C. prior to their 9 o'clock news on Sundays. They were played as usual on Sunday, July 6, but the *Internationale*, the Soviet National Anthem, was not included. When the subject was raised in the House of Lords, July 8, 1941, Lord Snell replied on behalf of the Government that the Soviet Anthem was not played because in the accepted sense of the term the U.S.S.R. was not our ally.

The Anglo-Soviet Agreement of July 12, 1941, was broadcast by the B.B.C. as a special announcement on the afternoon of Sunday, July 13, and it was widely expected that when the National Anthems of the Allied Governments were played as usual at 8.45 p.m. on that day, the Soviet National Anthem would be included. But no, a Soviet march was played and then followed the various National Anthems. When a representative asked why, he was told: " The B.B.C. was acting on instructions from the Foreign Office."

Enquiries were made by the competent authorities whether the Soviet Embassy would be satisfied with some other Russian song in lieu of their chosen National Anthem and they naturally replied,

"No." The B.B.C., or those who were responsible for this ridiculous behaviour, were in a dilemma. The Soviet Union was now our ally. Discrimination against the U.S.S.R. would be insulting to that country and would be emphatically rejected by the British people. A solution had to be found and the solution made the ridiculous still more absurd. Mr. Duff Cooper, Minister of Information, announced in the House of Commons, July 16, 1941, that the National Anthems would not be played in future.

> "No wonder the House of Commons hooted with mirth," commented the *News Chronicle*, July 17, 1941, "when Mr. Duff Cooper announced yesterday that all National Anthems are to be discontinued on the wireless on Sundays. He was so ridiculously solemn about it. 'The increase in the number of National Anthems,' he said, 'renders it impossible to do full justice to them in the time allotted.' . . . Chuck it, Duff! You know perfectly well that you have decided to scrap a whole building because you don't like the colour of the proposed roof. Your action has made you a laughing stock, and it serves you jolly well right—except, of course, that it's not really your fault, but the fault of that mysterious High Authority."

We shall return to this subject later.

From the first there was no question as to the British nation's approval of the British Government giving full support to the Soviet Government; Sir Archibald Sinclair, Secretary of State for Air, expressed what was in many minds when, at a Liberal meeting on July 19, he said that the Nazi attack on the U.S.S.R. "brings Russia where Liberals believe she would have been long ago but for the follies and vagaries of British and French policy before the war—fighting alongside us against the common Nazi enemy."*

II. Atlantic Charter. Anglo-Soviet-Iran Agreement. Anglo-Soviet Trade Union Agreement

After Parliament rose for the summer recess, the tireless Mr. Churchill met Mr. Roosevelt somewhere in the Atlantic, and Prime Minister and President hammered out the famous "Atlantic Charter" which was announced to the world on August 14, 1941.

In the course of their meeting, they sent a joint message to Premier Stalin suggesting a Conference in Moscow to discuss the best possible use of available and potential war supplies. The message concluded:

> "We realise fully how vitally important to the defeat of Hitlerism is the brave and steadfast resistance of the Soviet Union, and we feel therefore that we must not in any circumstances fail to

* *Times*, 21.vii.41.

act quickly and immediately in this matter of planning the programme for the future allocation of our joint resources."

M. Stalin replied two days later, thanking the Governments of both countries and welcoming the proposal of a Three-Power Conference in Moscow, and on the same day an Anglo-Soviet Agreement was signed in Moscow under which the British Government granted the U.S.S.R. a credit of £10,000,000 for five years. It was agreed that when this credit was exhausted the Governments would negotiate for a further sum.

It is pertinent to our narrative to take a swift glance here at the position as it existed on the Soviet-German front about mid-August, 1941. The courageous and skilful fight put up by the Soviet forces had astounded the general public throughout the world, had confounded many military experts in all countries and had dragged unwilling encomiums from the Hitlerite forces and military commentators.

Goebbels essayed a war of nerves. He declared, on July 12, 1941, that "the Stalin Line" was broken at all material points and that the Axis forces were advancing rapidly on Leningrad, Moscow and Kiev. But this had about as much effect on the morale of the Soviet forces and peoples as the proverbial water on a duck's back. True, the Soviet forces had had to give ground and the Axis forces had taken Smolensk and were knocking at the gates of Odessa. But in retreating the Soviet forces had inflicted enormous losses on the Axis, and Leningrad, Moscow and Kiev were still in Soviet hands.

By this date, mid-August, 1941, the Blitzkrieg had been proved to be a failure in the U.S.S.R., so much so that a Berlin military spokesman asserted that "German strategy never knew the term blitzkrieg."

Meanwhile, the British and Soviet Governments were becoming increasingly uneasy about the large number of German "specialists and tourists" in Iran, and friendly warnings were repeatedly addressed to the Iranian Government.

On August 16, 1941, the British and Soviet Governments presented a memorandum to the Iranian Government requesting the latter to expel a large number of German Intelligence Service Agents, terrorist groups and others then in the country and working against British, Soviet and Iranian interests. Unfortunately, this friendly warning was unavailing and on August 25, British and Soviet troops entered the country. A pledge was given to the Iranian Government that the two Governments had no designs on Iranian territory or independence, and that their troops would be withdrawn as soon as the danger threatening Iran, Great Britain and the U.S.S.R. had been removed. A new Government was formed in Teheran on August 28, 1941, and the

Premier ordered his troops not to oppose the British-Soviet forces. On September 10, Mr. Eden, the Foreign Secretary, was able to inform the House of Commons:

> "The terms put forward by His Majesty's Government and the Soviet Government, and now accepted by the Iranian Government, provide that the German Minister and his staff must leave Teheran at once and that the German Legation must be closed. This also applies to the Italian, Hungarian and Rumanian Legations. The Iranian Government state that the four Legations have been informed of this decision and requested to comply forthwith. Orders have also been given by the Iranian Government to stop the facilities of the Axis Legations for communicating in cypher or by wireless. I take this opportunity to add that steps are being taken by the Iranian Government to hand over the German community in Iran to the British and Soviet Governments."*

Safe conduct to the frontier was given to the Axis diplomats, but the other Axis nationals were handed over to the British and Soviet representatives for internment. It is outside the scope of this work to deal further with developments within Iran except to add that since then a number of important questions have been settled. Transport across the country from the Persian Gulf to the Caspian for supplies to the Soviet Union has been considerably improved and all this has been achieved without friction. Iranian independence has been scrupulously respected, British and Soviet troops are still in the country and the most cordial relations exist between them. They will, of course, be withdrawn at the conclusion of hostilities.

On September 2, 1941, the British T.U.C. adopted unanimously and with the greatest enthusiasm a resolution "for the establishment of an Anglo-Russian Trade Union Council composed of an equal number of representatives from both countries, and providing for regular meetings alternately in Russia and Britain for the exchange of views and information on matters of common concern."

Mr. Jack Tanner, President of the Amalgamated Engineering Union, in supporting the resolution, among other things said:

> "There is a point of view held in certain quarters which may result in a nullification of the whole war effort. There are people in high places who declare that they hope the Russian and German armies will exterminate each other, and while this is taking place we, the British Commonwealth of Nations, will so develop our Air Force and other armed forces that, if Russia and Ger-

* *Hansard*, 10.ix.41, col. 159.

many do destroy each other, we shall have the dominating power in Europe. That point of view has been expressed quite recently by a Cabinet Minister—a member of the present Government—a gentleman who holds a very important position—none other than the Minister for Aircraft Production, Colonel Moore-Brabazon.

I think every one will agree that such an attitude is a terrible danger, and it is a crime against the people of this country and the people of Russia."

In replying to the debate, Sir Walter Citrine, Secretary of the General Council of the Trades Union Congress, said:

"I was startled at Mr. Tanner's statement. I have known there are people in high places who do not agree either with the Soviet system or with what happens in Russia generally. I have never heard myself any evidence that would have caused me to think that anyone was ready deliberately to sabotage the efforts which this country is making to give help to Russia. Mr. Tanner, of course, did not go so far as to say that, but it is a very serious position if the fact can be substantiated."

Mr. Tanner: It can.

Sir Walter Citrine continued:

I think you are bound to be called upon to substantiate it. I do not think Mr. Tanner would have made that statement without satisfying himself he could. I feel sure that the person impugned will have to pursue the matter, and I feel I had better not make any comment beyond saying that it is an extraordinary situation if such a statement can be made by a Cabinet Minister in a Government whose Prime Minister had so fully pledged his country to render every possible help to Soviet Russia."

Mr. Tanner's charge was, of course, a very serious one and attracted very widespread attention and on the following day a statement was issued on behalf of the Minister concerned:

"The statement alluded to by Mr. Tanner evidently refers to a passage in a recent extempore speech which was open to misinterpretation. Colonel Moore-Brabazon's views on Russia are those recently announced by him in public at Chertsey. His words then were: 'Every one fighting there was fighting Britain's battle, and for that reason they should give all the help they could. By helping them they were helping themselves; for every life sacrificed against the Nazis was being lost in fighting our battle.'"*

* *Times*, 4.ix.41.

To which Mr. Tanner replied:

> " My allegation related to a speech made in private at a meeting in the North-Western area presided over by Sir Ernest Simon. Two officers of my union were present, and one of them afterwards wrote to Sir Ernest on the subject. This letter seems to have been shown to Colonel Moore-Brabazon, who replied to this union official expressing his regret for an extempore speech which, he claimed, was open to misinterpretation. I have seen the letter sent by the official and the Minister's reply, and it was on this evidence that I based my allegations and said I could substantiate them."*

When the matter was raised in the House of Commons, September 11, 1941, the Prime Minister said:

> " The versions which have been given to the public of the remarks made at a private gathering at the end of July by the Minister of Aircraft Production bear a construction which represents neither the policy nor the views of my Right Hon. and Gallant Friend."†

Colonel Moore-Brabazon did not issue a verbatim report of his remarks to the press after Mr. Tanner's disclosures. It is, of course, possible that the Colonel was misunderstood as he definitely claimed, but it cannot be questioned that the views attributed to him were held by a section of the ruling class in this country.

III. Visitors to Moscow

The war in the East was pursuing its relentless course and on September 9, 1941, the Prime Minister, in one of his periodic war reviews to the House of Commons, paid a very high and well merited tribute to the fighting forces of the U.S.S.R. Among many other things he said:

> " The magnificent resistance of the Russian armies and the skilful manner in which their vast front is being withdrawn in the teeth of Nazi invasion make it certain that Hitler's hopes of a short war with Russia will be dispelled. Already he faces the certainty of having to maintain his armies on the whole front from the Arctic to the Black Sea, at the end of long, inadequate, assailed and precarious lines of communication, through all the severity of a Russian winter, with the vigorous counter strokes which may be expected from the Russian Armies. From the

* Ibid. † *Hansard*, 11.ix.41, col. 296.

moment, now nearly 80 days ago, when Russia was attacked, we have cast about for every means of giving the most speedy and effective help to our new Ally. I am not prepared to discuss the military projects which have been examined."*

Then turning to Russia's loss of territory, he added:

> "A considerable part of the munition industry and iron and steel production of Russia has fallen into the hands of the enemy. On the other hand, the Soviet Union disposes of anything from 10,000,000 to 15,000,000 soldiers, for nearly all of whom they have equipment and arms. To aid in the supply of these masses, to enable them to realise their long continuing force and to organise the operation of their supply, will be the task of the Anglo-American-Russian Conference."†

"The House cheered loudly," commented the *Times* next day, "his tribute to the magnificent resistance of the Russian armies."

"The cheers were as general as they were generous," stated the *Manchester Guardian*; "Lord Winterton outstripped everybody else in the House in the vehemence of his vocal effort. Nor was the general body of Tory members a bit behind the Labour and Liberal members in this demonstration."

The cheers in the House of Commons were a reflection, but in fact only a pale reflection of the tremendous enthusiasm and admiration aroused in this country by the sustained and courageous fight of the Soviet forces and the efficient and resourceful leadership of its High Command. Moreover, by this date, large sections of public opinion were calling on the British and Allied Governments to discharge honourably their moral obligation to the Soviet Union by creating a Second Front in Western Europe. The point of view of the U.S.S.R. was well expressed by her Ambassador at a luncheon given by the American Chamber of Commerce in London, September 22, 1941. After dealing with the tremendous losses suffered by his country in the common cause he said:

> "It is at this juncture that the other democratic and freedom-loving nations come into the picture.
>
> We need their co-operation in this great struggle against Hitlerite Germany, a co-operation which can find its expression in many ways.
>
> The Soviet people have the right to expect such co-operation, as they are fighting, all of them—men, women and even children—heroically, not only for themselves, not only for their Fatherland, but also for the freedom and security of other countries."‡

* *Hansard*, 9.ix.41, col. 77. † Ibid., col. 78. ‡ *Daily Herald*, 24.ix.41.

M. Maisky's speech had an exceptionally good press and the *Times* next day, after referring to the speech as a "timely appeal to his audience, and through them to the British and American peoples, for increased aid to Russia," added, "the issues now at stake on the eastern confines of Europe are issues which involve the future of all the English-speaking peoples."*

On the day following M. Maisky's speech, a meeting of the Inter-Allied Council was held in London at which the Soviet Ambassador, in the course of a declaration, expressed his Government's adherence to the Atlantic Charter. On this point he stated:

> "My Government proclaim their agreement with the fundamental principles of the declaration of Mr. Roosevelt, President of the United States, and of Mr. Churchill, Prime Minister of Great Britain—principles which are so important in the present international circumstances. Considering that the practical application of these principles will necessarily adapt itself to the circumstances, needs and historic peculiarities of particular countries, the Soviet Government can state that a consistent application of these principles will secure the most energetic support on the part of the Government and peoples of the Soviet Union."

Five days later, September 28, Lord Beaverbrook, representing Great Britain, Mr. Averell Harriman, representing the U.S.A., together with members of the delegations, arrived in Moscow for the Three-Power Conference referred to on previous pages. They were received by Premier Stalin, M. Molotov and M. Litvinov and had an exchange of views lasting over three hours, and next day the Conference proper opened. M. Molotov presided and Marshal Voroshilov came from the Front to attend. All the representatives, delegates and technical staffs worked with lightning speed and the work was concluded on the afternoon of October 1. The British and U.S.A. representatives, in the course of a joint statement, declared:

> "It has now been decided to place at the disposal of the Soviet Government practically every requirement for which the Soviet military and civil authorities asked.
>
> The Soviet Government has supplied Britain and the United States with large quantities of raw materials urgently required by those countries."†

M. Molotov, in winding up the Conference said:

> "There has at last emerged against Hitler a coalition of Powers

* 24.ix.41. † *Times*, 2.x.41.

which will know how to find the ways and means for the eradication of the Nazi poison in Europe."

So ended an historic Conference, the usefulness of which was not confined solely to its immediate purpose. The British and U.S.A. representatives on their return home did much to shatter many widespread but ill-founded ideas regarding the Soviet peoples. Lord Beaverbrook in a world broadcast on October 12, stated among other things:

> "What of the Russians? Will they be able to produce munitions for themselves? Yes, certainly! They have good factories with a big output. Capt. Balfour, Colonel Lyon, of the American Air Force, and Sir Archibald Rowlands, of the Aircraft Ministry, all members of the conference, visited factories where aircraft are produced.
>
> All three tell me they place the aircraft and engine factories for efficiency and capacity on the level of performance we have reached in this country and in the United States.
>
> In particular, the Russians have most skilfully developed two new types of aircraft. One is the M.I.G.3 fighter, which corresponds in excellence of design and performance to our Hurricanes and Spitfires. Just as these machines are superior to the German fighters in the West, so have the Messerschmitts on the Eastern front met their match in the M.I.G.3.
>
> There is another new type. It is the Stormovik dive-bomber. Heavily armoured, this aircraft has proved an outstanding success in attacking troop concentrations and breaking up enemy formations.
>
> Colonel Lyon tells of the decision to construct an airfield for the reception of the British and American aircraft we have been sending to Russia. A forest was cleared. A swamp drained. A road was driven. Two long and wide runways were built. Yet that airfield was completed within 30 days.
>
> Now you may ask, can the Russians use to the best advantage the weapons made for them at home and abroad, in Britain and the United States? Yes. Their pilots are of the very best. Just as much experienced as any pilots anywhere. And the mechanics who service their aircraft compare in all respects with the mechanics of Great Britain and the United States."

On this subject, Lord Beaverbrook concluded: "Indeed, the Russians have a genius for mechanisation. They can be relied on to make full use of the opportunities our forges and factories provide for them."

Mr. Harriman on the following day, in a broadcast to the American people, declared:

> "Well, what did we learn by all that we heard and saw? The members of our party inspected a number of factories producing large quantities of munitions of all types. Our American airmen had been working with the Russians for the past months, showing them how to fly and maintain American aircraft.
>
> They all reported the same. The Russian has become a first-class mechanic in this last generation. The American tractor on the farm has played its part. Factories are equipped with the finest and latest American machinery, well laid out and well organised. There is no better work done anywhere.
>
> Out on the airfields, where much has to be done with little equipment, our Army officers report that they have never seen 'such skill, ingenuity, resourcefulness and morale. The Russian mechanics work without shelter in sleet, rain and wind an average of 14 hours a day.' The pilots learn to fly American aircraft as quickly and as skilfully as our own or the British.
>
> And so we have our answer to why Hitler's time schedule has been dislocated. The clumsy Russian moujik has become a skilled mechanic. Russia has learned to use the machine."

As for the leaders of the Soviet Union, Mr. Harriman stated: "Incidentally, we discovered that a lot of popular notions about the Russians were wrong. Anyone who still thinks they are slow does not know the leading men of this Government. Beaverbrook and I worked principally with Stalin. No man could work more quickly or with greater intensity."

Lord Beaverbrook and Mr. Harriman did an important international public service by these broadcasts, because an understanding of the peoples of the U.S.S.R. is a *sine qua non* to a permanent Alliance of Great Britain, the U.S.A. and the U.S.S.R.

It came perhaps as a surprise to many that the British and U.S.A. representatives promised the Soviet Government all that they asked for. The explanation was given by Lord Beaverbrook: "We [Beaverbrook and Harriman] saw at once that Stalin was determined to ask only for the goods he urgently required and that he was not just going to take all he could get hold of."*

Meanwhile, as a consequence of the decision reached at the T.U.C., a delegation from that body visited the U.S.S.R. and an Anglo-Soviet Trade Union Committee was formed whose main objectives were thus defined and announced on October 26, 1941:

> "1. The joining together of the trade unions of Britain and the

* House of Lords 23.x.41.

Soviet for organisation of mutual assistance in war against Hitlerite Germany.

2. Every possible support to the Governments of the U.S.S.R. and Britain in their common war.

3. Strengthening the industrial efforts of both countries, with the aim of maximum increase of production of tanks, aeroplanes, guns, ammunition and other arms.

4. Assistance in the rendering of the utmost help in arms to the U.S.S.R. by Britain.

5. To make use of all means of agitation and propaganda, press, broadcast, cinema, workers' meetings, etc., in the fight.

6. All possible support to the people of the occupied countries who are fighting for deliverance from oppression, for their independence and the re-establishment of their democratic liberties.

7. Organisation of mutual assistance of the trade unions of Britain and the Soviet, and mutual information.

8. Strengthening of satisfactory contact between representatives of the trade unions of the U.S.S.R. and Britain through the Central Council of Trade Unions of the U.S.S.R. and the British Trades Union Congress."

On the 24th anniversary of the coming to power of the Soviet Government, the British Foreign Secretary, for the first time since the establishment of that Government, sent a telegram of congratulation to the People's Commissar for Foreign Affairs ; in this, after expressing warm admiration for the bravery of the Soviet forces and sorrow at the sufferings of the civilian population he declared: "His Majesty's Government have pledged their utmost support to the Soviet Government and they and the British people will ensure that this pledge is fulfilled."

M. Molotov, in reply, November 10, 1941, warmly thanked the Government of Great Britain, stressed that their "thoughts and feelings" had been expressed by M. Stalin's speech of November 6, and concluded:

> "We swear to go forward on this glorious road until we fulfil this world task, and we believe unshakably in the victory of our just cause."

On November 6, on the eve of the 24th anniversary of the November Revolution, M. Stalin made an important review of the war, emphasising that the potential war production of the Allied Nations was much higher than that of Hitlerite Germany and her

"Allies," and, referring with satisfaction to the recent Three-Power Conference in Moscow, he added:

> "We can say with certainty that the coalition of the U.S.A., Great Britain and the U.S.S.R. is a reality which is growing and will continue to grow to the benefit of our common cause of liberation."

Two weighty speeches were made on November 21, by Mr. Eden, the Foreign Secretary, and M. Maisky, the Soviet Ambassador, at a luncheon in London.

Mr. Eden highly praised the work of M. Maisky as his country's Ambassador, warmly welcomed the appointment of M. Litvinov as Ambassador to Washington, acclaimed the conclusion of the Anglo-Soviet Alliance of July 12, 1941, asserted that Hitler had made a fatal mistake when he attacked the Soviet Union, that it was useless for Goebbels to try to resurrect the "Bolshevik bogey," and added:

> "I am fully convinced of the fundamental truth that on the main issue of international policy there is no reason for a conflict of interests between the Soviet Union and Great Britain. I felt that proposition to be true in 1935. It has certainly proved to be true in fact in 1941, and it will be proved true in the future. We in this country want the closest co-operation with the U.S.S.R. now and after the war, when our energies will be turned again to the cause of peace.
>
> I can think of a number of spheres in which the interests of the Soviet Union and those of the British Commonwealth are complementary to one another. I can think of none where they need be rivals."

Turning to the question of mutual aid between the two countries he said: "In this struggle, there is only one cause, and in such conditions, mutual help is self-help. Our resources are Russia's resources, and Russia's resources are our resources. All of you know the efforts being made to-day to despatch arms, munitions, tanks, aeroplanes and raw materials to Russia. Perhaps you do not know that these same ships that carry these munitions to Russia are now bringing back to us valuable raw materials from Russia for our own war effort. So is unity made complete."

M. Maisky disclaimed his title to Mr. Eden's praise, but added that no laudation could be too high for the Soviet peoples who were so magnificently resisting the Axis' attack. As usual he had no use for facile optimism:

> "There is no use in shutting our eyes to the grim realities of

the situation. We have had many difficulties in the course of these five months. We lost one and three-quarter million men in killed, wounded and missing. We lost large tracts of territory with a very considerable population. We lost a certain portion of our industrial resources—although, of course, the boast of Hitler that two-thirds of Soviet industry are now out of action fully corresponds to his usual standard of veracity!

We have had to evacuate millions and millions of our civil population, which inevitably caused inconvenience, hardships and suffering to our people. In strict pursuance of the 'scorched earth' policy we had to destroy, with our own hands—and this was perhaps one of the most tragic aspects of the situation—many of the proudest creations of our Five-Year Plans, all those great industrial undertakings, power stations, magnificent buildings, etc., which had sprung up all over the Soviet Union as a result of the heroic efforts and the great sacrifices on the part of the entire people."

But there were important items on the credit side, also. "On the other hand, Hitler's plans for a blitzkrieg in the east have completely failed. We have ample evidence that he sincerely believed in the possibility of overrunning my country up to the Urals in six to eight weeks."

How cocksure Hitler had been, said M. Maisky, was proved, *inter alia,* by the statement of Dr. Dietrich, Chief of Hitler's Press Department, to the press in Berlin on October 9, 1941, when he declared:

"The campaign against Russia has virtually been decided with the destruction of Timoshenko's army groups. Remnants of the defeated Russian armies are now in headlong retreat along a front which stretches from the sources of the Volga to the Black Sea. Russia as a military power is finished."

"Well," continued M. Maisky, "in the light of the situation as it is to-day, one has to admit that Hitler may be quite human, at least in one respect: he can indulge, like so many others, in wishful-thinking."

How was the common victory to be brought nearer? As usual, M. Maisky was downright:

"In the first place, all the Allies, and more particularly Great Britain and the U.S.S.R., have to unite their efforts in the great fight against Nazi Germany and to think of it in terms of one common front. All the military, political, and economic resources of the two great Powers, together with their Allies and friends, should be pooled and shifted from one part of the front to another as the military situation demands. I am glad that Mr. Eden spoke about our common cause and our united front. This is the kind of approach which is able to solidify our alliance and to bring victory nearer."

How and where should this general principle be applied?

"It remains an undeniable fact: the terrible menace of Hitlerism which now overhangs the world will be finally removed only when the German army is utterly destroyed and crushed. There is no other way to complete victory. Who thinks differently lives in a fool's paradise. I repeat once more: Germany can be finally beaten only on land, and every one of the Allies has to contribute to this end. Hence the necessary practical consequences must follow in building and training armed forces, in producing armaments, in preparing strategic plans."

Finally, referring to the post-war period, M. Maisky said: "I warmly welcome Mr. Eden's announcement that the British Government would like to base its post-war policy on the principle of the closest possible collaboration with the U.S.S.R. I fully reciprocate this desire. My Government would like also to base its post-war policy on the closest possible collaboration with Great Britain. It would be futile to gainsay that there are still certain difficulties in the way of this being accomplished, but with goodwill on both sides, they can and should be overcome."

On December 6, 1941, the British Foreign Office at length announced that a state of war existed between Great Britain on the one hand and Finland, Hungary and Rumania on the other. These three States had been at war with the U.S.S.R. since June, 1941, and Moscow had repeatedly asked London to declare war on them; the declaration, though belated, was welcomed in the Soviet capital.

By December, 1941, the magnificent fight put up by the Soviet forces had won for them the admiration of the world and in the course of this month the British Prime Minister, Mr. Winston Churchill, paid three public testimonials to the Red forces. Speaking in the House of Commons, December 11, he declared: "In Hitler's launching of the Nazi campaign upon Russia, we can already see, after less than six months of fighting, that he made one of the outstanding blunders of history, and the results so far realised constitute an event of cardinal importance on the final decision of the war."

Speaking to both Houses of the United States Congress, December 26, 1941,* the British Prime Minister, according to the *Times* report, " roused a tempest of cheers " when he stated:

> " Mighty strokes of war have already been dealt against the enemy; by the glorious defence of their native soil by the Russian armies and people—wounds have been inflicted upon the Nazi tyranny and system which have bitten deep, and will fester and inflame not only in the Nazi body but in the Nazi mind."†

And four days later, addressing the Canadian Parliament, an audience which showed equal enthusiasm, he said:

> " Russia's army, under their warrior leader, Josef Stalin, are waging furious war with increasing success along the thousand-mile front of their invaded country."‡

Also during the course of this month important and practical steps were taken—to quote Mr. Eden, the British Foreign Secretary—to put Anglo-Soviet relations " on a sound permanent basis now and for after the war." The British public read no doubt with surprise—because the visit to Moscow was a well-kept secret—but with immense pleasure and interest an official communiqué published December 29, stating that in the second half of December, Mr. Eden had had exhaustive and friendly talks in Moscow with MM. Stalin and Molotov on questions " relating to the conduct of the war and to post-war organisation of peace and security in Europe."

M. Maisky and Sir Stafford Cripps were present and at some of the meetings the British Permanent Under-Secretary of State for Foreign Affairs, Sir A. Cadogan and the Vice-Chief of the British Imperial General Staff, Lieutenant-General Nye, also attended.

The Moscow conversations, which were complementary to those in Washington and of which the U.S.A. Government had been kept fully and continuously informed, were enthusiastically hailed by the peoples and press of both countries. We quote two comments typical of the press as a whole:

> " A new and important step forward has been taken towards a further rapprochement between the U.S.S.R. and Great Britain," stated *Pravda*. " This strengthens still further the confidence of the peoples of the U.S.S.R. and Great Britain in the fruitful development of Anglo-Soviet collaboration, and the con-

* Following the attack by Japan on Pearl Harbour and British Pacific bases on December 7, 1941, the U.S.A. and Great Britain declared war on Japan, December 8. On December 11, Germany and Italy declared war on U.S.A. and on December 22, 1941, it was announced that Mr. Churchill had arrived in Washington for consultations with President Roosevelt on the future conduct of the war.

† *Times*, 27.xii.41. ‡ Ibid., 31.xii.41.

fidence that the hour of decisive victory over Hitlerite Germany, over the worst enemy of mankind, is approaching."*

"Collaboration between the United States, Soviet Russia, and Great Britain for the purposes of war is the one sure guarantee that the Axis threat to civilisation will be repelled and broken," commented the *Times*. "Its continuance after the war affords the best—perhaps the only—hope of rebuilding our civilisation on a new and securer basis of ordered freedom and shared prosperity."

Mr. Eden and M. Maisky were accompanied on their return journey from the U.S.S.R. by a delegation of 14 Soviet Trade Union leaders, headed by Mr. N. M. Shvernik, who had been invited by the British Trades Union Congress to visit this country.

CHAPTER XXIX

ANGLO-SOVIET RELATIONS IN 1942

I. First stages of co-operation

It is not easy to compress into a limited space all that passed between London and Moscow, and between the British and Soviet peoples in the course of 1942.

By the dawn of the New Year the enthusiastic admiration of the British public had been won both by the courageous and skilful fight of the Soviet forces against the self-styled "invincible" German Army and by the fortitude of the Soviet peoples.

Dr. Lang, the Archbishop of Canterbury, in a New Year's message, in a broadcast service, well summed up what very many were thinking:

> "How great their sufferings have been and are we cannot even imagine, but these have been met, not by fear or depression, but rather by a wonderful exaltation of spirit, because even in the darkness they kept the light burning of indomitable faith and resolution. They are now turning their suffering into victories."

"A great concourse of people filled the Albert Hall yesterday, for a New Year pageant of Empire and Allies, which was attended by members of the Royal Families, the Governments or the Ambassadors of all the nations engaged in the fight for freedom. Nothing so rich in symbolism and colour, so challenging in its manifestation of unity, has been seen since the war began."† When M. Maisky, the

* *Pravda*, 30.xii.41. † *Times*, 2.i.42.

Soviet Ambassador, was introduced by Admiral Sir Edward Evans, he received " a tumultous welcome " and the entire audience gave him the " V " salute. The Archbishop of Canterbury addressing the vast gathering said:

> " There is a beacon shining through the vast clouds of destiny. That is Russia, who is fighting as one man; not for any system or party but for the cause of freedom and for the soil which her people passionately love."*

Mr. Eden, the Foreign Secretary, lost little time in giving a report of his mission to Moscow to an attentive but impatient country. In a broadcast, January 4, 1942, he dealt at length with his visit to Moscow, his talks with M. Stalin and M. Molotov, on the feats of the Red Army, on future collaboration after the war, on the confidence which he found in the Soviet Union, on Hitler's miscalculations respecting the U.S.S.R. on the Soviet's loss of territory, and concluded:

> " The Soviet Union is determined to do all that is in its power to ensure that Germany cannot launch further wars upon the world, so are we. Out of the untold human suffering of the present war the Soviet Union wishes to gain a lasting peace for all its peoples; so do we.
>
> For these common objects we must work together to win the war and to win the peace. With the experience of our Moscow talks fresh in my mind, I am convinced that we can do both."†

Four days later, in the House of Commons, after dealing with the same subjects again, he declared: " I believe that the march of events is bringing our nations together. It is the task of statesmanship to ensure that the future is a happy one for the peoples of both countries, is a victorious one for the Allied war effort, and is an enduring one for the peace of the world."

When the delegation of Soviet Trade Unionists (p. 696) arrived in this country with Mr. Eden, as the guests of the British Trades Union Congress, Trade Union Conferences were held in many of the important industrial centres and were addressed by members of the delegation and members of the General Council of the T.U.C. Members of the Soviet delegation visited many munition and other engineering works and often addressed the workers in the canteens during the lunch-time break. Everywhere the Soviet representatives were received with unbounded enthusiasm.

After their return to Moscow on February 22, 1942, the members of the delegation gave full reports to keenly interested mass meetings on their impressions gained in this country. The results of all this

* Ibid. † *Daily Telegraph*, 5.i.42.

undoubtedly were: a better mutual understanding and a strengthening of the bonds between the Trade Unions of both countries.

The tremendous enthusiasm for the Soviet Union manifested at this period among industrial workers was well brought out by the Bishop of Bradford, who in an open letter to the War Cabinet signed by himself and 23 others, stated:

> "Those of us who have done any speaking in public, especially to the workers in the war factories, have noticed recently one very significant fact, that the only reference that immediately evoked enthusiastic applause was a reference to Russia. Why? Not because many of the workers were Communists, but because here was a supreme war effort that they could understand, a people fighting and toiling heroically for all they had created and owned themselves."*

Sir Stafford Cripps resigned his position in Moscow and returned to this country on January 21, 1942, Sir Archibald Clark Kerr being appointed in his stead as Ambassador to the Soviet capital. Sir Stafford, after his return home, made a number of declarations explaining the efforts, policy and aims of the Soviet Government. In an interview with the press, January 24, 1942, he stated: "The strength of the Russian Army at the end of the winter will be twice as large as when the war started—about nine million men."†

And in answer to the question: "Why did Hitler attack the Soviet Union?" he replied:

> "Hitler saw the growing strength of the Russian Army and felt that unless he struck at once he would be too late. He is too late, anyway. Some Russians expected the attack; others thought Germany would make another effort to get more material from Russia by negotiation, thus giving the Nazis more time to prepare."‡

Addressing his constituents, February 8, 1942, Sir Stafford stated:

> "We have got to have the same 100 per cent. concentration on winning the war as they have in the Soviet Union if we are to join in the victory. I think the Russian Army will defeat Hitler, but only if we give them every ounce of help in our power."§

He spoke of a possible German spring offensive and the urgent need Russia would have of our whole-hearted help, then turning to post-war collaboration he added: "Either we have a partnership with

* *Manchester Guardian*, 23.ii.42. † *Sunday Express*, 25.i.42.
‡ Ibid. § *Times*, 9.ii.42.

Russia in the reconstruction of Europe or we plunge the world into chaos."*

And in reply to a question on the following day, Sir Stafford declared: "I am perfectly convinced that the Soviet Government have no desire to interfere in any way with the other Governments of Europe."†

Referring to the German-Soviet Non-Aggression Pact of August, 1939, Sir Stafford said:

> "I told the British Government in the preceding June that the agreement would be made by September 1. . . . Stalin tried, I think quite genuinely, early in 1939 to get agreement with France and Britain. When it failed he was not ready himself to take on the Germans. He signed the agreement with Germany, and immediately production went ahead on a full war basis for the time when the Russians knew they would have to fight Germany."‡

The appointment of Sir Stafford Cripps as Lord Privy Seal, Leader of the House of Commons and a member of the War Cabinet was announced on February 19, 1942. His new status gave added weight to his next utterances. Speaking at an Anglo-Soviet Youth Conference, March 1, 1942, he said:

> "You and I are filled to-day with enthusiasm and gratitude for the magnificent exploits of the Soviet forces. . . . Past trials have steeled the youth of Russia, and from them has emerged a brave and resourceful people. Its confident and courageous youth is going to play a great part both in the victory over Nazidom and in the construction of a new world civilisation after the victory. . . . It is vital that the youth of Britain and the Soviet Union should work together in a common partnership with the youth of China, America and the oppressed European countries."

And in an article in the American magazine *Life*,§ Sir Stafford declared that the security of the U.S.S.R. demanded that after the war her territorial frontiers should be substantially those of June, 1941, although it was possible that there might be some friendly readjustment of the Soviet-Polish frontier, which had been fixed temporarily, before the German attack on the U.S.S.R.

We think that these quotations taken together give an accurate picture of the efforts, policy and aims of the Soviet Government as Sir Stafford saw them. The fact that the Soviet Government would insist on the 1941 frontiers had been well known in diplomatic and political

* Ibid. † *News Chronicle*, 10.ii.42.
‡ *Daily Telegraph*, 10.ii.42. § Reprinted by the *Daily Mail*, 7.iii.42.

circles in this country prior to the date of the article just quoted, and in this connection the *Times* had commented:

> "Public pronouncements give no justification for any apprehension of vast Soviet ambitions of territorial aggrandisement. Recent events have shown that the imperative necessities of Russian defence provided a more solid foundation for some past claims than most people in this country were prepared to concede to them at the time."*

Relations between the two countries were certainly becoming more cordial. The Prime Minister reviewed the war situation in the House of Commons, January 27, 1942, and referring to the victories of the Red forces and British supplies to the U.S.S.R. said:

> "Our munitions were of course only a contribution to the Russian victory, but they were an encouragement in Russia's darkest hour. Moreover, if we had not shown a loyal effort to help our Ally, albeit at a heavy sacrifice to ourselves, I do not think our relations with Premier Stalin and his great country would be as good as they are now. There would have been lack of comradeship, and the lack of comradeship might have spread reproaches on all sides. Far from regretting what we did for Russia, I only wish it had been in our power—but it was not—to have done more."

Again, in the course of a broadcast, February 15, he declared: "It is little enough we have done for Russia considering all she has done to beat Hitler and for the common cause."

It had become a common-place, so common as to pass almost unnoticed, that the courageous and skilful fight of the Soviet forces, as well as the fortitude of the Soviet peoples, had completely swept away from the majority—we use the word *majority*, not the word *all* deliberately—of the British people, the evil veil of anti-Soviet prejudice, and the better understanding of the peoples of the Soviet Union found expression in many ways.

A Gallup Poll published in the *News Chronicle*, February 10, 1942, showed that in reply to the question: "Would you like to see Great Britain and Russia continuing to work together after the war?", 86 per cent. answered "Yes," 6 per cent. said "No," and 8 per cent. replied "Don't know." In reply to the further question, "Do you think they will"?, 53 per cent. answered "Yes," 18 per cent. "No," and 29 per cent. "Don't know."

On the previous day, the *News Chronicle* had stated editorially:

> "There are not wanting those, even in high places, who would

* *Times*, 12.ii.42.

still like, if they could, to-day or to-morrow, to sabotage the hopes of permanent understanding with Russia. Such men would prefer to work for a settlement after the war which would build up what they would doubtless call a 'strong Europe,' as a barrier against Russian 'encroachment.' Some of them would even be found ready, if the opportunity came, to champion the establishment of a strong de-Nazified Germany for this traitorous purpose.

Traitorous, because that way lies the certainty of another and still crueller and bitterer war, one that in truth might bring civilisation finally crashing down. Any man, therefore, who secretly harbours this intent in his heart is a dealer in the black market of human calamity."

It was revealed on March 2 that an R.A.F. wing which had been serving in the U.S.S.R. had returned to this country. The members spoke in glowing terms of the Soviet airmen; in the course of a graphic account of their stay in the U.S.S.R., one of the pilots who spoke Russian fluently, declared that "in a surprisingly short time they [the Soviet pilots] were most efficient." He also stressed that the ground mechanics were equally quick at mastering the intricacies of the new types of planes.

After describing the victories the British pilots scored over the Nazis, he remarked: "When the Russians saw we were there to kill Germans as well as to pass on our knowledge of the Hurricane, nothing was too much for them to do for us." "After one important joint operation," said the British pilot, "our aircraft had not even a single bullet-hole in them, and the Soviet bombers were able to do their job unmolested. The Russian General telephoned his thanks."*

On March 17, 1942, Major-General F. N. Mason-McFarlane, head of the British Military Mission in Russia, awarded on behalf of the British Government, the D.F.C. to four Soviet pilots, the first Russians to receive this British honour. They were Major Safonov, Capt. Tumanov, Capt. Novalenko and Capt. Kukharenko, and the awards were for "conspicuous bravery in combined operations." On March 25, M. Maisky, on behalf of the Soviet Government, awarded the Order of Lenin—the highest Soviet Order—to Wing-Commander H. N. G. Ramsbottom-Isherwood, Squadron-Leaders A. H. Rook and A. G. Miller, and Pilot-Officer G. Howes, for service with the R.A.F. wing in Russia.

When presenting the Orders, M. Maisky praised the valour of "the four brave members of the Royal Air Force," and stressed the great importance of close collaboration between the Allies, particularly the

* *Daily Telegraph*, 2.iii.42.

U.S.S.R. and Great Britain. He then gave the four fundamental characteristics of the present war:

> "The first is that we are now engaged in a *modern war,* not a war of the 19th century, not even the war of 1914-18, but in the war of 1939-42. The essence of modern war is, as Stalin recently put it, that it is 'a war of engines.'
>
> The high technique of modern war defeats time and space—top speed becomes the order of the day. Operations which in former times demanded many months for their execution are now completed within a few days. Distances which previously were considered to be prohibitive are now covered within a few hours.
>
> He who does not appreciate to the utmost the nature of those immense changes is bound to pay dearly for his inability to think and act in accordance with present-day conditions.
>
> The second thing which must never be forgotten is that the simple arithmetical preponderance of one side over the other in population, in territory, in natural wealth, in industrial resources, is in itself no guarantee of victory. . . .
>
> The secret of victory consists in having a decisive preponderance over the enemy at the decisive moment and in the decisive place.
>
> The necessary prerequisite for that is an offensive spirit that will penetrate the whole strategy of the war, including political and economic warfare. . . .
>
> The third thing, which is of the greatest importance, is the question of initiative in war. . . .
>
> For this to be achieved they must outwit the enemy in all respects. If the enemy is daring, they must be still more daring. If the enemy is obstinate, they must be still more obstinate. If the enemy is full of offensive spirit, they must have more of the same spirit. This is the only road to victory.
>
> Finally, the fourth thing which must be clearly understood is that the slogan "Time is on our side" is in no way axiomatic."

Turning to the conclusions to be drawn from the then military position, he declared:

> "Now all the Allies put together already have the essential implements for victory: troops, tanks, aircraft, arms. There is no time to wait until the last button is sewn to the uniform of the last soldier!
>
> The days are grim. History is not like the pavements of Piccadilly. Sometimes you have to fight not under conditions that are desired, but under conditions that are unavoidable. In

such a case you have quickly to change your plans and to adapt yourselves to the new circumstances.

The time is now ripe for this. The decisive moment is the year of 1942. The decisive place is the front of the U.S.S.R. We have to start from this if the Allies really desire to achieve victory (and I have not the slightest doubt that they do desire it). They have to throw into the battle everything they have got."

How was this to be done? M. Maisky did not shirk the issue: "How, when and in what form this can be done—these are matters for the Allied General Staffs. But the all-important thing is this. The whole work of the General Staffs must be imbued with one thought, one idea—1942 and not 1943.

"If, as I strongly hope, the Allies will take this road, then the backbone of Hitlerite Germany will be broken this year. There will then remain the task of finishing off the mad beast. Future generations will then be able to mark the year 1942 as the beginning of a new and better epoch in the history of humanity."

"M. Maisky speaks sound sense," remarked the *Daily Mail*:

> "He addresses realistic maxims to the High Commands of other United Nations. It is his right and privilege to do so. What he said yesterday has also been said by ourselves and many others in the past few weeks. What it comes down to is this: 'The whole work of the Allied general staffs must be imbued with one thought, one idea—1942, and not 1943.' . . . If we have planned an offensive for 1943 it must be adapted to meet the conditions of 1942. Speed and initiative are indispensable to victory. These and the offensive spirit."*

On the 24th anniversary of the foundation of the Red Army (February 23, 1942) warm greetings were sent from London to the Soviet capital. General Sir Alan Brooke, Chief of the Imperial General Staff, and Air Marshal Sir Charles Portal, Chief of the Air Staff, sent the following personal message to Marshal Shaposhnikov, Chief of the Soviet General Staff:

> "On the occasion of Red Army Day we send the heartiest greetings of the British Army and Royal Air Force to their gallant Russian comrades who are so relentlessly attacking and forcing back the German invader. We wish you and the Red Army and Air Force all possible success in your great task of liberating your country. Together we shall secure final victory over our common enemy."†

* *Daily Mail*, 26.iii.42. † *Times*, 24.ii.42.

And the Prime Minister sent the following message to M. Stalin:

> "The twenty-fourth anniversary of the foundation of the Red Army is being celebrated to-day after eight months of a campaign which has reflected the greatest glory on its officers and men and has enshrined its deeds in history for all time.
>
> On this proud occasion I convey to you, the Chairman of the Defence Committee of the U.S.S.R., and to all members of the Soviet forces an expression of the admiration and gratitude with which the people of the British Empire have watched their exploits, and of our confidence in the victorious end of the struggle which we are waging together against the common foe."

Equally warm greetings were sent to Moscow by Sir John Dill, the Lord Mayor of London, the Chairman of the L.C.C., etc., etc.

"Cabinet Ministers, Ambassadors, Allied Premiers, Admirals, Generals, Air Marshals and their wives crowded into the Soviet Embassy," reported the *Daily Express*,* "to honour the twenty-fourth anniversary of the Red Army" at a reception held by M. and Mme. Maisky. In all some 700 guests were present.

Meanwhile, Sir Archibald Clark Kerr, the new British Ambassador to the U.S.S.R. had taken up his post. Reaching Kuibyshev on March 15 and Moscow on March 20, he presented his credentials to M. Kalinin, President of the Soviet Union on March 24; on March 28, he had a two-hours' conversation with Premier Stalin, M. Molotov also being present. Commenting on this interview the diplomatic correspondent of the *Daily Telegraph* wrote:

> "There have lately been many evidences of a much warmer and more mutually confident spirit animating talks directed towards the closest practical collaboration between London and Moscow.
>
> On the British side there is a deep-seated desire, amounting to a determination, that every practicable step shall be taken to cement the bonds which now unite the two nations."†

II. The Second Front

Before dealing with the agitation for the speedy opening of a Second Front in Europe, it is germane to our purpose to recall that Hitler, in a speech to the Reichstag, April 26, 1942, revealed to the world that the German Eastern Front had been within an ace of catastrophe in the winter of 1941-42. He declared:

> "When I last spoke to you there was, over the east, a winter

* 24.ii.42. † 1.iv.42.

such as had not been known even in those parts for more than 140 years. In a few days the thermometer dropped from zero to minus 47 deg., and even lower. . . .

For months new highly-trained masses came from inner Asia and the Caucasus against our line, which, particularly at night, could be held only by strong points.

The problem, however, which at that time pressed most upon us was that of supply. For neither the German soldiers, their tanks, trucks or locomotives were prepared for such intense cold.

Yet the fate of our armies depended on the maintenance of our supply line.

You will, therefore, understand and approve that in one case or another I ruthlessly intervened with the grimmest determination to master the fate that might otherwise have overtaken us. . . .

Only when nerves were at breaking point, obedience wavered or where a sense of duty was lacking in mastering the task did I make stern decisions by virtue of the sovereign right which I believe I have received for the purpose from my German people."

Surely, the moral to be drawn from these sentences is clear. The fate of the German forces was swaying in the balance. A decisive stroke in Western Europe in the form of a Second Front might well have brought the scales firmly and definitely down in favour of the Allies.

During the first three months of 1942, numerous voices in the press, on the platform, in the munition works, in the ranks of the British and Allied fighting forces stationed in Great Britain, urged the British and Allied Governments to create a Second Front in Western Europe without a moment's unavoidable delay.

Taking the articles, speeches, resolutions, etc., as a whole, they stated in effect that "Honour, self-interest, expediency, sound strategy and clear-headed common-sense demand the earliest possible creation of a Second Front in Western Europe."

"The creation of a war front in another part of Europe to relieve Russia was advocated at Stafford last night by Sir Walter Womersley, Minister of Pensions. He declared that this was necessary because pressure would come again in the spring. Russia must be helped in more ways than by the supply of war materials."*

Major Philip Gribble† wrote:

"The next six months are fateful. This summer's campaigns

* *Daily Telegraph*, 17.ii.42. † *News Chronicle*, 23.iii.42.

will stretch Germany to breaking point. . . . What part can Britain play to help beat Hitler this year? Great Britain should continue to supply but not reinforce the armies already committed in the Middle East and India, and subject to fulfilling Russia's requirements, through Murmansk and Archangel, concentrate the whole of her remaining resources in carrying out whatever may be considered the best form of offensive in the West."

"Highly placed younger staff officers, who have been through some of the toughest fighting of the war, are urging a forward policy on the War Office," stated a *Daily Herald* reporter next day. "They want to forestall Hitler's spring offensive and have submitted a plan showing how it can be done. Their recommendations are now being considered by the Minister of War, Sir James Grigg." As to the representatives of the exiled Governments in this country, Mr. Vernon Bartlett wrote:

"All the Allied Governments in London have information that their people believe the war will be decided this year.

They therefore expect that British forces will intervene in some form or other in the European struggle within the next few months.

Their hope and confidence would be finally and utterly destroyed if Russia were defeated and Britain had done nothing in Europe beyond air raiding, to prevent that defeat."*

On Sunday, March 29, 1942, Trafalgar Square was jammed with a crowd estimated by a police inspector at 43,000 and was addressed by members of all political parties demanding the speedy opening of a Second Front in Western Europe. "Victory in 1942! London's largest and most tense war demonstration demanded it yesterday. Attack, attack, attack! That was the burden of all the speeches. Help Rusia more! Help Russia Now!" commented Mr. Hannen Swaffer,† who added: "Trafalgar Square was more crowded than I have seen it in an experience of forty years."

This meeting was typical of Great Britain as a whole. From every corner of the land the cry went up, "Strike quickly." "Open a Second Front in the West." "Defeat Hitler in 1942."

On the same day, from far off Florida, Lord Beaverbrook's voice was heard in a broadcast that attracted world attention, in the course of which, after referring to the achievements of the Anglo-Saxon and American peoples in former days, he stressed the debt we owed to Russia and the need to help her *now*, declaring:

"If the Russian armies were scattered beyond the Urals all

* *News Chronicle*, 25.iii.42. † *Daily Herald*, 30.iii.42.

our hopes would be scattered too. Nazi Germany would possess sinews to fight a war that would be long indeed and ravenous; Japan would see new and distant horizons."

"Attack," he insisted was the word. "Attack by sea, attack by air, attack in the field."

During April, 1942, some important Ministerial pronouncements seemed to indicate that the Government realised the need for speed and action, and the demand for the creation of a Second Front in Western Europe increased in volume.

Sir James Grigg, the Minister for War, speaking at Cardiff, April 5, 1942, said: "I am for all the greatest possible manifestation of the offensive spirit, and our training is largely devoted to that end."*

Speaking in the same city four days later, and referring to British aid to the Soviet Union, he said:

> "We must of course do more. There are all the signs that Germany is preparing one more mighty drive to knock Russia out of the war. We must do all we can in every direction to help Russia defeat this drive. In what direction we can help you will not expect me to say, but everything we can do you may be sure we shall do."†

Mr. Ernest Bevin, M.P., Minister of Labour and National Service, and member of the War Cabinet, "gave the nation," said the *Daily Herald,* "long-awaited news," when at a meeting in Shipley on April 12, 1942, he said: "The tide is on the turn. I cannot tell you when or how, but we shall soon be passing from defence to attack."

Mr. Amery, Secretary of State for India, speaking at Birmingham on April 24, 1942, went further:

> "The next few weeks may be more fateful for the future of the world than any since Dunkirk. They would decide whether our main enemy had shot his bolt and the end was in sight, or whether further years of uphill struggle lay before us."

These trenchant declarations naturally created the impression that in a matter of weeks, or at the outside, months, the Allied Governments would commence aggressive action on a large scale in Western Europe.

Here we cannot help noting the curious and indeed amazing fact that it was not until April 12, 1942, that the B.B.C. summoned sufficient courage to play the Soviet National Anthem, "The Internationale," although on one occasion at least, between June 22, 1941, and April 12, 1942, they actually played "God Save the Tsar"!

* *Daily Telegraph,* 6.iv.42. † *Times,* 10.iv.42.

Indicative of the interest in the U.S.S.R. by this time widespread in Great Britain, was the opening in London, on April 13, 1942, by M. Maisky, of a short course for teachers on the subject of the Soviet Union. Introducing the Ambassador, Mr. R. A. Butler, President of the Board of Education, said:

> "The course which had been arranged by the Board was designed to give an objective view of Soviet Russia in her various fields of attainment. To gain knowledge there was no need or place for a partisan or political approach. Education was an important medium for international understanding."*

M. Maisky, in the course of his address, said:

> "In the course of the past 20 years my country was subjected to a very regrettable misrepresentation in the world at large. This had separated the people of Russia from the rest of the world, including Great Britain, by a wall of ignorance and suspicion. To destroy that wall, to clear the air, to make the peoples outside the Soviet Union better understand my country was a matter of the highest importance. On this to a very large extent depended the possibility of close collaboration between Great Britain and Russia after the war. Without such collaboration between the Soviet Union and Great Britain and the friendly co-operation of the United States, there was no hope for mankind to establish a just and durable peace."†

The enormous change which had taken place in public opinion respecting the Soviet Union and its great founder, Lenin, was shown on April 22, 1942, when in Holford Square, Finsbury, London, M. Maisky unveiled a memorial bust of Lenin, placed opposite the house in which Lenin lived in 1902 and 1903. The Soviet Ambassador, referring to the Memorial and to the fact that the London County Council had recently placed a plaque on the blitzed remains of 30, Holford Square, where Lenin had actually lived, expressed the thanks of his country and said:

> "Lenin is the ideal embodiment of the Soviet people. His unforgettable image has been inspiring, and is inspiring our people with constant and unshakable determination in the struggle to achieve the best future for themselves and for the whole of humanity. His ideas, further developed by Stalin, have been giving and are giving our people an orientation in the most complicated situation of our time. At this very moment the orientation is as follows: the people of the U.S.S.R., together with the

* *Times*, 14.iv.42. † Ibid.

> people of Great Britain, together with the people of the United States and with the peoples of the other allies, must defeat and annihilate Hitlerite Germany and her satellites. They must do it and they will do it."

"Russia has been reborn and regenerated through Lenin's leadership," commented the *Times* next day. "He laid the foundation of an edifice whose solid strength, firmly based on a united and unshakable national spirit, has withstood the utmost fury of a rampant and hitherto victorious Hitlerism. . . . It was Lenin who first brought home to the consciousness of the western world the truth that a civilisation based on the antagonism of capital and labour inevitably carried within it the seeds of its own destruction. . . ."

During April, 1942, there was no question that the Government and peoples of the Soviet Union were looking towards Great Britain for the creation of a Second Front in Western Europe or that a very big section of the British press supported the Russians in their request. Lord Beaverbrook, in a broadcast from New York on April 23, 1942, declared:

> "Now the day has come when, in almost every quarter of Britain, the cry goes up, 'Attack, attack in support of Russia.' For the passion to set up a Western fighting front in aid of the Russians is deep in the hearts of our people.
>
> We know that Russians kill more Germans every day than all the Allies put together. We know they destroy more enemy tanks and bring down more enemy planes than any of us or all of us. Russia is the fighting front. That is the opportunity, the chance to bring Germans to battle. . . ."

"Russia," added Lord Beaverbrook, "may win victory in 1942. . . . That is a chance, an opportunity to bring war to an end here and now. But if the Russians are defeated and driven out of the war, never will such a chance come to us again. . . ." He urged that Britain must strike now and added: "How admirably Britain is now equipped in weapons of war for directing such an attack upon Germany I well know."

This speech made a great impression in the U.S.A. and Great Britain. "On both sides of the Atlantic," commented the *New York Times*, "the belief is strong that we cannot afford to waste the present opportunity and that the hour for attack lies near at hand." "Beaverbrook's demand for a Second Front," stated Mr. Swaffer in the *Daily Herald*,* "made him, during the week end, the most discussed man in the country. It encouraged hopes of an early offensive in all those quarters in which, for months, aggressive action has been urged—

* 27.iv.42.

hopes already aroused by the greater activity of the R.A.F. and the appointment of Lord Louis Mountbatten as chief of combined operations. These have stimulated workers in all the factories. They will be the subject, next Sunday, of many Labour Day speeches."

Meanwhile, armaments and other supplies were being shipped to the U.S.S.R., and gratefully received by the Soviet peoples. Premier Stalin, in his Order of the Day of May 1, 1942, declared:

> "The peoples of all freedom-loving countries regard the Soviet Union as a force capable of saving the world from the Hitlerite plague. The first place among these freedom-loving countries is held by Great Britain and the U.S.A., with whom we are bound by ties of friendship and alliance, and who are rendering our country constantly increasing military assistance against the German Fascist invaders."

During May, 1942, many high and well-deserved tributes were paid to the Soviet forces by members of the British Government, promises were made that everything humanly possible would be done to aid the Red Army, and the need and intention to work closely with the U.S.S.R. after the conclusion of the war was also stressed. The demand for the creation of a Second Front became ever more emphatic. The Foreign Secretary, Mr. Eden, speaking at Edinburgh, May 8, 1942, on the need to win not only the war but the peace, declared in forcible terms:

> "The United Nations together must possess sufficient force to provide the police to prevent highway robbery and the success of gangster methods. We have to aim at a state of affairs in which the four great world Powers represented by the British Commonwealth of Nations, the United States, the U.S.S.R. and China will together sustain this peace system. In peace they will look for aid from other peace-loving countries just as they do now in war. But upon them must fall the main burden for the maintenance of peace and the main responsibility for the economic reconstruction of the world after the war."*

Two days later, the Prime Minister, in a broadcast, after paying a high tribute to Premier Stalin and the Soviet forces and people, continued:

> "There is, however, one serious matter which I must mention to you. The Soviet Government have expressed to us the view that the Germans in the desperation of their assault may make use of poison gas against the armies and people of Russia. We

* *Manchester Guardian*, 9.v.42.

are ourselves firmly resolved not to use this odious weapon unless it is used first by the Germans. Knowing the Hun, however, we have not neglected to make preparations on a formidable scale. I wish now to make it plain that we shall treat the unprovoked use of poison gas against our Russian ally exactly as if it were used against ourselves, and if we are satisfied that this new outrage has been committed by Hitler we will use our great and growing air superiority in the West to carry gas warfare on the largest possible scale far and wide against military objectives in Germany.

It is thus for Hitler to choose whether he wishes to add this additional horror to aerial warfare.

We have for some time past been bringing our defensive and precautionary arrangements up to date and now give public warning so that there may be no carelessness or neglect. Of one thing I am sure—that the British people who have entered into the full comradeship of war with our Russian ally will not shrink from any sacrifice or trial which that comradeship may require."*

This threat was very opportune. "Mr. Churchill's poison-gas warning to Hitler," commented the military correspondent of the *Daily Express*, "follows reports that have been pouring into London in the last few days that this is the new weapon the Germans intend to employ in trying to beat the Red Army."†

The warning was greeted with grim but profound satisfaction in this country. "This is a threat which the British people will soberly approve," declared the *Daily Mail*. "The risk of such reply as it may be in the power of the Luftwaffe to give here we will take, in certain conviction that by our action we are powerfully sustaining, and it may be, revenging, Russia."‡

As always in dealing with the Nazi Government, the bold course proved to be the safest: the German press and wireless immediately began to declaim that the Reich Government never had any intention of using poison gas.

An episode occurred on April 29, 1942, which clearly demonstrated that the public was not satisfied with the British Government's policy towards the Soviet Union. On that date, Mr. W. J. Brown, an independent candidate, was returned for Rugby after a fortnight's campaign, against a Government nominee supported by the three parties. Mr. Brown, when he started, had no machine. The Government candidate declared for all aid for the Soviet Union in accordance with Government policy; Mr. Brown, who said the Government was not doing enough, was returned and after his victory wrote: "I fought

* *Manchester Guardian*, 11.v.42. † 11.v.42. ‡ 11.v.42.

this fight on the question of the Second Front. . . . My victory was in large measure due to my advocacy of the Second Front."

Among other Trade Unions, the Confederation of British Shipbuilding and Engineering Workers, about 2,000,000 in all, added its powerful voice to the demand for a Second Front. Mr. H. N. Harrison, in his Presidential address (May 18, 1942), declared:

> "There has grown up a belief that now Soviet Russia is fighting on our side everything is all right and we are winning. Russia cannot win this war for us by herself. We must therefore urge our Government to create and apply new attacks to compel Hitler to divert to some other front large numbers of his forces now being used in Eastern Europe against Soviet Russia. This would then ease the terrific strain that has been placed on the Soviet fighting forces."*

Many mass meetings were held throughout the country in May, 1942, at which the demand for a Second Front was unanimously accepted with enthusiasm. Here we need mention only two: one organised by the *Daily Express* in the London Hippodrome on May 24, when fourteen hundred people were present and the speakers included Lord Winster, Lord Strabolgi, Mr. E. Shinwell, M.P., and the editors of two London newspapers—Mr. John Gordon (*Sunday Express*) and Mr. Michael Foot (*Evening Standard*). The other, organised by the Communist Party, on the same day in Trafalgar Square, was attended by 50,000 people.

The troops also made their voices heard. *Reynolds News*,† published a letter signed by seven N.C.O.'s and 47 privates from a depot in Southern England:

> "We, the undersigned, 54 British soldiers, urge the speediest creation of a Second Front on land in the West, so that the United Nations can jointly achieve the defeat of Hitler in 1942. We know that the men and women in the factories will not let us down and we, too, are anxious to play our full part."

This letter reflected sentiments felt very widely in the ranks of Britain's fighting forces.

The Prime Minister, speaking at Leeds on May 16, referred "to the noble manhood of Russia, now at full grips with the murderous enemy, striking blow for blow and repaying better ones for blows struck at them," and reminded his listeners that "lately the enemy has not been so ready to come to this island, first, because a large portion of his air force is engaged against our Russian allies ; and, secondly,

* *Daily Herald*, 19.v.42. † 24.v.42.

because he knows our arrangements for meeting him," but made no specific mention of British assistance to the U.S.S.R.

However, the gap was filled by Sir Stafford Cripps, Lord Privy Seal, who speaking to his constituents next day, said:

> "Much has been said and urged about a Second Front in Western Europe and I can assure you that the Government are as keen and anxious for this to materialise as you are. The only difference between us is that you can talk freely about it, whereas we cannot because we have two responsibilities—to organise it at the proper time and place; and second, not to give the enemy any information of our intentions."*

Three days later, the Lord Privy Seal, winding up a debate on the war situation in the House of Commons, stated that "the Russian armies, with the most tremendous sacrifice, are holding the bulk of the German armies to-day and a great proportion of their air force too, and thereby saving us directly from the danger of attack and invasion in this country," and after pointing out that it was the policy of His Majesty's Government to do everything possible to aid our courageous Ally, continued:

> "The value of the bombing of Germany must not be under-estimated. Not only is it destructive of Germany's industrial effort, not only does it have a material effect upon the morale of the German people, but also it engaged in Germany and away from the Russian front great forces on air defences of all kinds and considerable forces of fighters, and, when possible for the Germans, of retaliatory bombers. It is, in our view, of material assistance to the Russian resistance, and it is the best way in which we can give that assistance, until such time as we are able to make a carefully planned attack upon the Continent of Europe, which we intend to do."†

"Sir Stafford Cripps declared," commented the *Times* next day, "with a more down-right emphasis than has yet been heard, the firm intention of the Government to invade the Continent."

Summing up the agitation for a Second Front, Mr. Hannen Swaffer wrote: "For weeks, millions of workers, massed at 'Aid to Russia' meetings, have demanded it (the Second Front)."‡

Two days later, the National Union of Manufacturers published a Memorandum,§ which showed that they realised the big rôle that the U.S.S.R. was destined to play in post-war trade.

> "Any plans for the future of world trade," stated this

* *Daily Express*, 18.v.42. † *Hansard*, 20.v.42, cols. 337–8.
‡ *Daily Herald*, 3.vi.42. § Dated May, 1942.

Memorandum, "can only be made effective if they have the cordial assent and co-operation of Russia, for if Russia, with the help of Britain and the United States, is able to smash Germany, Russia will probably be the most powerful single state in the world."

III. M. Molotov's visit to London. The Anglo-Soviet Alliance

June, 1942, was a notable month in the chequered history of Anglo-Soviet relations. It started well. On the 2nd, the British Admiralty announced that "Another large convoy consisting of merchant ships of the United Nations carrying important supplies to Russia has fought its way through to a north Russian port."* True, there were losses, but they were not excessive.

The high light of the month came from the House of Commons on June 11. As Sir Stafford Cripps wound up a two days' debate on coal, the Treasury Bench filled up, the Prime Minister, the Foreign Secretary and the other Ministers took their places and an air of expectancy pervaded the Chamber. Then the Foreign Secretary, Mr. Anthony Eden, debonair, capable, self-confident, announced in quiet tones that on May 26, 1942, the British Government had concluded a Treaty with the U.S.S.R. which confirmed the Anglo-Soviet Alliance against Germany and provided for collaboration between Britain, the U.S.S.R. and the other United Nations after the war "on the basis of the principles of the Atlantic Charter."

Mr. Eden also referred to his own visit to Moscow in December, 1941, and to the fact that he had then invited M. Molotov to visit Britain; M. Molotov had subsequently accepted this invitation as well as one from Mr. Roosevelt to visit the U.S.A., and had arrived in London on May 21, 1942.

Mr. Eden then gave the following brief outline of the Anglo-Soviet Treaty:

> "The United Kingdom and the Union of Soviet Socialist Republics reaffirm their determination to afford one another all possible assistance in the war and
>
> 'not to enter into any negotiations with the Hitlerite Government or any other Government in Germany which does not clearly renounce all aggressive intentions and not to negotiate or conclude except by mutual consent any armistice or peace treaty with Germany or any other State associated with her in acts of aggression in Europe.'
>
> The two countries also agree that they will, when peace is re-established, work together for the organisation of security and economic prosperity in Europe. In doing so, they will take into

* *Times*, 3.vi.42.

account the interests of the united nations, and they undertake to be guided by the two principles of not seeking territorial aggrandisement for themselves and of not interfering in the internal affairs of other States. The two Governments go on to declare their desire

'to unite with other like-minded States in adopting proposals for common action to preserve peace and resist aggression in the post-war period.'

Meanwhile, when the war is ended they will take

'all measures in their power to render impossible a repetition of aggression and violation of the peace by Germany or any of the States associated with her in acts of aggression in Europe.' "*

"There is, of course," continued Mr. Eden, "bound to be some interval after the victory has been gained before an effective international system can be built up for preserving peace and for the prevention of further aggression. The two Governments accordingly have agreed that should one of our countries during the post-war period become involved in hostilities with Germany or any of her European associates in consequence of an attack by one of them, the two Governments will at once give each other 'all the military and other support and assistance' in their power."

In the absence of a mutual agreement to the contrary, this undertaking would remain in force for 20 years and thereafter until terminated by one of the contracting parties.

Mr. Eden next stated that the conversations had not been confined to the Treaty alone, and quoted an official communiqué† issued the same day (June 11) which contained the following passage:

> "Full understanding was reached between the two parties with regard to the urgent tasks of creating a Second Front in Europe in 1942. . . ."

He referred to "this happy result through the establishment, by our contact with Mr. Stalin and Mr. Molotov, of complete mutual confidence," and paid a well-deserved tribute: "This is the time to mention the valuable contribution to Anglo-Russian understanding made by Mr. Maisky over a long period of years." The Treaty, explained Mr. Eden, was not exclusive. In the maintenance of the peace of Europe and the settlement of the economic questions which would arise after the war had been won, all the United Nations must bear their share but "without the closest understanding between Great Britain and the Soviet Union there can be no security and stability in Europe either for ourselves or for any of our Allies."

* For full text of the Treaty, see Appendix.

† This communiqué is given more fully on p. 718.

Mr. Eden concluded:

"The problems of peace are not, of course, for Europe alone, and I hope with assured confidence, that the good work which our two Governments have accomplished will be welcomed by the President and people of the United States, and will enable our three great countries to work together in the years of peace as now in the hard times of war."

In reply to a question by Mr. Arthur Greenwood, Mr. Eden stated that there were "no secret engagements or commitments of any kind whatsoever" attached to the Treaty.

It was very fitting that Mr. Lloyd George closed the day's proceedings with the following weighty words:

"As one who has laboured for over 20 years to establish a good understanding between Soviet Russia and this country, I felicitate the Prime Minister and the Foreign Secretary and the Government upon the accomplishment of this Treaty. Had it been a fact some years ago many grave blunders in foreign policy would have been avoided. Not only that, this war could never have occurred."

The tremendous historical significance of this Treaty or, to quote the *Times*, "the full breadth and force of the Treaty" was quickly realised as the news flashed round the world. "The news went out all through last night in 44 languages—28 in Europe alone. For another 24 hours, 600 writers and speakers will continue to spread it."*

The Treaty was given a hearty and unanimous reception by the British press and this was "supported and amplified in the messages of satisfaction coming in from all the capitals of the allied nations. . . . Many Governments—the Dominion, United States, Polish and others—had been told of the discussion as it went on day by day. Their congratulations are now unstinted."†

As to the Soviet public: "The news of a closer comradeship in war and peace with their British and American allies has been warmly welcomed by the Russian public," cabled the Moscow correspondent of the *Times*. "When at intervals throughout yesterday evening there was read through street amplifiers the terms of the Anglo-Soviet Treaty and the accompanying documents, people formed large groups and listened intently. The phrase "a Second Front" gave rise to an animation that was unlike anything I have seen in Russian streets before."‡

The details of M. Molotov's visit became known after Mr. Eden's announcement in the House of Commons: M. Molotov, accompanied

* *Daily Mail*, 12.vi.42. † *Times* Diplomatic Correspondent, 12.vi.42.
‡ *Times*, 13.vi.42.

by a staff of diplomatic and military advisers including Maj.-Gen. Issayev and M. Sobolev, Secretary General of the People's Commissariat for Foreign Affairs, alighted from a giant Soviet bomber early on the morning of May 20, at a British airport where he was met by M. Maisky. After inspecting a guard of honour, the party proceeded by special train to a London suburban station where they were cordially greeted by Mr. Eden, Sir Alexander Cadogan, Permanent Under-Secretary at the Foreign Office, and Lt.-Gen. A. E. Nye, Vice-Chief of the Imperial General Staff. Soon afterwards they drove to Chequers, which the Prime Minister had placed at their disposal.

Negotiations began next day at 10, Downing Street, in the Cabinet Room, with the Prime Minister in the Chair. Several meetings were held in Mr. Eden's room at the Foreign Office, where the clauses of the instrument were hammered out.

Each day the Soviet representatives motored to and from London, and in all, seven meetings were held. During his stay in this country, M. Molotov, accompanied by M. Maisky and Mr. Eden, had an audience with the King at Buckingham Palace. There were few formal engagements: one lunch at 10, Downing Street and the other at the Soviet Embassy where M. Molotov was introduced to members of the War Cabinet. During his stay M. Molotov was taken by the Prime Minister to a Fighter Command Headquarters whilst operations were in progress. Also M. Maisky conducted M. Molotov and his staff through areas which had been devastated by German bombers as well as through various parts of London.

On one occasion at Chequers, M. Molotov, Mr. Eden, Mr. Churchill and M. Maisky—the latter acting as interpreter—talked into the early hours of the morning. At last the Treaty was completed:

> " About 5.30 on that historic Whit Tuesday, Mr. Eden's room at the Foreign Office was all prepared for the ceremony.
>
> Great cinema lights flooded the table. R.A.F. photographers in uniform were standing by to take pictures.
>
> On the British side sat Mr. Churchill, Mr. Eden, Mr. Attlee, Sir Archibald Sinclair and Foreign Office officials. M. Molotov was flanked by his own delegation, M. Maisky and members of the Soviet Embassy staff.
>
> Short speeches, the signature and a glass of wine to celebrate the occasion brought the proceedings to an end. Britain and Russia had become partners in an alliance for war and for peace.
>
> There were two texts of the Treaty—one in English and one in Russian. The actual document was bound in thin blue ribbon gathered together in the red seals of the signatories."*

* *Daily Telegraph*, 12.vi.42.

"Half an hour after the signing of the Treaty, M. Molotov and his party left London and were on their way to the United States by plane."*

The film taken of the arrival of M. Molotov in this country, of the signature of the Treaty and the departure of the Foreign Commissar,† was shown throughout the country and the commentator's remark as the giant Soviet plane rose into the sky, "Come again soon and bring Premier Stalin with you next time" always drew hearty cheers, for it expressed the feeling of the British people, deeply grateful for the great part the Soviet Union had played and was playing against the Axis forces in Europe.

Mr. Eden, in his speech in the Commons on June 11, had, as we noted, quoted from a communiqué issued by the Foreign Office, and the paragraph to which he referred is of such vital importance regarding the question of the Second Front that it must be given in full here:

> "Full understanding was reached between the two parties with regard to the urgent tasks of creating a Second Front in Europe in 1942. M. Molotov, M. Maisky, Major-Gen. Issayev and Rear Adml. Kharlamov and Mr. Churchill, Mr. Attlee, Mr. Eden and the British Chiefs of Staff took part in the conversations on this subject. Discussions also took place on the question of further improving the supplies of aeroplanes, tanks and other war material to be sent from Great Britain to the Soviet Union. Both sides were gratified to note the identity of their views on all the above questions."‡

No dubiety there—a Second Front in 1942 and increased supplies, and that is how the Agreement was interpreted by the press and public both here and abroad.

The Second Front decision was emphasised in M. Molotov's farewell message to Mr. Churchill. It read:

> "I consider it my duty to express my sincere gratitude to the British Government and to you personally for the sincere reception and the warm hospitality which was shown to me in your country. I am convinced that the mutual treaty concluded between the Soviet Union and Great Britain, and the agreement reached concerning the opening of a Second Front in Europe in 1942, will considerably hasten the complete destruction of Hitlerite Germany and is the expression of the deep union existing between our peoples in honest friendship and wide co-operation."§

* Ibid.
† This refers to his departure from Great Britain after his return from the U.S.A.
‡ *Daily Telegraph*, 12.vi.42 § *Times*, 15.vi.42.

Simultaneously with Mr. Eden's announcement to the House of Commons, June 11, 1942, a statement referring to Soviet-American conversations was issued from the White House, warmly welcoming M. Molotov's arrival in Washington, May 29:

> " Among those who participated in the conversations were the Soviet Ambassador (Mr. Maxim Litvinov), Mr. Harry Hopkins, General Marshall, the U.S. Chief of Staff, and Admiral King, Commander-in-Chief of the United States Navy. Mr. Cordell Hull, U.S. Secretary of State, joined the subsequent conversations on non-military matters.
>
> In the course of conversations a full understanding was reached with regard to the urgent tasks of creating a Second Front in Europe in 1942.
>
> In addition, measures for increasing and speeding up supplies of planes, tanks and other kinds of war materials from the United States to the Soviet Union were discussed.
>
> Further were discussed fundamental problems of co-operation between the Soviet Union and the United States for safeguarding the peace and security of freedom-loving peoples after the war. Both sides state with satisfaction the unity of their views on all these questions."

The statement ended: " At the conclusion of the visit, the President asked Mr. Molotov to inform Mr. Stalin on his behalf that he feels that these conversations have been most useful in establishing a basis for fruitful closer relationship between the two Governments in pursuit of the common objectives of the United Nations."

A few days later, summing up the views of Great Britain, the U.S.A. and the U.S.S.R., the *Times* diplomatic correspondent wrote respecting M. Molotov's visits:

> " Writers and speakers in the three great allied countries still dwell upon the many decisions reached during his conferences, the Russians emphasising the 'complete' agreement with regard to the urgent tasks of creating a Second Front in Europe in 1942, the Americans especially welcoming the agreement on lend-lease, and opinion in this country dwelling equally on the 20-year treaty of alliance and the recognition that whatever can be done in the west will be done."*

The Treaty of Alliance was ratified by the Presidium of the Supreme Soviet on June 18 and by the King on June 24, 1942.

Londoners gave the Treaty an enthusiastic welcome when the great Empress Hall was packed from floor to ceiling at a British-Soviet

* 15.vi.42.

Alliance anniversary demonstration on June 20, 1942. Sir Stafford Cripps, speaking as the representative of the Government and the War Cabinet, expressed " whole-hearted support for our ever gallant Soviet Allies " and, turning to the question of the Treaty, declared:

> " The two countries and the world owed a deep debt to four men—M. Molotov, M. Maisky, the Russian Ambassador, Mr. Churchill and Mr. Eden.
>
> Future generations will hail their work as the laying of a great foundation stone for the structure of the post-war world."*

Then after dealing with the course of the war, Nazi atrocities, the determination of the British and Soviet peoples to continue the war till final victory, he came to the subject for which his huge audience was particularly waiting:

> " The time will come when we shall be able to launch a great and successful attack upon Hitler in the West. But it is success that is the essence of the help that we can render to our Allies, failure would damage and would not assist our common cause. When we strike, let us strike hard and with the determination to march through to Berlin before we call a final halt.
>
> When that moment will come we cannot say. I am not going to help Hitler by telling you or him. It may be sooner or later, though Hitler had apparently guessed that it may not be too far ahead. As we make our preparations, so, no doubt, he will try to make his, too, and this in itself may influence the time factor. The matter, as you know, was discussed with M. Molotov when he was in England and I can assure you that he knows much more about it than I can tell you! "†

Finally, Sir Stafford made an earnest and necessary plea for a better understanding of the U.S.S.R.

IV. Supplies to the U.S.S.R. and the Second Front

The question of the opening of a Second Front in Western Europe was never absent from the mind of the country and the subject was being constantly raised in public. " Certain people were impeding war production in their own financial interests," said Mr. Jack Tanner, in his Presidential address to the National Committee of the Amalgamated Engineering Union, June 15, 1942. " Such people had a very close connection with those who were trying to stifle the demand for a Second Front." The National Committee sent a telegram to the

* *Sunday Times*, 21.vi.42. † *Reynolds News*, 21.vi.42.

Prime Minister, on behalf of 650,000 engineers, pledging themselves to secure 100 per cent. production in order to ensure the necessary munitions of all kinds for the opening of a Second Front.

Lord Beaverbrook, speaking at an Anglo-Soviet demonstration at Birmingham, June 21, 1942, attended by 30,000 people, including men and women in the uniform of the services, as well as from the foundries and factories, warned the country:

> "There is that little group in this country who opposed the shipment of munitions to Russia, who had circulated obscure magazines, made vague speeches, and carried on furtive conversations. There was a book privately printed and widely circulated* which attacked the Russians and raised doubts about Russian policy. There were people who said we gave everything to Russia and got nothing back."†

Lord Beaverbrook quickly answered the last-mentioned complaint:

> "Anglo-Soviet trade is a two-way traffic. Tanks, guns, aircraft, munitions, raw materials were provided for the Russians; timber, pitch, chrome and other products were provided for us. We have been promised a Second Front by the Government," he proceeded: "Now the need is for urgency. There must be no unnecessary delay in sending forthwith a second expeditionary force to fight on the Second Front, and we must work, every one of us, with all our strength, in the factories and the foundries and the shipyards."‡
>
> "Let no man doubt how very near the Russians came to defeating the Germans last winter. It was a close thing, so close that with a little more the Germans would have been defeated. The German army would now be invading Britain if the Russian army had broken down last autumn. For the future we must work together in the war and in the peace."§

June 22, 1942, the first anniversary of the German attack on the U.S.S.R., naturally evoked many comments on the course of the struggle and on the present and future relations of Great Britain and the U.S.S.R. We quote two:

> "One of the weak points in Hitler's make-up is that he thinks he knows when he doesn't. He thought that Russia *couldn't* fight—just as he believed that Britain *wouldn't* fight. . . . Looking back upon the gigantic efforts the German Wehrmacht has made in Russia, we realise far better how desperate our situation

* *With Sikorski to Russia*, by Major Victor Cazalet.

† *Times*, 22.vi.42. ‡ Ibid. § *Daily Herald*, 22.vi.42.

would have been if its attack had been concentrated on us, and how greatly the stubborn Soviet resistance has helped our cause."*

"Great Britain and Soviet Russia," stated the *Times*:

> "will emerge from the war as the two great European countries whose resources and determination have enabled them to withstand German might.
>
> The structure of European peace must be truly international, and must be founded upon the freedom and co-operation of the peoples of Europe. But Great Britain and Russia will remain the essential pillars on which the whole framework rests. So long as they are intact and erect, the structure of peace will stand unshaken. If they fall asunder, nothing else will avail. . .
>
> The widespread popular enthusiasm in this country both for the achievements and for the ideals of Soviet Russia may sometimes outrun knowledge and understanding. But it is based on a far more real comprehension of the needs and of the realities of the future than those narrow and backward-looking prejudices which are still sometimes found lurking in unexpected quarters."

In these lucid sentences, Mr. Ward Price and the *Times* summed up what the press in general wrote and what the British public was thinking.

The Church also made its contribution. The new Archbishop of Canterbury, Dr. Temple, wrote: †

> "I hope that on Sunday, June 21, our people will be led to prayer on behalf of the nation and people of Russia. Our debt to them already is beyond estimate; their cause is ours, and much in our hope for the future depends on the springing up of a real friendship between our two peoples, who have so much both to give and to receive in mutual intercourse."

And he gave the wording of a special prayer for Russian success. Ministerial pronouncements were warm and appreciative. "But all the aid we had been able to give had been small compared with the tremendous efforts of the Soviet people," declared Mr. Bevin, Minister of Labour. "Our children's children would look back, through their history books, with admiration and thanks for the heroism of the great Russian people."‡

"You can count on us to assist you by every means in our power," cabled Prime Minister Churchill to Premier Stalin.

"During the year which has passed since Hitler fell upon your

* Ward Price, *Daily Mail*, 22.vi.42. † *Canterbury Diocesan Gazette and Notes.*
‡ *Times*, 22.vi.42.

country without warning, friendly relations between our two countries and peoples have been progressively strengthened. We have thought not only of the present, but of the future, and our Treaty of Alliance in the war against Hitlerite Germany and of collaboration and mutual assistance in the post-war period, concluded during M. Molotov's recent visit to this country, has been welcomed as sincerely by the British people as I know it has been welcomed by the Soviet people. That treaty is a pledge that we shall confound our enemies and, when the war is over, build a sure peace for all freedom-loving peoples."*

An indication of the sympathy and admiration in this country for the Soviets was shown by the success of the Red Cross "Aid to Russia" Fund sponsored by Mrs. Churchill. When that fund was launched, £1,000,000 had been asked for, but on June 23, 1942, Lord Iliffe announced that the total on that morning was just over £2,000,000.

At this time a dark cloud of disappointment and frustration was hanging over Great Britain. Our forces in Libya had suffered a series of defeats and Egypt was imperilled. Naturally the question was asked whether this would affect Great Britain's pledge to the Soviet Union on the Second Front. Many were of the opinion that the threat to Egypt was a reinforced argument for striking in Western Europe and thus relieving pressure on the Russian and Egyptian fronts.

Mr. Churchill paid another visit to the U.S.A. in June, 1942, and had conferences there with President Roosevelt and Mr. Maxim Litvinov. A communiqué issued in London and Washington on June 27, stated:

> "While our plans, for obvious reasons, cannot be disclosed, it can be said that the coming operations which were discussed in detail at our Washington conferences, between ourselves and our military advisers, will divert German strength from the attack on Russia."

The declaration of June 27 was generally interpreted as a double guarantee of the British Foreign Office statement of June 11, to open a Second Front in Europe in 1942.

Later (November 11, 1942), Mr. Churchill disclosed that both an invasion of the European Continent and operations in North Africa had been discussed and that "preparations were made for both possibilities either alternatively or simultaneously"—but that finally it had been considered advisable by the military experts to launch the African campaign first. We shall deal with this more fully later (p. 741 *et seq.*)

* *Times*, 23.vi.42.

The question of payment for military supplies from Great Britain, the Dominions and Colonies to the U.S.S.R. and Soviet exports to this country had for a time been under review, and finally, on June 27, an agreement was signed in Moscow under which retrospective as from June 23, 1941, deliveries of military supplies should be on "Lend Lease" without payment, but on a reciprocal basis. Further, the original British credit of £10,000,000 having been used up, the sum was increased by an additional £25,000,000. Civilian goods to the U.S.S.R. were to be paid for partly by credit created by the British Government and partly by Soviet exports to this country.

During July, 1942, the questions of supplies to the U.S.S.R. and a Second Front were again much canvassed. Lord Beaverbrook scotched a pernicious canard that the allied forces in Libya were short of tanks because of the number sent to the Soviet Union. "It was untrue to say," he stated in the House of Lords, July 1, 1942, "that tanks for Russia had interfered with tanks for Libya," and on the following day the Prime Minister told the House of Commons that although the British Govenment had sent over 2,000 tanks to the Soviet Union, it had sent 4,500 altogether to the Nile Valley. However, despite these categorical denials the whisper was passed on by mischief makers, some of them at least, in high places.

But supplies, though important, were not all. The Soviet Government was undoubtedly expecting her Allies to open a Second Front and never hesitated to put the case forcibly: "The Second Front must be created," stated Moscow radio on the morning of July 15. "Its creation will entail great sacrifices by the American and British peoples, but these sacrifices would be much greater if the Eastern front did not exist. Battles on the Eastern front are battles for New York and London."*

Neither was there any question that the majority of the British people desired that the pledge given on June 11, 1942, should be honoured promptly and effectively. The Conference of the Mineworkers Federation on July 21, and the Conference of the Electrical Trades Union on the following day called for the opening of a Second Front; and the Gallup poll published on July 27, revealed that in reply to the question: "Do you think that the Allies should or should not try to invade Europe this year?" 60 per cent. answered, "Should," 12 per cent., "Should not" and 28 per cent. answered "Don't know."

The *Daily Herald*, *Daily Telegraph* and *Daily Mail*, in leading articles on July 28, stated that there was a powerful and sustained demand in the country for the opening of a Second Front in Europe, but declared that the Government was second to none in their desire to speed this consummation and urged their readers to leave the

* *Daily Herald*, 15.vii.42.

matter to those who alone knew all the pertinent facts. The *Times*, on the following day, however, concluded with a serious warning to the Government:

> " In the end the effectiveness of the support given to Russia in her hour of peril will, quite inevitably, be taken—and on the whole rightly taken—as the acid test of the ability and foresight with which the conduct of the war has been planned and developed."

Next day, July 30, " thousands of women war workers in London factories were represented by a deputation which went to the House of Commons and 10, Downing Street, to appeal for the opening of the Second Front. ' We will not draw back from any sacrifice,' their petition declared. ' Unless we open a Second Front our menfolk will have to face a much longer and bloodier war against the full force of the German military machine.' "*

On the afternoon of that day, " M. Maisky, the Soviet Ambassador, addressed a big all-party meeting of Members of Parliament at the House of Commons on the war situation, and made a considerable impression," wrote the Parliamentary correspondent of the *Times*. " Sir Percy Harris was in the chair. A statement issued after the meeting said that M. Maisky ' gave a full and frank statement on the progress of the war, particularly on the Russian front,' and that he afterwards gave equally frank replies to questions."†

Mr. Lloyd George said afterwards that it was the biggest meeting of its kind that he had ever seen. More than 300 members were present.

In view of the appeals from Moscow for an Allied invasion of Europe and of the fact that Rostov and Novocherkask had been evacuated by the Soviet forces and that the Don Bend was threatened, it is not difficult to divine the content of the frank statement and serious warning about the grave situation on the Eastern Front which the Ambassador made to the assembled M.P.'s. There can be no doubt that M. Maisky's exposition made a profound impression in political and Government circles and had important repercussions.

Many present at that gathering may have thought that M. Maisky's admonition was unduly sombre, but unfortunately it was fully justified by the course of the war on the Soviet-German front during the following two months, viz., August and September.

On August 16, the Soviet official communiqué announced the evacuation of Maikop. Three days later it announced the evacuation of Krasnodar and on August 25, for the first time, fighting north-west of Stalingrad. In the first week of September it was estimated that

* *Daily Herald*, 31.vii.42. † 31.vii.42.

so severe was the continuous fighting that the Soviet forces were losing from 6,000 to 7,000 men per day on the front. On September 11, the Soviet official communiqué announced the evacuation of Novorossisk. To sum up, by the end of September the Axis forces were fighting both in the suburbs of Stalingrad and in the area of Mozdok ; they were in occupation of Novorossisk, Maikop, Elista and Kotelnikovo and were stretching out their hands towards the important oil centre of Grozny.

Hitler, in the course of a speech, September 30, 1942, claimed that his armies had occupied all the territories they had set out to conquer in the Soviet Union and that Stalingrad would be taken. To quote his exact words: " We have made a thrust to the Volga and an attack on Stalingrad—and it will be taken, you may be sure of that. You may rest assured that once there, no one will ever get us out of this position."

It had been felt for a long time in responsible quarters in Great Britain that an effort should be made to depict to the Soviet people, life in this country and the aims of Great Britain as an ally of the U.S.S.R., but it was only after considerable delay that the first issue of *Britansky Soyuznik* (" British Ally ") was at length published in Kuibyshev on August 15, 1942. This journal is on sale in all the large cities of the Soviet Union and large numbers are sent to various societies, universities, students and units of the fighting forces ; most of the articles are issued from London. Some of the early numbers were sharply criticised by British and other foreign journalists in the U.S.S.R. but the criticisms were taken to heart and later there was a noticeable improvement in the publication.

Soon after the U.S.S.R. and Britain first became Allies, a daily Bulletin in English, *Soviet War News*, had been published in London by the Press Department of the Soviet Embassy and this was later followed by a weekly journal *The Soviet War News Weekly*. Both publications were much appreciated by British readers.

V. Mr. Churchill's visit to Moscow and after

Many competent observers in this and other countries, disquieted at the evident dissatisfaction in the Soviet Union with the support they were receiving from Great Britain and the U.S.A. had been hoping that at least the heads of the British and Soviet Governments, accompanied by capable service advisers, could meet around a table for a heart to heart talk ; such observers, as well as the general public, were delighted when, on the night of August 17, 1942, it was announced that the Prime Minister had visited Moscow and had had personal consultations with M. Stalin, in which Mr. Harriman, representing Mr. Roosevelt, had participated. These discussions had been also attended by the People's Commissar for Foreign Affairs, V. M. Molotov, by Marshal K. E. Voroshilov, the British Ambassador, Sir A. Clarke Kerr, the Chief of the Imperial General Staff, Sir A. Brooke and other responsible representatives of the British armed forces, and by the Permanent Under-Secretary of State for Foreign Affairs, Sir A. Cadogan. The British delegation included General Sir Archibald Wavell and Air Chief Marshal Sir Arthur Tedder, Chief of the Air Command, Middle East. The United States delegation included, in addition to Mr. Harriman, Major-General Maxwell, Commander-in-Chief, American Forces in Egypt, and Brigadier S. P. Spalding. The British and American delegations totalled 20 persons in all.

The announcement stated that a number of decisions relating to the war had been reached, that the discussions had been conducted in an atmosphere of cordiality and complete sincerity, and that both Governments were determined to carry on with all their power and energy until the complete destruction of Hitlerism and any similar tyranny had been achieved.

Three great Liberator bombers, accompanied by fighter escort, had landed on a Moscow aerodrome about 4 p.m. on August 12. Mr. Churchill and Mr. Harriman, on alighting, were welcomed by M. Molotov, by Marshal Shaposhnikov, the Soviet Chief of Staff and other Soviet representatives, and by the Ambassadors of Great Britain and the U.S.A. and General Bradley of the American Army. The Soviet Guards' band played the British, American and Soviet National Anthems, Mr. Churchill took the salute, inspected the guard of honour and then walked into an airport building where he and Mr. Harriman made short broadcast records.

Mr. Churchill said:

> "We are fully determined, whatever sufferings and difficulties lie ahead of us, to continue the struggle hand-in-hand with our comrades and brothers, until the last remnants of the Hitler régime have turned to dust and remain in our memories as a warning and example for the future."

Mr. Harriman stated:

> "The President of the United States entrusted me with the task of accompanying the British Prime Minister on his most important journey to Moscow during this decisive moment of the war. The President of the United States will agree to all decisions taken by Mr. Churchill. Americans will stand hand-in-hand together with the Russians."

Immediately afterwards. the distinguished delegation were conveyed in a fleet of cars to the Kremlin where the same evening Mr. Churchill and Mr. Harriman had a talk with Premier Stalin lasting nearly four hours. Next day (August 13), Mr. Churchill had a long talk with M. Molotov and later another long conference with Premier Stalin. On the evening of August 14, after a full day of business discussions, the Soviet Government gave one of their famous Kremlin dinners. " M. Stalin presided," cabled the *Times* correspondent. " All members of the Soviet Government were present, including all the members of the Defence Committee and Politburo. The maximum of friendliness and the minimum of formality were the features of this dinner. M. Stalin himself proposed half a dozen of the total of 25 toasts. Others were proposed by Mr. Harriman, Sir Archibald Clark Kerr, the British Ambassador, and Admiral Standley, the United States Ambassador. The dinner went on until well after midnight."*

Despite the friendly atmosphere which prevailed at the dinner, the Soviet representatives were very far from satisfied with the British reply to the Soviet request for the opening of a Second Front in Europe. This was very natural in view of the undue share of the common burden which the forces and the civil population of the Soviet Union had borne and were bearing and because her Service Chiefs were convinced of the practicability of a Second Front in 1942.

Mr. Churchill and Mr. Harriman spent the following day (August 15) in the country and at 7 p.m. the former called on Premier Stalin to take his leave. The feeling of strain still persisted. However, M. Stalin invited the British Prime Minister to have supper with him and the latter promptly accepted. The two statesmen supped, smoked and talked into the early hours of the morning. At 1 a.m. Sir A. Cadogan and M. Molotov were called in and the talks continued until 3 a.m. When finally the gathering broke up a very much better atmosphere prevailed than when it began. Mr. Churchill had had no sleep that night because two hours later, at 5 a.m., the British and American delegations started by air on their long journey home via Egypt. On leaving Moscow, Mr. Churchill sent the following message to Premier Stalin:

> " I take the opportunity of thanking you for your comradely attitude and hospitality. I am very glad to have visited Moscow, firstly because it was my duty to express myself, and secondly because I am certain that our contact will play a useful part in furthering our cause. Please convey my kind regards to M. Molotov."

This meeting naturally attracted profound world-wide interest and was recorded in thick headlines in the press. Were important decisions taken? That was the question asked from the Atlantic to the Pacific,

* 18.viii.42.

from the Arctic to the Antarctic. The British correspondents in Moscow were unanimous in stating that the decisions arrived at were of the greatest importance.

The British press of August 18, 1942, greeted the Conference in the warmest terms. " Nothing but good can come of this conference " (*Daily Mail*). " The alliance is further cemented. The military results will show themselves in good time " (*Manchester Guardian*). " It is an immense benefit to the cause of full understanding between the United Nations " (*Daily Express*). " This news from Moscow is big and heartening " (*Daily Herald*). These were typical comments. As for the British public—when the newsreel of the Moscow conversations was shown in the cinemas throughout this country, it invariably drew long and warm applause.

The comments of the Soviet press were very downright. That of *Izvestia* was typical of the rest:

> " Now, when the struggle has reached the highest tension and the war against Hitler's Germany and her associates in Europe has entered upon a decisive stage, the leaders of the Allied countries have reached decisions covering the field of the war which both Governments are determined to carry on with all their power and energy. The most important and historical significance of the conference is that the war will be prosecuted with all the forces of the entire coalition."

The Soviet peoples were interested, extremely interested—all the British correspondents were unanimous on this point—as to how far the conversations would hasten the establishment of a Second Front in Western Europe.

" Every reaction I have got so far," cabled the Moscow correspondent of the *Daily Telegraph*, " and I have no doubt that it will prove to be the real one, is 'Does this meeting mean a Second Front in Europe at once? ' "

Mr. Churchill arrived back in London at 11.25 p.m. on August 24, and was photographed at the station with Mrs. Churchill and M. and Mme. Maisky ; he was asked by a woman if he was tired and replied: " Tired? Why should I be tired? I have been refreshed."*

The British press was all persuaded that the personal meeting between the heads of both Governments had done immense good, that each side now understood better the needs and difficulties of the other and that confidence between the two Governments had been widened and deepened, but, to quote the *Times*, " the proof of their efficacy [that of the Moscow conversations] must be sought in reports from the battlefields." " Now the public awaits a sign," commented

* *Times*, 25.viii.42.

the *Daily Herald*, "that the talks between Stalin and Churchill were the prelude to action."

Mr. Churchill gave his long awaited report to the House of Commons on September 8, 1942. After dealing with his visit to the Middle East and a number of other matters, the Prime Minister came to "the main purpose of his journey," his visit to Premier Stalin:

> "We spent four days in conferences, with Premier Stalin and Mr. Molotov, sitting sometimes for five and six hours at a time, and we went into everything with the utmost candour and thoroughness. At the same time, the Chief of the Imperial General Staff and General Wavell, who accompanied me, had further conferences with Marshals Voroshilov and Shaposhnikov and dealt with the more technical aspects of our joint affairs. Naturally I should not give any account of the subjects we discussed or still less of the conclusions which we reached. I have reported all these to the War Cabinet, and Mr. Harriman has reported them to President Roosevelt, but all must remain secret.
>
> I may say, however, that the Russians do not think that we or the Americans have done enough so far to take the weight off them. This is not at all surprising, in view of the terrific onslaught which they are enduring and withstanding with such marvellous tenacity. No one in the last war would have deemed it possible that Russia could have stood up as she has been doing to the whole weight of the Teutonic armies. I say the whole weight, because although there are 40 to 45 Germans divisions facing us in the west and holding down the subjugated countries, these numbers are more than made up against Russia by Finnish, Hungarian, Rumanian and Italian troops who have been dragged by Hitler into this frightful welter.
>
> It is a proof of the increased strength which Premier Stalin has given to Russia that this prodigious feat of the resistance of Russia alone to the equivalent of the whole of the Teutonic army has been accomplished for so long and with so great a measure of success. It is difficult to make the Russians comprehend all the problems of the sea and of the ocean. We are sea animals and the United States are to a large extent ocean animals. The Russians are land animals. Happily, we are all three air animals. It is difficult to explain fully all the different characteristics of the war effort of various countries, but I am sure that we made their leaders feel confidence in our loyal and sincere resolve to come to their aid as quickly as possible and in the most effective manner without regard to the losses or sacrifices involved so long as the contribution was towards victory.

It was an experience of great interest to me to meet Premier Stalin. The main object of my visit was to establish the same relations of easy confidence and of perfect openness which I have built up with President Roosevelt. I think that, in spite of the accident of the Tower of Babel which persists as a very serious barrier in numerous spheres, I have succeeded to a considerable extent. It is very fortunate for Russia in her agony to have this great rugged war chief at her head. He is a man of massive outstanding personality, suited to the sombre and stormy times in which his life has been cast; a man of inexhaustible courage and will-power and a man direct and even blunt in speech, which, having been brought up in the House of Commons, I do not mind at all, especially when I have something to say of my own. Above all, he is a man with that saving sense of humour which is of high importance to all men and all nations, but particularly to great men and great nations. Stalin also left upon me the impression of a deep, cool wisdom and a complete absence of illusions of any kind. I believe I made him feel that we were good and faithful comrades in this war—but that, after all, is a matter which deeds not words will prove.

One thing stands out in my mind above all others from this visit to Moscow—the inexorable, inflexible resolve of Soviet Russia to fight Hitlerism to the end until it is finally beaten down. Premier Stalin said to me that the Russian people are naturally peaceful people, but the atrocious cruelties inflicted upon them by the Germans have roused them to such a fury of indignation that their whole nature is transformed."

Mr. Churchill concluded: "As I flew back to Cairo across the vast spaces, back across the Caspian Sea and the mountain ranges and deserts, I bore with me the conviction that in the British Empire, the United States and the Soviet Union, Hitler has forged an alliance of partnership which is strong enough to beat him to the ground and steadfast enough to persevere not only until his wickedness has been punished, but until some at least of the ruin he has wrought has been repaired."*

When the Prime Minister had risen to speak, the House was packed, but less than an hour after the opening of his speech Members started to drift away. To quote the Parliamentary Correspondent of the *Daily Mail*, Mr. Percy Cater:

"The House, which had been packed and intent—M.P.'s whose journeys had all been necessary and converged on Westminster straight from the recess for this—had started to thin when the

* *Hansard*, 8.ix.42, cols. 94–5.

Prime Minister was two-thirds of the way through his speech.

When Mr. Churchill finished there were yawning gaps in the benches."*

What was the explanation? The *Manchester Guardian* asserted that the Members who left were " bored," but there can be little doubt that it was hardly boredom—a big section of the House of Commons, not by any means limited to those who drifted out, was very dissatisfied with the general war situation and had also expected to hear something much more concrete after Churchill's visit to Moscow.

When the Prime Minister sat down, Mr. Arthur Greenwood immediately rose and, after declaring that the public had heard of the Prime Minister's visit to Russia with pleasure and gratitude, said:

> " In the first place, the British people feel in their hearts that, however much we have done for the U.S.S.R. in material of all kinds—and it is not negligible—somehow it is not enough." . . . Secondly the public " know that Anglo-Russian relations have been clouded for many years by mutual suspicion, created very largely on this side, but which, having regard to their treatment in the press, the Russians maintained up to very recent days. If we can do something, as the Prime Minister has told us he has endeavoured to do with some success, to give the impression that we are not going to let the Russians down but are going to play fair by them, and that we are standing in with them in this struggle, it will not only add powerfully to the successful prosecution of the war but will lay the foundation of a permanent friendship after the war. In the years of the interregnum after the war, this will be vital to the maintenance of peace in Europe."†

After the Prime Minister had spoken there was a general exodus of Members, and although two days had been allotted to the debate, since opposition had been expected and in fact prepared, discussion completely collapsed about an hour after Mr. Greenwood had sat down.

Mr. Churchill's speech was widely read and welcomed so far as it went, but it was easy to detect a strong undercurrent of anxiety, particularly in view of the seriousness of the Soviet position at Stalingrad at that time; as to the attention the speech attracted in the U.S.S.R. there can be no question. " Mr. Churchill's speech has been reproduced extensively, and given great prominence in every central Russian newspaper," cabled the *Times* Moscow correspondent:

> " It is safe to say that the more complete version will be read

* 9.ix.42. † *Hansard*, 8.ix.42, col. 100.

by more people in the Soviet Union than in Great Britain itself. It will be a subject of discussion among groups, and will become part of that essential knowledge of the war which it is the aim of the Soviet Government that every citizen should possess."*

But the Second Front did not materialise and on October 4, 1942, M. Stalin dealt with this subject in reply to three questions put to him by Mr. Henry Cassidy, Associated Press Correspondent in Moscow:

"1. What place does the possibility of a Second Front occupy in Soviet estimates of the current situation?

Answer: A very important place. One might say, a place of first-rate importance.

2. To what extent is Allied aid to the Soviet Union proving effective and what could be done to amplify and improve this aid?

Answer: As compared with the aid which the Soviet Union is giving to the Allies, by drawing upon itself the main forces of the German Fascist armies, the aid of the Allies to the Soviet Union has so far been little effective.

In order to amplify and improve this aid, only one thing is required: That the Allies fulfil their obligations fully and on time.

3. What remains of the Soviet capacity for resistance?

Answer: I think that the Soviet capacity of resisting the German brigands is, in strength, not less, if not greater, than the capacity of Fascist Germany or of any other aggressive Power to secure for itself world domination."

"M. Stalin's public statements are exceedingly few and far between," cabled the Moscow correspondent of the *Daily Telegraph*. "They are eagerly scanned and analysed by scores of millions here for insight into Russia's real situation and light on Allied intentions. His written answers to the three questions put by Mr. Henry Cassidy . . . were broadcast this morning by all stations, not only in Russian, but in many other Soviet languages."

The subject of the interview was at once raised in the House of Commons by Mr. Greenwood, but Mr. Churchill declared that the matter did not call for a British Government statement. The press generally seized on the vital and disquieting fact that, to put it very mildly, much was lacking in the relations between the Allied Governments.

"M. Stalin's recent letter to an American journalist is a disturbing document, obviously intended to disturb," commented the *Times*,† ". . . the fact that such a debate should be carried on, in the enemy's

* 11.ix.42. † 7.x.42.

hearing, between allies in a life and death struggle implies that something is wrong in the organisation of the United Nations for war."

Premier Stalin had only expressed what was in the minds of the Soviet peoples. "The Russians have been bitterly disappointed in our conduct this year," wrote a Moscow correspondent in the *New Statesman and Nation*, October 24, 1942, "with all the humming and hawing and hair-splitting over the Second Front communiqué, the unsatisfactory state of the deliveries to Russia—not only their quantity but their quality, as in the case of the over-slow Allied planes delivered to Stalingrad, about the half-hearted tone (as the Russians see it) of the British press on the Second Front issue, about 'I've nothing to add to what I've said before.' . . . They think that the people who have been hesitating about the Second Front this year may also hesitate about a Second Front next year—why not?"

We may add one comment, namely, that the Soviet press in its criticism of affairs at home and abroad has never been afraid to call a spade a spade, a fact that was not and is not widely understood in this country.

Interest in the Soviet Union grew rapidly in this country as the British people watched with increasing admiration the unparalleled fight of the Red forces against the Axis forces in Europe. The Army Bureau of Current Affairs which the British War Office had set up in September, 1941, for the promotion of discussion groups among the troops, found that Russia was an always popular subject. One officer remarked to a correspondent:

> "We can't give them enough about Russia. The soldiers feel these Russians must be wizards to stand up like this to the Boche, and their curiosity is multiplied, of course, by the fact that Russia has been as remote to us as Tibet all these years."*

It may seem a far cry from Army lectures to public-houses, but the habitués of these places of refreshment—a large cross-section of the British public—were also keenly interested in the course of the war on the Eastern Front. "A country acquaintance," said Mr. A. J. Cummings, "who visits a local public-house for his nightly glass of beer and a general gossip with soldiers and civilians says the wireless knob is turned always on the stroke for the news of the day. All listen in absolute silence to the announcements about the siege of Stalingrad and then the wireless is switched off. Nobody wants to hear a word about anything else—it is Stalingrad and only Stalingrad all the time."†

During September and October, 1942, the question of the urgency of a Second Front in Europe was never long absent from the British

* *Times*, 22.x.42. † *News Chronicle*, 2.x.42.

press and other public forums; the press, with perhaps some unimportant exceptions, supported and even stressed the need for the Second Front, but argued that only the Government with all the facts at its disposal could decide the "when" and "where."

The subject was debated at the Trades Union Congress, September 10, 1942, on a Resolution submitted by the General Council and an amendment sponsored by the Amalgamated Engineering Union. The Resolution declared:

> "The Congress, sharing the general desire to give maximum assistance to Soviet Russia and to hasten the decisive military action which will bring about the defeat of the enemy pledges the fullest support of the British trade union movement so soon as the competent authorities decide that the time has come to launch an effective offensive action in Europe."

The amendment called for "the immediate organisation" of a Second Front. The spokesmen for the Resolution protested that they were as keen as the protagonists of the amendment for the establishment of a Second Front at the earliest possible moment, but argued that these were matters of high military strategy and not for the man in the street. The Resolution was finally carried by 3,580,000 votes to 1,526,000. Many delegates afterwards expressed regret that a form of words had not been found which would have made a unanimous vote possible. The *Daily Herald* commented "If there is reason to believe that the offensive is delayed by timidity, stupidity or prejudice, the Trade Union Movement will not be reluctant to protest."*

One of the Unions which supported the Resolution, the Transport and General Workers' Union, affiliating about 500,000 members to Congress, passed a Resolution at a Delegate Conference in London, October 16, 1942, "regretting the delay in opening a combined offensive against the Fascist forces," and calling on the British Government "to proceed as soon as possible with their launching of an Allied offensive in Europe to which we stand pledged."†

The British, Soviet and Allied peoples read with considerable satisfaction and relief—relief because of Nazi rumours—an Admiralty communiqué issued on September 23, 1942:

> "Another important convoy, carrying large quantities of war material, has arrived in northern Russian ports.
>
> Losses were suffered among the ships in convoy, but despite heavy attacks by enemy aircraft and U-boats, the great majority of the ships have arrived at their destination. The convoy consisted of British, American and Russian merchant ships.

* 12.ix.42. † *News Chronicle*, 17.x.42.

It is not intended to assist the enemy by informing him of the extent of his lack of success against this convoy, but it is possible to state that his claims on this occasion have been even more exaggerated than usual.

No ship of the escort of this convoy was lost."

Speaking four days later at Leamington, Mr. Eden, the Foreign Secretary, said that so immense was the convoy that it had required 75 British warships to protect it; and on the following day, Mr. P. Noel-Baker, Joint Parliamentary Secretary of the Ministry of War Transport, added that "this last convoy took the greatest quantity of arms, tanks and aircraft which Russia has ever received."*

In connection with convoys in general it is pleasant to record that on September 7, the Moscow radio announced the following awards made to British sailors for services rendered on convoys taking war supplies to the Soviet Union: "Cmdr. Maxwell Richmond, Cmdr. Richard George Onslow, Cmdr. Eric Percival Hinton and Capt. John Laurie have been awarded the Order of the Red Banner. Petty Officer Cornelius Stephen Dollins, Engineer Officer Robinson and Ship's Officer V. Prance have been awarded the Order of the Patriotic War (First Degree). Seaman Henry James Woodward and Boatswain F. G. Kendle have been awarded the Order of the Patriotic War (Second Degree)."

Another award which the British press and public warmly welcomed was that of the Order of Lenin to M. Maisky, on the tenth anniversary of his Ambassadorship to Great Britain. "M. Maisky's latest honour, the Order of Lenin, will be very widely welcomed here," commented the *Daily Telegraph*†:

"His popularity is the result of his personal qualities as well as of our admiration for the country he represents.

The importance of this award, the highest honour the Soviet Government can bestow, is heightened by the fact that it has been given to mark the tenth anniversary of his ambassadorship in London.

During those ten years, M. Maisky has had to face many and various problems. His professional skill, coupled with an unruffled urbanity, has carried him successfully through them all.

In any appreciation of M. Maisky's work, the help he has received from Mme. Maisky must be mentioned. Mrs. Churchill's description of her as 'the complete Soviet woman' cannot be bettered."

Mrs. Churchill's tribute to Mme. Maisky had been made at the opening of the Artists' Aid Russia Exhibition on July 1, when 900

* *Manchester Guardian*, 29.ix.42. † 28.ix.42.

sculptures and drawings were on view and the Wallace Collection attracted the largest crowd in its history:

> "To me Mme. Maisky is the complete Soviet woman and, as such, we salute her. During the time I have known the Ambassador's wife, I have found her full of fervent nationalism and patriotism, with a natural enthusiasm and a cultured taste for the architecture, music and literature of all countries. . . ."*

We would add that the wife of an Ambassador plays an important rôle in his work. In this respect M. Maisky has been very fortunate. Mme. Maisky is not only a charming woman but she is also highly cultured, keenly interested in and with a clear understanding of the economic, political and cultural development of her country. Sharing as she does M. Maisky's views, she has always been a real companion to her husband and has been an invaluable help to him throughout the years of his Ambassadorship, both as hostess at Embassy functions and in many other ways.

When Germany attacked the U.S.S.R., Mme. Maisky, like so many of her countrywomen, rallied enthusiastically to the Soviet cause. With characteristic energy and drive and without thought of self, she threw herself into the work of the Russian Red Cross, the organisation of the collection of various funds, the ordering and supervising of supplies and all the numerous duties this involved.

When we reflect what a great part the women of the U.S.S.R. have played in the development of their country, how noble has been their response to the call of their Motherland when attacked by the Nazi barbarians, Mrs. Churchill's description of Mme. Maisky as the "complete Soviet woman" is high praise indeed—praise which is not mere flattery but well-deserved.

General Smuts, world-famous soldier-statesman, when he addressed both Houses of Parliament on October 21, 1942, paid a pointed and warm tribute to the pre-eminent part played by the Soviet forces in the joint effort against the Axis forces in Europe and urged that every effort should be made to lighten the tremendous and undue share of the common burden which the Soviet Union was being compelled to shoulder.

> "Baulked in his air attack on London," said the General, "Hitler saw that it was unsafe to attempt an invasion of Britain before first clearing his rear in Russia. The magnitude and duration of Russian resistance have surprised not only Hitler but everybody else. Probably no such losses on both sides have ever been suffered in the history of war. If the Russian losses

* *Times*, 2.vii.42.

> must be terrible, it is equally true that the German Army is bleeding to death in Russia.
>
> The appalling bloodletting which is necessary for Hitler's ultimate defeat is being administered by the Russians, and they alone can do it. In spite of their losses in men and material and territory the Russians show not the least sign of giving in, and the bitter defence will go on to the bitter end. . . . The course for the allies to follow is clear. Whatever help in whatever form we can give to Russia to sustain her in her colossal effort should be given in fullest measure and with the utmost speed. She is bearing more than her share at present of the common burden."*

And later in his notable speech, General Smuts underlined a doctrine which the Soviet Government had been urging for many months: "Once the time has come to take the offensive and to strike while the iron is hot it would be folly to delay, to over-prepare, and perhaps miss our opportunity."

The attitude of the Soviet Government on the war situation and towards Great Britain and the U.S.A. was expressed in a frank, friendly and objective manner in Premier Stalin's 25th anniversary speech, on November 6, 1942. He pointed out that Germany and her satellites, owing to the absence of a Second Front in Europe, had been able to concentrate 240 Divisions on the Soviet-German front. The majority of the remaining Axis divisions were doing garrison duty in the occupied countries. On the Egyptian-Libyan front, where the Allied forces had launched their notable attack just two weeks earlier, M. Stalin pointed out that in all only four German and eleven Italian divisions were being employed. It was crystal clear from Premier Stalin's speech, that the Soviet Government was deeply disappointed that a Second Front had not by that date been opened in Western Europe, a point which the press and public immediately recognised, and Stalin left no doubt as to what precisely he meant by a Second Front and what the result would have been had a Second Front been opened in the Spring of 1942:

> "Let us assume that a Second Front existed in Europe, as it existed in the first World War and that a Second Front diverted, let us say, sixty German divisions and twenty divisions of Germany's allies. What would have been the position of the German troops on our front then?
>
> It is not difficult to guess that their position would have been deplorable. More than that, it would have been the beginning of the end of the German Fascist troops, for in that case the Red

* *Times*, 22.x.42.

> Army would not be where it is now, but somewhere near Pskov, Minsk, Zhitomir and Odessa.
>
> That means that in the summer of this year the German Fascist army would already have been on the verge of disaster. If that has not occurred, it is because the Germans were saved by the absence of a Second Front in Europe."

In other words, Stalin said that what he understood by a Second Front was such military action as would result in the diverting of 80 enemy divisions, i.e., one-third of the Axis forces, from the Eastern Front, and in effect he added that had this been done the Allies would already have brought the Axis forces to " the verge of disaster."

But Premier Stalin had no doubt that his British and American Allies would shoulder their honourable obligations and fulfil their solemn pledges. He continued:

> " It is often asked: But will there be a Second Front in Europe after all? Yes, there will be, sooner or later, there will be one. And it will be not only because we need it, but because above all our allies need it no less than we do.
>
> Our allies cannot fail to realise that since France has been out of action, the absence of a Second Front against Fascist Germany may end badly for all freedom-loving countries, including the Allies themselves."

The Soviet Premier did not slur over the existence of differences in the social systems within the Anglo-Soviet-American coalition:

> " It would be ridiculous to deny the difference in the ideologies and social systems of the countries composing the Anglo-Soviet-American coalition. But does this preclude the possibility and expediency of joint action on the part of the members of this coalition against the common enemy who hold out the threat of enslavement for them? It certainly does not preclude it.
>
> More than that, the existence of this threat imperatively imposes the necessity of joint action upon the members of the coalition in order to save mankind from reverting to savagery and medieval brutality."

Then, turning to the extremely important question of Anglo-Soviet relations, he declared:

> " In July, 1941, several weeks after Germany attacked the U.S.S.R., Great Britain concluded with us an Agreement on ' Joint action in the war against Germany.' At that time we had not yet any Agreement with the United States of America on this subject.
>
> Ten months later, on May 26, 1942, during Comrade Molotov's

visit to Great Britain, the latter concluded with us a 'Treaty of Alliance in the war against Hitlerite Germany and her associates in Europe and of collaboration and mutual assistance thereafter.'

This Treaty was concluded for a period of twenty years. It marks an historic turning point in the relations between our country and Great Britain. In June, 1942, during Comrade Molotov's visit to the United States, the United States of America concluded with us an 'Agreement on principle applying to mutual aid in the prosecution of the war against aggression,' an Agreement representing a substantial advance in relations between the U.S.S.R. and the United States.

Lastly, one should mention so important a fact as the visit to Moscow of the Prime Minister of Great Britain, Mr. Churchill, which established complete mutual understanding between the leaders of the two countries."

Stalin concluded this section of his speech with the following statement: "There can be no doubt, that all these facts point to a progressive *rapprochement* between the U.S.S.R., Great Britain and the United States of America, and to their uniting in a fighting alliance against the Italo-German coalition. It follows that the logic of things is stronger than any other logic. There can be only one conclusion, namely that the Anglo-Soviet-American coalition has every chance of vanquishing the Italo-German coalition and certainly will vanquish it."

Stalin's speech was carefully studied in this country and the U.S.S.R. and for that matter throughout the world. The British press and public welcomed his frankness on the question of a Second Front, feeling it far better that Soviet disappointment should be openly stated, rather than that it should fester like a neglected wound and infect the whole body of Anglo-Soviet relations. Stalin's frank admission of the existence of ideological differences was also welcomed and his emphatic assertion that these did not constitute an obstacle to the closest co-operation between the three countries was recognised as realistic and far-seeing statesmanship; his final declaration regarding the result of Mr. Churchill's visit to Moscow, the Alliance with Great Britain and the "progressive *rapprochement*" between the two countries, was warmly received.

"Premier Stalin's speech on the eve of the twenty-fifth anniversary of the Russian revolution was blunt and realistic," wrote Mr. J. L. Garvin, well summing up British reaction.

As regards Soviet opinion: "Stalin's speech has brought about a decisive and unexpected change in the atmosphere," cabled the Moscow correspondent of the *Times* and *Manchester Guardian*.

"It swept away all doubts in people's minds that differences in ideology between Britain, the United States and the Soviet Union were an obstacle to the full mobilisation and employment of the total Allied strength; it underlined the full understanding reached during Mr. Churchill's visit to Moscow, and it was a reminder that far from growing worse inter-Allied relations were improving. . . ."*

Five days after this speech, Mr. Churchill gave one of his periodic war reviews to the House of Commons. After referring to the crushing Allied victory in Egypt over the German-Italian forces he proceeded to deal with the question of Anglo-Soviet relations and the Soviet Union's part in the war. The Red forces, he said, had rendered an incomparable service to the common cause by "permanently putting out of action far more millions than Germany lost during the whole of the last war," and continued:

> "I recognise the force of all that Premier Stalin said in his last speech about the enormous weight that has been thrown on Russia. . . . Everything that he said about the burden thrown on them, the disproportionate burden, is perfectly true.
>
> The Russians have borne the burden and the heat of the day, and I think it absolutely natural on their part, and fully within their rights, for them to make the very strong and stark assertions which they have made."†

The Prime Minister next dealt at length with the great and complicated tasks involved in invading the Continent of Europe and added that the Chiefs of Staff finally came to the conclusion that the feat would not be possible in the summer or autumn of 1942. Members of Parliament and visitors hanging on the Prime Minister's words were by this time asking themselves, "What about the promise made to the Soviet Government in June?" Mr. Churchill faced the issue squarely; he continued:

> "Why then, it will be said, did you allow false hopes to be raised in Russian breasts? Why then, did you agree with the United States and Russia to a communiqué which spoke of a Second Front in Europe in 1942? I must say quite frankly that I hold it perfectly justifiable to deceive the enemy even if, at the same time, your own people are for a while misled.
>
> There is one thing, however, you must never do and that is to mislead your ally. You must never make a promise which you do not fulfil. I hope we shall see we have lived up to that standard.

* *Manchester Guardian*, 10.xi.42. † *Hansard*, 11.xi.42, cols. 24–5.

> All British promises to Russia have been made in writing or given across the table in recorded conversations with the Soviet representatives.
>
> In June, I gave the Russian Government a written document making it perfectly clear that while we were preparing to make a landing in 1942 we could not promise to do so.
>
> Meanwhile, whether or not we were going to attack the Continent in August or September, it was of the utmost importance to Russia that the enemy should believe we were so prepared and so resolved. Only in this way could we draw and keep the largest number of Germans pinned in the Pas de Calais, along the coast of France, and in the Low Countries."

Mr. Churchill, knowing that the Soviet leaders and people would be bitterly disappointed at the British Government's decision not to open a Second Front on the Continent in 1942, had, like the outstanding man that he is, decided to go to Moscow and in a heart-to-heart talk with Premier Stalin, explain the reasons of the Government's decision, a course which, he said, "prevented a great deal of friction and ill feeling between us and our Russian Allies."

The Prime Minister then cited with satisfaction Premier Stalin's reference to the Moscow visit (quoted on p. 740) adding:

> "I assure the House I have a solid belief in the wisdom and good faith of this outstanding man, and although the news that I brought was not welcome and was not considered by them adequate, nevertheless the fact remains that we parted good friends and, in the words which Stalin uses, a complete understanding exists between us.
>
> The Russians bore their disappointment like men. They faced the enemy, and now they have reached the winter successfully, although we were unable to give them the help they so earnestly demanded and, had it been physically practicable, we would so gladly have accorded."

Mr. Churchill's explanation as to why a Second Front had not been opened was in the main accepted by Parliament and the British press. However that was not quite the case in the U.S.S.R. The speech was extensively quoted in the press of the Soviet Union and evoked much comment among the public, partly favourable, partly critical. The Soviet people fully understood the importance of the Allied operations which had just begun in North Africa; they also realised that an ill-prepared and frustrated landing on the Continent would not bring them relief, but they were surprised and disappointed that the Allies —in view of the long respite that they had been given by the powerful resistance of the Red forces—rated their own chances of creating a Second Front on the European Continent so poorly.

On the 25th anniversary of the Russian Revolution, November 7, 1942, congratulatory cables poured into Moscow from people in all spheres of public life, of all shades of politics in Britain, as from all corners of the globe. The press of all shades of political opinion paid tributes to the unparallelled progress registered by the U.S.S.R. in the short space of 25 years, to the courage and skill of its fighting forces, to the fortitude of its peoples, and to the ability and sincerity of its leaders.

At the joint diplomatic reception given by M. and Mme. Maisky and M. and Mme. Bogomolov* at the Soviet Embassy in London, November 7, 1942, for this anniversary, 1,500 guests, "representing every phase of the United Nations war effort," were present, including members of the Diplomatic Corps, statesmen, writers, artists, scientists, trade union officials, etc. A Cabinet Minister, as he surveyed the closely packed guests, remarked to the authors: "Had this reception been held in 1938 and had the same atmosphere then prevailed, this terrible war would never have occurred." A sentiment with which we fully concur.

Many of the guests as they took leave of M. and Mme. Maisky, and M. and Mme. Bogomolov, must have realised the tremendous change which had taken place in Anglo-Soviet relations from bitter enmity, profound suspicion, cruel war, to a friendly, well-founded Alliance. On the maintenance, deepening and widening of the relationship between Great Britain and the Union of Soviet Socialist Republics depend the peace and happiness of mankind.

CHAPTER XXX

CONCLUSION

STUDYING the history of Anglo-Soviet relations, one thing stands out very clearly, i.e., the fact that British policy towards Soviet Russia was throughout ridden by inner contradictions. The State interests of Britain undoubtedly required the speedy establishment and maintenance of good diplomatic and trading relations with Soviet Russia; on the other hand, the class prejudices of sections of the British ruling classes against a workers' Government intervened. These two tendencies were constantly making themselves felt and were in perpetual conflict with one another, sometimes one, sometimes the other gaining ascendency.

* M. Bogomolov is Soviet Ambassador to the Allied Governments in London.

There never was and there is now no conflict of interests between the two countries—economic or territorial. On the contrary, Britain and the U.S.S.R. are economically complementary to one another. The mineral resources, raw materials and foodstuffs which the U.S.S.R. possesses in such abundance over her vast territory are of the highest value to the British people and manufacturers. On the other hand, with her teeming millions she provides an immense market for British machinery and finished products, as well as for a variety of Commonwealth and Colonial goods. In the early days of Soviet Russia all these were indeed even urgently needed by that country.

Nor were there or are there any frontier or territorial disputes. No calm study of the facts could deny this, but circles hostile to the Soviet régime endeavoured to camouflage their hostility by attributing to the Soviet Government imperialist and expansionist aims dangerous to the British Empire; they talked of Soviet designs on India, etc. This was always entirely without foundation; in any case, the danger of this was very real during the existence of Tsarist Russia which was frankly Imperialist, and yet this did not prevent the existence of quite normal diplomatic and trading relations between Britain and Tsarist Russia, nor did it prevent the formation of the Anglo-French-Russian Entente, which, in effect, though not in name, was a military alliance.

It should also be added that from the first there was undoubtedly strong sympathy for the Soviets—sometimes instinctive, sometimes reasoned, often indeed both—on the part of the British Labour and Trade Union movement, but unfortunately neither State nor foreign policy was wholly under their control even during the time when the Labour Governments were in office—being minority Governments, these Governments were in office but not in power.

After the conclusion of the first world war, both British State interests and the interests of world peace required the establishment of peace and good relations with Soviet Russia, but class prejudices intervened and we had instead British participation in foreign armed intervention in 1918-1921. During this period the opposite tendency which put British interests before class prejudices struggled to come to the fore and finally became sufficiently strong to induce the negotiation in 1920-21 for an Anglo-Soviet trading agreement.

However, so strong was still the other tendency—the influences against even trading relations with the Soviets—that the negotiations for the trading agreement which started on May 31, 1920, were not concluded until March 16, 1921, i.e., ten months. The opposition of the two tendencies was illustrated very markedly during these negotiations.

Mr. Lloyd George was strongly in favour of coming to an understanding with the Soviets and under his direction and active participation Sir Robert Horne, President of the Board of Trade, carried on the negotiations with M. Krassin who acted on behalf of the Soviet Government. On the other hand, Lord Curzon, the Secretary of State for Foreign Affairs was vehemently opposed to any understanding with the Soviets. Although unable to prevent them, he attended some of the meetings, but he took little active part in the proceedings.

The signature of the agreement signified that State interests had prevailed over class prejudice, but the latter was sufficiently strong to prevent *de jure* recognition for some years.

The conflict between the two tendencies was also illustrated vividly when although some British statesmen at international congresses desired to establish normal relations with Soviet Russia, class prejudices were sufficiently strong again to force them, at any rate to acquiesce in decisions of these conferences which sought to treat the U.S.S.R. only as a fourth-rate Power, and even to try and force on her, in some cases, a system of capitulations. The unbending attitude of certain British, French and other ruling circles towards Soviet Russia was, no doubt, also occasioned by the hope that if she were sufficiently humiliated and economically boycotted, the Soviet Government would founder and capitalism as well as the power of foreign capital in Russia might be restored.

In Britain class prejudices made themselves felt in a vigorous agitation for the rupture of the Anglo-Soviet Trade Agreement (1921) and they nearly succeeded in 1923, when Lord Curzon sent a curt ultimatum to Soviet Russia on a matter on which it would have been unthinkable for a rupture of relations to have been threatened, had the country concerned been other than the Soviet Union. The Soviet Government, however, refused to play the game of the British diehards and the rupture was avoided this time.

Even when the Labour Government took office—pledged as they were to the *de jure* recognition of the U.S.S.R.—there was much hesitation and delay—why ? Not because the majority of the Labour Government and their supporters were not anxious that such recognition should be granted immediately, but because the class prejudices of powerful forces in " the highest society " exercised heavy pressure behind the scenes.

When at length *de jure* recognition was granted, February 1, 1924, these same influences prevented the mutual appointments of Ambassadors as the Soviet Government desired, and for some years the two Governments were represented in one another's countries only by Chargés d'Affaires. Moreover, during this time, except when the Labour Government was in power, the Foreign Office boycotted Soviet Embassy receptions.

The Labour Government and those ruling circles which put State interests above class prejudices undoubtedly desired to regularise relations completely between the two countries, but when after prolonged negotiations a General Treaty and a Treaty of Commerce and Navigation were signed in London on August 8, 1924, the clamour let loose against them and the misrepresentations of their terms was, as we have shown in the chapter dealing with the subject, absolutcly unprecedented.

What might be called a classic example of class prejudice gaining ascendency over British State interests was the Arcos raid. In 1925-1927, the class prejudice tendency was expressed in a crescendo of anti-Soviet propaganda carried on by certain sections of the press and well-known politicians. On the other hand, the opposite tendency was expressed by the activities of those who, realising the needs of British industry and trade, sought to find ways and means of extending Anglo-Soviet trade, and this finally resulted in the conclusion of an agreement for financing Soviet orders in Britain between the Soviet Trade Delegation and the Midland Bank. The operation of this agreement which would have meant the end of the financial blockade of the Soviet Union would undoubtedly have consolidated Anglo-Soviet relations, but the diehard class prejudices got their blow in first; the day following the signature of the agreement came the thunderbolt of the Arcos raid which was subsequently followed by the rupture of diplomatic relations.

With the advent of the second Labour Government, June 5, 1929, it was thought that the course was set more fair—that State interest was taking precedence over class prejudice, but no! again there was hesitation; it was sought to lay down conditions for a renewal of relations and it was not till October 3, 1929, that a protocol was signed establishing full diplomatic relations. Early in December the two Governments appointed Ambassadors to one another's country, and on April 16, 1930, a temporary Commercial Agreement was signed. However, lest normal diplomatic and trading relations might have followed these steps, the anti-Soviet elements in Britain let loose a continuous flood of anti-Soviet lies, alleging religious persecution, forced labour, imminent financial collapse, etc., etc.

This agitation paved the way for the denunciation by the British "National" Government of the Anglo-Soviet Temporary Commercial Agreement on October 7, 1932, following the Ottawa Conference. No other country was treated in the same way, however real had been their dumping, however much they indulged in forced labour, etc., and the reason for this was given quite unashamedly by Mr. Neville Chamberlain in the House of Commons, October 21, 1932, as we pointed out in Chapter XV—viz., in effect, because the U.S.S.R. economy was organised on a Socialist basis.

It was the same bitter class prejudices that singled out the U.S.S.R. as the one country which was excluded from the Trade Facilities Acts and at first also from the Export Credits Guarantee Scheme, in spite of the fact that the U.S.S.R. had never defaulted on any commitments the Soviet Government had themselves undertaken and that the developing Soviet economy, particularly under the Five-Year Plans, had put the Soviet Government in a position to place valuable orders in Britain, which would have provided ample work for idle factories, and wages instead of the dole for very large numbers of unemployed workers.

This class antagonism was also illustrated vividly in the report issued January 14, 1933, by the Executive Committee of the Association of British Chambers of Commerce, which frankly advocated discrimination against the U.S.S.R., objected in particular to their monopoly of foreign trade, etc., and it was again apparent in the amazing attitude of the British Government and press towards the trial of the Metro-Vickers engineers in Moscow in 1933. Indeed, up to July 1933, Great Britain's relations with Soviet Russia had no parallel in British diplomatic history. Even in the Houses of Parliament, where precedent plays such an important rôle in governing proceedings, precedent was thrown to the winds when the question of Anglo-Soviet relations was under discussion.

For instance, it was a rule of both the Lords and the Commons that no member was permitted to denounce a foreign Government with which His Majesty's Government was in diplomatic relations. This rule was repeatedly violated, the most abusive epithets being hurled against the Soviet Government without the slightest rebuke from "Mr. Speaker," or the Lord Chancellor.

The attitude of successive British Governments towards the Soviet Union was so unprecedented that it is no exaggeration to state that the normal state of Anglo-Soviet relations up till the time when the Nazi menace began to throw its ugly shadow over Europe was abnormal.

With the closing of the incidents arising out of the trial of the Metro-Vickers engineers in the late summer of 1933, Anglo-Soviet relations assumed a more normal aspect. In the first place, sections of the British governing classes which previously had been motived by class prejudice, now realised that the Soviet Government had come to stay; secondly, many, among them prominent statesmen, for instance, Mr. Churchill and the late Sir Austen Chamberlain who had been bitterly anti-Soviet, now began to realise the deadly menace of Nazidom to Europe in general, and to Britain in particular, and the essential part which the U.S.S.R.—which was becoming more and more powerful without being aggressive—could play in meeting this danger.

Common sense won the day and with the signing of a new Anglo-Soviet Commercial Agreement, February 16, 1934 (negotiations had started December 5, 1932), a definite improvement in Anglo-Soviet relations set in, but even then the interplay of the two tendencies still made itself felt; not all the anti-Soviet diehard elements in British public life had given up the struggle, but those who put British State interests and the interests of world peace before class prejudice had, for the time being gained the upper hand. The entry of the U.S.S.R. into the League of Nations and Mr. Eden's visit to the U.S.S.R. in 1935 resulted in a further improvement.

Unfortunately, this improvement was again not maintained. The Anglo-German Naval Agreement, June 18, 1935, was viewed with suspicion in Moscow, as showing that pro-Nazi elements in Britain were again coming to the fore and the hesitant attitude of the British Government towards trade and political relations with the U.S.S.R. at that time lent colour to this suspicion. The complacency with which the British Government seemed to view the successive Nazi violations and abrogation of international Treaties, the pandering to Italian Fascism as illustrated in the Hoare-Laval plan against Abyssinia in December, 1935, the tolerance with which the British Government met the direct intervention of Germany and Italy on behalf of the Fascist leader Franco against Republican Spain—all this and more indicated that the elements in Britain which stood for an understanding with Nazi Germany, rather than with the U.S.S.R. were still extremely powerful, and that the policy of friendly understanding and co-operation with the U.S.S.R. inaugurated by Mr. Eden was not being followed up, even though, on the whole, Anglo-Soviet relations continued to be more or less normal.

The great need of the time was undoubtedly a close understanding between the U.S.S.R. and the Western democracies for the organisation of collective security against the ever-increasing Nazi-Fascist aggression. Only the organisation of such a united peace front could have averted the present war, but Mr. Chamberlain, who became Prime Minister in May, 1937, and his closest friends and advisers had other views—they were, as we have shown in the preceding chapters, far more bent on appeasing Nazi Germany and Fascist Italy than forming a peace front with the U.S.S.R. Shortsightedly they hoped in this way to turn Germany's eyes East and keep her from British shores—they did not realise that even if Hitler had turned East first it would have been only in order to prepare the better for his jump West later.

It is characteristic that Lord Londonderry (ex-Secretary of State for Air) in a book* covering the period 1933—to the outbreak of the war and discussing international policy and ways and means of

* "Wings of Destiny," by the Marquess of Londonderry (MacMillan).

averting war, only mentions the U.S.S.R. a few times in passing. There is not a word in the book to indicate that the Soviet Union was a great Power or the need for an understanding with her. Indeed, by implication, he even regrets the entry of the U.S.S.R. into the League of Nations. For instance he declares: " It occurred to me that one useful move would be to bring Germany back to the League, but that had not been made any easier by the admission of the Soviet Union to a seat on the Council."* Lord Londonderry was all for an understanding with Germany because as he explained in a letter to Mr. Winston Churchill: " I feel that if the Nazi régime in Germany is destroyed then the country will go Communist."†

Lord Londonderry's attitude was typical of all those whose narrow class interest and prejudices blinded them not only to the barbarous predatory nature of Nazidom and Fascism, but to the real menace they presented to Britain and the British Empire itself.

With Mr. Neville Chamberlain and his friends in power, it is small wonder that no agreement was reached on the formation of a strong peace front during the negotiations of 1938 and 1939. Instead we had the famous " scrap of paper " brought back by Mr. Chamberlain from Munich. Convinced of the British Government's hostility to a real Pact with the Soviet Government, the latter concluded a Non-Aggression Pact with Germany.

With the outbreak of the war in 1939, the Munich policy collapsed and when Germany perfidiously attacked the U.S.S.R., Mr. Churchill, who, luckily for Britain, the U.S.S.R. and the peace-loving world had become Prime Minister in May, 1940, at once realised the importance of the U.S.S.R. as an Ally and grasped her hand frankly and cordially as such in his famous speech of June 22, 1941. This was followed by an Anglo-Soviet Agreement, July 12, 1941, and later by the Anglo-Soviet Alliance of May 26, 1942, for a term of 20 years after the conclusion of the war.

This co-operation in the war and the co-operation after the war envisaged in the Alliance is pregnant with immense benefits not only for the two countries concerned, but for the world in general. But the importance of Treaties depends not merely on their terms, but on how they are carried out. The elements which prevented an understanding with the U.S.S.R. to safeguard peace before the outbreak of the war are now quiescent, but they are by no means dead.

In 1941 and 1942 there was deep disappointment in the U.S.S.R. at the failure to relieve the terrific pressure on them by the organisation of a second land front in Europe. More than once Soviet statesmen have pointed out that a second land front in Europe when the Nazis were being battered by the Red Forces during the winter of 1941-1942

* p. 118. † p. 171.

and again in the winter of 1942-43, would in all probability have sent the Nazi military machine crashing to perdition. It may also be recalled, as we have recorded in foregoing pages, that Nazi spokesmen, too, after these winter campaigns referred to the fact that only a hair's breadth separated them from disaster both in the winters of 1941-42 and 1942-43.

If in the course of 1943 really big scale and effective co-operation in the field of battle materialises, if those interests which put their class prejudices before the interests of their country and of world peace are not permitted to play their old game once again and British co-operation with the Soviets is sincere and effective, the disappointments of 1941 and 1942 will be eradicated and a new era of friendship and co-operation between the peoples of Great Britain and the U.S.S.R. will have been inaugurated, which will be of lasting benefit to the peace and prosperity of both countries and of the world.

POSTSCRIPT

Since the above was written the dissolution of the Communist International—whose existence, status and activities formed, as our readers are well aware, a constant matter of dispute between the British and Soviet Governments—has been proposed in a resolution of the Presidium of the Executive Committee of the Communist International, and the resolution has already been endorsed by most of the national sections.

The dissolution of the Communist International which has been rightly greeted in Britain, the U.S.A. and other countries as of the utmost historic significance, undoubtedly paves the way for far more cordial Anglo-Soviet relations, if only because it deprives the diehard elements of a convenient " Red Bogey " with which to frighten the timid or less intelligent of their followers. Given good will, there are now still greater possibilities of obtaining unity of purpose and action in sweeping away the Nazi and Fascist menace to peace and prosperity.

When peace has been restored the world will still be faced with tremendous economic and political problems, the solution of which will demand the co-operative efforts of all peace-loving nations and in which Great Britain, the U.S.S.R., the U.S.A. and China will be bound to play the foremost part.

But the present generation owes it to the millions of victims of the present war and to posterity to do all in its power to make a recurrence of the present world tragedy impossible. For this it is essential that Britain, the U.S.S.R., U.S.A. and China should take the lead in forming a united peace front against aggression, an object for which the Soviet Government strove so valiantly for many years before the outbreak of the present war.

APPENDIX I

TRADE AGREEMENT BETWEEN HIS BRITANNIC MAJESTY'S GOVERNMENT AND THE GOVERNMENT OF THE RUSSIAN SOCIALIST FEDERAL SOVIET REPUBLIC.

London, March 16, 1921.

WHEREAS it is desirable in the interests both of Russia and of the United Kingdom that peaceful trade and commerce should be resumed forthwith between these countries, and whereas for this purpose it is necessary pending the conclusion of a formal general Peace Treaty between the Governments of these countries by which their economic and political relations shall be regulated in the future that a preliminary Agreement should be arrived at between the Government of the United Kingdom and the Government of the Russian Socialist Federal Soviet Republic, hereinafter referred to as the Russian Soviet Government.

The aforesaid parties have accordingly entered into the present Agreement for the resumption of trade and commerce between the countries.

The present Agreement is subject to the fulfilment of the following conditions, namely:—

(*a*) That each party refrains from hostile action or undertakings against the other and from conducting outside of its own borders any official propaganda direct or indirect against the institutions of the British Empire or the Russian Soviet Republic respectively, and more particularly that the Russian Soviet Government refrains from any attempt by military or diplomatic or any other form of action or propaganda to encourage any of the peoples of Asia in any form of hostile action against British interests or the British Empire, especially in India and in the Independent State of Afghanistan. The British Government gives a similar particular undertaking to the Russian Soviet Government in respect of the countries which formed part of the former Russian Empire and which have now become independent.

(*b*) That all British subjects in Russia are immediately permitted to return home, and that all Russian citizens in Great Britain or other parts of the British Empire who desire to return to Russia are similarly released.

It is understood that the term "conducting any official propaganda" includes the giving by either party of assistance or encouragement to any propaganda conducted outside its own borders.

The parties undertake to give forthwith all necessary instructions to their agents and to all persons under their authority to conform to the stipulations undertaken above.

I

Both parties agree not to impose or maintain any form of blockade against each other and to remove forthwith all obstacles hitherto placed in the way of the resumption of trade between the United Kingdom and Russia in any commodities which may be legally exported from or imported into their respective territories to or from any other foreign country, and not to exercise any discrimination against such trade, as compared with that carried on with any other foreign country or to place any impediments in the way of banking, credit and financial operations for the purpose of such trade, but subject always to legislation generally applicable in the respective countries. It is understood that nothing in this Article shall prevent either party from regulating the trade in arms and ammunition under general provisions of law which are applicable to the import of arms and ammunition from or their export to foreign countries.

Nothing in this Article shall be construed as overriding the provisions of any general International Convention which is binding on either party by which the trade in any particular article is or may be regulated (as for example, the Opium Convention).

II

British and Russian ships, their masters, crews and cargoes shall, in ports of Russia and the United Kingdom respectively, receive in all respects the treatment, privileges, facilities, immunities and protections which are usually accorded by the established practice of commercial nations to foreign merchant ships, their masters, crews and cargoes, visiting their ports, including the facilities usually accorded in respect of coal and water, pilotage, berthing, dry docks, cranes, repairs, warehouses and generally all services, appliances and premises connected with merchant shipping.

Moreover, the British Government undertakes not to take part in, or to support, any measures restricting or hindering, or tending to restrict or hinder, Russian ships from exercising the rights of free navigation of the high seas, straits and navigable waterways, which are enjoyed by ships of other nationalities.

Provided that nothing in this Article shall impair the right of either party to take such precautions as are authorised by their respective laws with regard to the admission of aliens into their territories.

III

The British and other Governments having already undertaken the clearance of the seas adjacent to their own coasts and also certain parts of the Baltic from mines for the benefit of all nations, the Russian Soviet Government on their part undertake to clear the sea passages to their own ports.

The British Government will give the Russian Soviet Government any information in their power as to the position of mines which will assist them in clearing passages to the ports and shores of Russia.

The Russian Government, like other nations, will give all information to the International Mine Clearance Committee about the areas they have swept and also what areas still remain dangerous. They will also give all information in their possession about the minefields laid down by the late Russian Governments since the outbreak of war in 1914 outside Russian territorial waters, in order to assist in their clearance.

Provided that nothing in this section shall be understood to prevent the Russian Government from taking or require them to disclose any measures they may consider necessary for the protection of their ports.

IV

Each party may nominate such number of its nationals as may be agreed from time to time as being reasonably necessary to enable proper effect to be given to this Agreement, having regard to the conditions under which trade is carried on in its territories, and the other party shall permit such persons to enter its territories, and to sojourn and carry on trade there, provided that either party may restrict the admittance of any such persons into any specified areas, and may refuse admittance to or sojourn in its territories to any individual who is *persona non grata* to itself, or who does not comply with this Agreement or with the conditions precedent thereto.

Persons admitted in pursuance of this Article into the territories of either party shall, while sojourning therein for purposes of trade, be exempted from all compulsory services whatsoever, whether civil, naval, military or other, and from any contributions whether pecuniary or in kind imposed as an equivalent for personal service and shall have right of egress.

They shall be at liberty to communicate freely by post, telegraph and wireless telegraphy, and to use telegraph codes under the conditions and subject to the regulations laid down in the International Telegraph Convention of St. Petersburg, 1875 (Lisbon Revision of 1908).

Each party undertakes to account for and to pay all balances due to the other in respect of terminal and transit telegrams and in respect of transit letter mails in accordance with the provisions of the International Telegraph Convention and Regulations and of the Convention and Regulations of the Universal Postal Union respectively. The above balances when due shall be paid in the currency of either party at the option of the receiving party.

Persons admitted into Russia under this Agreement shall be permitted freely to import commodities (except commodities, such as alcoholic liquors, of which both the importation and the manufacture are or may be prohibited in Russia) destined solely for their household use or consumption to an amount reasonably required for such purposes.

V

Either party may appoint one or more official agents to a number to be mutually agreed upon, to reside and exercise their functions in the territories of the other, who shall personally enjoy all the rights and immunities set forth in the preceding Article and also immunity from arrest and search provided that either party may refuse to admit any individual as an official agent who is *persona non grata* to itself or may require the other party to withdraw him should it find it necessary to do so on grounds of public interest or security. Such agents shall have access to the authorities of the country in which they reside for the purpose of facilitating the carrying out of this Agreement and of protecting the interests of their nationals.

Official agents shall be at liberty to communicate freely with their own Government and with other official representatives of their Government in other countries by post, by telegraph and wireless telegraphy in cypher and to receive and despatch couriers with sealed bags subject to a limitation of 3 kilograms per week, which shall be exempt from examination.

Telegrams and radiotelegrams of official agents shall enjoy any right of priority over private messages that may be generally accorded to messages of the official representatives of foreign Governments in the United Kingdom and Russia respectively.

Russian official agents in the United Kingdom shall enjoy the same privileges in respect of exemption from taxation, central or local, as are accorded to the official representatives of other foreign Governments. British official agents in Russia shall enjoy equivalent privileges, which, moreover, shall in no case be less than those accorded to the official agents of any other country.

The official agents shall be the competent authorities to visa the passports of persons seeking admission in pursuance of the preceding Article into the territories of the parties.

VI

Each party undertakes generally to ensure that persons admitted into its territories under the two preceding Articles shall enjoy all protection, rights and facilities which are necessary to enable them to carry on trade, but subject always to any legislation generally applicable in the respective countries.

VII

Both contracting parties agree simultaneously with the conclusion of the present Trade Agreement to renew exchange of private postal and telegraphic correspondence between both countries as well as despatch and acceptance of wireless messages and parcels by post in accordance with the rules and regulations which were in existence up to 1914.

VIII

Passports, documents of identity, Powers of Attorney and similar documents issued or certified by the competent authorities in either country for the purpose of enabling trade to be carried on in pursuance of this Agreement shall be treated in the other country as if they were issued or certified by the authorities of a recognised foreign Government.

IX

The British Government declares that it will not initiate any steps with a view to attach or to take possession of any gold, funds, securities or commodities not being articles identifiable as the property of the British Government which may be exported from Russia in payment for imports or as securities for such payment, or of any movable or immovable property which may be acquired by the Russian Soviet Government within the United Kingdom.

It will not take steps to obtain any special legislation not applicable to other countries against the importation into the United Kingdom of precious metals from Russia whether specie (other than British or Allied) or bullion or manufactures or the storing, analysing, refining, melting, mortgaging or disposing thereof in the United Kingdom, and will not requisition such metals.

X

The Russian Soviet Government undertakes to make no claim to dispose in any way of the funds or other property of the late Imperial and Provisional Russian Governments in the United Kingdom. The British Government gives a corresponding undertaking as regards

British Government funds and property in Russia. This Article is not to prejudice the inclusion in the general Treaty referred to in the Preamble of any provision dealing with the subject-matter of this Article.

Both parties agree to protect and not to transfer to any claimants pending the conclusion of the aforesaid Treaty any of the above funds or property which may be subject to their control.

XI

Merchandise the produce or manufacture of one country imported into the other in pursuance of this Agreement shall not be subjected therein to compulsory requisition on the part of the Government or of any local authority.

XII

It is agreed that all questions relating to the rights and claims of nationals of either party in respect of Patents, Trade Marks, Designs and Copyrights in the territory of the other party shall be equitably dealt with in the Treaty referred to in the Preamble.

XIII

The present Agreement shall come into force immediately and both parties shall at once take all necessary measures to give effect to it. It shall continue in force unless and until replaced by the Treaty contemplated in the Preamble so long as the conditions laid down both in the Articles of the Agreement and in the Preamble are observed by both sides. Provided that at any time after the expiration of twelve months from the date on which the Agreement comes into force either party may give notice to terminate the provisions of the preceding Articles, and on the expiration of six months from the date of such notice those Articles shall terminate accordingly.

Provided also that if as the result of any action in the Courts of the United Kingdom dealing with the attachment or arrest of any gold, funds, securities, property or commodities not being identifiable as the exclusive property of a British subject, consigned to the United Kingdom by the Russian Soviet Government or its representatives judgment is delivered by the Court under which such gold, funds, securities, property or commodities are held to be validly attached on account of obligations incurred by the Russian Soviet Government or by any previous Russian Government before the date of the signature of this Agreement, the Russian Soviet Government shall have the right to terminate the Agreement forthwith.

Provided also that in the event of the infringement by either party at any time of any of the provisions of this Agreement or of the conditions referred to in the Preamble, the other party shall immediately be free from the obligations of the Agreement. Nevertheless it is agreed that before taking any action inconsistent with the Agreement the aggrieved party shall give the other party a reasonable opportunity of furnishing an explanation or remedying the default.

It is mutually agreed that in any of the events contemplated in the above provisos, the parties will afford all necessary facilities for the winding up in accordance with the principles of the Agreement of any transactions already entered into thereunder, and for the withdrawal and egress from their territories of the nationals of the other party and for the withdrawal of their movable property.

As from the date when six months' notice of termination shall have been given under this Article, the only new transactions which shall be entered into under the Agreement shall be those which can be completed within the six months. In all other respects the provisions of the Agreement will remain fully in force up to the date of termination.

XIV

This Agreement is drawn up and signed in the English language. But it is agreed that as soon as may be a translation shall be made into the Russian language and agreed between the Parties. Both texts shall then be considered authentic for all purposes.

Signed at London, this sixteenth day of March, nineteen hundred and twenty-one.

DECLARATION OF RECOGNITION OF CLAIMS.

At the moment of signature of the preceding Trade Agreement both parties declare that all claims of either party or of its nationals against the other party in respect of property or rights or in respect of obligations incurred by the existing or former Governments of either country shall be equitably dealt with in the formal general Peace Treaty referred to in the Preamble.

In the meantime and without prejudice to the generality of the above stipulation the Russian Soviet Government declares that it recognises in principle that it is liable to pay compensation to private persons who have supplied goods or services to Russia for which they have not been paid. The detailed mode of discharging this liability shall be regulated by the Treaty referred to in the Preamble.

The British Government hereby makes a corresponding declaration.

It is clearly understood that the above declarations in no way imply that the claims referred to therein will have preferential treatment in the aforesaid Treaty as compared with any other classes of claims which are to be dealt with in that Treaty.

Signed at London, this sixteenth day of March, nineteen hundred and twenty-one.

APPENDIX II

TEMPORARY COMMERCIAL AGREEMENT BETWEEN HIS MAJESTY'S GOVERNMENT IN THE UNITED KINGDOM AND THE GOVERNMENT OF THE UNION OF SOVIET SOCIALIST REPUBLICS.

London, April 16, 1930.

HIS Majesty's Government in the United Kingdom of Great Britain and Northern Ireland and the Government of the Union of Soviet Socialist Republics, being mutually desirous to conclude as soon as possible a formal Treaty of Commerce and Navigation between the United Kingdom of Great Britain and Northern Ireland and the Union of Soviet Socialist Republics, have meanwhile agreed upon the following temporary Agreement to serve as a *modus vivendi* pending the conclusion of such a Treaty.

ARTICLE I

For the purpose of developing and strengthening the trade relations between the United Kingdom of Great Britain and Northern Ireland and the Union of Soviet Socialist Republics, the Contracting Parties agree that, without prejudice to any more favourable provisions contained below, all facilities, rights and privileges which in the United Kingdom and the Union of Soviet Socialist Republics respectively are or may be accorded with respect to trade to the subjects or citizens of any other foreign State or to juridical persons including companies constituted under the laws of such State or to the property of such subjects, citizens or juridical persons including companies shall be extended reciprocally to citizens or juridical persons including companies of the Union of Soviet Socialist Republics and to British subjects, British protected persons or juridical persons including companies of the United Kingdom respectively and to their property. The natural produce and manufactures of the United Kingdom shall enjoy in the Union of Soviet Socialist Republics and the natural produce and manufactures of the Union of Soviet Socialist Republics shall enjoy in the United Kingdom, all the facilities, rights and privileges which are at present or may be hereafter accorded to the natural produce and manufactures of any other foreign country, in all that relates to the prohibition and the restriction of imports and exports, customs duties and charges, transport, warehousing, drawbacks and excise.

Nothing in the present Agreement shall apply to—

(*a*) the special provisions relating to trade contained in treaties which the Union of Soviet Socialist Republics has concluded, or may conclude, hereafter with those States, the entire territory of which on the 1st August, 1914, formed in all respects an integral part of the former Russian Empire or with the continental border States in Asia;

(*b*) the rights which have been accorded or may be accorded to any third country forming part of a customs union with the Union of Soviet Socialist Republics;

(*c*) the privileges which the Union of Soviet Socialist Republics has accorded, or may accord, to border States with respect to local trade between the inhabitants of the frontier zones.

NOTE.—The expression " British protected persons " in this Agreement is understood to mean persons belonging to any territory under His Majesty's protection or suzerainty or in respect of which a Mandate has been accepted by His Majesty. It is understood, however, that the stipulations of Article 1 do not apply to persons belonging to any such territory to which the present Agreement is not extended in accordance with the provisions of Article 5.

ARTICLE 2

1. In view of the fact that, by virtue of the laws of the Union of Soviet Socialist Republics, the foreign trade of the Union is a State monopoly, His Majesty's Government in the United Kingdom agree to accord to the Government of the Union of Soviet Socialist Republics the right to establish in London a Trade Delegation, consisting of the Trade Representative of the Union of Soviet Socialist Republics and his two deputies, forming part of the Embassy of the Union of Soviet Socialist Republics.

2. The head of the Trade Delegation shall be the Trade Representative of the Union of Soviet Socialist Republics in the United Kingdom. He and his two deputies shall, by virtue of paragraph 1 of the present Article, be accorded all diplomatic privileges and immunities, and

immunity shall attach to the offices occupied by the Trade Delegation (5th Floor, East Wing, Bush House, Aldwych, London) and used exclusively for the purpose defined in paragraph 3 of the present Article. No member of the staff of the Trade Delegation, other than the Trade Representative and his two deputies, shall enjoy any privileges or immunities other than those which are, or may be, enjoyed in the United Kingdom by officials of the State-controlled trading organisations of other countries.

3. The functions of the Trade Delegation shall be—

(*a*) to facilitate and encourage the development of trade and commerce between the United Kingdom and the Union of Soviet Socialist Republics;

(*b*) to represent the interests of the Union of Soviet Socialist Republics in all that pertains to the foreign trade of the Union, and to control, regulate, and carry on such trade with the United Kingdom for and on behalf of the Union of Soviet Socialist Republics.

4. The Trade Delegation acting in respect to trade for and on behalf of the Union of Soviet Socialist Republics, the Government of the latter will assume responsibility for all transactions lawfully concluded in the United Kingdom by the Trade Representative or by persons duly authorised by him. The Government of the Union of Soviet Socialist Republics will not, however, accept any responsibility for the acts of State economic organisations which, under the laws of the Union of Soviet Socialist Republics, are exclusively responsible for their own acts, except in cases where responsibility for such acts has been clearly accepted by the Trade Representative, acting for and on behalf of the Government of the Union of Soviet Socialist Republics.

5. The names of the Trade Representative, and of the persons empowered to represent him shall be periodically published in the "Board of Trade Journal" and in addition shall in other ways be clearly made known to the public. The authority of these persons to represent the Trade Delegation shall continue until such time as notice to the contrary has been similarly published.

6. Any questions which may arise in respect of commercial transactions entered into in the United Kingdom by the Trade Delegation shall be determined by the Courts of the United Kingdom in accordance with the laws thereof.

7. The property of the Union of Soviet Socialist Republics in the United Kingdom shall be subject to such measures as may lawfully be taken to give effect to the Orders of the Courts of the United Kingdom, in so far as these Orders have been issued in connexion with transactions referred to in paragraph 6, unless it is property which, according to international law, is immune from such measures

as being necessary for the exercise of the rights of State sovereignty or for the official functions of the diplomatic or consular representatives of the Union of Soviet Socialist Republics.

ARTICLE 3

British vessels and their cargoes and passengers and vessels of the Union of Soviet Socialist Republics and their cargoes and passengers shall enjoy in the ports and territorial waters of the Union of Soviet Socialist Republics and of the United Kingdom respectively, the same rights, privileges and facilities as are enjoyed, or may be enjoyed hereafter, by national vessels, their cargoes and passengers, or the vessels of the most favoured foreign country and their cargoes and passengers.

The provisions of this Article do not extend to the coasting trade. The Contracting Parties reserve the right to limit to national ships the coasting trade between ports on the same coast. In regard to trade between ports not on the same coast they undertake to accord to the ships of each other treatment not less favourable than that accorded to the ships of any other foreign country.

The provisions of the present Article shall not extend to—

(*a*) The application of special laws for the safeguarding, renewal and development of the national merchant fleet.

(*b*) Privileges granted to marine sports societies.

(*c*) Port services, including pilotage; towage and life-saving and maritime assistance.

(*d*) Navigation on inland waters closed to foreign vessels in general, even though such navigation may be open to the vessels of limitrophe States.

NOTE 1.—Nothing in this Article shall be deemed to confer on the vessels of either Party the right to carry on fishing operations in the territorial waters of the other, or to land their catches in the ports of the other, nor shall it entitle British vessels to claim any privileges which are, or may be, accorded by the Union of Soviet Socialist Republics to the fishing fleets of countries situated on the Arctic Ocean.

NOTE 2.—Nothing in this Article shall affect the right of either Party to apply regulations in accordance with its national legislation for the transportation of immigrants, emigrants and pilgrims.

NOTE 3.—The provisions of the present Article do not apply to ships registered at the ports of His Majesty's self-governing Dominions and to their cargoes and passengers unless and until the present Agreement is extended to them in the manner provided in Article 4.

ARTICLE 4

The provisions of the present Agreement may by mutual agreement be extended with any modifications agreed upon to any of His

Majesty's self-governing Dominions (including any mandated territories administered by the Governments of such Dominions) or to India, by means of an Exchange of Notes between the Government of the Union of Soviet Socialist Republics and the Government of any such Dominion or of India.

Article 5

The provisions of the present Agreement may also be extended on condition of reciprocity to any of His Majesty's colonies, possessions or protectorates or to any mandated territory administered by His Majesty's Government in the United Kingdom if a notification to that effect is given to the Government of the Union of Soviet Socialist Republics by His Majesty's Ambassador at Moscow or, in his absence, by His Majesty's Chargé d'Affaires.

The Contracting Parties agree that in case a notification is made by His Majesty's Ambassador at Moscow (or, in his absence, by His Majesty's Chargé d'Affaires) extending, in accordance with the provisions of the foregoing paragraph, the present Agreement to any of His Majesty's colonies, possessions, or protectorates or to any mandated territory administered by His Majesty's Government in the United Kingdom, the trading organisations of the Union of Soviet Socialist Republics shall be accorded the right to send to the respective colony, possession, protectorate or mandated territory, agents, who shall be acceptable to the Government concerned, for the purpose of carrying out the commercial transactions of the Union of Soviet Socialist Republics in such colony, possession, protectorate or mandated territory.

It is understood that any such agent will in all cases be subject to the ordinary law relating to aliens in the colony, possession, protectorate or mandated territory in which he resides and will not be entitled to enjoy any diplomatic or consular privileges or immunities.

Article 6

So long as in any territory referred to in Articles 4 or 5 which is not bound by the present Agreement the natural produce and manufactures of the Union of Soviet Socialist Republics are accorded treatment as favourable as that accorded to the natural produce and manufactures of any other foreign country, the natural produce and manufactures of such territory shall enjoy in the Union of Soviet Socialist Republics complete and unconditional most-favoured-nation treatment. At the same time, however, the Government of the Union of Soviet Socialist Republics reserves to itself the right to denounce this Article at any time in respect of any particular Dominion or India.

ARTICLE 7

The present Agreement comes into force on this day and shall remain in force until the coming into force of a commercial treaty between the United Kingdom and the Union of Soviet Socialist Republics, subject, however, to the right of either Party at any time to give notice to the other to terminate the Agreement which shall then remain in force until the expiration of six months from the date on which such notice is given.

So far as concerns any of His Majesty's self-governing Dominions, India or any colony, possession, protectorate or mandated territory in respect of which notes have been exchanged in virtue of Article 4 above or in respect of which notice of the application of this Agreement has been given in virtue of Article 5 above, the Agreement may be terminated separately by either Party at the end of the sixth month or at any time subsequently on six months' notice to that effect being given either by or to His Majesty's Ambassador at Moscow or, in his absence, by or to His Majesty's Chargé d'Affaires.

In witness wherof the undersigned, duly authorised for that purpose, have signed the present Agreement, and have affixed thereto their seals.

Done in duplicate at London in the English language the sixteenth day of April, 1930.

A translation shall be made into the Russian language as soon as possible and agreed upon between the Contracting Parties.

Both texts shall then be considered authentic for all purposes.

PROTOCOL

In concluding the present Agreement the Contracting Parties are animated by the intention to eliminate from their economic relations all forms of discrimination. They accordingly agree that, so far as relates to the treatment accorded by each Party to the trade with the other, they will be guided in regard to the purchase and sale of goods, in regard to the employment of shipping and in regard to all similar matters by commercial and financial considerations only and, subject to such considerations, will adopt no legislative or administrative action of such a nature as to place the goods, shipping, trading organisations and trade in general of the other Party in any respect in a position of inferiority as compared with the goods, shipping and trading organisations of any other foreign country.

In accordance with the above principle, trade between the United Kingdom and the Union of Soviet Socialist Republics shall be eligible for consideration on the same basis as trade between the United Kingdom and other foreign countries in connexion with any legislative or administrative measures which are or may be taken by His Majesty's

Government in the United Kingdom for the granting of credits to facilitate such trade. That is to say, that in considering any given transaction, regard shall be had to financial and commercial considerations only.

London, 16th April, 1930.

Additional Protocol

With reference to paragraph 6 of Article 2, it is understood that the privileges and immunities conferred on the head of the Trade Delegation and his two deputies by paragraph 2 of Article 2 of the present Agreement shall not be claimed in connexion with any proceedings before the Courts of the United Kingdom arising out of commercial transactions entered into in the United Kingdom by the Trade Delegation of the Union of Soviet Socialist Republics.

London, 16th April, 1930.

APPENDIX III

TEMPORARY COMMERCIAL AGREEMENT BETWEEN HIS MAJESTY'S GOVERNMENT IN THE UNITED KINGDOM AND THE GOVERNMENT OF THE UNION OF SOVIET SOCIALIST REPUBLICS.

London, February 16, 1934.

The Government of the United Kingdom of Great Britain and Northern Ireland and the Government of the Union of Soviet Socialist Republics considering it desirable, pending the conclusion of a formal Treaty of Commerce and Navigation between them, to enter into a temporary Agreement to regulate trade and commerce, have accordingly agreed as follows:—

Article 1

(1) For the purpose of developing and strengthening trade relations between the United Kingdom of Great Britain and Northern Ireland and the Union of Soviet Socialist Republics, the Contracting Parties agree that, without prejudice to any other provisions of this Agreement according more favourable treatment, all facilities, rights and privileges, which in the United Kingdom and the Union of Soviet Socialist Republics respectively are or may be accorded with respect to trade to the subjects or citizens of any other foreign State or to juridical persons including companies constituted under the laws of

such State or to the property of such subjects, citizens or juridical persons including companies shall be extended to citizens of the Union of Soviet Socialist Republics or juridical persons including companies constituted under the laws of the Union of Soviet Socialist Republics and to British subjects, British-protected persons or juridical persons including companies constituted under the laws of the United Kingdom respectively and to their property. The natural produce and manufactures of the United Kingdom shall enjoy in the Union of Soviet Socialist Republics, and the natural produce and manufactures of the Union of Soviet Socialist Republics shall enjoy in the United Kingdom, all the facilities, rights and privileges which are at present or may be hereafter accorded to the natural produce and manufactures of any other foreign country, in all that relates to the prohibition and the restriction of imports and exports, customs duties and charges, transport, warehousing, drawbacks and excise.

(2) The expression "British-protected persons" in this Agreement is understood to mean persons belonging to any territory under the protection of His Majesty the King of Great Britain, Ireland and the British Dominions beyond the Seas, Emperor of India, or under His Majesty's suzerainty or in respect of which a Mandate has been accepted by His Majesty.

Article 2

(1) If either Contracting Party shall give notice to the other that there is reason to believe that, in respect of any class of goods produced or manufactured in the Union of Soviet Socialist Republics or the United Kingdom, as the case may be, and imported for consumption in the United Kingdom or the Union of Soviet Socialist Republics respectively, such prices are being created or maintained by the other Party, or by its State economic organisations, as are likely to frustrate preferences accorded, or detrimentally to affect the production of such goods, in the United Kingdom or the Union of Soviet Socialist Republics respectively, the two Parties agree to enter immediately into negotiations.

(2) Failing a settlement by negotiation, the Party giving the notice under paragraph (1) of this Article may intimate to the other that the provisions of Article 1 will as from a specified date cease to apply in the United Kingdom or the Union of Soviet Socialist Republics as the case may be, in so far as the prohibition and the restriction of imports are concerned, to goods produced or manufactured in the Union of Soviet Socialist Republics or the United Kingdom, respectively, of the class in respect of which notice has been given. On and after the date so specified the first Party may cease to apply the provisions of Article 1 in accordance with the intimation so given.

(3) The date specified in the intimation under paragraph (2) of this Article shall not be earlier than three months from the date on which notice was given under paragraph (1) of this Article.

(4) A Party who has given a notice under paragraph (1) of this Article shall consider any assurances which the other Party may give to the effect that action has been taken which will prevent a recurrence, in respect of those goods, of the position which led to the giving of the notice, and, if satisfied that such action has in fact been taken, shall again extend to those goods the full benefits of Article 1 of this Agreement, if effect has already been given to the intimation under paragraph (2) of this Article, or shall withdraw the intimation if it has not already been put into effect.

ARTICLE 3

The Government of the Union of Soviet Socialist Republics, being desirous of applying in an increasing proportion the proceeds of the sale in the United Kingdom of goods imported from the Union of Soviet Socialist Republics to payments for goods purchased in the United Kingdom and for the utilisation of British shipping services, will give effect to the arrangements with regard to an approximate balance of payments set out in the Schedule to the present Agreement.

ARTICLE 4

Trade between the United Kingdom and the Union of Soviet Socialist Republics shall be eligible for consideration on the same basis as trade between the United Kingdom and other foreign countries in connection with any legislative or administrative measures which are or may be taken by the Government of the United Kingdom for the granting of credits to facilitate such trade ; that is to say, that, in considering any given transaction, regard shall be had to financial and commercial considerations only.

ARTICLE 5

(1) In view of the fact that, by virtue of the laws of the Union of Soviet Socialist Republics, the foreign trade of the Union is a State monopoly, the Government of the United Kingdom agree to accord to the Government of the Union of Soviet Socialist Republics the right to establish in London a Trade Delegation, consisting of the Trade Representative of the Union of Soviet Socialist Republics and his two deputies, to form part of the Embassy of the Union of Soviet Socialist Republics.

(2) The head of the Trade Delegation shall be the Trade Representative of the Union of Soviet Socialist Republics in the United

Kingdom. By virtue of paragraph (1) of the present Article he and his two deputies shall be accorded all diplomatic privileges and immunities, and immunity shall attach to the offices occupied by the Trade Delegation (5th Floor, East Wing, Bush House, Aldwych, London) and used exclusively for the purpose defined in paragraph (3) of the present Article. No member of the staff of the Trade Delegation, other than the Trade Representative and his two deputies, shall enjoy any privileges or immunities other than those which are, or may be, enjoyed in the United Kingdom by officials of the State-controlled trading organisations of other countries.

(3) The functions of the Trade Delegation shall be—

(*a*) to facilitate and encourage the development of trade and commerce between the United Kingdom and the Union of Soviet Socialist Republics;

(*b*) to represent the interests of the Union of Soviet Socialist Republics in all that pertains to the foreign trade of the Union and to control, regulate and carry on such trade with the United Kingdom for and on behalf of the Union of Soviet Socialist Republics.

(4) In view of the fact that the Trade Delegation is acting in respect of trade for and on behalf of the Union of Soviet Socialist Republics, the Government of the latter assume responsibility for all transactions concluded in the United Kingdom by the Trade Representative or either of his two deputies. The Government of the Union of Soviet Socialist Republics will not, however, accept any responsibility for the acts of State Economic Organisations which, under the laws of the Union of Soviet Socialist Republics, are exclusively responsible for their own acts, except in cases where responsibility for such acts has been clearly accepted by the Trade Representative or either of his two deputies, acting for and on behalf of the Government of the Union of Soviet Socialist Republics. All obligations undertaken in the United Kingdom by the Trade Representative or either of his two deputies, acting for and on behalf of the Union of Soviet Socialist Republics, in addition to being signed by the Trade Representative or either of his deputies, must be countersigned by a person to be specially authorised by the Union of Soviet Socialist Republics for the purpose.

(5) The names of the Trade Representative, of his two deputies and of the person authorised as aforesaid shall be supplied to the Government of the United Kingdom from time to time and shall be published in the *Board of Trade Journal,* and the authority of any such Trade Representative, deputy or person authorised to bind the Government of the Union of Soviet Socialist Republics shall be deemed to continue until such time as notice to the contrary is published in like manner.

(6) Any question which may arise in respect of any transaction entered into in the United Kingdom by the Trade Delegation, the Trade Representative or either of his two deputies, acting for and on behalf of the Union of Soviet Socialist Republics, and duly signed in accordance with the provisions of paragraph (4) of the present Article, shall be determined by the Courts of the United Kingdom in accordance with the laws thereof, and, for the purpose of any proceedings which may be instituted in respect of any such transaction, service of the Writ of Summons or other process shall be deemed to be good service if such Writ or process is left at the office in London of the Trade Delegation.

(7) The Union of Soviet Socialist Republics will accept the jurisdiction of the Courts of the United Kingdom in respect of any question referred to in paragraph (6) of the Present Article and will not claim any privilege or immunity in connection with any proceedings which may be instituted in pursuance of the said paragraph. Where any writ of summons or other process is served upon them in accordance with the said paragraph (6), the Union of Soviet Socialist Republics will cause the Trade Representative or other person acting on their behalf to take the necessary steps to enable the questions involved in the proceedings to be determined by the Courts of the United Kingdom and to ensure that an appearance to those proceedings is entered on their behalf. Equally, the Trade Delegation, the Trade Representative and his two deputies will accept the jurisdiction of the Courts of the United Kingdom in respect of any question referred to in paragraph (6) of the present Article and will not claim any privilege or immunity, whether under paragraph (2) of the present Article, or otherwise, in connection with any proceedings which may be instituted in pursuance of the said paragraph (6).

(8) All the property of the Union of Soviet Socialist Republics in the United Kingdom shall, notwithstanding any privileges or immunities, be subject to such measures as may lawfully be taken to give effect to the orders of the Courts of the United Kingdom made in any proceedings which may be instituted in pursuance of paragraph (6) of the present Article, other than such property as is necessary for the exercise of the rights of State sovereignty or for the official functions of the diplomatic or consular representatives in the United Kingdom of the Union of Soviet Socialist Republics.

ARTICLE 6

British ships and their cargoes and passengers, and ships of the Union of Soviet Socialist Republics and their cargoes and passengers shall enjoy in the ports and territorial waters of the Union of Soviet Socialist Republics and of the United Kingdom respectively treatment not less favourable in any respect than that accorded to ships of the most favoured nation and their cargoes and passengers.

The provisions of the present Article do not apply to ships registered at the ports of the self-governing Dominions of His Majesty the King of Great Britain, Ireland and the British Dominions beyond the Seas, Emperor of India, which are separate members of the League of Nations, or of the mandated and other territories administered under the authority of His Governments in those Dominions, or to the cargoes and passengers of such ships.

Nothing in this Article shall entitle British ships to claim any privileges which are or may be accorded by the Union of Soviet Socialist Republics to the fishing fleets of countries situated on the Arctic Ocean.

ARTICLE 7

(1) Nothing in this Agreement shall entitle the Union of Soviet Socialist Republics to claim the benefit of any treatment, preference or privilege which may at any time be in force exclusively between territories under the sovereignty of His Majesty the King of Great Britain, Ireland and the British Dominions beyond the Seas, Emperor of India, or under His Majesty's suzerainty, protection or mandate.

(2) Nothing in the present Agreement shall apply to—

(*a*) the special provisions relating to trade contained in treaties which the Union of Soviet Socialist Republics has concluded, or may conclude hereafter, with Estonia, Latvia or Lithuania, or with States on the continent of Asia whose territory borders on the territory of the Union of Soviet Socialist Republics ;

(*b*) the rights which have been accorded or may be accorded to any third country forming part of a customs union with the Union of Soviet Socialist Republics ;

(*c*) the privileges which the Union of Soviet Socialist Republics has accorded or may accord to border States with respect to local trade between the inhabitants of the frontier zones.

(3) Nothing in this Agreement shall preclude the right of either of the Contracting Parties to enforce special sanitary or other provisions for the purpose of securing the safety of persons or the protection of animals and plants against diseases and pests, of regulating the trade in arms and ammunition, or of regulating the trade in any particular article under the provisions of any general international convention which is binding on that Contracting Party.

ARTICLE 8

So long as in any territory under the sovereignty of His Majesty the King of Great Britain, Ireland and the British Dominions beyond the Seas, Emperor of India, or under His Majesty's suzerainty, protection or mandate, other than the United Kingdom and the self-governing Dominions which are separate members of the League of Nations, and the mandated and other territories administered under the authority of His Governments in those Dominions, goods the produce and manufacture of the Union of Soviet Socialist Republics are accorded most favoured nation treatment, subject only to the exception specified in paragraph (1) of Article 7, then goods produced and manufactured in such territory shall enjoy in the Union of Soviet Socialist Republics, completely and unconditionally, treatment as favourable as that accorded to goods the produce and manufacture of the most favoured nation.

Goods the produce or manufacture of Palestine shall not be debarred from the benefits of this Article by reason only of any special customs privileges which may be accorded in Palestine to goods the produce or manufacture of any State the territory of which in 1914 was wholly included in Asiatic Turkey or Arabia.

Article 9

The present agreement shall be ratified and the ratifications shall be exchanged at Moscow as soon as possible. It shall come into force on the date of the exchange of ratifications and shall remain in force until the expiration of six months from the date upon which either of the Contracting Parties shall have given notice of intention to terminate it.

In witness whereof the undersigned, duly authorised to that effect, have signed the present Agreement and have affixed thereto their seals.

Done in duplicate at London in the English language the sixteenth day of February, 1934.

A translation shall be made into the Russian language as soon as possible and agreed upon between the Contracting Parties.

Both texts shall then be considered authentic for all purposes.

Schedule

Balance of Payments

1. The payments of the Union of Soviet Socialist Republics in the United Kingdom as hereinafter defined shall bear to the proceeds of

the Union of Soviet Socialist Republics in the United Kingdom as hereinafter defined the following proportions:—

In the year ending December 31, 1934	...	1:1·7
In the year ending December 31, 1935	...	1:1·5
In the year ending December 31, 1936	...	1:1·4
In the year ending December 31, 1937	...	1:1·2

Thereafter an approximate balance of payments measured by the ratio 1:1·1 shall be maintained.

2. For the purposes of this Schedule—

(*a*) the proceeds of the Union of Soviet Socialist Republics in any year shall be the value of imports of merchandise (excluding goods transhipped under bond) recorded in that year in the Trade Accounts of the United Kingdom as consigned to the United Kingdom from the Union of Soviet Socialist Republics,* subject to the deduction of 97 per cent. of the value of canned salmon not handled by the trading organisations of the Union of Soviet Socialist Republics; and

(*b*) the payments of the Union of Soviet Socialist Republics in the United Kingdom in any year, subject to the provisions of paragraphs 3 and 4 of this Schedule, shall be the sum of the four following amounts:—

(i) the value of exports of United Kingdom produce and manufactures and of imported merchandise (excluding goods transhipped under bond) recorded in that year in the Trade Accounts of the United Kingdom as consigned from the United Kingdom to the Union of Soviet Socialist Republics subject to the deduction of the value of goods exported or re-exported in that year from the United Kingdom to the Union of Soviet Socialist Republics for which payment is not made in the year in which the export or re-export takes place;

(ii) the amount of credits repaid by the Government or trading organisations of the Union of Soviet Socialist Republics in that year (excluding interest) in respect of exports or re-exports of the United Kingdom in previous years;

(iii) the amounts paid by the Government or trading organisations of the Union of Soviet Socialist Republics in that year in respect of the chartering of British ships registered at ports in the United Kingdom; and

(iv) an amount equal to 6½ per cent. of the sum of the imports of the United Kingdom from the Union of Soviet Socialist Republics in that year (as defined in paragraph (*a*)

* Goods passing under bond through the territory of the Union of Soviet Socialist Republics will not be recorded among imports consigned to the United Kingdom from the Union of Soviet Socialist Republics unless they are reconsigned from the Union of Soviet Socialist Republics.

above, and excluding 97 per cent. of the value of canned salmon not handled by trading organisations of the Union of Soviet Socialist Republics) and the exports and re-exports of the United Kingdom to the Union of Soviet Socialist Republics in that year (as defined in sub-paragraph (i) above) to represent the excess of all payments of the Union of Soviet Socialist Republics not otherwise specifically provided for over similar payments of the United Kingdom.

3. If in any year the payments of the Union of Soviet Socialist Republics differ from the amount which they should have reached in accordance with the provisions of paragraph 1 above, the amount of any deficiency will be deducted from and the amount of any excess will be added to the sum of the four amounts referred to in the preceding paragraph in computing the payments of the Union of Soviet Socialist Republics in the following year, and the payments of the Union of Soviet Socialist Republics in that year shall be deemed to be the amount arrived at after the deduction of the amount of that deficiency or after the addition of the amount of that excess, as the case may be.

4. The Government of the United Kingdom agree that expenditure incurred by the Government or trading organisations of the Union of Soviet Socialist Republics upon the purchase for export of British ships registered at ports in the United Kingdom, the export of which, being old vessels, is not recorded among the exports of the United Kingdom, is a proper addition to the payments of the Union of Soviet Socialist Republics, and the Government of the Union of Soviet Socialist Republics will from time to time supply the Government of the United Kingdom with a statement showing the names of any such ships, the amounts paid in respect of each ship, and the dates upon which such payments were made.

5. The trading operations of the Union of Soviet Socialist Republics shall be so conducted that the amount by which the payments of the Union of Soviet Socialist Republics in the United Kingdom fall short, in any year, of the amount which they should have reached in accordance with the provisions of paragraph 1 above shall not be more than 7½ per cent. of the latter amount.

6. The Government of the Union of Soviet Socialist Republics will supply to the Government of the United Kingdom the following information in respect of each year:—

(i) A statement of payments (excluding interest) made in that year in respect of exports of United Kingdom produce and manufacture to the Union of Soviet Socialist Republics showing separately payments made in respect of goods exported during that year and goods exported during each previous year.

(ii) A statement of payments (excluding interest) made in that year in respect of re-exports from the United Kingdom to the Union of Soviet Socialist Republics (excluding goods transhipped under bond) showing separately payments made in respect of goods re-exported during that year and goods re-exported during each previous year.

(iii) A statement showing the British ships registered at ports in the United Kingdom chartered during that year and the amounts paid in that year by the Government or trading organisations of the Union of Soviet Socialist Republics in respect of any such ship chartered in that or any previous year.

(iv) A statement showing the declared value at the time of importation of canned salmon imported into the United Kingdom from the Union of Soviet Socialist Republics which has been handled by trading organisations of the Union of Soviet Socialist Republics.

7. The Government of the Union of Soviet Socialist Republics will also furnish the Government of the United Kingdom with a statement showing the payments (excluding interest) made by the Government and trading organisations of the Union of Soviet Socialist Republics in the year ending the 31st December, 1933, in respect of (i) exports to the Union of Soviet Socialist Republics of United Kingdom produce and manufactures, and (ii) exports to the Union of Soviet Socialist Republics of imported merchandise (excluding goods transhipped under bond) which were exported during that year to the Union of Soviet Socialist Republics.

8. In this Schedule, unless the context otherwise requires, the expression " year " means a year beginning on the 1st January and ending on the 31st December. The expression " merchandise " has the same meaning as in the Trade Accounts of the United Kingdom.

APPENDIX IV

TREATY FOR AN ALLIANCE IN THE WAR AGAINST HITLERITE GERMANY AND HER ASSOCIATES IN EUROPE AND PROVIDING ALSO FOR COLLABORATION AND MUTUAL ASSISTANCE THEREAFTER CONCLUDED BETWEEN HIS MAJESTY IN RESPECT OF THE UNITED KINGDOM AND THE PRESIDIUM OF THE SUPREME COUNCIL OF THE UNION OF SOVIET SOCIALIST REPUBLICS.

London, May 26, 1942.

No. 1

TREATY OF ALLIANCE IN THE WAR AGAINST HITLERITE GERMANY AND HER ASSOCIATES IN EUROPE AND OF COLLABORATION AND MUTUAL ASSISTANCE THEREAFTER CONCLUDED BETWEEN THE UNION OF SOVIET SOCIALIST REPUBLICS AND THE UNITED KINGDOM OF GREAT BRITAIN AND NORTHERN IRELAND.

His Majesty The King of Great Britain, Ireland, and the British Dominions beyond the Seas, Emperor of India, and the Presidium of the Supreme Council of the Union of Soviet Socialist Republics ;

Desiring to confirm the stipulations of the Agreement between His Majesty's Government in the United Kingdom and the Government of the Union of Soviet Socialist Republics for joint action in the war against Germany, signed at Moscow on the 12th July, 1941*, and to replace them by a formal treaty ;

Desiring to contribute after the war to the maintenance of peace and to the prevention of further aggression by Germany or the States associated with her in acts of aggression in Europe ;

Desiring, moreover, to give expression to their intention to collaborate closely with one another as well as with the other United Nations at the peace settlement and during the ensuing period of reconstruction on the basis of the principles enunciated in the declaration made on the 14th August, 1941,† by the President of the United States of America and the Prime Minister of Great Britain to which the Government of the Union of Soviet Socialist Republics has adhered ;

Desiring, finally, to provide for mutual assistance in the event of an attack upon either High Contracting Party by Germany or any of the States associated with her in acts of aggression in Europe.

* "Treaty Series No. 15 (1941)." Cmd. 6304.

† "United States No. 3 (1941)." Cmd. 6321.

Have decided to conclude a treaty for that purpose and have appointed as their Plenipotentiaries:—

His Majesty The King of Great Britain, Ireland, and the British Dominions beyond the Seas, Emperor of India,

For the United Kingdom of Great Britain and Northern Ireland:

The Right Honourable Anthony Eden, M.P., His Majesty's Principal Secretary of State for Foreign Affairs;

The Presidium of the Supreme Council of the Union of Soviet Socialist Republics:

M. Vyacheslav Mikhailovich Molotov, People's Commissar for Foreign Affairs,

Who, having communicated their Full Powers, found in good and due form, have agreed as follows:—

PART I

ARTICLE I

In virtue of the alliance established between the United Kingdom and the Union of Soviet Socialist Republics the High Contracting Parties mutually undertake to afford one another military and other assistance and support of all kinds in the war against Germany and all those States which are associated with her in acts of aggression in Europe.

ARTICLE II

The High Contracting Parties undertake not to enter into any negotiations with the Hitlerite Government or any other Government in Germany that does not clearly renounce all aggressive intentions, and not to negotiate or conclude except by mutual consent any armistice or peace treaty with Germany or any other State associated with her in acts of aggression in Europe.

PART II

ARTICLE III

(1) The High Contracting Parties declare their desire to unite with other like-minded States in adopting proposals for common action to preserve peace and resist aggression in the post-war period.

(2) Pending the adoption of such proposals, they will after the termination of hostilities take all the measures in their power to render impossible a repetition of aggression and violation of the peace by Germany or any of the States associated with her in acts of aggression in Europe.

ARTICLE IV

Should one of the High Contracting Parties during the post-war period become involved in hostilities with Germany or any of the

States mentioned in Article III (2) in consequence of an attack by that State against that Party, the other High Contracting Party will at once give to the Contracting Party so involved in hostilities all the military and other support and assistance in his power.

This Article shall remain in force until the High Contracting Parties, by mutual agreement, shall recognise that it is superseded by the adoption of the proposals contemplated in Article III (1). In default of the adoption of such proposals, it shall remain in force for a period of twenty years, and thereafter until terminated by either High Contracting Party, as provided in Article VIII.

Article V

The High Contracting Parties, having regard to the interests of the security of each of them, agree to work together in close and friendly collaboration after the re-establishment of peace for the organisation of security and economic prosperity in Europe. They will take into account the interests of the United Nations in these objects, and they will act in accordance with the two principles of not seeking territorial aggrandisement for themselves and of non-interference in the internal affairs of other States.

Article VI

The High Contracting Parties agree to render one another all possible economic assistance after the war.

Article VII

Each High Contracting Party undertakes not to conclude any alliance and not to take part in any coalition directed against the other High Contracting Party.

Article VIII

The present Treaty is subject to ratification in the shortest possible time and the instruments of ratification shall be exchanged in Moscow as soon as possible.

It comes into force immediately on the exchange of the instruments of ratification and shall thereupon replace the Agreement between the Government of the Union of Soviet Socialist Republics and His Majesty's Government in the United Kingdom, signed at Moscow on the 12th July, 1941.

Part I of the present Treaty shall remain in force until the re-establishment of peace between the High Contracting Parties and Germany and the Powers associated with her in acts of aggression in Europe.

Part II of the present Treaty shall remain in force for a period of twenty years. Thereafter, unless twelve months' notice has been given by either Party to terminate the Treaty at the end of the said period of twenty years, it shall continue in force until twelve months after either High Contracting Party shall have given notice to the other in writing of his intention to terminate it.

In witness whereof the above-named Plenipotentiaries have signed the present Treaty and have affixed thereto their seals.

Done in duplicate in London on the 26th day of May, 1942, in the English and Russian languages, both texts being equally authentic.

(L.S.) ANTHONY EDEN. (L.S.) V. MOLOTOV.

APPENDIX V

STATISTICAL TABLE OF ANGLO-SOVIET TRADE

Year.	*Imports consigned from Soviet Russia.* £.	*Exports and Re-exports consigned to Soviet Russia from the United Kingdom.* £.
1921	2,694,674	3,391,290
1922	8,102,829	4,611,027
1923	9,266,100	4,481,126
1924	19,773,842	11,072,529
1925	25,322,033	19,256,929
1926	24,130,217	14,401,366
1927	21,051,633	11,289,775
1928	21,576,107	4,800,752
1929	26,487,499	6,542,033
1930	34,235,002	9,291,301
1931	32,285,563	9,203,214
1932	19,645,130	10,619,687
1933	17,491,099	4,298,770
1934	17,326,619	7,545,900
1935	21,763,984	9,726,057
1936	18,903,385	13,345,741
1937	29,124,460	19,504,856
1938	19,543,030	17,419,518
1939 (Jan.-June).	3,851,667	5,903,090
Total.	372,575,073	186,704,961

Thus, according to the Board of Trade figures, Soviet imports to this country for the 18½ years under review amounted to £372,575,073; but British exports and re-exports to the Soviet Union amounted to only £186,704,961. At first sight it would seem that the Soviet Union had a favourable trade balance of £185,870,112. However, that was not the case. The sum total of Soviet exports to Great Britain represented the sum total of what the Soviets received for their exports to this country; but the sum total of British exports and re-exports to the Soviet Union did not represent by any means the sum total expended by the Soviet representatives on the British market. The Soviet trading organisations in Great Britain spent in addition very considerable sums on such items as precious metals, freight, loading and unloading operations, storage, sorting, packing, insurance, trading and administrative expenses, interest on credit, and goods purchased on the London market for direct shipment from British Dominions and Colonies and foreign countries to Russia.

The amounts spent under these heads—they then covered the period 1920-1928—were last published in 1929. They amounted to about two-thirds of the Soviets' favourable trade balance. There is no reason to think that the proportion would not have been about the same in the period now under review, viz., 1921-1939. On this calculation the Soviets' favourable balance would be reduced from £185,870,112 to about £61,000,000. This is a proportionately small trade balance as compared with the favourable trade balances which countries such as Belgium, Canada and the U.S.A. had in their total trade turn-over with Great Britain in the period under review.

No statistics of British-Soviet trade have been published by the Board of Trade since the outbreak of the war, September 3, 1939.

INDEX

NOTE.

All entries referring to one person are brought under the title which he bore at the end of the period referred to. Earlier or later titles are included in brackets. Thus we have BRENTFORD, Lord, (Sir W. Joynson-Hicks), but MOORE-BRABAZON, Lt.-Col. J. T. C. (Lord Brabazon).